The making of the Irish poor law, 1815–43

MANCHESTER
1824
Manchester University Press

The making of the Irish poor law, 1815–43

Peter Gray

Manchester University Press
Manchester and New York
distributed in the United States exclusively by Palgrave Macmillan

Published by Manchester University Press
Oxford Road, Manchester M13 9NR, UK
and Room 400, 175 Fifth Avenue, New York, NY 10010, USA
www.manchesteruniversitypress.co.uk

Distributed in the United States exclusively by
Palgrave Macmillan, 175 Fifth Avenue, New York,
NY 10010, USA

Distributed in Canada exclusively by
UBC Press, University of British Columbia, 2029 West Mall,
Vancouver, BC, Canada V6T 1Z2

British Library Cataloguing-in-Publication Data
A catalogue record for this book is available from the British Library

Library of Congress Cataloging-in-Publication Data applied for

ISBN 978 0 7190 7649 7 *hardback*

First published 2009

18 17 16 15 14 13 12 11 10 09   10 9 8 7 6 5 4 3 2 1

Typeset by SNP Best-set Typesetter Ltd., Hong Kong
Printed in Great Britain
by CPI Antony Rowe, Chippenham, Wiltshire

In memory of my father, Henry Gray, 1937–1999

Contents

Acknowledgements

I am grateful to the Marquess of Normanby for permitting me to quote from the Normanby Papers at Mulgrave Castle. Quotations from the Castle Howard Papers are by kind permission of the Howard family; those from the Broadlands Papers are by that of the Trustees of the Broadlands Archives. I am grateful to the staffs of the following libraries, record offices and archives for assistance and permission to use the collections in their keeping: the Bodleian Library, British Library, Cambridge University Library, Devon Record Office, Doncaster Archives Department, Durham University Library, Hartley Library (Southampton), Lambeth Palace Library, Liverpool Record Office, National Archives (Kew), National Library of Ireland, National Library of Wales, Public Record Office of Northern Ireland, Queen's University Library, Staffordshire Record Office, UCL Archives, West Sussex Record Office.

The writing of this book was supported by financial assistance and research leave awarded by the Arts and Humanities Research Council, the British Academy, the Burns Library at Boston College, the University of Southampton and Queen's University Belfast. Earlier versions of sections of the book were presented as papers to the Social Science History Conference, Amsterdam, 1998, the Research Institute of Irish–Scottish Studies, Aberdeen, 2004, the 'History of Welfare in the Peripheries' conference at Glasgow Caledonian University, 2006, and the International Economic History Congress, Helsinki, 2006. I am grateful to organizers and participants for useful feedback.

Particular thanks are due to Virginia Crossman, for commenting critically on several of the draft chapters; and to Sara Jan for reading and correcting some errors in the text. Anthony Malcomson graciously shared his knowledge of the Clements correspondence in the Killadoon papers. I am grateful for various forms of assistance, advice, encouragement and criticism to a large number of people, including Tom Boylan, Inga Brandes, Alison Brisby, Melissa Calaresu, Sean Connolly, Neil and Alison Gregor, David Hayton,

Boyd Hilton, Andrew Holmes, Janice Holmes, Joanna Innes, Elizabeth Keaney, Kevin Kenny, Tony Kushner, Shirley Matthews, Joy Moorhead, Hiram Morgan, Deb Mortlock, Ros Oates, Cormac Ó Gráda, Kendrick Oliver, Robert O'Neill, Gearoid Ó Tuathaigh, Robert Portsmouth, Olwen Purdue, Jennifer Regan, Richard Smith, Allan Warren and Chris Woolgar. Thanks also to my family, and to past and present colleagues at Southampton University and Queen's University Belfast.

List of abbreviations

BL: AP	British Library, London: Althorp Papers
BL: BP	British Library, London: Bowood Papers
BL: GP	British Library, London: Graham Papers
BL: PP	British Library, London: Peel Papers
CHP	Castle Howard, N. Yorkshire: Castle Howard Papers
DAD: BWP	Doncaster Archives Department: Battie-Wrightson Papers
DRO: FP	Devon Record Office, Exeter: Fortescue of Castle Hill Papers
DUL: GP	Durham University Library: Grey Papers
MC: NP	Mulgrave Castle, N. Yorkshire: Normanby Papers
NA: HOP	National Archives, Kew: Home Office Papers
NA: PLCP	National Archives, Kew: Poor Law Commission Papers
NA: RP	National Archives, Kew: Russell Papers
NA: TP	National Archives, Kew: Treasury Papers
NLI: KP	National Library of Ireland, Dublin: Killadoon Papers
NLI: MP	National Library of Ireland, Dublin: Monteagle Papers
NLI: SOBP	National Library of Ireland, Dublin: Smith O'Brien Papers
NLW: HCP	National Library of Wales, Aberystwyth: Harpton Court Papers
NLW: NSP	National Library of Wales, Aberystwyth: Nassau Senior Papers
PP	Parliamentary Papers
RA: MP	Royal Archives, Windsor: Melbourne Papers
SRO: HP	Staffordshire Record Office, Stafford: Hatherton Papers
SUL: BP	Southampton University Library: Broadlands Papers
SUL: WP	Southampton University Library: Wellington Papers
UCL: CP	UCL Archives, London: Chadwick Papers

1

Introduction: the Irish poor and public charity before 1838

The extent and depth of early nineteenth-century Irish poverty frequently provoked both natives and visitors to the island into expressions of outrage or despair. Ireland, it appeared to many commentators, displayed a singularity of social suffering that distinguished it from every 'Christian' country, and perhaps also those of other faiths. The French traveller and sociologist Gustave de Beaumont expressed this sentiment following his first visit to the country in summer 1835:

> Misery, naked and famishing, that misery which is vagrant, idle, and mendicant, covers the entire country; it shows itself everywhere, and at every hour of the day; it is the first thing you see when you land on the Irish coast, and from that moment it ceases not to be present to your view; sometimes under the aspect of the diseased displaying his sores, sometimes under the form of the pauper scarcely covered by his rags; it follows you everywhere, and besieges you incessantly; you hear its groans and cries in the distance; and if the voice does not excite profound pity, it importunes and terrifies you. This misery seems inherent to the soil, and one of its natural products; like one of those endemic scourges that pollute the atmosphere, it blights everything which approaches it, smites the rich man himself, who cannot, in the midst of his joys, separate himself from the miseries of the poor, and makes vain efforts to rid himself of the vermin which he has produced, and which cling to him.[1]

Such visceral shock at the sight of Irish poverty, expressed by a man who had travelled widely in Europe and North America, is striking, if perhaps somewhat overstated for rhetorical effect. Recent historical research suggests that living standards in Ireland may on average have been rising in the pre-Famine decades, even while significant proportions of the rural classes were facing growing immiseration.[2] De Beaumont's preoccupation with evidence of the

1 Gustave de Beaumont, *Ireland: Social, Political and Religious* ([1839] Cambridge, MA, 2006), p. 128.

2 See Cormac Ó Gráda, *Ireland: A New Economic History 1780–1939* (Oxford, 1994), pp. 80–97.

latter did not, however, incline him or his travelling companion Alexis de Tocqueville towards a resigned fatalism in the face of Irish destitution. Both displayed an intense interest in the developing debate in the 1830s about whether Irish poverty could or should be alleviated by state intervention, and about the modalities this might take.

Once having decided to visit Ireland, the pair prepared themselves in London by sitting in on a conversation on the question of policy responses to Irish poverty, between de Tocqueville's friend, the political economist Nassau Senior, and John Revans, then secretary of the Irish Poor Inquiry Commission. De Tocqueville, who found Revans 'a very intelligent young man', belonging to 'the radical party', was evidently impressed by his confident responses to critical questioning by Senior, and recorded the exchange verbatim in his diary entry for 7 June 1835:

> S[enior]. To what do you principally attribute the poverty of Ireland?
>
> R[evans]. To a landlord system that profits from the intense competition of labourers [for land] to exact from the farmers an excessive rent. From the moment a farmer begins to make a profit, the landlord raises the price of his lease. The result is that the farmer is afraid to make improvements, for fear of being taxed by his master for a much higher sum than his improvement would be worth to him, and he confines himself strictly to subsisting.
>
> S. Do you think that a good poor law would by its nature diminish this evil?
>
> R. Yes, by diminishing the competition of labourers and by putting the common man in a position to lay down, up to a certain point, the law to the proprietor of the soil.
>
> S. Is the poverty as great as they say?
>
> R. The poverty is horrible. The people live only upon potatoes, and often they lack them.

The discussion then proceeded to review the opportunities and obstacles to Irish economic development:

> S. Could an agriculturalist who imported a large amount of capital into Ireland be sure of reaping the fruits of his industry?
>
> R. No, the people are faced by evils too great, and kept because of this in too great and continual a state of agitation for property to be secure there: the lack of security for property is the greatest evil in Ireland.
>
> S. Do you not believe that this inferiority of the Irish to the English derives from a racial inferiority?

> R. I do not know. But I am not disposed to believe it. In the districts where property is secure and where poverty reigns less, the peasant shows himself steady and progressive.[3]

This (staged) conversation established some of the principal themes for further investigation by the Frenchmen, which would later be developed in the account prepared by de Beaumont and published in 1839. On their tour they visited the old Dublin poorhouse and the famine-ravaged district of Newport in Co. Mayo, and questioned a range of sources (especially from among the Catholic clergy) on the subjects of poverty and poor relief.[4] Ultimately, both de Beaumont and de Tocqueville came down against a poor law for Ireland, endorsing the contemporary critique of state welfare institutions, and preferring a range of alternatives focused on political and land reforms, which they believed would liberate individual exertions, as the best way of addressing the problem of poverty.[5] However, their observations clearly reflect two central concerns common to Irish, British and foreign commentators on the state of Ireland in the 1830s – the prevalence of poverty, and the belief that it could and should be (at least in part) remedied by public policy.

The present study seeks to set the Irish Poor Law Act of 1838, one of the most controversial pieces of legislation for nineteenth-century Ireland, into the context of the intense political and ideological debates observed by the travellers and the sweeping inquiry carried out into Irish poverty and its alleviation in 1833–36. The exchange between Senior and Revans, and the subsequent interviews that the travellers conducted with Irish Catholic clergymen, establish some of the central themes of this investigation, just as it did for de Tocqueville and de Beaumont in the 1830s. Senior and Revans embodied two quite distinct and opposed positions on Irish poor relief within British (and Irish) liberalism. The former, like his mentor and friend Archbishop Whately, adhered to an orthodox economic perspective on Ireland that stressed the Malthusian peril of excessive population, and opposed any transfer of resources from private investment to public welfare; in contrast, Revans

3 Emmet Larkin (ed.), *Alexis de Tocqueville's Journey in Ireland July–August, 1835* (Dublin, 1990), pp. 19–22.

4 *Ibid.*, pp. 24–5, 30, 40, 63, 78–9, 93–4, 116–18, 129–36. See also Hugh Brogan, *Alexis de Tocqueville: A Biography* (London, 2006), p. 307.

5 De Beaumont, *Ireland*, pp. 281–9. De Beaumont's analysis drew on personal experience, but was probably also influenced by English writings on Irish society, most notably J. E. Bicheno's *Ireland and its Economy* (London, 1830). For de Tocqueville's critique of the English poor law and his preference for private charity, see his *Memoir on Pauperism* (Chicago, IL, 1997 [1835]).

explored ideas of welfare entitlement and social security alongside an economic analysis that proposed the state should stimulate investment through punitive taxation of landed 'neglect' of poverty. These rival positions attracted differing political sponsors within the governing Whig-liberal coalitions of the 1830s. At the same time, de Tocqueville's record of his conversation with the bishop of Kildare and Leighlin in July 1835 revealed significant Catholic clerical interest in an Irish poor law: 'I believe the adoption of "poor laws" indispensible', Bishop Nolan told him; '[t]he natural link that should unite the upper and lower classes is destroyed. The latter have nothing to expect from the former if the law does not come to their aid.'[6] The bishop's opinion was strongly contested by other voices in Ireland, but formed part of a growing lobby there for a new legal dispensation in favour of the poor. The outcome of these debates, the 1838 Irish Poor Law Act, was a messy compromise that dissatisfied the supporters while only partially (at best) reconciling opponents of such a measure, but it cannot be understood without being located within the contestations over the nature of Irish poverty and the responsibilities of the state that were rife in these decades.

Both the 1838 measure itself and the more general debates surrounding poor relief in Ireland in the 1820s and 1830s have been ill-served by historians. In contrast to the poor laws of England and Scotland, the Irish poor law has, until very recently, been seriously under-researched.[7] The intense historiographical focus on the Great Famine in the 1980s and 1990s did give rise to a considerable number of local studies (of varying quality) of the impact of that catastrophe on individual poor-law unions, and to several studies of national policy-making and relief administration in the later 1840s, in which the poor law played a prominent role.[8] This attention to the study of the institution in crisis, in the context of the worst peacetime social and

6 Larkin (ed.), *Tocqueville's Journey*, p. 40.

7 The English literature is very extensive, but for recent overviews, see Alan Kidd, *State, Society and the Poor in Nineteenth-Century England* (Basingstoke, 1999); Steven A. King, *Poverty and Welfare in England 1700–1850: A Regional Perspective* (Manchester, 2000); Lynn Hollen Lees, *The Solidarities of Strangers: The English Poor Laws and the People, 1700–1948* (Cambridge, 1998). For Scotland, see Rosalind Mitchison, *The Old Poor Law in Scotland: The Experience of Poverty, 1574–1845* (Edinburgh, 2000).

8 For general studies of poor law policy, see James S. Donnelly, jr, '"Irish property must pay for Irish poverty": British public opinion and the Great Irish Famine', in Chris Morash and Richard Hayes (eds), *Fearful Realities: New Perspectives on the Famine* (Blackrock, 1996), pp. 60–76; Peter Gray, *Famine, Land and Politics: British Government and Irish Society 1843–50* (Dublin, 1999); and Christine Kinealy, *This Great Calamity: The Irish Famine 1845–52* (Dublin, 1994).

demographic disaster in modern European history, is understandable, but has nonetheless tended to distort our understanding of the place of the institution in modern Irish history more generally. Apart from the Famine-related studies, only isolated aspects of Irish poor law history have thus far received scholarly attention. The medical charities of Ireland, temporarily excluded from the purview of the poor law in 1838, but despite vigorous resistance on the part of the medical lobby eventually subordinated to it from 1851, have been the subject of two excellent monographs.[9] Pioneering work on the practical operation of the system in the later nineteenth and early twentieth centuries, coloured by the changing political and ideological context of that period, has recently been undertaken by Virginia Crossman.[10] In addition, a number of other younger scholars are engaged on research projects on the comparative aspects of poor relief in Ireland.[11] Individual voluntary relief institutions dating from before the 1838 act also have their own histories.[12] The one (and very recent) short survey of the poor law throughout its lifetime from 1838 to 1922 (in Northern Ireland to 1948) serves more as a guide to future research agendas than as a summation of a significant body of existing scholarship.[13]

The establishment of the institution, a process spanning the formation of the Irish Poor Inquiry Commission in 1833, the enactment of the poor relief bill in 1838, and its implementation in the years preceding the onset of famine in 1845, has been the subject of a number of disparate accounts, but there is

9 Ronald D. Cassell, *Medical Charities, Medical Politics: The Irish Dispensary System and the Poor Law, 1836–1872* (Woodbridge, 1997); Laurence M. Geary, *Medicine and Charity in Ireland 1718–1851* (Dublin, 2004).

10 Virginia Crossman, *Politics, Pauperism and Power in Late Nineteenth-Century Ireland* (Manchester, 2006); 'The New Ross workhouse riot of 1887: nationalism, class and the Irish poor laws', *Past & Present*, 179 (2003), pp. 135–58.

11 Inga Brandes, '"Odious, degrading and foreign" institutions? Analysing Irish workhouses in the nineteenth and twentieth centuries', in Andreas Gestrich *et al.* (eds), *Being Poor in Modern Europe: Historical Perspectives 1800–1940* (Bern, 2006), pp. 199–228; Ina Scherder, 'Galway workhouses in the nineteenth and twentieth centuries: function and strategy', in *ibid.*, pp. 181–98.

12 e.g. Audrey Woods, *Dublin Outsiders: A History of the Mendicity Institution 1818–1998* (Dublin, 1998); R. W. M. Strain, *Belfast and its Charitable Society: A Story of Urban Social Development* (London, 1961). See also Joseph Robins, *The Lost Children: A Study of Charity Children in Ireland 1700–1900* (Dublin, 1980).

13 Virginia Crossman, *The Poor Law in Ireland 1838–1948* (Dublin, 2006). Another academic account that attempts an extended survey relies heavily on evidence from the important (but unrepresentative) South Dublin union: Helen Burke, *The People and the Poor Law in Nineteenth-Century Ireland* (Littlehampton, 1987).

nothing in the format of Anthony Brundage's seminal monograph on the formation of the English Poor Law Amendment Act of 1834, which examines the preparation, passage and introduction of the new English law as a 'pre-eminently political process'.[14] Brundage's approach – modified to take account of the very different political context and dynamics of the Irish case – has been adopted as a general model for the present study. It has been supplemented by reflection on the significance for the Irish case of the stimulating work of Peter Mandler on the complex ideological dimensions of the English poor law debates of the 1820s–30s and the legislation of 1834, and on Boyd Hilton's emphasis on the role of Christian economic thought in English social and economic policy-making in the early nineteenth century.[15]

By the far the most thoroughly researched account of the intellectual and political origins of the Irish measure can be found in R. D. Collison Black's *Economic Thought and the Irish Question, 1817–70*, first published in 1960, and still the starting point for any study of Irish policy-making in the first two-thirds of the nineteenth century. Black's account manifests both the strengths and potential weaknesses of his general approach.[16] As a survey of economic thought on poverty (and the associated questions of population, development and the legitimate functions of the state), it is erudite, extensively researched and powerfully constructed. The limitations arise in part from the brevity of his account of the process of relief policy-making (which necessitates some generalization), and in part from his failure to offer a persuasive explanation of the interrelationship between economic thinkers and political actors, and to give sufficient weight to non-economic motivations in policy-making. The question of poverty in Ireland, as de Beaumont and de Tocqueville recognized, was intensely politicized, and gave rise to complex and cross-cutting responses that were subject to change over time. Any persuasive attempt to explain the origins and passage of the Irish poor law needs to go further in combining an analysis of the range and complexity

14 Anthony Brundage, *The Making of the New Poor Law: The Politics of Inquiry, Enactment and Implementation, 1832–39* (London, 1978).

15 Peter Mandler, 'The making of the new poor law *redivivus*', *Past & Present*, 117 (1987), pp. 131–57; 'Tories and paupers: Christian political economy and the making of the new poor law', *Historical Journal*, 33 (1990), pp. 81–103; Boyd Hilton, *The Age of Atonement: The Influence of Evangelicalism on Social and Economic Thought, 1785–1865* (Oxford, 1988).

16 R. D. Collison Black, *Economic Thought and the Irish Question, 1817–1870* (Cambridge, 1960), pp. 86–112. Thomas G. Conway, 'The approach to an Irish poor law 1828–33', *Éire-Ireland*, 6 (1971), pp. 65–81, while a useful summary, fails to get far beyond the printed primary records.

of attitudes towards poverty and poor relief in Ireland in the years preceding and following 1838 with a detailed narrative of the political appropriation and utilization of the themes of 'poverty' and 'poor relief' as applied to the Irish case in the public life of both islands.

Some accounts of the passage and implementation of the measure have tended to suffer from oversimplification and rhetorical excess. Frederick Powell offers a challengingly theoretical social-scientific approach to the development of poor-relief policy in Ireland; while his book contains a number of useful critical observations on the developments of the 1830s, it is erratic in its use of primary sources and occasionally inclined towards reductionist and ahistorical speculations.[17] In an otherwise sophisticated and detailed account of post-Famine workhouse riots in Dublin, Anna Clark similarly seeks to shoehorn the complex origins of the Irish act into the problematic categories of 'Foucauldian govermentalism' and 'colonial modernity'.[18]

In contrast to these theoretically-driven approaches, most modern historical surveys of British–Irish relations in the nineteenth century opt to follow McDowell in treating the 1838 measure as the conventional transfer of a deeply-flawed English institution to a country to which it was wholly unsuited – in essence echoing Nassau Senior in his depiction of it as an example of unthinking anglicization. This interpretation relies too uncritically on George Nicholls' own (self-serving) assertion that 'the Irish Poor Law was in its origin no more than a branch or offshoot of the English law', and on George O'Brien's oversimplistic but influential claim that the poor law was carried at the behest of English public opinion and in the face of universal Irish opposition.[19] The accepted narrative lauds the 1836 Whately Commission report into Irish poverty as offering an imaginative and innovative alternative menu of ameliorative measures, which was suppressed by the Whig ministry because it 'cut across British assumptions and interests'. The (indisputable) failure of the poor law during the Great Famine, and its utilization in the late 1840s as the agent of a putative capitalist social revolution in the countryside, is read backwards to condemn the 1838 act as a counter-productive distraction from

17 Frederick W. Powell, *The Politics of Irish Social Policy 1600–1990* (Lampeter, 1992).

18 Anna Clark, 'Wild workhouse girls and the liberal imperial state in mid-nineteenth century Ireland', *Journal of Social History*, 39 (2005), pp. 389–410.

19 R. B. McDowell, *Public Opinion and Government Policy in Ireland, 1801–46* (London, 1952), pp. 192–3; George Nicholls, *A History of the Irish Poor Law* (London, 1856), p. v; George O'Brien, *An Economic History of Ireland from the Union to the Famine* (London, 1921), pp. 173–4.

the radical agrarian reforms that alone might have prevented disaster.[20] While perhaps emotionally satisfying, this reading bears a problematic relationship to the evidence, fails to interrogate what precisely were the objectives and underlying assumptions of Richard Whately and his colleagues, or how 'British interests' were conceptualized (and debated) in the 1830s, and ignores the place of the poor law initiative in the wider Irish policy strategy of the 1835–41 administration. Rather than a straightforward colonial imposition, the motivation behind the 1838 act, for all its flaws and limitations in practice, might better be read as the product of a negotiation between reformist British ministers and significant sections of Irish public opinion, and as part of what was anticipated as being a larger strategy of economic development paralleling the administrative and political reforms of the later 1830s. The idea of a poor law for Ireland was intimately related to the concepts of welfare entitlement and social citizenship, similar to, albeit in a radically different political context, the traditional association of these themes with the poor laws of England explored by Lynn Hollen Lees.[21] While the post-1838 Irish system fell far short of the aspirations of many of its advocates – for reasons of contingency as well as policy – any assessment of its significance or evaluation of its 'success' or 'failure' needs to be located within these wider interpretive frameworks. Close attention to the political as well as the administrative archives is also necessary in plotting the patterns of motivation and response in the making of poor-law policy and the public reactions to policy initiatives.[22]

The crisis of poverty in Ireland that both attracted the attention and repelled the sensibilities of de Beaumont and de Tocqueville in 1835 was neither new nor unprecedented. 'Poverty' was a characteristic long associated

20 Oliver MacDonagh, 'The economy and society, 1830–45', in W. E. Vaughan (ed.), *A New History of Ireland, v: Ireland under the Union, i, 1801–70* (Oxford, 1989), pp. 225–8. A similar version, albeit with greater nuance in treating the O'Connellite and government positions, can be found in Angus Macintyre, *The Liberator: Daniel O'Connell and the Irish Party, 1830–47* (London, 1965), pp. 201–26.

21 Lees, *Solidarities of Strangers*, pp. 11–12.

22 Several essays by Gerard O'Brien offer by far the most comprehensive survey of the implementation of the Irish poor law from 1838, but lack a persuasive political context and come to rather sweeping conclusions regarding the 'failure' of the measure: Gerard O'Brien, 'The establishment of poor-law unions in Ireland, 1838–43', *Irish Historical Studies*, 23 (1982), pp. 97–120; 'Workhouse management in pre-Famine Ireland', *Proceedings of the Royal Irish Academy*, 86C (1986), pp. 113–34; 'A question of attitude: responses to the new poor law in Ireland and Scotland', in Rosalind Mitchison and Peter Roebuck (eds), *Economy and Society in Scotland and Ireland 1500–1939* (Edinburgh, 1988), pp. 160–70.

with Ireland in the eyes of overseas observers, most especially those from the colonial power, and which had long been employed to signify that country's inherent barbarism and hence to justify its conquest, plantation and subordination. By the early nineteenth century, however, Irish poverty was increasingly seen (especially by liberals) as both remediable and a legacy of past misgovernment or neglect by Britain and its Anglo-Irish proxies. Such criticisms came easily to even otherwise anglophile continental travellers, but were also increasingly attractive to British critics of erstwhile 'aristocratic', 'corrupt' or 'illiberal' modes of governance, and allowed for potential common ground with Irish reformers of various stamps, including many repealers. The communications revolution of the early nineteenth century enhanced this awareness of Irish poverty in several ways – by rendering travel easier for both the social commentator and the migrant labourer, and by promoting an ever more widely-read print media. The 'condition of England question' so prominent in British public consciousness after 1815, itself part of a wider European reaction to the social challenges thrown up by a new urban-industrial environment, could not be isolated from the 'condition of Ireland question' once that country began to export its impoverished migrants in droves to the neighbouring island in the following decade.

In seeking explanations and answers for the specific nature of Ireland's 'crisis of poverty', Irish, British and overseas commentators were drawn to delineate and theorize on the country's 'social constitution' and draw contrasts with that of other societies. Explanations of Irish 'backwardness' grounded on its religious or racial difference, on its political subordination, or on the deviant characteristics of its agrarian structures were long established, but from 1815 were increasingly joined by debate on the consequences of its lack of provision for poor relief. For some commentators the root of its socio-economic malaise, for others the one glimmer of hope amid the encircling Malthusian gloom, the absence of a poor law in Ireland came to be a focus of developmental as well as humanitarian controversy in these decades.

What welfare provision existed for the poor of Ireland before 1838? The agreed absence of a national legislative framework for poor relief in Ireland, on the model of the English Poor Law Act of 1601, was the key to the debates of the late 1820s and 1830s, being defended by the detractors, and denounced by the supporters of such an institution. This did not mean that Ireland was wholly without an 'old poor law' of a more disparate and diverse character. David Dickson has made the case that the accumulated melange of vagrancy acts, voluntary institutions (often established with parliamentary encouragement), and parochial collections for poor relief undertaken by the established Church, amounted to something of the sort for at least a portion of the island from the later seventeenth century.[23] Rosalind Mitchison adds that while Scotland may have had a formal poor law on the statute book from 1579, in practice this too was voluntarist and 'permissive', making provision dependent on local circumstances, and hence that Scotland shared a similar experience to Ireland for most of the eighteenth century at least.[24] This may be true, although both the anglicization of Scottish poor law practice denounced by Thomas Chalmers in the 1810s–20s, and the near-collapse of many of the older Irish institutions under the pressure of population growth, advancing immiseration, and greater sectarian tensions from the 1790s, problematizes the comparison for the early nineteenth century. Annual charity sermons, parochial relief, the badging of 'deserving' paupers and clerical oversight of alms-giving may indeed have been significant in the larger boroughs and in east Ulster (where Dickson has identified Scottish alongside English modes of relief in operation) in the eighteenth century, but these appear to have become severely attenuated, if not wholly extinct, by the 1820s–30s.[25] A study of the 'poor books' of St Mark's parish in Dublin for 1772–1820 indicates that the parochial funds raised by charity sermons and other levies increased from the 1770s to 1800s, before falling away in later years. These alms went disproportionately (but not exclusively) to Protestant parishioners.[26] In 1825 an Ulster resident noted that to become truly 'like Scotland', a series of reforms were needed, including a 'system of poor laws' based on the 43rd Elizabeth of England to 'annihilate the humiliating spectacle of swarms of beggars' that so afflicted even that relatively prosperous province.[27]

23 David Dickson, 'In search of the old Irish poor law', in Mitchison and Roebuck (eds), *Economy and Society*, pp. 149–59.

24 Rosalind Mitchison, 'Permissive poor laws: the Irish and Scottish systems considered together', in S. J. Connolly *et al.* (eds), *Conflict, Identity and Economic Development in Ireland and Scotland 1600–1939* (Edinburgh, 1995), pp. 161–71.

25 One parish in which an elaborate parochial relief system, involving 'visitations' of the poor by the resident gentry and the provision of employment in a parochial 'workroom', survived into the 1830s was Dalgany, Co. Wicklow: see Rev. W. Cleaver, 'Plan for benefiting the poor pursued in the parish of Dalgany', *Royal Commission for inquiring into the Condition of the Poorer Classes in Ireland [Poor Inquiry Commission]: Appendix C, Part ii, Addenda*, PP 1836 [35], xxx.35, pp. 40e–43e.

26 Ruth Lavelle and Paul Huggard, 'The parish poor of St Mark's', in David Dickson (ed.), *The Gorgeous Mask: Dublin 1700–1850* (Dublin, 1987), pp. 86–97.

27 Anon., 'Remarks on some of the evils of Ireland, and their removal', *The Pamphleteer*, 25 (1825), pp. 141–59. For the case that the Scottish poor law operated similarly to that of England by the later 1820s, see George Strickland, *A Discourse on the Poor Laws of England and Scotland, on the State of the Poor of Ireland and on Emigration* (London, 1827), pp. 57–66.

Places outside the older urban centres were only sporadically covered by old or new forms of charity. Writing to the poor inquiry in 1833 on behalf of the Sisters of Charity at Sandymount – a relatively prosperous district then on the edges of Dublin – Mary Aikenhead observed that 'there are no public establishments in this populous district for the relief of the poor', and that the small charitable means of her convent were swamped by the extent of local distress.[28] A number of historians have documented the emergence in early nineteenth-century Ireland of an enthusiastic and predominantly female-led philanthropic drive to address the problem of poverty of women and children.[29] Aikenhead's comments serve as a reminder not only of the serious resource constraints that operated on such agencies in the face of the scale of pre-Famine destitution, but that active philanthropists did not necessarily regard some form of state intervention as incompatible with their own mission.

The problem of policing the perceived hordes of 'idle poor', as well as a desire to facilitate parochial initiatives for the relief of the 'deserving poor', led to a number of abortive legislative initiatives in sixteenth- and seventeenth-century Ireland. As Patrick Fitzgerald has observed in his survey of early-modern provision, each met concerted resistance to any form of compulsion from the landed classes, who preferred to blame poverty on English mercantilism and native idleness.[30] It was not until 1703 that the Irish parliament finally endorsed (and partly funded) a municipal workhouse for Dublin. Initially intended both to incarcerate mendicants and to house the virtuous 'parish poor' of the city, it was rapidly overwhelmed by the growing scale of need in Dublin and by the influx of 'strange' paupers from the surrounding counties propelled by the famines and dislocations of the early eighteenth century; it had evolved by 1750 into a hospital for the reception of foundling children, and was specifically redesignated as such in 1772.[31]

28 Mary Aikenhead to the Poor Inquiry Commissioners, 30 Dec. 1833, *Poor Inquiry Commission [PIC]: Appendix C, Part ii*, pp. 25e–26e.

29 Maria Luddy, *Women and Philanthropy in Nineteenth-Century Irel*and (Cambridge, 1995); Margaret H. Preston, *Charitable Words: Women, Philanthropy, and the Language of Charity in Nineteenth-Century Dublin* (Westport, CT, 2004).

30 In 1640 a bill for a compulsory parochial provision was introduced into the Irish parliament, but never enacted: Patrick Fitzgerald, 'Poverty and vagrancy in early-modern Ireland' (unpublished PhD thesis, Queen's University of Belfast, 1994).

31 Until at least the late 1760s the discourse of municipal poor relief in Dublin appears to have been dominated by the themes of social control and the threat of vagrancy to public order and health: Joseph O'Carroll, 'Contemporary attitudes towards the homeless poor 1725–1775', in Dickson (ed.), *Gorgeous Mask*, pp. 64–85.

Cork followed Dublin in securing legislation to establish a 'workhouse ... for employing and maintaining the poor, punishing vagabonds, and providing for and educating foundling children' in 1735; it was financed from the proceeds of a coal tax, but also had become solely a foundling hospital by the end of the century.[32] In 1757 the developing commercial town of Belfast introduced its own municipal poor law as a response to food rioting during the subsistence crisis of that year, the corporation initially levying a tax on householders to fund outdoor relief, before opening its own poorhouse in 1774, funded by a local lottery and later by the grant of a monopoly over water rates.[33] This was emulated in the provision of municipal institutions by other Ulster towns such as Lisburn and Coleraine. Local pride in the efficacy and local control of this system made these areas reluctant to accept its supersession by a national relief framework, although there were demands for greater self-assessment powers along Scottish lines.[34] The great bulk of the country's population remained untouched by these urban initiatives.

After a campaign led by Rev. Richard Woodward from the later 1760s, an act of the Irish parliament in 1772 permitted (but did not compel) county grand juries to make grants-in-aid for county houses of industry to relieve the 'helpless poor'. Simultaneous attempts to revive the badging of 'legitimate' beggars (i.e. those resident in their localities for a year and certified as 'helpless') were of limited success, and new houses of industry were established in only six counties as well as the city of Dublin. The house of industry in the capital had become entirely dependent on parliamentary grants by the late 1770s, which rose to an annual peak of £49,000 in 1814, partly due to its recognition (along with its associated hospitals) as a 'national' rather than simply a municipal establishment.[35] The provincial houses of industry did not share in this largesse. While these played an important role in providing local relief during the subsistence crisis of 1783–84, they were always seriously under-funded and over-stretched, and even the Dublin house had been reduced by 1800 to serving principally as a refuge for the aged and sick, and lunatics and orphans.[36]

32 Nicholls, *Irish Poor Law*, pp. 42–5; *Return of Number of Beggars, Vagrants and Foundlings relieved in Cork, Waterford, and Limerick*, PP 1831–32 (565), xl, p. 2.

33 Strain, *Belfast and its Charitable Society*.

34 [John Macausland], *A Letter to the Right Hon. Lord Goderich, on the Deplorable Condition of the Helpless Poor in Ireland, with a Plan of Relief, as at Present partly in operation in several Districts of the Province of Ulster* (Dublin, 1827).

35 Nicholls, *Irish Poor Law*, p. 84. For Woodward, see below, pp. 21–3.

36 Dickson, 'In search of the old Irish poor law', pp. 154–6; R. B. McDowell, *The Irish Administration, 1801–1914* (London, 1964), pp. 169–70.

The epidemic of distress that broke out in the wake of 1815, caused by traumatic economic dislocation accompanied by the abrupt demobilization of tens of thousands of servicemen, called forth a renewed voluntarist response, alongside the *ad hoc* government efforts to stave off famine in 1817 and 1822. Mendicity associations were established in Dublin and other provincial centres from 1817, now with the aim of giving indoor (daytime) employment to the destitute. Public subscriptions for these were sought on the grounds that the structured and disciplined charity provided at these mendicity institutions would remove beggary from the streets, provide a labour test to determine real need, and hence allow a reduction in the total amount of alms doled out privately.[37] The concept of 'less eligibility' was thus not unknown in Ireland before 1838, as the Poor Law Commissioner George Nicholls was later to point out.

The voluntary mendicity institutions initially attracted the patronage of the civic and religious elites in their respective towns, and evolved active voluntary administrations to investigate the conditions of the poor, collect subscriptions, and supervise the institutions' staff. As non-proselytizing establishments they received some Catholic as well as Protestant support. Crucially, however, despite some public lobbying, the Dublin institution failed to gain any legal powers to punish and suppress mendicancy, mainly due to fear that this must be followed by the introduction of compulsory poor-rates, then regarded as politically impossible. The double consequence was that the mendicity institution in Dublin had no power to compel beggars to enter its house, and that it was constantly dependent on the fluctuating subscriptions of the city's public. The Dublin body was financially embarrassed right from its inception, and within three months of opening in summer 1818 the committee was obliged to take the desperate step of parading its paupers through the city's streets in order to shame the citizenry into payment. This spectacle became part of an established pattern in the following years; while the threat of a poor law measure in 1836–38 may have further reduced contributions, it certainly did not initiate the problems of the capital's leading voluntary relief institution. 'The Mendicity' came perilously close to bankruptcy on several occasions (especially in 1831).[38] Dublin and the other major towns had a plethora of other charitable bodies, of varying

37 Woods, *Dublin Outsiders*, pp. 10–11.

38 *Ibid.*, pp. 16–17, 21, 74–109. For the abortive case made for granting coercive powers against vagrants, see Anon., *Arguments in Proof of the Necessity and Practicability of Suppressing Street Beggary in the City of Dublin* (Dublin, 1817).

degrees of effectiveness, such as the Sick and Indigent Roomkeeper's Society, and a number of charitable loan societies.[39]

The one area in which pre-1838 Ireland had a relatively well-developed welfare infrastructure for its time was in public health. In response to growing fears of epidemic disease (which could attack the rich as well as the poor), as well as a developing consciousness that incapacitating illness was predominantly a result of ill-fortune rather than providential retribution, a network of medical charities was created through a series of legislative enactments and local initiatives. A number of 'voluntary hospitals' providing gratuitous medical assistance to the poor were founded in Dublin, Cork, Limerick and Belfast in the wake of the setting up of the Dublin Charitable Infirmary in 1718. These were mostly reliant on voluntary philanthropy for their formation and maintenance, and imbued with a strong Anglican bias.[40] In 1765 parliament enacted that each county should have a general infirmary; where established, these hospitals offered limited treatment, of highly varying standards, to the poor in the district adjacent to the county town. They were supported in part by charitable subscriptions, and, increasingly, by a series of parliamentary and county grand jury grants.[41] A larger number of dispensaries, offering out-patient assistance and medicines to the poor, were established from 1782, initially by private subscription in the urban centres, and later also in the rural areas after an 1805 act allowing them to be grant-aided by the grand juries. Some 660 dispensaries were in operation across the county by the 1840s.[42] Finally, fever hospitals were founded sporadically by local initiative in the later eighteenth century and increased in number under the 1807 and 1818 fever acts, which empowered grand juries to erect them and assist in their maintenance; these were largely restricted to Leinster and Munster. The Dublin Castle administration had powers to appoint district boards of health during epidemics, and established a national board in 1832 on the arrival of the cholera pandemic, but this mode of direct intervention was *ad hoc* and short-lived, as the government preferred to work through advice and encouragement to local bodies.[43]

39 Anon., *Resolutions of the Committee for managing the Charitable Fund, for the Relief of the Industrious Poor, in St George's Parish* (Dublin, 1814); Deirdre Lindsay, 'The Sick and Indigent Roomkeepers' Society', in Dickson (ed.), *Gorgeous Mask*, pp. 132–56.

40 Geary, *Medicine*, pp. 2–3, 13–39. Three Dublin hospitals received annual parliamentary grants from 1765, rising to seven by 1828: McDowell, *Irish Administration*, pp. 166, 171.

41 Geary, *Medicine*, pp. 40–53.

42 McDowell, *Irish Administration*, p. 166.

43 *Ibid.*, pp. 167–8; Geary, *Medicine*, pp. 54–92.

The first state asylum for the insane in Ireland was established at Cork in 1788, with an additional institution in Dublin opened in 1815. District asylums for the poor were provided for under an act of 1817 which had been promoted by the Irish Whigs Sir John Newport and Thomas Spring Rice, but construction of these was slow before the 1830s, as initiative rested again with the county grand juries.[44]

While impressive on paper, and in comparison to some other European societies, the Irish medical charities were unevenly distributed, poorly funded, and confusingly organized.[45] The idea advanced by some commentators that they offered an acceptable alternative to a poor law was highly controversial. While the dispensaries and hospitals were fairly effective in providing a basic provision of medical assistance to the poor (at least in certain districts), the restriction of aid to medicine, where food and shelter might have been more effective in preventing illness, frustrated some practitioners. The physician to the Roscrea, Co. Tipperary, dispensary and fever hospital complained in 1828 that his work was severely hampered by the absence of a 'Mendicity Association . . . to afford the starving population wholesome food, clean straw beds, and quick-lime for whitewashing cabins to free them from contagion'.[46]

In most of Ireland, the main source of relief for the destitute was the traditional charity of the poor themselves. This was widely acknowledged by observers, but closer examination suggests that there were overlapping but distinct cultures of mendicancy in pre-Famine Ireland and a range of popular opinions about the endemic practice of begging. Perceptions of mendicancy, as Larry Geary notes, were shaped by the variables of class, religion, gender and domicile; but most rural dwellers drew a line between the casual or occasional beggars forced into the practice by short-term distress or life circumstances, and the professional beggars or 'boccoughs' who were associated with imposture and dissolute behaviour.[47] Many of the former were women and children, the widows or families of labouring men who had migrated in search of harvest employment in the summer or were unemployed, and who sought to support themselves by seeking alms in kind, usually in a neighbouring

44 Joseph Robins, *Fools and Mad: A History of the Insane in Ireland* (Dublin, 1986), pp. 60–74.

45 The inadequacies and abuses of the medical charities were identified by the medical inquiry under the Whately Commission, *PIC: Appendix B*, PP 1835 (369), xxxii, part ii.

46 William Kingsley, *The Annual Medical Report of the Roscrea Fever Hospital and Dispensary, for the year 1827* (Roscrea, 1828).

47 Laurence M. Geary, '"The whole country was in motion": mendicancy and vagrancy in pre-famine Ireland', in Jacqueline Hill and Colm Lennon (eds), *Luxury and Austerity* (Dublin, 1999), pp. 121–36.

rather than their own district of residence (to minimize the public shame of begging). Customary and religious motivations lay behind the traditional generosity of the peasantry to these members of 'God's poor', although some degree of social stigma was always associated with casual mendicancy, and some of the poor chose hunger rather than endure the shame of begging.[48] It was estimated in 1830 that the farming classes donated up to a million pounds' worth of potatoes annually to the poor as alms.[49]

The 'professional' mendicancy undertaken by vagrants was, in contrast, usually regarded more negatively by the rural poor themselves, and was more commonly seen at fairs and in urban areas. Niall Ó Ciosain's survey of the evidence given to the Poor Inquiry Commission indicates that countrypeople drew sharp distinctions between the 'deserving' and 'undeserving' beggars determined by the above categories, suggesting that (while not identical), the difference between elite and popular views of mendicancy was less wide than is sometimes assumed. This distinction appears in particular to have inflected the opinions of the Catholic clergy in constructing their case for state intervention.[50] For their part, 'professional' mendicants evolved their own distinct culture and 'moral economy', and proved remarkably resilient in the face of the state's attempts to control their activities in the eighteenth and nineteenth centuries.[51]

Traditional forms of charity were always to some degree conditional and came under growing strain in the adverse economic conditions following 1815. Regional famines and the fever epidemics of 1817–19, 1822 and 1831 not only greatly increased the numbers of 'casual mendicants' rendered destitute by crop failure and unemployment, but slashed the small local surpluses available for relief in kind and created a universal terror of the fever carried by vagrants. This led to attempts to curb vagrancy and to a temporary drying up of alms in the affected areas, and threw the burden of relief much more

48 See, for example, the evidence of the Widow Kilboy and others, Ballina, in [PIC], *Selection of Parochial Examinations relative to the Destitute Classes in Ireland* (Dublin, 1835), pp. 104–6.

49 *First Report of the Select Committee on the State of the Poor in Ireland*, PP 1830 (589), vii.278, p. 46.

50 Niall Ó Ciosain, 'Boccoughs and God's poor: the deserving and undeserving poor in Irish popular culture', in Tadgh Foley and Sean Ryder (eds), *Ideology and Ireland in the Nineteenth Century* (Dublin, 1998), pp. 93–9. For Bishop James Doyle's sharp distinction between these classes of beggars, see below, p. 70.

51 Gerard O'Brien, 'Cosherers, wanderers and vagabonds: the treatment of the poor and insane in Ireland', *Saothar: Journal of the Irish Labour History Society*, 13 (1988), pp. 45–8.

squarely onto the government.[52] Even in 'non-crisis' seasons the evidence suggests that growing disparities of wealth in the countryside left more cottier and conacre-labourer families on the verge of destitution while the incomes and consumption patterns of other portions of the farming community improved.[53] Those dependent on an 'economy of makeshifts' for survival found themselves increasingly dependent on exploitative credit relationships with local money-lenders ('gombeen men') or stronger farmers for the food they needed to survive.[54] Various loan funds did offer 'microcredit' on better terms to small farmers, but these were less often available to the poorest families, and (according to their advocates) had insufficient resources to meet the growing demands upon them.[55]

At the same time, growing population, the rapid collapse of the proto-industrial textile sector in much of the country in the 1820s, and the accelerating pace of land clearance for pasture, created new classes of paupers who were neither 'casual' nor 'professional' but structural, and whose expanding numbers were only partially offset by increased emigration.[56] Traditional social relationships and the patterns of relief associated with them came under growing pressure in the countryside, at the same time as Irish elites and British opinion were obliged to confront the problem due to the financial and political costs of famine relief and increasingly alarmist reactions to Irish migration to Great Britain.

The consequence of this was a widespread sense by the later 1820s in both Ireland and Britain that the Irish crisis was fundamentally one of poverty, and that radical remedies could no longer be postponed. The failure of Catholic emancipation in 1829 to stem social or political unrest, the subsequent outbreak of a rural 'tithe war', and the eruption of what was to many in Britain the incomprehensible campaign for the repeal of the Union in 1830, strengthened the case that the underlying socio-economic issues must be addressed if political and religious agitation was to be tackled successfully. Both moral and

52 Geary, 'The whole country', p. 126.

53 Joel Mokyr and Cormac Ó Gráda, 'Poor and getting poorer? Living standards in Ireland before the famine', *Economic History Review*, 37 (1988), pp. 209–35.

54 For resentment of this by labourers, see for example, [PIC], *Selection of Parochial Examinations*, pp. 235, 259.

55 Aidan Hollis and Arthur Sweetman, 'Microcredit in prefamine Ireland', *Explorations in Economic History*, 35 (1998), pp. 347–80. One supporter proposed the state take responsibility for and finance the microcredit sector as an alternative to a poor law: Matthew Barrington, *An Address to the Inhabitants of Limerick, on the Opening of the Mont De Piété* (Dublin, 1836).

56 Timothy P. O'Neill, 'Poverty in Ireland 1815–45', *Folk Life*, 11 (1973), pp. 22–33.

practical considerations compelled the formulation of some novel response to the problem. In this context the trope of Ireland's singularity in lacking a coherent national system for the relief of poverty became almost universal. One Irish pamphleteer in 1830 lamented his country's deviation from what he believed to be universal norms of social responsibility:

> Look also to China . . . in that wise country, Poor-Laws are in as active operation as they ever were in England; for there it is not a mere moral precept to protect the poor, but an absolute law of the land that the poor should be taken care of; and shame, and fie for shame! in this Christian country that there is no protection for the poor, that they should be allowed to starve, pine and rot; when in the very country of the Ottomans, ay! the very 'country of dogs,' there is not a village without its caravansary, where Turk, Jew, ay! and Atheist, black man and white man, Christian and Pagan, without the remotest inquiry, are provided with an asylum – where they are not only fed but housed besides. Quere? I ask, have not at all times, and in the present time, Poor-laws been in existence, even in this country, namely, the poor laws of the human heart?[57]

The dilemma to be resolved was what form of poor laws should or could be introduced for a country in so distressed a condition as Ireland.

57 Anon., *A Letter to the Right Hon. the Lord Mayor of Dublin, proposing an Wholesome and Improved System of Poor-Laws for Ireland* (Dublin, 1830), p. 10.

2

Positions stated: the cases for and against an Irish poor law, *c.*1737–1833

The controversy over the desirability of an Irish poor law developed momentum in the years of economic hardship after the end of the French wars in 1815. The subject attracted particular interest in both Ireland and Britain during the crisis years of 1816–17, 1822–23, 1826–27 and 1830–32. However, the roots of the case made for a poor law in Ireland lay much further back, and the language and preoccupations of its eighteenth-century advocates and detractors continued to be echoed into the following century. This chapter considers the genealogies of the campaigns for an Irish poor law, as manifested in the variant traditions of paternalist Anglicanism, liberal Catholicism, Irish radicalism, English meliorism and labour protectionism. It also reviews the contrary arguments which these campaigns provoked among members of the Irish and British elites, and the crucial role played by the discourse of political economy in both countries in supporting this opposition before the mid-1830s.

Swift, Woodward and the Anglican case

As David Dickson has noted, one influential eighteenth-century group that expressed an interest, albeit partial and intermittent, in improving the provision for the poor of Ireland, was the clergy of the established Church.[1] The Anglican clergy were traditionally expected to be involved in raising and distributing parochial funds for the local poor, and to participate on the governing bodies of the various voluntary relief institutions that had emerged from the later seventeenth century. However, the ideal of universal parochial relief under the aegis of the Church establishment was rarely realized in reality in a society in which the Anglican community outside the major urban centres and east Ulster was frequently small and isolated, and in which clerical non-residence was a recurrent problem. Even where parochial or municipal relief

1 Dickson, 'In search of the old Irish poor law', p. 157.

institutions did operate with some coherence (as to some extent was the case in Dublin), their narrow scope, and the absence of effective settlement regulation, posed recurrent problems. It was these discrepancies that drew Jonathan Swift, then dean of St Patrick's Cathedral in Dublin, into print on the subject of the regulation of the poor in 1737. His principal motivation on this occasion was defensive and retributive. The Dublin poor-house and other forms of parochial relief in the city were, he thundered, rapidly becoming overwhelmed by the influx of hordes of 'foreign beggars' – chiefly from other Irish parishes, but also, he alleged, shipped over from England. The only suitable remedy was to revive and enforce the ancient practice of 'badging' the native paupers, and to forcibly expel the others, 'after the practice in England, send[ing] them from one parish to another, until they reach their own homes'. Whether from ignorance or wishful thinking, Swift believed such a process of forcible return to a place of settlement to be legally justified, as '[b]y the old laws of England still in force, and I presume by those of Ireland, every parish is bound to maintain its own poor.'[2] This was not the case, and Swift's pamphlet appears more an angry protest against the 'country 'squires' exporting their pauper colonies to the capital, and the 'vicious race' of sturdy beggars he perceived around him, than a sustained argument for a comprehensive national relief system.

Nevertheless, the writings of Swift and his contemporary Bishop George Berkeley went some way towards identifying the Catholic as well as Protestant poor as part of a civic (if not political) community of Ireland, and drawing attention towards the relief provisions that did or should exist for them. Berkeley, bishop of Cloyne from 1734, developed his thinking on the socio-economic state and prospects of Ireland in *The Querist* (1735–37), motivated, he asserted in the preface, by a desire to 'to feed the hungry and clothe the naked, by promoting an honest industry'.[3] Berkeley's principal concern was to establish the moral responsibility of the ruling classes of Ireland for the employment of the currently 'indolent and supine' population and for the development of the Irish economy. His concerns were multiple, but a number of the queries indicated a clear, if rather unfocused, interest in the principles of a poor law; query 370 asked, rhetorically, '[w]hether it would be a great hardship if every parish were obliged to find work for their poor?', this being rapidly followed by implicit praise of the beneficial operation of the Dutch workhouses. Would it, he continued, 'be a hardship on people destitute of all

2 Jonathan Swift, 'A proposal for giving badges to the beggars in all the parishes of Dublin', in Temple Scott (ed.), *The Prose Works of Jonathan Swift* (12 vols, 1897–1908), vii, p. 328.

3 George Berkeley, *The Querist* (2nd edn, London, 1750), 'advertisement'.

things, if the public furnished them with necessaries which they should be obliged to earn by their labour?' (even if this required temporary servitude on the part of the 'study beggar').[4] The latter aside reflected contemporary preoccupations with disciplining the 'idle' able-bodied pauper.

It was, however, a successor of Berkeley in the see of Cloyne who would make a case for an Irish poor law in a more coherent and systematic form. Richard Woodward, an Oxford-educated Englishman, came to Ireland as dean of Clogher in 1764, subsequently receiving preferment to the chancellorship of St Patrick's Cathedral, Dublin, in 1772, and to the bishopric of Cloyne in 1781. Evidently appalled by the misery he witnessed in his adopted country (and by the indifference of the establishment towards it), Woodward advocated a modified form of England's relief institutions for Ireland. In 1766 he published, under the auspices of the Dublin Society, a plan for the construction of county workhouses to house the sick and aged and employ vagrant beggars, to be funded by taxation and placed under the direction of the grand juries.[5] Two years later he expanded his argument to incorporate a case for such a compulsory provision grounded on natural rights as well as expediency. In making this case, Woodward was now careful to distinguish the deserving poor, who 'though willing to work, cannot subsist through labour', from the 'those idle vagrants who are a pest to society'.[6] The plight of the former was not, he insisted, self-induced, but the product of systematic oppression by the landed classes of the country; the good example of a few exceptional proprietors could not compensate for the general rule of neglect or exploitation. Voluntarist parochial charity he found to be, in most places, 'too trivial to be worth mentioning', and by no means proportionate to the needs of the country. Yet the reciprocal bonds of society required an equitable recognition of the right of the poor to relief:

> Every friend to the common rights of mankind will readily admit, that no political system can be wisely and equitably constructed, without giving such attention to the welfare of every class of its members, as will render their situation in that society preferable to what is called . . . a state of nature. Now as every citizen (who has not forfeited his right by civil guilt) hath this claim on the community to which he belongs, some writers on natural law have had recourse to the idea of a certain compact, as the origin of government; which though it never fully took place, serveth well to illustrate the right inherent in every man

4 *Ibid.*, pp. 39–40.

5 [Richard Woodward], *A Scheme for Establishing County Poor-Houses in the Kingdom of Ireland* (Dublin, 1766); Dickson, 'In search of the old Irish poor law', p. 152.

6 Richard Woodward, *An Argument in Support of the Right of the Poor in the Kingdom of Ireland to a National Provision* (Dublin, 1768), p. 11.

> to subsistence and protection, in return for his services to the publick, and submission to its laws.[7]

If, as Woodward admitted, the idea of the social contract was a fiction, it was nevertheless a useful one; the rich who ruled in all societies through laws serving their own interests could not legitimately subordinate the poor without the *quid pro quo* of admitting their right to a legal subsistence at public expense.

Woodward's Irish initiative coincided with a brief reformist moment in attitudes towards the poor, and led to a 1772 Irish statute which combined enforcement of the badging the mendicant poor (which had so preoccupied Swift) with the introduction of permissive powers for local authorities to establish houses of industry funded from subscriptions and grants. While this was welcomed, it fell well short of Woodward's aspirations, and the 'moral panic' over increased poor-law expenditure in England in 1775–85 appears to have had a negative impact on Irish elites.[8] Woodward responded with another pamphlet criticizing the voluntarist limitations of the 1772 legislation and defending the old English model in principle against its critics.[9] The formation of the Dublin house of industry under the 1772 act had marked, Woodward argued, a major step forward towards relieving the needy and suppressing idle vagrancy, but it continued to be hampered by irregular charitable funding. The successful experiment in Dublin had demonstrated both the efficiency and deterrent effect of the system, but still the great majority of county grand juries refused to imitate it, citing the critique of the English law recently published by the Scottish jurist Lord Kames in their defence. Woodward was well aware of the negative associations beginning to attach to the English law, but retorted through the twin strategies of undermining Kames's theoretical reasonings, and emphasizing that his Irish proposals – which would deny a legal right to relief to the poor and would abandon the law of settlement – would evade the specific problems witnessed across the Channel. Ultimately, however, Woodward's case was grounded in enlightenment moral theology. Kames was, he believed, self-evidently wrong in denying the moral truth embodied in a poor law:

> Is the law of nature to be found in chance or in reason, in confusion or in order? Is the Plan of Providence to be traced in cruelty, idleness, misery, and vice, or

7 *Ibid.*, p. 24. For the novelty of this argument in Ireland, see O'Carroll, 'Contemporary attitudes', pp. 64–85.

8 Boyd Hilton, *A Mad, Bad and Dangerous People? England 1783–1846* (Oxford, 2006), p. 593.

9 Richard Woodward, *An Address to the Publick, on the Expediency of a Regular Plan for the Maintenance and Government of the Poor* (Dublin, 1775).

> in benevolence, industry, happiness and in virtue? The law of nature is the law of reason: every benevolent exertion of which is part of the great *Plan of Providence.*[10]

Woodward's pamphlets prefigured many of the arguments that would recur in various formulations through to the 1830s, but interest in his proposals rapidly faded away from the mid-1770s. As bishop of Cloyne he was increasingly distracted by what he perceived to be the threat posed to the Church establishment by Whiteboyism and resurgent Catholicism, and these questions rather than the poor law preoccupied him in his final years. He never had the full support of members of his own denomination in the 1760s–70s, and paternalist Anglican interest in the subject more generally appears to have faded rapidly in the face of the social and political crises that dominated the final decades of the century in Ireland, and the growing antipathy towards poor laws generally in English public discourse. In the context of intense political polarization, literature blaming poverty on the moral failings of the poor appears to have become more widespread.[11]

Woodward's thoughts on the poor law (along with Berkeley's more elliptical queries) were revived for a later generation by William Parker of Passage West, Co. Cork. Parker was an evangelical country gentleman, serial pamphleteer, and leader of an abortive Irish colonization project in the Cape Province in 1820.[12] In 1816 he had advocated, as a rider to a proposed reform of the grand jury system, that the government respond to the escalating social crisis in the countryside by providing a system combining aid and discipline funded from absentee and other taxes.[13]

Searching for theoretical support for his proposals, he appears to have lighted on Woodward's works, and in 1819 published a long annotated commentary on Woodward's *Argument*, augmented with relevant extracts from Berkeley.[14] In rather disjointed fashion, Parker struggled to render the arguments of half a century earlier relevant to the age of Malthus. While he could not deny the salience of the writings of the latter on the evils of early marriage

10 *Ibid.*, pp. 77–8.

11 See R. B. McDowell, *Irish Public Opinion 1750–1800* (London, 1944), pp. 34–5. In 1772 the dean of Armagh countered Woodward with an appeal to the poor to submit passively to the will of Providence and the laws of political economy, *ibid.*, p. 36.

12 William Parker, *Letter from William Parker, to Earl Bathurst* (n.p., [1825]).

13 William Parker, *Observations on the Intended Amendment to the Irish Grand Jury Laws* (Cork, 1816), pp. 138–9.

14 William Parker, *A Plea for the Poor and Industrious. Part the First, the Necessity of a National Provision for the Poor in Ireland* (Cork, 1819).

and overpopulation (and indeed he advocated assisted emigration as a partial remedy), he sought to reconcile this with the moral case made for a compulsory poor law by Woodward. Parker continued to lobby intermittently for an Irish poor law – in 1833 a petition prepared by him was discussed by the London Corporation at the instigation of the city's MP George Grote – but his major contribution may have been in rescuing Woodward's ideas from oblivion.[15] In this he was not entirely unsuccessful – in 1830 the English Tory-radical M. T. Sadler quoted Woodward at length in a speech in support of an Irish poor law, and the prelate's opinions were also endorsed by the commentators Frederick Page and Montgomery Martin.[16] Of course, an awareness of Woodward did not always mean support for his poor-law proposals; the 1822 prospectus of one 'improving' agricultural society – which included both pro- and anti-poor-law figures, and which justified its activities as essential not least because of the absence of poor laws – opted to cite approvingly his more ecumenical *Word to the Wise* rather than his potentially divisive poor law tracts.[17]

A number of other Irish Protestant clergymen carried on, consciously or unconsciously, the tradition associated with Woodward. In 1796 Rev. Michael Sandys of Powerscourt urged Henry Grattan to take up the cause of the labouring poor in Ireland. Although vague as to specific remedies, like Berkeley he praised the relief system of Holland and reiterated the scriptural proofs of the 'divine condemnation of those who grind the faces of the poor'.[18] In 1824 Bishop William Bisset of Raphoe was prepared to offer strong endorsement to a petition from Kilmore in Co. Armagh (signed, he noted, by the Anglican, Catholic and Presbyterian clergy as well as many householders),

15 By 1833 Parker was proposing a national rather than parochial structure of poor relief. His petition praised the support for such a provision evinced by three bishops of Cloyne – Berkeley, Woodward, and the present incumbent, John Brinkley: *The Times*, 7 May 1833.

16 *Hansard's Parliamentary Debates*, 2nd ser., xxiv, 1312–17 [3 June 1830]; Frederick Page, *Observations on the State of the Indigent Poor of Ireland, and the Existing Institutions for their Relief* (London, 1830), pp. 23–4, 42; R. Montgomery Martin, *Poor Laws for Ireland, a Measure of Justice to England; of Humanity to the People of both Islands; and of Self-preservation for the Empire* (London, 1833), pp. 13–14. In 1836 G. C. Lewis, then preparing his tract on Irish disturbances and the poor law, also tried to obtain a copy of Woodward's book, NLW: HCP, C/3685, McCullagh to Lewis, 9 Jan. 1836.

17 Anon., *Society for Improving the Condition and Increasing the Comforts of the Irish Peasantry* (London, 1822).

18 Michael Sandys, *A Letter to the Right Honourable Henry Grattan, on the State of the Labouring Poor in Ireland* (Dublin, 1796).

calling for a permissive act allowing the vestry to make an assessment for the relief of the parish poor. This localized approach fell far short of Woodward's vision – which Bisset thought impracticable – but it did reflect a consciousness that private charity was failing to meet the social needs of rural Ulster, and demonstrated a preference for a 'local option' which became typical of opinion in that province in the following decades.[19]

Outside Ulster something less dependent on local initiative was requisite if the magnitude of the temporal, and to some also the spiritual, crisis was to be addressed. An Irish evangelical layman, who had served as an agent for distributing the proceeds of the London Tavern Committee's relief collections in the west in 1822, warned his audience that such *ad hoc* generosity, while welcome, could never be enough. With landlords either absentee or exploitative, the middle class virtually non-existent, and the peasantry being ground down into paupers, some permanent intervention was essential. The author was vague as to what this might be, suggesting colonization or waste-land reclamation, but appealed to the 'benevolent' English reader through the 'lamentation' of a 'poor Irishman', which was evidently modelled on the rhetoric of the anti-slavery campaign:

> I am a slave of the lowest cast, a slave in mind and body. Look at my person; I am but half fed, and not half clothed; dirty and ragged; my poor wife and numerous children are still more filthy and naked; we lie down together on a bed of straw and heath, with little more to cover us at night, than the rags we wear by day. Look at my cabin; it is a sooty hovel, without chimney or window. My pig, if I am rich enough to have one, is the companion of myself and my family; we sleep under the same roof; we all fare alike. True, I am indolent; but I have no stimulus to exertion; all the fruits of my labour go to the landlord and tax-gatherer; and after my greatest industry, I have not enough to pay my charges. There is nothing left for my own enjoyment; my food is potatoes, and nothing but potatoes; if they are plenty, I can barely live; if they are scarce, I have to lie down and die. I am not treated with kindness. . . . My mind is degraded; I have no light of true knowledge; I am kept in ignorance; I am in the worse bondage; I am a poor heathen, a miserable idolater. I live in a land of liberty and of plenty, of Christian knowledge and virtue; but I am shut out from their blessing; I have them not. O you, who have compassion on the wretched African slave, have pity on me also! Come over and help me!

19 *Hansard*, 2, xi, 1098–9 [10 June 1824]. Embarrassingly, this was closely followed by a counter-petition signed by a number of landholders from the same locality, who claimed that it was 'manifestly false' that the majority had approved of the original paper, and stated that they opposed a poor-rate as an unsupportable burden on farmers: *Journals of the House of Commons* [*JHC*], lxxix (1824), pp. 419, 533.

This appeal to the British evangelical conscience was heartfelt, if unfocused.[20]

A more general argument for compulsion in assistance to the poor was later made by the leading Irish evangelical Rev. Robert Daly, rector of Powerscourt from 1814, and after 1843 the first bishop of the united sees of Cashel, Emly, Waterford, and Lismore.[21] Daly admitted himself in 1829 a convert on the subject of poor laws, and was now convinced that it was a national duty to introduce such a provision; he believed it was essential that landlords be given a direct pecuniary interest in managing their estates to produce the smallest amount of poverty, and that the injurious system of 'sturdy mendicancy' should be replaced by the equitable relief of the deserving poor. This should be the role of the state, not the clergy – whose focus should be on the spiritual rather than the temporal needs of the community – indeed, ministerial neglect of the poor could be construed as a form of national sin.[22] This did not, he believed, preclude simultaneously encouraging the poorer classes to help themselves through provident societies, one of which he established at Powerscourt in the same year.[23]

This evangelical take on the moral duty of the state to the poor was probably shared by Daly's landed patrons. The fifth Viscount Powerscourt and his second wife, Theodosia Anne, presided over an intensely evangelical salon in the 1820s and 1830s, in which Daly played an active part. Their son Richard, the sixth viscount, made an impassioned speech in the Commons in 1838 in defence of the government's poor law bill as embodying the 'fundamental principle of the Christian faith, as a great rule of enlightened policy, the doctrine of charity'.[24] This was, however, a minority view within Irish Protestant evangelicalism. The third Earl of Roden, the younger Powerscourt's father-in-law, took, as we shall see, quite a different view on the question, and many evangelicals appear to have been more preoccupied with proselytism, and to have identified the miseries of the poor with the influence of 'popery'. The confrontational convert Rev. Samuel O'Sullivan, for example, denounced

20 Anon., *Lachrymae Hibernicae, or, The Grievances of the Peasantry of Ireland, especially in the Western Counties* (Dublin, 1822), pp. 22–3.

21 The living of Powerscourt, under the patronage of the Wingfield family, was one of the most influential in the country: Donald Harman Akenson, *The Church of Ireland: Ecclesiastical Reform and Revolution, 1800–1885* (New Haven, CT, 1971), p. 133.

22 Robert Daly, *A Letter to the Editor of the Christian Examiner, on the Subject of a Legal Provision for the Poor of Ireland* (Dublin, 1829).

23 Rev. R. Daly, 'A proposal for an improved plan of benefiting the poor, by inducing them to endeavour to assist themselves', *PIC: Appendix C, Part ii, Addenda*, PP 1836 [35], xxx.35, pp. 39e–40e.

24 *Hansard*, 3, xlii, 690–3 [30 Apr. 1838].

suggestions for a poor law on the English model as merely a 'concession yielded to fierce insubordination, [which] might be accepted only as a means of rendering conspiracy stronger'.[25] His brother Mortimer similarly rejected any measure that might appear a concession of a legal right to relief, while supporting allowing parish vestries to voluntarily assess themselves and proffer both alms and (Protestant) moral guidance to the poor.[26] Proselytizing Bible societies likewise looked to the distribution of tracts and Bibles as the primary mode of eradicating the 'depravity' that underpinned poverty.[27] Woodward's legacy may have survived, but by the 1830s it was as a decidedly minority strand in the social thought and policy of Irish Anglicans.

James Doyle and liberal Catholicism

The central figure on the Catholic side in the campaign for an Irish poor law was Bishop James Doyle of Kildare and Leighlin (who wrote as 'JKL'), the leading liberal-Catholic churchman of his generation. Doyle, who was elevated from the principalship of Carlow College to the bishopric in 1819, was heavily involved in Catholic charitable activities; combating poverty, 'the leprosy which covered Ireland', was the theme of many of his pastoral letters, and he was at the forefront of collecting alms for the poor of both the diocese and western counties in seasons of crisis, and in promoting employment initiatives for those without work. He had participated in the dispensary committee in his native New Ross, and in the operation of both the Sick Poor Institution and a short-lived Mendicity Association at Carlow.[28] It was, at least in part, the evident limitations or outright failure of these voluntarist bodies that led Doyle towards embracing the demand for state provision to meet the needs of the poor. The context lay in his sense of a moral as well as an economic crisis in the early 1820s, which had given rise to what he regarded as the immoral and self-defeating violence of the Ribbonmen and to millennialist popular excitements.[29] While fully committed to the campaigns for

25 [Samuel O'Sullivan], 'How is Ireland to be governed?', *Dublin University Magazine* [*DUM*], 4 (Oct. 1834), p. 362.

26 *Third Report of the Select Committee on the State of the Poor in Ireland*, PP 1830 (665), vii.649, pp. 547–61.

27 Luddy, *Women*, pp. 55–6.

28 Thomas McGrath, *Politics, Interdenominational Relations and Education in the Public Ministry of Bishop James Doyle of Kildare and Leighlin, 1786–1834* (Dublin, 1999), pp. 85–9; Thomas McGrath (ed.), *The Pastoral and Education Letters of Bishop James Doyle of Kildare and Leighlin, 1786–1834* (Dublin, 2004), p. 11.

29 James Doyle, *Pastoral Letter addressed to the Roman Catholic Clergy of the Deanery of Kilcock* (Dublin, 1823).

Catholic emancipation, tithe abolition and the extension of education, Doyle appears to have come to the conclusion that these alone would not curb the social crisis afflicting his country. If the government educated the people without providing for their physical distress, he warned in 1824, they would merely be placing the 'sharpest weapons into the hands of men who, as they learn to read, will also learn to calculate their strength, and to devise . . . schemes of retaliation and revenge'.[30]

By early 1825 Doyle had developed a theoretical justification and a rough plan for an Irish poor law and published this in his *Letters on the State of Ireland*, alongside his critique of the Church establishment and the continuing exclusion of Catholics from political life. His moral case for a welfare measure was grounded in a generally positive analysis of Ireland's economic and demographic structures. Denying that the country was overpopulated relative to its productive potential, he attributed the undeniable evidence of distress to the economic dislocations of the wars and the oppression of the poor by rack-renting landlords and the established Church. These contingencies had rendered Ireland highly vulnerable – should dearth occur, he prophesied, 'famine and pestilence will set in together, and rid us probably of a million'.[31] Only the state, he concluded, possessed the power of agency competent to prevent such a disaster, and it was the duty of the Catholic clergy, as 'advocate[s] of the poor', to 'check the insolence of power, [and] plead the cause of the oppressed' before the government. A practical opportunity to do so came later that year when Doyle was summoned to give evidence before two parliamentary inquiries into the state of Ireland.[32]

Doyle constructed his case for a poor law on a paternalist social model. As God had determined the social body on the model of the family, it followed that its head – the state – had been divinely charged with securing provision for 'such of its members, as by the visitation of God, the ordinary laws of providence, or the working of social institutions, are rendered unable, physically or morally, to provide for themselves', and that this should be operated on paternal as opposed to economic lines.[33] While the poor could not safely be granted a formal legal right to relief, they nevertheless had a moral right to support from their richer neighbours, a right that could not be guaranteed

30 [James Doyle], *Important Letter from Bishop Doyle to – Robertson* (Dublin, [1824]).

31 [James Doyle], *Letters on the State of Ireland: Addressed by J. K. L. to a Friend in Ireland* (Dublin, 1825), p. 114.

32 *Select Committee of House of Lords appointed to inquire into State of Ireland*, PP 1825 (181, 521) ix.1, pp. 223–48, 308–16.

33 Doyle, *Letters*, p. 318.

by the irregular proceeds of voluntary charity. Enforcement of this moral right was not only the common practice of truly civilized societies from antiquity to the present, but reflected the divine law of redistributive social justice. Distressed and underdeveloped Ireland, whose poor had never received recompense for the loss of entitlement consequent on the dissolution of the monasteries (which had possessed a social welfare function in their localities) and the appropriation of the Catholic church's property by the colonizing minority, needed a poor law now more than any other country:

> That in a country so abundant as Ireland there cannot at any time be a dearth of provisions, is almost certain: that by a system of poor's laws these provisions would be prudently and justly distributed, so as to prevent the recurrence of famine in the midst of plenty, is a truth that cannot be contested: that God and Christ, and the nature of society, as well as the circumstances of Ireland, require that some legal provision be made for our poor, seems to me to be also sufficiently obvious.[34]

It is unclear whether Doyle was aware of Woodward, but possible that he was conjoining the latter's moral theology with his own version of social Catholicism. In the wake of such a strong justification for a poor law by divine law and natural right, Doyle's specific proposals appear somewhat limited. Concerned at what he saw as the abuses and legalism of the English poor law, and aware how negatively these were regarded in Ireland, in 1825 he declared a preference for the Scottish model, granting the parish clergy a leading role in parochial administration and in the 'testing' of applicants, and seeking voluntary contributions in the first instance (although resorting, as he believed generally likely, to compulsory assessment where this was found to be necessary). This model would also restrict the deserving objects of relief to the 'impotent' poor who did not 'form a class having a political place in the community'.[35]

Doyle's understanding of the 'Scottish model' was at odds both with the reality in Scotland and its construction by Scotland's leading theorist Thomas Chalmers, and was adopted here for tactical rather than ideological reasons. Doyle clearly wanted the poor law to play, alongside this humane purpose, another, more dynamic role. If the poor law was, as he projected, to give the Irish people 'a new and settled character', to force the proprietor and occupier to give employment to the people and thus stimulate production, and to save the country from famine, its practical scope would have to be considerably greater than the measure sketched out in the *Letters*. These ambiguities in

34 *Ibid.*, pp. 337–8.
35 *Ibid.*, p. 322.

Doyle's texts allowed his readers to interpret him in quite different ways. He himself was obliged to clarify what he intended, and how a rights-based theory could be reconciled with a restricted set of proposals, when the subject of an Irish poor law (and the suitability of the Scottish and English models for emulation) came under more intense public scrutiny in 1830–31.[36]

Doyle's widely-read *Letters*, and subsequent elaboration of his opinions, appear to have had a significant impact on the social as well as the political thinking of much of the Catholic clergy in Ireland, and to have moved the moral case for a poor law towards the forefront of their concerns. It was almost certainly Doyle who persuaded twenty-three of his fellow bishops in synod to agree to an 1831 petition reminding parliament of the 'starving' condition of the Irish poor and requesting a poor law as an act of Christian justice. One parish priest, Matthew Horgan of Whitechurch, Co. Cork, organized his parishioners into sending an annual petition for a poor law to parliament from 1828. Their 1832 petition urged the Lords

> [T]o protect the Poor of Ireland from their Oppressors; and enact some Plan of Poor's Rates by which the rich Church, the Absentee, and unfeeling Landlord will be obliged to contribute; and . . . whereby Mendicity will be suppressed, the lame, the feeble and the blind supported, and lucrative Employment afforded those in their Native Country, who must otherwise, through Distress and absolute Want, emigrate to England, to return at the End of the Season with their scanty Earnings.[37]

In his evidence to the 1832 select committee on Irish disturbances, Rev. James Delaney, parish priest of Ballinakill and a protégé of Doyle, repeated Doyle's warning that the only effective response to the Rockite disturbances would be 'to give to Ireland a poor-rate in some shape or other'.[38] Doyle's successor in the see of Kildare, Edward Nolan, adopted his predecessor's views wholesale, and similar opinions were expressed in 1835 by Bishop William Kinsella of Ossory, who hoped a poor law would compel landlords to reverse the shift from tillage to pasture, and made impassioned complaints that the poor alone supported the poor while the landowners escaped untaxed.[39]

36 See below, pp. 67–73.

37 *JHC*, lxxxiii (1828), p. 325; *Journals of the House of Lords* [*JHL*], lxiv (1831–32), pp. 78–83.

38 *The Times*, 7 Jan. 1833.

39 Larkin (ed.), *Tocqueville's Journey*, pp. 40, 63, 78–9. Bishop Thomas Coen of Clonfert was less enthusiastic about poor laws, but echoed the anti-Malthusianism of Doyle, denounced assisted emigration as unnecessary, and pointed to the availability of 'vast tracts' of reclaimable waste-land in the west as an alternative answer to poverty, *PIC: Appendix C, Part ii*, p. 34e.

Other socially-engaged clergymen, such as Fr Thaddeus O'Malley, would also take up Doyle's agenda and develop it in a more radical direction. For the 'popular' Catholic advocates of such a measure, both lay and clerical, the case made by 'JKL' became the most frequently cited authority. By 1831 an enthusiastic advocate of the social necessity of poor laws as Ireland's first political priority, both as a guarantee to the poor of an entitlement to life which was inherent in true Christianity, and as a means of introducing effective discipline against vagrancy, was praising Doyle as his inspiration.[40] Not all members of the Catholic clergy were so enthusiastic. Dean Patrick McNamara of Limerick in 1835 privately expressed distaste for the sort of measures approved by Doyle, while acknowledging that the clergy generally favoured them (a fact he believed likely further to alienate most of the landed class from the concept of poor laws).[41] For his part, Archbishop John MacHale of Tuam observed a general feeling in the country for a poor law, but would support it only if it transferred all the costs of poor relief from the tenant farmers to the landowners and Church establishment.[42]

Other, lay, members of the Irish Catholic political movement also began to adopt an argument for social provision alongside political emancipation from the mid-1820s, although rarely with the focus and rhetorical power displayed by Doyle. Nicholas Sheahan, who had trained for the priesthood at Maynooth but had chosen to return to his native Cork to engage in radical politics and journalism, used his paper the *Cork Mercantile Chronicle* to promote an Irish poor law in 1826; he continued to advocate the right of the destitute poor to state relief in print and at public meetings through to his death in 1836.[43] Eneas MacDonnell, the London agent for the Catholic Association, argued in 1825 that – alongside the standard demand for extensive public works – cautious consideration ought to be given to some form of modified poor law. His comments were spurred less by wholehearted conviction than by a gut reaction against what he regarded as the 'cold indifference' of the recommendations made by the 1825 committee of inquiry into the state of the Irish poor, which had been coloured by the Co. Limerick landowner and MP Thomas Spring Rice's Malthusian preoccupations, and an orthodox and sweeping dismissal of the English relief system engineered by Vesey Fitzgerald and the other Irish gentry members.[44] Michael Staunton, editor of

40 Anon., *The Desideratum, or Ireland's Only Remedy*; *'Poor Laws and Education'* (Dublin, 1831).

41 NLI SOBP, Ms 427, fol. 276, McNamara to Smith O'Brien, 25 Feb. 1835.

42 [PIC], *Selection of Parochial Examinations*, pp. 133–5.

43 Fintan Lane, *In Search of Thomas Sheahan: Radical Politics in Cork 1824–1836* (Dublin, 2001), pp. 13–14.

44 [Eneas MacDonnell], *Practical Views and Suggestions, on the Present Condition and Permanent Improvement of Ireland* (Dublin, 1825).

the *Morning Register*, and later a leading supporter of a poor law within the O'Connellite movement, also responded angrily to the 'dogmas' of the economists which he believed lay behind the 'mischievous' official reports of 1825 and 1830. Priority must, he concluded, be given to providing the poor with 'food and raiment', although his preferred mode for doing this was through the reclamation of the waste-lands and subsequent settlement thereon of the 'unemployed and suffering poor'.[45] This preference for poor relief by employment in land reclamation, which became highly popular among Irish reformers (as well as sympathetic British figures such as Poulett Scrope), drew heavily on the model of the Dutch 'pauper colonies' established by the voluntarist Dutch Benevolent Association in 1818. Although the Dutch project was generally unsuccessful (a point highlighted by Nassau Senior's report on continental welfare regimes in 1834), its applicability to Irish conditions (especially if under state direction) remained a point of faith for many.[46] However, reformers such as Staunton increasingly sought to reconcile this model with other welfare ideas, especially in the wake of the debates of 1830–31.

Doyle's social thought was not entirely unparalleled, and it bears comparison with contemporary themes in European liberal Catholicism. Doyle inclined strongly towards the reformist tradition within the Church and had visited both France (where he assisted Archbishop Murray in re-establishing the Irish College in Paris in 1828), and the Low Countries. In both he had observed that, in harsh contrast to Ireland, 'the poor [were] either collected in charitable institutions, or exhibit[ed] even in their relative poverty no signs of squalid misery, or shameless nakedness, or extreme distress'.[47] His enthusiastic defence of political liberty and an extensive franchise was echoed in the radicalism of the Abbé Félicité de Lamennais and his followers, who founded the journal *L'Avenir* in 1830 to promote the cause of liberal Catholicism under the new Orleanist regime in France. The promotion of political ties between the O'Connellites and the French liberal

45 Michael Staunton, *Hints for Hardinge* (Dublin, 1830), pp. 54–62, 113.

46 W. Jacob, *Observations on the Benefits arising from the Cultivation of Poor Soils, by the Application of Pauper Labour; as exemplified in the Colonies for the Indigent, and for Orphans in Holland* (Lindfield, 1828); John Hinchy, *General Observations on the State of Ireland, and Plans for its Improvement, with Remarks on Poor Laws* (Dublin, 1835); W. E. Brady, *A Letter and Suggestions for the Employment of the People, and the Amelioration of the Poor in Ireland* (London, 1835).

47 McGrath (ed.), *Pastoral Letters*, pp. 7–8, 32; William John Fitzpatrick (ed.), *The Life, Times and Correspondence of the Right Rev. Dr Doyle, Bishop of Kildare and Leighlin* (new edn, 2 vols, Dublin, 1890), ii, p. 101.

Catholics by Count Charles de Montalembert is well known.[48] Less explored are the potential interconnections between liberal-Catholic clergy and laymen in the realm of social thought and action. *L'Avenir* took a practical as well as political interest in Ireland, and launched a subscription which raised 70,000 francs for famine relief in the Irish west in 1831, printing a number of grateful letters from Irish clergymen in response.[49] French and Belgian liberal Catholicism had, to some extent, emerged in response to the perceived crisis of urban destitution, but through the Christian political economy of Alban de Villeneuve-Bargemont, Charles de Coux and others, it also took an interest in the question of rural poverty, both at home and in Ireland.

Villeneuve-Bargemont was among the more radical of the social-Catholic writers, and had extensive experience of the practical development of public health relief as a prefect under both Napoleon and the French restoration regimes before developing his economic theories in print after 1830.[50] He had sought to alleviate poverty in the distressed Nord by promoting poor-colonies on the Dutch model, but lost his position following the 1830 revolution before this could be fully implemented. In his *L'Économie politique chrétienne* (1834), which was influenced by Sismondi's critique of Malthusianism and the adverse social consequences of capitalism, he argued that the scale of destitution in France (and other European societies) was now so great that direct state action to provide employment and relief, alongside moral regeneration, was required to ameliorate it. Charles de Coux, who had contributed to *L'Avenir* on economic and social affairs and who held the chair of political economy at the Catholic University of Louvain from 1834, shared Villeneuve-Bargemont's critique of classical political economy and moralistic concern at the extent of poverty in modern society, but was less convinced of the need to replace Catholic charitable action and proletarian self-help with state intervention. What united the rather amorphous liberal-Catholic school was less agreement on positive proposals than shared antipathies towards social ills

48 Pierre Joannon, 'O'Connell, Montalembert and the birth of Christian democracy in France', in Maurice R. O'Connell (ed.), *Daniel O'Connell: Political Pioneer* (Dublin, 1991), pp. 89–109.

49 W. G. Roe, *Lamennais and England: The Reception of Lamennais's Religious Ideas in England in the Nineteenth Century* (Oxford, 1966), p. 11. Lamennais was, however, closest theologically to John MacHale on the Irish hierarchy, probably because they shared a common doctrinal ultramontanism, *ibid.*, pp. 89–90.

50 Ann F. La Berge, 'A Restoration prefect and public health: Alban de Villeneuve-Bargemont at Nantes and Lille, 1824–1830', *Proceedings of the Annual Meeting of the Western Society for French History*, 5 (1977), pp. 128–37.

and an expectation that the active agency of the Catholic clergy was central to amelioration.[51]

The role of Irish liberal Catholicism in influencing French thought is easier to document than the reverse. Doyle received high praise from Montalembert as a 'solid pillar of the true faith', and his vigorous defence of the principle of a poor law against O'Connell's waverings was highlighted positively in Michaud's *Biographie universelle*, but direct French influences on Doyle are more difficult to identify.[52] However, there is evidence for some dissemination of French ideas among educated Irish Catholics after his death. In 1837 the newly-established voice of intellectual liberal Catholicism in Ireland and Britain, the *Dublin Review*, commissioned de Coux to review Villeneuve-Bargemont's *L'Économie politique chrétienne* for its anglophone readership.[53] De Coux set out to establish the central concerns of the 'school' and demonstrate the relevance of its economic thought in the Irish context, although in doing so he could not avoid demonstrating the difference between Villeneuve-Bargement's anti-industrial agrarianism and his own more positive attitude towards a (moralized) form of industrial development. There was concord, however, on the denunciation of Malthus as both anti-scriptural and empirically wrong on population, and on the desideratum of raising wages to improve the condition of the labouring poor. While Catholics were conscious that temporal power could never eliminate poverty from society, they were equally clear that – led by the unfettered moral force of the priesthood – they could pressurize the state into measures of amelioration, while promoting moral regeneration among the rich and poor alike. It was this combination of ethical and rational dimensions in political economy that de Coux sought to stress:

> He [Villeneuve-Bargemont] has a real respect for the poor; he respects them as a Catholic, who sees in them the suffering members of Jesus Christ: and here again the school to which he belongs reasons upon utilitarian principles. They maintain that the arguments made use of to demonstrate the necessity of depriving the lower orders of all resources but what they may find in their wages, can have no effect but that of exasperating and driving them to a sanguinary retaliation. As the insults continually offered to their improvidence or their

51 Peter N. Stearns, 'The nature of the *Avenir* movement (1830–31)', *American Historical Review*, 65 (1960), pp. 837–47; see also H. A. C. Cunningham, *The July Monarchy: A Political History of France 1830–1848* (London, 1988), pp. 306–8.

52 Fitzpatrick (ed.), *Doyle*, ii, p. 399; M. Michaud, *Biographie universelle, ancienne et moderne* (Paris, 1855), xi, p. 285.

53 [Charles de Coux], 'Christian political economy', *Dublin Review* [*DR*], 3 (July 1837), pp. 165–98.

> distress, and the empty threat of leaving them to their fate cannot in reality save the country a farthing, they ask if it would not be wiser to seek to inspire them with a sincere affection for the richer classes.[54]

For Villeneuve-Bargemont such a paternal economy would combine a national network of Catholic parochial charities with state-funded asylums for the aged and infirm poor, and waste-land colonization projects, eliminating indigency through employment and the subsequent redistribution of small plots to the needy. Although de Coux expressed strong doubts on the latter point, this combination of measures to address poverty undoubtedly appealed to much of Irish Catholic clerical opinion, and it is comparable, both in form and tone, to Fr Thaddeus O'Malley's project of 1836–37.[55]

Irish radicalism and the poor

There were other contributions to the debate on poverty than those emanating from the Anglican and Catholic traditions. Radicalism had enjoyed a brief but catastrophic blossoming in the Ireland of the 1790s. While the United Irish movement was never uniform or consistent in its social thought, sections of it – especially the 'northern radical' group around Samuel Neilson, Henry Joy McCracken, Thomas Russell and Jemmy Hope – were attracted towards Paineite egalitarianism and sought to promote the idea of a social alongside a political revolution, not least to broaden the movement's appeal to agrarian radicals and the urban working classes. While the radical message was principally concerned with emancipation from the state – in the form of the reduced taxation and the abolition of tithes that would follow the overthrow of the established order – the 'northern radicals' at least were prepared to hint at a more positive role for the state as well. *The Union Doctrine or Poor Man's Catechism* (*c.*1796) proposed not only confiscating and dividing up the great estates to alleviate the land hunger of the peasantry, but the state regulation of rent, and the sale of church lands to create a national fund for public welfare, especially 'to relieve old age, [and] to give education and protection to infancy'.[56] This Paineite ideal of welfare, only crudely developed before 1798 and restricted to only a section of the republican revolutionaries, barely survived the defeat and dispersal of the United Irishmen. It may, however,

54 *Ibid.*, p. 190.

55 For O'Malley, see below, pp. 227–30.

56 James Quinn, 'The United Irishmen and social reform', *Irish Historical Studies*, 31 (1998), pp. 188–201. For Paine's proposals of social security payments to the young and elderly in place of a poor law, see Gareth Stedman Jones, *An End to Poverty? A Historical Debate* (London, 2004), pp. 23–5.

have lingered in parts of the urban radical underworld of the early nineteenth century, such as that associated with the radical weaver Jemmy Hope in Belfast.[57]

A rather different sort of Irish radical case for the creation of welfare entitlements was revived in response to external stimuli in the 1820s and 1830s. Robert Owen's visionary proposals to 'relieve and remoralize the poor and unemployed working classes' through the medium of co-operative villages were taken up with enthusiasm by his Irish admirers in the wake of the subsistence crisis of 1822 and his lecturing tours of the country in that and the following year. If such an experimental system were introduced as a form of poor law in place of the fallacious workhouse principle, Owen argued, agricultural productivity would rapidly transcend the artificial constraints currently imposed upon it, and prosperity would be disseminated equitably. As Owen's message tended to remove the responsibility for distress from individual proprietors, and to stress the remedial power of voluntarist class collaboration, a number of Irish 'improving' landowners (including Spring Rice, Lucius O'Brien and Lord Cloncurry) were prepared to toy with the idea through the medium of the Hibernian Philanthropic Society. The *Freeman's Journal* was also generally sympathetic, but interest from these quarters was not sustained.[58] Cloncurry warned Owen that although he had 'zealous and grateful friends, . . . unless Parliamentary or private munificence of the British public assist us, nothing effectual can be done, and ruin stares us in the face'.[59] Owen's proposals were given close attention by the 1823 Commons committee on the state of Ireland over which Spring Rice presided, but its report criticized Owen's egalitarianism as visionary, and excluded the state from any participation in a scheme which appeared 'so irreconcilable with the nature and interests of mankind, and the experience of all ages'. Despite the efforts of Spring Rice and Lords Clare and Leinster to interest their fellow Irish landowners in appropriating elements of the plan, and the attempts of the radical Benthamite William Thompson to revive popular interest in the

57 Hope later expressed an Owenite interest in self-governing rural communes as a means of equalizing wealth: see John Newsinger (ed.), *United Irishman: The Autobiography of James Hope* (London, 2000), pp. 94–8.

58 Anon., *A Report of the British and Foreign Philanthropic Society, with Other Statements and Calculations explanatory of Mr Owen's Plan for the Relief of Ireland* (Dublin, 1823); Fintan Lane, *The Origins of Modern Irish Socialism, 1881–1896* (Cork, 1997), pp. 6–10.

59 Cloncurry to Owen, 2 Jan. 1823, in William John Fitzpatrick (ed.), *The Life, Times and Contemporaries of Lord Cloncurry* (Dublin, 1855), pp. 341–2.

scheme in Cork in 1826, little assistance was forthcoming, and the appeal of Owenism faded.[60]

Ultimately only a handful of landowners were prepared to experiment along Owenite lines, most notably John Scott Vandaleur, who established an Owenite co-operative village at Ralahine, Co. Clare, in 1831–33. Despite some initial achievements in providing stable employment and raising the living standards of its members, the colony folded under the weight of Vandaleur's private debts and thus failed to provide the successful high-profile alternative to a poor law that its supporters had hoped. William Thompson had plans to initiate a similar experiment on his Rosscarbery estate, but died in 1833 before these could be implemented.[61] An effort was made by a Belfast doctor to interest the town's Charitable Association in Owen's and Thompson's ideas, but to no avail.[62] Subsequently Irish radicals looked more to the populist arguments of Cobbett, the ethical interventionism of Doyle and the productivist case of Poulett Scrope in support of a labour-based poor law rather than an Owenite alternative of co-operation. Cloncurry, for example, became a regular supporter of the idea of extending the English poor laws to Ireland, along vaguely Cobbettite lines, from around 1825.[63]

British demands for an Irish poor law

The idea of extending the English poor law to Ireland appears to have played little or no part in pre- or post-Union debates in Great Britain. However, the later 1820s witnessed an upsurge in British interest in an Irish poor law. This campaign drew on a number of different strands – some sympathetic and

60 *Report of the Select Committee on the Condition of the Labouring Poor in Ireland*, PP 1823 (561), vi.331, pp. 9–10; *Hansard*, 2, ix, 1021–2, 1039 [18, 19 June 1823]; Lane, *Sheahan*, p. 14.

61 Cormac Ó Gráda, 'The Owenite community at Ralahine, County Clare, 1831–33: a reassessment', in Edward Thomas Craig, *An Irish Commune: The Experiment at Ralahine, County Clare 1831–1833* (Blackrock, 1983), pp. 193–208; Lane, *Origins*, pp. 11–19.

62 Henry McCormac, *A Plan for the Relief of the Unemployed Poor* (Belfast, 1830). He was more successful in establishing the Belfast Co-operative Company in 1829: see Vincent Geoghegan, 'Robert Owen, co-operation and Ulster in the 1830s', in Fintan Lane and Donal Ó Drisceoil (eds), *Politics and the Irish Working Class, 1830–1945* (Basingstoke, 2005), pp. 6–26.

63 Fitzpatrick (ed.), *Cloncurry*, pp. 373–5. Doyle also had expressed interest in Owen's scheme in 1823, but had moved beyond it by 1825: Fitzpatrick (ed.), *Doyle*, i, p. 260.

others overtly hostile towards Ireland and the Irish – but for the most part mutually compatible in seeking a common end. In 1827 George Strickland, a Yorkshire landowner and later reforming MP for that county and subsequently the West Riding, advocated an Irish poor law within the context of what he saw as the necessary reform of both the English and Scottish laws. A system that returned to the original (restricted) principles of 43rd Elizabeth, as still operated in practice in much of the northern counties of England, would, he hoped, prove applicable throughout the United Kingdom.[64] Strickland's case for extending a reformed English poor law to Ireland was based on a number of elements. Firstly, he was prepared to cite Doyle and other sympathetic sources on the moral case for state provision to address the virtually unequalled misery of Ireland. Quoting Lord Stourton on Irish absenteeism, he observed that

> Even the last shield of self-interest, which protects the West Indian slave, does not cover the Irish peasant. Not only does no poor law of human origin notice him; not only has he no proper hold on the divine, and almost universal law of nature, which governs in other countries the relations of rich and poor; but self interest, that best friend to other men, is often directly and strongly opposed to him: for that labour which is his only property, his only marketable commodity, if not wanted, becomes a drag and burthen to the community.[65]

Secondly, Strickland rejected the then fashionable remedy of assisted emigration as counter-productive, on the grounds that Malthus had been right in his original argument that emigration merely created a rapidly-filled vacuum.

While Strickland was not without some sympathy for the plight of the Irish poor, it is clear that, in common with very many British observers, his main concern was with the adverse consequences of Irish impoverishment for Britain itself. As a reformer he had no hesitation in pointing out that there was an element of just retribution for past misgovernment in this situation: 'It is the means in the hands of Providence by which the people of England and the government will be taught, that the rights and happiness of a great and powerful people, in a fruitful and productive country, cannot be trampled upon with impunity.'[66] Britain must now, however, protect itself from the influx of Irish paupers by raising the character and situation of the Irish labourer. Despite this robust argument, Strickland's mechanism for doing so,

64 Strickland, *Discourse on the Poor Laws of England and Scotland, on the State of the Poor of Ireland*, pp. 1–9, 122. For the importance of regional 'regimes' under the old English poor law, see King, *Poverty and Welfare in England*.

65 Strickland, *Discourse*, pp. 89–90.

66 *Ibid*., p. 69.

a poor law limited to the aged and infirm poor, appeared (like Doyle's 1825 proposals) to many to be incommensurate with its larger objects. By 1832 the logic of his arguments (and perhaps also the petitions of his constituents) had propelled him into supporting Sadler's much more radical demand for an Irish measure, while at the same time he continued to call for a major reform of the English laws.[67]

Similar demands for an Irish poor law to protect the English and Scottish poor appeared with growing frequency from provincial centres from the mid-1820s. William Bruce, a Bristol evangelical and anti-Malthusian defender of the English law, adverted to a poor law as the 'panacea' for Ireland's woes, but reserved his purple prose for reminding his readers of the folly of creating a free trade in labour under the Union without the equitable protection offered by a national poor law. While the corn laws regulated the rental of land in both countries, the absence of poor-rates had allowed Irish landowners to reduce wages there to the absolute minimum necessary for subsistence. This not only gave them an unfair competitive advantage in the English grain market, it drove the impoverished peasantry into seasonal migration, thereby undermining the wages of English labourers. The question, he asked rhetorically, was

> Whether the Irish landholder, for the sake of an exorbitant rental, is to be allowed to send over by steam packets sixty thousand potatoe-raised labourers annually, to lower the wages, the comforts, and the mental tone of the English peasantry, and to keep an entire population on the lowest verge of subsistence, '*The husks which swine did eat*,' and consequently liable (during the germinating season of the potatoe) to famine, and its concomitants, pestilence and rebellion; – or, is a system of parochial contribution to be introduced, that will raise the price of labour in Ireland to its fair and proper height, and cause a market for, and consequently an internal manufacture of (throughout the Irish villages) all the different articles of domestic use, comfort, enjoyment and luxury of the English day-labourer, that form the basis of England's internal prosperity, and employment of her population[?][68]

At the same time as protecting England, the introduction of a poor law would grant the Irish peasant the social entitlement – in Bruce's words the 'parochial relief which forms such an integral part of that Commonwealth to which he is so material a contributor' – currently lacking under the Union. It would

67 *Hansard*, 3, ix, 709–10 [23 Jan.], xiii, 843 [19 June 1832]. Strickland had opposed the same motion the previous year and was clearly uneasy over Sadler's motives, *ibid*., vi, 816–18 [29 Aug. 1831].

68 [William Bruce], *Poor Rates, the Panacea for Ireland* (2nd edn, Bristol, 1828), p. 5.

oblige the landlords to provide employment as a means of evading poor-rates, and provide the security necessary for artisans and skilled labourers to survive temporary stoppages of employment without being driven to flight. Belfast, Ireland's sole industrial success story, had, he noted, a municipal poor-rate, albeit an inequitable and unsatisfactory one.

Bruce's and Strickland's arguments had the potential to appeal to a broad constituency of anxious British agriculturalists and industrialists, working-class radicals and earnest reformers. The argument for a unified national system of poor laws was attractive to those who believed in the principle of equitable economic opportunities and welfare rights, although many were uneasy about using the current English regime as a suitable model.[69] Other commentators, such as an organizer of a petition of Wiltshire landowners and farmers in 1830, were more openly chauvinistic in defending the 'glorious institution' of the English poor law and focused more brazenly on penalizing Irish landowners and impeding Irish labour migration. The agricultural crisis of 1829–31, which saw the eruption of Swing rioting in the southern English countryside, appears to have given a particular stimulus to the populist theory that Irish immigration and unfair competition by Irish grain-growers were at the root of the problem. In a voice not dissimilar in tone to more recent tirades against economic migrants, the Wiltshire petitioner demanded to know:

> WHY are we to submit longer to this biting inequality? Had *we* been the conquered nation, and the Irish our victors, they could scarcely have imposed harder terms than we have voluntarily submitted to, seemingly out of a desire for self-mortification, and philanthropic disinterestedness . . . How long will [the English landed interest] continue thus to pay tribute to the landowners of Ireland; to maintain their poor, and give them command of their own markets?[70]

Another pamphleteer calculated that migrant Irish labourers drained over a million pounds annually from the English wages-fund and floated the idea of a punitive passenger tax on Irish Sea crossings to deter them.[71]

69 e.g. Anon., *Hints suggesting the Possibility of essentially altering and amending the Poor Laws of Great Britain and Ireland* (London, 1830).

70 Anon., *A Letter to the Agriculturalists of England on the Expediency of extending the Poor Law to Ireland* (London, 1830), p. 16. See also *The Times*, 5 Apr. 1828.

71 John Ede, *Reflections on the Employment, Wages, and Condition of the Poor* (London, 1829). *The Times* (8 Jan. 1831) observed that this remedy, and the imposition of an import tariff on Irish grain, could be legitimate only in the aftermath of a repeal of the Union.

Some elements of the British press, particularly *The Times*, endorsed these fears. In 1829 the paper warned that the disfranchisement of the Irish forty-shilling freeholders would lead to clearance and expulsion of masses of poor peasants to England unless checked by an Irish poor law. Only such a measure, it insisted, could save the English labourers from being reduced to the squalor of Irish conditions, and would oblige the Irish landowners to stop trafficking their poor across the channel and raise them instead to a civilized standard through care and employment.[72] The years 1830–33 saw a significant increase in the number of parliamentary petitions from England imploring an Irish measure, with the Wiltshire petition being joined by others from Chatham, London, and Greenwich, and from Kent landowners, as well as from the northern industrial towns of Carlisle, Leeds, Halifax and Dewsbury.[73] Other petitions complained about the cost to parishes of repatriating Irish vagrants to their country of origin.[74] The session of 1833 appears to have marked the climax of this petitioning campaign in England, with the Commons' *Journals* listing twenty petitions from Great Britain (many from parochial authorities) in favour, alongside eight from Ireland.[75] At least some successful parliamentary candidates, such as the Tory William Bolling at Bolton, had also inserted the demand for an Irish poor-rate into their election hustings in 1832.[76]

Similar questions were asked by many Scots, who had to deal with a proportionately much larger annual influx of Irish seasonal labourers and permanent migrants than their southern neighbours. The *Scotsman* observed in August 1827 that the Irish were 'spreading like locusts over the whole surface of the country', and turning to begging where they could not get employment.[77] John Douglas of Glasgow demanded protection for the labourers of Clydesdale from this invasion of people with 'the mobility and fecundity of wild animals'. The British nation, he asserted, would no longer submit to supporting the Irish poor in addition to their own, while granting the Irish landlords and established Church the 'monopoly price of our supplies of grain and provisions'. He located the introduction of a poor law within a wider Unionist rhetorical framework. Irish elites would

72 *The Times*, 30 Apr., 30 May, 18 Dec. 1829.

73 *Hansard*, 2, xxxiii, 961; xxv, 1117; 3, v, 1257–60; ix, 709; xvii, 960–2; xviii, 108; xx, 191; *The Times*, 4 July 1831. The Leeds petition of 1831 attracted 800 signatures, while that of the following year – which incorporated a call for the appropriation of Church property for welfare purposes – drew 6,000.

74 *The Times*, 9 Mar. 1830; *Hansard*, 2, xvii, 1126 [12 Mar. 1828]; *ibid.*, 3, xv, 311–12 [7 Feb. 1833].

75 *JHC*, 88 (1833).

76 *Manchester Guardian* [*MG*], 23 June 1832.

77 *Scotsman*, cited in Strickland, *Discourse*, pp. 66–7.

find that the same power which plucked up their corrupted separate parliament, by the rotten roots which had lost every hold on its native soil, will, for the sake of the interest of both countries, adopt the only effectual means of raising the Irish common people to the condition of the British, and, while it is yet time, protecting our people from sinking to a level with the ragged lazzaroni who infest the streets and high-ways of Ireland.[78]

Douglas subsequently made the historicist case that as Church property in tithes had originally been instituted in part to meet the physical as well as the spiritual needs of the poor, a portion of the tithe should be appropriated for poor relief.[79]

Caledonian alarms at the scale of Irish migration and the implications it held for the already overstretched poor-relief systems of the central lowlands gave rise in 1828 to petitions and legislative initiatives to curb the access of migrants to Scottish parochial funds. Several Scottish MPs took advantage of the subsequent debate to press for an Irish poor law; the reformer T. F. Kennedy assured the Commons that his aim in seeking to increase the minimum period for settlement to seven years was not to impede legitimate labour movement, but to protect Scots against the unjust transfer of welfare costs.[80] Liberal Scottish opinion tended to favour the extension of the Scottish poor law to Ireland, and criticized those Irish landowners who opposed this.[81] Scottish landowners also remained among the vocal advocates of an Irish poor law in 1833, although even here opinion was divided, with some adhering to the orthodox case that mobile Irish labour had contributed greatly to the wealth of Scotland.[82]

The classical economists were generally hesitant about endorsing any such demonization of Irish labour migration. However, it was perhaps no accident that the one who did so most forcefully was the Scotsman J. R. McCulloch, who warned in 1828 that

Great Britain has been overrun by half-famished hordes, that have by their competition, lessened the wages of labour, and, by their example, degraded the habits and lowered the opinions of the people with respect to subsistence. But great as the mischief is that has already been occasioned by this barbarian

78 John Douglas, *Observations on the Necessity of a Legal Provision for the Irish Poor* (London, 1828), p. 8.

79 This argument was quoted at length by Doyle in his *Letter to Thomas Spring Rice . . . on the Establishment of a Legal Provision for the Irish Poor* (Dublin, 1831), pp. 126–33.

80 *Hansard*, 2, xix, col. 375 [6 May 1828].

81 *Scotsman*, 17 Mar. 1830.

82 *Hansard*, 3, xvii, 960–3 [6 May 1833].

> immigration, it is trifling indeed to what we may confidently predict will be furnished by it, if no efforts are made to put a stop to it.

The solution in his view lay in compulsory passports (which could be denied to Irish labourers), until the remedial measures of assisted emigration and a poor law had made an impact on existing Irish conditions.[83] While philanthropists might place the welfare of the Irish poor at the forefront of their concerns, the perceived necessity of self-protection was clearly predominant in the minds of many of the advocates of an Irish poor law, and the theme of a racialized 'Irish threat' coincided with claims of humanitarian concern. Conveniently, a poor law would, many claimed, both protect British self-interest and reclaim the Irish poor from their sub-human mode of living.

Both themes could be given a radical coloration. William Cobbett, the leading figure in English popular radicalism and a vocal defender of the old English poor law, entered the fray in early 1832 in an aggressive public letter attacking O'Connell for his inconsistency on the question. The withholding of poor laws from Ireland in the reign of Elizabeth was, Cobbett asserted, the 'original sin' of misrule in Ireland – the root of the gulf between the manners, habits and condition of the working classes in the two countries. It was not the English people but their corrupt and self-serving governors who had made Ireland poor, not least by failing to compel the landowners to pay poor-rates. Alongside his idealization of the English poor law – the 'Magna Carta of the working people' – and the implication that it would have the same socially bonding effect in Ireland, Cobbett could not restrain himself from taking anti-O'Connellite and chauvinist swipes at the condition of the Irish poor at home and abroad:

> When did you, or anybody else, ever see or hear of *Englishmen* prowling about, in bands of half-naked beggars, in any country upon earth; when did you ever hear of the necessity of taking *them* up by force, and carrying them like malefactors and tossing them back upon their native shores: when did you ever hear of *them* being an incumbrance to any people among whom they went . . . when, since you talk of the 'naked cells' of the poor-house did you ever hear of thousands of *them* living on stinking shell-fish, sea-weed, and nettles, and of thousands at a time receiving the last offices of religion as preparatory to death by starvation . . . when, lastly (not to suffer the provocation to urge me further), did you ever see or hear of an '*English* slave' *disowning the country of his birth*, and wherever found, and under whatever circumstances, not forward to proclaim himself an *Englishman*, and to boast of the *honour of the name*?[84]

83 [J. R. McCulloch], 'Poor laws', *Edinburgh Review* [*ER*], 47 (May 1828), p. 327.

84 'Letter to Mr O'Connell on his speech against poor-laws for Ireland', 14 Jan. 1832, in *Cobbett's Manchester Lectures* (London, 1832), pp. 176–7.

Irish admirers of Cobbett were obliged to tread carefully in extracting his rights-based prescriptions from the populist-nationalist rhetoric in which they were embedded, but they were aided by the more sympathetic rhetoric Cobbett employed during his Irish tour of 1834.[85] Cobbett's exhaustive series of public lectures may have done much to stimulate Irish popular enthusiasm for a poor law, but he was as much concerned with attacking the 'Scotch monsters of the school of the parson MALTHUS', whom he held responsible for the English amendment act of that year, as he was with promoting an Irish measure.[86]

Not all British commentators adopted such a reductionist line. One important supporter of a poor law, who utilized his own eyewitness testimony in support of theory, was Colonel Frederick Page. In the summer of 1829 Page went on a rambling tour of Ireland with a companion, James Ebenezer Bicheno. Although personal friends (Bicheno dedicated his own account of the tour to his 'intelligent and agreeable companion'), the pair differed radically in their published opinions on the theory and practice of the English poor laws. They presumably saw their journey as an opportunity to test out their rival ideas on the applicability of a poor law to Ireland. Page had been a parish overseer in Berkshire, and in 1822 had published an essay offering a historicist and comparative justification for the legal relief of indigence, a defence of both the socially beneficent and providential principles of the English poor laws (albeit reformed along the lines of the Sturges Bourne recommendations of 1817), and a preliminary case for their extension to Ireland. Page's case was, at root, ethical, and justified by reference to the liberal theology of William Paley's *Natural Theology* and Richard Price's sermons. Poor laws had in his opinion been ordained to provide the essential counterweight to the 'natural' inequalities of society:

> Indigence in its varied forms must always exist under the present constitution of society and dispensation of Providence. Humanly speaking, division of property is the necessary consequence of the principle of population, and indigence

85 Cobbett's first experience of Ireland confirmed his opinion that the country 'wants THE LAW, the *Christian* law, the *holy* law of England, which says that no human being shall, on English ground, *perish from want*', *Political Register*, 27 Sept. 1834.

86 Cobbett to the members of the Meath Club, *Political Register*, 4 Oct. 1834. Ireland continued to serve an instrumental purpose; he warned his English readers that if the old poor law was 'put down' there, they would be reduced to the appalling condition of Irish labourers, and declared his intention to publish the proceedings of his tour as 'Ireland's woes; a warning to Englishmen', *ibid.*, 11 Oct., 1 Nov. 1834.

> the necessary consequence of the division of property. They follow in that order, which the wisdom of the ALMIGHTY seems to have appointed for the preservation of Civil Society. But from the actual constitution of Civil Society arise duties which, properly performed, appear capable of preventing indigence from degenerating into misery or crime, from that cause only.[87]

It is unclear how far the actual experience of Ireland modified Page's preconceptions. Spring Rice, while decidedly sceptical about the utility of such tours, noted approvingly that both Page and Bicheno had been 'very much pleased and surprized at the state of Ireland and above all at the extreme morality of our people'. Yet, while he expressed optimism about the island's economic potential, Page was not dissuaded from his conviction that a poor law was both practicable and essential. While he admitted that he had not seen 'excessive mendicancy', he attributed this to the successful (albeit financially precarious) operation of mendicity associations in the major towns, and the 'astounding' fact that the rural destitute were relieved by the poor themselves.[88] Nevertheless, Page appealed to the evidence presented to the 1825 select committee on the state of Ireland, and to the arguments of bishops Woodward and Doyle, in support of his case for a legal measure replacing the 'failing' mendicities with a compulsory local assessment, accompanied by auxiliaries of employment and colonization. Page was at odds with other advocates in denying that this necessity arose principally from English self-interest. Complaints about Irish labour migration to Britain were, he assured his readers, exaggerated, for such population transfers were the result of growing British demand rather than Irish oversupply. It was the power loom rather than Irish labour that had reduced wages in English manufacturing. The chief benefit that would flow from poor-law extension would be political, so long as it was 'treated not as a measure of defensive war, but of reconciliation and peace'.[89] Some British politicians would subsequently be prepared to develop this idea of poor laws as an element of 'justice to Ireland' rather than simply a sop to British protectionism.

Further backing for the poor-law case came from the pen of the economist and MP George Poulett Scrope. Although a radical Whig, Scrope made his first argument for an Irish poor law in the pages of the Tory *Quarterly Review* in 1831, perhaps because the Whig *Edinburgh Review* was antipathetic to his heterodox brand of economic thought and preoccupation with 'welfare economics', and also because Scrope identified the Tory gentry readers of the

87 Frederick Page, *The Principle of the English Poor Laws illustrated and defended* (3rd edn, London, 1830), p. 129.

88 Page, *Observations on the State of the Indigent Poor in Ireland*, pp. 12–28.

89 Page, *Observations*, p. 49.

Quarterly as potential political supporters for his crusade.[90] For Scrope, the Elizabethan poor law needed to be understood as both a measure of justice – securing to those confronted with the vicissitudes of life the right not to starve in the midst of plenty – and of policy – protecting society against the evils of mendicancy and its associated crimes, and equitably distributing the burden of relief.[91] While the English law had evidently been subjected to such abuses as the allowances system by interested parties, which had reduced it to a 'deformed and knavish piece of jugglery' in some of the southern counties, this distortion was relatively recent (since the advent of the 'Speenhamland system' in 1795) and hence capable of reform. Both justice and policy, combined with the evidence presented to the recent parliamentary inquiries (especially that of Doyle in 1830) dictated that Ireland receive the boon of a reformed poor law, shorn of the excrescence of the allowance system which so preoccupied and misled its opponents.

In a previous outing in the *Quarterly* Scrope had argued that political economy in Britain had deviated from the broad principles established by Adam Smith in becoming preoccupied with the production of national wealth to the exclusion of all other considerations. The Malthusian paradigm was particularly at fault in exaggerating the extent and ignoring the potential resolution of the problem of overpopulation.[92] This distortion he held to be most evident in commentary on the poor laws, which had neglected the central question of whether the happiness of the population tended to increase alongside the aggregate wealth of the country. A broader vision of political economy revealed, Scrope assured his readers, that both interests could be reconciled: an unprejudiced review of poor laws demonstrated not only that they secured the interests of the poor, but that they prevented 'the waste of the great and principal instrument of all production, *labour*', and thus promoted reproductive capital formation. Having exposed the errors of the orthodox economists and their followers, and indicated the unquestionable benefits likely to accrue to Ireland, Scrope sought to engage his English readership further by flagging the likely consequences for England. Not only would the Union be cemented and completed (and O'Connell thereby confounded) by introducing poor

90 For the difficulty of categorizing Scrope's idiosyncratic blend of political economy, moralist paternalism and entitlement-based social theory, see David Stack, 'The "Secret Concatenation" in the mid-nineteenth century: the case of George Poulett Scrope, a still neglected political economist', *History of Political Economy*, 32 (2000), pp. 553–84. For Scrope's attitude towards the readers of the *Quarterly*, see Mandler, 'Making of the new poor law', pp. 150–1.

91 [G. Poulett Scrope], 'Poor laws for Ireland', *Quarterly Review* [*QR*], 44 (Feb. 1831), pp. 511–54.

92 [G. Poulett Scrope], 'The political economists', *QR*, 44 (Jan. 1831), pp. 1–52.

laws, but it would address the problem of the 'hordes of Irish who thus flock to England, as a refuge from famine, undersell the native labourers in every corner of the country, but especially in the towns, and drive them to be maintained in idleness from the poor-rate'. This theme, repeated in Scrope's torrent of comments in the press and in parliament, may have been calculated to arouse political interest in Britain, but his revival of the language of labour protectionism posed potential problems for his Irish admirers.

Political economy and the poor law

Opposition to an Irish poor law flowed from two principal sources. The first was the opinion shared by most political economists in both countries that poor laws in general were undesirable and the extension of an English-style poor law to such a 'backward' country as Ireland was likely to be disastrous. The second was the conviction of the majority of Irish landowners that any additional burden placed on property would have a detrimental effect on the rural economy and further damage the already unsatisfactory state of class relations in Ireland. In practice these became interrelated, with Irish landowners finding ammunition in the more abstract writings of the economists to complement and justify their more interested arguments. A combination of these elements is evident as early as 1773, when a Dublin-published pamphlet attacked Bishop Woodward's proposals as certain to curb what 'spirit of industry' existed in Ireland and emulate the English poor laws in augmenting rather than diminishing poverty. National indolence was, the author asserted, the true cause of poverty, and was grounded in the tendency of farmers to occupy more land than they could properly till. Only the stimuli of higher rents could free the country from its slothful habits.[93]

Debate on the poor laws in both countries was fundamentally shaped by the appearance of Thomas Malthus' writings on the principle of population from 1798, and their rapid incorporation into the core of orthodox economic discourse. Malthus' swingeing critique of the English poor laws as a stimulant to improvident reproduction, and hence a primary source of the pauperism they affected to relieve, proved attractive both to advocates of abolition or fundamental reform in England, and to opponents of poor-law extension to Ireland. To the orthodox economists and their followers, the social crisis so evident in post-1815 Ireland arose self-evidently from the tendency of the rate of population increase to outstrip that of capital-formation in the context of an extensively subdivided cottier-peasant agricultural structure. The

93 Anon., *Remarks on a Pamphlet recommending a National Provision for the Poor of Ireland* (Dublin, 1773).

consequence was a redundancy of population that a poor law could only augment rather than alleviate. While both Ricardo and Malthus were initially sceptical about the effectiveness of reducing population through mass emigration, they agreed that for Ireland to escape the poverty trap the cottier system must be swept away and replaced with the English system of a tripartite division of agricultural society into improving landowners, capitalist farmers and landless wage-labourers. Only this structure would promote capital accumulation, check population growth, augment the wages-fund and create demand for luxuries and expectations of material betterment through self-exertion.[94]

Malthus, who had visited Ireland in 1817, explicitly opposed the idea of extending poor laws to Ireland in evidence he gave before the 1827 Commons Emigration Committee. Such an act would, he was certain, aggravate rather than diminish the misery all too prevalent there. However, he had now become persuaded that assisted emigration, if accompanied by measures to promote social 'transition' within Ireland, such as the sub-letting act of 1826, would be desirable. The 'colonization' of Canada had been enthusiastically advocated for Ireland (and Britain) since 1817 by Col. Robert Torrens and was promoted as an alternative to the poor law in parliament and within the administration by the under-secretary for the colonies, R. J. Wilmot Horton, from 1822. The 'conversion' of Malthus and other economists, such as J. R. McCulloch, on this subject by the mid-1820s may have been in part the consequence of a reconsideration of the likelihood of Ireland undertaking the desired social transition unaided, and a new sense of urgency following the economic crises of 1822 and 1826.[95] By 1833 Malthus remained convinced that poor laws must be resisted for the sister island not least because it would 'fix the surplus and unemployed population in Ireland instead of putting them upon means of providing for it by emigration'.[96]

Malthus' opinions on the subject had a formative impact on the leading English economist of the next generation, Nassau Senior. The younger man's first journey to Ireland, in 1819, convinced him that the solution to that country's problems lay in church reform and the encouragement of landlord residency rather than any poor-relief policy; Ireland's 'freedom from our

94 Black, *Economic Thought*, pp. 86–99; Peter Gray, 'The peculiarities of Irish land tenure 1800–1914: from agent of impoverishment to agent of pacification', in Donald Winch and Patrick K. O'Brien (eds), *The Political Economy of British Historical Experience, 1688–1914* (Oxford, 2002), pp. 139–62.

95 Black, *Economic Thought*, pp. 203–11; Malthus to Wilmot Horton, 8 Mar. 1827, in R. N. Ghosh, 'Malthus on emigration and colonization: letters to Wilmot-Horton', *Economica*, n.s., 30 (1963), p. 49.

96 Extract from J. L. Mallet's diary, 6 Dec. 1833, in [Political Economy Club], *Political Economy Club . . . Minutes of Proceedings, 1899–1920* (London, 1921), p. 253.

great drawback, the Poor Laws' was to him a source of some consolation.[97] This was to remain a central element of Senior's thinking on Ireland, and was reflected in his extended public commentary on the subject of 1831. In 1835 he corrected Alexis de Tocqueville's misapprehensions on the questions of relief expenditure (which Senior held to be positively correlated with 'despotism' and 'aristocracy') and on the principle of population:

> I cannot think that population is an element of wealth. It may rather be said to be an element of poverty. The wealth or poverty of the *people* of a country depends on the proportion between their numbers and the aggregate wealth of a country. Diminish their numbers, the wealth remaining the same, and they will be, individually, richer. The people of Ireland, and indeed of England, would be richer if they were fewer.[98]

Senior's Malthusian concerns about Irish overpopulation, and his conviction that a poor law could only worsen the situation, proved influential with many in the 'educated' classes.

Although most serious political economists remained staunchly opposed on Malthusian grounds to a poor law for Ireland at least until the mid-1830s, there were a few significant exceptions. McCulloch was one who changed his stance on the question over time. In 1825 he had given evidence critical of both the general principle of poor laws and their applicability to Ireland, but at the 1830 inquiry he commented that 'further reflection upon their operation in England' had convinced him 'that this opinion was not well founded, and that poor laws may be administered so as to be made productive of good rather than evil'. Prior to 1795, he now believed, the English law had operated to check excessive population growth by giving landowners both an interest and the means to restrict access of labourers to the land. The same effect might be expected if a suitable system could be devised and applied to Ireland.[99] While continuing vigorously to denounce what he regarded as the folly of the anti-Malthusian agitators for a rights-based law, he had come to consider a minimal poor law a useful safeguard in facilitating the transition to capitalist agriculture.[100]

97 Senior, memo on the Irish Church Question, 1819, in S. Leon Levy, *Nassau W. Senior 1790–1864* (Newton Abbot, 1970), pp. 218–19.

98 Senior to de Tocqueville, 17 Feb. 1835, in M. C. M. Simpson (ed.), *Correspondence and Conversations of Alexis de Tocqueville with Nassau William Senior from 1834 to 1859* (2nd edn, 2 vols, London, 1872), i, pp. 2–4. For his 1831 commentary, see below, pp. 75–8.

99 Black, *Economic Thought*, pp. 103–4. For McCulloch's growing confidence in the less eligibility principle, see 'Poor Laws', *ER*, 47 (May 1828), pp. 303–30.

100 [J. R. McCulloch], 'Sadler on Ireland', *ER*, 49 (June 1829), pp. 300–17.

In the wake of the devising of the new English poor law of 1834 other economists also came to share this opinion. Perhaps the most clearly considered case for the introduction of a limited, workhouse-based system of relief to all classes of destitutes in Ireland was made by the Irish economist Mountifort Longfield in that year.[101] While careful to distance himself from the 'dangerous doctrines' of Scrope and Doyle, Longfield's lectures on the subject, given in his capacity as Whately professor of political economy at the University of Dublin, placed him at odds with his eponymous patron, the archbishop of Dublin, who remained implacably opposed to such a concession. The editorials of John Black in the *Morning Chronicle* are also credited with persuading some economists (including James Mill) of the utility of an Irish poor law, although his influence has probably been exaggerated.[102]

The effects of these 'conversions' among the classical economists should not be overstated. Although public opinion had unquestionably shifted over the decade preceding 1835, orthodox political-economic opinion was now divided rather than fully persuaded, and some of the most prominent and respected public economists, such as Malthus, Senior and Robert Torrens, remained as intensely opposed to an Irish poor law as before. At a meeting of the Political Economy Club in December 1833 (i.e. after the report of the English poor inquiry and while the Irish inquiry was sitting), McCulloch found himself in a decided minority in opposing a hostile motion on the question moved by Spring Rice and endorsed by Malthus, Senior and others. However, a later meeting in 1835 reversed this consensus in the absence of the latter figures and under pressure from Edwin Chadwick.[103] Even so, some of the 'converts', such as McCulloch, remained lukewarm, and others, like Longfield, were clearly uneasy at finding themselves in the same camp as the poor-law enthusiasts. The initiative for an Irish poor law ultimately came from a political rather than a theoretical source, and while it now found some allies in the ranks of the economists, it also faced acute antagonism from those who held to a more hard-line Malthusian position, even in the wake of the English Poor Law Amendment Act of 1834.

Irish landed opposition

The wisdom of the economists was disseminated to a wider audience in both Ireland and Britain through journal literature and anti-poor-law pamphleteering. The theme of Ireland's 'redundant population' and the danger it

101 Mountifort Longfield, *Four Lectures on Poor Laws, delivered in Trinity Term, 1834* (Dublin, 1834).

102 Macintyre, *Liberator*, p. 208.

103 Extracts from Mallet's diary, 6 Dec. 1833, Mar. 1835, *Political Economy Club*, pp. 250–3, 266–7.

posed to social stability was quickly taken up as a counterweight to moralist arguments for a poor law. Irish Anglican supporters of a poor law were countered by the clergymen such as William Hickey and M. I. Keating who echoed a reductive Malthusian line and looked to moral education to promote preventive checks to population growth, or to emigration draining off the surplus to the colonies, as desirable alternatives. There was, Hickey insisted in 1820, no more injudicious law than the 43rd Elizabeth; it required gradual abolition in England and total exclusion from Ireland.[104] Another Protestant clergyman asserted that poor laws could only safely be granted in the wake of an effective demarcation of the farming from the labouring classes; any premature introduction must lead to widespread abuse, and actually subsidize rackrenting landlords at the expense of the industrious agriculturalists.[105] The rector of Derryvullan in Fermanagh recommended in the place of poor laws the consolidation of holdings and adherence to the motto '*laissez nous faire*'.[106]

Representatives of the landed interest in Ireland frequently fell back on the arguments of orthodox economics, while distancing themselves from responsibility from the state of the country's poor. Lord Carbery, a resident landowner in west Cork, wrote to the *Munster Farmer's Magazine* in 1818 with a dire warning that acute subdivision now threatened a Malthusian catastrophe. His solution lay not in poor laws, but in a ban on further subdivision, provisions against the erection of the 'mudwalled cabin[s]' in which the Irishman 'rears a brood of children in a hovel', the gradual consolidation of holdings, and the provision of reproductive employment by landowners.[107]

Another southern landlord, a self-confessed absentee, blamed the 'diseased state of Irish society' on past misgovernment, while warning that poor laws in the current demographic conditions would confiscate the bulk of rents and thus stifle works of improvement. Any such measure must follow and not precede a thinning of the population.[108] Others denounced the idea as an Owenite plot to check the beneficial operations of emigration and rejected

104 [William Hickey], *The State of the Poor of Ireland briefly considered and Agricultural Education recommended, to check Redundant Population and to promote National Improvement* (Dublin, 1820); M. I. Keating, *A Letter to Wilmot Horton . . . on Emigration from Ireland* (Limerick, n.d.). Hickey, who was incumbent of a series of parishes in Co. Wexford, also wrote on economic and agricultural issues as 'Martin Doyle'; Keating was rector of Ventry, Co. Kerry.

105 Richard Ryan, *A Letter to the Right Hon. E. G. Stanley . . . in Answer to Doctor Doyle's Letter, to Thomas Spring Rice . . . on the Subject of Poor Laws* (Dublin, 1831).

106 Rev. George Miller, 'Observations on the circumstances and habits of the people of Fermanagh', *PIC: Appendix C, Part ii*, pp. 28e–29e.

107 Parker, *Plea for the Poor*, pp. 146–56.

108 Anon., *A Letter to a Friend, on the State of Ireland; with some Observations on the Best Mode of introducing Poor Laws into that Kingdom* (Bristol, 1830).

the claim that Irish labour migration was the cause of English distress; or rebutted Scrope through reference to Malthus' case that a poor law must lead to yet further demoralization.[109] George Hampden Evans, a Co. Dublin landowner and a generous philanthropist in his own neighbourhood, warned that a poor-rate could only (as in England) increase the number of paupers by holding out a bounty to indolence and draining the productive capital of the country. McCulloch's evidence to the 1825 inquiry had, he (rather overhastily) asserted in 1829, never been contradicted, and Irish advocates of the measure were simply doing the dirty work of the self-interested labour protectionists in England. Evans would adhere to the case for active paternalism in place of a poor law through the following decade.[110] A rather cruder Malthusianism was voiced with predictable regularity in parliament by the Earl of Limerick in reaction to any suggestion of an Irish poor law.[111]

There was also an alternative, anti-Malthusian case against a poor law made by Irish landowners. George Ensor, the prolific commentator on political and economic questions and subsequently a Repealer, published in 1823 *The Poor and their Relief*, a general treatise on the history and theory of poor relief, which identified the internal contradictions in Malthus' argument on population and dissected the multiple 'vain remedies' that had been proposed for pauperism. While rejecting the standard Malthusian arguments as unproven or erroneous, Ensor made clear his own opinion that the poor laws, as a 'fraudulent and inhuman policy', were tolerable where they existed only as a necessary evil in the absence of more sweeping changes. His interpretation of the real causes of poverty were those of a populist radical (although more of the Humeite than Cobbettite stamp); 'old corruption' had imposed high taxation, tithes, corn laws and high rents on the people in both islands, reducing them to distress. Once these pauperizing oppressions had been removed by political change, poor laws would be replaced by 'the tenderness and generosity of relations – of friends – of neighbours – of the public . . ..'[112]

109 Henry Flood, *Poor Laws. Arguments against a Provision for Paupers, if it be Parochial or Perpetual* (Dublin, 1830); Anon., *Remarks on an Article in the Quarterly Review, for February, 1831; entitled 'Poor Law for Ireland'* (Dublin, 1831).

110 G. H. Evans, *Remarks on the Policy of introducing the System of Poor Rates into Ireland* (London, 1829). Evans was MP for Co. Dublin 1832–41, and voted consistently against the government poor law bills.

111 *Hansard*, 2, xiv, 408–9 [15 Feb. 1826]; xvii, 129–30 [29 Mar. 1827], xix, 251–3 [1 May 1828].

112 George Ensor, *The Poor and their Relief* (London, 1823). A decade later Ensor was still declaiming his opposition to poor laws and urging abolition of tolls and charges in their place, NLI: MP, Ms 13,375/2, 14, Ensor to Spring Rice, 7 Mar., Spring Rice to Ensor, 18 Mar. 1833.

Although highly erratic in his pronouncements on the subject, a similar combination of landed paternalism and a reductively constitutional reading of the causes of poverty would also mark the opinions of his friend Daniel O'Connell.[113]

Other landed commentators who may not have endorsed Ensor's radicalism shared his unease with both the state of society and the doctrines of orthodox economics. One option was to propose paternalist voluntary initiatives as a substitute for a poor law. One landowner suggested the formation of companies of gentlemen raising subscriptions to settle poor families on reclaimed waste-lands. Another, fearing that 'parliament may impose a system of poor laws from mistaken policy and the selfish considerations of the English people', urged instead a self-imposed system of labour (or emigration) rates under local control.[114] This positing of a morally regenerated landlordism as an alternative to poor laws was also promoted by William Hickey and was taken up by the doyen of Dublin Toryism George Alexander Hamilton, and would have an impact on the deliberations of the Poor Inquiry Commission of 1833–36.[115] Such exhortations to landed voluntarism did little, however, to dissuade those already convinced that a poor law was required to compel the class as a whole to alter their behaviour.

English opposition to an Irish poor law

Many English observers also responded to the growing demands for an Irish poor law in both countries with hostility. For those committed to the abolition or severe pruning of their own relief institutions, the campaign for a translation of the '43rd Elizabeth' to Ireland appeared contrary to both sound economic doctrine and common sense. One spokesman for northern commercial interests challenged the alarmism over Irish labour migration and argued that full freedom of trade and the dynamics of private enterprise must extend manufacturing industry to Ireland and thereby resolve its crises.[116] The 1826 trade depression and failure of Ireland (outside the north-east) to

113 See below, pp. 87–90.

114 Charles T. Waller, *A Plan for the Relief of the Poor in Ireland (Bath, 1826); Anon., A Letter to the Right Hon. the Earl of Darnley, on the Introduction of a Labour Rate for the Employment of the Poor in Ireland* (Dublin, 1831).

115 Martin Doyle [William Hickey], *An Address to the Landlords of Ireland, on Subjects connected with the Melioration of the Lower Classes* (Dublin, 1831); George Alexander Hamilton, 'Memorandum on the state of the labouring classes, Balbriggan, County of Dublin', *PIC: Appendix C, Part ii*, pp. 26e–28e.

116 James Cropper, *Present State of Ireland: with a Plan for improving the Condition of the People* (Liverpool, 1825).

respond as expected to the total abolition of trade barriers cast doubts on such naïve optimism, but Irish labour migration continued to find defenders among those who believed that it was demand rather than supply led, and that it benefited the English economy. Commentators convinced that the English laws were the source of demoralization were unlikely to recommend them for a society that was regarded as infinitely more wretched and 'barbarous' to begin with. Although some provision was legitimate for the 'impotent' categories of the poor, one writer noted in 1830, the only remedies for able-bodied labourers were voluntary charity in cases of acute distress, and education in the virtues of self-dependence.[117] The *Manchester Guardian* similarly echoed the concerns of the orthodox economists over the stimulus to reproduction and the drain on the reproductive wages-fund inherent in any poor law for the able-bodied in Ireland, while defending the utility of Irish labour-migration to England.[118]

A more considered and lengthy critique was provided by Sir John Benn Walsh, a landowner and magistrate in Berkshire, Cumberland and Radnorshire and a Tory MP.[119] Walsh admitted in 1830 that the question had recently attracted considerable attention in Britain, due both to the greater diffusion of knowledge about the sister island as well as to the alarm aroused by the influx of large numbers of Irish labourers. While Britain deserved blame for the consequences of its previous neglect or misgovernment of Ireland, the greatest danger now was, he warned, any precipitate and irrevocable action respecting poor laws. The case for a poor law must, he continued, be argued from Irish rather than British premises, as any selfish step to protect British labour or agriculture from Irish competition would amount to a gross betrayal of the already unpopular Union. In any case, any advantages to Britain would prove wholly imaginary given the implacable laws of the market, the cheapness of steamship travel, and the likelihood that a poor law would increase rather than reduce labour migration by promoting clearances. The logic of Malthus' doctrine that poor laws tended only to augment pauperism and prove a dead weight on the energies of the community was incontrovertible. Indeed, Malthus had simply delineated the beneficent wisdom of divine providence, which the utopian enthusiasts for human perfection ignored at their peril. The principles of population proved:

117 George A. Grierson, *The Circumstances of Ireland considered with Reference to the Question of Poor Laws* (London, 1830).
118 *MG*, 19 Apr. 1828, 1 Feb. 1834.
119 John Benn Walsh, *Poor Laws in Ireland, considered in their Probable Effects upon the Capital, the Prosperity and the Progressive Improvement of that Country* (London, 1830).

> that the Great Author of Nature had introduced a powerful spring into the moral machinery of the world, that its uncontrouled effects would be boundless, but that, compressed, and regulated by other causes, it continues a chief agent in his government, and imparts a regular and sustained impulse to the course of mankind.[120]

This classic liberal-Tory formulation of the intimate relationship between natural and divine laws in regulating human affairs was the motto of Walsh's discussion. These truths were recognized by 'all the most eminent statesmen, [and] by all the most profound and reflecting writers of every party', leaving only the deluded and popularity-seeking to argue the opposite. In England, where the poor laws were acknowledged to be 'an increasing, an almost irremediable evil, gnawing, like a canker, into the heart of her prosperity', the difficulties that lay in the way of abolition from social convulsion were, regrettably, great. But while that country possessed sufficient wealth and civilization to withstand the drain on her capital, energy and social cohesion, the same could not be said of 'backward' Ireland, and any arguments made on the grounds that what had worked in one country was therefore applicable to the other, as in McCulloch's recent statements, were not only problematic in themselves, but highly dangerous given the profound differences between the countries. Ireland lacked the rural middle class essential to provide the machinery of any workable system, and the peasant secret societies that so disturbed the country would ignore it as a distraction from their demands for more land and lower rents. The imposition of a poor law would destroy both the ability and the desire of the bulk of Irish landowners to improve the condition of the people, and would check the existing signs of social and economic improvement. Beneath any claims to rationality, he concluded, the campaign was, in the manner of the French Revolution, a form of class warfare, as 'Poor Rates in Ireland are a translation of "guerre aux chateaux"'.[121]

The most extended negative commentary on the idea of an Irish poor law was provided in 1830 by James Ebenezer Bicheno. The son of a premillennialist Baptist minister from Newbury and an overseer of the poor for that parish, Bicheno was something of a polymath; a barrister, secretary to the Linnaean Society, and Fellow of the Royal Society, he wrote with equal zeal on legal reform, economics, zoology and botany. In 1817 he had published a treatise on poor laws in general in which he announced his support for a 'bold measure of extinguishing' them in England, albeit by stages. Bicheno's case was grounded less in economics than in evangelical

120 *Ibid.*, p. 15.
121 *Ibid.*, p. 123.

moralism and a concern for the ethical implications of Malthus' writings. The disjuncture between the rapid progress in middle-class morality and the 'vicious tameness' of the increasingly separate order of the poor he attributed to the 'mistaken benevolence' of the poor laws. These had originated in 'mistaken notions of Christian precepts' that had arisen 'during the corrupted state of the Roman Church' and had unfortunately lingered in England after its incomplete Reformation. True Christians should now seek to complete a moral reformation and bring society into tune with God's beneficent natural laws:

> The laws, having given the right of subsistence to every man, contrary to the natural order of Providence, attempt something which they cannot attain. They destroy the essential properties of benevolence, by taking away the moral liberty and judgement; – and can it be any wonder then that the object of it is not obtained? The law, in consequence of its precise and positive nature, cannot discriminate between the deserving and the undeserving, the industrious and the idle, those whom a little pecuniary assistance would encourage to virtue, and those who would squander it in vice. The charity that is compelled to dispense its benefits thus at random, like a state lottery, will care as little how its ill-gotten provision is lavished. . . . That which is a matter of conscience cannot be governed by any power but its own. Civil law can never determine an obligation that depends on the choice and preference of the individual; and it would be as impotent to make men pious, grateful, or merciful, by acts of parliament, as it had been to make them charitable.[122]

Clearly Bicheno was as much concerned with reclaiming the sacred activity of charity from state regulation as he was with the economic consequences of the poor laws, and in this he shared much of the evangelical Christian economics associated most prominently with Thomas Chalmers.[123]

This was the baggage Bicheno brought with him on the tour he made of Ireland in 1829 in the company of Frederick Page. The outcome, *Ireland and its Economy*, which appeared the following year, was, he assured his readers, the product of detailed empirical research. Ireland's state was, he began, as anomalous to the English political and moral philosopher as Australia was to the naturalist. At root the backwardness of the country arose from the partial and flawed conquest and Reformation. As a consequence of the continuing conflict that ensued Ireland lacked both the paternalism of feudal social

122 J. E. Bicheno, *An Inquiry into the Poor Laws, chiefly with a View to examine them as a Scheme of National Benevolence, and to elucidate their Political Economy* (2nd edn, London, 1824), pp. 148–50.

123 For the intellectual parallels between Bicheno and Chalmers, see Hilton, *Age of Atonement*, pp. 78–80, 217–18.

relationships and the dynamic of capitalist agriculture that had emerged in Britain. The exploitative and irresponsible Irish gentry were (with some individual exceptions) chiefly responsible for the current crisis.

While Bicheno was prepared to acknowledge that the shocking reality of Irish distress appeared to render something like a poor law necessary, his chapter on the subject made explicit the constraints that needed to be imposed. Some augmentation and co-ordination of the existing institutions for relieving the impotent, aged and sick poor he regarded as legitimate – as embracing the classes initially envisaged as 'deserving' under the Elizabethan act – and hence uncontroversial. However, consistently with his previous comments, he insisted that any further intervention must not damage the existing forms of charitability and familial responsibility that were the saving graces of Ireland (and to a great extent also of Scotland). The business of the true statesman was, Bicheno opined, 'to keep the natural affections active in society as long as he can'; the happiness of society rested on maintaining its moral character.[124] His concern was as much about the morally sapping consequences of compulsory relief on the giver as on the receiver. The centrality of this consideration had not been grasped by those who had approached the subject from a purely political-economic perspective:

> [T]o paralyse the noble virtue of charity by the calculations of prudential reason, or the statistics of political economy, can never be the wish of any wise or good man; and it is far better that some abuse of indiscriminate relief should exist, than that we should extinguish our best feelings by a cold and frigid philosophy. My arguments are chiefly intended to caution the world against ministering to its own deception, by the encouragement they at present give to philanthropic enthusiasts, who imagine the world will never go on well but under their direction, and to the second-hand and spurious charity of committees, boards, vestries, and other bodies of men acting in a collective or corporate capacity. . . . Charity, to bless him who gives and him who receives, must be impelled by sympathy of heart, directed by a sound discretion.[125]

Bicheno's animus was not against political economy *per se*, but against those practitioners (such as McCulloch) who ignored the moral dimension of economic life stressed by Christian political economists such as Malthus and Chalmers. Like the later Malthus, Bicheno was favourably inclined towards mass emigration as a remedy, so long as the responsibility for behavioural change was brought home to the Irish landowners by making the land bear the expenses of transplantation.[126]

124 Bicheno, *Ireland and its Economy*, p. 255.
125 *Ibid.*, pp. 266–7.
126 *Ibid.*, pp. 273–4.

Bicheno had by 1830 come to the attention of Lord Lansdowne's political circle, which also included Spring Rice. Conveniently for the development of a patronage relationship, Bicheno had exempted Lansdowne from his charges against clearing landlords. This connection, along with the favourable reception of his book, would ensure that Bicheno was called (along with Page) before Spring Rice's Commons committee on the state of Ireland in 1830, where he gave greater emphasis in his evidence than he had in his book to the need for an agrarian 'transition' towards capitalist, large-farm agriculture, in line with the orthodoxies of classical economic thought in Ireland. His well-known views and good connections ultimately led to his belated appointment to the Irish Poor Inquiry Commission in 1834.[127] Bicheno's was to become a privileged, and an influential, voice in the Irish poor law debates.

By 1830 the main arguments for and against an Irish poor law had been established and were well aired before the political publics of both countries. A vigorous lobby for an Irish poor law had emerged, but had stimulated an equally vigorous counterweight, and failed to attract much political support. Providentialist theological cases had been deployed on both sides. A number of developments over the following six years would bring the question to a head and lead to the formulation of a highly contested legislative response in 1837. Principal among these were the growing intensity of public pressure for legislation in both Ireland and Great Britain, the assertiveness of much of the Catholic clergy on the matter, the changing of the parameters of the debate in the wake of the English poor law inquiry report and the reform measure of 1834, and the shifting balances of power and Irish strategy within the Whig-liberal administrations after 1830.

127 Ibid., p. 93; *Second Report of the Select Committee on the State of the Poor in Ireland*, PP 1830 (654), vii.451, pp. 377–8.

3

The campaigns for an Irish poor law, 1826–35

The intellectual, moral and pragmatic cases for and against a poor law for Ireland were well established in print by 1830. From the later 1820s parliamentary and outdoor pressure for such an enactment began to increase, tentatively at first, but reaching a significant level of intensity by 1830–31. This chapter considers the parliamentary initiatives led by Irish Whig-liberals and British popular and Tory radicals; the attempts by the anti-poor-law lobby to stifle this movement through the mechanism of a committee of inquiry giving precedence to the rival philanthropic philosophy of Thomas Chalmers; the restatement of the orthodox economic position by Nassau Senior; and the conflict between Bishop James Doyle and Daniel O'Connell over the place of the politics of poor relief in the 'outdoor' politics of post-emancipation Ireland.

Lord Darnley and the Irish Whigs

Parliamentary interest in an Irish poor law was slow to develop in the 1820s, but had become a prominent matter for debate in both Houses by 1830. The initial, rather tentative, advocates of an Irish poor law were a group of 'popular' Irish Whig-liberals, principally the Earl of Darnley in the Lords, and James Grattan (MP for Co. Wicklow), Charles Brownlow (Co. Armagh) and Henry Villiers Stuart (Co. Waterford), in the Commons. Darnley was a significant landowner in Meath and Kent, and a regular advocate of state provision of employment for the Irish poor. While he argued that such aid was vital, he also believed the landowners were also under the obligation of spending some part of their income on employing the poor on their estates (as he himself had done around Athboy).[1] Initially hostile towards a compulsory poor law, Darnley appears to have been gradually won over, perhaps by Bishop Doyle, with whom he was in correspondence on the state of the Irish poor in the later 1820s. Doyle later lamented that 'all the efforts made by your

1 *Hansard*, 2, ix, 1043–6 [19 June 1823], xi, 236–61 [8 Apr. 1824].

lordship . . . to better the condition of the Irish poor, were coldly received or in no ways attended to'.[2]

By 1826 Darnley was, rather uncertainly, calling for the consideration of 'some modified provision' shorn of the abuses of the English relief system. In 1827, 1828 and 1829 he again raised the subject in the Lords, making clear his preference for relief to the impotent poor alongside employment provision for the able-bodied, and citing in support a range of arguments, including the danger Irish emigration posed for Britain, Doyle's evidence on the extremity of distress, M. T. Sadler's refutation of the assisted-emigration schemes preferred by the ministry, the collapse of voluntary relief, and the ethical case for state intervention.[3] These interventions led *The Times* to praise Darnley as the acme of Irish landlordism (and to denounce his opponent Lord Limerick as his moral opposite).[4] By 1830 Darnley was more self-confidently proposing the introduction of a modified system of poor laws into Ireland, in the wake of 'a great revolution . . . in the opinion of all persons' on the subject.[5]

Initiatives in the Commons were at first equally tentative. In 1825 James Grattan, son of the deceased patriot leader, was prepared only to propose an experimental bill to allow parishes to assess themselves (rather along the lines of the Kilmore petition of the previous year and echoing Scottish practice). Despite his insistence on distancing this mild suggestion from the abuses of the English system, the mere mention of the subject drew fundamentalist hostility from the Irish Tories William Vesey Fitzgerald and Maurice Fitzgerald and the Whig Sir Henry Parnell, all of whom regarded it as a wedge that must rapidly open the door to a ruinous and sweeping expansion of relief along English lines.[6]

A stronger line of advocacy appears to have been stimulated by the petitions for a system of compulsory relief drawn up in the major urban centres (outside Ulster) in the wake of the industrial crisis of 1826. Despite vigorous

2 *Ibid.*, xi, 1099–1100 [10 June 1824]; Darnley to Doyle, 20 Feb. 1827, 17 Nov. 1828, Doyle to Darnley, 30 Dec. 1830, in Fitzpatrick (ed.), *Doyle*, ii, pp. 92, 370–2, 236–8.

3 *Hansard*, 2, xiv, 407–8 [15 Feb. 1826]; xvii, 128–32 [29 Mar. 1827]; xix, 239–51 [1 May 1828]. The latter motion was phrased in religious language: 'Would their lordships call themselves the followers of the benevolent Jesus, who taught them to feed the hungry and to clothe the naked, and who spent his whole life in going about doing good, when they refused to take this subject into their consideration, because it was opposed to the political notions of some persons?'

4 *The Times*, 2 May 1828, 30 May 1829.

5 *Hansard*, 2, xxiii, 366–76 [16 Mar. 1830].

6 *Ibid.*, xii, 1136–8 [22 Mar. 1825].

resistance from local Tory and shopkeeping interests, a series of public meetings in Cork city resolved to demand some form of poor law. This was in the context of the catastrophic collapse of the county's linen and cotton industry in that year.[7] When the Cork petition was debated in parliament in 1827, Grattan declared that he was now of the opinion that a poor law could not be worse than the present situation. His brother Henry, MP for Dublin city, agreed that the state of the Irish towns now rendered some modified system indispensable, but in the face of widespread hostility from other Irish MPs and government indifference, the brothers decided they could not proceed.[8] The continuing social crisis in Dublin and other depressed manufacturing districts sparked further petitions and resolutions in 1828–29, including an appeal from the Trades Union to the people of England protesting (in an interesting inversion of the English assumption) that the English poor laws were ruining the Irish manufacturers by allowing the underselling of goods, while unchecked absenteeism was starving the rural poor.[9] A growing number of petitions for a poor law on the Elizabethan model came from the unemployed proto-industrial workers of Leinster. One demanded that parliament

> assimilate the laws of *England* and *Ireland*, as they have reference to the poor, whereby a provision may be made certain for the aged and infirm, the widow and the orphan protected from impending danger, the balsam of relief stretched forth to the weary stranger, and the heartless lord and their contracted gentry compelled to bear their proportionate burthen of these works of mercy.

Others also insisted on employment relief for the able-bodied, and expressed regret that the poor were obliged by destitution to flock to England.[10] A petition from the Society for the Improvement of Ireland calling for a relief law was introduced enthusiastically in 1828 by Charles Brownlow (who was

7 Lane, *Sheahan*, pp. 13–14; David Dickson, *Old World Colony: Cork and South Munster 1630–1830* (Cork, 2005), p. 491. The petition from the 'inhabitants of Cork' was countered by one from its Protestant parishioners expressing 'alarm' at the proposal of 'the obnoxious measure of a Poor Law system', *JHC*, lxxxii (1826–27), p. 300.

8 *Hansard*, 2, xvi, 1086–91 [9 Mar. 1827]. For Henry Grattan's previous ambivalence, see *Report of the Select Committee on the Condition of the Labouring Poor in Ireland*, PP 1823 (561), vi.331, p. 131.

9 Address from the Trades of Ireland to the People of England, 17 Mar. 1828, *Political Register*, 27 Sept. 1834. For the devastating and sustained effect of the 1826 depression on living conditions in Dublin, see David O'Toole, 'The employment crisis of 1826', in Dickson (ed.), *Gorgeous Mask*, pp. 157–71.

10 *JHC*, lxxxiii (1828), pp. 169, 221, 238, 246, 319, 383: petitions from the weavers, manufacturers and traders of Dublin, Kilmanaghan, Ballycumber, and Clara, King's Co., and Moate, Co. Westmeath, etc.

Darnley's son-in-law as well as a member of that society) and supported by the Grattan brothers, who endeavoured to tie the desideratum of waste-land reclamation to a poor law in a manner advocated by a number of Irish pamphleteers.[11]

By 1829 Brownlow was prepared to go further than the still cautious Grattans, and endorsed Henry Villiers Stuart's motion for a measure based on the 43rd of Elizabeth that would include statutory relief for the able-bodied destitute. Crucially, he argued, the bill must act penally against his fellow landowners. Only a compulsory assessment would force the absentees to return and oblige landowners to employ the labourers on their estates rather than see them thrown on the poor-rates. In his opinion, the passage of Catholic emancipation should now allow attention to shift to the social question, which the disfranchisement of the forty shilling freeholders threatened to render yet more precarious.[12] For his part Villiers Stuart sought to play on English fears about the spillover effects of Irish distress and the inevitability under the Union of both societies finding either a higher or a lower equilibrium of living standards, while also stressing the positive advantages of the English model: the poor law would raise the poor man by giving him a modicum of independence from his employer, and free him from the 'potatoe-minimum' that entailed constant vulnerability to famine.[13]

For the first time, this more forceful motion of 1829 drew serious responses from the ministerial front benches. Lord Palmerston, then secretary at war (as well as an extensive Irish landowner in counties Sligo and Dublin), denounced poor laws along orthodox economic lines as a tax on industry and production and hence a waste of capital. The Irish chief secretary Lord Francis Leveson Gower claimed that the evidence relating to a poor law for Ireland was solidly against it. More circumspectly, home secretary Robert Peel conceded that the matter was worthy of discussion, but believed the great difficulties lying in its way must render such a measure impracticable. Villiers Stuart's motion was withdrawn, but the growing interest both within and without parliament (in both countries) was leading the government and other parliamentary opponents towards identifying a strategy for managing the Irish poor-law question.[14]

11 *Hansard*, 2, xix, 1036–49 [6 June 1828]. Brownlow introduced a bill to promote waste-land reclamation the following year.

12 *Ibid.*, xxi, 1149–54 [7 May 1829]. He subsequently made clear his objection to the labour-protectionist case for an Irish poor law made by figures such as the Liverpool MP General Gascoyne, *ibid.*, xxiii, 209–11 [11 Mar. 1830].

13 *Ibid.*, xxi, 1123–30 [7 May 1829].

14 For the impact of these arguments in 'converting' at least one English provincial newspaper, see *MG*, 23 May 1829.

Sadler and Tory-radicalism

For several years from 1829 the most prominent torch-bearer for an Irish poor law in parliament, albeit of a rather different description to that envisaged by the Irish 'popular' Whigs, was the English evangelical Tory-radical Michael Thomas Sadler. Given the controversial and polarizing nature of Sadler's rhetoric and politics, this may have been a mixed blessing for Irish advocates; certainly the liberal-Protestant Villiers Stuart sought to disassociate himself from the controversial and violently anti-Catholic orator in 1829. A vigorous, if eccentric, opponent of Malthus' population theory, Sadler developed an interest in Ireland in reaction to the 1827 Commons emigration committee report, and the apparent ministerial sympathy given to Wilmot Horton's colonization proposals for both islands. In 1828 he entered the lists with a pamphlet attacking the emigration project and the Malthusian propositions underlying it, and was provided with a public platform the following year when he was returned to parliament for the ultra-Tory duke of Newcastle's pocket borough of Newark.[15]

In a series of rambling, if impassioned, speeches, Sadler introduced motions calling for the straightforward extension of the 'old' English poor law to Ireland in June 1830, August 1831 and June 1832. His commitment to the subject was, he affirmed, grounded in his conviction that the condition of English labour could not be ameliorated without the simultaneous elevation of the working classes in Ireland. Natural law theory, the logic of the Union, the practice of virtually all European and American polities, and true Protestant religion all dictated that the 'rights of the poor' enshrined in the English law be extended to the Irish. Sadler's European models were the 'humane provisions' of Protestant states, for 'in every country where it had prevailed, Catholicism had carried its charity to the poor to an excess that was almost culpable, inasmuch as it tended to create the very evil which it aimed at removing'.[16] The regular horrors of Irish famine and pestilence (and their impact on England through crisis migration and constant calls for financial assistance) were, he claimed, directly attributable to the absence of compulsory poor relief and the social injustice this permitted, rather than to any excess of population over productive resources.[17] Sadler's claims to economic expertise were treated with withering contempt by orthodox political

15 M. T. Sadler, *Ireland: its Evils, and their Remedies: Being a Refutation of the Errors of the Emigration Committee and Others* (London, 1828). This in turn drew a spirited riposte from Wilmot Horton in *Causes and Remedies of Pauperism in the United Kingdom considered* (London, 1830).

16 *Hansard*, 2, xxiv, 1294–327 [3 Jun. 1830].

17 *Ibid.*, 3, vi, 783–816 [29 Aug. 1831].

economists and philosophical radicals, but he drew support from a coalition of assorted Tory-radicals and paternalists, Irish reformers and populist radicals, and despite clear government hostility, his 1831 motion was lost by only sixty-four to fifty-two votes.[18] After a highly repetitive debate his 1832 motion was also lost, although by the larger margin of seventy-seven to fifty-eight.[19] While indicative of a bloc of support for an Irish poor law in the Commons, these small divisions were not necessarily representative.

The growing volume of demands for an Irish poor law from both countries did, however, put pressure on the administration and the parliamentary opponents of such a measure to offer some form of concrete response. There is little evidence to suggest that the Tory ministers in 1828–30 (with the possible exceptions of the lord lieutenant Lord Anglesey and the secretary to the Admiralty J. W. Croker) had any sympathy for such an initiative, and certainly Wellington as prime minister made his opposition explicit in the Lords in 1828 and again in 1830.[20] The ministry discussed the possibility of tinkering with the laws relating to the medical charities and grand jury presentments, but preferred the encouragement of self-help to state intervention on behalf of the poor, and to this end in 1829 extended to Ireland legislation promoting and regulating friendly societies.[21] Core Tory thinking on the economic problems of Ireland changed little thereafter, and is expressed succinctly in Lord Ellenborough's private comments in response to the 1833 coercion bill:

> I see no hope of amendment in that country without a gradual enlargement of farms, the undertaking of great works, emigration and the return of absentees. Of these all but emigration depend upon tranquillity.[22]

Spring Rice, Chalmers and the 1830 Committee

The most committed, and increasingly anxious, Irish opponents of poor laws were becoming rattled by this upsurge in parliamentary attention. Thomas Spring Rice's case against poor laws in both countries was rigidly Malthusian,

18 *Ibid.*, 816–54.

19 *Ibid.*, xiii, 831–73 [19 June 1832].

20 *Ibid.*, 2, xix, 257–9 [1 May 1828]; xxiii, 367–8 [16 Mar. 1830]. The Irishman Croker favoured the extension of poor laws to Ireland, but appears not to have pressed this on his colleagues: see Croker to Drummond, 26 Feb., 4 Mar. 1825, Louis Jennings (ed.), *The Croker Papers: The Correspondence and Diaries of the late Right Honourable John Wilson Croker* (3 vols, London, 1884) i, pp. 283–4.

21 Brian Jenkins, *Era of Emancipation: British Government of Ireland 1812–1830* (Kingston, Ont., 1988), pp. 281–5.

22 Ellenborough diary, 18 Feb. 1833, in A. Aspinall (ed.), *Three Early Nineteenth Century Diaries* (London, 1952), p. 305.

although he made the case for assistance to the country through emigration and public works. He had also made a strong emotional investment in the principle of voluntarism, having served as a governor of the Limerick house of industry. He had warned parliament in 1829 that even the public discussion of the matter was dangerous as it raised unrealizable expectations in Ireland.[23] Alarmed by the noise Sadler had raised, he took the trouble to write to Bishop Doyle to warn him against the 'childish errors' of reasoning in Sadler's book, and to assure the prelate that his own opposition to an Irish poor law was grounded on true concern for its likely effect on the conditions of the poor rather than mere landed prejudice.[24] In September he wrote to Lansdowne that, while the feeling in Ireland 'is on all sides adverse to the Poor Laws', he feared that Peel and the chancellor of the exchequer, Henry Goulburn, might both be 'bit'. An 'enquiry into the state of our poor and the best means of improving it' would be desirable, he added, implicitly as a defensive mechanism to fend off any danger of undesirable legislation.[25]

The precedents for such a step were well established. In 1804, 1819, 1823 and 1825 select committees on the state of Ireland, dominated by 'experts' on political economy and Irish conditions, had recommended against any extension of poor laws to Ireland, and suggested other measures of improvement in their place. The Waterford MP Sir John Newport, who had chaired the inquiries of 1804 and 1819, had taken a particularly strong line against a parochial rate, and was succeeded by Spring Rice as the voice of liberal landed opposition from 1823.[26] Spring Rice, having been assured that the government would have no objection, moved in March 1830 that a new select committee of inquiry be formed to consider the state of the labouring poor in Ireland, free from the rhetorical excesses of the Commons chamber. He was well aware that some might be sceptical as to the real purposes behind such a manoeuvre, but assured the House of his sincerity in seeking to elucidate and adjudicate between all opinions. At the same time, he took the opportunity to establish his own views. The distress of the poor in Ireland had, he

23 *Hansard*, 2, xxi, 1142–3 [7 May 1829].

24 NLI: MP, Ms 13,345, Spring Rice to Doyle, 26 Apr. 1829. He sought to refute the heresies of the 'Sadlerian school' more generally in 'Mr Sadler's school – Italian economists', *ER*, 50 (Jan. 1830), pp. 344–63.

25 BL: BP, B/95, Spring Rice to Lansdowne, 23 Sept. 1829.

26 *Report of the Select Committee on Legislative Provisions for Support of Aged and Infirm Poor of Ireland, Punishment of Vagrants, and Care of Lunatics*, PP 1803–04 (109) v.771; *Second Report of the Select Committee on State of Disease, and Condition of Labouring Poor, in Ireland*, PP 1819 (409), viii.457; *Report of the Select Committee on the Condition of the Labouring Poor in Ireland*, PP 1823 (561), vi.331; *Reports from the Select Committee on the State of Ireland*, PP 1825 (129), viii.1.

insisted, been grossly exaggerated by interested parties; they were, in fact, in a better position than the pauperized labourers of the south of England, and likely to advance further as Irish agriculture continued in its improving trajectory. Moreover, Ireland already had a magnificent system of asylums and hospitals for the sick, destitute and insane, which were a tribute to the charitable character of the Irish gentry; in contrast, the institutions closest to those of England – the houses of industry – had proved a costly and demoralizing failure. Citing Malthus and Walsh, he proceeded to rebut Sadler's claims about the likely effects of a poor law, and to urge tax rebates in the form of lightening the grand jury cess, and the provision of reproductive public works, as more suitable alternatives.[27]

Although this speech received a mixed response from those already committed on the subject, it was welcomed in essence on behalf of the administration by Leveson Gower, who agreed that the question of a poor law was irrelevant to the phenomena of labour migration to Great Britain and landlord absenteeism, even if he thought Spring Rice had sought to extend the scope of his inquiry too widely.[28] Peel added that 'mature consideration' of the subject was essential, and urged Spring Rice to ensure that the committee's proceedings were focused and practical. He proceeded to give a clear indication of his own views. While the assimilationist case appeared plausible, it was not in his opinion to be taken seriously. General Gascoyne, the Liverpool MP who had urged extension of the full England law to protect his constituents from Irish immigration, was, Peel observed, like 'a fox who had lost its tail, and who wanted to persuade all other foxes that tails were an encumbrance'. Even if introduced in reformed shape, he continued, the constant tendency of any such legislation granting the poor any right to relief was towards abuse and ultimately an agrarian law. Reproductive work could not be found artificially without draining the wages-fund, he went on, and the ill-defined Scottish system was no more applicable than the English law to Ireland. Any attempts to impede the natural, market-driven flow of labour from one place to another were bound to fail, but an Irish poor law would almost certainly artificially stimulate rather than impede the supply of mobile labourers.[29]

After previous rumours of Peel's ambivalence on the subject, this clear rejection must have come as a relief to the opponents of a poor law for Ireland. No realistic measure could proceed without government support, and with both the leading figures in the Tory administration openly against

27 *Hansard*, 2, xxiii, 183–202 [11 Mar. 1830].
28 *Ibid.*, 212–13.
29 *Ibid.*, 216–20.

it, any immediate danger was diminishing.[30] Now confident of official approval, Spring Rice proceeded to constitute his committee with hand-picked members in March 1830. Of those appointed, the majority (it was alleged) had previously made comments hostile to an Irish poor law; they included Sturges Bourne, Althorp, Peel, Parnell and Newport. Brownlow was the only sympathetic MP who took an active part.[31]

Spring Rice sought to neutralize the demand for an Irish poor law based on the English model by giving space to leading advocates of such a measure, including Doyle and McCulloch, while countering them with witnesses he was confident would effectively undermine them. One of these was Bicheno, who reprised his warning that a compulsory poor-rate would 'break up what is of vital importance to a good state of society, the virtuous exercise of the social feelings'. Bicheno also argued that the only effective and acceptable state aid to the necessary agricultural transition in Ireland lay in modest assistance to landlord efforts to emigrate their surplus tenantry.[32] Other 'hostile' witnesses who had already contributed to the poor law debate were Ensor and Hickey.

However the committee's 'star' witness – then approaching the peak of his public influence in England as well as Ireland – was the leading Scottish evangelical divine, Thomas Chalmers. What Bicheno and Chalmers had in common was a Christian political economy grounded in Malthus' pessimistic concern about lower-class immorality and overpopulation, and scepticism about secular progress and human perfectibility. Both located the fundamental cause of poverty and misery in the moral failings of the poor – their lack of foresight, self-help and sexual restraint, in the moral indifference of the upper classes, and in the existence of ill-designed institutions that had encouraged such attitudes (principally the poor law in England – which was now also threatening Ireland, as well as absentee, non-paternalist landlordism).

30 Peel had previously shown little interest in the question, although in 1816 he had proposed the imposition of a strict labour test on able-bodied paupers in the Dublin house of industry to tackle the problem of overcrowding. He lacked sympathy for the argument that Irish labour migration damaged the British economy: McDowell, *Irish Administration*, p. 169; Jenkins, *Era of Emancipation*, p. 287.

31 *Hansard*, 2, xxiv, 1294–333 [3 June 1830]; [Thomas Spring Rice], 'Proposed introduction of the poor laws into Ireland', *ER*, 59 (Apr. 1834), pp. 234. One openly pro-poor-law member, W. H. Trant, appears to have boycotted the proceedings, while Sadler refused to give evidence as he believed himself to have been black-balled from membership.

32 *Second Report . . . on the State of the Poor in Ireland*, PP 1830 (654), vii.451, pp. 380, 382–3.

Chalmers, moreover, had the additional authority garnered from having pioneered an experiment in voluntary poor relief, aimed at 'purifying' the traditional Scottish relief system from its subsequent accretions, in the Glasgow parish of St John's in 1819–23. Stewart Brown describes this as a determined attempt to recreate an ideal 'Godly Commonwealth' amid the social dislocation consequent on the rapid and unsettling industrialization and urbanization of the Scottish lowlands. It is clear, moreover, that Chalmers believed his Glaswegian model readily exportable to both Ireland and England.[33]

Chalmers' objectives in his evidence given before the committee were to justify the superiority of the traditional Scottish system of poor relief over its English rival, to challenge the inroads the latter was starting to make in the practice of the Scottish borders and cities, and to advocate his own perfection of the Scottish approach in the St John's experiment as the optimum system for Ireland. For Chalmers, the chief merit of the traditional Scottish system lay in its minimalism: 'the excellence of our system', he opined, 'when compared with that of England, is altogether of a negative kind. Our parochial charity, from the extreme moderation of its allowances, does not seduce our people from a due dependence on themselves, or to a neglect of their relative obligations.'[34] But its true superiority, and indeed universal applicability, resided in its close approximation to the providential natural laws of creation, which Chalmers, as an evangelical Christian political economist, was convinced had been divinely ordained for the regulation of human society. Whereas public relief to the sick, insane and incapable was legitimate and scripturally defensible, assistance to the able-bodied destitute (or indeed to the aged, to abandoned children and even to orphans) was not, and was likely to impede vital behavioural change by offering inducements to dependency, wantonness or immorality.

In St John's parish, he continued, the traditional Scottish system had been perfected through a total abandonment of charitable aid to the destitute (except for the sick and insane, and a dying remnant of 'old' parish paupers), and the introduction of a regime of moral inspection by the lay deacons of the parish who had distinguished the deserving from the undeserving poor and promoted self-help among the urban poor through advice and paternal moral care. The effect, he claimed (although this was disputed by other observers) was a sharp fall in destitution and beggary as well as in parish expenditure on relief – allowing the transfer of resources to the more positive agencies of moral education and church extension.

33 Stewart J. Brown, *Thomas Chalmers and the Godly Commonwealth in Scotland* (Oxford, 1982), pp. xiv–xv.

34 *Second Report . . . on the State of the Poor in Ireland*, p. 287.

The allegedly positive response of Irish immigrants in the parish to this system, despite its being founded on the established Church of Scotland infrastructure, convinced Chalmers of its transferability. Indeed the absence of any pre-existing and corrupting expectation of state relief in Ireland, and the lauded charitability of the rural poor to each other, would make its introduction more straightforward. Contrariwise, the introduction of any compulsory assessment for the poor in Ireland would be disastrous, creating the false expectation of a 'right' to relief, and impeding the necessary socio-economic transition to capitalist agriculture and industry that had been so successful in Scotland but still faced obstacles in Ireland. If such a transition in the absence of any compulsory poor relief might entail short-term suffering, this was preferable to the alternative of moral abasement, which preceded and must determine the socio-economic condition of a people. Chalmers rejected the environmental meliorism typical of many Whigs and radicals, and the Tory-radical paternalism of evangelicals such as Sadler, and replaced these with a more reductive and individualizing 'moderate' evangelical moralism:

> The pervading fallacy in the speculations of those who advocate the establishment of a poor rate in Ireland, . . . is founded on the observation of a connection between a high state of character and a high state of economic comfort . . . It is often conceived that comfort is the cause, and character is the effect; now I hold that character is the cause, and that comfort is the effect. . . . [I]f instead of taking hold of the man, and attempting to elevate him by the improvement of his economic condition, you take hold of the boy, and attempt to infuse into him another element, which I conceive to be the causal one, by means of education, then you will, through the medium of character, work out an improvement to his economic condition. What I should advise is, that education be made universal in Ireland, and that you should weather for a season the annoyance of Ireland's mendicity, and the annoyance of that pressure, which I conceive to be altogether temporary. This appears to me to be the only principle on which Ireland can be securely and effectually brought to a higher standard of enjoyment, and into the state of a well habited and well conditioned peasantry.[35]

Reconsidering this bleak short-term scenario, Chalmers conceded that some temporary relief to immediate suffering through assisted emigration would be acceptable, but doubted that there was much demand for this, and demoted it from the role of panacea that some of its advocates claimed, to that of a useful auxiliary to a developmental strategy based on moral rearmament rather than state intervention.

35 *Ibid.*, p. 315.

Doyle *versus* Chalmers and Senior

If Chalmers and Bicheno had received sympathetic (if leading) questioning from the committee, the foremost pro-poor-law witness, Bishop Doyle, had a rougher ride, and was confronted with a series of a mostly antagonistic cross-examinations. Doyle's evidence was largely in line with his public pronouncements of 1825, although in the aftermath of Chalmers' statements he now downplayed the applicability of any 'Scottish' model for Ireland. The bishop's practical suggestions remained relatively cautious: he still rejected both the workhouse system and any grant of a right to relief to the able-bodied (whom he would relieve only in seasons of 'extraordinary distress'); relief committees would otherwise have the power to levy parochial rates to assist family emigration, give outdoor relief to the 'impotent' poor principally through assistance for rent and clothing, and grant licences to beg to 'resident' paupers only. In ordinary seasons the able-bodied poor would be relieved indirectly through the transfer of the burden of maintaining their 'impotent' dependents to the state. Echoing Swift's preoccupation of a century earlier, Doyle argued that three years' domicile in a parish should give a settlement, and that relief committees should distinguish between the deserving 'settled' beggars, and the wandering 'gypsies, and fortune-tellers, and strumpets and thieves, who go from parish to parish vending all manner of lies, disseminating vice, and troubling the minds of the people with false prophesies [sic] and stories'. Despite its limitations, Doyle understood his proposal as embodying the substance of the 43rd of Elizabeth in a form appropriate to Ireland.[36]

The effect of the incessant critical questioning of Doyle in the committee was, however, to spur him to offer an impassioned defence of the principle of a poor law for Ireland, in a form that transcended these limited concrete proposals. His concise argument for state responsibility could, for example, be used to support a much more extensive relief measure:

> I know that the degree of misery in the present system is such in Ireland as, in my opinion, to demand from the Government of the country a remedy; because I think the first duty of a government is to watch over the lives of its subjects, next over the honour of its subjects, and lastly over their property; and I think where thousands of lives of those subjects are sacrificed, Government is called upon to devise means whereby those lives can be saved; and I think that could be done by an assessment to be imposed (whether permanently, or whilst the transition lasts), upon the property of the country.[37]

36 *Ibid.*, pp. 401, 405.

37 *Ibid.*, p. 399. For criticism of the committee's style of cross-examination made by Doyle's allies, see *Hansard*, 3, i, 409–12, 415–16 [11 Nov. 1830: J. Grattan, Smith O'Brien].

Contra Chalmers, Doyle insisted that the great efforts the Irish poor made in supporting their destitute family and neighbours represented not the epitome of charitable morality, but an index of endemic immiseration. It followed that, imperfect as it was, the introduction of even the current English system would be preferable to the status quo: 'We have . . . a disorganized population becoming by their poverty more and more immoral, and less and less capable of providing for themselves; and we have besides that, the frightful, and awful, and terrific exhibition of human life, wasted with a rapidity and to a degree such as is not witnessed in any civilized country upon the face of the earth.'[38] Rather than offering an opportunity for the active remoralization of society through enlightened private agency, the extremity of Irish poverty threatened social disintegration and the complete collapse of moral values into barbarism in the absence of any preventive interposition of public agency.

The secular responsibility to provide welfare entitlement was derived, Doyle maintained, from the 'evangelical' and natural law on which the legitimacy of any Christian state must be founded. The 'positive law of the gospel' directed that equity rather than equality be the objective of true statesmanship; prudence indicated that this moral requirement could be met without the concession of unregulated and unlimited rights on the part of the poor.[39] Constant prodding by his interlocutors, however, led the bishop into outbursts that deflected from such attempts at measured proposals. Most notably, he reacted angrily to a suggestion that the extent of distress in parts of England under the old poor law might undermine his interpretation of the requirements of divine law:

> It is not compatible in my mind with the attributes of the Deity that any case of the kind could possibly exist. I know that the Almighty in the dispensations of His providence towards nations sometimes does permit plague, famine, war and pestilence to ravage states, so in like manner by a particular infliction of the providence of God, a state may be overrun with pauperism so as to almost destroy the people; but if that did happen, it would be a special visitation of Divine wrath for some violation of the Divine Law, or the omission of some duty which that State should have performed. . . . If therefore a case of that kind of evil to which reference has been made were to happen at any time in this State, it would, in my judgment, be reasonable to consider it not as the result of the laws of pauperism, but as a special punishment from God for having neglected the poor, whose cries are said to ascend to Heaven, and to become the forerunners of Divine wrath.[40]

38 *Second Report . . . on the State of the Poor in Ireland*, p. 415.
39 *Ibid.*, p. 454.
40 *Ibid.*, p. 462.

The implications of this pronouncement were clear; the governors of Ireland, and not the poor themselves, were morally responsible for the visitation of divine providence manifest in endemic poverty and outbreaks of famine. Atonement could come only from the acknowledgement of state responsibility and the adoption of appropriately penitent (and socially redemptive) policies.

While Doyle was not drawn publicly into advocating a measure which would extend a right to relief to the able-bodied poor, the logic of his argument increasingly pointed in this direction. He confessed as much in a private letter in 1832. His proposed restrictions were, he admitted, prompted by political expediency and the desirability of attaining state relief to the 'helpless' poor in the first instance:

> I thought hitherto it would be vain, to attempt in Ireland such a measure as you contemplate, and therefore contented myself with urging a provision for the helpless poor, and a power to relieve by assessment the able-bodied in times of extraordinary distress. I had no serious doubt at any time, and I have no doubt at all at present, but that the able-bodied poor will in a little time extort a provision for themselves; but I would be exceedingly glad that the Legislature anticipated the coming necessity by the adoption of your plan, which I believe is just and feasible. However, as the urging of it at present might interfere with that provision for the helpless poor which is the primary object of my solicitude – and for the adoption of which the Government, the country, and the Legislature are nearly if not fully prepared – I should think it unwise for me to encumber or embarrass it by proposing or advocating a measure of compulsory relief for the able-bodied, such as yours would be.[41]

This was a commitment to the stadial development of poor laws from a limited beginning – much as Spring Rice and other opponents feared.

Spring Rice may have miscalculated in hoping that by subjecting Doyle's ideas to a critical public grilling and by juxtaposing them to the radically different moral construction of poverty proposed by Chalmers and Bicheno, the case for an Irish poor law would be neutralized. The final report of the committee in July 1830 sought further to bury the matter by warning that any false step would have fatal consequences, and sidelining it in preference for a lengthy list of nineteen practical measures of amelioration. These included provisions for consolidating and aiding existing charitable institutions, carrying out public works under reformed direction, giving some assistance to

41 Doyle to William Stanley, 29 Oct. 1832, in Fitzpatrick (ed.), *Doyle*, ii, pp. 429–30.

emigration, reforming the grand jury and vestry systems, and introducing national education.[42]

This postponed the poor-law question for the session, and – presumably with the same object in mind – Spring Rice successfully moved for the re-appointment of the committee with the same personnel at the start of the next session in November 1830. The motion was approved despite the observation of James Grattan that it would again prove a waste of time and expense and a manoeuvre for putting off the debate on a real poor law.[43] In fact the rapidly changing political circumstances prevented the committee reconvening. Spring Rice's admission to the new Grey administration as secretary to the Treasury at the end of the year, and the inclusion of powerful allies such as Lansdowne in the new cabinet, must have reassured him on the matter after the unsettled period of Wellington's administration. The clear statement made by the government's leader in the Commons against Sadler's 1831 motion was particularly reassuring; any such measure to relieve immediate suffering in Ireland (and England), Viscount Althorp declared, 'must subject them to future evils of greater malignity'. Only the 'feelings of honour and independence which prevailed amongst the labouring classes' had, until very recently, preserved England from the evil effects of parish relief to the able-bodied. The absence of such saving virtues in Ireland, he concluded, rendered extension extremely unwise.[44] The new chief secretary, Edward Stanley, was equally dismissive of any initiative that might open the door to able-bodied relief, while acknowledging the growing clamour for change from Ireland.[45] His answer, broadly following Spring Rice's promptings, was to introduce in 1831 measures for national education and public works under the supervision of national boards. For Spring Rice and many other moderate Irish Whig-liberals, the regeneration of Ireland depended on the successful implementation of such initiatives, and could only be hampered by the introduction of a poor law.[46]

42 *Report of the Select Committee on the State of the Poor in Ireland*, PP 1830 (667), vii.1, pp. 55–7. The recommendations appear to have been personally drafted by Spring Rice, see NLI: MP, Ms 13,365, Spring Rice memo 'On state of the Irish poor' [1830].

43 *Hansard*, 3, i, 409–20 [11 Nov. 1830]. Sadler's 1830 motion, which sought to evade the net through its ambiguous titling, was quickly curbed by the government, *ibid.*, 2, xxiv, 1294–1333 [6 June 1830].

44 *Ibid.*, 3, vi, 825–8 [29 Aug. 1831].

45 *Ibid.*, 833–6.

46 For his endorsement of Stanley's policies, see [Spring Rice], 'Ireland', *ER*, 57 (Apr. 1833), pp. 248–79.

Parliamentary reform dominated the attention of the political public during the sessions of 1831 and 1832, but the Irish poor law debate remained lively, not least against the backdrop of the escalating 'tithe war' in Ireland and the questions it posed about the legitimacy (and possible alternative uses) of established Church revenues, and the relationship between agrarian unrest and poverty. Doyle entered the public lists again in March 1831, with his *Letter to Thomas Spring Rice*, intended as a rebuttal to the 'leading questions' which had been put to him the previous year, the contrary evidence presented to the committee, and the anodyne conclusions which its chairman had penned. The pamphlet repeated much of what Doyle had already argued, but with greater coherence and framed in yet more impassioned rhetoric. He identified nine core arguments against an Irish poor law manifest in the 1830 report, and proceeded to refute them. Doyle reiterated his fundamentally moralistic case, but added a more aggressive swipe at the 'selfishness, odious alike to God and man' of those who denied its necessity out of self-interest.[47] The dogma that a poor law would drain investment capital from the wages-fund he dismissed as simultaneously subverting the Gospel's injunction to mercy, and ignoring the likely consequences of the introduction of a genuine measure of social security to the poor: 'It would establish that peace and security which, more effectually than laws, prisons, and police, teach the small capitalist that he may embark his money in trade, or in productive labour, without fear or apprehension.'[48] His harshest criticisms were reserved for the hypocrisy of those who preached the moral superiority of private charity, while evading the requirements of effective relief. While refraining from mentioning Chalmers by name, Doyle denounced his doctrines and those who sought to hide behind them:

> These men abet a system which is proved in evidence to sends thousands prematurely out of life – the victims of famine – the prey of disease; but they are pious withal, and are anxious that no encroachment be made on that divine commandment to which is annexed the promise of 'a long life upon the earth.' They will take care that the child honour the father, that the child may live long; but they will, should he be reduced to poverty, leave him to the care of that Providence which feeds the sparrow on the house top. He may like the lily of the field be clothed better than Solomon, but if they see him naked they will not cover him: if he be poor and a wanderer they will not take him into their house: if he be an orphan they will not break their bread to him: nor wipe away the tear from the cheek of his widowed mother.

47 Doyle, *Letter to Spring Rice . . . on the Establishment of a Legal Provision for the Irish Poor*, p. 12.

48 *Ibid.*, p. 20.

Chalmers and his ilk were not true Christians but 'Pharisees':

> The originals of this class relying on their absurd and impious traditions, made void the commandments of God. – The copyists of our days relying on theories, often the creatures of a heated fancy, or on the doctrines of supply and demand, violate the first duty of statesmen and transgress its precepts – no – but subvert the foundation of the whole Christian law. Yes! for the first duty of a statesman is to secure the necessaries of life to the bulk of the people committed to his care, and Christianity has no characteristic, unless it be that of those who profess it loving one another, and each of them doing to the other as he would have that other do unto him.[49]

Most importantly, in his own eyes, Doyle refuted at length the argument that 'the poor have no claim founded on justice to a provision' at the expense of the propertied.[50] He had, he declared, previously reined in his opinions on this matter so as to avoid exciting uncontrollable anger on the part of the dispossessed against those who continued to deny their moral entitlement. His patience had now snapped. Far from being absolute, the rights of property (albeit necessary) were rendered by Scripture and natural justice inferior to the right to life; the state which ignored this great fact brought social anarchy upon itself. In place of Chalmers' theological defence of the primacy of private charity, Doyle offered the opposite – a theological justification of state relief. This sat easily with a pointed rejection of the conventional economic notion of a necessary transition of Ireland towards a socially-anglicized future – a vision which he also thought based on an un-Christian pursuit of unrestricted capital accumulation that ignored the true interests of the people and must end in revolution and social convulsion. To avoid such a disaster he would 'adopt a sumptuary law, or a law of *ostracism*, or if not those laws, I would surely seek for a Poor Law, if for no other purpose, to check the progress of society on its "road to ruin".'[51]

This full-blooded reaction to Chalmers was not without public effect, not least among the more radical strand in British Whiggery associated with the *Morning Chronicle*, which asked: 'Who is there of the established clergy, either of England, Ireland, or Scotland, to compare with Dr Doyle? Compare his evidence on the Poor Law Committee with that of Dr Chalmers, and his superiority appears immense.'[52] But Doyle's latest outburst also provoked a heavyweight response – explicitly in defence of Chalmers – from one of the leading political economists of his generation, Nassau Senior, then professor of

49 *Ibid.*, pp. 34–6.
50 *Ibid.*, p. 65.
51 *Ibid.*, p. 60.
52 *Morning Chronicle* [*MC*], 18 Jan. 1831.

political economy at King's College London.[53] Senior had already turned his attention to the possibility of reforming the English poor laws, and had sent the incoming home secretary a lengthy memo on the subject in January 1831.[54] He clearly regarded Doyle as the principal opponent of 'sound doctrine' on the Irish poor-law question, and did not stint in his indictment of the prelate (in contrast he was much more reserved in his criticism of his fellow economist McCulloch, whose mistaken opinions he believed based on incorrect data). Doyle's views were 'tinctured by the peculiarities of his religious tenets', and his evidence and pamphlet filled with 'clap-traps on the rights of the poor and duties of the state'. The prelate's dogmatism had led him

> to affirm, like a Turkish fatalist, who sees no distinction . . . between filthiness and plague, that if, under a system of poor laws, a state were overrun with pauperism, it ought reasonably to be considered not the result of those laws, but a particular infliction of Providence, a special visitation of Divine wrath, a special punishment from God, for having neglected the poor.[55]

Such oriental-like credulity needed to be contrasted with English Protestant rationality in political economy and moral philosophy.

Senior placed particular emphasis on the discrepancy between the allegedly limited system of relief Doyle envisaged for Ireland, and the expansionist implications of the rationale he provided for state relief. If, as Doyle had asserted, the poor of Ireland were unable to subsist by their own labour without state assistance, and an effective poor law must 'shelter the homeless, clothe the naked, feed the hungry, comfort the afflicted, relieve the distressed, end vagrancy, separate the impostor, compel the idler to work, and remove the food of sedition', it could not long be restricted to the 'impotent' poor. The logic of Doyle's case, combined with the violence endemic in Irish society, must be the rapid extension of relief as a 'right' – rapidly rendering Ireland 'one vast house of industry'.[56] The bishop's pronounced opinions on the appropriation (to Senior, the 'confiscation') of established Church property for welfare and education purposes merely confirmed Senior's conviction that Doyle represented a strand of quasi-socialist Catholicism that deserved summary dismissal: 'Doyle is almost a St Simonist. His beau ideal of civil society is Paraguay under the Jesuits, where law punished idleness and sinfulness, and priest divided among the people the whole produce of the soil.'[57]

53 Nassau W. Senior, *A Letter to Lord Howick on a Legal Provision for the Irish Poor* (London, 1831), p. 3. It appears that Howick, under-secretary for the colonies and son of the prime minister, had approached Senior for a private opinion on the question.

54 SUL: BP, 35/91, Senior, memo on poor laws and population, 31 Jan. 1831.

55 Senior, *Letter to Howick*, pp. 18, 26–7.

56 *Ibid.*, pp. 35–6.

57 *Ibid.*, p. 38.

In contrast, Senior offered his own proposals, largely endorsing the conclusions of the Spring Rice committee. These he located within a theoretical structure balancing and interrelating concern for both 'physical' and 'moral' considerations. The former, following Malthus, concerned the protection (and augmentation) of the wages-fund of capital available for productive investment and employment. Secondly, and more prominently in this pamphlet, Senior stressed the crucial importance of 'moral' values in wealth-creation. Echoing Chalmers (whose 1830 evidence he extracted in an appendix), Senior identified the centrality of 'industry' and 'forethought' to social improvement and any real diminution of poverty; all human institutions should be judged according to their positive or (more frequently) negative impact upon these cardinal moral virtues. English and, as Chalmers had testified, recent Scottish experience had demonstrated the disastrous moral consequences of poor laws, threatening the very destruction of society if not summarily remedied. Only unmediated exposure to the direct consequences of immoral behaviour could produce behavioural improvement on the part of individuals; universal experience 'in all ages and countries', Senior concluded, proved that 'idleness and improvidence can be prevented only by leaving them to the punishment inflicted by nature – want and degradation'.[58]

It followed that, to evade the dependency trap, state relief could only safely be granted in cases where no such adverse moral consequences could follow. Senior offered a moral typology of poverty to guide legislators: victims of 'unforeseeable' calamities such as infectious disease, crippling accidents, blindness and madness could be safely relieved through state-funded fever hospitals and asylums, but other bodily infirmities should be anticipated and assistance restricted to charity and some public aid to dispensaries and infirmaries. Assistance to the elderly, however, merely placed a premium on improvidence and undermined familial bonds and private charity. Orphans were a more difficult case, but Senior (again following Chalmers) concluded that the evils of public provision outweighed the benefits; aid to deserted children more straightforwardly promoted vice and profligacy on the part of their parents. Relief to the able-bodied poor without employment would be the greatest evil, except in the exceptional case of famine arising from unforeseen crop failure (and even here Senior favoured a county rate-in-aid and strict checks to prevent abuses). The condition of the poor would only effectually be improved by development, not by welfare; modest amounts of public money could be usefully employed in facilitating this through assistance to emigration and public works for constructing roads, canals and harbours, as well as transferring the burden of supporting the Catholic clergy to

58 *Ibid.*, p. 35.

the public purse. In short, every experiment for relief should be tried, except that of a poor law.[59]

Although very different in its language and short of overt providentialist commentary, Senior's pamphlet shared many of the preconceptions that had motivated both Chalmers and Bicheno. Significantly, it had been prepared in summer 1831 in consultation with Senior's close friend and mentor, and fellow Oxford 'Noetic', Richard Whately, then Drummond professor of political economy at Oxford, and from October of that year archbishop of Dublin. While generally agreeing with Senior, Whately (in common with his chaplain Samuel Hinds, who had also read the draft) warned him of the anger of many in England over the perceived drain of English resources to support Irish migrant labourers:

> [t]o which must be added the frequent and large contributions made in the country to relieve Irish distress . . . Perhaps also in speaking of Irish *labourers*, it would be right to consider also that of Irish *beggars*: some who are incapable of work, some who prefer begging. Some who cannot find work, at least not for a great part of their time. And they are the more freely relieved, on account of the want of a poor-law in Ireland, because a man cannot say, as to an Englishman, 'Go to your parish.' This is certainly a heavy evil . . . May it not be said that the Irish labourers, whose standard of decencies is so low, tend to bring down the English to the same level? If I am an English labourer, and am outbid by an Irishman, who lies on straw and lives on potatoes, I must accept the same wages (unless I go to the parish), and live the same piggish kind of life.[60]

This appears to have been Whately's first engagement with a question that would occupy such a large place in his concerns over the following years. Like other Protestant Christian economists he was also preoccupied with the moral causation of poverty, although he would ultimately place a higher emphasis on 'colonization' from Ireland than others, reflecting his concern that something more constructive needed to be done to neutralize the immediate threat to England of being 'swamped' by Irish paupers. With this partial exception, the report on Irish poverty over which Whately would preside in 1836 closely mirrored both Senior's recommendations of 1831 and Spring Rice's proposals of the previous year.[61]

59 *Ibid.*, p. 44.

60 Whately to Senior, 21 Aug. 1831, in E. J. Whately (ed.), *Life and Correspondence of Richard Whately, DD* (2 vols, London, 1866), i, pp. 94–7.

61 Whately strongly endorsed Senior's proposal for payment of the Catholic clergy, on the dual grounds that it would be the simplest way of relieving the Catholic poor from a heavy (and unproductive) burden, while simultaneously tending to weaken 'Romanism' by bringing the clergy under state control: Whately to Copleston, 21 Sept. 1831, Whately (ed.), *Life*, i, pp. 106–9.

Not surprisingly, Senior's hostile commentary provoked a further impassioned response from Doyle, who accused the Englishman of ignorance of real Irish experience: '[I]s he or I the better judge? and who is Mr Senior and who am I, why he should presume to question a statement vouchsafed by me?'[62] Raising the rhetorical bar yet higher, the bishop denounced that perversion of political economy that excused those guilty of the 'murder' of the Irish poor through the denial of relief. How could an Irishman, he thundered, look on unmoved 'at the systematic murder of millions of his fellow-men!'[63]

Doyle was certainly not alone in his emotive reaction to Senior's pamphlet. Neither was such antagonism restricted to Irishmen. The Tory *Fraser's Magazine* attacked the 'unsound and inhuman' Malthusianism inherent in the argument, and dismissed the applicability of Chalmersian charitable methods to Ireland (or to England – which was still subjected to the influx of 'half-naked savages' from Ireland).[64] *The Times* acknowledged that Senior had exposed the vagueness of what Doyle meant by a 'poor law', but denied that the ingenuity of his arguments had altered its own opinions on the matter. It was, the paper concluded, fruitless to restrict a poor law to the impotent if the great object was the mitigation or prevention of absolute famine, and giving an assurance to society that men and women, and helpless children, would no longer die of hunger. Chalmers' concerns were misplaced; if charity cooled, this was because it would be superseded as the exclusive hope of the miserable.[65]

The exchanges of 1830–31, when combined with the escalating tithe war and renewed threat of regional famine in summer 1831, further polarized opinion in Ireland. For supporters of a poor law, Doyle's religiously-grounded and passionate advocacy now provided a new point of reference. One Dublin pamphleteer asserted that Doyle had convincingly proved Chalmers wrong on the crucial question of the entitlement of the poor.[66] Daniel Callaghan, the Catholic MP for Cork city, declared in 1832 that he had subsequently heard nothing 'that could shake his confidence in the opinion of the view he had heard delivered . . . by Dr Doyle, that the 43rd of Elizabeth, which gave a

62 [James W. Doyle], *The Rt. Rev. Dr Doyle's Letter on Poor Laws in Reply to Mr Senior of London* (Dublin, 1831), p. 4.

63 *Ibid.*, p. 10; McGrath, *Politics*, pp. 93–4.

64 Anon., 'Senior on the introduction of Poor-Laws into Ireland', *Fraser's Magazine*, 4 (1831), pp. 554–65.

65 *The Times*, 29, 31 Aug. 1831. With typical acerbity, Doyle took the opportunity offered by this half-criticism of him to pen a letter ticking off the leader writer and taking another swipe at Senior for his 'ignorance' and 'absurd bigotry in his estimate of the Catholic clergy', *ibid.*, 3 Sept. 1831.

66 Anon., *The Desideratum, or Ireland's Only Remedy.*

system of Poor laws to England, was the Magna Charta of the poor'. Co. Wexford's Whig-liberal MP Henry Lambert agreed that 'Doyle had so fully exposed the cant and hypocrisy of the objection to Poor laws' as to make further objection impossible.[67] The Dublin-born imperial publicist Robert Montgomery Martin also cited Doyle at length in support of his case that a poor law was essential to give justice to both Ireland and England, and to preserve the empire by undercutting social unrest and the repeal movement it fuelled.[68] Even more sceptical observers, such as the Catholic Whig Thomas Wyse, felt that while 'poor laws, even among the Quakers, are losing partizans', widespread distress and discontent rendered imperative some alternative initiative.[69]

Petitions in favour of a substantive measure from Ireland also increased in number. In 1829 a further petition for a poor law similar to England's, from Clara in King's County (not coincidentally, the residence of the tireless advocate of such a measure, Samuel Robinson), offered the occasion for Sadler's first parliamentary foray on the subject.[70] The following year saw petitions in favour from King's County weavers and from Tullamore (also in King's County) endorsed by 100 individuals whose total property was worth £100,000. A more demotic petition was signed by 2,000 artisans, shopkeepers and inhabitants of Dublin, calling simply for the 'immediate extension of the principle of the *English* Poor Laws to *Ireland*'.[71] These in turn provoked counter-petitions from landowners and magistrates in counties Cavan, Roscommon and Fermanagh against such a measure.[72] The local notables at Clara had previously objected vociferously to Robinson's efforts to stir up enthusiasm for the subject, complaining to the Commons that

> [I]t did not express the sentiments of any educated or respectable person in that neighbourhood; it was . . . the offspring of Mr *Samuel Robinson*, of *Clara*, a

67 *Hansard*, 3, xiii, 858–60 [19 June 1832].

68 Martin, *Poor Laws for Ireland.*

69 NLI: MP, Ms 13,371/2, Wyse to Spring Rice, 12 Jan. 1831. Wyse was too hasty on the last point; the Quakers Samuel Robinson in King's County, Ebenezer Shackleton in Kildare, and Joseph Harvey in Limerick remained active local campaigners for an Irish poor law: see Ebenezer Shackleton, *Poor Laws the Safest, Cheapest and Surest Cure for Boyism of Every Kind in Ireland* (Dublin, 1832); NLI: MP, Ms 13,372/1, Harvey to Spring Rice, 13 June 1832.

70 *Hansard*, 2, xxi, 1114–15 [7 May 1829]. See also Samuel Robinson, *To the Right Honourable John Edward Littleton . . . Remarks on the Advantages to be expected from a Compulsory Rate in Ireland* (n.p., 1833).

71 *Hansard*, 2, xxiii, 389 [16 Mar.], xxiv, 428 [6 May], 533 [11 May 1830]; *JHC*, lxxxv (1830), p. 446.

72 *Hansard*, 2, xxiii, 365 [16 Mar.], xxiv, 706 [14 May], xxv, 81 [8 June 1830].

> miller, who has for some years applied himself with great ardour to political pursuits; and the signatures thereto annexed are . . . those of the lowest orders of the people (even of children,) who congregated at the sound of a bell rung through the streets to sign, on the top of a barrel, something which they were taught to believe would in some way or other give them a share in the property of their betters[.][73]

Despite (and perhaps even because of) such overt hostility from county elites the idea of a poor law was clearly attracting wider support within Ireland.

A pro-poor-law petition from Waterford in 1831 allowed (or persuaded) the veteran MP for the county, Sir John Newport, to announce his conversion on the subject, while in August Brownlow introduced another petition on behalf of the twenty-four Catholic bishops of Ireland in synod, in support of their colleague, Doyle.[74] The assertive, even threatening, tone of that text strongly suggests that prelate's authorship:

> Petitioners have never ceased to hope that . . . your Honourable House would, without delay, devote its attention to the wants which prey upon the laborious and destitute classes of the Irish poor; that you would not suffer famine to ravish a country not only fertile and productive, but abounding with provisions; nor permit disease to grow and spread itself amid a healthful and vigorous population intrusted by Providence to your superintending care; for petitioners humbly submit that to you it most especially appertains to so apportion the burdens of the several classes in the commonwealth, as that the poor be not goaded by wants into acts of outrage, or left to perish unheeded by those whom their toils have enriched. . . . God . . . is the father of the indigent: it is by His power you legislate. He is provoked to anger when the poor are neglected or oppressed; 'He transfers kingdoms from one people to another, because of injustices, and wrongs and injuries, and divers deceits.' Your Honourable House should fear Him, and ensure His protection to this mighty Empire by extending your care to His poor.[75]

In the same year even the ambivalent Daniel O'Connell was prepared to introduce a petition for a poor law, from the householders of the Dublin parish of St Michans.[76] In 1832 a meeting at Castledermot in Co. Kildare resolved to petition parliament for a poor law to assist in restoring peace to the county. A petition from Limerick in 1833, proposed by one of the city's MPs, insisted that full justice to Ireland was impossible without such a measure.[77] These petitions were few in number compared with those for tithe

73 *JHC*, lxxxiv (1829), p. 360.
74 *Hansard*, 3, v, 390 [27 July], 1105–7 [10 Aug. 1831].
75 Fitzpatrick (ed.), *Doyle*, ii, pp. 320–1.
76 *Hansard*, 3, vi, 157–8 [17 Aug. 1831].
77 Shackleton, *Poor Laws*, p. 3; *Hansard*, 3, xvii, 910–13 [3 May 1833].

abolition, parliamentary reform and repeal of the Union – topics which dominated popular politics in Ireland in the early 1830s. Yet they were not insignificant and provide evidence of some popular as well as elite engagement with the question.

Smith O'Brien, Musgrave and Poulett Scrope's bills

Given his reactionary views on Catholicism and parliamentary reform, and romantic attachment to the unaltered form of the 'old' English poor law, Sadler was always at best an ambiguous leader of the parliamentary campaign, and other politicians had sought to displace him even before his electoral defeat at Leeds in 1832.[78] The motions of 1826–31 had been vague as to details and few (Doyle excepted) had been prepared to specify precisely what their poor law would feature. One of the first to attempt a draft bill, and hence to put himself at the head of the campaign, was William Smith O'Brien, then MP for Ennis. Smith O'Brien introduced his opinions on the matter in a pamphlet published in early 1831, which he circulated for comment to Doyle, Grattan, Villiers Stuart, Brownlow and others. O'Brien's approach was generally similar to Doyle's, but embodied a different emphasis typical of a 'patriotic' improving landowner, stressing the need for relief for those necessarily displaced by the consolidation of farms, and for the equalization of the burden of relief and development on the neglectful absentee as well as the active resident proprietor.[79] Although he thought Chalmers' ideals inapplicable to Ireland, he nevertheless felt the Scottish system more appropriate than the English, and proposed that assessment be voluntary – by the decision of the householders of the parish – rather than universal. Where such a determination was entered into, an elected committee of 'better' ratepayers in a parish (with the local clergy as *ex-officio* members) would manage the poor fund raised by a rate borne equally by landlord and tenant, and prepare monthly lists of the parish poor. The committee would have the power to deny relief to 'strangers', and mendicancy would be banned. No relief would be given in 'ordinary' circumstances to those able to work, although O'Brien favoured a separate and extensive colonization measure to alleviate the problem of excessive labour competition.[80]

78 Sadler retired to New Lodge, Belfast, where his family owned linen works. He died in 1835.

79 William Smith O'Brien, *Plan for the Relief of the Poor in Ireland* (2nd edn., Dublin, 1831), pp. 15–16. O'Brien took up the question during his period of political transition from liberal Tory to moderate reformer: see Robert Sloan, *William Smith O'Brien and the Young Ireland Rebellion of 1848* (Dublin, 2000), pp. 24–42.

80 O'Brien, *Plan*, pp. 48–59.

O'Brien's attempt to bring in such a bill in February 1831 met a point-blank rebuff from Althorp.[81] Three months later he was obliged (for family reasons) to give up his seat, and he remained out of parliament until 1835. Nevertheless, he continued as a private individual to campaign for a limited Irish poor law alongside an emigration project. In 1832 he collaborated with John Musgrave of Cappoquin, Co. Waterford, to have a bill introduced by Sir Richard Musgrave, then Whig-liberal MP for that county.[82] The Musgraves expressed doubts over O'Brien's suggestion for a society to promote the idea of a poor law among the, as yet largely unconverted, landed classes, and favoured instead the discussion of a concrete measure in parliament.[83] However, Richard Musgrave's defeat at the elections of 1832 curtailed this option; the bill was forwarded to the chief secretary, who ignored it, and when Musgrave returned to the Commons in 1835 he would propose it as an alternative (albeit similar) measure to O'Brien's to relieve the 'helpless and impotent poor' only.[84] Musgrave believed that as his bill involved only the power to allow voluntary assessment it did not contradict the principles evinced by Chalmers in 1830.[85]

Doyle and Villiers Stuart were sympathetic to O'Brien's proposed society, although the bishop regretted that the deteriorating state of his health would preclude his active participation. There was a danger that the many competing political campaigns then in existence might crowd out that for the poor law, but Doyle hoped that by connecting the demand of a labour-rate for the able-bodied labourers with a poor law for the incapables, a broader coalition might be formed. Nothing could be expected from the government without pressure: 'We can hope for nothing new or efficient from the Government', he wrote to O'Brien in 1832. 'They possessed all my confidence and affection and I am now forced to think of them as you yourself do. But it gives me pain

81 *Hansard*, 3, ii, 246 [8 Feb. 1831]; *A Bill to make provision for the Relief of the Poor in Ireland, in Certain Cases*, PP 1831 (237), ii.

82 NLI: SOBP, Ms 427, fol. 182, John Musgrave to Smith O'Brien, 19 Oct. 1832. John Musgrave, who was probably the uncle of the MP, had previously criticized O'Brien's bill for its failure to place the bulk of the rate on the landlords and the unlikelihood that it would curb clearances, but seems subsequently to have regarded it more pragmatically, see NLI: MP, Ms 13,371/2, Musgrave to Spring Rice, 12 Mar. 1831.

83 NLI: SOBP, Ms 427, fol. 183, John Musgrave to O'Brien, 31 Oct. 1832.

84 Liverpool Record Office, Derby Papers, 920 DER (14), 18/3, John Musgrave, 'Draft of a bill to authorize the relief of the poor in Ireland in certain cases'; *Hansard*, 3, xxvii, 202–4 [24 Mar.], xxix, 308–12 [8 July 1835].

85 *Ibid.*, xxxi, 226–9 [9 Feb. 1836].

to write or hear of them.'[86] For whatever reason, O'Brien's own interest in the subject temporarily waned from late 1832 as he turned instead to promoting emigration through his involvement with the Limerick Emigration Society. It was restored only by the activities of the Poor Inquiry Commission; he pressed his views upon the commissioners and gave evidence before them in late 1833 and again in early 1835, and hosted them at Dromoland during their tour of the country.[87] O'Brien's reintroduction of his motion in July 1835 (and again as a bill in 1836) drew public support from some quarters, but the debate had moved on since its drafting in 1831 and his measure now appeared too moderate to meet the heightened expectations of the poor-law lobby in Ireland.[88]

In the aftermath of Sadler's defeat, and the interrupted efforts of O'Brien and the Musgraves, the leading parliamentary advocates for an Irish poor law were the English radical Whig George Poulett Scrope, who represented Stroud from 1833, and the MP for Knaresborough, John Richards. Both took a strong line for a comprehensive law based on the 43rd Elizabeth. Richards' 1833 motion – in support of which he quoted Doyle – drew support from Henry Grattan, who insisted that the Union had given Ireland the right to a poor law and threatened to support repeal if it was denied.[89] However, it was Scrope who was to have the greater influence on the subsequent debates. He had already stated his more advanced views on the subject in the *Quarterly Review* in 1831, and he subsequently responded to Senior's intervention in the same periodical, invoking the natural-right case for poor laws associated with Paley and Blackstone against the Malthusianism of Senior and Chalmers.[90]

Scrope developed his proposals more fully in an 1833 pamphlet. Although well intentioned, the imperfect measures proposed by Musgrave and O'Brien (and endorsed by Doyle) would, he argued, prove as delusive as the sixteenth-century English legislation that preceded the 43rd Elizabeth. Only a true poor law on the principle of that measure could meet the extent of Irish distress, begin the process of unlocking Ireland's vast productive capacities, and protect

86 NLI: SOBP, Ms 427, fols. 186, 189, Doyle to O'Brien, 6 Nov., Stuart to O'Brien, 18 Nov. 1832.

87 O'Brien to Revans, 12 Nov. 1833, *ibid.*, fol. 246; Corrie to O'Brien, 2 Jan. 1835, *ibid.*, fol. 275; Hort to O'Brien, 26 Jan. 1835, *ibid.*, fol. 274.

88 *Hansard*, 3, xxvi, 1206–11 [19 Mar. 1835], xxxiii, 833–4 [11 May 1836]; NLI: SOBP, Ms 427, fol. 279, George Howell to O'Brien, 4 Mar. 1835. O'Brien's bill was criticized as meeting only half the evil as it would exclude relief to the able-bodied: *Freeman's Journal* [*FJ*], 7 Mar. 1836.

89 *Hansard*, 3, xvii, 846–67, 882–6 [2 May 1833].

90 [G. Poulett Scrope], 'Senior's *Letter on the Irish Poor*', *QR*, 46 (Jan. 1832), pp. 390–410.

England from the scourges of unfair competition and the permanent labour migration that was crowding out the English poor.[91] Scrope revived the now well-established case for an Irish poor law grounded on the various arguments of social justice, humanity, and security for capital investment; but his main concern was to establish that any meaningful measure must be both compulsory and incorporate relief by employment for the unemployed able-bodied. The rationale for the latter was as much developmental as welfarist, and aimed at drawing out Ireland's 'vast latent resources' through government enforcement.[92] The parochial and county poor-law boards he envisaged would also have the power to use rates to assist emigration and (foreshadowing what would become Scrope's great preoccupation in future years) to resettle evicted families on reclaimed waste-land allotments.

Scrope's more advanced opinions led him to publicly criticize the introduction of the workhouse test, although not the principles of central supervision and less eligibility, in the English amendment poor law bill of 1834.[93] His parliamentary campaign for an Irish measure began with a proposed amendment to the renewal of the Irish Coercion Act in 1834, in which he urged the provision of 'the means of securing life by peaceful and honest industry' as the only mode of eradicating agrarian violence.[94] However, his preference for an amended form of the 'old' English act put him into conflict with other supporters of a 'poor law' for Ireland. He rejected Musgrave's bill in 1835, and introduced his own measure in 1836. His bill was not, he insisted, in conflict with the more valuable aspects of the amended English act of 1834; it incorporated the principle of centralized supervision, while adapting the model to fit the circumstances of Ireland, by allowing for an outdoor labour test of destitution.[95] The crucial development since 1831 had been, he informed the Commons, the rejection of voluntarism by the English poor law inquiry in its 1833 report, and its acknowledgement that a poor law was expedient

91 Although denying that English interests lay at the forefront of his concerns, Scrope made clear his support for the claim that Irish migration was adversely affecting the English labour market and 'throwing back' onto rural parishes labourers who would otherwise be absorbed by urban employment: G. Poulett Scrope, *Plan of a Poor-Law for Ireland, with a Review of the Arguments for and against it* (2nd edn, London, 1834), pp. 17–19.

92 *Ibid.*, pp. 12–13.

93 For Scrope's interventions in 1834, see Brundage, *Making of the New Poor Law*, pp. 59–60.

94 The amendment was seconded by Feargus O'Connor, and lost by 34 votes to 89, *Hansard*, 3, xxv, [21 July 1834].

95 *Ibid.*, xxix, 320–4 [8 July 1835], xxxi, 429–30 [15 Feb. 1836], xxxiii, 590–8 [4 May 1836].

in every civilized country; '[f]rom that moment I felt that the question of a Poor-law for Ireland was virtually carried, and that all that remained was a question of time.'[96] He was fully aware that only government could carry a successful bill, but felt it requisite to express in legislative form the impatient frustration of the Irish poor-law lobby with ministerial inaction.

Scrope was certainly correct in recognizing the importance of the English inquiry report of 1833 and the subsequent legislation of 1834 in opening the way for an Irish measure, although over-sanguine in believing that his own proposals would be preferred to a system more closely modelled on the English act. The negative associations of the 'old' English poor law in the eyes of much of parliamentary and wider political opinion in Britain and Ireland had long proved a stumbling-block for the Irish lobby. Although the populist defence of the 'old' English system, and the case for its virtually unmoderated extension to Ireland made by 'patriotic' and Tory radicals such as Cobbett and Sadler, may have had some popular appeal, they unquestionably proved counter-productive for any legislative initiative, and inclined parliamentary advocates to stress the limitations and 'safeguards' of their proposals for Ireland. The official declaration that the 'old' English system was reformable, and that its underlying principle was sound (although what this was continued to be contested), paved the way for removing this obstacle. The new centralized administration established in 1834 also created an institutional lobby with a potential interest in extending its purview and in applying its expertise to the Irish problem.

It should be stressed, however, that these developments did not render an Irish poor law (or the precise measure enacted in 1838) inevitable. The applicability of the new English system to Ireland was also to be fiercely contested, and the bulk of the landed class in Ireland remained as unpersuaded as before. Even after 1834 a number of significant obstacles to the enactment of an Irish poor law remained to be overcome. The most important of these were the hostile stance of the administration, and the fluctuating, if generally negative, attitude of the predominant political figure in the country, Daniel O'Connell.

The ministers most concerned with Irish policy had differed little in their responses to their Tory predecessors. Althorp, Stanley and Spring Rice had on a number of occasions made clear their antagonism towards a poor law, and despite the concession of a commission of inquiry into the condition of the Irish poor in 1833 there is no evidence that they, or the other dominant figures in the cabinet, seriously entertained the idea before the break-up of Grey's government in 1834. The social and economic perspective of the administration was dominated by the paradigm of 'moderate liberal' thought,

96 *Ibid.*, 591. See also Scrope, *Plan*, p. 13.

close to (and informed by) the orthodox economic thinking of Nassau Senior.[97]

If there were doubts about the position of the ministry on the Irish poor-law question in 1834, Spring Rice sought to put them to rest in an article in the party's house journal, the *Edinburgh Review*. Spring Rice, soon to be promoted to the cabinet as colonial secretary, and subsequently to serve as chancellor of the exchequer in 1835–39, insisted in the face of changing economic fashion that the wisdom of Senior, Malthus and Chalmers remained paramount on the subject. Utilizing evidence presented to the 1830 committee, he sought to undermine Scrope's case and restate the practical and ethical superiority of Chalmersian voluntarism, modified by the limited forms of relief to the impotent poor and aid to public works and emigration endorsed by Senior in 1831.[98] Spring Rice made no reference to the English report or legislation, which suggests that for him (and his allies) the compromise worked out for the 'English problem' had no ramifications for the quite separate Irish case. A different political approach to the Irish poor law would have to await the rise to prominence of a different grouping within the Whig-liberal leadership from 1835 onwards.

The ambivalence of Daniel O'Connell

The take-off of any mass campaign for an Irish poor law was to a considerable degree dependent on the stance taken by O'Connell. A combination of concern for political tactics and the promptings of his personal ideology inclined O'Connell towards scepticism at best. He had made vague statements of support for such a measure at the Catholic Association in 1824 and 1828, but evidently did not feel himself bound by this, and on his entry to the Commons in 1830 made clear his view that tithes rather than poor-rates should be employed for the relief of the poor.[99] A poor law, especially if associated with the claims made by a number of its advocates that it would prove a panacea for Ireland's social inequalities and unlock its productive capabilities, had the capacity to impede his campaign for repeal. As a divisive issue within Ireland itself, the poor law also had the potential to alienate a number of landed sympathizers from the repeal movement if endorsed as part of its platform.

97 See Peter Mandler, *Aristocratic Government in the Age of Reform: Whigs and Liberals 1830–1852* (Oxford, 1990), pp. 123–56.

98 [Spring Rice], 'Proposed introduction', pp. 227–61.

99 Fitzpatrick (ed.), *Doyle*, ii, p. 368; *Hansard*, 3, i, 420 [11 Nov. 1830]; *MC*, 1 Aug. 1838.

O'Connell's own socio-economic ideology was, as Joe Lee has observed, an undisciplined amalgam of unresolved elements. It is clear that he placed great emphasis on the regenerative power of the resident gentry (whose numbers he believed would be augmented by repeal), less as 'modernizing' economic agents than as paternalistic employers and improvers of their dependent populations.[100] If he was indeed influenced by Jeremy Bentham on some matters, this certainly did not extend to the Benthamite vision of rational poor-law management embodied by Edwin Chadwick.[101] Modelling his ideal of the resident gentleman on his own practice as a paternalist Kerry proprietor, O'Connell tended to denigrate the desirability of legislative compulsion or centralized state supervision in determining the behaviour of these agents. He also confessed himself particularly sensitive to the argument that poor laws modelled on that of England tended to promote immorality, most especially in the form of sexual laxity.[102] He was personally engaged in a wide range of voluntary charitable activities – including the management committee of the Dublin Mendicity Institution from 1822 – and was strongly committed to 'moral' action of this description. Yet he was never fully consistent in his stance and would prove highly eclectic in adopting or rejecting arguments and evidence when convenient.

O'Connell was susceptible to argument grounded in Catholic moral theology and was, at least temporarily, won over by Doyle in 1831. The *Letter to Spring Rice* had, he confessed, touched him personally in a way other arguments on the subject had not:

> You have convinced me – your pamphlet on the necessity of making a legal provision for the *destitute* Irish poor has completely convinced me. The candour and distinctness with which you state the arguments . . . have quite overpowered my objections, and rendered me an unwilling, but not the less sincere, convert to your opinions. I candidly acknowledge that you have done more – you have alarmed me, lest, in the indulgence of my own selfishness as a landowner, I should continue to be the opponent of him who would feed the hungry and enable the naked to clothe themselves.

100 Joe Lee, 'The social and economic ideas of O'Connell', in Kevin B. Nowlan and Maurice R. O'Connell (eds), *Daniel O'Connell: Portrait of a Radical* (Belfast, 1984), pp. 70–84.

101 The case for a 'Benthamite' O'Connell is made in James E. Crimmins, 'Jeremy Bentham and Daniel O'Connell: their correspondence and radical alliance, 1828–1831', *Historical Journal*, 40 (1997), pp. 359–87.

102 O'Connell to Doyle, 19 Mar. 1830, in Maurice R. O'Connell (ed.), *Correspondence of Daniel O'Connell* (8 vols, Dublin, 1972–80), iv, pp. 141–2. He was particularly incensed on this occasion by the government's introduction of an Irish bill based on the bastardy clauses of the English poor laws, which would, he believed, remove the necessary 'moral and legal restraint over the female sex'.

The apocalyptic scenes which Doyle had invoked had, he assured his correspondent, had a transformative effect on his conscience:

> The scenes which you have *actually* witnessed – the misery which you have *actually* beheld – the woe which you have actually wept over – the famishing children – the starving parent – the perishing youth – the young blood running cold, chilled by penury – the aged sinking into the grave under the pressure of hunger – avaricious cruelty thinning the folds of the population, and starvation filling the churchyards with emaciated victims! I cannot, my Lord, endure to look at the picture you have drawn from the life, and strewed with real dead. I will not bear it without at least a struggle, and now I offer myself – all that I have of energy and perseverance – to the cause that you support and ornament – the cause of the poor, the destitute, the famishing – the cause of the unjustly afflicted man – the cause – am I here at liberty to say it without profaneness? – the cause of God[.][103]

This seemingly sincere and heartfelt 'conversion' was not to last; but he did adopt a conciliatory approach in the 1831 session, requesting that Doyle assist him in formulating a parliamentary case, welcoming the bishops' petition as the harbinger of a necessary poor-rate, and promising Sadler the support of the Irish party in return for the postponement of his motion until the reform bill was passed.[104] Sadler's refusal to do so, and the overtly anti-Catholic and anti-repeal language which he (and some other English advocates of the measure) adopted, unquestionably strained O'Connell's already shaky attachment to the campaign.

By the following session, however, O'Connell had completely reneged on his pledge to Doyle and reverted to a fundamentalist antagonism towards poor laws in principle. He would now, he proclaimed in response to Sadler's latest motion, exert all his influence in Ireland to guard the people against the delusion that they 'ought to rely upon the pockets of their more wealthy neighbours for support, instead of their own exertions'. Patient and minute investigation had now disabused him of his earlier mistaken views, and convinced him that compulsory poor laws inevitably destroyed the morality of the poor, stoked class antagonisms, and distracted from the real means of improving the people. Rather than conveying natural rights, a poor law 'as implying slavery on the part of those who thus obtained relief under their provisions, was . . . prejudicial to the independence of the national character'.[105]

103 O'Connell to Doyle, 29 Mar. 1831, in Fitzpatrick (ed.), *Doyle*, ii, pp. 285–6.

104 O'Connell to Doyle, 16 June 1831, in O'Connell (ed.), *Correspondence of O'Connell*, iv, pp. 334–6; *Hansard*, 3, v, 1109–10 [10 Aug.], vi, 225 [18 Aug. 1831].

105 *Ibid.*, xiii, 853–6 [19 June 1832]. He had expressed similar views at a meeting of the National Political Union on 3 January 1832: McGrath, *Politics*, p. 99.

Such an abrupt volte-face was not without cost. Fully engaged in the repeal campaign as he was in 1832–33, he could, perhaps, afford to shrug off the waves of hostility and allegations of heartless cruelty it provoked from British radicals and Tories. More problematic was the rift that it threatened with the Catholic clergy, which he regretted publicly in 1833.[106] With Doyle now openly sceptical about the value of repeal and concerned that it might distract from substantive reforms such as a poor law, the rift may have been a tactic to force the clergy to choose between rival political leaders, just as it may have been no coincidence that O'Connell's 'conversion' in March 1831 had accompanied his decision to put repeal aside to campaign for parliamentary reform. The 'Liberator' proclaimed to a public meeting in January 1832, 'I have my system of poor laws for Ireland – a Repeal of the Union.'[107] Doyle reacted with a stinging public letter published in the *Dublin Evening Post*, denouncing his former ally for his vacillating weakness, for misrepresenting his plan through inappropriate reference to the abuses in the English system, and for adopting a position flagrantly in defiance of divine law. Privately, he added that O'Connell was doing 'immense injury to this country by deceiving the public on the subject of poor laws'.[108]

O'Connell was also bolstered in his scepticism by, rather belatedly, encountering Chalmers' moralistic voluntarism. When Chalmers visited London in July 1833, O'Connell made the effort to meet and thank him. '[He] shook me most cordially by the hands,' Chalmers wrote to his daughter, 'complimenting me on my evidence about the Irish Poor-Laws, saying he was a disciple of mine upon that subject, and not of his own priest, Dr Doyle.'[109] This was no empty gesture. O'Connell incorporated Chalmers' vision into his parliamentary rhetoric that year. While the economic consequences of poor laws were everywhere negative, he declared, it was their moral effects that posed the greatest dangers:

> [H]e was satisfied that no laws could be devised better calculated to destroy the feelings of humanity in the breasts of the population than this system of Poor-laws. These feelings, he was happy to say, yet existed in Ireland. God had planted them deep in the hearts of the people; and the voice of revealed religion, at least told him that it was a duty to perform acts of charity – that if he expected to be rewarded hereafter, he must wipe away the tear from the eye of the widow and orphan – and that he must relieve those who were in affliction and distress.[110]

106 *Hansard*, 3, xvii, 871–9 [2 May 1833].

107 Fitzpatrick (ed.), *Doyle*, ii, p. 367.

108 Doyle to O'Connell, 6 Jan. 1832, Doyle to Parnell, June 1832, in *ibid.*, ii, pp. 362–5, 417–18; McGrath, *Politics*, pp. 99–100.

109 Brown, *Chalmers*, pp. 192–3.

110 *Hansard*, 3, xvii, 877–8 [2 May 1833].

Such an overt identification with the ideas of the Scottish evangelical drew harsh criticism even from sections of the O'Connellite press in Dublin.[111] It also, rather unusually, placed O'Connell into an alliance with the mouthpiece of the Irish Conservative landed interest, which also endorsed the morally and practically superior 'Scottish system', as most applicable to Ireland.[112]

O'Connell's certitude about the poor law in 1833 appeared as intensely held as his earlier, and quite opposite, convictions expressed to Doyle in 1831. In fact, although at heart he may have leaned towards moralistic opposition, he appears to have been swayed by both immediate arguments and calculations of political advantage. After Doyle's death, and with repeal again suspended in preference to a renewed Whig alliance from 1834, he became for a time more amenable on the subject. This may have been in part an attempt to heal a developing rift with his parliamentary following, nearly all of whom (according to at least one Westminster observer) were opposed to his rejection of a poor law in principle.[113] His reactions to the 1835 motions, inflected with sarcastic reactions to those who had used the question to beat him, were generally antagonistic, although he was now prepared to admit that a case could be made 'out of necessity' for doing something for the indigent poor of Ireland.[114] At the same time, he was shifting his domestic rhetoric towards the acceptance of such a measure as right in itself. This second 'conversion' was ultimately to prove no more lasting than the first, but opened up a window in which it appeared to some that an Irish poor law might serve as part of a 'justice to Ireland' platform shared by a rejuvenated and reformist Whig-liberal administration, the liberal-Catholic clergy and the tribune of Irish popular politics.

111 *FJ*, 23 Mar. 1835.

112 Anon., 'The Scottish system of poor laws', *DUM*, 3 (May 1834), pp. 508–22. Some Scottish commentators, however, criticized his apparent deviation from the Scottish model in excluding the aged poor from an entitlement to relief: *Scotsman*, 2 Mar. 1833.

113 *Ibid.*, 6 Apr. 1833.

114 *Hansard*, 3, xxvi, 1212–14 [19 Mar.], xxix, 335–9 [8 July 1835].

4

The rise and fall of the Whately Commission, 1833–36

The Commission for Inquiring into the Condition of the Poorer Classes in Ireland (better known in abbreviated form as the Poor Inquiry Commission, or, after its chairman, as the Whately Commission) has received a remarkably good press. Richard Whately, rightly regarded as the guiding force behind the commission's reports, has been praised by historians of the Irish poor law as 'clear-headed and independent', a master of the complexities of poverty in a manner unmatched by the English Poor Law Commissioners. His commission has been praised for working prodigiously hard to produce the three reports accompanied by volumes of supporting evidence which were published in 1835–37.[1] The output of the commission was impressive, filling five volumes of parliamentary blue books with some 5,000 pages of text, much of it comprising transcripts of oral and written testimonies taken from about 1,500 witnesses drawn from all social classes. The volumes of evidence offer a wealth of information on social and economic conditions and perceptions, unparalleled for Ireland (or indeed most other countries) in the nineteenth century, and as such continue to serve as a principal resource for Irish historians. The commission's policy recommendations, however, remain more controversial.

For Whately's modern biographer, the report embodied the abandonment of the prescriptions of classical economics in 'an extraordinarily farsighted scheme', representing the triumph of realism over theory. One Irish welfare historian describes the proposals as 'generally enlightened and not hampered by currently held economic doctrines'; another as 'imaginative and constructive . . . its recommendations were too radical for contemporary economic thinking' – and they agree this rendered them distasteful to the government. In his magisterial survey of economic thought and policy relating to Ireland, Collison Black comments that as a scheme for economic development, the

1 e.g. Burke, *People and the Poor Law*, pp. 17–37.

proposals were 'comprehensive and far-sighted'.[2] This chapter casts a more critical eye over the formation, operations and conclusions of the Whately Commission between its establishment in 1833 and the completion of its labours in spring 1836.

The origins and formation of the commission

The decision to establish a commission of inquiry into the problem of Irish poverty and the desirability of a poor law (of whatever description) appears to have been taken in March 1833.[3] Although evidently still reluctant to countenance the idea, the administration found itself under increasing pressure in the first post-Reform parliamentary session from the series of motions and bills proposed from the backbenches and a rising volume of petitions from both Great Britain and Ireland. Significantly, their own lord lieutenant had also revived his demands for an Irish poor law and labour-rate, and in March had transmitted a draft plan, prepared for him by Richard Griffith and Anthony Blake, for discussion at Whitehall.[4] Anglesey was persuaded that Lord Holland would support these measures in cabinet, and urged the new chief secretary, John Cam Hobhouse, to do the same.[5]

Pressure mounted higher still when, on 2 April, the leader of the opposition, Sir Robert Peel, suggested that the government establish an Irish inquiry in the wake of the forthcoming English poor-law report. Peel was no convert to the principle of an Irish poor law, but recognized the desirability of heading off incessant parliamentary agitation through the well-tried expedient of instituting an official inquiry.[6] It should have come as no surprise, therefore, that such a commission should have been announced a month later during the debate on John Richards' motion for an Irish poor law by Lord Althorp, the leader of the House and chancellor of the exchequer. Althorp's comments on proposing the commission were intended to avoid offering any hostages to fortune. The House could not be pledged by such an initiative, he declared, and indeed the consequent report might be as likely to recommend reasons for not adopting a poor law as the contrary.

2 Donald Harman Akenson, *A Protestant in Purgatory: Richard Whately, Archbishop of Dublin* (Hamden, CT, 1981), p. 128; Robins, *Lost Children*, p. 158; Geary, *Medicine*, pp. 157–8; Black, *Economic Thought*, p. 107.

3 In March the *Morning Chronicle* announced 'on good authority' that, despite ministerial denials, such an initiative was imminent, cited in *Pilot*, 29 Mar. 1833.

4 PRONI (Public Record Office of Northern Ireland), Belfast, Anglesey Papers, D/619/27/D, pp. 47–9, Anglesey to Grey, 27 Mar. 1833.

5 SRO: HP, D/260/M/O/1, fols 32–3, Anglesey to Hobhouse, 10 Apr. 1833.

6 *Hansard*, 3, xvii, 36 [2 Apr. 1833].

While claiming that the government would not give the commission a 'go-by' or seek to direct its conclusions, he made manifest his personal scepticism towards an Irish poor law, which was founded on his reading of the evil consequences of the English poor laws.[7]

Aware of the government's lack of enthusiasm, the two major London dailies, both of which favoured an Irish poor law, reacted antagonistically. To *The Times*, the new commission would undoubtedly prove as much an Irish landlord job as that of 1830; Althorp's association at the Treasury with Spring Rice, the chair of the 1830 exercise, was cited in evidence. The paper read the very extensive terms of reference proposed for the inquiry as a conspiracy to evade the more pressing and direct issue of a poor law: 'Such an inquiry, if skilfully managed, may last until the millennium.'[8] The pro-government *Morning Chronicle* also thought a further inquiry redundant and was disappointed by the negative terms with which Althorp had prefaced his announcement. Much would depend on the choice of commissioners, and, the paper warned, the commission must not 'be named as a screen'.[9]

The *Chronicle*'s editorialist was right; while ostensibly 'neutral', the tenor and orientation of the commission would be determined by the selection of its active members. The power of appointment lay with the British government, and more specifically with the proposer, Althorp, and the home secretary, Melbourne, who had ultimate responsibility for poor-law related matters and outranked the Irish ministers Anglesey (whose judgement on this matter was suspect), and the recently appointed chief secretary Edward Littleton. Melbourne privately revealed just what he intended the commission to do in a letter summarizing the principal achievements of the government to summer 1833, including the 'Ground laid for the establishment in Ireland of a provision for the old, infirm, and infants by the appointment of a Commission to enquire'. The able-bodied labouring poor are notable by their absence from this list.[10] While it was expedient that the commission appeared impartial, the key policy decision on Irish welfare provision had already been taken by the senior ministerial team of 1833.

The ministers' first preference to head the inquiry was the English country gentleman and liberal-Tory MP Thomas Frankland Lewis. Lewis had claims to expertise on both poor laws and Ireland, having been a leading figure in

7 *Ibid.*, 867–71, 893 [2 May 1833]. Richards later claimed that he had withdrawn his motion only after Althorp had promised to exclude Spring Rice from the appointment of the commissioners: *The Times*, 24 Nov. 1836.

8 *Ibid.*, 4 May 1833.

9 *MC*, 3, 6 May 1833.

10 NLI: MP, Ms 13,375/6, Melbourne to Spring Rice, 25 Aug. 1833.

the 1817 Sturges Bourne inquiry into the English poor laws, and a prominent advocate of its recommendations for drastic reductions in poor relief; he had subsequently served on the Irish revenue commission in 1821 and the education commission in 1825–28, and had been offered the Irish chief secretaryship in 1828. His opinion that the poor laws of both England and Scotland were inapplicable to Ireland had been cited as authoritative by the duke of Wellington in 1828.[11] Lewis was approached in summer 1833, but, after some hesitation, declined the offer. He rightly suspected that the exercise was likely to be protracted and would require a 'tedious' residence in Dublin, and feared that his previous position on the pre-1831 education commission might raise embarrassments in any working relationship with Archbishop Whately.[12] Lewis was to find the subsequent offer of the chairmanship of the English Poor Law Commission in 1834 more agreeable, but the overtures of 1833 at least opened the possibility of a subordinate position on the Irish commission for his son, George Cornewall Lewis.[13]

As chairman of the Irish national education board, the most prominent liberal churchman in Ireland, and a significant figure in wider political-economic debates, Archbishop Richard Whately of Dublin was always likely to be a serious contender for membership, if not the chairmanship, of the Poor Inquiry Commission. If there was any doubt over this, it was put to rest by the intervention of Nassau Senior, who, in the immediate aftermath of Althorp's announcement, urged ministers in forthright terms to place their confidence in his former teacher and intimate friend. Given Senior's authoritative position on the inquiry into the English poor laws, and his close personal connections with senior ministers, his advice would have been difficult to reject, and Whately was promptly selected as chairman.[14] Although he had

11 *Hansard*, 2, xix, 257–9 [1 May 1828]. In his evidence to the 1825 inquiry Lewis had admitted in the abstract that a poor law might incline landowners to check population growth in Ireland, but could not see how the problems of excessive demand for relief and the absence of suitable machinery could be overcome: *Select Committee of House of Lords appointed . . . into State of Ireland*, PP 1825 (181) ix.1, pp. 41–2. In 1830, however, he recommended Spring Rice's committee consider the Scottish model for Ireland: *Hansard*, 2, xxiii, 204–5 [11 Mar. 1830].

12 NLW: HCP, C/2746, C/2748, George Cornewall Lewis to E. Villiers, 24 July, 7 Aug. 1833.

13 Whately's reluctance to answer the younger Lewis's letters suggests a certain (in hindsight justifiable) reluctance to take him on board, Lewis to Villiers, 20 Oct. 1833, *ibid*., C/2750.

14 BL: AP, Add Ms 76,419A, Senior to Spring Rice, 5 May 1833. Mandler suggests that had he not been in Dublin, Whately would almost certainly have been appointed to the English inquiry: Mandler, 'Tories and paupers', p. 98.

something of a reputation as a dominant personality – one observer at a meeting of the Political Economy Club noted that the archbishop was 'a bad listener, interrupts conversation, and seems to be going on, giving vent to the current of his own thoughts, without any regard to his company' – his sceptical stance towards an Irish poor law was already well known, and he was undoubtedly regarded by the ministers as a safe pair of hands.[15]

The appointment of the remaining commissioners remained to be resolved. Littleton was impatient to complete the preliminaries and set the body to work, but found Melbourne characteristically preoccupied. His journal dryly relates:

> Tried a second time to see Lord Melbourne, with a view to induce him to settle the commission for enquiring into the state of the Irish poor. The first time, I found Lady [. . .]'s carriage at the door; and this morning I was interrupted in the middle of my conversation by the announcement of the Countess of S—, with whom I shook hands in the audience room as I immediately retired.[16]

Despite these setbacks, Littleton was ultimately successful in lobbying for the inclusion of his friend the Rev. John Corrie as one of two paid commissioners on the Irish inquiry. A member of Littleton's West Midlands political connection, Corrie was a non-practising Unitarian minister from Birmingham, 'an excellent man of business . . . a powerful writer [who] would be very useful in digesting matter procured by others'.[17] He was also a pronounced poor-law sceptic.

Having settled on a chairman to his liking and agreed to the inclusion of Corrie, Melbourne encouraged Whately to suggest names for the remaining places. Whately's choices reflected a desire to combine setting an ecumenical balance with securing a working majority compliant with his own opinions. The Catholic archbishop of Dublin, Daniel Murray, was proposed with an eye to religious equity. Several of Whately's other nominees had worked closely with him before, on charitable bodies, on the education board, or on the establishment of the Whately chair of political economy at Trinity College Dublin. He named Fenton Hort of Leperstown, a country gentleman active in charitable affairs; Dr Charles Vignoles, the chaplain to the lord lieutenant; Dr James Wilson of Trinity College Dublin; Mountifort Longfield, the first holder of the Whately chair of political economy at Trinity; and Matthew Barrington, the crown solicitor for Munster.[18]

15 Extract from J. L. Mallet's diaries, 9 Mar. 1833, in [Political Economy Club], *Political Economy Club*, p. 248.

16 SRO: HP, D/260/M/F/5/26/9, p. 31, Littleton Journal, 1 Aug. 1833.

17 RA: MP, 96/2, Littleton to Melbourne, 6 May 1833.

18 Melbourne to Anglesey, 16 Aug. 1833, *ibid.*, 94/129.

Whately had a particularly strong and fruitful relationship with Murray, who had co-operated enthusiastically with him on the education board, despite the hostility of other Catholic prelates. Murray's presence on the Poor Inquiry Commission may have been meant as primarily decorative, but Whately was unlikely to encounter much criticism from that side. Murray's personal opinions on poverty were serious – on rising to the episcopate he vowed 'to cherish and protect the poor', which he understood to involve the encouragement of voluntary Catholic charitable bodies. He was instrumental in the establishment of the Sisters of Charity, the Society of St Vincent de Paul and other Catholic charitable bodies in Ireland, but took little interest in the creation of a state entitlement to relief as advocated by other Catholic clergymen in the period.[19] The ministers regarded Murray's appointment as unproblematic, but thought he should be balanced by the inclusion of a senior Presbyterian to satisfy the northern Dissenters. The obvious choice was Whately's other clerical collaborator on the education commission, Rev. James Carlile, minister of the Abbey Church in Dublin.

Anglesey was alarmed by Whately's other suggestions. With opinions running so high in Ireland, he warned, any appearance of the commission being 'packed' would be disastrous. Wilson was Whately's private chaplain and therefore 'entirely his man'; Longfield as a political economist (and holder of the archbishop's eponymous chair) would be considered as entirely against poor laws. Barrington, as a close Limerick associate of Spring Rice, would also be suspect. Whately himself was already well known for being 'decidedly against poor laws'.[20] Senior had already pre-empted the latter criticism of Whately by suggesting that in fact he had publicly disapproved only of 'any provision that should destroy industry and providence', and Whately retorted that Anglesey's views reflected both his own countervailing bias and an ignorance of political economy.[21] Nevertheless, it was clear that the administration's purposes would be ill served by so evidently lop-sided a selection, and several of Whately's names had to be sacrificed.

19 For Murray's charitable activities, see William Meagher, *Notices of the Life and Character of His Grace, Most Rev. Daniel Murray* (Dublin, 1853), pp. 37–42, 137–44; Luddy, *Women*, p. 37.

20 RA: MP, 94/130, Anglesey to Melbourne, 22 Aug. 1833. Longfield's views were in fact more nuanced than the viceroy allowed, but were available publicly only in the following year as *Four Lectures on Poor Laws, delivered in Trinity Term, 1834* (Dublin, 1834).

21 BL: AP, Add Ms 76419A, Senior to Spring Rice, 5 May 1833; NLI: MP, Ms 13,375/6, Melbourne to Spring Rice, 30 Aug. 1833.

The relatively little-known Fenton Hort and Charles Vignoles were retained,[22] but were now joined by two members who the government calculated would appeal to (and neutralize opposition from) different political constituencies in Ireland. Richard More O'Ferrall had been an active member of the Catholic Association but by the mid-1830s was Whig-liberal MP for Co. Kildare. James Naper of Loughcrew, Co. Meath, was a Protestant Tory landed gentleman who had already contributed to the poor-law controversy in print, and whose plans had been approvingly summarized in an 1831 Commons debate on Irish poor relief.[23]

The last member of the original commission was, in contrast to these 'political' appointments, intended to be an active agent. William Battie Wrightson, a Yorkshire landowner and barrister, was already heavily involved in poor-law affairs in Doncaster, and had good political connections, having been a Whig MP in 1826–32, and later sitting for Northallerton for thirty years from 1835. Wrightson was appointed (probably on Althorp's nomination), alongside Corrie as the second 'salaried' commissioner (the Irish-based commissioners were non-stipendiaries).[24] These two, with Whately, would be the central figures within the commission proper, and, although not part of his patronage network, were to prove his ideological soul-mates on the Irish poor-law question. On arrival in Dublin, Corrie expressed delight at the final make-up of the group, which he thought would both prove popular and 'answer all the objects of Government'.[25] This may have been true for the ministry of 1833 – it was demonstrably not the case for that in power from April 1835.

Of the original commissioners, More O'Ferrall was to resign in autumn 1834 (although his signature appeared on the first report, published in early 1835). His reasons for withdrawal are unclear, but O'Ferrall seems to have taken little active part in its early operations, and was unhappy that it had failed to recommend decisive intervention in the face of the public health and starvation crisis he discerned in parts of western Ireland in summer 1834.[26]

22 Fenton Hort (1794–1873) was a junior member of the Kildare landed family headed by Sir Josiah Hort. In 1833 he was serving with Whately on the managing committee of the Dublin Mendicity Institution. Vignoles (1789–1877) was subsequently dean of Ossory.

23 James Naper, *Practical Hints for the Relief and Employment of the Poor of Ireland* (Dublin, 1831); *Hansard*, 3, vi, 836–46 [29 Aug. 1831: Leader].

24 The stipendiary commissioners were to receive a fixed sum of £600 each, BL: AP, Add Ms 76,384, Melbourne to Althorp, 24 Sept. 1833.

25 Corrie to Drummond, 8 Nov. 1833, *ibid.*, Add Ms 76,419A.

26 SRO: HP, D/260/M/OI/2604, More O'Ferrall to Littleton, 14 July 1834. A number of assistant commissioners had been asked to report to Dublin Castle on the extent of the distress; on the strength of their reports the under-secretary and 'most of the commissioners' agreed that extraordinary government assistance would be counter-productive: Gossett to Littleton, 23 July 1834, *ibid.*, D/260/M/OI/359.

By August he was privately recommending the commission be wound up and restarted under the authority of its secretary (John Revans); a parting of the ways was thus inevitable.[27] In keeping with the public-relations priority of maintaining a politico-religious balance, O'Ferrall was replaced by Lord Killeen, heir to the Catholic Earl of Fingall, who was also close to the government interest in Ireland.

Additional commissioners were added at moments when it appeared the progress of the inquiry was stalling. Lord Lansdowne had been lobbying since spring 1833 for the inclusion of his protégé, the self-appointed expert on Ireland and the poor laws, James Ebenezer Bicheno. Bicheno had first suggested himself on hearing of the prospective inquiry, and had previously been nominated unsuccessfully by Lansdowne.[28] When the opportunity arose for additions to the commission, on its renewal in September 1834, Lansdowne again pressed his case, and was outraged when an apparent administrative mix-up at the Home Office led to the two additional names, Bicheno and Sir Charles Grey, being omitted from the reissued commission. Lansdowne suspected a conspiracy by the new home secretary, Duncannon, and proceeded through threats of resignation to bully Melbourne (now prime minister) into adding Bicheno as a third paid member.[29] This was a significant addition given Bicheno's ultra-negative position on the Irish poor-law question, and his public stance as an advocate of gradual abolition of the English poor laws.

The final addition to the commission was Anthony Blake, the chief remembrancer to the exchequer in Ireland and the leading 'Castle Catholic' advisor to all Irish administrations between the 1820s and 1840s. Blake's belated inclusion in October 1835 was by the express desire of the commissioners themselves, at a time when it appeared that the voluminous materials and proposals collected could only with great difficulty be moulded into a coherent final report, and after the commissioners had lost confidence in the ability of their secretary to undertake this role to their satisfaction. Blake's role was to be chiefly a technical one, but his opinions on the ethical undesirability of compulsory poor relief had been put on the official record in his evidence before the 1830 committee:

> [T]he people have not yet sufficiently learned to venerate themselves as men, [and] it is by teaching them to do so, and affording them means of profitable

27 NLW: HCP, C/445, G. C. Lewis to T. F. Lewis, 6 August 1834.

28 BL: BP, B/107, Bicheno to Lansdowne, 6 Apr. 1833; BL: AP, Add Ms 76,419A, Memo: Candidates for Irish Poor Commission [1833].

29 BL: BP, B/91, Melbourne to Lansdowne, 4, 10, 12 Sept., Lansdowne to Melbourne, 11 Sept. 1834. Charles Grey was the 2nd earl's son and until November 1833 his private secretary; his appointment was not proceeded with.

> employment, that you can effect a solid improvement in the country; a compulsory provision for the poor would tend to prevent the growth of those independent feelings and industrious habits, through which alone I look for the regeneration of Ireland.[30]

Blake was evidently trusted by Whately and his colleagues to convey their opinions most effectively, and the physical drafting of the third report was undertaken by him, with some assistance from Bicheno.[31]

Alongside the commissioners proper, the other crucial role in the inquiry was that of secretary. Several names were considered, but in the end the choice was an obvious one. John Revans, a man who had first come to ministerial attention as a critic of the navigation laws, had already served as secretary to the English poor law inquiry in 1832–33.[32] He had won the confidence of Nassau Senior for his management of that monumental exercise, and on its conclusion he was seconded to Ireland to play the same role in the Whately inquiry. He had placed under him an assistant secretary, Hamilton Dowdall, five clerks and two messengers.[33] Revans' position as secretary was ostensibly subordinate and technical – on the English inquiry he had been, according to Senior, 'zealous . . . but docile: [he] never attempted to originate, but followed . . . directions actively and intelligently', and the same behaviour was expected in Ireland.[34] Subsequent events would reveal just how wrong these assumptions were.

As with the English inquiry, the Irish commission would have to rely on the industry of considerable numbers of travelling assistant commissioners in acquiring the corpus of information on poverty, social conditions, economic development and charitable institutions on which any report of recommendations would ostensibly be based. Senior was of the opinion that the choice of assistant commissioners should be left to the commission itself, citing both the need for mutual confidence and Whately's mastery of 'the art of selecting

30 *First Report . . . on the State of the Poor in Ireland*, PP 1830 (589), vii.278, p. 343.

31 NA: HOP, HO 100/246, fol. 369–70, 371, Morpeth to Russell, 29 Oct. 1835, Whately to Morpeth, [Oct. 1835]. Bicheno's remuneration was increased to £800 to reflect his efforts in the drafting of the final report, NA: TP, T1/4100/590, Spring Rice memo, 11 Oct. 1836.

32 Revans was born in 1804, the son of a London surgeon and brother of the colonial radical Samuel Revans. After publishing a pamphlet attacking the Baltic timber duties in 1831, he had been commissioned by Althorp to write for the *Westminster Review* against the navigation laws: see John Revans, *England's Navigation Laws no Protection to British Shipping* (London, 1849).

33 *Return of Numbers of Existing Commissions of Inquiry*, PP 1834 (291), xli.349, p. 10.

34 NLW: NSP, C/549, Senior to Whately, 21 Dec. 1835.

good tools, and sharpening, as well as using them'. He thought unpaid assistant commissioners, ideally younger barristers seeking no pecuniary gain or subsequent employment, would be best for the job, although the specific circumstances dictated the desirability of a balance of Irishmen and Englishmen, and of Protestants and Catholics.[35] While agreeing that English assistants would be more experienced, Melbourne accepted that the existence of cultural differences made the inclusion of some Irishmen desirable, and that this 'would render the enquiry itself more complete and accurate. Much, that would escape a stranger, would be detected by a native of the country, and the latter would not be so liable to be deceived or misled as the former.'[36]

Inundated with requests for employment from applicants and their sponsors from the moment the inquiry was announced, the ministers were inclined to agree with Senior's suggestions.[37] However, the difficulty of persuading experienced English candidates to commit to extended periods in Ireland without salaries proved a handicap, and a decision was taken to allow these a fixed sum of £200 each, payable in arrears. Irish-based assistant commissioners, however, were to receive only their expenses – although these turned out (for most) to be relatively generous at a minimum of fifteen shillings per day.[38] The opportunity to exercise some patronage proved difficult to eschew, and the English ministers did not in the end allow Whately to choose any of the first nine English assistants.[39] Whately reluctantly accepted this so long as Whitehall allowed him the liberty to appoint as many Irish assistant commissioners as he felt necessary. The English commission, he reminded Littleton, had selected all their own assistants, 'who were, in fact their servants', and this had ensured internal concord. Despite concerns expressed by Corrie and Littleton that allowing the commission to select its Irish assistants would promote favouritism and inefficiency, Whately was allowed to retain de facto control over this area. In the end Littleton conceded this so long as Dublin Castle retained a consultative role in these appointments.[40] Given Whately's

35 BL: AP, Add Ms 76,419A, Senior to Spring Rice, 5 May 1833.

36 RA: MP, 96/59, Melbourne to Littleton, 24 Oct. 1833.

37 For the lengthy list of applicants and sponsors, see BL: AP, Add Ms 76,419A, Memo: Candidates for Irish Poor Commission [1833].

38 Melbourne to Althorp, 24 Sept. 1833, *ibid.*, Add Ms 76,348; *Commission and Instructions to the Commissioners on the State of the Poor in Ireland*, PP 1834 (175), xliii.407, p. 1. For Irish anger at the discrepancy in payments, see *FJ*, 30 Jan. 1834.

39 SRO: HP, D/260/M/OI/2, pp. 212–13, Littleton to Whately, 29 Oct. 1833.

40 Whately to Littleton, 30 Oct. 1833, *ibid.*, D/260/M/OI/2369, Littleton to Melbourne, 21 Oct. 1833; RA: MP, 96/58, 96/59, Melbourne to Littleton, 24 Oct. 1833; SRO: HP, D/260/M/OI/2, p. 227, Littleton to Whately, 1 Nov. 1833.

association with the ministry, this arrangement inevitably led to some complaints from Tories about political bias in the appointment of assistant commissioners.[41]

Whately's frank admission that he regarded the assistants as occupying a servile role within the exercise is revealing: already denied the sole nomination of commissioners he had originally sought, he now feared loss of control over the subordinate agents. This may indicate a touch of paranoia on the part of the archbishop (he was equally intolerant of dissent in his other domain, the education board), unnecessary so long as ministerial opinion was in parallel with his own desires, but not wholly unwarranted should the political balance shift in a direction which might undermine his own authority. By February 1834 thirty-nine assistant commissioners had been named, nine of them English (including G. C. Lewis).[42] These numbers (and the associated costs of the exercise) subsequently escalated; up to June 1835 fourteen English assistants had served with the commission, and a further four were added by order of Lord John Russell as home secretary later that month.[43] Assistant commissioners were drawn from a range of backgrounds – the Rev. Charles Clarke was a clergyman, extensive practical farmer and former poor-law guardian in Suffolk, and had formerly served on the English inquiry.[44] Jonathan Binns – who followed his official tour covering twenty-two Irish counties in eighteen months with a 'private' visit to another four, and who published his personal memoir of his experiences in 1837 – was a Lancaster Quaker and land surveyor with radical opinions on England's responsibility for Ireland's 'anomalous condition'.[45] Another 'English' assistant commissioner was Frederick Solly Flood (1801–88), a London-based lawyer who had inherited his grandfather's Wexford estates in 1824 and was subsequently attorney-general of Gibraltar. A number of the English and Irish assistants, such as Captains White and Pringle, Major Ninian Crawford and Lt-Col. Burke, were half-pay army or navy officers. Whately was able to deploy at least some patronage in the 'Irish' appointments; his domestic chaplain and private secretary Charles Dickinson was appointed (albeit temporarily and without remuneration) in

41 Anon., 'The state of the Irish poor', *DUM*, 7 (Apr. 1836), p. 362.

42 Commission and Instructions, p. 2.

43 *Accounts of Expenses of Commission for Inquiring into the State of the Poor in Ireland*, PP 1835 (559), xlvii, p. 1. The final cost of the inquiry was just under £16,000: see *Return of Commissions issued since November 1830*, PP 1836 (528) xxxvii.491, p. 37.

44 John Revans, *Evils of the State of Ireland: Their Causes and Their Remedy – A Poor Law* (2nd edn, London, 1837), pp. 63, 131. Several others, including Captain Pringle and Patrick Johnston, were also veterans of the English inquiry.

45 Jonathan Binns, *The Miseries and Beauties of Ireland* (2 vols, London, 1837).

1833.[46] A Catholic priest, Fr M. Flanagan, was also put to work on the Dublin investigation. Ultimately, in the light of the length of the inquiry – one assistant commissioner complained that he had suffered from excessive workload for two and a half years – additional payments were made by the Treasury to both 'English' and 'Irish' assistant commissioners on a case by case basis.[47]

The commission in action, 1833–36

The Whately Commission was formally instituted by the Crown on 25 September 1833, charged with inquiring into and recommending remedial measures to ameliorate the condition of the Irish poor, within a period of one year. The last condition was wholly unrealistic given the anticipated extent of the inquiry's fieldwork, but it is unlikely that either Whately or the responsible ministers regarded the conclusion of the exercise as in any way urgent. Wrightson and Revans did not arrive in Dublin until early November, and the few assistant commissioners then available were put to work first on a 'minute examination' of the state of the poor in Dublin. Corrie observed that the Irish commissioners had been erratic in attending the early board meetings (a pattern which was to continue), but was confident that he, Wrightson and Revans would make its daily operations effective, so long as Littleton did not press for impossible completion targets.[48]

The next few weeks saw the resolution of outstanding issues relating to the housing of the commission's offices in Dublin and the provision of necessary funding from the Treasury.[49] In October–December 1833 five sets of preliminary queries, prepared separately for notables in urban and rural districts, for medical officers of dispensaries, magistrates at petty sessions and ministers of congregations of all creeds, were published and posted out to their respective recipients.[50] Of the 7,600 sets circulated, some 3,100 were returned, covering about 1,100 parishes, or some 47 per cent of the total number in Ireland. As replies to these missives began to come in, a 51-page booklet of instructions

46 *Return of . . . Commissions of Inquiry*, p. 10; Dickinson (1792–1842) had been heavily involved in voluntary charity in Dublin as chaplain to both the Magdalene Asylum and the Female Orphan House; he later served briefly as bishop of Meath.

47 NA: TP, T1/4100/590, T. N. Vaughan to Treasury, 6 June 1836, and general correspondence in this file.

48 BL: AP, Add Ms 76,419A, Corrie to Drummond, 14 Nov. 1833. He noted that Vignoles and Hort were the most regular Irish members in attendance.

49 RA: MP, 96/89A, Melbourne memo, 29 Nov. 1833; SRO: HP, D/260/M/OI/2, pp. 278–9, Littleton to Spring Rice, 1 Dec. 1833.

50 *Pilot*, 23, 28 Oct., 11 Dec. 1833.

to the assistant commissioners was drawn up to direct their follow-up activities in the localities.[51]

By the end of the year several specialist inquiries had also been initiated. George Cornewall Lewis, who had previously served as an assistant commissioner on the English inquiry, was allocated the responsibility of reporting on the condition of Irish immigrants in Great Britain, an onerous task (in his own opinion) which he had completed by late March 1834. His findings would be published as appendix G of the third report.[52] Four medical assistant commissioners, Sir David Barry, J. R. Corrie, William P. Borrett and Cusack Roney, were to spend five months in 1834 investigating the medical charities and county infirmaries throughout Ireland; their report would be appended to the commission's first report in 1835.[53] Like Lewis and some of the other assistant commissioners, Borrett resented the servile status expected of them by Whately, and later entered the print controversy, challenging the policy recommendations ostensibly based on the foundations of these reports.[54]

The great majority of the assistant commissioners were allocated the task of touring the localities of Ireland to follow up and expand on the written returns made in response to the commissioners' queries. The methodology of investigation was to be social-scientific: assistant commissioners were to sample popular feeling through public meetings in one parish in each barony. They were instructed to be strictly impartial in collecting evidence, to avoid giving offence or endorsing any personal opinion, to encourage persons of opposite opinions to state their cases, and to record all proceedings in 'a regular and minute journal', abstracts from which would be regularly forwarded to Dublin. The categories for investigation were prescribed in some detail in the document, although the assistant commissioners were accorded flexibility in pursuing topics of local interest in greater detail. Assistants were to review firstly the 'circumstances which must have a general influence on the condition of the poorer classes', including education, charitable institutions and alms-giving, benefit societies, loan funds, emigration, combinations, alcoholic consumption, pawnbroking, landlord–tenant relations and

51 Poor Inquiry Commission [PIC]: *First Report*, pp. viii; BL: AP, Add Ms 76,419A, Corrie to Drummond, 14 Nov. 1833; [Poor Inquiry Commission], *Instructions given by the Commissioners appointed to inquire into the State of the Poor in Ireland, to the Assistant Commissioners* (n.d. [1833]); *Commission and Instructions*, pp. 3–13.

52 NLW: HCP, C/2754, Lewis to Villiers, 13 Jan, 1834; *PIC: Appendix G: Report on the State of the Irish Poor in Great Britain*, PP 1836 [40], xxxiv.1.

53 Geary, *Medicine*, pp. 47–8; *PIC: Appendix B*, PP 1835 (369), xxxii.1, part II.

54 See W. P. Borrett, *Three Letters upon a Poor Law and Public Medical Relief for Ireland to Daniel O'Connell* (London, 1838), and below, pp. 265–6.

landholding, absenteeism, the judicial and penal system, local taxes and levies, and public works. Having done this, they were, secondly, to report on the actual condition of the poorer classes, both the 'impotent poor' and the 'able-bodied' (the latter subdivided into five classes). Finally, the existing institutions for the relief of the poor were to be investigated.[55] These categories in themselves give an indication of the limitations of the 'neutrality' of the inquiry, and the predetermined palette in which it would depict Irish poverty.

Nevertheless, within its own discursive parameters it did seek to prioritize the collection of not only the largest possible volume of material, but also the widest range of opinions about the problem under review, and record these with a relatively light degree of editorial intervention. This was to be an information-gathering exercise with a significantly wider remit than the English commission of 1832–33, or indeed any previous Irish inquiry. While the final policy recommendations may have been largely in the leading commissioners' minds from the outset, they felt it important that the data collected should be as far as possible above public criticism; an authoritative body of evidence was likely to cast a glowing empirical aura around any proposals associated with it.

Revans subsequently promoted the Irish inquiry as a model for future investigations of the physical and moral conditions of the poor. A 'balanced' set of questions had been attained by denying any commissioner the power of veto in preparing them. The obligation on assistant commissioners to report verbatim the evidence given, and insistence that all present be allowed to speak, was an advance on the English commission's methodology. Most importantly of all, the poor themselves had been the focus of consultation; Revans commented that the best evidence came 'either from the poor themselves, or from those who are most near to them in circumstances, the small farmers; the farmers of six or eight acres; but so difficult is it for the persons of one class to know the circumstances of those of other classes, that even the small farmers were in many cases incapable of answering questions closely connected with the state of the labourers'. Such information, he concluded, was the only sound basis for any legislation affecting the working classes.[56]

This commitment to both scale and depth was to ensure that the Whately Commission's collection of evidence ultimately confounded those critics who argued that it could not add anything to what had previously been presented to parliament or 'what could be furnished by any MP or peer of Ireland'.[57]

55 Commission and Instructions, pp. 2–10.

56 *Select Committee on the Education of the People of England and Wales, and Grants in Aid*, PP 1835 (465), vii.763, pp. 47–51.

57 BL: AP, Add Ms 76,419A, Thomas Conroy to Althorp, 18 May 1833.

Other observers had, more reasonably, questioned whether, given the existing power-relationships in the Irish countryside, any reliable information would be proffered by those in the lower rungs of the social pyramid. One Armagh correspondent warned:

> The knowledge you derive from public investigations is defective as the poor farmers are so much under the controul [sic] of their landlords, that they dare not tell the truth, and the facts generally communicated through private channels are distorted by party feelings and interests. Unfortunately there are very few resident in Ireland whose motives are not governed by interest of party. They are connected with the oppressors, the oppressed, or are designing knaves who live by discord[.][58]

Given the fractured social, religious and political nature of the country, this was a fair comment, and questions have subsequently been raised about both the balance and reliability of the Poor Inquiry Commission's evidence. As one historian has noted, both the issue of the transcription (and often also the translation from Irish) of interview statements into 'official' English, and the public character of testimony, have to be taken into account in assessing the recorded evidence. However, these constraints were to some considerable degree counteracted by the 'variety of opinions recorded, the extent of disagreement between witnesses, and the clear expression of different types of conflict within rural society'.[59]

Several examinations, chosen at random, might serve to illustrate the range of persons whose voices were recorded. At Ballina, Co. Mayo, twenty-five witnesses appeared before the duo of assistant commissioners in public session. They comprised two gentlemen, seven men drawn from the middle classes (a merchant, two doctors, a constabulary officer, the Catholic and Protestant clergymen and a 'classical teacher'), two farmers, nine labourers and a labourer's widow, two beggars and two men described as 'broken down', presumably labourers afflicted by chronic ill health. Only three – the two beggars and the widow – were female, but the lion's share of the recorded evidence on this occasion was given by the agricultural labourers Thady Carnan, James Browne and Pat Cooper.

At Burrishoole, Co. Mayo, the social and gender range of the witnesses was similar, and the examinations were held in 'a public room, which was crowded during the greater part of the time that they lasted'. As before, an attempt

58 SRO: HP, D/260/M/OI/2364, Daniel Dowling to Littleton, 16 Oct. 1833.

59 Niall Ó Ciosain, 'Introduction', in Maureen Comber (ed.), *Poverty Before the Famine: County Clare 1835* (Ennis, 1996), pp. iii–vii. Ó Ciosain notes that the choice of witnesses was more skewed by gender than by class or occupation, with women severely under-represented.

seems to have been made to collect the evidence of the poorer witnesses verbatim and to allow them at least as long to make their case as their social superiors.[60] At Kilkee, Co. Clare, much of the recorded testimony was that of a labourer, James McMahon. Despite the presence of the landowner, Crofton Vandeleur, and numerous farmers, McMahon openly denounced to their faces the latter for imposing exploitative credit relations on the labouring poor, and the landlords for clearances and heartlessness: 'We are worked harder and worse treated than the slaves in the colonies. I understand they are taken care of by their masters when they are sick or old. When we are sick, we must die on the road, if the neighbours do not help us.'[61] It seems that most assistant commissioners took seriously the view that the value of their returns would be enhanced by the range of perspectives recorded, and it is this that gives the Whately report evidence its particular character and historical value. The authority thus awarded to the voice of individuals from the lower classes caused some unease among Irish elites, especially when they criticized their social superiors in public.[62]

Not all contemporaries were, however, persuaded of the 'objectivity' of the information thus collected. The Scottish travel writer Henry Inglis, who toured Ireland simultaneously with the operation of the inquiry in spring–autumn 1834, argued that a single private traveller would always have the edge in eliciting the truth 'over a posse of government commissioners'. Unlike those hampered by their official status, he insisted, a traveller could enter ordinary people's houses, socialize with them, and win their confidence. Inglis also observed a gendered dimension to such social knowledge; unlike any of the official commissioners, he had been accompanied by his wife, whose visits to cabins had been welcomed by the peasantry 'as a particular condescension, and met by a proportional confidence'.[63] Inglis proceeded to provide his own answers to the sets of queries circulated by the commission, and to include his own summary recommendations, based on his assertedly superior access to the true social conditions of the country and his political independence: he concluded that the state should impose the 'imperative and sacred duty' of obliging the landowners to provide for the aged, impotent and infirm poor through compulsory rates, while the able-bodied labourers should be relieved

60 Extracts in *The Times*, 9, 13 Sept. 1836.

61 [Poor Inquiry Commission], *Selection of Parochial Examinations*, pp. 233–4.

62 Anon., 'The state of the Irish poor', *DUM*, 7 (Apr. 1836), p. 358.

63 Henry D. Inglis, *A Journey throughout Ireland, during the Spring, Summer and Autumn of 1834* (3rd edn, 2 vols, London, 1835), ii, pp. 287–93. Inglis's attitude to the gendered issue of travel writing was nevertheless ambivalent: the presence of his wife on the tour had not been acknowledged until late in the second volume of his narrative.

through employment on the state colonization of the waste-lands 'for the benefit of the people'.[64] Given the great popularity of Inglis's work in Britain (it went through eight editions between 1835 and 1838, and was quoted at length in parliament by both Smith O'Brien and Poulett Scrope), these criticisms and proposals were likely to have been influential, although perhaps not entirely subversive of the commission's evidence and recommendations.[65]

Assistant commissioners, working usually in pairs, began to arrive in the provinces from early 1834. In the interests of political balance, where possible, an Englishman was to be accompanied by an Irishman. Two assistants had the power to co-opt a third member of each local team if they thought this appropriate (such as to provide a religious balance), but were not to allow any local resident to participate in the interrogations. They were instructed to seek out and give equal attention to the testimony of individuals from all classes and creeds, which was to be given 'in open court'.[66] Six weeks was regarded by one of their number as the minimum period for a thorough investigation of the town of Limerick;[67] rural parishes are likely to have occupied a shorter period of time. In Limerick, an English (John Spencer) and an Irish (L. M. Stewart) assistant commissioner worked together, with the assistance of a third (unspecified) figure – a pattern replicated elsewhere. The local press in this instance gave the work its full support, expressing its 'perfect confidence that everything will be investigated by the commissioners to the very source, so as to give satisfaction to all parties'.[68] The reception of investigators elsewhere must have been to some extent dependent on the attitudes of local elites and their readiness to mediate between the officials and the populace. However, the support of most of the clergy of all denominations for the exercise (as manifested by the inclusion of their senior representatives on the commission's board) must have smoothed the way in many localities. Nevertheless, the particular deference shown by some assistant commissioners to the Catholic clergy aroused the ire of some Protestant commentators, and the commissioners were acutely aware that the intense political divisions dividing the clergy and resident proprietors, and the suspicion with which the

64 *Ibid.*, pp. 322–6.

65 *Hansard*, 3, xxvi, 1207–8 [19 Mar.], xxix, 320–4 [8 July 1835]. His opinions were less popular among Catholics, who objected to his more dogmatic observations on religion: see [John O'Connell], 'Miseries and beauties of Ireland', *DR*, 4 (Apr. 1838), pp. 409–10.

66 *Pilot*, 4 Nov. 1833.

67 SRO: HP, D/260/M/OI/881a, L. M. Stewart to Littleton, 26 Feb. 1834.

68 *Limerick Chronicle*, 22 Feb. 1834.

constabulary was regarded by much of the populace, rendered reliance on such intermediary agents problematic.[69]

As Littleton had feared, however, not all of the Irish assistant commissioners could avoid becoming embroiled in local controversies, with some embarrassment to the inquiry. L. M. Stewart, who was already well known in Limerick as former secretary to the local corporation commissioners, unintentionally ran foul of these expectations and was the subject of a complaint from Lord Milltown. This elicited a formal warning from the Home Office, and in July his removal on Corrie's recommendation. Stewart's alleged behaviour, it was noted, had been 'absurd', obliging his fellow assistant commissioners to disassociate themselves and Revans to undertake an investigation, but his dismissal was made discreetly so as to avoid undermining the public standing of the commission.[70]

Not content with awaiting the reports from the travelling investigators, Corrie, Wrightson and several of the other commissioners made occasional forays from headquarters and participated in the collection of testimony, especially in response to specific claims made about localities in parliament.[71] In July 1834 Corrie and Vignoles were at Balbriggan, Co. Dublin, where they heard enough to satisfy themselves that accounts of unusual distress that summer had been greatly exaggerated, and that if anything the people were in a better condition than usual. Quoting Whately as his source, Corrie declared such hands-on investigations to be essential, as 'truth lies at the bottom of a well, and in Ireland that well is a very deep one.'[72] In January 1835 the commissioners undertook a 'figure of S' tour of the country, presumably for the same purpose, visiting proprietors such as Smith O'Brien en route.[73]

Despite this seeming hive of activity in 1834, some privileged observers were less than impressed by the organization and energy of the inquiry.

69 Anon., 'The state of the Irish poor', p. 362; *PIC: First Report*, p. vi. However, cf. the claim of a chief constable in Listowel, Co. Kerry, that the intermediary role played by the stipendiary magistrates and constabulary had ensured that accurate local information had been made available: Brady, *Letter and Suggestions*, pp. 11–12.

70 NA: HOP, HO 122/15, fols 205–6, J. M. Phillipps to Revans, 17 Mar. 1834; SRO: HP, D/260/M/OI/882, Corrie to R. D. Craig, 28 July 1834.

71 Wrightson ultimately claimed for £400 in travelling expenses, NA: TP, T1/4100/590, Wrightson to F. Baring, 10 Oct. 1836.

72 SRO: HP, D/260/M/OI/356, 882, Corrie to Littleton, 11 July, Corrie to Craig, 28 July 1834.

73 NLI: SOBP, Ms 427, fol. 274, Hort to Smith O'Brien, 26 Jan. 1835.

Arriving in Ireland after completing his research in the 'Little Irelands' of Great Britain, G. C. Lewis was extremely critical of what he saw. In April he wrote to his friend Edward Villiers:

> There is an immensity of work to be done and scarcely anybody to do it. Nobody seems to like work, either at the Board, or among the Assistant Commissioners. They sadly want a couple of such men as Senior and Chadwick. Having once established it, I feel anxious that the thing should not altogether fail, but I must say its present aspect is very unpromising. Whately does absolutely nothing.[74]

Lewis, of course, had both personal ambition and an agenda; he had also cut his academic teeth while at Oxford in picking holes in Whately's *Elements of Logic* and he lacked the awed admiration of the bishop's intellect that other contemporaries appear to have held.[75] His views on the dilatoriness and inefficiency of the investigation were, however, increasingly shared by other close observers as the exercise approached its second year. Littleton took the opportunity presented on Melbourne's replacement by Duncannon as home secretary in August 1834 to vent his frustration at the lack of progress made so far. Not a single rural parish had been investigated, he complained, and thus there was now no chance of a report in time for the next parliamentary session. In his opinion, the plan of investigation had been over-elaborate and needed fundamental revision.[76]

Revans as secretary had responsibility for the smooth running of the operation, but rather than blame him Lewis pointed the finger at Whately's indolence and the culture shock encountered by English 'men of business' on encountering Ireland. 'Revans', he commented, 'seems to have been struck aghast at the jobbing propensities of the Irish: he seems, like many other innocent Englishmen, to have expected to find the same standard of morality on both sides of the channel.'[77] By September 1834, however, Lewis was reporting that Revans had imposed a greater degree of personal authority and order over the operations of the commission.[78] The change of occupancy at the home office may have contributed to this; Revans appears to have become more assertive from this point onwards and entered upon the collision path with Whately and his associates.

74 NLW: HCP, C/2762, Lewis to Villiers, 27 Apr. 1834.

75 George Cornewall Lewis, *An Examination of Some Passages in Dr Whately's Elements of Logic* (Oxford, 1829).

76 SRO: HP, D/260/M/OI/883–4, D/260/M/OI/3, pp. 410–12, Littleton to Duncannon, 9 Aug., Littleton to Gossett, 14 Aug. 1834.

77 NLW: HCP, C/2760, Lewis to Villiers, 30 Mar. 1834.

78 Lewis to Villiers, 7 Sept. 1834, *ibid.*, C/2766.

On behalf of the commission, Revans was prepared to admit in September 1834 that the first eight months of operations had been largely wasted, although he insisted that major progress had been made in the subsequent four months and that a robust plan was now in place to deliver a significant corpus of information on social conditions throughout the island for publication in early 1835. Numbers of better-qualified assistants had lately been taken on, and a review of destitution and modes of relief carried out in a sample of one or two parishes per barony for sixteen counties would soon be complete. A separate investigation of agricultural practices and employment in six dispersed counties was on the point of being initiated. It was unfair, he concluded, to compare the Irish inquiry unfavourably with that of England, given the much wider frame of reference and the lack of competent personnel in the former.[79]

Further detailed sets of questions were drawn up to be used by the assistants, although Revans insisted that these were intended for guidance rather than being prescriptive. If individual discretion was not allowed to assistant commissioners on how to shape interviews, he noted, the exercise would become mechanical and ineffective. However, Revans continued to insist that the scale of the survey must not be curtailed, not just for the sake of completeness, but with an eye to practical outcomes. In a long letter to Lewis he reiterated both the modified methodology and the ends he desired:

> It is not to satisfy a few highly intelligent men that such an enquiry is made but to satisfy those who have prejudices, are sceptical, [or] are not in the habit of deep thinking. Such persons require every parish in a kingdom to report the fact before they believe its universality and unless it be universal they will admit of no law. In like manner such people (the great mass of society) require assent to a self evident proposition from what they call practical people, otherwise if as clear as that 3 and 3 make 6 they will [resort?] in any conclusion to which it may be necessary. If none but the highly enlightened and thinking portion of society are to be informed by this Commission, then I think the Commission a farce because a man who is well acquainted with human nature will in two months consideration frame you regulations, as foreseeing consequences, just as perfectly as if he were never acquainted with every separate instance under his rule. Not only facts but even immediate inferences must be multiplied to the utmost extent in the evidence or the cavillers in Parliament and out of Parliament – the self interested on either side will quickly destroy all the calculations.

The commission's initial operations had been, in his opinion, unfocused and desultory, but crucially now they had divided the investigation into two

79 SRO: HP, D/260/M/OI/2078, [Revans?], Memo on Irish poor inquiry, [Sept. 1834].

categories of analysis – firstly an inquiry into how the destitute were currently supported and whether this could be improved, and secondly, into the causes of poverty and underemployment and the means of redressing these. While these were not unrelated, Revans insisted that the categorical distinction be retained. Given that Ireland, like every European country, was always likely to have a destitute fraction of its population, the key question became what was

> the best mode of subsisting such, for they will subsist by worse means if you will not subsist them by better. In order to do this you must enquire what are the evils[,] what the advantages of each particular system – of leaving them to beg or steal on the one hand, or of giving them a subsistence on the other.[80]

While not neglecting the importance of 'the causes of destitution' or remedial action to address them, Revans' musings pointed in one direction. As Lewis approvingly observed, 'Revans thinks the evidence will be strongly in favour of a poor law, and that the English members will carry it against the Irish landlords.'[81]

Writing the report: Whately *versus* Revans

The fall of the Whig ministry in November 1834 and its replacement by the short-lived first Peel administration appears to have made little difference to the operations of the Whately Commission. Lewis, who had been transferred to the Irish Church commission (which, among other things, was engaged in taking a 'religious census'), was concerned that this more politically sensitive inquiry (he had privately referred to his role as that of 'demolishing the Church') might fall prey to party expediency, but in the end the new government failed to take the 'counter-revolutionary' step of suppressing it, just as it ignored the continuing workings of the poor inquiry.[82]

However, the restoration of the Whigs to office in April 1835 ushered in a very different political atmosphere. The incoming home secretary, Lord John Russell, promptly directed his attention to the Whately Commission and demanded explanations for the continuing delay in producing the final report of recommendations. The new lord lieutenant, Lord Mulgrave, was instructed to question the secretary and ascertain the regularity of board meetings and

80 NLW: HCP, C/2312, Revans to Lewis [Sept. 1834].

81 Lewis to Villiers, 16 Oct. 1834, *ibid.*, C/2767.

82 G. C. Lewis to T. F. Lewis, 13 Oct., 22 Nov. 1834, G. C. Lewis to Villiers, 17 Mar. 1835, *ibid.*, C/446, C/447, C/2778; G. C. Lewis to Mrs Austin, [1834], in Gilbert Frankland Lewis (ed.), *Letters of the Rt. Hon. Sir George Cornewall Lewis, Bart., to Various Friends* (London, 1870), pp. 38–9.

their attendance.[83] Evidently dissatisfied with the response from Dublin and determined to make the poor-law question a political priority, Russell threatened the dissolution of the commission and its replacement by an efficient body of three, excluding the bishops and political appointments.[84] July 1835 saw the publication of the first report, with its extensive transcriptions of parochial examinations on the state of the poor arranged under various classifications, but lacking any policy recommendations. Public consumption of this evidence, which the commissioners also had published in a cheaper volume of extracts and which were widely reprinted in the press, tended to draw attention to the absence of any concrete proposals for addressing the misery so thoroughly documented, while raising expectations that something extensive would have to be proposed to rescue Ireland from such 'an extent of destitution unparalleled in human suffering'.[85]

Prevarications on the part of the commissioners, and the eventual addition of Blake to draft the final report, appear to have bought more time, but in September 1835 Spring Rice, now chancellor of the exchequer, warned that it would be utterly disgraceful if (as appeared likely) no such report was forthcoming that year. If the government failed to table something early in the 1836 session in answer to the three or four 'absurd' bills already before the House, he told Whately, it would lay itself open to charges of bad faith.[86]

Whately's response was either studied evasion – a long interview with the new chief secretary Lord Morpeth in July led to nothing – or veiled threats that any hurried report might produce disastrous and irrevocable legislation.[87] This was enough to satisfy Spring Rice, who shared Whately's general approach and accepted his plan to bring the 'interminable' inquiry to a completion by spring 1836.[88] The commission's second report, providing a lengthy discussion of the history and condition of the existing charitable institutions in Ireland, but again making no significant recommendations, was completed in January 1836 (but not published in full until the following

83 MC: NP, M/916, Russell to Mulgrave, 15 May [1835].

84 Russell to Mulgrave, 3 June 1835, *ibid.*, M/781.

85 *PIC: First Report*, PP 1835 (369), xxxii.1; Anon., 'The state of the Irish poor', pp. 349–64.

86 NLI: MP, Ms 551, pp. 132–3, 135, Spring Rice to Drummond, 13 Sept., Spring Rice to Whately, 13 Sept. 1835.

87 MC: NP, M/465, Morpeth to Mulgrave, 17 July 1835; NLI: MP, Ms 551, p. 135, Whately to Spring Rice 13 Sept. 1835. Morpeth's account stressed Whately's eccentricity; throughout their conversation, the archbishop 'stuck his legs in the air and was very much occupied with hitting the flies on his head'.

88 NLI: MP, Ms 553, p. 106, Spring Rice to Whately, 18 Jan. 1836.

year).[89] There were, however, sufficient hints in this report to alert critics to the fact that the commission would recommend 'no public provision for the destitute poor', and dismiss its 'mountains of irrelevant testimony' as a smoke-screen. Important sections of the press demanded urgent action to redress the 'slow starvation' of the poor revealed especially in evidence given by the Catholic and Protestant clergy.[90] This further delay in producing definitive final recommendations also clearly frustrated and antagonized Russell and the Irish administration. Another deadline for completion of the substantive report by 31 January was exceeded despite Russell's threats to wind it up if nothing had been produced, and it was not until the end of March 1836 that the recommendations of the third report were finally delivered.[91]

In the changed political climate of 1835–36, Revans had become much more assertive and his relationship with Whately deteriorated markedly. In early 1835 the archbishop complained that Revans had become involved with factional differences between groups of assistant commissioners and had begun to rub certain commissioners up the wrong way.[92] By the end of the year the rift was irrevocable. Whately's explanation veered between accusing Revans of self-interested careerism and misplaced political enthusiasm. He complained to Senior:

> Revans who is in actual solicitation of a place from Lord Roi-seul [Whately's deprecating nickname for Russell] has completely veered round in his views respecting poor laws: me he alone excepted in speaking to you with contempt of the Commissioners, and with especial contempt of Dr Vignoles; whom he is now cajoling, and supplying him underhand with everything that can be urged in opposition to me. It all looks like a conspiracy; not least because the O'Connell papers have now, for the first time, opened their batteries on me.[93]

Having excluded Revans from the preparation of the final report on the expectation that he would seek to 'blow up all the resolutions we have passed', Whately then complained that he was spending too much time at Dublin Castle, and asked Senior to put ministers on their guard against 'that viper R[evans]', who has caught 'the infection of the mob-radicals'.[94] The latter

89 *PIC: Second Report*, PP 1837 [68], xxxi.587.

90 *The Times*, 19, 23 Jan. 1836.

91 NA: HOP, HO 100/246, fol. 365, Russell memo, 3 Nov. 1835; CHP, J/19/1/10, fol. 52, Russell to Morpeth, 4 Jan. 1836; MC: NP, M/536, Morpeth to Mulgrave, 5 Apr. 1836. The recommendations can be found in summary form in an undated memo, NA: RP, PRO30/22/2D, fols 372–8.

92 Lambeth Palace Library, London [LPL], Whately Papers, Ms 2164, fols 140–1, Whately to Senior, 17 Jan. 1835.

93 NLW: NSP, C/548, Whately to Senior, 6 Dec. 1835.

94 Whately to Senior, [Jan. 1836], [Feb. 1836], *ibid.*, C/552, C/558.

charge was supported by the 'strong suspicion' within the board that Revans had leaked portions of the unpublished evidence, 'selected for a purpose', to Poulett Scrope.[95] There is circumstantial evidence to support this allegation; Revans certainly colluded with Scrope in October 1835 in lobbying Morpeth to extend the inquiry's remit to the collection of evidence on agrarian crimes – an addition that Scrope was convinced would highlight the need for a full relief measure.[96] Whately's warnings came too late; Russell and his ministerial circle had already absorbed Revans' alternative opinions on the forthcoming report and had decided to reward him by promoting his appointment to a permanent assistant commissionership under the English Poor Law Commission.[97]

If the relations between Whately and the commission's secretary had completely broken down in the crucial period of report-drafting, those with his fellow commissioners were more mixed. Whatever indolence the archbishop may have demonstrated in the earlier, information-gathering, stages of the inquiry was now dispelled, and he demonstrated a determination to stamp his own vision on the final document. It was now the inattentive attitude of his fellows he found galling:

> We have been much impeded by [Blake's] attack of illness; and more by several of the Commissioners who had been absent for many weeks during our most interesting debates, and then drop in one by one, just at last, each requiring the whole discussion to be gone thro' over again. It is a tedious dinner where several guests drop in just as the dessert is coming in, and require soup, fish and all to be replaced.[98]

When the other commissioners did attend in numbers, other stresses revealed themselves. Whately expressed strong dislike of Bicheno's rhetorical style; he was, the archbishop punned, 'a perfect Erymanthian' (a bore), whose constant appeals to humane feelings and ancestral wisdom had 'neither head nor tail'.[99] This may reflect, as Hilton suggests, less a difference over policy than a discursive tension within Christian political economy between 'pessimistic' evangelicals such as Bicheno, and more 'optimistic' neo-Paleyans such as

95 Whately to Senior, 26 Dec. 1835, *ibid.*, C/550.

96 Poulett Scrope to Morpeth, Oct. 1835, and Morpeth's memo on this letter, in R. Barry O'Brien (ed.), *Thomas Drummond, Under-secretary in Ireland 1835–40* (London, 1889), pp. 205–7. Despite Morpeth's approval the commission does not appear to have undertaken such an investigation.

97 NA: PLCP, MH19/63, Russell to T. F. Lewis, 19 Nov. 1835. Revans was gazetted on 4 February 1836, at a salary of £700, *Return of Commissions issued*, p. 11.

98 NLW: NSP, C/558, Whately to Senior, [Feb. 1836].

99 Whately to Senior, 6 Dec. 1835, *ibid.*, C/548.

Whately.[100] Despite Whately's suspicions that he had been introduced to the commission as a spoiler, Bicheno did not dissent from the fundamentals of Whately's stance on poor-law provision in Ireland, and he assisted Blake in the preparation of the final report. He did insist, nonetheless, on the inclusion of an appendix to the report setting out his personal grounds for agreeing to its conclusions, and which adopted a distinctly sceptical tone towards the role of active state intervention in mitigating Irish distress through works of agricultural improvement better undertaken by the proprietors themselves.[101]

Corrie and Wrightson appear to have been more reliable allies for the chairman, and it was the authoritative voice of Wrightson in particular which carried the crucial debate in the commission in December 1835. Whately noted approvingly that, after a long struggle, relief to the able-bodied and the workhouse system had been negatived.[102] This rejection of a poor law for the able-bodied destitute would form the basis of the final report presented in 1836.

Resistance to this within the commission proper came from three members, Vignoles, Killeen and Naper. The three appear to have agreed only that reliance on voluntary charity was inadequate, rather than on any definite alternative plan. Their minute of 'dissent' explicitly rejected the voluntary principle as an efficient and equitable mode of relieving 'able-bodied' destitution, citing religious antagonisms and the lamentable condition of the existing mendicity institutions in support of their position. As a consequence of this disagreement, the section setting out an elaborate scheme of voluntary associations on the 'Scottish' model, on which Whately had placed much weight, had to be relegated to appendix H of the report, and was signed by only eight of the eleven commissioners. The 'dissent' by Vignoles, Killeen and Naper was also included, but at least thereby excluded from the main report.[103]

This disaccord was potentially highly embarrassing to Whately, especially in the context of his falling out with Revans and his deteriorating relations with the ministry. In an effort to achieve unanimity on the main report he proceeded to accept various amendments from the dissentient members in

100 Hilton, *Age of Atonement*, pp. 79–80.

101 *PIC: Appendix H, Part ii. Remarks by J. E. Bicheno*, PP 1836 [42], xxxiv.657.

102 NLW: NSP, C/548, Whately to Senior, 6 Dec. 1835. For Corrie's unreserved endorsement of the final report, see [John Corrie], *Remarks on a Bill for the more effectual Relief of the Destitute Poor in Ireland* (2nd edn, London, 1837).

103 *PIC: Appendix H, Part i: Containing Reasons for recommending Voluntary Associations for the Relief of the Poor and Reasons for Dissenting from the Principle of raising Funds for the Relief of the Poor by the Voluntary System, as recommended in the Report*, PP 1836 [41], xxxiv.643.

return for the exclusion of the 'dissent' from the report proper – and it was this necessity which both prolonged the final drafting and led to the inclusion in the final report of a series of additional schemes to provide employment for the able-bodied poor as a means of heading off compulsory relief. Naper was insistent that the solution to Irish poverty lay in mass public and private employment of the agricultural population, a position he subsequently underlined through the publication of a pamphlet protesting against the government's bill.[104] If the price of obtaining Naper's and Killeen's signatures was the inclusion of such schemes in the final report, Whately was prepared to pay it, although this did not mean that he felt any obligation towards the implementation of these added elements. Indeed Senior clearly believed that the 'concessions [made] to inferior members of the board', including the imposition of a tax on mortgages, could safely be buried at the legislative stage.[105]

Whately's strategy was largely successful; Killeen and Naper subsequently defended the report *in toto*, and only one commissioner – Vignoles – refused to sign the third report.[106] Whately's explanation for this, which he passed to Lansdowne for dissemination, was disingenuous. Vignoles' private reason for dissenting was, the archbishop alleged, an objection to the inclusion of the statement that the penal laws had played a part in reducing the Irish peasantry to their debased condition; public endorsement of this would mean Vignoles breaking 'the wand of peace with the Orangemen', a step he dared not take.[107] Vignoles himself subsequently refuted this imputed sectarian motive in letters to Russell and the Irish press, but the immediate damage to his reputation had been done. In the end his individual recalcitrance had no impact on the reception of the report.[108] He was, however, ultimately to relish the later 'censure' of his fellow commissioners at the hand of George Nicholls.[109]

104 J. L. W. Naper, *An Address to the Landlords and Landholders of the County of Meath . . . on the New Poor Law Bill* (2nd edn, Dublin, 1837).

105 NLW: NSP, C/568, Senior to Whately, [May 1836]. For Killeen's doubts about voluntarist aspects of the report but enthusiasm for the measures to employ the labouring poor, see NA: RP, PRO30/22/2A, fols 207–9, Killeen to Russell, 5 Feb. 1836.

106 *Hansard*, 3, xxxviii, 1448 [13 June 1837].

107 BL: BP, B/130, Whately to Lansdowne, 14 Feb. 1836.

108 Vignoles to Russell, 28 Mar. 1836, Vignoles to *Morning Register*, 9 June 1836, in A. H. Lynch, *An Address to the Electors of Galway on the Poor-Law Bill for Ireland* (London, 1838).

109 MC: NP, M/576, Morpeth to Mulgrave, 11 Dec. 1837.

The Whately report, 1836

The third report was formally presented to parliament in early June 1836, but had already been widely leaked in the press from early April.[110] It set out what its authors understood to be the root causes of Irish poverty along with the most appropriate and legitimate modes of alleviating it. The underlying problem, they concluded, was the backwardness and inefficiency of the Irish agricultural economy, and the absence of adequate forms of alternative employment. The rural population was excessive for the amount of employment available, leading to an underdeveloped division of labour and low and erratic wages. Ireland was compared unfavourably with Great Britain: there were five agricultural labourers in Ireland for every two on the same quantity of land in Britain, whose agricultural output was more than four times greater. It followed that some institutions applicable on one side of the Irish Sea would simply not be suitable on the other, so long as they threatened to impede the necessary 'levelling up' of Ireland and the anglicization of its social and economic structures.

The report posited that Ireland's economic backwardness and adverse population to employment ratio explained the overt manifestations of its poverty – the extent of its mendicancy, the wretched quality of its housing, its dietary dependence on potatoes. The scale of the 'problem of poverty' in Ireland was constantly emphasized. Notoriously, the number of labouring men whom the commissioners estimated as 'out of work and in distress during thirty weeks of the year' was given as 585,000, which, when 1.8 million family dependents were added, gave a total number of persons in need of annual relief of 2,385,000 (more than 30 per cent of the 1831 population of 7.7 million). This statement of numbers was crucial – it provided the basis for the commissioners' rejection for Ireland of a poor law on the English model; however, the calculation proved highly controversial subsequently. Even the sympathetic Spring Rice was later to lament that the 'studiedly exaggerated' numbers of destitute recorded by the commission had embarrassed its case.[111]

It followed from the numerical analysis that only certain categories of the 'poor' could safely be granted an entitlement to relief based on a compulsory property assessment. First were the 'impotent poor', already partially relieved by voluntary or specialized institutions – comprising 'incurable as well as curable lunatics, . . . idiots, epileptic persons, cripples, deaf and dumb and blind poor'. These should in future be relieved in hospitals, infirmaries or convalescent establishments, or externally through distribution of food and

110 *PIC: Third Report*, PP 1836 [43], xxx.1; *Observer*, 3 Apr. 1836.
111 NLI: MP, Ms 545, pp. 18–19, Spring Rice to Ensor, 15 Jan. 1837.

medicines. The 'sick poor' could also safely be relieved through continuing state support of (the existing network of) hospitals and dispensaries. A mixture of national and local rates overseen by both the English Poor Law Commissioners and elected local boards of guardians would finance this provision on a sounder basis than the existing grand jury grants in aid.

A larger category of the poor comprised 'the aged and infirm, orphans, helpless widows with young children, and destitute persons in general'. On this head a difference of opinion among the commissioners was recorded, although the majority opinion was firmly endorsed: relief for these classes should be offered by a plan of voluntary associations, relying on charitable donations aided where necessary by rates raised by a public levy on the land. The Poor Law Commission was to regulate the network of alms houses and mendicity institutions created by voluntary initiatives, and make grants in aid out of the rates, but was not to take responsibility for the direct provision of relief by these institutions. This option the commissioners approvingly cited as being modelled on the 'Scottish system' of poor relief principally through voluntary agency. They envisaged that any public aid necessary to support the system in the first instance would gradually be reduced as the improved system of voluntarism in Ireland took hold and the relief system came progressively more into line with the Scots ideal (or rather the impression of it derived from Thomas Chalmers). The view of the majority was that

> although the system of providing for the poor by means of voluntary associations, aided by the public purse, and constructed upon well-digested principles, may not succeed at once in every part of the country – yet that, so far as it does succeed, it will tend to bring the population into a sound state with respect to the poor, and will we trust gradually work its way over the face of the island, and probably supersede in many places, as the Scottish system does so extensively, the necessity of a compulsory rate . . . [for] although a compulsory rate might be rendered general more rapidly, and be administered by artificial means, it would every day become more difficult to manage, and tend to bring the country into a worse state than our inquiry has found it.[112]

The final statement indicated that any rate-aid to the voluntary bodies would be marginal at best.

The last category of poor were the 'able-bodied' – those capable of supporting themselves and their dependents through work, but unable to find sufficient regular employment to avoid destitution. These were to receive no direct state assistance from the rates. However, the more general problem of poverty in the labouring population was to be tackled by a number of initiatives separate from a poor law. Foremost amongst these was a plan of

112 Nicholls, *Irish Poor Law*, p. 150.

state-assisted emigration, with half the costs coming from the Treasury and the other half divided between a national rate for Ireland and individual landlord contributions (either voluntary or imposed by the commission on 'clearing' landlords – the details were left vague). A network of emigration depots would be established to give temporary shelter to those willing to leave under the scheme, the costs of emigration granted to all selected as fit for the journey, while the Colonial Office would supply them the 'means of settling themselves in an approved British colony'. Alongside this 'voluntary' emigration, two other categories of poor would be exported. Vagrants would be detained and subsequently 'removed as free labourers to such colony, not penal, as shall be appointed for them by the Colonial Department', with their subsequent wages being docked to reclaim of the costs of their passage. Foundling and orphan children would also be sent to the colonies at public expense. The commission was anxious that all of these schemes should be disassociated from the taint of penal transportation, the latter being a particular bugbear of Archbishop Whately; for the latter groups it would be, nevertheless, compulsory.

While the key sections of the report were thus inflected by a Malthusian perspective that the adverse population–employment ratio rendered an extensive poor law unaffordable and required a thinning of the 'surplus population' through emigration, this was paradoxically balanced by recommendations for the promotion of reproductive employment within Ireland by state assistance and facilitation. A labour-rate was ruled out, but the state was to facilitate and stimulate private employment in agriculture through various initiatives. A central 'Board of Improvement' was to be established for this purpose, with powers to survey the Irish waste-lands and improve them by arterial drainage and road-building (in return for a portion of each waste being appropriated from its owner for public use), as well as to enforce the proper fencing and drainage of private lands (in return for generous improvement loans being made available to private landowners), and to establish agricultural schools in each district. The board would also co-ordinate the provision of other public works, while responsibility for local works presentments would be transferred from county grand juries to more efficient local fiscal boards.

In addition to these main heads the report also contained a series of rather disjointed additional recommendations, including measures to promote temperance, to tax mortgage interest on landed property, and to purchase the tithe composition of Ireland for vesting in the Poor Law Commissioners to offset the rates. Despite the alarming calculations as to the scale of poverty in the country, the report ended surprisingly optimistically. On the whole, the commissioners felt, there was a rising spirit of improvement in Ireland, which legislation should encourage and not stifle. Wealth would trickle down as economic activity increased, so long as excessive welfare transfers did not impede growth.[113]

The multifarious character of the commission's recommendations was to a considerable extent the result of horse-trading between its members in the lead-up to completion. Its character as a 'compromise' document, attempting to 'reconcile as much, and repel as little, of [the commissioners'] diverging views as possible', was identified by its critics.[114] Further evidence for the belated addition (or augmentation) of the statist developmental elements can be traced by comparing the 'summary recommendations' (undated, but certainly delivered to Russell before the completion of the report) with the published version. The memo in the Russell Papers is much more abrupt in distinguishing the classes of poor who were and who were not to receive rate-based relief, and in constraining the aid which might be given to voluntary charitable bodies to a 'fixed sum . . . never to exceed a certain proportion of the voluntary contributions'. It explicitly rejected public works as a mode of relieving the destitute, and insisted that 'location upon waste lands in Ireland cannot be effectually undertaken by the government as a means of relief'; instead the state might provide 'facilities and encouragement . . . for bringing such lands into the market and enabling enterprising individuals and associations to invest capital beneficially therein'. While agricultural education and assisted emigration (albeit partly funded from landlord contributions and repayable loans to labourers) featured prominently, this earlier version contained no reference at all to a 'Board of Improvement', and limited the improving activities of the commissioners to the facilitation of sales and divisions of encumbered estates, foreshadowing the measure to introduce 'free trade in land' to Ireland would that eventually become law in 1849.[115]

The subsequent inclusion of the more statist developmental recommendations associated with the 'Board of Improvement', along with the employment of more ambivalent language in several places, tended to render the published report more popular (with both many contemporaries and subsequent historians) than might have been expected had it been confined to the summary recommendations on poor relief, emigration and land transfer. It should also be noted that a number of the recommendations for public works, including those for the promotion of waste-land reclamation under the Board of Works, had already been proposed the previous year by the Select Committee on Irish Public Works chaired by the Galway MP A. H. Lynch, and

113 *PIC: Third Report*, PP 1836 [43], xxx.1.

114 *Hansard*, 3, xlii, 688 [30 Apr. 1838: Morpeth].

115 NA: RP, PRO30/22/2D, fols 372–8, 'Irish Poor Law Commissioners: Summary Recommendations' [1836].

had been well received in Ireland.[116] On the other hand, some hostile commentators, including one former assistant commissioner, regarded the myriad of proposals in the third report as a deliberate smoke-screen: 'their real object', he alleged, 'was to deter Parliament from entertaining any project of relief, by the abortiveness of some of their expedients, and the inapplicability of others.'[117] While some other (mostly Irish) assistant commissioners were more enthusiastic about the auxiliary measures, this internal dispute within the wider commission, once exposed to public view, raised embarrassing questions.[118]

It did not follow that the 'core' group of commissioners (including Whately, Corrie, Wrightson and Blake), or their political allies, were equally committed to the implementation of all the elements of their final report. Indeed Wrightson later anonymously declared that the conflation of employment with poor relief had been a mistake, and noted that even the promotion of emigration, though necessary, had been pushed beyond its proper limits in the final report.[119] Senior was also subsequently to cast doubt on whether the emigration proposals were at all practicable or whether a centralized system of land improvement could have lasted more than a year.[120] Lansdowne himself was dismissive of the details of the 'Irish poor law budget', but approved of it generally as an elaborate smoke-screen: 'It in some degree makes up for what it recommends, by what it omits and I suppose the quantity of nostrums is intended to reconcile to abstinence from the most mischievous part of the quackery.'[121]

116 *First and Second Reports of the Select Committee appointed to inquire into the Amount of Advances made by the Commissioners of Public Works in Ireland*, PP 1835 (573), xx. 169. The committee promoted reclamation as an alternative to internal or external migration for the labouring poor of the west.

117 Anon., *Remarks on the Application of the Workhouse System with Other Modes of Relief to the Irish Poor* (London, 1837), p. 6.

118 More favourable responses from assistant commissioners include James O'Flynn, *Extracts from a Pamphlet on the Present State of the Irish Poor* (London, 1836), W. T. McCullagh, *Letter to the Representative Peers of Ireland, on the Ministerial Measure of Irish Poor Laws* (Dublin, 1838). One assistant commissioner rejected the emigration proposals and their Malthusian rationale, but opted for wasteland reclamation schemes over a workhouse-based poor law: Binns, *Miseries and Beauties*.

119 [W. B. Wrightson], 'The workhouse system: the Irish poor law', *ER*, 66 (Oct. 1837), pp. 186–208.

120 [Nassau W. Senior], 'Proposals for extending the Irish Poor Law', *ER*, 84 (Oct. 1846), pp. 283–4.

121 BL: BP, B/96, Lansdowne to Spring Rice, 27 Dec. [1835]. This suggests that the draft report dated from December 1835 at the latest.

An incomplete printed draft bill 'for the relief of the poor of Ireland', lodged in the Russell Papers, but clearly authored by one of the Whately commissioners (possibly Blake), in an effort to see their proposals turned into legislation, provides further support for this reading of priorities. The full text is not extant, but the preface to this bill makes no reference to any public works or 'Board of Improvement' which might accompany the introduction of legal provision for 'the sick and infirm poor' of Ireland; instead it highlights the urgent need for thinning the rural population if the state of the poor in general was to be alleviated:

> [T]here is a redundant number of agricultural labourers there, whereby the whole class is injuriously depressed, and that many poor persons do in consequence thereof suffer severe distress: and . . . there is a want of agricultural labourers in several of his majesty's possessions abroad, and it is therefore expedient to facilitate the emigration of such poor inhabitants of Ireland as being unable to support themselves and their families by industry [that] are desirous of emigrating to some of his majesty's said possessions abroad[.][122]

Even if not by Whately himself, this document unquestionably embodied his own order of priorities.

Richard Whately: theology, political economy and Irish poverty

Whately's own position can be identified by locating his personal commentary on the drafting of the report within the context of his wider views on political economy, poverty and the state. As a member of the 'Noetic' group of Christian political economists that emerged in Oxford in the 1820s, Whately was concerned with reconciling universal truths of classical political economics with the moral teaching of Christianity, arguing that the two were complementary and must be united in the service of good governance. Despite occupying the Drummond chair of political economy at Oxford 1829–31, he was not principally a theoretical economist, but rather a tireless propagandist for the new science. On becoming archbishop of Dublin in 1831 he self-consciously carried this 'mission' of economic education to Ireland, simplifying his Oxford lectures on political economy for inclusion in the texts used throughout the new national education system, establishing the Whately chair of political economy at Trinity College in 1832, and later

122 NA: RP, PRO30/22/2E, fols 89–120, Memo: 'A bill for the relief of the poor of Ireland'.

inspiring the Barrington lectures on economics and the Dublin Statistical Society.[123]

Like most Protestant Christian political economists, he was grounded in Malthus, although Whately was generally more 'optimistic' in outlook – rejecting for example the 'Malthusian' idea of the invariability of diminishing returns to the application of labour and capital to land – and leaned towards a more beneficent providentialism in his understanding of the divine purpose behind the 'natural laws' governing the economic world. Yet he continued to hold to an underlying Malthusian concern about excess population growth, and to develop the emphasis of Malthus' later writings (especially as refracted through Thomas Chalmers) on the importance of moral action in both the public and private spheres in fending off the catastrophes inherent in over-population.[124] Whately's adherence to and proclamation of these ideas in the face of widespread unpopularity have prompted one commentator to describe him as 'Ireland's only Malthusian martyr'.[125]

Whately was convinced of the universal scientific truths revealed by orthodox economic methods and that these needed to be internalized by the Irish. The field of poor-relief policy, which required the combination of these economic truths with the ethical guidance available only from revealed religion, was thus one he found particularly attractive. Economic truths were, in his opinion, deductive rather than inductive; correct theory must proceed from reflection rather than the acquisition of facts.[126] Given these preconceptions, it would be surprising if Whately did not approach the Irish Poor Inquiry Commission with a predetermined theoretical schema in mind, one which relegated the role of the 'facts' revealed by the commission to that of shaping the application of predetermined principles.

123 For his educational 'mission' to diffuse orthodox economics in Ireland, see Thomas A. Boylan and Timothy P. Foley, *Political Economy and Colonial Ireland: The Propagation and Ideological Function of Economic Discourse in the Nineteenth Century* (London, 1992); J. M. Goldstrom, 'Richard Whately and political economy in school books, 1833–80', *Irish Historical Studies*, 15 (1966–67), pp. 131–46.

124 See A. M. C. Waterman, *Revolution, Economics and Religion: Christian Political Economy, 1798–1833* (Cambridge, 1991), pp. 204–14.

125 Norman Vance, 'Improving Ireland: Richard Whately, theology and political economy', in Stefan Collini *et al.* (eds), *Economy, Polity and Society: British Intellectual History 1750–1950* (Cambridge, 2000), p. 187. In his discussion of the contributions 'Noetics' such as Whately and Senior made to the debates on poor laws, Mandler argues that Hilton overstates the distinction between their thinking and that of evangelical economists such as Chalmers. The Irish case tends strongly to support his contention: see Mandler, 'Tories and paupers', p. 86.

126 Salim Rashid, 'Richard Whately and Christian political economy at Oxford and Dublin', *Journal of the History of Ideas*, 38 (1977), pp. 147–55.

Given Whately's intimate relationship with Nassau Senior, it is hardly surprising that he should have strongly endorsed the English Poor Law report of February 1834. Indeed, his privileged relationship with the most active member of that commission had, he informed a correspondent, resulted in his being 'repeatedly consulted' during the preparation of the English report.[127] His own experience of local administration of the poor laws, acquired as the incumbent of the parishes of Halesworth, Suffolk and Chediston, Norfolk in 1822–31, had convinced him that a radical reform of the English law was essential. In 1823 he had penned a broadside to the directors of the district's House of Industry, denouncing the Speenhamland system of allowances and gratuitous outdoor relief to the able-bodied, citing both the moral and economic hazards involved. He had subsequently pushed through parochial reforms in the face of stiff local opposition.[128] It was in these rural parishes that he also developed and advocated the principle of emigration to the colonies as the optimum solution to the poverty concomitant with a 'redundant population'.[129] His enthusiasm for the English recommendations was palpable, and he was convinced the proposed act would ultimately prove popular.[130] It follows that Whately's position on the Irish inquiry arose not from any rejection of the principles that underpinned the new English Poor Law Amendment of 1834, but from a conviction that the system thereby created, although essential for England, was not applicable to the sister kingdom. This conclusion was founded mainly on Malthusian premises.

Whately's preoccupations in constructing the Irish report can be traced in his lengthy and candid correspondence with Senior. The relationship continued to be one of collaborators, with Senior frequently proffering advice during the drafting of the commission's report, and supplying insider advice on the positions adopted by key political figures in London.[131] It is thus no accident that in essence the core recommendations of the report chimed with Senior's conclusions of 1831, that 'public money should be advanced to facilitate emigration, and for the formation of roads, canals, and harbours', and that every experiment for relief should be tried except a poor law.[132]

127 BL: BP, B/130, Whately to Lansdowne, 15 Mar. 1834.

128 [Richard Whately], *Letter to the Directors of the House of Industry at Bulcamp* (Halesworth, 1823).

129 He had already rejected Malthusian scepticism about the power of emigration to alleviate excessive population in England: [Richard Whately], 'Emigration to Canada', *QR*, 23 (July 1820), pp. 373–400; Akenson, *Protestant in Purgatory*, pp. 49–50.

130 BL: BP, B/130, Whately to Lansdowne, 15 Mar. 1834.

131 NLW: NSP, C/549, C/555, C/559, C/558, Senior to Whately, 21 Dec. 1835, 19 Jan., 9 Feb. 1836, Whately to Senior, [Feb. 1836].

132 Senior, *Letter to Howick*, p. 44.

Whately was concerned with seeing off the danger of a poor law for the able-bodied poor, especially when 'the persons most likely to take their tone from Government' began 'raving in favour of a provision by law for the able-bodied'; such a 'vicious measure' had to be resisted at all costs, not least because it might be carried for the sake of 'temporary popularity'.[133] A memo forming a first draft of his report, sent by Whately to Senior in late 1835 and then circulated to some cabinet members, set out his preoccupation with nailing down the costs of any provision for the poor. Workhouses were inadmissible in Ireland because the principle of less eligibility in diet could not be maintained within them, and poor-rates would be ratcheted up under political pressure 'till the country was drained, while the claimants for relief, instead of diminishing, were daily increasing'. Voluntary mendicity asylums were preferable and any state aid could be capped at a low level, leaving the bulk of funding to be raised by local charity. While prepared on humanitarian grounds to see almshouses provided with 'decent apartments for a more comfortable class of old people', the necessary resources must not come from taxation but from charity. Assisted emigration was highly desirable, but Whately hoped it could be done cheaply (on Wakefieldian lines), through the creation of a 'colonial chest' fund which would be recovered through appropriating the wages of assisted emigrants – a sort of revived indenture system with the state as creditor.[134] Home-colonization (the reclamation of waste-lands for re-settlement) might be desirable, but should be left to individual enterprise:

> assisted it may be, by government loans: but not at government-expense, nor again do I deny that a comfortable provision for the aged poor is desirable; but I dare not recommend it to come from any source but charity. An attempt to relieve our compassionate feelings at the public expense by compulsory rates, would lead I am convinced, to serious results: and to that determination I shall adhere, unless – which is hardly to be expected – I should hear of something quite distinct from what I have ever yet heard.[135]

Whately's insistence on the repayment of any advances made to emigrants was repeated in a memo summarizing his main recommendations sent to ministers before formal submission of the report. In this draft, cleared tenants were also to be assisted to emigrate, so long as their landlord gave them 'a

133 NLW: NSP, C/548, Whately to Senior, 6 Dec. 1835.

134 NLW: NSP, D/19, Whately memo [Dec. 1835].

135 *Ibid*. Whately hoped his scheme to buy up Irish tithes would provide the bulk of the funds for poor relief and education in Ireland, BL: BP, B/130, Whately memo on Irish Tithe, [1835].

certificate of good character' and made some monetary contribution.[136] There is little in either of these papers of the 'flexibility' and 'imagination' with which Whately has been credited by his admirers. There is no mention here, or elsewhere in this correspondence, of the statist developmental proposals that attracted so much attention in the final report, confirming that these were added as afterthoughts – part of the 'Penelope's-web-work' of final drafting necessary to bring the largest possible number of signatories on board.[137] At least one cabinet member upbraided Whately for completely omitting employment measures (along with any right to relief) from this first draft of the report, and this may also have had some influence in shaping the final version.[138]

Whately's initial emigration suggestions had been modest and grounded on the self-supporting theories of Edward Gibbon Wakefield and Robert Torrens. The more extensive and expensive emigration scheme found in the published report was probably the consequence of Senior's warning that, in the current political climate, it would be impossible to 'avoid giving a right to the alternative of either workhouse support, or emigration'.[139] For Whately the slippery slope of able-bodied relief had to be evaded at all costs – at least for the foreseeable future – and hence state-assisted emigration acquired a greater prominence in his repertory. The stimulus to emigrate must not, he warned, be impeded by other provisions: '[I]f you begin by offering emigration to the able bodied who cannot get work, you may afterwards descend to supplying work or aid at home; but to begin by offering them home-relief precludes you from offering what they would call sentence of transportation.' Despite this stronger stance, however, he remained persuaded that assisted emigration would not pose an excessive burden on Britain or Ireland, and both he and Senior remained in close contact with Torrens, who was continuing to press the feasibility of 'self-supported colonization'.[140]

Whately's principal concern was always the protection of the wages-fund, the primary source of capital for any sustainable development of the Irish economy, which he believed to be vulnerable to any 'ruinous experiment' of

136 NA: RP, PRO30/22/2D, fols 372–8, Memo: 'Poor Inquiry Commission, Summary Recommendations', n.d. [1836].

137 NLW: NSP, C/557, Whately to Senior, 26 Jan. 1836.

138 Howick to Senior, 5 Jan. 1836, in Levy, *Senior*, pp. 263–6.

139 NLW: NSP, C/559, Senior to Whately, 9 Feb. 1836.

140 Torrens to Senior, 3 May 1836, *ibid.*, Ms 23858/I/E, fols 228–9; DAD: BWP, DD/BW/F7/57, Whately to Wrightson, [1838]; Robert Torrens, *A Letter to the Right Honourable Lord John Russell on the Ministerial Measure for Establishing Poor Laws in Ireland* (2nd edn, London, 1838).

a grant of welfare entitlement to the able-bodied poor, which must increase incrementally if introduced, and squeeze out investment:

> Ireland is not sinking into a worse state as regards the distress of the poor; but the reverse. Why take this time to make an experiment, which I think must, but which all men of judgement and knowledge agree may, throw it back above two centuries? Let time be given at least to see what education can do when introduced; what can be done by taking away some of the power of agitators, by settling the Church question, and by paying the priests: let a good wholesome plan of emigration be set on foot . . . let facilities be given to land-improvements; let relief be given to all the blind, cripples, deaf and dumb, and incurable etc and then I don't say do nothing more, but – wait to see the effects of these which ought in all reason to be the first steps[.][141]

The order in which Whately listed the reforms he thought most beneficial to Ireland is important: education, as always with this most pedagogically-minded of men, took precedence, followed by the comprehensive tithe reform and concurrent endowment plans which he hoped would produce sectarian pacification; only then were assisted emigration and improvement loans included, before he concluded with the minimal state provision for poor relief. This ranking reflects Whately's dictum, made in his Oxford lectures on political economy, that the harmony produced under *laissez-faire* is evidence for the existence of Divine wisdom.[142] His proposals for intervention in emigration and land improvement might appear to contradict this, but less so when it is understood that what Whately believed Ireland needed was merely some state pump-priming to produce the virtuous circle of largely self-financed colonization and agricultural development, and then only to avoid the ruinous consequences of a more overt welfare intervention.

To the archbishop, the precepts of political economy were, naturally, in conformity with those of scripture. It followed that the recommendations and classifications of the third report could, in essence, be traced to the practice of Christ himself. Indeed, in several charity sermons preached in the Dublin diocese in 1835, Whately came close to claiming Christ as the first political economist:

> It is now generally acknowledged that relief afforded to want, as mere want, tends to increase that want; while the relief afforded to the sick, the infirm, and the disabled, has plainly no tendency to multiply its own objects. Now it is remarkable, that the Lord Jesus employed His miraculous power in healing the sick *continually*, but in feeding the hungry only twice; which the power of multiplying food, which He then manifested, as well as His directing the

141 BL: BP, B/130, Whately to Senior, 28 Sept. [1836].
142 Rashid, 'Richard Whately', p. 152.

> disciples to take care and gather up the fragments that remained that nothing might be lost, served to mark that the abstaining from any like procedure on other occasions was deliberate design. In this, besides other objects, our Lord had probably in view to afford us some instruction, from His example, as to the mode of our charity. Certain it is, that the reasons for this distinction are now, and ever must be, the same as at that time.[143]

If Christ had given regular indiscriminate relief to 'mere poverty' through food and clothing, he would have adversely affected the labour market of ancient Palestine and thereby worsened the condition of the poor. This moral lesson needed to be learned by his contemporaries.

The moral and providential connotations of Whately's vision are clear, and help explain his intense and emotive attachment to the main provisions of the 1836 report. The ministry's rejection of the menu of measures, and with them the underlying precepts of the report, was to drive the archbishop into fits of despairing fury over the following years. His marginalization led him to adopt the persona of a despised but ultimately vindicated prophet, warning against the consequences of short-sighted ignorance in social policy.[144]

143 Richard Whately, 'Sermon XIV: Christ's example', in *Sermons on Various Subjects* (London, 1835), pp. 362–92. Whately may have been inspired by Thomas Chalmers' similar commentary on this scriptural incident, in the evidence he gave to the Spring Rice committee, *Report of the Select Committee on the State of the Poor in Ireland*, PP 1830 (667), vii.1, p. 320. For his admiration of Chalmers as an economist, see Whately to Senior, 24 Oct. 1830, in Whately (ed.), *Life*, i, p. 84.

144 See, for example, Richard Whately, *Introductory Lectures on Political Economy* (3rd edn, London, 1847), pp. 279–80.

5

Russell, Nicholls and the making of the Irish poor law bill, 1835–37

The government's Irish poor law bill, hammered out in 1836–37, and presented to parliament in the foreshortened 1837 session, could not have been more different from the menu of policy recommendations presented in the third report of the Whately Commission. The latter had rejected state relief for the able-bodied and would have limited assistance to all but the most 'helpless' classes of the poor to grants in aid of voluntary charity. The government's bill, on the other hand, proposed to relieve all those in a state of 'destitution', constrained by a strict enforcement of a workhouse test and the granting of discretion to elected boards of guardians in determining the 'fit' objects for admission to the workhouse. Moreover, while the Whately recommendations on relief had been surrounded by a myriad of related proposals on assistance to emigration and agricultural employment, and local government and other reforms, the government's bill was stark in its apparent isolation and relative simplicity. This chapter investigates the reasons for this abrupt and highly controversial volte-face, considering the motivations of Lord John Russell and other Whig ministers, and the influence of the commentaries penned by George Nicholls, Nassau Senior, G. C. Lewis and John Revans. It also reviews the political contestations within the cabinet in 1835–37, and the place of the proposed poor-law measure within the wider public policy agenda for Ireland.

A number of explanations have been proposed for the government's rejection of the Whately report: unimaginative adherence to economic orthodoxy, a wish to avoid the costs involved, political cowardice in the face of a restive parliament, blind adherence to the new English poor-law system, and the zealous advocacy of the Benthamite ideologues Nicholls and Chadwick. While each is worth exploring, none of these is entirely convincing in isolation. Much of the critique assumes that the third report had the character of a coherent and uniform vision, rather than, as we have seen, emerging as an amalgam of 'core' and 'peripheral' recommendations held together by the necessity of producing unanimity (or near-unanimity) between the commissioners. It also conveniently ignores the close political and ideological relationships between certain key ministers in 1833–34 (including Melbourne, Althorp, Littleton, Lansdowne and Spring Rice) and the core group of 'working' commissioners, and the evidence for a substantially shared perspective on the problem of Irish poverty between these parties. After 1835 Whately continued to find allies in the government among the survivors of this 'moderate liberal' grouping, but this was insufficient to counteract other political forces pushing in a contrary direction. Whately's personal idiosyncrasies and lack of practical 'business-sense' occasionally put some strain on this relationship, but this was partially offset by the mediation of the more politically savvy Nassau Senior.[1]

George Nicholls and Irish poverty

It is widely assumed that George Nicholls' role in the making of the Irish poor law was both crucial and the product of his own Benthamite vision for the extension of the 'enlightened' forms of the new English poor law to the 'backward' social environment of Ireland. There is no doubting the importance of his contribution, or the basic convictions that informed it, but the precise place of both in the formation of the act would benefit from closer examination. The initial reluctance of Nicholls to propose the measures that would later be so strongly associated with his name raises serious questions about the interpretation of the act as simply a centralizing and uniformizing Benthamite exercise.

Rather like his future antagonist Richard Whately, Nicholls was initially drawn into the English poor law controversy through localized personal experience, in his case as the consequence of residence as a small landed proprietor in Nottinghamshire.[2] Nicholls' active reforms as overseer of the poor at Southwell, which centred on the introduction of a less-eligibility test for pauperism through use of the workhouse, were subsequently published and proved an important influence on the English poor-law inquiry commission of 1832–34.[3] Nicholls' later narrative of the reforms stressed both his success

1 Frustration with Whately's impracticalities led Melbourne to complain that '[i]t is impossible to be with the Archbishop of Dublin for ten minutes upon affairs without perceiving not only that he can do no business, but that no business can be done where he is', SUL: BP, MEL/RU/403, Melbourne to Russell, 19 Sept. 1837.

2 Nicholls had bought the property with the proceeds of his voyages as an East Indian ship captain; his nautical background would later be used by O'Connell to mock him: *Hansard*, 3, xxxviii, 705 [8 May 1837].

3 [George Nicholls], *Eight Letters on the Management of the Poor* (Newark, 1822); H. G. Willink, 'Life of Sir George Nicholls', in George Nicholls, *A History of the English Poor Law* (new edn, 2 vols, 1898), i, pp. xi–xv, xxxii–xxxv.

(at least in his own eyes) in persuading the poor themselves of the beneficial effects of the retrenching reforms, and in improving in the moral condition of the community. The latter outcome, he admitted, had not been initially envisaged in what had started as an economy drive, but had come on reflection to represent the most important consequence. The workhouse test, he now realized, offered the means of providential escape from the Malthusian trap through its impact on the moral faculties of the working classes:

> The workhouse thus acted instead of – in a mitigated shape, it is true, but still in accordance with – that law of *necessity* wisely imposed by Providence upon mankind, and a neglect of which is ever followed by punishment in some shape – among an uncivilised people by entailing misery, disease, destitution and death; under our civilised and more perfect institutions, by the improvident or the idle being cast upon the parish, and forced to shelter into a workhouse, where, although screened from the extreme penalties of his neglect, the pauper is yet subjected to so many disagreeable circumstances that the desire to escape from these constantly urges him on to renewed exertion, and to an observance of those virtues a neglect of which had entailed upon him privations so hard to be borne.[4]

This was not so dissimilar from the opinions on the reform of the English law entertained by Whately and other 'Noetics'. Nicholls' achievements and well-publicized views impressed Senior, and led to his nomination by the latter as one of the triumvirate of English Poor Law Commissioners in 1834.[5]

It was in the latter capacity that Nicholls first observed the workings of the Irish Poor Inquiry Commission. Although the English commission was not formally involved in the Irish exercise, Senior operated as a conduit of ideas and information between the two bodies, and in December 1835 he ascertained that the English commissioners would also be prepared to act as the superintending body for Ireland, which both he and Whately thought highly desirable, despite their preference for a very different mode of relief there.[6]

Nicholls' first Irish initiative came in the wake of the publication of the volumes of evidence accompanying the first report of the Irish inquiry; he submitted a memo on the subject to the government, probably via Senior, in January 1836. In the absence of any official recommendations made by the commission thus far, he felt it his duty to offer some suitable remedies for consideration. His objective position at Somerset House, he argued, allowed

4 Willink, 'Nicholls', pp. xiii–xiv.

5 The others were Thomas Frankland Lewis and John Shaw Lefevre, a protégé of Althorp. Nicholls worked well with the latter but found the former frustratingly inactive: *ibid.*, pp. xl–xli.

6 NLW: NSP, C/549, Senior to Whately, 21 Dec. 1835.

him to make useful comparative observations between the pauperism of the two islands, and to suggest recommendations in a manner more specific and focused than the much larger scope of the Irish commission permitted.[7]

What is striking about this document, given Nicholls' well-known later stance, is just how similar it was to the essentials of the Whately–Senior position on Irish poor relief. In the memo Nicholls explicitly ruled out relief for the able-bodied and cast doubt on the suitability and applicability of the workhouse test in Ireland, while advocating indoor relief of the 'impotent poor' funded by public rates (although he went considerably further than Whately and Senior in including the elderly, widows with young children, and orphaned children in this category). This limited concession of relief would, he believed, have a beneficial effect on the vast mass of the labouring population who 'stood on the very brink of destitution and but just raised above its level', as it would offer the best means of lifting the burden of relieving the 'impotent poor' from their shoulders and redistribute it equitably through the whole community, while also connecting the property and poverty of the country through the taxation nexus. Granting any more formal right of relief to the able-bodied would, he argued at this time, be unsafe and contravene the principle introduced in England in 1834 (if not yet fully implemented), that it was best 'to leave the able bodied to their own resources and efforts in the great mart of capital and labour'. At the same time, mendicancy and vagrancy should be suppressed by law in Ireland as in England.

Nicholls leant more towards Benthamism in his belief that the basic tenets of poor relief were rooted in universally-applicable principles: 'Mankind is always essentially the same, in every clime and under every variety of circumstances, and we shall rarely be wrong if we take a sound general principle for our guide, provided only, that we modify its application by the sure test of experience, and due attention to local peculiarities.' However, the sheer scale of Irish poverty rendered necessary, in his view, some deviation from the English model. The excess ratio of population to available capital rendered the assisted emigration of the 'surplus' population necessary, and should be supported by a combination of local rates and national loans; public works would be an undesirable substitute for the additional employment created by the anticipated influx of British capital. The diffusion of education and the greater availability of wage-labour employment would, he concluded, combine to eliminate the moral deviations which had promoted early marriage and its concomitant of unsustainable population growth.[8]

7 Nicholls memo, 'Suggestions for the relief of the poorer classes in Ireland', 21 Jan. 1836, *ibid.*, D/20.

8 *Ibid.*

Nicholls' intervention received a rather mixed response, paradoxically inverting the reactions that would meet his much better-known official reports of 1836–37. Nassau Senior recommended it to Whately as a paper deserving of much consideration.[9] On the other hand, George Cornewall Lewis, who had already made his support for an able-bodied poor law explicit, denounced Nicholls fiercely. To Lewis the memo was 'a weak worthless paper . . . recommending a meagre measure of relief for the Irish poor', which he feared might be seized on by a timid government to avoid a substantial measure.[10] Only later would Lewis revise his opinion of Nicholls in the wake of extensive discussions between the two men and Nicholls' defection to a position more amenable to the convictions of both Lewis and the home secretary. Nicholls' first commentary casts into serious doubt the widespread assumption, still extant in the scholarly literature, that he was the sole initiator of the 1837 poor law bill, and that the ministers merely followed his determined lead.[11]

The Senior and Lewis commentaries on the Whately report

Lord John Russell was evidently unhappy with both Whately's report and the conclusions of Nicholls' memo. In the immediate aftermath of the submission of the third report in March 1836 he sought expert advice on its recommendations from two individuals intimately connected with it. The first commentary, from Senior, was rapidly penned and presented to the cabinet in mid-April 1836.[12] Senior was strictly briefed to prepare a report setting out the problems of implementing the proposals of the third report – a fact that led to some strain in the relationship with his old friend Richard Whately. He defended himself to the latter by stating that he had been obliged to write more rapidly than he had wished and that he had needed to adopt the veneer of total impartiality in commenting on the individual recommendations. It was unstated but mutually understood that Senior's professional advancement was dependent on government patronage and that any refusal on his part to report along the lines dictated by the Home Office would have been impossible.[13] If, as one scholar has argued, it was about this time that Senior

9 NLW: NSP, C/559, Senior to Whately, 9 Feb. 1836.

10 NLW: HCP, C/2790, Lewis to Villiers, 25 Aug. 1836; see also Villiers to Lewis, 4 Sept. 1836, *ibid.*, C/2579.

11 See, for example, O'Brien, 'Establishment of poor-law unions', p. 103.

12 *Confidential Letter from Nassau W. Senior . . . on the Third Report from the Commissioners for inquiring into the Condition of the Poor in Ireland*, PP 1837, [90], li.241.

13 Senior was then lobbying for a lucrative mastership in chancery, a position he secured in May 1836: Levy, *Senior*, p. 101.

was losing confidence in the efficacy of a Hortonian assisted-emigration scheme to address the problem of poverty in both islands, this may also have had a detrimental impact on the enthusiasm with which he was prepared to support the positive as opposed to the negative elements of the report.[14]

However, apart from his rejection of the proposal to purchase tithes to offset poor-rates, which he declared to be politically unfeasible, Senior endorsed the core recommendations of the report while raising questions about the details of implementation and dismissing what he regarded as the 'minor' recommendations. He submitted a copy of his 1831 pamphlet (which had included support for assisted emigration) along with the official letter to remind ministers of the consistency of his own opinions. In Senior's own mind he was simply strengthening the core of the third report by stripping away the extraneous and impractical accretions. At the same time he assured Whately that the government would stick to the report's foundations in preparing legislation.[15] While this turned out to be erroneous, it should serve as a reminder that the fate of the Whately report was (at least in the eyes of this Whitehall insider) by no means predetermined in 1836. Any differences in tone or detail with Whately were rapidly patched up in the face of an agreed threat to these 'core' elements in the following months, with the archbishop accepting that the terms of the commentary had been imposed upon Senior and that it by no means represented his 'final decision' on the subject.[16] Nevertheless, Senior was embarrassed by the official publication of his letter in June of the following year without any contextualizing correspondence, and may have leaked his unhappiness concerning Russell's use of his name to the government's critics.[17]

Despite the somewhat ambivalent tone of his commentary, Senior's fundamental stance on the 'problem of Ireland' and the remedial measures it required had not altered since 1831. These were vigorously restated in private letters to Howick in 1836–37. His opposition to a poor law for Ireland was founded on two pillars: a conviction that it must enhance rather than alleviate the 'redundancy of population' there, and a certainty that the infringement of *laissez-faire* involved would prove disastrous. Any suggestion of a right to relief

> would increase the insecurity of *persons*, by rendering the Government the great insurer responsible for all the results of private misconduct and improvidence,

14 R. N. Ghosh, 'The colonization controversy: R. J. Wilmot-Horton and the classical economists', *Economica*, n.s. 31 (1964), pp. 396–8.

15 NLW: HCP, C/568, Senior to Whately, n.d. [May 1836].

16 NA: RP, PRO30/22/2F, fols 276–7, Whately to Russell, n.d. [1837].

17 *The Times* (20, 22 June 1837) accused the government of attempting to fool parliament into thinking Senior supported the government bill.

> and by giving to the poor a sort of joint property with the richer orders, and therefore a constant subject of dissatisfaction, if they thought themselves defrauded of their right share.

Real social security could only be attained by rendering the Catholic clergy the agents of social control in the countryside through state provision for their livelihoods.[18]

The other official commentary on the third report, submitted by the former assistant commissioner George Cornewall Lewis on 22 July 1836, suffered from no such ambivalence.[19] It was almost certainly commissioned by the Home Office precisely because Lewis's antipathy towards the report's conclusions was already well known. Lewis launched a full-frontal attack on the fundamentals of the Whately–Senior position, questioning both the justice and practicality of the exclusion of the able-bodied destitute from state relief. The schema of classification upon which the commissioners based their plan was, Lewis declared, radically unsound. Any attempt to define entitlement by category of recipient, rather than by the absolute need of the individual, and which excluded the able-bodied indigent as such, would prove an inducement to fraud and engineer its own collapse. The moral evils likely to follow – importunate feigning of sickness, the desertion of children and the elderly, the break-up of family ties – would not be the fault of the desperate poor, but of the mechanism that obliged them to resort to such dodges for survival. English experience, he insisted, had demonstrated that the only legitimate and effective test was that imposed upon the individual applicant of making relief conditional on entry into the workhouse.

The Whately report's objections to workhouses for Ireland were summarily dismissed by Lewis, who argued that Irish circumstances rendered that institution more rather than less necessary there. Despite claims that Irish ethnic difference rendered workhouses unsuitable, his experience indicated that they would also be 'safe'. The principle of less eligibility rested not on diet (which indeed could not be safely lowered beyond what Irish cottiers were accustomed to), but on restraint, in the form of the compulsory labour, discipline and internal classification (the separation by sex and age), inseparable from the new English workhouse model. The tractability of Irish paupers at the Liverpool workhouse demonstrated that in cases of sufficient need, internal discipline was also not likely to pose a serious problem. Lewis was able to provide evidence from English assistant commissioners to assert the success of the introduction of the workhouse system there, and was unable to discern

18 Senior to Howick, 8 Jan. 1836, 30 May 1837, in Levy, *Senior*, pp. 266–73.

19 *Remarks on the Third Report of the Irish Poor Inquiry Commissioners . . . By George Cornewall Lewis*, PP 1837 [91], li.253.

sufficient grounds for its inapplicability to Ireland. Given the desirability of integrative legislation and institutions within the United Kingdom, the English model should be adhered to as far as possible, with the English commission overseeing its implementation in Ireland.

Significantly, Lewis did not dispute Whately's conclusion that Ireland was overpopulated and that the 'redundant' labouring population required some thinning. He differed in declaring that emigration and workhouse-relief for the able-bodied were not (as the third report had implied) incompatible, but rather complementary – as the English report had also found. He savaged the particularities of the Irish report's emigration scheme, finding the proposed emigration depots likely to encourage fraud, and the penal aspects of the transportation of vagrants and orphans both unjust and unworkable. Some system of structured colonization was desirable, but certainly not the one Whately had placed on the table.

With a proper scheme of assisted emigration and the disincentive to the abuse of relief created by the workhouse test, Lewis concluded that an Irish poor law would not be overwhelmed by what he regarded as the exaggerated numbers of paupers enumerated by the third report. However, he agreed that economic development was essential if the general condition of the poor labourer and his dependants was to be improved. Here again, Lewis inverted Whately's reasoning. He concluded that, rather than acting as a barrier to investment in agricultural improvement, an effective poor law would serve as a stimulus to the socio-economic 'transition' that Ireland must undergo. The cottier system of peasant agriculture must be swept away and replaced by an anglicized social structure of waged labour, substantial capitalist tenant farmers and improving landowners. Given that the main obstacle to this transition rested in the alienation between landlord and peasant – which gave rise to exploitation and indifference to suffering on one hand and to the retributive violence of Whiteboyism on the other – a mechanism was required to compel them to pursue their common interest. This *deus ex machina* would take the form of the poor law, loosening the peasant's desperate hold on the soil by granting him a security against starvation, while at the same time restoring to the landlord both the interest and the power to improve his estates and the people on them. This self-acting poor-law mechanism, rather than the complex and interfering improvement boards suggested by the third report – which Lewis thought most likely to promote self-interested jobbing and wasteful expense in Ireland – was best calculated to drag Ireland into modernity. This argument owed something to McCulloch's revised opinions on an Irish poor law of 1829–30, but the case was stated much more aggressively and pointedly by Lewis.[20] It also reflected something of the zeal

20 *Ibid.*, pp. 17–19, 27–31.

of the convert. Before arriving in Ireland, Lewis confessed, he had leaned towards a racialized interpretation of Irish social backwardness. Careful social observation, and comparing notes with Gustave de Beaumont, had converted him to an environmentalist position:

> [W]hen I came to look at things more nearly, and to see all the demoralizing influences to which they have been subjected, I asked myself whether a people of Germanic race would have turned out much better; and I really could not answer in the affirmative . . . *Caeteris paribus*, I would rather have a German than a Celt, a Protestant than a Catholic; but I have no doubt that a peasantry of Catholic Celts may be so governed and placed under such moral influences as to be peaceable, industrious and contented; and I have no doubt that a peasantry of Protestant Germans might, if properly oppressed and brutalized, be made as bad as the Irish.[21]

A poor law should form part of the ameliorative strategy vital to counterbalance the ethnographic backwardness of the Irish.

Lewis's stark and uncompromising attack on the Whately report paved the way for the subsequent Nicholls reports, privately as well as publicly. As a former assistant commissioner in Ireland (and son of the English commissioner T. F. Lewis), and author of a successful analysis of Irish rural violence, Lewis had some claims to attention. However, his official position was insecure: having been turned down for a permanent assistant commissionership in England in 1835, he did not receive a commission to inquire into the social condition of Malta until later in the following year.[22] It seems probable that the decision to commission from him a commentary on the third report, and to employ it in support of the 1837 measure, was predicated on Lewis's usefulness as an attack dog who could be set upon Whately. Russell later urged wavering MPs to read Lewis's remarks, in which a poor law was 'enforced with a power of argument which had hardly been surpassed by any paper of that kind'.[23] Lewis certainly relished the confrontation, joking to his friend, the assistant Poor Law Commissioner Edmund Head, that the commissioners would send over 'a detachment of Whiteboys to despatch me if they found out I criticised their performance in so insidious a manner', while boasting that he had 'made a complete smash of them'.[24]

21 Lewis to E. W. Head, 9 Apr. 1836, in Lewis (ed.), *Letters*, pp. 48–51.

22 Lewis came to believe that Malta suffered from the same structural problem as Ireland – overpopulation promoted by a Catholic religious culture favouring early marriage, and mendacious and non-entrepreneurial landlordism – although he did not propose a poor law for the islands: G. C. Lewis to T. F. Lewis, 25 Oct., 8 Nov. 1836, G. C. Lewis to Head, 31 July 1837, in *ibid.*, pp. 62–4, 67–8, 83–5.

23 *Hansard*, 3, xxxviii, 1586 [23 June 1837].

24 Lewis to Head, 15 July 1836, in Lewis (ed.), *Letters*, pp. 53–4.

Lewis's opinions on the poor law had been addressed to a wider audience in the section on 'remedies for Irish disturbance' in his *On Local Disturbances*, which had appeared earlier in 1836. Here a compulsory poor law was posited as the only effective alternative to repeated coercion in Ireland, as essential to facilitate the necessary transition from the current feudal state of rural society to a dynamic capitalized agriculture. Irish circumstances nullified the 'naked theory' of orthodox political-economic antagonism towards state relief. Rather, Lewis proclaimed, the poor-law principle could be inverted to serve as the instrument for the attainment of the classical economic objective of 'facilitating the transition to large farms and a systematic mode of cultivation'.[25] This was an important theoretical intervention, and attractive to some members of the administration, but it would be a distortion to see Lewis's commentaries as the sole or perhaps even as the principal source of ministerial commitment to an Irish poor law. Certainly in the aftermath of completing his report Lewis himself was pessimistic as to whether the government would take any account of his opinions.[26] By the time his report was published in June 1837, however, the situation had been transformed, and it was received rapturously by parts of the liberal press: 'This paper', proclaimed the *Morning Chronicle*, 'grapples with first principles, and shows such clearness and coolness of thought as must be accompanied by superior powers for administrative action.'[27]

John Revans and Irish poverty

A figure with more direct access to the ministerial ear was the former secretary of the Irish inquiry, John Revans.[28] Although Revans had left Ireland before the winding up of the Whately Commission, having been appointed to an English assistant commissionership for the northern region in February 1836, he continued to influence the Irish debate, principally through the publication later that year of a 160–page pamphlet, *Evils of the State of Ireland*. Although now on the English Poor Law Commission's payroll, Revans had been retained by the government in London between mid-February and late March 1836, possibly to give him time to draft this manifesto.[29] This text,

25 George Cornewall Lewis, *On Local Disturbances in Ireland* (London, 1836), p. 324.

26 NLW: HCP, C/2790, Lewis to Villiers, 25 Aug.; Lewis to Head, 6 Dec. 1836, in Lewis (ed.), *Letters*, pp. 69–72.

27 *MC*, 23 June 1837.

28 NA: RP, PRO30/22/2A, fols 156–60, Mulgrave to Russell, 1 Feb. 1836.

29 NA: PLCP, MH32/65, Morpeth to Nicholls, 13 Feb. 1836, Revans to Nicholls, 2 Apr. 1836. For the period of composition, see Revans, *Evils of the State of Ireland*, p. 4.

which drew heavily on selections from the evidence the collection of which Revans had overseen, was welcomed by some sympathetic commentators as an alternative (and more acceptable) report of the Poor Inquiry Commission. It provided, to some extent, the proposed extracts of evidence for easier public consumption that Morpeth had endorsed the previous September; although in its location of extracts within a clear interpretive analysis, Revans may have gone considerably further than was originally intended.[30] Revans insisted his text's authority as both evidential summary and interpretation arose from his unique combination of experience on both the English and Irish inquiries.[31]

In his uncompromising adherence to a compulsory provision for the able-bodied destitute of Ireland and emphasis on the instrumental value of a poor law for transforming Irish rural society, Revans shared much with Lewis. However, in both the tone adopted and the tenor of his social vision, Revans deviated in significant ways. Like Lewis, he identified the dependence of the labouring poor on access to land for their subsistence and the extortionate rents extracted for this as lying at the root of Ireland's malaise and disorder. However, for Revans it was the specific plight of the casual labouring families dependent on conacre lettings, rather than that of the equally poor but less vulnerable small tenant farmers and cottiers, that lay at the crux of the problem. The conacre-labourers lacked adequate employment to sustain the necessaries of life, especially during the unavoidable 'hunger months' of the summer when the previous season's potato crop was exhausted and agricultural labour was scarce, and were obliged to resort for survival to seasonal vagrancy (on the part of the women and children) and labour migration or theft (on that of the men). Despite the social stigma against beggary in Irish rural society, the aged, sick and helpless were also often driven to vagrancy and dependence on the charity of the marginally less badly-off. Some able-bodied men and women (a minority), demoralized by acute poverty, also took to vagrancy as a more regular source of sustenance.

Revans admitted that agrarian crime was endemic throughout the lower classes of Irish rural society, and that it arose from their absolute determination to maintain their holdings, but concluded that this would best be curbed by removing the pressure from below that underpinned the vicious circle of desperation and violence. Revans deviated from Lewis's more economically orthodox position in denying that Ireland was necessarily overpopulated and rejecting the idea that the small tenant farmers and cottiers were intrinsically an impediment to viable agriculture and capital accumulation. Remove the pressure placed upon these 'peasant' classes to offer extortionate rents by the cut-throat competition for holdings by desperate casual labourers, he asserted,

30 CHP, J/19/11/2, pp. 108–9, Morpeth to Russell, 28 Sept. 1835.
31 Revans, *Evils of the State of Ireland*, p. 1.

and the invidious system of 'nominal rents' would collapse. Incremental self-improvement and small-scale accumulation would follow from the diffusion of social security in the countryside. No sweeping agricultural revolution was necessary; an effective poor law would forestall rather than facilitate it. This 'small farm' vision of the Irish agricultural future predated that articulated by John Stuart Mill and W. T. Thornton in the 1840s. Like them, Revans saw Belgium rather than England as a suitable model for Irish social development, and placed greatest emphasis on peasant rather than capitalist-farmer agency in this process. Unlike the sceptical Mill, however, Revans envisioned the poor law as the main engine of social change.[32]

For Revans, the most important impact of the introduction of a workhouse-based poor law into Ireland would be in enforcing a minimum wage for agricultural labour. Generous relief of the destitute in local establishments (Revans favoured the less offensive terms 'asylum' or 'house of refuge') would have the beneficial effects of setting a lower limit on wages, as he claimed it had always done in England, of banishing the fear of starvation that underlay the cut-throat competition for conacre and cottier plots, and removing the justification for vagrancy and hence the financial burden this placed on the peasantry. The abhorrence of confinement would ensure the operation of the less-eligibility principle among the able-bodied; workhouse diet and conditions should be comfortable enough to avoid degradation, while not greatly exceeding the levels attainable to an independent labourer on prevailing rates of wages. The standard of workhouse relief could be raised incrementally 'to force an improving rate of earnings', in line with agricultural recovery, until the conditions of Irish rural labourers approached those of England.[33]

The fears of those who opposed such a measure were summarily dismissed. The Irish wages-fund already supported the destitute, albeit through the distorting and demoralizing medium of alms to vagrants; despite annual 'hungry months', starvation was rare and a Malthusian crisis seemed unlikely. A regularized poor law would redirect that wages-fund into more beneficial channels, while removing the existing obstacles to the incremental growth of that fund to the mutual benefit of all classes. The number of persons cited as 'destitute' in the Whately report was dismissed by Revans as the result of a series of calculating errors, which included classifying the conacre-labourer as 'destitute' when out of work, whereas he and his family only became so when their stock of potatoes ran out. It followed that the 'able-bodied' requiring relief were mostly the victims of seasonal or accidental rather than continuous

32 For Mill's citation of Revans as an authority on the cottier economy, see John Stuart Mill, *The Principles of Political Economy* (3rd edn, 2 vols, London, 1852), i, pp. 388–9. See also Gray, 'Peculiarities of Irish land tenure', pp. 145–9.

33 Revans, *Evils of the State of Ireland*, pp. 133–4.

destitution, requiring short-term rather than extended assistance. Moreover, it was not necessary for large numbers to enter the workhouses for social conditions to change, as the moral effect of the certainty of admission *in extremis*, arising from a legal right to relief, would act as a preventive factor.

Revans went on to sketch, somewhat superficially, the practicalities of the poor law he envisaged for Ireland. A national network of workhouses was essential. For optimum effect these needed to be easily accessible to the poor (no more than ten miles apart), which equated to a total of around 500. Each should have a capacity of around 200 inmates except for large towns, providing a national provision of not much above 100,000 places. Revans expected this to be more than adequate for the fluctuating numbers of the able-bodied destitute; the additional 2–300,000 infirm and aged destitute, and perhaps also the families of able-bodied male inmates, could safely be relieved in their homes without imposing a workhouse test.[34] The cost of construction or purchase of existing buildings for workhouses would not exceed one million pounds, while the anticipated maximum annual expenditure for relieving 400,000 persons (about five per cent of the population) through indoor and outdoor relief would be half a million per annum. Given the condition of Ireland and the likelihood that increased burdens would provoke an anti-poor-law backlash, Revans felt that the provision of the former by grant was the least Britain could do. Recurrent costs were best met by a national rate on all forms of property in Ireland that addressed the localized imbalance between destitution and the ability to relieve it; Ulster and Leinster could hardly complain at this as they were currently bearing the brunt of western destitution through the seasonal influx of vagrants.[35] The practical administration of the system could be shared between a limited number of contractors undertaking to supply the needs of groups of workhouses, under the supervision of local boards of guardians and the ultimate surveillance of the London-based Poor Law Commission through its corps of assistant commissioners.

Revans' vision for an Irish poor law was in a number of ways at odds with the more conventional Benthamite approach maintained by his superiors Chadwick and Nicholls. These tensions extended to his practice as an English assistant commissioner, and would lead to a formal reprimand from the Poor Law Commission and the threatened resignation by Revans from the service in 1838.[36] The tone of *Evils of the State of Ireland* was markedly

34 *Ibid.*, pp. 134–7.

35 *Ibid.*, pp. 134–46.

36 For the deteriorating relationship between Revans and Chadwick from 1836, see S. E. Finer, *The Life and Times of Sir Edwin Chadwick* (London, 1952), pp. 105, 109. In July 1838 Revans' diaries and reports were critically examined by the commissioners, and although they were found satisfactory, he offered his resignation, NA: PLCP, MH1/15, pp. 75, 113, 322–3, PLC Minutes, 30 July, 17 Aug., 20 Sept. 1838.

more sympathetic towards the plight of the poor than most other contemporary commentaries, while at the same time it avoided slipping into a diatribe against Irish landlords (whom Revans held to be largely powerless to change a land system that damaged their real interests as much as those of the rural poor). Part of this sympathy might be attributed to his visceral shock at witnessing the depths of Irish suffering, which he viewed as being on a different plane from that of the neighbouring island; 'I have smiled at English horrors when witnessing Irish scenes', he confided. Even a short exposure to Irish poverty tended to induce despair and to blunt private charity.[37] But Revans was also explicit about the interpretive schema through which he read his experience. There were, he declared, three sects of political economists – those who saw the getting of wealth as the only purpose of human activity; those who admitted that this should be subordinated to human happiness but took account only of the happiness of the wealthy; and those who regarded the creation of wealth as solely a means to the end of increasing the happiness of the aggregate of mankind. It was with the latter position, which refused to regard the working classes as mere machinery or cattle, and which refused to treat labour as just another marketable commodity, that Revans identified himself. From this followed his conviction that the right to relief under a universal poor law was a fundamental requirement of civilized society. Smithian economics ignored the fundamental power imbalance in labour relations:

> The capitalist can generally lower wages in any part of Europe to a mere subsistence. He can at most times delay his work, whether in agriculture or manufactures, a week or a fortnight, without great inconvenience, but the labourer's stomach cannot be kept without food two days. It is very common to talk of wages being regulated by the proportion which the supply of labour bears to the demand for it. Labour is treated as a marketable commodity, and as if the workman was as able to withhold his labour as the employer is to delay his work. The fact is, however, that the labourer and the employer are in the same position towards each other when making a bargain for wages as would two dealers, the one holding a quantity of corn and wanting a quantity of oranges, the other holding a quantity of oranges and wanting a quantity of corn. The oranges will be rotten in a fortnight, the corn will keep two or three years.[38]

This was not an indictment of the principles of free trade (of which Revans remained an enthusiastic advocate), but of the unreflective application of English social models to Ireland. Experience everywhere had shown that only the existence of an effective poor law granting a degree of social security could redress the negotiating imbalance between capital and labour. The failure of

37 Revans, *Evils of the State of Ireland*, p. 142.
38 *Ibid.*, pp. 122, 146.

remedial projects in Ireland likewise indicated that its regeneration could only begin with such a legislative enactment.

Whately had animadverted on Revans' radicalism as early as 1835, and had expressed fear both about the growing self-consciousness with which it was being articulated and the access which Revans had secured to key ministerial figures. The appearance of the pamphlet merely confirmed the archbishop's suspicions of 'his real (revolutionary) principles' and desire for 'a dissolution of the union, a civil war, and a final loss of half the crown'.[39] This outburst reflected not only Whately's rather fevered paranoia, but a real fear of Revans' influence on this key legislative question. Revans was not, of course, the sole or perhaps even the principal influence on ministerial thinking about Ireland, and the measure eventually introduced was in many ways distant from his suggestions. Nevertheless, the importance of his contribution has been overlooked in most discussions of the origins of the bill, and repays closer examination. His intervention not only helped shape the views and rhetoric (if not always the actions) of the 'Foxite' ministers, but was received positively by a range of observers, from Lewis – who thought it one of the best descriptions he had read on the question – to liberal Catholic journals such as the *Dublin Review* – and even the editorial writers of *The Times*, and the previously sceptical *Spectator*.[40]

Lord John Russell and the Foxite Whigs

Why were the critiques of the Whately report by Lewis and Revans so eagerly sought and utilized by the administration? What had become of the relatively comfortable relationship between Whately and the ministers of 1833–34? To answer these questions it is necessary to review the internal politics of the governing party. The ministerial group that exercised greatest control over Irish policy from the formation of Melbourne's second administration in April 1835 was centred on Lord John Russell. This circle, described by Peter

39 Whately to Senior, 14 Nov. 1837, in Whately (ed.), *Life*, i, pp. 396–7. Revans continued to adhere to radical causes. In 1847 he proposed a steeply progressive expenditure tax to replace customs and excise duties, and in the mid-1850s was honorary secretary and a propagandist for several reformist associations: see John Revans, *A Per Centage Tax on Domestic Expenditure, to Supply the Whole of the Public Revenue* (London, 1847); *Working Plan of the Administrative Reform Association* (London, 1856); *List of the Present House of Commons, with the Degree of its Subjection to the House of Lords* (London, 1858); *The Times*, 17 June 1857.

40 NLW: HCP, C/2809, Lewis to Villiers, [Dec. 1837]; [Mark Perrin], 'A poor law for Ireland', *DR*, 2 (Dec. 1836), pp. 51–95; *The Times*, 9 Dec. 1836; 'The only reform for 1837', *Spectator*, 28 Jan. 1837.

Mandler as 'Foxite Whigs' from their shared devotion to the memory and political style (if not always to the policies) of Charles James Fox, had distinct policy orientations in a number of areas, including social reform and Irish policy.[41] They were the protégés of Fox's nephew Lord Holland, and sought to follow his commitment to the precept of aristocratic government on behalf of 'the people', pursuing 'balanced' constitutional and social reform on their behalf and engaging in dialogue with constitutionally-voiced manifestations of mass opinion in shared opposition to a 'corrupt' and class-interested Toryism.

Russell, as Holland's adoptive political heir, was the leading Foxite of his generation. Closely associated with him was Viscount Duncannon, heir to the Earl of Bessborough and to large estates in Kilkenny and other Irish counties. Also in this aristocratic faction were Viscount Ebrington (son of Earl Fortescue), the Earl of Mulgrave (later first marquess of Normanby), and Viscount Morpeth (heir to the earldom of Carlisle). This was a group united not by regional interest (Morpeth and Normanby had Yorkshire bases, but the others had principal interests in Bedfordshire, South Leinster and Devon), nor even solely by cousinhood (Ebrington and Normanby were originally from Tory families; Morpeth's father was a Canningite), but by shared political convictions. This did not mean that members of this political grouping held identical opinions on all political questions, either substantial or tactical, but it did incline them towards shared positions on a range of prominent issues between the 1820s and 1840s. More loosely associated with Russell (although he was to go his own way after 1839 and acquire his own factional associates) was Lord Howick, son of Earl Grey.

Ireland was amongst the foremost issues of concern to the Foxite Whigs from the 1810s. They differed from other liberals in forging a constructive (even cordial) relationship with Daniel O'Connell, mainly through the personal friendship between the agitator and Duncannon.[42] The group did not, however, restrict their Irish connections to O'Connell. In summer 1832, at the height of the 'tithe war', Duncannon made a point of visiting the Catholic bishop of Kildare and Leighlin, James Doyle, to discuss the state of the country and prospects of the ministry. Doyle recorded that he 'expressed [his] opinions freely enough to [Duncannon]', albeit in the belief that neither men's opinions would be much attended to by the ministry then in office.[43]

41 Mandler, *Aristocratic Government*, esp. pp. 13–43. For the application of Mandler's typologies of Whig-liberalism to Irish policy in the 1830s–40s, see Gray, *Famine*, pp. 18–22.

42 Dorothy Howell-Thomas, *Duncannon: Reformer and Reconciler 1781–1847* (Norwich, 1992), pp. 117–18.

43 Doyle to Sir Henry Parnell, June 1832, in Fitzpatrick (ed.), *Doyle*, ii, p. 418.

The ascendancy of Edward Stanley as Irish secretary in 1830–33 frustrated the Foxite group, who found his unmitigated coercive policy particularly offensive.[44] Foxite apologists subsequently denounced this episode of a 'government liberal in theory and Tory in practice', which had undermined the Irish people's confidence in British liberalism.[45] The failure of Catholic emancipation to resolve Irish unrest deeply troubled the group, and led them to the conviction that the British government needed to win the allegiance of its Irish subjects, not by piecemeal concessions, but by demonstrating to the Catholic majority that it was possible to attain civil and religious equality, and social amelioration, within a reformed British state. This alternative political project, summarized by the phrase 'justice to Ireland', involved accommodation rather than confrontation with the political leadership of the Irish majority community. Precisely what should be encompassed by 'justice' remained creatively ambiguous, but what differentiated the Foxite Whigs from other groups prepared to flirt with killing Repeal with kindness was an acceptance of O'Connell's legitimate position in political life, and a degree of responsiveness to the grievances of Irish mass opinion as articulated by O'Connell and other popular representatives, including members of the Catholic clergy.

Russell's 1834 bid to commit the ministry to the appropriation for non-denominational use of the 'surplus' revenues of the Irish Church was intended to reformulate policy on Foxite lines; instead it split the party and brought down the government. Duncannon's negotiating tactics during the short-lived Peel administration of 1834–35 led to the 'Lichfield House compact', whereby the O'Connellites and radicals were accommodated to a new, more advanced, Whig-liberal programme founded on the principle of appropriation.[46] The second Melbourne government formed in April 1835 was thus qualitatively different from the Whig-liberal administrations of 1830–34, not least because of the advancement of Foxites to prominent ministerial positions. Russell took the Home Office and the leadership of the Commons; Mulgrave became lord lieutenant of Ireland with Morpeth as his chief secretary; as chief commissioner of woods and forests (a cabinet post), Duncannon occupied a position from which he could exert influence over many areas of policy; Ebrington went on to succeed Mulgrave as viceroy in 1839.

The strategy of 'justice to Ireland' entailed the necessity of engagement with Catholic popular opinion in Ireland, and was based on a belief that support

44 Mandler, *Aristocratic Government*, pp. 123–8; McDowell, *Public Opinion*, pp. 142–3.

45 Anon., 'Ireland', *Monthly Chronicle*, 2 (1838), p. 32.

46 West Sussex Record Office, Chichester, Bessborough Papers, F/150, Holland to Duncannon, 20, 23 Jan. 1835; A. H. Graham, 'The Lichfield House Compact, 1835', *Irish Historical Studies*, 12 (1960–61), pp. 209–25.

for Repeal was conditional and that good government would have to 'please the people of that country', the 'only way of governing Ireland [which] had not yet been tried'.[47] This assumption that Irish and English interests were reconcilable, or even identical, was a heroic one, but nevertheless sincerely held. The feasibility of the strategy was dependent on O'Connell and other spokesmen for Irish majority opinion suppressing their scepticism on this head and choosing to collaborate with the new ministry. Lichfield House at least offered a breathing space to experiment in this new form of political engagement.

The Foxites had strong support on Irish policy from the *Morning Chronicle* under the editorship of John Black, who had developed advanced ideas on both an Irish poor law and land reform. This shift in governing style and substance from 1835 was identified by many observers both in Ireland and Britain. One Scottish supporter praised Melbourne's administration, comprised of members of the 'old Whig families' as 'thoroughly imbued with the Whig principles of Fox'. This was manifest both in Irish conciliation and British reforms (although regrettably, in his opinion, stopping short of overthrowing the 1834 Poor Law Amendment Act).[48]

While the Whig administration of Ireland in 1835–41 achieved only limited legislative success, its relative popularity rested on the partial revolution it imposed in the personnel and practice of the Irish executive. Emancipation was to be rendered complete through the promotion of Catholics to responsible positions under the Crown. The Foxites were of the opinion that past misgovernment and support for religious discrimination was responsible for both the social unrest and the economic malaise that characterized the island. Their liberal constitutionalism inclined them to regard the popularization of the instruments of administration and the restoration of confidence in the rule of law as basic requirements for social progress.

At the root of 'justice to Ireland' was an integrationist conception of the Union, ultimately owing much to Edmund Burke. If the ministers were conscious of Ireland's history of colonial subordination to Britain, and of certain parallels with such restless parts of the empire as Canada, India and Jamaica, they chose to emphasize instead the ideal of 'completing the Union' through the accommodation of emerging Irish elites, and the 'elevation' of the Irish people to British standards. If this vision was ultimately compromised both by its own internal contradictions and by political and economic constraints

47 Russell to Holland, 20, 30 Sept. 1833, cited in Mandler, *Aristocratic Government*, pp. 152–3.

48 John Douglas, *Life and Property in Ireland assured as in England by a Poor-rate on Land to provide Employment for the Destitute Poor on the Waste Lands of Ireland* (London, 1846), pp. 10–11, 18.

over which the ministry had no control, it nevertheless appeared to many (in Ireland, Britain and abroad) to offer the hope of a new relationship in the later 1830s.[49]

'Justice to Ireland' involved not only the absorption of some Irish Catholics into the Irish administration, but the use of the Irish executive in novel ways. The expanding activities of the Dublin Castle departments, already substantially more interventionist than their English counterparts, offered an opportunity to circumvent the obstruction and local monopoly of the established Protestant landed elite. The appointment as under-secretary in July 1835 of the Scotsman Thomas Drummond – previously an officer on the Irish Ordnance Survey and private secretary to Althorp – ensured that a vigorous and efficient (as well as politically engaged) hand would guide the Irish departments.[50] While 'justice to Ireland' in 1835–41 was concerned primarily with redressing Catholic political, legal and religious grievances, there was a recognition that the tithe issue involved more demotic concerns, and that 'justice' must also extend into the economic sphere. Mulgrave's overt use of the viceregal prerogative of mercy, especially in agrarian cases, and his promotion of Catholics to judicial office was widely regarded (and condemned by their opponents) as reversing the previous bias in the judicial system towards upholding the economic interests of the landed establishment. This reflected in part a more general Foxite antagonism towards Irish landlords as a class, which had mainly a political rather than an economic root. Believing the Protestant ascendancy had abused its powers and responsibilities as property-owners and thereby alienated the Catholic farming and labouring masses, the Foxites held that 'justice' would have to be imposed on this class from without. This had particular implications for the role of the state as a regulatory agency in Irish society.

Probably the most coherent single statement of the Foxite position on the social dimensions of the 'Irish question' can be found in the celebrated letter written by Drummond, on behalf of the Irish government, to the Tipperary magistrates in May 1838. After rejecting the magistrates' appeals for additional coercive powers as unnecessary and provocative, Drummond lectured them on their class culpability for agrarian disturbances, and on the indispensability of a measure of poor relief. The causes of praedial crime lay, he insisted, in the land tenure system, and the 'lamentably destitute condition of a cottier tenantry, possessing no adequate means of continuous support'.

49 For the idealization of the 'Pacata Hibernia' allegedly created after 1835 by such reforms, see Anon., 'Ireland', *Monthly Chronicle*, 2 (1838), pp. 31–9 and [David Leahy], 'Ireland and Lord Normanby', *ibid.*, 3 (1839), pp. 289–301.

50 M. A. G. Ó Tuathaigh, *Thomas Drummond and the Government of Ireland, 1835–40* (Dublin, 1978).

If the proprietors had evidently been at fault in permitting or encouraging the emergence of this class for their own economic and political interests, they had no moral right summarily to remove them by clearance now that circumstances had changed. Indeed it was this precipitate rush to clear, without counterbalancing actions, that was at the root of violence in Tipperary: in the absence of any alternative to starvation, the principle of self-preservation on the part of the peasantry was understandable, if lamentable.

If the people were to be weaned away from such erroneous manifestations of agrarian law, the state must insist that the landowners shoulder their just responsibilities, rather than assist them in repressing popular anger:

> Property has its duties as well as its rights; to the neglect of those duties in times past is mainly to be ascribed that diseased state of society in which such crimes take their rise; and it is not in the enactment or enforcement of statutes of extraordinary severity, but chiefly in the better and more faithful performance of those duties, and the more enlightened and humane exercise of those rights, that a permanent remedy for such disorders is to be sought.

It remained to be seen how such an agenda for the reform of social relationships in Ireland might be put into force.[51]

Russell's own Foxite instincts were strongly reinforced when he visited Ireland in September 1833 to observe conditions at first hand. The brief diary he kept of his visit is useful in giving some clues as to the formation of his thought on the subject. On arrival in Dublin he was quick to endorse the critical attitudes of English residents in Ireland towards the Irish gentry *per se*: 'The general tone of officers who had been serving in the country, was that of pity for the peasantry, and dislike of the gentry.'[52] However, he excepted from condemnation the sympathetic and improving Whig landowners whose properties he visited. On viewing the duke of Leinster's estate at Carton, he noted both the industrious labour of workers on good piece rate wages, and the success of the duke in conciliating those previously agitated against him by O'Connell through kindness and good feeling.[53] After visiting St Patrick's

51 Drummond to Donoughmore, 22 May 1838, in O'Brien (ed.), *Drummond*, pp. 276–87. O'Brien's book established a rather distorted picture of the administration of the later 1830s focused almost solely on Drummond, which has persisted in the historical literature. In reality, Drummond was a subordinate (albeit a determined and highly efficient) official. The political strategy, drive and style of the administration were determined by the 'popular' aristocrats who held ministerial posts.

52 University College London Archives [UCL], Russell Diary, Ms Ogden 84 (6 Sept. [1833]).

53 *Ibid.* (7, 9 Sept. [1833]).

College, Maynooth (where he met the president and future archbishop of Cashel, Michael Slattery), he travelled on to Duncannon's estates in south Kilkenny, noting en route cases of both wretched and improving agriculture and peasant cabins. On the Bessborough estates he saw examples of the possibility of amelioration of peasant living conditions.[54] Duncannon himself attributed this improvement, and the development of the habit of savings, principally to the paternalistic efforts he had made to provide blankets, clothing and other goods at subsidized prices and on credit through the estate 'poor shop', and to provide employment specifically to the women and children of poor families.[55]

Russell's main lesson from his Irish sojourn related to the immediate political concern of the year: although the 1833 Coercion Act had worked effectively in quieting the country, the 'present terror' was unsustainable and the radical reform of tithe, including the payment of the Catholic clergy out of the revenues of the established Church, was urgently required. At the same time, however, he formed lasting opinions concerning landlord–tenant relations and the situation of the rural poor: 'Poor people!', he noted in his diary, 'alternatively the anvil and the hammer of others.'[56] On returning to England he concluded that in order to put an end to the system whereby exorbitant rents were extracted 'by the distress of the landlord, from the distress of the tenant', a scheme should be devised enabling the state to purchase and improve land on a large scale.[57] Poor relief may not as yet have been at the top of Russell's agenda, but another undated memo from 1833 makes clear his view that some form of provision would be desirable, if only to make good use of any surplus raised by taxation to provide for the costs of the churches: 'Apply surplus to the relief of the aged, suppression of mendicancy etc, in the way Commrs shall point out.'[58] Russell and his colleagues increasingly came to interpret Irish grievances not solely in terms of the need to grant civil equity to the middle classes or payment to the Catholic clergy, but also to secure the peasant 'justice' against his landlord.

Russell's thinking on the subject of an Irish poor law appears to have become much clearer and more pronounced in the course of 1834, possibly because of his participation in the cabinet committee involved with drafting

54 *Ibid.* (8, 11, 12 Sept.). For contemporary opinion on the Bessborough estates as a model for the improvement of cottier tenants without resort to clearance, see Doyle [William Hickey], *Address to the Landlords of Ireland.*

55 Duncannon in *PIC: Appendix C, Part ii*, pp. 29e–30e.

56 UCL, Ms Ogden 84, Russell Diary (9 Sept. 1833).

57 Memorandum on Irish policy, 18 Oct. 1833, Rollo Russell (ed.), *Early Correspondence of Lord John Russell, 1805–40* (2 vols, London, 1913), ii, p. 43.

58 UCL, Ms Ogden 84, Russell memo, n.d. [1833].

the English poor law bill and the parliamentary focus on the minutiae of the legislation.[59] By September 1834 he was urging on Melbourne the necessity of calling an immediate session of parliament to forestall renewed O'Connellite agitation through a programme of Irish reforms and amendments of the existing coercion bill. Crucially, he now placed an Irish poor bill second after a tithe and church bill in this incipient 'justice to Ireland' menu, urging Melbourne to act quickly in the face of urgent necessity.[60] While Melbourne acknowledged the immediacy of the tithe question, he could not see the same need respecting the 'difficult and doubtful question' of poor relief, a potential source of embarrassment for the ministry (and of course still the subject of a royal commission).[61] While the prime minister preferred adhering to the official fiction that an opinion on the matter should be formed only in the wake of the commission's report, Russell insisted on his right to state his own views on the matter to parliament at the earliest opportunity.[62] In the event parliament was not recalled in November 1834 and the ensuing political crisis altered the context.

During the 'hundred days' of the first Peel ministry of 1834–35 Irish issues acquired yet greater prominence. The principal Irish 'question' remained that of the church. However, there is evidence that Russell and his allies also saw an Irish poor law bill as forming part of the 'justice to Ireland' strategy. Their conviction that such a measure would be politically popular was in part a matter of timing. In the spring of 1835, almost simultaneously with the Lichfield House discussions, O'Connell publicly declared his latest 'conversion' to an Irish poor law, perhaps not coincidentally as multiple public meetings in the country seemed unanimous in demanding it.

At a meeting in Dublin of the Anti-Tory Association on 28 April 1835, O'Connell announced that he now regarded a poor law as the only effective (albeit risky) mechanism for curbing politically-motivated clearances by landlords and preventing the retaliatory violence they provoked. He told an appreciative audience: '[W]e must protect the people. I care not what the consequences are, if it be necessary to have poor laws, I am for poor laws. (Cheering.) Orangemen of Ireland, you have driven me to it, and Orange landlords, look to yourselves!' He assured his audience that Ireland would already have had poor laws if only he had been convinced of this sooner;

59 Although Mandler notes that Russell was the 'least active' member of the cabinet committee and not strongly committed to the terms of the 1834 act: *Aristocratic Government*, pp. 139, 173.

60 RA: MP, 13/35, Russell to Melbourne, 2 Sept. 1834.

61 Melbourne to Russell, 4 Sept. 1834, *ibid.*, 13/36.

62 Melbourne to Russell, 8 Sept., *ibid.*, 13/38; Russell to Melbourne, 6 Sept. 1834, *ibid.*, 13/37.

nothing, certainly not emigration, would now suffice.[63] In June he went so far as to warn he might introduce his own bill if the ministry failed to act.[64] His adherence to the campaign was welcomed with enthusiasm by the pro-poor-law press, which saw the new unity between the leader and the 'people' as a guarantor of legislative success.[65]

O'Connell may have been responding in part to electoral pressures on the ground. In the fiercely contested Co. Carlow election in June 1835, the Whig-liberals Raphael and Vigors were returned (although later unseated on petition) with the strong support of the Catholic clergy. Fr James Maher, now bearer of the flame of his late patron and friend Bishop Doyle, proclaimed this a victory for an anti-aristocratic movement that was demanding legal provision for the poor. In his words, the anti-Tory patriot demanded that the legislature

> [t]ake the burdens . . . from the overloaded shoulders of the peasantry; put clothes on their backs, flesh on their bones, supply wholesome food for their hungry stomachs, in a word, remove the causes of turbulence and outrage, and you can at once break up that beautiful machinery for degrading the people, of treadmills and barracks, and police establishments.[66]

The logic of the 'anti-Tory'-alliance of 1835 was that repeal be set aside in pursuit of practical reforms that would benefit the masses of Ireland.

At a Dublin dinner in January 1836 O'Connell was reported as toasting 'A Poor-law for Ireland!' This came at a crucial moment in policy development, and was regarded as of profound importance by supporters of such a measure, and as an unforgivable betrayal by its opponents.[67] While O'Connell's second conversion was also not to be sustained, the sense that a poor law would prove a 'popular' measure remained strong for Foxite ministers. Even as late as September 1836, as the ministers were preparing their poor law bill, it appeared that O'Connell, while now 'less sanguine' of such a measure's success, would not oppose an initiative proposed by a popular ministry and for which there was, he acknowledged, a great cry in Ireland.[68]

As home secretary and leader of the Commons from April 1835, under the increasingly disengaged Melbourne as prime minister, Russell pressed for a

63 *The Times*, 4 May 1835. He subsequently strongly endorsed a petition for a poor law prepared by a Catholic priest for the Registry Association, *ibid.*, 11 May 1835.

64 *The Times*, 30 June 1835.

65 *FJ*, 4 May 1835.

66 Speech by Maher, June 1835, in Patrick Francis Moran (ed.), *The Letters of Rev. James Maher* (Dublin, 1877), pp. xliii–xlvii.

67 'O'Connell's new toast', *Spectator*, 30 Jan. 1836, p. 105.

68 O'Connell to the electors of Kilkenny, 28 Sept. 1836, in *The Times*, 4 Oct. 1836.

speedy conclusion of the Whately Commission. It is clear, however, that he had decided long before the submission of the third report that a more direct and summary measure of poor relief for Ireland was both expedient and correct in principle. This commitment chimed with Russell and his circle's generally proactive and interventionist attitude towards the role of government in promoting social improvement in both Britain and Ireland. There is evidence that the Foxite Whigs regarded the recently established central poor law administration as a potential engine for expanding the reformist scope of government, and established a constructive, if uneasy, collaborative relationship with Chadwick and other Benthamite officials to promote this.[69]

The Irish poor-law question in Dublin Castle and Whitehall

The newly appointed Irish ministers were also inclined to place poor relief high on their list of political priorities. As a Yorkshire MP, Morpeth had previously introduced and spoken in favour of petitions for an Irish poor law sent from several West Riding towns.[70] His interest in the subject extended beyond the (arguably selfish) concerns of his constituents, and he was one of the very few Whigs prepared to support Sadler's 1831 resolution in principle, on the grounds that 'it was the duty of the resident gentlemen of Ireland, to look after the comfort of those persons by whom they were surrounded'.[71] His views on Irish social questions may also have been influenced by his friendship with his Oxford contemporary Lord Clements, the Whig-liberal MP for Co. Leitrim. Clements urged Morpeth to visit him at his Lough Rynn estate to see the real problems of the Irish countryside:

> [W]e have . . . plenty of the most miserably wretched poor people to visit, to prepare your nerves for poor laws. If you would submit yourself to my guidance I would give you as detailed an insight into their condition in 24 hours as volumes of blue books could convey to you in a month . . . and you would make me very happy if you would come and lionize my squatting and clearing[.][72]

Although Morpeth appears not to have journeyed to Leitrim, Clements was keen to convey, by other means, 'the lesson on what poverty really is – which is a very painful lesson and one that makes the heart both sore and hard'.[73] His influence may, perhaps, be discerned in the speech Morpeth delivered to

69 Mandler, *Aristocratic Government*, pp. 170–99.
70 *Hansard*, 3, v, 1257–60 (12 Aug. 1831); ix, 709 [23 Jan. 1832], *ibid*., v, 1113 [10 Aug. 1831].
71 *Ibid*., vi, 846–7 [29 Aug. 1831].
72 CHP, J/19/1/13/51, Clements to Morpeth, 18 Oct. 1836.
73 Clements to Morpeth, 27 Dec. 1836, *ibid*., J/19/1/12/77.

his West Riding constituents at Leeds in January 1837, one which Clements assured him was 'the best I have read since Melbourne became prime minister'. The chief secretary had framed the government's intention to introduce an Irish poor law within the rhetoric of 'justice to Ireland':

> No question can approach, whether we take it in reference to their duties as statesmen or their feelings as philanthropists . . . in its urgency for early consideration and for deep importance of complicated detail to the introduction of Poor-laws into Ireland (loud cheers). And it is by legislating thus, in the spirit of kindly consideration for the sufferings of that country – of just recognition of her rights – of generous confidence in her gratitude, that we may most hope, because we shall best deserve, to make her, instead of what she has too long been to us – a thorn, a burden, and a blot – our pride and our health, an ornament in all the arts of empire and in all the paths of glory (cheers).[74]

Soon after their appointments, Morpeth and the lord lieutenant were confronted with an immediate and pressing crisis of poverty in Ireland that appears to have made a significant impact on both men. Summer subsistence crises in the west of Ireland were hardly a new phenomenon, but the summer dearth of 1835 that affected Connacht, Kerry and Donegal drew an instant reaction from the Castle. One of Morpeth's first acts in his new office was to order an inquiry into 'the causes, temporary or permanent, of the existing distress'.[75] Mulgrave immediately consulted the Poor Inquiry Commissioners on the subject, but it was Revans who made himself available for a lengthy interview with the viceroy in late May, and who was then dispatched to the Irish Office in London with papers for urgent delivery to Morpeth.[76]

The relationship between Revans and the Irish ministers was thus forged from the latters' concern that the more rambling investigations of the Whately Commission be replaced with a focused plan combining the immediate relief of hunger with the targeting of its underlying causes. Both Mulgrave and Morpeth saw their roles as proactive agents in the relief of distress; Mulgrave dug deep into his own pocket to provide urgent relief in aid of local subscriptions in the west, while Morpeth lobbied the Treasury for state relief funds and local discretionary powers for the viceroy in their expenditure.[77] While anxious to avoid creating disincentives to local initiative, the ministerial correspondence relating to the crisis reveals a readiness to take it seriously,

74 Clements to Morpeth, 24 Jan., *ibid.*, J/19/1/13/110; *MC*, 21 Jan. 1837.

75 CHP, J/19/11/2, pp. 8–9, 11–12, N. Macdonald to Gossett, 25 May 1835, Macdonald to W. H. Wyatt, 28 May 1835.

76 Mulgrave to Morpeth, 31 May 1835, *ibid.*, J/19/1/9, fol. 41.

77 Mulgrave to Morpeth, 5 June, *ibid.*, J/19/1/9, fol. 49; MC: NP, M/449, Morpeth to Mulgrave, 10 June 1835.

and an emotive reaction to accounts of human distress. Mulgrave found Archbishop John MacHale's accounts of Mayo, conveyed in a private interview, 'quite heart-rending and extraordinary', and was continually pushing the government for more money on humanitarian grounds. He wrote to Morpeth: 'They throw everything on the Govt but . . . that is no reason why thousands should be permitted to starve.'[78] This might be contrasted with Spring Rice's conviction that 'the present distress is very partial indeed and has been in many cases exaggerated'.[79]

Certainly, sympathetic observers in Dublin concluded not only that the Irish ministers were genuinely concerned with alleviating the western food crisis, but that they had made an explicit connection between the annual near-famine of the summer months and the necessity of a permanent and extensive poor law. The *Freeman's Journal* editorialist claimed that sources close to the Castle had revealed that both ministers were now committed to such a measure, and urged them to state this publicly.[80] One of them would come very close to doing so less than two weeks later.

In July 1835 Morpeth was obliged to respond in the Commons to the backbench motions for an Irish poor law pressed by Smith O'Brien, Poulett Scrope and Musgrave. While welcoming the earnest activities of these individuals, he was obliged to insist on patience until the Poor Inquiry Commission had completed its operations and formally reported. While critics may have regarded this as yet another ministerial delaying tactic, Morpeth hinted at a ministerial commitment to an initiative in the 1836 session, in declaring that the government was 'in no way inclined to shrink from taking that part in the introduction of Poor-laws into Ireland to which a sense of their duty might lead them'.[81] This statement of apparent intent drew a quick rebuke from Spring Rice, foreshadowing an intra-ministerial conflict over Irish poor laws that would rumble on through the following years.[82]

These tensions first came to a head at a cabinet meeting to discuss the content of the King's Speech that would open the 1836 session. The insistence of Russell and the Irish government on including a commitment to legislate

78 CHP, J/19/1/9, fols 50, 64–5, 84–5, Mulgrave to Morpeth, 8 June, 29 June, 20 July 1835. MacHale had just published a public letter stating that temporary relief of distress would be inadequate in the absence of a comprehensive poor law, *FJ*, 10 June 1835.

79 NLI: MP, Ms 551, Spring Rice to Morpeth, 11 July 1835.

80 *FJ*, 29 June 1835.

81 *Hansard*, 3, xxix, 314–16 [8 July 1835]. Smith O'Brien also privately lobbied the chief secretary to take up his measure as a ministerial bill, NLI, Larcom Papers, Ms 7,698, Smith O'Brien to Morpeth, 23 Jan. 1836.

82 MC: NP, M/463, Morpeth to Mulgrave, 9 July 1835.

along lines cognate with the English act of 1834 (i.e. incorporating relief to the able-bodied destitute through workhouses), drew the fire of moderate liberals, especially those with Irish landed interests. It was clear that the Foxites and their allies would no longer wait for, or accede to, Whately's well-flagged (yet still undelivered) recommendations. John Cam Hobhouse noted in his diary:

> What gave us most trouble was the recommendation of poor laws for Ireland, and the [allusion?] to the poor law amendment act. Palmerston contended that the circumstances of the two countries were dissimilar and not having the abuses of a previous poor law to remedy the new act could scarcely be applied or at least referred to as a model for imitation. Ld Lansdowne and Rice seemed to take the same view – after a good deal of talk I proposed some words which were adopted. . . . When going away Thomson came up to me and said 'these Irish Poor Laws will break up our Cabinet[;] Lansdowne[,] Rice and Palmerston will never consent to a compulsory law, and I will never consent to a voluntary Law'.[83]

Charles Poulett Thomson, the president of the board of trade, was one of the more radical members of the government and politically close to Howick. He represented Manchester and was sympathetic to English middle-class demands for a punitive measure directed at Irish landowners. On this question he agreed substantially with his populist-radical brother George Poulett Scrope, and was confirmed in this by a two-month tour of inspection he made of Ireland in summer 1837.[84]

Howick himself had already emerged as a committed advocate of an Irish poor law. Dismissing Whately's draft report in January 1836, he demanded a system modelled on the English workhouse principle and the award of a legal right of the destitute poor to relief charged on the produce of the land, along with employment of the able-bodied paupers. Only this, he asserted, could create the social security that would attract development capital to Ireland, unleash its productive potential, and render mass emigration redundant. Subsidiary employment measures would, however, be necessary to assist its introduction.[85] Senior attempted to refute Howick's case by denying that the vital supervisory agency of 'enlightened public opinion' existed in Ireland, and stressing the inapplicability of English social institutions to a country 'in

83 BL: Broughton diary, Add Ms 56,558, fol. 73 (27 Jan. 1836).

84 G. Poulett Scrope, *Memoir of the Life of . . . Charles Lord Sydenham* (2nd edn, London, 1844), pp. 74–5.

85 Howick to Senior, 5 Jan. 1836, in Levy, *Senior*, pp. 263–6; DUL: GP, 155/1, Howick memo, 'Paper on reasons for making legal provision for relief of poor in Ireland' [1836].

which the local aristocracy is less numerous, more ignorant and more jobbing, the recklessness and improvidence more barbarous, and the average of subsistence lower than any Christian country, except perhaps Mexico and Hayti'. Such hyperbole merely further convinced Howick of the correctness of his own original opinions.[86]

Of the originators of the Whately Commission, Althorp had left the government on his succession as Earl Spencer in 1834, and Melbourne – perhaps to avoid confrontation on an issue from which he felt increasingly disengaged – later affected to have had insufficient time to read enough on the matter to make any useful observations.[87] Resistance to the Russell–Thomson–Howick initiative came most strongly from Spring Rice as chancellor of the exchequer, Lansdowne as lord president and Palmerston as foreign secretary, although Senior feared that even this formidable group, while 'quite sound' in their views, faced an uphill struggle in preventing unwelcome legislation.[88]

The compromise wording worked out by Hobhouse defused an immediate rift by combining caution with commitment and fudging the question of whether Whately's report or the 1834 English law would form the template for Irish legislation. In the end the King was to urge parliament to approach the subject with due caution, while noting that the new English act might assist their deliberations.[89] The final appearance of Whately's report did nothing to resolve the impasse. It had long been clear that the Foxite and radical members of the administration would not accept his exclusion of relief from the able-bodied destitute. After an interview with Revans in early February, the lord lieutenant had concluded that its terms would be unworkable:

> [T]he archbishop has done incalculable mischief . . . the Report will disappoint everyone. I understand that it is only to recommend appointment of a central board which is to have no other authority than to authorise the levying of voluntary subscriptions upon local application being made for this purpose. This you will see is absolutely nugatory for any object either of the Philanthropists or the English landowner who objects to the unchecked inroad of Irish labourers. The provision to satisfy them or indeed to mean anything (whatever may be its extent) must be compulsory in its nature.[90]

While relieved at Whately's rejection of compulsory relief, his moderate allies had problems with the sprawling and ill-focused character of the report. They

86 Senior to Howick, 8 Jan., in Levy, *Senior*, pp. 266–8; NLW: NSP, Ms 23,858/I/E, fols 128–9, Howick to Senior, 23 Jan. 1836.

87 MC: NP, MM/101, Melbourne to Mulgrave, 8 Sept. 1836.

88 NLW: NSP, C/555, C/559, Senior to Whately, 19 Jan., 9 Feb. 1836.

89 *Hansard*, 3, xxxi, 4 (4 Feb. 1836).

90 NA: RP, PRO30/22/2A, fols 156–60, Mulgrave to Russell, 1 Feb. 1836.

were also decidedly uneasy at the implied centralizing powers of the Board of Improvement – which aimed to drain 'everything except patience' – and the likely costs of implementing the proposals.[91] At the same time, they were no more ready than in January to accede to the sort of alternative compulsory measure being contemplated by Russell and Duncannon.[92] Feelings were so strong on the matter in March 1836 that Senior also feared the question might fatally split the government.[93]

The result was a temporary impasse, with the cabinet deciding on 16 April, after considering Senior's commentary, to postpone the question for the remainder of that session.[94] As Morpeth had predicted, when announced this further delay led to an outcry in parliament and the Irish and English press.[95] Russell's explanation to the Commons stressed the excessive complexity and legislative incoherence of the third report and requested time for the preparation of alternative bills. As his impatient critics observed, however, this clashed with the promise given in the King's Speech. Damaging accusations of ministerial duplicity followed and Scrope and Smith O'Brien reinitiated their backbench campaigns.[96]

Nicholls' first report, 1836

Clearly, if progress was to be made on the measure, a way would have to be found to break first the cabinet, and then the potential parliamentary, logjam. It appears to have been this consideration which motivated Russell to select George Nicholls to carry out a further official investigation for the purpose of paving the way for an Irish poor law bill. Nicholls had several attractions for the mission. As an English commissioner with a background in practical administration he possessed the experience necessary to draft a report on which legislation could be constructed. Perhaps more importantly, he had, through his first intervention in January 1836, gained the confidence of Senior and Whately (and by extension their ministerial allies). He was also highly regarded by the opposition leader Sir Robert Peel.[97] Yet Russell must have believed him malleable enough to entrust him with a commission which

91 NLI: MP, Ms 553, p. 229, Spring Rice to Morpeth, 4 Apr. 1836.
92 MC: NP, M/103, Duncannon to Mulgrave, 25 Mar. 1836.
93 NLW: NSP, C/563, Senior to Whately, 17 Mar. 1836.
94 BL, Broughton diary, Add Ms 56,558, fol. 117, 16 Apr. 1836.
95 MC: NP, M/536, M/537, Morpeth to Mulgrave, 5, 13 Apr. 1836; *FJ*, 21 Apr., *The Times*, 20 Apr. 1836.
96 *Hansard*, 3, xxxii, 1167–8 [18 Apr.: Russell]; xxxiii, 590–602 [4 May 1836: Scrope, O'Brien].
97 Willink, 'Nicholls', pp. xxix–xxx, xxxvii–xxxviii.

would have been useless to the home secretary unless it came to a conclusion quite different to the one Nicholls had previously entertained – that a compulsory workhouse-based poor law for Ireland was practicable and desirable and that it could be modelled on the amended English system. Russell approached him in late July with a view to carrying out a short tour of inquiry of six to eight weeks restricted to the consideration of several 'chief points to which I shall draw your attention'.[98] After several interviews with the home secretary in early August, Nicholls was left in no doubt as to the real purpose and intended outcomes of his journey. Well before meeting Lewis in early September, Nicholls had shifted his ground on the fundamental question of the applicability of the workhouse system to Ireland.[99] He wrote candidly to his wife on 14 August:

> It (the Irish journey) really is anything but desirable, and it will very probably end in my being made a kind of scapegoat; whilst the labour, responsibility, and anxiety will be quite enough for what Georgie calls my 'figurehead.' Well, I see it all – the danger, the difficulty, the little chance of success, the great chance of failure; but I'll go on resolutely, fearlessly, and, if I live, will hope to succeed. There shall be nothing wanting on my part, if the Government will be firm and do their duty.[100]

A formal letter of appointment from Russell followed on 22 August, instructing Nicholls to proceed to Ireland in early September, there to direct his attention to those parts of the third report relating to relief of the poor by money payments and the resource of emigration: the possibility of relief to whole classes of poor without tests to guard against imposture, the practicability of rate-funded workhouse relief and applicability of the less-eligibility principle to Ireland, and the practical questions concerning rating and local administration of relief. He was also to review the existing relief bills in parliament, and one being prepared by one of the former commissioners.[101]

Russell's intentions were clearly telegraphed in his letter, and evidently understood by Nicholls, but if he was in any doubt he was instructed to liaise with Mulgrave and Morpeth at Dublin Castle before proceeding to the provinces. In turn the Irish ministers were told to facilitate his inquiries to the best of their abilities. There was no ambiguity in Russell's expectation of the outcome or Nicholls' role in it: 'I wish him to see how a poor law is likely to

98 Russell to Nicholls, 28 July 1836, in *ibid.*, p. xlv.

99 Lewis typically attributed Nicholls' conversion to his own powers of persuasion, but the timing of the encounter does not bear this out: NLW: HCP, C/2792, Lewis to Villiers, 8 Sept. 1836.

100 Nicholls to his wife, 14 Aug. 1836, in Willink, 'Nicholls', p. xlvi.

101 NA: HOP, HO122/17, fols 15–18, Russell to Nicholls, 22 Aug. 1836.

grow on Irish soil before we plant it.'[102] The executive decision had been taken – Nicholls' place was to rationalize the decision and prepare a practical plan for legislation and implementation.

By the time Nicholls arrived in Dublin in the second week of September, the lord lieutenant had already taken the opportunity of engaging on his own tour of inquiry into Irish distress. Potato failures in the north-west of the country had again given rise to acute distress and dire warnings of famine.[103] The confidential reports which Mulgrave received from Donegal in June revealed conditions so 'frightful and heartrending' that he concluded state intervention to prevent the starvation of twenty thousand people was urgently required. Drummond added that the 'cold-blooded indifference' of Lord Conyngham and other landowners was greatly to blame for the state of the poor.[104] Deciding to investigate the situation for himself, Mulgrave toured the famished districts of Donegal on horseback, reporting initially to Russell from Doe Castle in late August, before compiling a full report the following month. The tour had a political as well as an investigative purpose, with the viceroy's personal popularity doing much to counteract the negative impression created by the dropping of the poor law, along with other Irish measures, for that session.[105]

Writing at length to Russell, the lord lieutenant explicitly rejected the orthodox political-economic explanation for Ireland's poverty, at least so far as it applied to the north-western districts he had just observed:

> The North West coast of that county is as you are aware a district where the wretchedness and want of the people have most often reached the point of periodical destitution and starvation. It is rather curious that this lamentable effect has been here produced by distinct if not opposite causes from those which in the desire to generalize have been usually cited as the universal [origin] of the misery of the Irish people. Excess of population with absence of capital producing a demand for land disproportioned to the reward for labour has in other parts of Ireland directly caused most of the wretchedness and indirectly most of the crime of the population. But in Donegal there is no excess of population, nor any scarcity of very fine rich (though hitherto uncultivated) land. Nor is there in consequence any serious competition for it nor any disposition on the part of the landlords to let it nominally for much more than they know they can ever receive. They are nevertheless principally to blame for the wretched

102 NA: RP, PRO30/22/2C, fols 40–1, Nicholls to Russell, 3 Sept. 1836; MC: NP, M/840, Russell to Mulgrave, 12 Sept. 1836.

103 *FJ*, 28, 30 May 1836.

104 CHP, J/19/1/11, fols 72, 82, Mulgrave to Morpeth, 8 June, Drummond to Morpeth, 21 June 1836.

105 *FJ*, 29 Aug. 1836.

> uncivilized state of a fine country of which so much might be made. But their faults here are all [passion?] but action and consist of an utter neglect of their own interests as well as those of their tenants . . . It happens unfortunately that almost all the land here is in the hands of great absentee proprietors no one of whom depends upon his Donegal property.

He expressed a degree of personal shock at the conditions he had witnessed – 'the condition of the people in all these parts as to subsistence partakes more of the precarious nature of the savage state than I had previously supposed existed in any portion of the civilized world' – before passing on to discuss possible remedies. Emergency aid and infrastructural development were both desirable and within the realm of state action, but would not in themselves be sufficient. He concluded, 'local cooperation is the one thing wanted and strange to say the difficulty seems to be to get the landlords to act as if they had any interest in their properties . . . Any person in that position who began by showing interest in the welfare of their serfs (for they are little more) might do what he pleased with them.'[106] Mulgrave had prefaced this discussion by stating that he was currently devoting all his spare time to studying the poor-law question; although he still lacked a draft plan, he was now clearly of the opinion that an extensive measure was vital to oblige landowners to 'take an interest' in the rural poor on their estates. Russell evidently agreed that landlord neglect or oppression was 'in most parts the real cause of the misery degradation and consequent disorganization of the peasantry', and this shared opinion was forcibly communicated to Nicholls on his first meeting with Mulgrave the following week. In turn, the viceroy was 'much pleased with the temper in which he seemed disposed to commence his enquiries'.[107]

After these official interviews and visits to the Mendicity Institution and House of Industry in Dublin, Nicholls proceeded on a circular tour of Ireland, before finally returning to Dublin on 16 October 1836.[108] His interim reports contained very upbeat assessments of both the practicability of a workhouse-based poor law and the widespread popularity of such a measure, not only among the clergy and medical professionals, but also amongst 'the people', who he claimed to have interviewed in their cabins, as well as in the markets

106 NA: RP, PRO30/22/2B, fols 324–5, 2C, fols 114–19, Mulgrave to Russell, 27 Aug., 13 Sept. 1836. Compare with Nicholls' more orthodox reading in *Second Report of Geo. Nicholls . . . on Poor Laws, Ireland*, PP 1837–38 [104], xxxviii.657, pp. 12–13.

107 NA: RP, PRO30/22/2C, fols 166–7, Mulgrave to Russell, 22 Sept. 1836.

108 *Report of George Nicholls . . . on Poor Laws, Ireland*, PP 1837 [69], li.201, p. 3; CHP, J/19/1/13, fol. 45, Macdonald to Morpeth, 15 Oct. 1836. Nicholls kept a journal of all his dealings with the Irish poor-law question from August 1836 onwards, which is now unfortunately lost: see Nicholls, *Irish Poor Law*, p. 221.

and fields of the south. While some of his interviewees, including the Catholic Bishop Kinsella of Ossory, might have been 'a little unsound upon a point or two', Nicholls was typically confident in his own ability to persuade Irish opinion to accept the details of his plan of implementation. It was these impressions of a poor law as a rung of a popular 'justice to Ireland' policy that Morpeth endorsed in his covering letter to Russell as 'very satisfactory, very much perhaps because they coincide with those which I have ventured to form'.[109]

On returning to Dublin, Nicholls was again impressed with the urgency of the case in his meetings with officials and ministers. Duncannon arrived at Dublin Castle 'full of the necessity of beginning the "great measures" at once' and had several lengthy discussions with the commissioner, during which they appear to have reached substantial agreement on most points.[110] Duncannon was persuaded that Nicholls possessed the administrative knowledge vital for the drafting of a practical measure, and that his proposal was 'free . . . from all those fanciful and theoretical proposals, we have so often had promoted to us'.[111]

Nicholls was given one last, and less savoury, task to complete before returning to London to write up his report. On hearing of Nicholls' appointment, Whately had, understandably, regarded it as a calculated snub to himself and an attempt to undermine his commission's recommendations, and had, in the words of the viceroy, '*phophoed* him unmercifully', speaking of him 'with sovereign contempt as indeed he does of every one who crosses his path and refuses to mount behind him on the [back] of the hobby he happens to be then riding'.[112] Nevertheless, Russell was anxious that an attempt be made by Nicholls to persuade the former commissioners of the errors of their conclusions, if only for the sake of form. Morpeth suggested individual interviews rather than a potentially disastrous round-table conference, and Nicholls eventually called upon Vignoles, Killeen (now Earl of Fingall), Blake, Murray and Whately.[113] In the end, only the latter was openly hostile; despite Nicholls' optimistic hope that he might 'reconcile jarring opinions and bring about a

109 NA: RP, PRO30/22/2C, fols 188–9, 186–7, Nicholls to Morpeth, 23 Sept., Morpeth to Russell, 29 Sept. 1836; CHP, J/19/1/12, fol. 36, Nicholls to Morpeth, 10 Oct. 1836.

110 CHP, J/19/1/13, fols 45, 49, Macdonald to Morpeth, 15 Oct., Nicholls to Morpeth, 17 Oct.; NA: RP, PRO30/22/2C, fols 273–4, Nicholls to Russell, 17 Oct. 1836.

111 NA: RP, PRO30/22/2C, fols 287–8, Duncannon to Russell, 19 Oct. 1836.

112 Mulgrave to Russell, 22 Sept. 1836, *ibid.*, fols 166–7.

113 Morpeth to Russell, 5 Oct., *ibid.*, fols 218–19; CHP, J/19/1/13, fol. 43, Russell to Morpeth, 8 Oct.; NA: RP, PRO30/22/2C, fols 273–4, Nicholls to Russell, 17 Oct. 1836.

unity of action for the promotion of this great measure', their encounter was, in the words of one eyewitness, 'rather stormy'.[114]

For his part, Whately again demonstrated his talent for vituperation in his denunciation of Nicholls to his friends in England. His charge that Nicholls had simply confirmed his pre-existing 'ready made theories and plans' on his hurried tour, while substantially true, was somewhat disingenuous:

> The abuse of the public is in pretending that their opinion is, when it is not, derived from what they have observed here. 'Oh, but they have seen the state of things!' They have seen, that is, that there is distress, and dirt, and drunkenness – just what nobody in or out of Ireland doubts. But that on which the doubts exist, viz., whether this or that mode of remedy for those evils would be safe and effectual – have they seen this? or do they expect to see it before the trial is made? . . . They often, I believe, deceive themselves, as well as others, in the same way as the believers in ghost and fairy stories . . . [Nicholls] is, as far as I can judge, 'gone to listen to the bells.'

Taking a cynical view of the motivations of ministers on the matter, he feared something rash was in the offing, while hoping his political allies might yet be able to annul it, or that (as Senior suggested) the ministry would collapse before any measure came before parliament.[115]

Russell was evidently very pleased with the outcome of the exercise and welcomed the verbal report he received from his emissary in late October; with 'one or two essential limitations' (for example, setting a maximum rate), it would provide the basis for the long-desired legislative measure.[116] Nicholls formally submitted his first report to the home secretary on 15 November 1836.[117] The tone in which he expressed himself was rather different from that adopted by the Foxite ministers, and there were clear borrowings from Lewis, and to a lesser extent, Revans, but at the core of the report was a clear articulation of the principles agreed with Russell before his journey, and the proposals hammered out in his Dublin Castle meetings in October with Duncannon, Drummond and Mulgrave. In prefacing his recommendations Nicholls did not repudiate his previous conviction that Ireland was overpopulated, but

114 CHP, J/19/1/12, fol. 39, Macdonald to Morpeth, 29 Oct. Nicholls' optimism may have arisen from the apparent ease with which Archbishop Murray had shifted his ground on the question: Nicholls to Morpeth, 17 Oct. 1836, *ibid.*, J/19/1/13, fol. 49.

115 NLI: MP, Ms 13,382/1, Whately to Senior, 2 Oct. 1836; NLW: NSP, C/571, Senior to Whately, 5 Nov. 1836.

116 MC: NP, M/844, Russell to Mulgrave, 30 Oct. 1836.

117 *Report of George Nicholls*. Nicholls was subsequently to prepare two subsidiary reports on the same subject in 1837, see below, pp. 192–4.

now endorsed Lewis's and Revans' contention that it was the absence of legal provision for the destitute that had promoted excessive subdivision of holdings and early marriage. Also with the former, but against the latter, he endorsed the conventional economic opinion that agricultural consolidation and assimilation of the 'social and agricultural system of the two countries' was essential and that a poor law was necessary to underpin such a 'transitional period'.[118] He agreed with Revans, however, that it would break the 'circle of evils' presently depressing the Irish economy, by giving real security for the investment of capital and the creation of employment.[119] Nicholls' preoccupation with the morally debilitated condition of the Irish poor, verging at times on negative ethnic stereotyping but checked by his conviction that the national character was malleable and not determined, echoed his own background as an English poor-law reformer. Irish behavioural flaws, he asserted, closely resembled those of the English peasantry in the pauperized districts under the old English poor law; an Irish poor law based on the principles of the English reform act of 1834 could not fail to have the same beneficial moral effects.[120]

At the heart of the document lay an authoritative refutation of the central elements of the Whately report. The purported merits of voluntarism were undermined by an examination of the actual (as opposed to theoretical) operation of the Scottish system, and yet more so by the dismal failure of the Dublin Mendicity Association in practice. Irish public opinion was, Nicholls continued, strongly in favour of an extended poor law based on the proven model of the amended English system, not least because it would lift a significant portion of the current burden from the poor themselves and compel economic engagement and co-operation on the part of all classes.[121] The workability of the workhouse test in Ireland had been proven both by the tractability of the Irish poor in English workhouses (as well as within the existing houses of industry in Ireland), and the requirement that less eligibility be enforced through confinement and regulation (providing all relief was indoors) rather than through diet or clothing.[122] Any practical problems relating to the establishment of a suitable structure could easily be overcome so long as the existing English model was adopted (with a few modifications) as a template, and considerable latitude given to the central authority in the formation of unions and establishment of regulations. The most important

118 Lewis welcomed Nicholls' report as being in agreement with his own 'on all the main points', NLW: HCP, C/2798, Lewis to Villiers, 5 Feb. 1837.

119 *Report of George Nicholls*, p. 12.

120 *Ibid.*, pp. 5–7.

121 *Ibid.*, pp. 7–9.

122 *Ibid.*, pp. 12–15.

'modifications' included some elements which Chadwick and Senior may have wished to incorporate into the English reform, but lacked the political support to impose in one step upon the existing infrastructure. These included the denial of all outdoor relief, the legal recognition that relief should be at the discretion of the guardians rather than 'of right', the exclusion of a law of settlement, and of the bastardy laws associated with the English poor law, and the requirement that applicants enter as family units rather than as individuals. All were justified as necessary in Irish existing circumstances, but also reflected an ideal form of the English law to which the Poor Law Commissioners (with the exception of T. F. Lewis) may have aspired. Their application to Ireland would subsequently be the focus of significant controversy in the following years.

Although later denounced for adopting a reductively narrow view of the question of Irish poverty, Nicholls was careful not to present his proposal as a panacea or to rule out auxiliary measures. 'A system of Poor Laws', he insisted, 'must not be expected to work miracles. It would not immediately give employment or capital; but it would, I think, serve to help the country through what may be called its *transition period*; and in time, and with the aid of other circumstances, would effect a material improvement in the condition of the Irish people.'[123] Poor laws could not be expected to cope with conditions of famine (although they might serve to address the underlying causes of such crises).[124] A subsidiary memo prepared with Chadwick's assistance stressed that the system would be both relatively cheap and manageable in numbers in 'ordinary' seasons. Workhouse accommodation would only 'occasionally' be required for 1 per cent of the population, or 80,000 persons. One hundred workhouses, each accommodating up to 800, would be required. Assuming three-quarters occupancy throughout the year, at a weekly maintenance cost of one shilling and sixpence per head, the entire system would cost the ratepayers no more than £260,000 annually.[125] These had something of back-of-the-envelope calculations about them and would subsequently be subjected to acute scrutiny. The clear preference for large unions, which followed Chadwick's conviction that these would always prove more cost-effective and capable of superior management, would also prove controversial in Ireland.[126]

123 *Ibid.*, p. 9.
124 *Ibid.*, p. 21.
125 NA: HOP, HO100/247, fols 340–1, Nicholls memo, 20 Jan. 1837. Nicholls based his calculation of need on the percentage on indoor relief in the four southern English counties formerly most pauperized and now most completely under the new poor law regime.
126 [Edwin Chadwick], 'The New Poor Law', *ER*, 63 (July 1836), esp. pp. 509–11.

Nicholls did not wholly reject the alternative remedial measures which the Whately Commission had advocated, but separated them from the question of poor relief and subordinated them to the introduction of a poor law. Assisted emigration might, he concluded, be desirable in certain overpopulated regions, but it should never be forced unnaturally. Any abstract benefits from emigration risked being offset by the export of the active and healthy, leaving a residuum of the less robust or resolute at home. Only the workhouse test could prove the existence of a permanent surplus of able-bodied labourers in a district; where this was the case, the state and the poor law union should share the costs of assisted emigration of these to a British colony.[127] Nicholls was vaguer on other 'auxiliaries'. Large amounts of additional employment could, he claimed, be created through the application of capital to the reclamation of the vast tracts of waste and bog land in Ireland, and to a lesser extent in the development of fisheries and forestries. He was reluctant, however, to recommend any direct state intervention in these fields beyond permissive legislation.[128] Nicholls had become persuaded during his visits that the underlying problem of Irish poverty could best be addressed by improving the modes of agricultural production. Although not opposed to consolidation, he appears not to have been as persuaded as Lewis that the optimal future lay in a transition to large-scale farming; indeed, in his subsequent period as resident Poor Law Commissioner in Ireland, he prepared an agricultural manual for small farmers (largely modelled on William Blacker's essays) advising on methods of increasing productivity on existing holdings, and came to regard the poor law as an educative engine for promoting agricultural improvement.[129]

The Nicholls report provided in its recommendations a definite and authoritative plan upon which the ministers could construct a legislative measure. It does not follow that Nicholls' rationalizations or indeed his ultimate vision of the poor law were identical with those of Russell and his circle. Nicholls had begun the year with a very different 'take' on the question from that which he formally presented in November. While this shift may have partially arisen from the evolution of his own thought, the evidence points to its arising substantially from the political influence and pressure placed upon him by the ministers, and to some extent also from Lewis. However, there

127 *Report of George Nicholls*, pp. 30–2.

128 *Ibid.*, pp. 10–11, 30–1.

129 [George Nicholls], *The Farmer's Guide: Compiled for the Use of the Small Farmer and Cottier Tenantry in Ireland* (2nd edn, Dublin, 1842). For Nicholls' promotion of the creation of an agricultural improvement society connected with the unions, see *Seventh Annual Report of the Poor Law Commissioners*, PP 1841 [327], xi.291, p. 62.

was a price to be paid for the workable legislative plan with which Nicholls presented his patrons. While he may have been quite right to enthuse on the popularity of a putative poor law in Ireland, the restrictive template based on a streamlined version of English poor law practice was not likely to produce the 'popular' social welfare measure which the Foxites so craved.

Following the presentation of Nicholls' report, Russell lost no time in proceeding to make it the foundation of legislation for the forthcoming parliamentary session. Not delaying to have it printed, the home secretary had manuscript copies distributed to the cabinet in mid-November 1836, along with a memo prepared by Morpeth and approved by Duncannon and Mulgrave, containing a series of heads for a poor law bill.[130] The lord lieutenant endorsed this sense of urgency, declaring the poor law now to be the 'question of questions' in Ireland.[131]

Morpeth's paper came to broadly similar conclusions as Nicholls' report, but used markedly different language. Whately's bundle of ameliorative measures he rejected as being not wrong in themselves, but as an inadequate and expensive answer to the recurring ethical question of destitution: 'Will you suffer a person, able bodied though he be, to die of starvation in a Christian land?' The employment proposals should be considered as distinct measures in their own right, but as subsidiary to rather than substitutes for a comprehensive poor law. There were also some differences of substance between Morpeth's paper and Nicholls' report: Morpeth favoured an Irish Poor Law Commission sitting in Dublin rather than incorporation of Irish business into that of the London commission, and he followed the Whately report in opting for a 2 : 1 ratio in allocating the rates burden between the landlord and the occupying tenant, as opposed to Nicholls' proposal of 1 : 1.[132] Although there was significant support in Ireland for allowing the ratepaying tenant to deduct the higher proportion of rate from his rent, it was the formula of equal shares that would find its way into the bill.[133]

Nicholls, meanwhile, had received strong support for his proposals from Chadwick, technically his subordinate as secretary to the English commission, but in practice the chief architect of the English central administration and a crucial figure in poor-law policy-making. Chadwick had expressed with some vigour his support for extending the reformed poor law to Ireland as early as March 1835, arguing that the less-eligibility principle was easily transferable,

130 NA: RP, PRO30/22/2D, fol. 40, Russell memo, 16 Nov.; Morpeth to Russell, 19 Nov. 1836, *ibid.*, fols 42–3.

131 Mulgrave to Russell, 5 Nov. 1836, *ibid.*, fols 14–23.

132 NLI: MP, Ms 13,385/5, Morpeth memo, [Nov. 1836].

133 Smith O'Brien urged the government to retain the original ratio as a greater incentive to the landlord, *Hansard*, 3, xxxviii, 401 [28 Apr. 1837].

as 'living in workhouses was extremely irksome to the poor, and particularly to the Irish, who loved rambling and quarrelling and drinking whisky, and would prefer even labour to the regularity and confinement of the workhouse'.[134] Chadwick and Nicholls had exchanged correspondence while the latter was in Ireland in which they expressed complete agreement with each other's views, although Chadwick did not see the finished report until sent a copy by Howick.[135] Support from quite a different political quarter was provided by the King, whom Russell represented to his colleagues as being very interested in the Irish poor-law question and supportive of Nicholls' approach of a workhouse-based system.[136] The King's endorsement may, as Russell later suggested, have been grounded his persuasion that co-operation on the boards would tend to 'soften religious animosities, and teach the members of the different creeds to act together in harmony for a work of charity'.[137]

Drafting the bill, 1836–37

With his forces thus marshalled, Russell was now ready to take the matter to the cabinet in early December. Lansdowne and Spring Rice continued to resist, and proposed that any poor law be partial and experimental (i.e. restricted to certain localities), but other opponents this time kept a discreet silence. While it may have swayed some waverers, Nicholls' report had failed to persuade the chancellor that his previous resistance had been wrong – the objections to relief of the able-bodied remained, in his mind, 'insuperable'. Such an enactment would 'strike a blow at the whole social system of the country – check industry, retard civilization and introduce an uncertainty with respect to all property. It supplies the only element of mischief from which we have hitherto been protected.'[138] Lansdowne was soon to be armed against the Nicholls report by a 130-page memorandum rejecting the workhouse system on the grounds of Ireland's social backwardness, almost certainly penned by his associate, the Poor Inquiry Commissioner J. E. Bicheno.[139]

134 Extract from J. L. Mallet's diaries, March 1835, in *Political Economy Club*, p. 267.

135 DUL: GP, 80/17, Chadwick to Howick, 19 Nov.; UCL: CP, 1733/127, Chadwick to Russell, 21 Nov. 1836.

136 MC: NP, M/850, Russell to Mulgrave, 1 Dec. [1836].

137 John, Earl Russell, *A Letter to the Right Hon. Chichester Fortescue, MP, on the State of Ireland* (3rd edn, 1868), pp. 13–14.

138 NA: RP, PRO30/22/2D, fol. 49, Spring Rice to Russell, 20 Nov. 1836.

139 BL: BP, B/145, [J. E. Bicheno], 'Memorandum on the state of Ireland and on the applicability of the workhouse system to its relief, 1837'. See below, pp. 248–9.

The report's enthusiastic supporters took the opposite view; for Howick a bill based on Nicholls' recommendations would finally 'begin the work (which cannot be said to be as yet commenced) of really civilizing Ireland'. He endorsed Lewis's developmental vision of an Irish poor law, but located this within his own anti-Malthusian economic 'optimism'. The 'only escape' from this poverty-trap lay in 'a good system of poor laws', which would not directly relieve all the distresses of Ireland, but bring about 'the removal of the causes which prevent society from proceeding in a natural and healthy course'.[140] Therein lay the core of Howick's subsequent 'moralist' attitude towards the role of the poor law in Ireland.

A cabinet committee was appointed to resolve the issue, containing the sceptics Lansdowne and Palmerston, but with a strongly pro-poor-law majority of Howick, Thomson, Duncannon and Russell.[141] Several issues were quickly resolved. Mulgrave and Morpeth had a strong preference for a Dublin-based supervisory commission, combining the political popularity of a local institution with the expertise of Nicholls or other English appointees, but did not protest when overruled by a majority which favoured the allocation of formal responsibility to the established English commission.[142] Duncannon's observation that an English-staffed commission sitting in Dublin would be of no political benefit may have been decisive.[143] At the same time, it was recognized that the regular conduct of Irish business from Somerset House would prove problematic. The compromise found was that Ireland would have a poor law board sitting in Dublin, presided over by an English commissioner (or an assistant commissioner deputizing for him), and reporting to the London commission and home office.[144]

On the more substantial issue, Lansdowne and his allies thought better of trying to oppose outright the Nicholls proposals in the cabinet or its committee at this point; Lansdowne was absent at Bowood when the cabinet discussed the question again on 10 December, while Senior made a point

140 UCL: CP, Ms 887, Howick to Chadwick, 21 Nov. 1836; DUL: GP, Howick memo 'Paper on reasons for making legal provision for relief of poor in Ireland' [1836].

141 BL: Broughton diary, Add Ms 61,827, fols 89–90 (4 Dec. 1836).

142 NA: RP, PRO30/22/2D, fols 117–21, 129, 131, 133, 141–2, Mulgrave to Russell, 4 Dec., Morpeth to Russell, 12 Dec., memos by Howick, Thomson and Spring Rice, 7 Dec. 1836.

143 Duncannon memo, [Dec. 1836], *ibid.*, fol. 127.

144 This arrangement was inserted in the draft bill despite the scepticism of Duncannon and Howick: see marginal comments in NA: HOP, HO100/247, fol. 46, Draft Bill for the Relief of the Destitute Poor in Ireland [1837].

of giving 'assent' to the plan on meeting Russell several days later.[145] This represented not surrender, but a shift of tactics. Any attempt to introduce the poor law partially and 'experimentally', Lansdowne observed, while desirable, could only delay the inevitable. A better tactic would be to outflank it by launching 'the emigration system so as to let it work a head [sic] of the workhouse system, and it should if possible be made sweet . . . as the other must be made bitter to the national taste.'[146] Nevertheless, certain concessions would still have to be made to the sceptics to facilitate the formation of an agreed bill and its passage through parliament; especially when Lansdowne hinted that otherwise it must be considered an open question within the cabinet and potentially the cause of its dissolution.[147]

The cabinet formally adopted Nicholls' report on 13 December and directed him to prepare a bill based on its recommendations the following day.[148] He was assisted in this by John Meadows White, the parliamentary solicitor, who had also participated in the drafting of the English Amendment Act, and whose views on Ireland were in parallel with his own. White supported the immediate introduction of a comprehensive workhouse network, on the grounds that a staged introduction would be more dangerous. He rejected settlement and a right to relief (which he glossed as 'a right to be idle'), and endorsed the grant of extensive discretionary powers to the central body charged with establishing the system in Ireland.[149] These points were agreed with the exception of the first; Irish unions would be declared when ready, but with the understanding that the commission would proceed rapidly to extend a uniform system throughout the country.

Russell also contributed to the shaping of the measure in detail through a lengthy memo he prepared in December and regular supervision of the drafting process at the home office. After discussions with Nicholls and the cabinet, Russell was now of the opinion that if the poor law for Ireland could only pass the legislature in a limited and tentative form, this was best acknowledged in the preamble so as not to raise false expectations. Such an act would deviate from the English act in the denial of an absolute right to relief, and restrict its attentions to the most distressed and suffering members of the community through workhouse relief only. This emphasis on providing a safety net for those *in extremis* ruled out (at least in the first instance) any poor-law expenditure on emigration or apprenticeships. At the same time, it also, by

145 BL: Broughton diary, Add Ms 61,827, fols 90–1, 10 Dec.; NLI: MP, Ms 13,382/11, Russell to Spring Rice, 17 Dec. 1836.

146 NLI: MP, Ms 13,382/8, Lansdowne to Spring Rice, 15 Dec. 1836.

147 NA: RP, PRO30/22/2D, fols 216–18, Lansdowne to Russell, 18 Dec. 1836.

148 Nicholls, *Irish Poor Law*, pp. 188–9.

149 NLW: NSP, D/21, John Meadows White, memo on Irish poor, 28 Dec. 1836; Brundage, *Making of the New Poor Law*, pp. 48–51.

its very limitation, made it impossible for the state to take any further legal action against mendicancy or vagrancy; the absence of a right to relief would also negate the necessity and hence the complication of settlement regulations. Russell was insistent that rates should be determined and levied locally rather than nationally to ensure local interest in their expenditure and active participation in the representative boards of guardians. He agreed with Nicholls on the crucial importance of a regulatory central authority, favouring an Irish board with a staff of assistant commissioners, responsible both to the central commission in London and to ministers in London and Dublin.[150]

Russell's memo represented a pragmatic scaling down of the more extended aspirations of both the ministerial and extra-parliamentary advocates of an Irish poor law. The decision not to grant a right to relief ran contrary to the emphasis placed on this point by both Morpeth and Revans, but was in line with Nicholls' more cautious proposals. However, Russell's opinion that mendicancy could not be outlawed without granting such a right contradicted the Nicholls report and (given the strong desire for criminalization of vagrancy on the part of sceptics such as Senior and Lansdowne) could be regarded as the creation of an incentive towards a future extension of the scope of the poor law.[151] Although the vagrancy clauses and the explicit statement that the measure's aim was to suppress mendicancy were reinserted into the 1837 bill, Russell (along with Howick and Duncannon) obviously doubted their legitimacy, and the suppression of mendicancy was omitted from the preface of the reintroduced bill of 1837–38, and the vagrancy clauses dropped in the course of that bill's passage through the Commons.[152]

This scaling down of the scope of the poor law may have been a rational recognition of the forthcoming legislative difficulties facing the measure (pre-echoed by the dogged opposition of its opponents in cabinet), but it inevitably entailed a mass of disappointed expectations both in Ireland and Britain. Feelers put out to leading figures in the parliamentary opposition had indicated their preference for a minimalist provision. Edward Stanley thought Nicholls' recommendations right in the main, if still insufficient to protect ratepayers from the seasonal influx of smallholding paupers into the wealthier districts of the country.[153] Sir James Graham was also generally welcoming,

150 NA: RP, PRO30/22/2D, fols 143–60, Russell memo, [Dec. 1836].

151 NLI: MP, Ms 13,385/5, Morpeth memo [Nov. 1836]; *Report of George Nicholls*, pp. 10, 21, 27–8; Willink, 'Nicholls', p. xlviii.

152 NA: HOP, HO100/247, fols 41, 133–52, Draft Bill, marginal comments by Howick and Duncannon expressing doubt over vagrancy clauses. See also below, pp. 179–80.

153 Stanley to Russell, 18 Dec. 1836, *ibid.*, fols 220–1. Stanley suggested a provision to prevent this 'abuse' which was similar to what would ultimately be enacted in 1847 as the 'quarter acre clause'.

but doubted the wisdom of omitting a law of settlement and consequently 'the *absolute* claim to relief, [which] will leave mendicancy with an excuse, and, I fear, unchecked'.[154] Despite these quibbles, the decision to base the bill on the recommendations of Nicholls, a man respected by moderate Conservatives as well as moderate Whig-liberals, proved a master-stroke. Unlike the government's other Irish measures, the poor law bill would not become the subject of party-political warfare in parliament.

Preparations of the Irish poor law bill continued through January 1837, with further contributions from Duncannon and Chadwick on the practical details of preparing a union-based workhouse system and estimating its likely costs. Chadwick made a strong case for triennial rather than annual elections of guardians, on the grounds that a rapid turnover of members imposed on the commission the frequent necessity of 'catching and taming a set of wild horses to work in team', but Russell appears to have overruled this preference for administrative efficiency over the principle of representation.[155] Although limited in scope, widespread and regular public participation in the operations of the act was still regarded as vital to its wider political success.

The cabinet met again on 4 February to review the draft bill, with Nicholls and Morpeth (who was not a cabinet member until February 1839) present by invitation. Emigration again appears to have been the main point of contention, with open dissension over the inclusion of emigration clauses within the bill only avoided by another uneasy compromise.[156] This issue could only be put off for so long, but the agreed wording was sufficient to allow the bill to be printed and proceed to its first reading in the Commons a week later. For his part, the prime minister expressed a weary indifference towards the initiative, declaring to Mulgrave that 'the great evil of Ireland is its hopeless . . . poverty – a Poor Law does not appear at first sight a remedy for this evil.'[157] Despite such scepticism, an Irish poor law bill, alongside the reintroduced tithes and municipal corporations bills, would form the principal Irish proposals for the 1837 session. At the same time it was no secret that the ministry remained acutely divided over the measure, and the evident reluctance of anti-poor-law ministers to defend the bill in parliament became a focus of regular commentary. Press critics chose to read their refusal to openly

154 Graham to Nicholls, 10 Feb. 1837, in Willink, 'Nicholls', p. l.

155 NA: RP, PRO30/22/2E, fol. 48, Duncannon to Russell, [Jan. 1837]; Chadwick to Russell, 19 Jan. [1837], *ibid.*, fols 26–9; UCL: CP, 1733/132, Chadwick to Russell, 2 Feb. 1837.

156 BL: Broughton diary, Add Ms 61,827, fols 104–6 (4 Feb. 1837). Lansdowne continued to press for a limited application alongside emigration provision, NA: RP, PRO30/22/2E, fol. 130, Lansdowne memo, [Mar. 1837].

157 MC: NP, MM/152, Melbourne to Mulgrave, 18 Apr. 1837.

oppose the hubristic fanaticism of Russell on the subject as a cynical prioritization of place over principle.[158]

Railways, emigration and Irish poverty

The Whig ministry has often been criticized for ignoring those aspects of the Whately report which recommended extensive state investment in infrastructural and agricultural improvement projects to promote employment. While Whately's proposal of such projects as an alternative to an extensive poor law was, as we have seen, rejected by the majority of ministers and their advisors from 1835, it does not follow that work-creation (or facilitation) projects were dismissed, and indeed 'auxiliary measures' were envisaged, with a greater or lesser degree of enthusiasm, by most members of the government as being essential to the successful introduction of a poor law. The reduced scope of the poor law bill that emerged in early 1837, alongside the continuing agitation for assisted emigration from Lansdowne and Senior, and the attempts by Whately and his associates to introduce their own schemes as backbench measures, may have rendered this more rather than less necessary in the minds of the Foxite ministers.

In fact, preparatory plans were already well under way for a landmark public works project that would, it was hoped, combine the desiderata of providing extensive employment for unskilled labourers across Ireland with a sustained stimulation of private employment, while remaining conceptually separate from the poor law. The Irish Railway Commission, which was to recommend in 1838 the establishment of an extensive state-constructed and controlled railway network, is rarely viewed as connected in any way with the poor-law question.[159] However, a closer examination of its chronology and the political considerations surrounding its establishment and operations suggests that it can legitimately be regarded as forming part of a common strategy with the poor law bill for the economic development of Ireland and the redressing of the structural problems of poverty in that country. Indeed, the contextual aspects of the railway report, setting out the socio-economic conditions of the country, might usefully be considered as an alternative poor inquiry report.

The first official suggestions that a railway inquiry be established for Ireland date from summer 1836, and followed pressure in parliament for the

158 *The Times*, 10 Feb. 1838.

159 MacDonagh treats it as an organic development emerging from the Board of Works: Oliver MacDonagh, 'Ideas and institutions, 1830–45', in Vaughan (ed.), *New History of Ireland*, v, p. 208.

government to consider the matter. Colonel John Burgoyne, the chairman of the Board of Works, was initially unsure as to what the government's intentions were, but recommended an expert inquiry that would forestall the wasteful competition that had characterized railway development in England, by producing an authoritative report setting out the optimal lines for development. He made no suggestion, however, that the state should undertake the construction of such a network by itself.[160]

Responsibility for the inquiry soon passed, however, to Drummond and the lord lieutenant. Both insisted that control should lie with Dublin Castle and the Home Office rather than at the Treasury (which had immediate oversight of the Board of Works). Their reasons were both political and strategic; it was important, they urged, that the Irish government and home secretary receive the popular credit for any major railway initiative. Mulgrave believed he now had sufficient knowledge of the country to direct its operations effectively, and had Burgoyne's support for this. Moreover, Irish government control would make it more likely that the outcome would be 'a great public work', unencumbered by the 'petit economies' likely to arise from Treasury oversight.[161] Russell endorsed this and Drummond proceeded to organize the railway commission; it was formally constituted on 20 October 1836 as a body of four commissioners – Drummond, Burgoyne, Richard Griffith and Peter Barlow, professor of mathematics at the Royal Military Academy, Woolwich (and Drummond's former tutor), with Captain Harry Jones of the Board of Works as secretary.[162] The bypassing of Treasury oversight may have been of crucial importance in shaping their work – the commissioners appear to have disregarded a Treasury minute of 3 November insisting that it was 'the duty of the Government to guard against any inference that it is their intention to interfere with private enterprize', and that it should be understood that 'no intention or pledge is either expressed or implied that works of this description should be undertaken at the public expense.'[163] In preparing the first, interim, report in March 1837, the commissioners explicitly linked the desirability of railway development in Ireland to the distressed conditions of the labouring poor, and defended the

160 NLI: MP, Ms 13,382/3, Burgoyne to Spring Rice, 29 Aug. 1836.

161 NA: RP, PRO30/22/2C, fols 70–1, 159–63, 168–71, Mulgrave to Russell, 7 Sept., Drummond to Mulgrave, 25 Sept., Mulgrave to Russell, 28 Sept. 1836.

162 MC: NP, M/842, Russell to Mulgrave, 29 Sept. 1836; *First Report of the Commissioners appointed to inquire into the Manner in which Railway Communications can be most advantageously promoted in Ireland*, PP 1837 [75], xxxiii.283, pp. 3–4.

163 *Treasury Minute, dated 3 November 1836, respecting the Railroad Commission for Ireland*, PP 1837–38 (654), xlvi. 481.

developmental function of public works.[164] This was a clear statement of intent. When a renewed commission was prepared following the King's death in summer 1837, the original clause proposing that the commission would aid joint-stock companies in selecting the best lines was quietly dropped.[165]

The second report, published the following year, featured an extensive plan for a state-sponsored railway infrastructure, again located within the context of the poor-law initiative. The commissioners pronounced:

> [A]n effective poor-law must greatly assist the object we are considering; and it is therefore most desirable that its provisions should be carried into effect promptly and fully. It should be recollected, however, that the landed interest will be taxed heavily for the support of the poor under the act, and it would, therefore, be a most auspicious introduction of so great a change in the social state of the country, if the pressure of the measure were lightened by the commencement of some works of great magnitude, which would last for a considerable time, and afford employment to large numbers of the people in various parts of Ireland. And if such undertakings were of a nature evidently calculated to open new avenues to industry, and thus hold out a reasonable prospect of constant occupation, even after the period of their completion, the anxiety which, both on the grounds of humanity and policy, must attend the adoption of so great a change, would be allayed, and the most formidable of its immediate inconveniences be effectually obviated.[166]

Other auxiliary measures involving the expansion of the powers and expenditure of the Board of Works relating to inland navigation and arterial drainage were also under consideration, and pushed by the Irish government on the chancellor.[167] The poor law was thus not intended by ministers to be a free-standing measure, but part of a comprehensive policy initiative involving considerable state intervention in the economy. Their difference with Whately was in thinking that these objects were complementary rather than contradictory.

The one area which remained highly contentious was assisted emigration – either on a national or local scale – as an auxiliary measure. In November 1836 Howick had noted that of the 'subsidiary measures' necessary to

164 *First Report of the Railway Commissioners*, p. 9.

165 Russell subsequently denied knowledge of this alteration: *Hansard*, 3, xlv, 1059–60 [1 Mar. 1839].

166 *Second Report of the Royal Commission appointed to Inquire into the Manner in which Railway Communications can be Most Advantageously Promoted in Ireland*, PP 1837–38 [145], xxxv.449. For a discussion of the operation of the railway commission, see A. R. G. Griffiths, *The Irish Board of Works, 1831–1878* (New York, 1987), pp. 42–6.

167 MC: NP, M/560, Morpeth to Mulgrave, 18 May 1837.

accompany the poor law, large-scale emigration would probably be required as a one-off step rather than as forming part of the poor law itself.[168] Over the following months he hardened his stance against any form of assisted emigration, and was joined in this by Russell. This put them onto a collision course with Lansdowne and Spring Rice on an issue that needed to be resolved by the cabinet before the poor law bill's clauses received detailed scrutiny in parliament.

Howick explained his thinking in an exchange of letters with Senior in spring 1837. What Ireland needed now, he wrote, was short-term employment for the able-bodied poor on public works, while other classes of destitutes were taken into the new workhouses. The social peace created by this double-pronged approach would create the conditions for the influx of investment capital, which in turn would obviate the necessity of sustained state intervention in the labour market, or assisted emigration. The latter was undesirable for three reasons – it would be less cost-effective, would arouse antagonism in the colonies, and would be unpopular in parliament and with British opinion.[169] While Howick was prepared to admit Senior's authority as a political economist, he would not be budged in his conviction that the solution to Ireland's problems did not lie in emigration.[170] Russell and his associates appear to have taken an equally clear decision that any assistance to emigration under the poor law would be marginal, and that the principal auxiliaries would involve employment within Ireland itself. Assisted emigration was omitted from the 1837 bill, although it was restored, in a minimal form permitting guardians to raise a supplementary rate to aid union emigration, in the subsequent bill of 1837–8.

Another area of the proposed poor law which received some clarification in the early months of 1837 was its relationship with the existing charitable institutions for the poor in Ireland. Nicholls had recommended their incorporation into the new poor-law structures and subordination to the controlling commission. This ran directly contrary to the views of the majority on the Whately Commission, which had envisaged the role of the state as that of an auxiliary supporter of the work of the voluntary sector. Nicholls' position was strengthened by the stance taken by the committee of the Dublin Mendicity Institution. This was the largest and most prominent of the existing charitable bodies, but had long suffered from severe funding crises, and had been saved from bankruptcy in September 1836 only by a personal donation from Morpeth.[171] A sub-committee of its governing body responded posi-

168 DUL: GP, 155/1, Howick memo, [Nov. 1836].

169 NLW: NSP, C/118, Howick to Senior, 14 Mar. 1837.

170 Howick to Senior, 18 May, Senior to Howick, 30 May 1837, *ibid.*, C/120, C/121.

171 *FJ*, 24, 27 Sept. 1836.

tively to the government's bill, and welcomed the early replacement of the Institution by a workhouse (although they questioned the wisdom of housing the able-bodied and infirm together, and thought it desirable that the system remain capable of enlargement if the initial form was found too narrow in operation). Russell's 'cautious' plan was desirable, they thought, not least because it 'admits without difficulty of the aid and co-operation of other remedial measures should it be found desirable to adopt them'. They also agreed with Nicholls that while the granting of outdoor relief in cash might appear 'merciful', the practice, once admitted, would be subject to unstoppable abuses.[172] Attempts by Blake and Hort to prevent the Mendicity's committee reporting adversely on the third report (which both had signed) had been overturned by majority vote.[173] This outcome no doubt strengthened Russell's hand in defending his bill in parliament, and the report was subsequently cited by Nicholls in support of the total exclusion of outdoor relief under the Irish bill.[174]

Other soundings by the Home Office on the likely operation of a workhouse-based poor law were less encouraging. One correspondent from Drogheda who had consulted a number of poor labourers in his district on the subject found (hardly surprisingly) that they would be extremely reluctant to enter the workhouse with their families, and would prefer the less degrading payment of an outdoor allowance in case of destitution.[175] Such confirmation of abhorrence of the workhouse may have endorsed Nicholls' case for the workhouse as a strict test of absolute destitution, but had obvious implications for its limitations as an engine for agricultural 'transition', at least under 'normal' circumstances, or its function as a 'popular' measure of 'justice to Ireland'.

By early 1837 a poor law bill based generally on Nicholls' first report had been prepared. It represented a partial compromise between different factions within the administration, but at the same time a clear defeat for Richard Whately and his allies within and outside the administration. However, this bill would have to be steered through the fractious and stormy seas of parliament before it could be turned into anything concrete.

172 NA: HOP, HO100/251, fols 78–83, 122–4, Thomas Abbott and Joseph Burke to Nicholls, 3 March 1837, Russell, 3 March 1837. In marginal notes, Russell commented that the separation of classes before the opening of new buildings would set a 'dangerous' precedent, and that the Mendicity Institutions would be rendered redundant on the opening of the union workhouses.

173 Report of AGM of the Dublin Mendicity Association, *FJ*, 10 Jan. 1837.

174 *Hansard*, 3, xxxviii, 452 [1 May 1837]; *Second Report of Geo. Nicholls*, p. 21.

175 NA: HOP, HO100/251, fols 110–11, Philip Mullan to Benjamin Ball, 2 Apr. 1837.

6

The poor law bills in parliament, 1837–38

The 'high political' history of the passage of the Irish poor law bills through parliament during the successive sessions of 1837 and 1837–38 is worthy of consideration in some detail. The legislation prepared by Russell and his advisors in 1836–37 already involved elements of compromise and was drafted with an eye to the difficulties of carrying such a contentious measure through a Commons in which the Whig-liberal government lacked disciplinary controls over a fractious following and was facing growing instability, and through a House of Lords dominated by its political opponents. Both the terms of the bill and the rhetoric with which it was invested needed to appeal to a range of political constituencies if it was to stand any chance of legislative success. Conservative and orthodox liberal scepticism on the desirability of any Irish poor law needed to be neutralized; British popular opinion in its favour enlisted but also held in check; and the pro-poor lobby in Ireland mollified over the limitations of the measure on the table. This required careful management and effective argument by ministers.

This chapter considers the modalities by which the bill was passed, the parliamentary rhetoric employed by ministers and supporters of the measure, the reasons for the failure of its parliamentary opponents, and the compromises involved in its passage. It also considers the fate of the 'auxiliary measures' associated with the poor law bills proper, most importantly the measures arising from the 1838 Railway Commission report. The following two chapters consider the parallel 'outdoor' debates in Ireland and Britain on the government's measures and the parliamentary proceedings associated with them.

The 1837 bill in the Commons

The Poor Relief (Ireland) Bill was introduced into the Commons by Lord John Russell on 13 February 1837.[1] His speech set out both the main terms of the bill and its underlying rationale and aspirations. The latter combined

1 *A Bill for the more effectual Relief of the Destitute Poor in Ireland*, PP 1837 (38), iii.451.

reference to the generic principles Russell took to characterize all effective poor laws, with a discussion of the specific problems and requirements of Ireland. Without adequate provision for destitution, he asserted, any country would remain subject to the moral hazards associated with unchecked mendicancy. A poor law would be in the first instance a measure tending to create social peace, and would thus allow the prohibition of vagrancy and its associated vices; this could not ethically or humanely be enforced without establishing an alternative provision.[2]

Secondly, a poor law was an instrument of social concord whereby the state and the community demonstrated their concern for 'the welfare of all classes', and, more specifically, placed property-owners under an obligation to concern themselves with the interests of their tenants and neighbours. By placing the financial responsibility for destitution principally upon them, it gave them a direct interest in preventing the impoverishment of their dependants. These, Russell asserted, were the fundamental principles underlying the Elizabethan poor law, which had brought incalculable social benefit to England, and which, he claimed, had been restored 'fully and fairly' rather than superseded by the amendment act of 1834.

This advocacy of the amended English act as the optimal model for an Irish measure obliged the home secretary to explain his reasons for the overthrow of the Poor Inquiry Commission's report. While careful not to dismiss the desirability of some of its proposals, Russell focused on the inutility of Whately's complex classification of the poor, and his attempt to exclude the able-bodied destitute from relief. Russell indentified the relief of the latter as fundamentally a question of humanity:

> If a person in the five-and-twentieth year of his age, in the full possession of his health and strength, be unable by his industry to obtain a livelihood, or if he have not the means of support, were to stand at the doors of one of these public institutions starving, in want of support, and who was likely, if not relieved, to die in a few days, I cannot understand the principle that would distinguish a person in that case, as one to whom you would not give relief, when you give relief to the young and the infirm. The real principle to be adopted on this subject is, to afford relief to the destitute – and to the destitute only[.][3]

This was a strong argument grounded on the moral right of the destitute to assistance from the community, but it begged the question of why the bill denied the able-bodied destitute an absolute legal right to relief. Russell suggested that the refusal of such a right (which he claimed was not in fact absolute even in England) was principally a temporary expedient to allow a

2 *Hansard*, 3, xxxvi, 454–5 [13 Feb. 1837].
3 *Ibid.*, 459–60.

staged introduction of workhouses across the country without subjecting those first opened to unsupportable pressure from peripatetic applicants. As a *quid pro quo*, he indicated that vagrancy could not legitimately be prohibited until the whole national system was in full operation.[4] This implied that the 1837 bill represented only the first step in a more lengthy process of introducing poor laws to Ireland; while Russell may have acquired the epithet 'finality Jack' in 1837 for his public stance on parliamentary reform, this was not appropriate to his position on an Irish poor law. At the same time, Russell may have been aware that the denial of a formal 'right' to relief, while politically expedient, may have meant little in practice. Privately, G. C. Lewis had endorsed the view that the refusal of 'an express right to relief will be quite illusory', as practice would soon establish what was absent in the legislation, and guardians would not be able to deny relief to any destitute applicant. Others would argue a similar line in the parliamentary debates.[5]

In justification of his rejection of Whately's report, Russell summarized and lauded Nicholls' mission and its conclusion that workhouse-based relief in Ireland was both practicable and 'safe'.[6] Following Nicholls and Lewis, he attributed the backward state of Ireland and any overpopulation there not to any moral failings on the part of the people, but to a social structure based on the potato-wage system. This sociological anomaly had, he observed, given rise to a customary poor law that inverted the bonds of social responsibility upon which any stable society must be founded. The poor tenantry currently supported the weight of Irish mendicancy to the tune of a shilling per acre annually, while the landowning class generally demonstrated indifference or neglect towards their tenants and labourers beyond what efforts were required for the extraction of rack-rents. *Pace* Whately, the state could not permit this dangerous injustice to continue.

Limitations were, of course, necessary. Outdoor relief would be, he asserted, unsupportable and uncontrollable if introduced under current Irish circumstances. In contrast, the safety of workhouse relief had already been demonstrated by the operation of the less-eligibility principle in the existing houses of industry. The specific circumstances of Ireland also required, as Nicholls had proposed, certain modifications to the machinery operating under the amended English poor law. While union boards of guardians would be elected and formed under roughly the same regulations and franchise, the number of *ex-officio* magistrate guardians would be restricted to one third of the number of elected guardians (i.e. one quarter of board membership) to

4 *Ibid.*, 468–9.

5 Lewis to Head, 3 Apr. 1837, in Lewis (ed.), *Letters*, pp. 75–6.

6 *Hansard*, 3, xxxvi, 461–2.

protect the elected element from being swamped by the narrow interests of property, and all clergymen would be excluded from membership, to preserve the boards from sectarian rancour and save the clergy themselves from pastoral conflicts of interest.[7] Also reflecting the specific requirements of Ireland, while the poor-rate would be paid by the occupying tenant in the first instance, half of the amount thus paid was to be deductible from the next rent due to his immediate landlord (thus giving the landowners an explicit interest in poverty), while the entirety of the rate was deductible by the poorest tenants holding land valued under five pounds annually (and consequently these would not have the vote in elections of guardians). The English Poor Law Commission would supervise the Irish system, but via a board sitting in Dublin, with an additional resident commissioner becoming responsible specifically for Ireland.

Russell was anxious to avoid giving the impression that such a poor law would be a panacea for all Irish problems. During the subsequent period of social 'transition' some assistance would be necessary from additional public employment schemes and assisted emigration, although Russell was quick to reject any Malthusian justification for the latter – the present eight million people of Ireland could, he claimed, be sustained with good and sufficient means from the soil of Ireland, although the pre-existing social system had indeed rendered a portion of this number temporarily and locally 'superabundant'.[8] Extended emigration schemes he dismissed as both impracticable and as unacceptable to the colonies; the best the state could do would be to employ emigration agents at the ports who would both assist and select those most suited to the challenges of life overseas. This was a far cry from Whately's vision of a mass (and semi-compulsory) removal of up to two millions from Ireland, and also represented some distancing from the views of Nicholls and Lewis on the subject.

While denying that it might serve as an alternative to a workhouse-based poor law, Russell was much less dismissive of public works employment. While sound discretion was imperative in selecting suitable projects, he thought it possible to identify projects that would both boost short-term employment and develop future industry.[9] The encouragement of private investment was also a desired outcome of the poor law, but these allusions to the proactive role of the state in assisting economic development had a

7 *Ibid.*, xxxvi, 469–70. The limitation of magistrates and exclusion of clergy had been strongly advocated by Duncannon and Morpeth, NA: RP, PRO30/22/2C, fols 287–8, Duncannon to Russell, 19 Oct. 1836; NLI: MP, Ms 13,385/5, Morpeth memo [Nov. 1836].

8 *Hansard*, 3, xxxvi, 473–4.

9 *Ibid.*, 474.

particular resonance in the context of the recent establishment of the Irish railway commission.

The home secretary's speech was well received across the political spectrum, although many later expressed disappointment at what they regarded as a marked discrepancy between the expansive themes of Russell's speech, and the heavily constrained contents of the published bill. Poulett Scrope declared he had felt 'intense gratification' on hearing Russell expound the principle of a poor law so clearly and emphatically, only to find that '[the bill's] perusal has grievously chilled the warm feelings which your speech excited, and blighted the anticipations I had entertained'.[10]

Russell was seconded in introducing the bill by the ever-enthusiastic Howick. Reflecting his 'optimistic' perspective on Ireland's potential for economic development, Howick pointed to the ample opportunities for the profitable employment of its existing labour force, if only obstacles to the safe investment of private capital could be removed, and quoted Lewis's *On Local Disturbances* on the indispensability of a poor law to stimulate this process. It would be the moral fact of the workhouses' existence, rather than their physical capacity and occupancy, that would turn Ireland around, he argued. Some auxiliary measures might also be necessary, but the growth of self-funded emigration from Ireland over recent years raised questions about the necessity and wisdom of any state interference on that head.[11]

The legislative success of the poor law bill depended on the reaction of several key groups in parliament, and the debate on the introduction of the bill offered the first public indications of how these would respond. The Whig-liberal government retained an increasingly precarious majority in the Commons (a situation which would deteriorate further after the general election of summer 1837), and was dependent for political survival on the radicals and O'Connellites failing to find common ground with the opposition Conservatives. The attitude of Peel and the Conservative leadership in the lower House was crucial for the success of the bill, not least because their stance would also influence the reaction of Wellington and the Conservative majority in the House of Lords. Given the place of the poor law bill within the political project of the government, the reaction of Irish MPs was also important: a solid rejection of the measure would render it meaningless as an

10 G. Poulett Scrope, *Remarks on the Government Irish Poor-law Bill, in a Letter to Lord John Russell* (London, 1837), p. 3.

11 *Hansard*, 3, xxxvi, 492–7 [13 Feb. 1837]. For Howick's 'moralistic' attitude towards Irish poverty and development, and hardening antagonism towards state interference with emigration, see Peter Gray, '"Shovelling out your paupers": the British state and Irish Famine migration 1846–50', *Patterns of Prejudice*, 33 (1999), pp. 47–65.

element of 'justice to Ireland' and wholly undermine its legitimacy on implementation.

Peel's personal opinions remained hostile to both the 'absurd' recommendations of the Whately Commission, and towards any more extended poor law. He had written to Goulburn warning that caution must be exercised in protecting landed property from the combined clutches of the Irish poor, priests, demagogues and a state relief bureaucracy.[12] Nevertheless, the Conservative leaders chose not to make the Irish poor law a 'political' question, much to the relief of some ministers.[13] While less than wholeheartedly enthusiastic, both Peel and Stanley in the Commons generally welcomed the government's proposal. Peel made clear his own antagonism towards the interventionist aspects of the Poor Inquiry Commission's report and his preference for free enterprise in both emigration and the provision of employment. Notwithstanding his personal admiration for Nicholls, he was sceptical about the effectiveness of the workhouse test in Ireland, and the possibility of excluding all domiciliary relief or really ending vagrancy, but was prepared to engage constructively with what had been brought forward by the ministry.[14]

As an Irish landowner, Stanley had more to lose personally from the proposed measure, and his previous opposition to an Irish poor law raised the question of consistency. However, it suited his purposes to contrast his own good conduct as a landowner with that of other, less conscientious, absentees, who he thought should be compelled to take a fair portion of the public burden of poverty. He welcomed the bill as a practical government initiative, and on the grounds that it would be restricted to the absolutely destitute, and calculated to improve the moral condition of the poor through eliminating vagrancy. At the same time he flagged some specific matters, such as the absence of a law of settlement and the proposed size of unions, with which he was unhappy. His stated preference for a 'right to relief' was offset by his insistence that small landholders seeking relief in the summer 'hungry months' should not be regarded as destitute so long as they remained in possession of land – a position that foreshadowed the 'quarter acre clause' inserted into the 1847 amendment act by Peel's protégé William Gregory.[15] This stance,

12 Peel to Goulburn, 12 Sept. 1836, in C. S. Parker (ed.), *Sir Robert Peel from his Private Papers* (3 vols, London, 1899), ii, p. 326. Wellington expressed similar concerns, BL: PP, Add Ms 40,310, fols 155–8, Wellington to Peel [1836].

13 BL, Broughton diary, Add Ms 61,827, fol. 113, 13 Feb. 1837.

14 *Hansard*, 3, xxxvi, 497–504 [13 Feb. 1837].

15 *Ibid.*, 504–17. Stanley later demonstrated he was not above playing some party politics with the bill, when he forced a division against the clause enabling the Commissioners to offer salaried workhouse chaplaincies to the Catholic clergy: *ibid.*, xxxviii, 1209–11 [5 June 1837].

acknowledging the inevitability of some such poor law, but hinting at substantial battles to come over the detailed terms of the bill, was echoed by the Irish Conservative leader Frederick Shaw.[16]

Behind the scenes, Peel and his shadow cabinet had ulterior motives for ensuring the Irish poor law bill absorbed significant amounts of parliamentary time in 1837 without being thrown out. With Graham and Stanley, he agreed that a strong case could be made for making the creation of a poor law valuation the necessary precondition for conceding reform of the corporate franchise in Ireland. Peel candidly advised Wellington that by linking the two measures as a 'manoeuvre' further delaying time could be bought respecting the Irish municipal corporations bill, which had already been thrown out twice by the Lords and which had become a touchstone of Tory resistance to the Whigs' Irish reform strategy.[17] Stanley was in no doubt that this poor law bill (as indeed any such) must be a practical failure, but that political advantage could still be extracted from the new valuation it would entail.[18]

This adoption of a position of neutrality on the Irish poor law bill may also have been politically beneficial for the Conservative leaders in appeasing their grass-roots agriculturalist supporters in Great Britain. In early 1836 Sir Thomas Fremantle, later Irish chief secretary in a Peel administration, publicly announced his conversion to an enthusiastic meeting of Buckinghamshire farmers. Responding sympathetically to the long-established populist themes that the absence of a poor law allowed Irish producers to undercut English arable farmers, and stimulated unwanted immigration, Fremantle declared the model of the 1834 amendment act in England had removed his objections to transferring the law to Ireland, and that he would support this in parliament.[19]

Irish reaction in the House to the introduction of the Irish poor bill was mixed, but not at this stage overtly hostile. O'Connell announced that he had serious doubts on both the principle and provisions of the bill, but that he would nevertheless support it as a government measure and an experiment. His attack on Nicholls' gross underestimation of the scale of destitution, and depiction of a poor-rate as an unproductive drain on the wages-fund and a

16 *Ibid.*, xxxvi, 479–82 [13 Feb.]. Shaw later voiced more significant doubts, but this was offset by stronger support for its principle (if not all its terms) expressed by the influential Irish Tory Edward Lucas, *ibid.*, xxxviii, 429–30, 441–5 [1 May 1837].

17 BL: PP, Add Mss 40,318, fols 40, 64–9, 423, fols 176–9, Graham to Peel, 27 Mar., Peel memo, 23 Apr.; Peel to Wellington, 9 Apr. 1837, in Parker (ed.), *Peel*, ii, pp. 344–7.

18 BL: PP, Add Ms, 40,424, fols 344–5, Stanley to Peel, 14 Feb. 1838.

19 *Scotsman*, 30 Jan. 1836.

disincentive to private charity, provided a clear sense of his real position, but in contrast to his recent treatment of the subject at public meetings in Ireland his restraint came as some relief to ministers.[20] Smith O'Brien was happier with the bill, if critical of its failure to conform to his own conception of what an Irish poor law should entail. The workhouse system did not, he complained, 'admit any of the kindlier feelings of human nature' which an allowance of outdoor relief would embody, and the number of workhouses anticipated would fall far short of the capacity required (after making due allowance for the exaggerations of the Whately Commission). Closer integration of both reproductive public works and emigration would, he thought, be vital to the measure's success.[21]

Importantly for the government, a number of other liberal Irish MPs were more enthusiastic. The O'Conor Don, MP for Co. Roscommon, welcomed the government's acceptance of the principle of a poor law for Ireland, and observed that many previously hostile observers had been converted by the success of the English Amendment Act in reducing abuses. The people of the country would, he believed, be grateful for the transfer of the burden of relief from the poor to the rich, while the latter were already realizing that they would benefit from greater social peace that would follow. If accompanied by suitable ancillary measures and education, the bill would be successful in its objects. James Grattan, a long-standing advocate for poor laws, endorsed this, adding (as an inducement to English members to support it) that it would be likely to stem the annual influx of Irish labourers. John Richards, who had moved the 1833 motion for extending the Elizabethan poor law to Ireland, was also quick to answer O'Connell's objections, and to welcome the bill as the fulfilment of Bishop Doyle's aspirations.[22]

A fuller range of opinions was voiced in the debates on the second reading of the bill, which occurred over the two nights of 28 April and 1 May 1837. As soon as O'Connell rose to give the opening speech it was clear that the government was in for a rougher ride. While recognizing that the combination of strong support from English public opinion and the Catholic clergy in Ireland now rendered a poor law inevitable, he launched an attack on the principle of the measure and the concomitant neglect of the real, political, causes of Irish poverty. O'Connell's central argument rested on the rejection of poor laws *per se*, which he claimed had failed universally and were being abandoned in America and the Low Countries as a consequence. While he dismissed the Malthusian underpinnings of the Whately report, he evidently shared its preoccupation with the ring-fencing of private charity and

20 *Hansard*, 3, xxxvi, 485–92 [13 Feb. 1837]; see also below, pp. 232–40.
21 *Ibid.*, 478–9 [13 Feb. 1837].
22 *Ibid.*, 482–5, 504, 519 [13 Feb. 1837]; *ibid.*, xvii, 846–64 [2 May 1833].

safeguarding the wages-fund, while he demanded lavish state expenditure on public works and emigration in atonement for centuries of English misgovernment. His denunciation of the terms of the bill was inconsistent but nevertheless ominous – it would be simultaneously too onerous on the ratepaying tenantry and too inhumane and minimalist towards the destitute poor to have any hope of popularity or even legitimacy.[23]

O'Connell's diatribe against poor laws in general spurred their Irish advocates into rebuttals. Yet while they queued up to criticize his arguments, they also – to greater or lesser degrees – now felt obliged to cast barbs at the limitations of the government's bill, which they had now had time to read and digest. Sharman Crawford reiterated his view that poor laws were essential instruments of social justice, and as such must address the seasonal need for assistance to the small landholders without punishing them through workhouse incarceration. Richards now criticized its reliance on Nicholls' preoccupation with extending the English workhouse system to Ireland. Like Crawford, he also denounced the 'despotic powers' reserved for the commissioners. Smith O'Brien joined the chorus of criticism against Nicholls and urged outdoor relief for the aged and infirm, but was still prepared to defend the bill as a fabian step forward.[24] The O'Conor Don, H. W. Barron and Thomas Wyse also endorsed the fabian argument, while insisting that suitable auxiliary measures must follow quickly. Lord Clements agreed, but warned that O'Connell had not overstated the unpopularity of the proposed scheme:

> In supporting the Bill he was sorry to say, that he did not speak to the wishes of his constituents. They were afraid of a Poor-Law. The idea of being locked up in a workhouse was so uncongenial to the disposition of the Irish, that not the destitute but the rate-payers and farmers were against it. He hoped this prejudice would wear away; but an Irish Member who supported this Bill could not be accused of aiming at popularity, as he was bound to say the measure was most unpopular.[25]

Privately, however, he praised the scheme as a 'very excellent one', while expressing concern at the counter-productive consequences of directly rating the small farmers. Despite its limitations he was 'glad for the sake of humanity, and for the landlords too, that the experiment is begun'.[26] A. H. Lynch of Galway, who had already been in discussion with the Irish government

23 *Ibid.*, xxxviii, 360–83 [28 Apr. 1837]. For the Irish political context of O'Connell's offensive, see below, pp. 232–40.

24 *Ibid.*, xxxviii, 383–402.

25 *Ibid.*, 420–3, 427–9, 430–41 [1 May 1837].

26 NLI: KP, Ms 36,035/37, Clements to Lady Leitrim, 13–14 Feb. 1837.

concerning his own public works proposals, was prepared to come to Nicholls' defence, while also stressing the necessity of measures of employment.[27] If the ministers derived any comfort from these less than resounding endorsements of their policy, it may have lain in the readiness of so many Irish liberals to confront O'Connell over the principle of state relief to the able-bodied, and at the same time their inability to articulate an agreed alternative to what was on the table (especially on the topic of emigration, which was forcefully opposed by Sharman Crawford and Lynch).

Peel's contribution to the second reading debate again appears to have been calculated to keep any significant Conservative opposition in check, while at the same time warning the government that any expansion of what was proposed, in terms of auxiliary measures or more extensive relief, would not be tolerated. He rebuffed Shaw for suggesting further delay to the legislation on the pragmatic grounds that this would be dangerous in the context of heightened expectations in Ireland. While questioning (not entirely consistently) some of the detailed provisions, he praised by name the presumed author of the bill: 'Mr Nicholls had drawn up his report with great ability and intelligence. He was a man of great personal integrity, and the whole tenor of his life disproved the assertion that he had any interest in party politics.' While Peel doubted that the bill would be very effective in the short term in improving the condition of the poor (and he believed it risked curbing private charity), he thought it was right that the experiment should be tried if 'as rigid as possible'.[28]

It again fell to Russell, supported by Morpeth, to justify both the principle and terms of the bill in the face of these conflicting criticisms. Both defended Nicholls and deprecated the Whately report, but were also now prepared to go further to assuage Irish critics. The chief secretary explicitly praised Lynch's public works bills as 'calculated to be of signal use in working out the objects of the present measure', and announced that the government would also be introducing a bill 'to extend, regulate and improve the system of medical charities now existing in Ireland'. He also held the door ajar for future extension of the poor law, confessing a hope that '[i]f, after the experiment had been tried a short time, it was found that the verge of relief could be extended, no one would be more rejoiced than himself.'[29] This was not mere rhetoric. Russell would be responsible for a major extension of the measure (albeit under catastrophic circumstances) in 1847, and as late as 1869 continued to advocate, alongside the retention of the workhouse test for the able-bodied, more sympathetic treatment for certain categories of the 'deserving' poor, in

27 *Hansard*, 3, xxxviii, 428.
28 *Ibid.*, 446–50.
29 *Ibid.*, 402–5 [28 Apr. 1837].

the form of outdoor relief to the elderly and infirm, and the transfer of younger children to convents. In both cases he proposed additional funding be found from appropriating a portion of the established church's income for charitable purposes.[30]

Russell's speech of 1 May 1837 was largely repetitive of that on the first reading of the bill, but he reacted sharply to Peel's suggestion that the bill might have the inadvertent effect of promoting clearances. The opposite would in fact be the case:

> At present when tenants are ejected they resort to towns and trust to public charity, but their numbers are eventually greatly diminished by fevers brought on by want and suffering, and they are not much heard of by those who ejected them because they are not burthened with their maintenance. But the case would be very different under a Poor-law such as that proposed. If the landlord ejected a number of persons from his estate they could go to the workhouse, and he would find from the increase of the rates that he gained no advantage by such an expedient; and besides, the fact would become so notorious that he would be obliged to desist from the force of public opinion.[31]

This calculus of the balance between individualizing responsibility for poverty and employing the leverage of 'public opinion' would determine the government's stance on a number of details relating to the bill, including the balance of the rate burden between landlord and tenant, and the determination of the size of unions and electoral divisions.

The Irish poor law bill passed the second reading without division, and entered its committee stage in the second week of May. Both Russell's explicit rejection of the idea that there was any intrinsic connection between this and the Irish tithes and corporations bills, and O'Connell's announcement that he would now oppose the indoor relief and other clauses on a line by line basis, pointed to a more difficult committee stage.[32] The home secretary's pledge that there would be a resident poor law board in Dublin, containing men of local knowledge, was enough to see off a revolt over the oversight of the English commission.[33] The size of rateable areas and settlement questions proved more difficult. A number of Irish members, including Sharman Crawford, Clements and Smith O'Brien, urged smaller unions and electoral districts than those which had been suggested by Nicholls and the ministers (although these were not actually specified in the bill), but did not press their

30 John, Earl Russell, *A Third Letter to the Right Hon. Chichester Fortescue, MP, on the State of Ireland* (London, 1869), pp. 46–8.
31 *Hansard*, 3, xxxviii, 450–2 [1 May 1837].
32 *Ibid.*, 690–7 [8 May 1837].
33 *Ibid.*, 705–7 [8 May 1837].

arguments against Russell and Morpeth's case that a workhouse-based system in Ireland would require larger units than in England and that the commissioners should be allowed complete discretion in making these practical arrangements.[34] Stanley, with the support of some Irish Conservatives, urged a different amendment for the limitation of units – making electoral divisions coterminous with townland and estate boundaries and avoiding the division of any estate between unions; Lucas asserted that only this alignment of proprietorial interest with poor-law boundaries would give the landowner a real interest in reducing pauperism. Russell failed to explain the administration's opposition to what would become one of the most long-standing grievances of Irish landowners against the poor law, but carried the original clause.[35] His main reasons may have been the preoccupation with the idea of promoting the formation of a 'public opinion' within each (large) union, stimulated by collective rather than individual rate burdens, and operating to pressurize recalcitrant proprietors into action, along with a concern to avoid creating too much proprietorial control over the representative boards of guardians.

On the following night Lucas brought forward another amendment to introduce a settlement clause into the bill, with broadly the same aim as Stanley's – 'so as more justly to apportion the pecuniary charges to be incurred and levied under the name of poor-rates'. He believed it possible to introduce the principle without the accompanying evils which had discoloured English practice, and that this need not imply any absolute 'right' to relief; it would, however, protect unions from being swamped by mobile paupers by enabling the guardians to remove such paupers to their place of origin, at the union's expense. The recent legislation for facilitating the removal of Irish and Scottish paupers from English unions provided the precedent, the census returns the mechanism for determining settlement.[36] Lucas was supported by the O'Conor Don and Thomas Wyse, and received heavyweight endorsement from Stanley, who supported something along the lines of the Scottish law of settlement as essential to prevent fraudulent and pernicious expenditure by guardians, and warned that without a law of settlement the poor law would tempt landlords to clear their estates without fear of the financial

34 *Ibid.*, 806–7, 812–15 [11 May 1837]. Nicholls' recommendation of unions of roughly 400 square miles was favoured by ministers; the Irish MPs proposed a maximum of 150 square miles (or 25,000 inhabitants) for unions and twenty square miles (or 6,000 inhabitants) for electoral districts.

35 *Ibid.*, 809–13, 815–16.

36 *Ibid.*, 827–33 [12 May 1837]. Robert Palmer's Irish and Scotch Vagrants Bill, rendering it cheaper for southern English unions to repatriate such paupers, had earlier been passed with little debate, *ibid.*, xxxvi, 583–5 [16 Feb. 1837].

consequences of increased rates.[37] However, the settlement lobby was weakened by the obvious reluctance of Lucas to allow any right to relief to the destitute, which distanced him from other supporters of settlement such as Poulett Scrope. It drew more fundamental rebuttals from Lynch, who denied that under a uniform workhouse system there would be any inducement to migrate to another union, and insisted that settlement must be accompanied by a right to relief which would require a system of outdoor relief which Ireland could not afford. Howick agreed that such a system was wholly impracticable, and undesirable (in England as much as in Ireland). By inhibiting the free migration of labour it would impede Ireland's improvement.[38] Russell endorsed the case for free labour markets and denied that settlement or an absolute right had been part of the original Elizabethan poor act, although he left the door open for a modified settlement if this was found necessary through experience. He dismissed Stanley's emotive argument about clearance as just another attempt to revive the defeated amendment for estate-based unions, and set out his case for the collective rather than individual responsibility of Irish landlords for tackling Irish poverty a little more clearly.[39] Lucas's amendment was lost by 68 votes to 120.[40]

The usually compliant Lynch subsequently moved that no magistrates should be included as non-elected *ex-officio* guardians, and this 'popular' gesture was echoed by similar amendments from O'Connell and the radical Hindley. Morpeth thought that in curbing the proportion of *ex-officio* guardians at one third of the elected number the bill had already gone well beyond the English act, while Russell piously hoped that regular interaction between the elected and unelected guardians might diminish the unpopularity of JPs. Both ministers may have really placed greater hopes for this in a future major revision of the bench. The amendments were defeated by significant majorities, as was Sharman Crawford's to remove the commissioners' powers to appoint vice-guardians to replace elected boards in specific circumstances.[41]

Despite Russell's personal readiness to concede Barron's proposal that the clause limiting the amount of land that unions could hire for agricultural labour be raised above twelve acres, this too was lost.[42] A more serious challenge came from Smith O'Brien, who moved that guardians should have the right to resort to other modes of relief outside the workhouse; this spurred

37 *Ibid.*, xxxviii, 837–8, 845–8, 850 [12 May 1837].

38 *Ibid.*, 833–5, 838–40.

39 *Ibid.*, 848–50.

40 *Ibid.*, 850–2. A number of radicals, including Buller, Sharman Crawford and Poulett Scrope, and liberals and O'Connellites, voted with the minority.

41 *Ibid.*, 1095–8 [26 May 1837].

42 *Ibid.*, 1162–4 [2 June 1837].

O'Connell into another denunciation of the bill as a whole as a delusion and a potential cause of agrarian disturbance in Ireland through its sole reliance on the 'prison' of the workhouse. Support for outdoor relief in Ireland also came from the English radicals Wakley and Ward.[43] Russell, as before, employed the carrot of characterizing the bill as an introductory experiment, with the stick of warning that outdoor relief would become uncontrollable and lead to the pauperization of the country. After a debate that extended long into the night, the division indicated the limited (if not insignificant) support for a more extensive poor law in Ireland – 50 supported Smith O'Brien, and 138 the government.[44]

The poor law bill of 1837 had proceeded to its fifty-ninth clause in committee with no significant amendment or concession on the part of the government, when it, along with all other parliamentary business, was halted by the King's death on 20 June. Despite the political exigencies created by the succession, Russell was extremely reluctant to give up the Irish poor law alongside the other 'great measures' of the session, but on 23 June he acceded to Melbourne's opinion that it would be impossible to carry it before a dissolution of parliament, not least because Irish members were likely to be unavoidably absent on the hustings.[45] This impromptu interruption of business wrecked not only the chances of a poor law being enacted that session, but also halted the public works employment bills which Morpeth had been committed to forwarding, and which the lord lieutenant had hoped would bring immediate relief amid another subsistence crisis in the west that summer.[46] A public works bill appropriating £50,000 in matching aid to sums raised locally on the baronial cess and which permitted three magistrates sitting in an open meeting of cesspayers rather than the established grand jury to initiate the presentment, had been proceeding through the Lords before the interruption.[47] Russell refused to undertake the responsibility of forwarding relief money on the security of prospective poor-rates, and the Irish

43 Ward was a strong supporter of schemes for 'systematic colonization': see H. G. Ward, *The First Step to a Poor Law for Ireland* (London, 1837). Wakley was a Cobbettite opponent of the new poor law in England and defender of the interests of the medical profession against state 'interference': *Hansard*, 3, xxxviii, 1211 [5 June 1837]. However, both voted for the third reading of the bill in 1838: *ibid.*, xlii, 717 [30 Apr. 1838].

44 *Ibid.*, xxxviii, 1165–9 [2 June]; BL: Broughton diary, Add Ms 61,828, fols 32–3, 5 June 1837.

45 SUL: BP, MEL/RU/346, Melbourne to Russell, 22 June; BL: Broughton diary, Add Ms 61,828, fols 48–52 (21, 23 June); *Hansard*, 3, xxxviii, 1585–6 [23 June 1837].

46 MC: NP, M/560, Morpeth to Mulgrave, 18 May 1837.

47 *Hansard*, 3, xxxviii, 1441–8 [13 June 1837].

government was again forced into a series of expedients (including another loan to the Dublin Mendicity Society) to stave off mortality.[48]

Interregnum: Nicholls' second report

Irish (especially O'Connellite) resistance to the poor law bill, and the potential problems of carrying the bill intact through a sceptical House of Lords, inclined Russell towards bolstering the case for the bill by sending Nicholls on a further tour of inquiry in Ireland, this time including the northern counties, which he had by-passed in 1836. He was not expected to alter his initial opinions in the light of further investigation, but to hone those details of the bill relating to the mechanism for implementation and to provide ministers with arguments on the resubmission of the bill. The decision to commission a second Nicholls report was taken in the wake of the elections in August, and Nicholls proceeded to Ireland in the final week of that month.[49] Nicholls, now a household name in Ireland, encountered more personal hostility than before, although the lord lieutenant noted that this was often softened by personal contact with his critics.[50] As before, the tour was co-ordinated by Dublin Castle – with Nicholls following in the viceroy's footsteps to 'witness the scenes of distress' again evident in Donegal – and the conclusions generally agreed with the lord lieutenant before Nicholls returned to England.[51] Predictably, Nicholls' renewed presence in Ireland sparked a further tirade from Whately, who had been for a while relatively quiet on the subject of the Irish poor law (perhaps because he was awaiting its arrival in the Lords or was preoccupied with his project for a new theological college in Dublin).[52]

48 *Ibid.*, 1607–8 [23 June]; MC: NP, M/180, Mulgrave to Drummond, 22 July [1837].

49 Russell to Nicholls, 12 Aug. 1837, in *Second Report of Geo. Nicholls*, p. 3; MC: NP, M/875, M/571, Russell to Mulgrave, 13 Aug., Morpeth to Mulgrave, 20 Aug.; CHP, J/19/1/15, fol. 48, Russell to Morpeth, 25 Aug. 1837.

50 NA: RP, PRO30/22/2F, fols 118–24, Mulgrave to Russell, 16 Sept. 1837.

51 Mulgrave to Russell, 7 Oct. 1837, *ibid.*, fols 143–6. Nicholls' reading of the structural problems of Donegal was more conventional than Mulgrave's, and emphasized emigration and consolidation to create a gradation of farm sizes, but they agreed that a poor law was requisite to compel proprietorial interest in welfare and improvement: *Second Report of Geo. Nicholls*, pp. 12–13.

52 NLW: NSP, C/575, Whately to Senior, 21 Sept. 1837. It was believed, however, that he had a hand in producing a savagely anti-Nicholls pamphlet, probably *Strictures on the Proposed Poor Law for Ireland* (London, 1837): see NLW: HCP, C/2804, Lewis to Villiers, 2 July 1837, Whately to Wrightson, 22 Feb. 1838, in [W. B. Wrightson (ed.)], *Irish Poor Laws: Additional Correspondence of Archbishop Whately 1837–1838* (n.p., [*c.*1867]), pp. 7–8.

The formal outcome was Nicholls' second report on Ireland, presented to the government on 3 November 1837. He also submitted in September a (very lightly) revised poor law bill for Morpeth to work up in detail. Not surprisingly, his latest tour had, he announced, confirmed his previous opinions concerning the indispensability of a poor law for Ireland based on the workhouse test and indoor relief. Optimistically, he reported that the 'minds of the people appear . . . to be generally better prepared for its reception', and that awareness of the aims and principles of the bill were now much better appreciated as a consequence of the parliamentary debates and pamphlet discussions. He admitted that the knock-on effects on Irish attitudes of the anti-new-poor-law campaign in England might render the introduction of the act more difficult, but was sure this would be temporary.[53]

A visit to Belfast and other Ulster towns, which had been omitted from his 1836 itinerary, had still not persuaded him of the truth of Spring Rice's claim that attitudes in the north would render the poor law inapplicable there. He told Morpeth:

> They have now a kind of petty poor law at Belfast, as at all the other towns of note in the north of Ireland. The means of affording relief to the destitute is now raised by voluntary contribution, and of course therefore very unequally, the most liberal paying most, and many paying nothing at all. This is a constant source of bickering and ill will, and the contributions are everywhere on the decline, as if to prepare the way for the imposition of an equal and universal rate – compelling every shoulder to bear a portion of the burthen which would then bear lightly upon all.

The finished report concluded that, rather than being inappropriate, the proposed poor law would better suit the circumstance and social habits of the north than any other part of the country, and face fewer difficulties of implementation. Morpeth rather triumphantly instructed Spring Rice to 'prune your trees with what alacrity you can' in consequence of these findings.[54]

53 *Second Report of Geo. Nicholls*, pp. 6, 34. Nicholls' final report took the form of a review of poor law practice in other countries, modelled on Senior's similar contribution to the English inquiry: see *Third Report of G. Nicholls, on Poor Laws, Ireland, containing Result of Inquiry into Condition of Labouring Classes, and Relief of Poor, in Holland and Belgium*, PP 1837–38 [126], xxxviii.713. In this he argued (*contra* Senior) that, despite some flaws, the public relief systems in the Low Countries had largely succeeded in eliminating pauperism, and in augmenting the general prosperity of small-scale agriculture.

54 CHP, J/19/1/15, fol. 90, Nicholls to Morpeth, 21 Sept.; NLI: MP, Ms 13,386/3, Morpeth to Spring Rice, 2 Oct. 1837; *Second Report of Geo. Nicholls*, pp. 10–13.

The prominence of Nicholls in the public debate remained both a source of strength and of weakness to the government. His membership of the English commission provided the necessary 'expert' authority on poor-law practicalities without which no scheme could hope to progress. At the same time his limited knowledge of Ireland and seemingly arbitrary calculations of the scale of Irish destitution remained the administration's Achilles heel. Mulgrave noted worryingly that persons of all classes and shades of opinion continued to question the accuracy of Nicholls' claims and hence the superstructure erected upon them.[55] Although rather diffident in defending his own estimations, Nicholls reasserted his confidence that these were of the correct order of magnitude, largely on the strength of the result of a further inquiry undertaken by the Dublin statistician, and future secretary of the Irish Poor Law Board, William Stanley. The latter's demolition of the Poor Inquiry Commission's 'exaggerations' was more persuasive than his positive claim that Ireland had a destitute population no greater than 83,000, which he calculated on the strength of evidence for a 2 per cent rate of destitution in the Dublin population and an assumption that the rural proportion was half of this. Stanley's assertions, first published in a private pamphlet, were given official sanction by their inclusion as an appendix to Nicholls' second report, but it is doubtful that they convinced many sceptics.[56]

Russell again persuaded a reluctant Melbourne to allow the Irish poor law bill precedence in the 1837–38 session; the prime minister was prepared merely to 'accede to . . . rather than approve' it, but recognized that reintroduction was politically expedient, and rejected Lansdowne's repeated appeal that it be made temporary, on the grounds that later amendment was preferable to repeated and vexatious parliamentary consideration of the whole.[57] While evidently unenthusiastic at best, Melbourne characteristically sought for the line of least resistance in dealing with countervailing pressures within his government. Morpeth sought to soften the blow for the sceptics with a promise that both he and Nicholls would seek to persuade the cabinet to accompany the measure with 'some more active encouragement to emigration', but it is unlikely that the poor law's antagonists put much faith in this.[58]

55 CHP, J/19/1/17, fol. 7, Mulgrave to Morpeth, 8 Feb. 1838.

56 *Second Report of Geo. Nicholls*, pp. 23–4, 42–55; William Stanley, *Remarks on the Government Measure for establishing Poor-laws in Ireland* (London, 1837).

57 SUL: BP, MEL/RU/395, Melbourne to Russell, 4 Sept.; BL: BP, B/92, Melbourne to Lansdowne, 28 Sept. 1837.

58 Morpeth to Lansdowne, 5 Oct. 1837, *ibid.*, B/108.

The 1837–38 bill in the Commons

The new parliament met on 10 November 1837 and was initially preoccupied with settling the civil list for the new monarch. The Irish poor relief bill was reintroduced by Russell at the earliest opportunity on 1 December. The bill was nearly identical to its predecessor, with some minor amendments and the addition (following Nicholls' strong recommendation) of a permissive assisted emigration clause, based on that in the English Poor Law Amendment Act. In fact the emigration clause went much less far than Nicholls' recommendations of a state grant in aid of union emigration rates and for the appointment of colonial emigration agents to assist with settlement; it was Russell rather than Nicholls who dismissed assisted emigration as a significant part of the 'answer' to Ireland's 'question'.[59] Despite the previously stated scepticism on Russell's part about the premature inclusion of clauses criminalizing vagrancy, these were again included after strong advocacy for them as an indispensable 'act of police' on the part of Nicholls.[60] Events would again prove that the home secretary felt little attachment to this aspect of the measure.

The home secretary's speech proposing the first reading followed the outlines of that given the previous season, but gave greater attention to two issues which had been highlighted by reactions to the previous bill in and out of parliament. Firstly he downplayed what he regarded as excessive expectations of the immediate effects of a poor law (and other state enactments) in Ireland – such legislation could offer no 'royal road to prosperity', but merely aid the destitute of a country in a 'recovering' state that had previously been subject to British misgovernment and denied full British freedoms. Yet if advocates of a poor law expected too much, its opponents had been too alarmist. Russell now took a much more confrontational stance vis-à-vis Whately and the Poor Inquiry Commission: their report, he declared, had confounded the question of measures desirable for the general welfare of the people with those which would directly address the plight of the destitute classes. The first could not be advanced by the state, but by the people themselves with suitable state assistance. The second was a direct state responsibility and must extend relief to the able-bodied in a situation where an excess of labourers to regular employment created involuntary unemployment. Provision for emigration beyond what was countenanced under the English poor law was unnecessary – and the commissioners' specific recommendation of emigration depots was potentially disastrous. Further investigations by Nicholls and William Stanley

59 *A Bill for the More Effectual Relief of the Destitute Poor in Ireland*, PP 1837–38 (15), v.305; *Second Report of Geo. Nicholls*, p. 22.

60 *Ibid.*, pp. 28–30.

had demonstrated the numbers given by the commission as 'destitute' (as opposed to those in comparative distress) to be distorted and exaggerated, in for example ignoring the considerable sums earned seasonally by migrant labourers in Great Britain. With a poor law and some (remunerative) auxiliary measures, Ireland would be put on the right path, but it would take perhaps ten years of good government before the evils of its social condition would be remedied.[61]

This speech provoked an angry reaction from Whately, whose readiness to take a strong public line against the bill had been bolstered by a decided (if not wholly uncritical) defence of the third report published by Wrightson in the *Edinburgh Review*.[62] Wrightson's return to the Commons at the 1837 election gave Whately an interested ally, and together they plotted parliamentary tactics for impeding the bill by amendments to exclude the able-bodied destitute. Additionally, they hoped to summon Nicholls, Revans, Lewis and others before a select committee of inquiry to interrogate all parties on the sources of their divergent 'facts' about Irish poverty. Whately also arranged for Wrightson to meet Robert Torrens to discuss pushing for an alternative 'colonization' measure for Ireland.[63] The archbishop was convinced that a combination of parliamentary resistance and mobilization of Irish public opinion in support of a petitioning campaign exposing the false simplicities of Nicholls and the bill would induce the Lords to halt it in its tracks.[64] If Russell's speech had been intended to silence Whately it had the opposite effect; the archbishop now warned Senior apocalyptically that

> [A]ll *your* labours in *England* will have been of no avail, if rash measures are adopted with respect to Ireland. For the dead corpse will poison the living body; and in fact, if such a system of providing food and employment at the public expense (*i.e.* of the empire) for all who want it in Ireland as some advocate, be adopted, I, for one, shall have nothing to say against repeal. It will be steering away from a ship on fire. By the help of Wrightson and Blake I hope we may avoid such extremities.[65]

If Whately failed to persuade Senior and his friends to break with the government over the poor law bill (and expressed frustration that they failed to grasp

61 *Hansard*, 3, xxxix, 477–92 [1 Dec. 1837].
62 NLW: NSP, C/576, Whately to Senior, 31 Oct. 1837; [Wrightson], 'The workhouse system', pp. 186–208. Whately was not originally aware that Wrightson was the author until apprised of this by Senior.
63 DAD: BWP, Dec. 1837, n.d. [1838]; NLW: NSP, C/584, Whately to Senior, 28 Dec. 1837; *Hansard*, 3, xl, 782 [5 Feb. 1838].
64 NLW: NSP, C/579, Whately to Senior, 13 Nov. 1837; Whately to Wrightson, 22 Feb. 1838, in [Wrightson, (ed.)], *Irish Poor Laws*, pp. 7–8.
65 Whately to Senior, [1837], in Whately (ed.), *Life*, i, pp. 399–400.

the primacy of the issue in the manner he did),[66] together they still represented a potentially powerful bloc around which other antagonistic elements might coalesce.

Whately's private protest to Russell against the 'misrepresentation' of his commission in the home secretary's speech of 1 December, and appeal for an alternative colonial emigration measure, met with little sympathy.[67] Russell thought that his comments might have been quoted out of context in the press, but did not apologize for refuting the third report's recommendations. Whately's retort that this attack on the commission reflected badly on the government which had appointed it is hardly likely to have had much leverage with Russell.[68] Morpeth had half-hoped that the letters sent to 'Dick' and Blake, along with Mulgrave's personal influence, might appease 'these stormy statists', but he was proved wrong.[69] The exchange put paid to any final faint hopes of reconciliation.

Whately's more overt opposition was echoed by that of a number of Irish members in the Commons. Shaw reacted to Russell by vigorously defending the Poor Inquiry Commissioners against Nicholls, as (on this occasion) did Fitzstephen French, the Whig-liberal MP for Co. Roscommon.[70] On the second reading, John Gibson of Belfast joined the chorus of criticism, and warned that the poor-rates would pauperize the Irish middle classes; it was better to leave Ireland to the 'natural course' of events than subject her to this.[71] O'Connell weighed in to force a vote against the principle of the bill on 9 February 1838. His criticisms were multiple (and, as his critics observed, not entirely consistent), but focused on his principal concerns: that Ireland was too poor to support able-bodied relief; that a compulsory poor law would extinguish Irish charity and the moral value system that underlay it; the rate would amount to an unsupportable tax of £1 million on the wages-fund, falling in the first instance on the occupying tenantry; and that imprisoning the poor in workhouses for no crime would be sowing dragon's teeth in Ireland.[72]

66 NLW: NSP, C/577, Whately to Senior, [Nov. 1837].

67 NA: RP, PRO30/22/2F, fols 213–14, Whately to Russell, 8 Dec. 1837.

68 Russell to Whately, 11 Dec., Whately to Russell, 13 Dec. 1837, *ibid.*, fols 215–16, 230–1.

69 MC: NP, M/576, Morpeth to Mulgrave, 11 Dec. 1837. 'Statist' here denotes a statistician – a reference to Whately's attacks on Nicholls' figures for Irish destitution.

70 *Hansard*, 3, xxxix, 492–6, 496–9 [1 Dec. 1837]. This was in sharp contrast to French's enthusiasm for Revans and support for Nicholls expressed earlier in the year: see below, pp. 242–4.

71 *Ibid.*, xl, 780–2 [5 Feb. 1838].

72 *Ibid.*, 947–65 [9 Feb. 1838].

O'Connell's intended opposition to the bill had already been pre-announced to the government through recent speeches in Ireland, and more directly through intermediaries such as the radical MP Henry Warburton, who transmitted O'Connell's letter on the subject to Russell. Given the underlying political strategy of which the poor law bill formed a part, it was hardly surprising that the cabinet took his opposition more seriously than Whately's, especially as it related to the point O'Connell had emphasized – the unpopularity and 'agrarian convulsion' likely to be stoked by the imposition of additional direct taxation on the tenantry.[73] Russell took this warning seriously enough to take the cabinet's views on the possibility of some form of direct rating of landowners rather than occupiers, although nothing came of this. Poulett Thomson, who had also toured Ireland the previous summer, identified the two main problems: firstly, tenants exempted from rates would lose their ratepayer franchise for the boards of guardians and the system as a whole would thus be denied political legitimacy; secondly, the occupiers as well as the landowners needed to come under the pressure of poor laws to ensure their proper operation. Duncannon strongly endorsed this, arguing that the active interest of the small farmers in the system – as ratepayers and electors – was essential to its success. Spring Rice highlighted O'Connell's objections as further evidence for the inevitable failure of the bill, but did not advocate alteration of the clause.[74]

O'Connell's sustained opposition on the poor law bill posed real problems for the administration, but ministers chose to persevere while doing their utmost not to break with him on the question. When Chadwick published (anonymously) a number of unauthorized and strongly anti-O'Connell articles in the *Morning Chronicle* in early January 1838, the government acted quickly to distance itself from these squibs. Nicholls, who had been suspected by a furious O'Connell of authorship of the articles, was prevailed on to write asserting his innocence, and his assurances were accepted by the Irish leader.[75] Drummond still hoped optimistically that O'Connell might yet be brought round by Duncannon and concessions, but believed the real battle for the legitimacy of the poor law must be fought elsewhere.[76]

The government's decision to proceed in the face of O'Connell's animosity was a calculated risk, but Russell privately insisted that it must be carried through whatever the threatened political backlash from the ratepaying classes

73 NA: RP, PRO30/22/2F, fols 187–8, Warburton to Russell, 16 Nov. 1837.

74 Thomson memo, 21 Nov., Duncannon memo, [Nov. 1837], Spring Rice memo, 17 Nov. 1837, *ibid.*, fols 189, 193–4, 195–6.

75 CHP, J/19/1/16, fols. 62, 77, 80, Nicholls to Morpeth, 10, 19 Jan., O'Connell to Morpeth, 21 Jan. 1838.

76 NA: RP, PRO30/22/3A, fols 30–5, Drummond to Morpeth, 6 Jan. 1838.

– his intention, he reminded Morpeth, was not to please the landlords or farmers, but 'to do good in Ireland'.[77] Nevertheless, O'Connell's out-and-out opposition in the Commons and repetition of his warnings led ministers to reassert the 'popular' aspects of the measure. On 5 February Russell sought to reassure Irish members that, despite the initial insistence on the workhouse test, greater flexibility in the mode of relief might be permitted in future:

> He was not prepared to say that in Ireland particular circumstances might not exist which might call for some modification of this principle. He was not prepared to say that in Ireland there ought to be no relief except in the workhouse. Neither did he say, that there might not be some other test framed; but that the principle must, he believed, at least with certain limitations, be adopted.[78]

He followed this up with a statement, made 'with more than usual emphasis', that stressed the extent to which the burden of relief would be transferred from the occupiers (as was currently the case through private charity) to the tenants and landowners in equal share. Although the poor law was no panacea and would not directly deal with general poverty or low wages, the initially prudent and cautious measure would also create the powers necessary for any future enlargement. Furthermore, he claimed the government's aim was to modify rather than totally reject the recommendations of the Poor Inquiry Commission.[79] This again left open the door for the 'auxiliary measures' so strongly demanded by Irish advocates of the poor law.

The combination of these soothing words from ministers and the uncompromising negativity of O'Connell's assault appears to have rallied a number of Irish members to the principle if not to every clause of the bill. For William Roche (MP for Limerick), the bill was only 'a beginning and a fragment' of what Ireland needed, but essential nonetheless. Sir Charles Style, despite being previously regarded as a fundamentalist opponent, signalled his reluctant acceptance of the measure, however insufficient and flawed it was.[80] Smith O'Brien was sure that, although amendments were necessary, the shopkeepers and small occupiers were (*pace* O'Connell) for the bill; the future under-secretary Thomas Redington believed extension beyond workhouse relief would be necessary, but that the bill was vital to replace the

77 CHP, J/19/1/17, fol. 8, Russell to Morpeth, 10 Feb. 1838.

78 *Hansard*, 3, xl, 789 [5 Feb. 1838].

79 *Ibid.*, 965–73 [9 Feb.]. The *Morning Chronicle* (10 Feb. 1838) observed apropos of this speech that 'Lord John Russell . . . always speaks best when a little excited and urged onward.'

80 *Hansard*, 3, xl, 774–8 [5 Feb.]. The Whig-liberal MP for Scarborough, Style was also a Donegal landowner.

inefficiencies of voluntarism and give security to the countryside. Barron added that the workability of less eligibility in Ireland had long been demonstrated by the operation of local institutions such as the Waterford House of Industry.[81] Clements summed up the sentiments of many Irish Whig-liberals: the proposed powers of the commissioners were excessive, outdoor relief would be essential and some system of settlement was unavoidable, yet the main features of the bill were right, and Ireland owed a debt of gratitude to the home secretary for promoting it.[82] Privately, however, he continued to lobby Nicholls and Russell to render the measure more 'popular' through concessions such as announcing they would appoint a majority of Irish assistant commissioners.[83]

The shape of Commons attitudes towards the bill were now clear. An uneasy alliance of O'Connell and certain of his supporters, parts of the Irish landed interest (both Tory and Whig), and English anti-new-poor-law radicals and Tories – a 'curious coalition' which some found laughable – would oppose the bill wholeheartedly.[84] A number of other Irish Whig-liberals and Repealers would challenge aspects of the bill rather than its principle. The difficulty this opposition would find in cohering was evident in the low support found for O'Connell's hostile motion – the division of 9 February was heavily defeated by 25 to 277. The fact that nearly three-quarters of the Irish contingent had voted for the bill on this occasion (including a majority of Repealers) would later be used to assert that it represented the will of the Irish people.[85] Others, including the Conservative leadership and pro-poor-law reformers, awaited the opportunities which might arise in the committee stages. The situation was astutely summarized by the lord lieutenant: there was no uniformity of objection to the bill, but, more worryingly, there also appeared to be no one who cordially approved of its provisions.[86]

81 *Ibid.*, 786–7 [5 Feb.]; 977–81, 985–8 [9 Feb. 1838].

82 *Ibid.*, 1007–9 [12 Feb.]. *The Times* (12 Feb. 1838) denounced such 'courteous deference' towards the home secretary as reflecting the unwillingness of Irish Whig-liberals to risk the government's safety.

83 NLI: KP, Ms 14,298, Clements to Nicholls, 8 Feb., Clements to Russell, 24 Feb. 1838.

84 BL: Broughton diary, Add Ms 56,559, fols 77–8 (30 Apr. 1838).

85 *Hansard*, 3, xl, 990–2 [12 Feb.]. The minority included a mixture of O'Connellites, Ulster MPs such as Gibson and Verner, 'popular' British radicals such as Thomas Attwood, and anti-poor-law fundamentalists such as the Cambridge political economist George Pryme. Attwood subsequently denounced the bill as a delusion and urged the House to vote £20 million to employ the 'white slaves' of Ireland on cultivating the waste-lands: *ibid.*, 1231–2 [16 Feb.].

86 CHP, J/19/1/17, fol. 10, Mulgrave to Morpeth, 12 Feb. 1838.

Much of the committee stage followed a similar pattern to the previous session. Despite the clear preference of the Irish ministers for a 'distinct management' in Ireland, the government again chose to insist on giving administrative responsibility and extensive discretionary powers to the English commissioners, albeit working through a Dublin-based board.[87] A number of Irish Whig-liberals, including Redington and the future chief secretary Sir William Somerville, voted for O'Connell's amendment for a separate commission, but most Irish MPs appeared to accept Russell's reassurances that distinct Irish circumstances would be recognized by a fourth commissioner resident in Dublin and acting with local knowledge, and this was subsequently written into the bill.[88] A number of other objections to the ill-defined and centralized powers allocated to the commissioners were easily overcome, with Peel vocally supporting the government, although the ministers also demonstrated a preparedness to make a few tactical concessions. Morpeth gave way, for example, to Irish pressure to allow guardians veto powers over the dissolution of their unions or the alteration of union boundaries.[89]

With O'Connell determined to force divisions on many clauses, especially those relating to the powers of the commissioners, and the exclusion of clerical and the inclusion of *ex-officio* guardians, progress was slow, although the bill suffered no material damage in committee. The government came closest to defeat when, in a thin House on 23 March, a majority of Irish MPs united to oppose the clause enabling the commissioners to appoint and remove paid officers when elected boards failed to carry out their responsibilities under the act – a matter which most closely affected the local interests of landed gentlemen and raised most directly the spectre of centralized control and patronage.[90]

The crucial moment in the Commons arrived when Shaw proposed the restriction of workhouse relief to the impotent and elderly poor only. His reassertion of the fundamentals of the Whately report on the exclusion of the able-bodied relief drew the support of Wrightson – who had previously (in collusion with Whately) prepared his own amendment to this end.[91] For Shaw the present bill was merely a 'screen' raised against the necessity of introducing the vital auxiliary measures of emigration and public works which the

87 MC: NP, M/581, Morpeth to Mulgrave, 24 Jan. 1838.

88 *Hansard*, 3, xl, 1021–5 [12 Feb.]; xli, 1180–1 [23 Mar. 1838].

89 *Ibid.*, xl, 1232–5 [16 Feb. 1838].

90 *Ibid.*, xli, 1185–94 [23 Mar. 1838].

91 However, the difficulties of practically defining 'the able-bodied' and those 'unable to work' for such a purpose had been raised by one correspondent to whom Wrightson had shown his draft amendment: DAD: BWP, DD/BW/F7/57, C. Bathurst to Wrightson, 7 Feb. 1838.

unfairly pilloried Poor Inquiry Commission had advocated. Wrightson insisted that the commission's system of classification was indispensable, and was founded on original English and Scottish statutes – a point previously asserted by the Sturges Bourne committee of 1817. In contrast the government's measure would inevitably increase destitution by creating an unproductive drain on the wages-fund.[92]

Morpeth responded by rejecting the classification system as practically unworkable, and, in a passage that O'Connell satirized as containing more oratory than political economy, stressed the moral case for an inclusive law. Referring to a report of a public meeting in Co. Clare where workhouse confinement had been criticized, the chief secretary paraphrased the humanitarian comments of (significantly) a Catholic priest in their defence:

> [He] mentioned the case of a poor woman, who, with three young children in a state of destitution, sought refuge in a waste house. In the course of the night, the youngest of the children, an infant, fell from off its mother's arms and perished of cold. The poor mother shared her fate, for she too perished in the course of the night, and the two surviving orphans had to be provided for by his parishioners. Now, was not the fate of those helpless beings worse than their being imprisoned in a workhouse, as it is called? Was not begging in the streets a greater degradation than seeking asylum in the walls of a workhouse?[93]

Morpeth's emotive case was well received by Irish Whig-liberals who had voted against certain clauses of the bill but supported its fundamental principles. Barron asked if Shaw really intended 'that the people were to starve – that they were not to live under equal laws?', while Clements flatly denied that the Irish wages-fund was incapable of supporting the destitute or of expanding under the stimulus of poor-rates, and denounced any emigration forced by the denial of relief at home as 'a species of transportation'. Russell himself reinforced the message by emphasizing, alongside the issue of costs, the ethical principle that those capable and willing to work, but unable to find employment, had an entitlement to relief.[94] Critics were sure that his allies, including Clements and Scrope, had been duped by ministerial hints at auxiliary measures that fell short of any concrete commitment.[95]

Crucially, while Shaw and Wrightson attracted support from O'Connell and his closest supporters, and from a significant number of Irish and English Tories, they failed to attract all the prominent Irish Conservatives (Edward Lucas spoke against the amendment), and were not supported by the party's

92 *Hansard*, 3, xl, 1265–8, 1272–5 [19 Feb. 1838].
93 *Ibid.*, 1268–70.
94 *Ibid.*, 1270–2, 1281–2.
95 *The Times*, 21 Feb. 1838.

leaders. Shaw's amendment was lost by a decisive 134 to 75. This was a serious setback to the bill's opponents, but there was still hope that the Lords would take a stronger line. As if in retaliation, Shaw refused to support Lucas's subsequent amendment to include settlement clauses in the bill, which the latter urged as necessary, amongst other things, to protect the industry of Ulster from being swamped by the mobile poverty of Connacht and Munster. Significantly, Lucas also argued that settlement should be included as the bill gave, in effect (if not *de jure*), a right to relief to the destitute. Clements agreed with the latter, but insisted that a 'practical settlement' implicit in the bill made any formal enactment unnecessary, while Wyse observed that such a 'practical settlement' already operated with respect to the Irish fever hospitals and houses of industry. Russell's insistence on maintaining the freedom of the labour market sealed the issue, and the amendment was lost by a majority of seventy-two.[96] Irritated by this setback, Lucas ultimately abstained on the final vote on the grounds that the bill, while right in principle, was seriously marred in its details.[97]

As with the previous year's bill, Smith O'Brien again moved that guardians be given the power to give outdoor relief to certain classes of the poor for whom the workhouse test was inapplicable. It was quite clear, he insisted, from the public meetings recently held in Ireland, that this alone would render the bill popular and allow MPs to return home 'to receive the blessings of their countrymen'. Yet, at the same time as making this clear case for 'popularizing' the bill, in which he was supported by Poulett Scrope and Daniel Callaghan of Cork, Smith O'Brien partially acknowledged the political difficulties preventing the government from so acting, by declaring that he could be reconciled to the present bill through a conviction that it 'must necessarily work out its own enlargement'.[98]

The emigration clause came under discussion on 2 March, with James Grattan denouncing it as a distraction from waste-land reclamation and an incentive to landowners to clear their estates at public expense, and O'Connell pointing out Russell's inconsistency in excluding it from the previous bill. In response, Russell downplayed its significance and declared it unlikely to be used except at the margin, and offered to alter the wording of the clause to remove the implication that the commissioners might have any emigration

96 *Hansard*, 3, xli, 61–73 [23 Feb.]. For Clements' lobbying for the admission of a flexible 'practice' of settlement, see NLI: KP, Ms 14,298, Clements to H. McCall, 16 Feb. 1838.

97 *Hansard*, 3, xlii, 703–5 [30 Apr.].

98 *Ibid.*, xli, 73–80 [23 Feb.]. A second attempt to allow outdoor relief by public works, moved by Poulett Scrope, also failed: *ibid.*, xlii, 538–40 [9 Apr. 1838].

powers over and above the decision of a board of guardians to raise a local rate for the purpose. Morpeth confirmed that the government's expectation was that the clause would only be used in exceptional circumstances (including in times of famine), but that it was required to assuage Irish opinion, and the clause, with amended wording, was retained.[99]

Discussion of the vagrancy and punitive clauses was initiated by Edward Sugden's objection to the liability placed by clause forty-nine on married women and widows, and on the mothers of illegitimate children, to maintain their children, which he declared to be an unfair punishment to women (as exonerating absent fathers), and which O'Connell thought calculated to encourage the breaking of family bonds. In response the solicitor-general announced that the government was prepared to strike out parts of clause fifty-three, which contained not only the sanctions against familial desertion but those against vagrancy also. In taking this opportunity to drop the vagrancy paragraph, Russell confirmed the opinion he had given privately in 1836 (and which Nicholls had strongly opposed): a vagrancy measure could not be expected to work until those who would operate it were prepared to do so, and that could not happen before it was clear that a poor law giving effective relief to all the destitute was in full operation. A separate vagrancy bill would, he now announced, follow only when these conditions were met.[100] In the end only the sanctions against those in receipt of relief who absconded from the workhouse, or broke its rules, or introduced or consumed alcohol therein, were retained, and the maximum penalty reduced from three to one month's imprisonment.[101]

Further debate touched on the rating clauses, with O'Connell and the radicals demanding that other species of property (including rents) be subjected to rate, while Irish landowners sought the exclusion or reduction of rates on bog-lands, mines and tithes. Again, only minor alterations to the original terms were approved. The ministers seriously considered Clements' suggestion that guardians might be paid allowances (thus facilitating the number of working farmers who might serve), but ultimately turned this down as likely to promote self-interested 'jobbery'.[102] In the end the only substantial amendments made in the Commons had been those fitting with the preconceptions of the home secretary, and which the expression of Irish opinion had facilitated him in making. Nevertheless, ministers were able to

99 Ibid., xli, 374–9 [2 Mar. 1838]; *A Bill [as amended in Committee and on Re-commitment] for the More Effectual Relief of the Destitute Poor in Ireland*, PP 1837–38 (238) v.345, p. 17.

100 *Hansard*, 3, xli, 379–85 [2 Mar. 1838].

101 *Bill [as amended in Committee]*, pp. 18–19.

102 NA: RP, PRO30/22/3A, fols 289–93, 306–7, Clements to Russell, 6 Apr., Duncannon to Russell, 11 Apr. 1838.

assert that of the twenty-five divisions that had taken place in committee, only eight had seen a majority of Irishmen vote against the government. They neglected to mention that these included the key votes on outdoor relief and settlement.[103]

Behind the scenes, however, ministers were evidently concerned at the unpopularity the measure was attracting both in parliament and in Ireland, and sought ways of softening the burden that would be imposed. The bill's strongest supporters insisted that the costs of workhouse construction must be underwritten by long, interest-free loans to the Irish unions (ten years without interest, with twenty annual instalments). In March Russell urged the cabinet to be generous, as '[t]he Bill requires some support to bear it up against the unjust odium exerted against it. If this is, as I believe, a very great measure for the United Kingdom (carried in its integrity) the cost is not too great.' Duncannon agreed that it would be impossible to ask that Ireland begin to repay the costs of construction at once and that some financial sacrifice by Britain was essential to carry it through.[104] This was generally supported by Howick and Thomson, but angrily rejected by Spring Rice and Melbourne. Both criticized what they regarded as the fiscal irresponsibility of the proposal, but the chancellor also revealed what was for him a more important consideration – it would strangle the availability of funds for public works and emigration.[105] In the end, however, Russell got most of what he had demanded.

The Commons debate on the third reading, on 30 April, saw the main arguments on the principle of the bill recapitulated. Irish country gentlemen, including the Repealer Sir William Brabazon and the Tories Sir Frederick Trench and Viscount Castlereagh, led the assault, citing the popular hostility towards it, the inadequacy of Nicholls' understanding, and (in the case of Ulster), the preferability of the existing 'Scotch system' of voluntary relief. O'Connell endorsed the statements made about the widespread unpopularity of the measure with the farmers and gentry, and expressed a hope that the Lords would dispatch it. Yet at the same time he was honest enough to acknowledge that his stance had put him into conflict with the Catholic clergy in their desire to 'make the rich feed the poor', although he believed their confidence in a poor law misplaced.[106]

103 *Hansard*, 3, xlii, 686 [30 Apr. 1838: Morpeth].

104 NLI: MP, Ms 13,398, Russell memo, 26 Mar., Duncannon memo [Mar. 1838].

105 Memos by Howick, Thomson, Melbourne and Spring Rice, 26 Mar. 1838, *ibid.*

106 *Hansard*, 3, xlii, 675–84; a string of Ulster Tories, including John Young, Henry Corry, Sir Edmund Hayes and Col. Conolly, also spoke and voted against the third reading. Castlereagh threatened that the bill would 'weaken the attachment of the Protestants of the north of Ireland to the English connection', *ibid.*, 718.

The speeches in this debate of three of the bill's supporters illuminate the different motivations and degrees of enthusiasm for the measure. Morpeth, in an address lauded in Whig journals as the best made on the question, vindicated the measure as one of 'justice to Ireland' and embodying the true will of the Irish people.[107] No government bill could be expected to satisfy in full the promoters of the range of rival bills, and a balance needed to be found between the excessive expectations of the proposed recipients of relief and the exaggerated alarms of those who would have to pay. It was true, he admitted, that numerous public meetings and petitions had been raised against the measure, but he questioned both their representativeness and the concern of their sponsors for those on the margins of society:

> [He] could not forget that the classes for whose benefit it was principally intended did not enjoy corresponding means of making their wishes known. From what, no doubt, were the honest and sincere, but he believed also the exaggerated, apprehensions of the contributors to the poor-rate, he could not help turning to the poorer classes of the Irish people, wandering on the highways, or perishing in their cabins. The cry of him that was ready to perish did not find its way to their table.

As before, it was the pastoral experience and authority of Catholic clergymen that the chief secretary invoked to provide justification for the measure. A Father Toole of Kildare, he related, had dared to answer O'Connell in a public meeting, reminding him that in that county 'there were annually hundreds of [the poor] who died of want, but who would have been saved by a poor law.' This simple but eloquent statement summed up, in his opinion, the heart of the bill. Clements echoed the sentiment that 'merchants and farmers in Ireland might be opposed to the measure, but there was another class which had not been consulted, the class of the destitute, the aged and the helpless.'[108]

In stressing the moral argument for a poor law, Morpeth had not neglected to mention his hope for its indirect operation in inducing the poor to seek work and the ratepayers to provide it. But this emphasis on the poor law as a mechanism for social engineering was taken much further by the president of the board of trade, Poulett Thomson. His recent visit to Ireland had, he asserted, convinced him both of the wide extent of 'imposition' on the part of mendicants evading honest employment, and the wholesale evasion by the wealthy of their social responsibilities that had caused the great increase in pauperism. The poor law involved, for him, chiefly the imposition of a system of compulsion – forcing all these classes to help themselves through self-

107 Anon., 'Ireland', *Monthly Chronicle*, 2 (1838), pp. 31–9.
108 *Hansard*, 3, xlii, 684–9, 702–3 [30 Apr.].

exertion.[109] This looked forward to the transformative expectations placed upon the Irish poor law in the later 1840s by moralists such as Howick and Charles Wood.

On behalf of the opposition front bench, Stanley gave the bill at best a very lukewarm endorsement, and did not hesitate to state his concern at the extensive powers reserved to the commissioners or his suspicions of Nicholls' false certainties about the scale of Irish destitution. Like Lucas, he felt that the bill could only be completed with the inclusion of vagrancy clauses and a particular settlement, but felt relieved that the responsibility for the consequences would rest on the ministers. His support was given 'reluctantly and hesitatingly', but this was enough to prevent a party division. Peel declined to speak and continued to give the bill his silent support. More usefully, Sugden denied the charge that the bill had been forced on Ireland by the weight of English numbers.[110]

The vote on the third reading was carried by 234 to 59. Embarrassingly for the government, however, and in contrast to the vote on the second reading, only twenty-five Irish members now voted with the majority (eighteen Whig-liberals, five Repealers and two Conservatives), while thirty-eight voted against, and at least eight (including Sheil, More O'Ferrall, and the O'Conor Don) abstained. Including the tellers, the heterogeneous minority comprised sixteen Irish Conservatives, twelve Repealers, ten Irish Whig-liberals, eighteen British Conservatives and five British Whig-liberals and radicals. This outcome allowed critics such as Castlereagh to bait an irritable Russell with the charge that it been passed on the back of the 'ignorant' vote of the English majority. *The Times* agreed that the English majority in the Commons were glad to be rid of such a 'tedious and difficult question', and cared little for the consequences in Ireland.[111]

The bill in the Lords

Attention now turned to the upper House. Some observers confidently expected the Conservative majority there to overturn the bill, but in reality this would depend on two factors: the extent to which a British protectionist argument for an Irish poor law acted as a counterweight to instinctive loyalty towards Irish landowners; and the stance taken by the Conservative leader in

109 *Ibid.*, 708–12.

110 *Hansard*, 3, xlii, 696–8, 712–15 [30 Apr.]; BL: Broughton diary, Add Ms 56,559, fols 77–8, 30 Apr. *The Times* (26 Feb. 1838) believed Stanley's illness during the committee discussion of settlement had prevented him throwing his weight behind Lucas's amendment.

111 *Hansard*, 3, xlii, 712–19 [30 Apr.]; *The Times*, 2 May 1838.

the Lords, the duke of Wellington.[112] The duke, who had Irish landed connections by birth and marriage, began to come under sustained pressure from the Irish anti-poor-law lobby during the course of the session. Copies of letters from Whately to Senior attacking the principle of the bill had been forwarded to him, but the question only really began to receive his serious attention towards the end of March 1838.[113] The active Irish Tory peers Glengall and Roden sent copies of the county grand jury resolutions and articles from Tory papers like the *Waterford Mail* against the bill, but the duke's initial response was to wait until it was clear what the Commons would do with this 'delicate' question, while warning his Irish correspondents of the difficulty posed by the support of most English proprietors for the bill.[114]

Once the Irish poor law bill arrived in the Lords on 1 May (introduced with a minimalist endorsement from Melbourne), the initial strategy on the part of its opponents, led by the maverick Whig-liberal Clanricarde, was to seek deferral of the second reading until after the more politically controversial tithe bill had been considered. Other vocal critics, such as Limerick and Londonderry, insisted that sufficient time must be allowed for the tabling of numerous hostile petitions from Ireland, and Wellington gave mild support to the request for postponement; in the end the second reading was put off until 21 May.[115] This breathing space allowed the anti-poor-law peers to prepare themselves.

Petitions from county grand juries were presented, 'read at length' and debated on 4, 7 and 21 May, allowing the Irish lords an opportunity to demonstrate to their English peers the extent to which the property of Ireland was 'uniformly' against the measure.[116] Meanwhile, the anti-poor-law Irish peers

112 *The Times* (21, 23, 24 May 1838) was sure that the 'still-born abortion' would be crushed or at least its chief deformities removed, but its editorialist badly misread Wellington's position.

113 SUL: WP, WP2/48/39, Copy of Whately to Senior, 13 Nov. 1837. For the duke's relations with the Irish Conservatives, see Peter Gray, 'Wellington and the government of Ireland, 1832–46', in C. M. Woolgar (ed.), *Wellington Studies, III* (Southampton, 1999), pp. 203–26.

114 SUL: WP, WP2/50/25–6, 32–6, 43, Glengall to Wellington, 25 Mar., Wellington to Glengall, 28 Mar., Edward Popham to Wellington, 28 Mar., Roden to Wellington, 31 Mar., Wellington to Roden, 3 Apr. 1838; *Waterford Mail*, 3 Mar. 1838.

115 *Hansard*, 3, xlii, 722–5 [1 May]. The reading had initially been postponed to 14 May, but put off by another week owing to Wellington's complaining of deafness, SUL: WP, WP2/51/61, Wellington to Melbourne, 14 May 1838.

116 *Hansard*, 3, xlii, 897–8, 943–4; xlii, 1–3. The Whig Fitzwilliam joined the Conservatives Wicklow and Londonderry in attacking Nicholls in these debates.

and MPs had met under the chairmanship of Clanricarde at the Carleton Club on 5 and 9 May to plan their tactics. There was general agreement that a measure for the relief of the aged and infirm would be acceptable, but not one embracing relief of the able-bodied, in or out of workhouses. They were, however, unable to resolve the differences between those who wished to oppose the second reading *in toto*, and those who (following Wellington's prompt) would hold their fire and concentrate on supporting amendments in committee. The latter would be drafted by Lord Fitzgerald, and include the resuscitation of Shaw's amendment to restrict relief to 'incapables'.[117]

Wellington met with the Irish Conservative leaders after the meeting of 9 May and discussed amendments proposed by them and Lord Ellenborough. The crucial one, which he was at first prepared to support, would (following Shaw in the Commons) insert into the workhouse clause the words 'for the necessary relief of the lame, impotent, old, blind, and such others among them being poor and not able to work' – thus pointing out 'the real objects of the bill'.[118] However, this did not receive universal support even from the Irish peers. Lord Devon, who owned extensive estates in Co. Limerick, and was close to Peel, thought Shaw's amendment unworkable, and assured Wellington that the bill could have the desired effect, in time, of improving the condition of the country. Lord Clancarty, a highly-respected young Irish peer, also came out in support of a 'comprehensive' poor law as necessary for the good government, future improvement and real safety of Ireland.[119] Perhaps more surprisingly, the ultra-Tory Earl of Wicklow also broke ranks to offer sustained support to the principle of the bill, which he thought had been rendered safe by the denial of a right to relief.[120] The arguments of these peers, and probably also of Peel – who was now seeking a political settlement of all the outstanding Irish questions – appear to have persuaded the duke to back away from his earlier commitment and ultimately to oppose the key amendment.[121] His irritable reaction to the ultra-Tory Lord Roden's excitable warnings that any substantial poor law bill would ruin the best resident gentry

117 SUL: WP, WP2/51/17, 32, Downshire to Wellington, 5 May, Clanricarde to Wellington, 9 May.

118 Wellington to Ellenborough, 11 May 1838, *ibid.*, WP2/51/39.

119 Devon to Wellington, 14 May, Clancarty to Wellington, 16 May, *ibid.*, WP2/51/56, 66–7. Devon was among the peers identified by Peel as 'our confidential friends' who met to discuss party strategy in the Lords: Peel to Wellington, 22 May 1838, *ibid.*, WP2/51/106.

120 *Hansard*, 3, xliii, 85–6 [22 May]; 354–5 [28 May 1838].

121 For Peel's desire for compromise and clearance of the Irish bills, see C. C. F. Greville, *The Greville Memoirs (Second Part)* (3 vols, London, 1885), i, pp. 100–1 [3–7 June 1838].

and rouse the anger of Irish loyalism, marked this shift. He shot back to Roden, warning him 'not to allow yourselves to be misled by any exaggerated representations of its enactments. . . . If you do not take this course you will expose the House of Lords to the imputation of throwing out a bill agreed to by all but a very small minority of the House of Commons composed principally of the *Tail*.'[122]

The second reading of the bill was debated in what one correspondent described as 'the fullest House I ever saw'.[123] Proposing the bill, Melbourne felt obliged to defend his evident inconsistency on the matter by appealing to the success of the amended English system and proposing its extension to Ireland. His advocacy, not unexpectedly, was less than overwhelming: 'I think it is worth trying the experiment,' he concluded, 'as it is more than probable that by degrees it may effect some amelioration.'[124] Hatherton took a stronger line in support of the bill, stressing its safety and economy, but nevertheless urging the addition of clauses relating to settlement and vagrancy. Devon was again its most enthusiastic supporter, rejecting any alternative to the workhouse test as unworkable and looking forward to the closer and more constructive social relationships the legislation would stimulate.[125]

In response, Fitzwilliam challenged not only the applicability of the English law, and the accuracy and intelligence of Nicholls, but also the generic principle of poor laws on Malthusian grounds: '[T]he laws for the benefit of the poor tended to rob the supreme Ruler of the Universe of one of his attributes, and to overthrow the law which he had promulgated in the beginning of the world – that "man should eat bread by the sweat of his brow."' This 'English bill' would destroy the growing prosperity of Ireland, he concluded.[126] This speech was acknowledged by many as particularly powerful; Lansdowne commented ruefully that he had never heard him speak better, and lamented the limitations of his own reaction.[127] Lord Brougham, long notorious as an antagonist towards 'that accursed law of Elizabeth', backed up this theoretical

122 SUL: WP, WP2/51/105, Roden to Wellington, 22 May; Wellington to Roden, 23 May 1838 [draft].

123 *Scotsman*, 23 May 1838.

124 *Hansard*, 3, xliii, 3–15 [21 May]. *The Times*'s (25 May 1838) sarcastic comment that he seemed happy to give the Lords 'sufficient elbow-room to carve and cut at pleasure', appears not far from the truth.

125 *Hansard*, 3, xliii, 44–8 [21 May].

126 *Ibid.*, 15–19. Despite the repeated claim that this was an 'English bill', it was also opposed *in toto* by a number of English peers, including Stanhope and Macclesfield: *ibid.*, 355–8 [28 May].

127 BL: BP, B/95, Lansdowne to Spring Rice, [May 1838].

hostility; but most of the bill's opponents gave greater stress to its unpopularity in Ireland and its unworkability. Clanricarde came closest to articulating a class interest in expressing the fear that the centralizing powers of the bill, in common with many other innovations under the present administration, would continue the process of 'gradually and by degrees superseding the resident gentry'.[128]

In his lengthy and highly sarcastic speech, Brougham, now bitterly opposed to his former colleagues in the ministry, goaded the still-silent Lansdowne to defend the bill of which he was the 'adoptive parent'.[129] Many observers were fully aware of the aversion towards the measure shared by Lansdowne and Spring Rice, and the Knight of Kerry had privately come to the conclusion that the government's real aim was to have the bill defeated in the Lords and thus transfer the obloquy for the loss of the current 'preposterous' measure.[130] While this was untrue, the illness of Duncannon and the 'idleness, busyness or carelessness' of other ministerial peers threw the responsibility for seeing the government's business through the House on the prime minister and Lansdowne. The latter appears at this point to have agreed with Senior, with whom he discussed the matter at length, that 'the present state of the English mind' rendered the bill unavoidable, and that all hope must be placed in the promotion of auxiliary measures.[131] Under these pressures, Lansdowne felt he had no choice but to speak in defence of the bill when 'dragged like a badger from his box, and baited into action' by Brougham and Lyndhurst. He did this by indicating the absence of feasible alternatives and the modest advantages he anticipated from the measure.[132]

Two opposition front-benchers spoke in the debate, employing markedly different tones. Lord Lyndhurst's acerbic comments amounted to a 'party speech' calculated to embarrass and undermine the government, and to delight hostile observers. Wellington's views were more important and more closely attended to. The duke went out of his way to echo Melbourne's case that the success of the English reform had paved the way for an Irish

128 *Hansard*, 3, xliii, 24–8, 40–4, 67 [28 May: Londonderry, Clanricarde, Westmeath].

129 *Ibid.*, 48–63 [28 May].

130 SUL: WP, WP2/51/52–3, Maurice Fitzgerald to Wellington, 12 May 1838. *The Times* (2 June 1837) had previously also advanced this interpretation.

131 NLW: NSP C/591, Senior to Whately, [May 1838]. Senior also appears to have softened his stance against the bill, as his doubts about the efficacy of emigration and public employment increased: Senior to Whately, 30 July 1838, *ibid.*, C/595.

132 *Hansard*, 3, xlii, 63–7 [21 May]; *The Times*, 25 May.

enactment, and that such a measure (without, he insisted, the iniquitous laws of settlement) was evidently required. He also stressed the size of the Commons majority for the bill and warned its opponents that if they rejected this, they must have an alternative measure ready for consideration.[133] This seriously disappointed the anti-poor-law Irish peers, and went far towards ensuring that the bill would pass the Lords with its essential attributes intact. Despite Wellington's private fear, expressed to Nicholls, that the bill might be lost, the second reading was carried by the unexpectedly large margin of 129 to 20. Lyndhurst, for all his denunciation of the measure, voted with the majority.[134]

For both its advocates and detractors the key clause in the bill was the forty-first, which offered workhouse relief to the destitute poor. The ministers agreed to postpone discussion of all other clauses in committee until this was resolved. Fitzwilliam moved a cosmetic alteration of the term 'workhouse' to 'poor-house', but also the more crucial omission of the word 'destitute' and the enumeration of classes of the 'impotent' poor deserving relief, and giving power to ratepayers to veto relief to able-bodied applicants. This rather upstaged Fitzgerald's similar amendment agreed at the meeting of Irish Tory peers – but Fitzgerald strengthened the case by cleverly flagging up the differences between the first Nicholls report and the present bill, especially in its omission of assisted emigration. Like most who spoke against the bill, he warned about the inflammatory consequences of disappointed expectations on the part of the poor, and the difficulties of imposing the law on recalcitrant ratepayers.[135] The west Cork landowner Lord Carbery combined the Malthusian concerns of many of his fellows about overpopulation and depletion of the wages-fund with a demand for assisted emigration and a warning that Catholic religious feelings would continue to obligate alms-giving with or without a poor law, meaning that mendicancy could never be suppressed.[136]

These attacks were answered without much conviction (as Brougham again sarcastically observed) by Melbourne and Lansdowne.[137] The English lord chancellor was more effusive – Cottenham (himself an Irish property-owner) cited the publications of Clements and Lynch in defence of the measure's suitability and ultimate popularity, while Lord Mulgrave, on a rare visit to Westminster, took advantage of a procedural point raised by Brougham

133 *Hansard*, 3, xlii, 19–24 [21 May], 358–60 [28 May]. The discrepancy between the speeches was stressed in *MC* (22 May), although denied by some Tory papers.
134 BL: Broughton diary, Add Ms 56,559, fols 102–3, 26 May 1838.
135 *Hansard*, 3, xlii, 364–9 [28 May].
136 *Ibid.*, 487–90 [31 May].
137 *Ibid.*, 370–5 [28 May], 493–3, 495–9, 499–500 [31 May].

to insist on the simple point that 'the property of Ireland should be made to bear its fair proportion towards the relief of a mass of misery; which, whilst it continued to exist in so large a limb of the empire, could not but be regarded as a national disgrace'.[138]

However, it was on Wellington's stance that the outcome of this motion would turn, and this turned out again to be unambiguously supportive of the clause as it stood. His dismissal of the efficacy of voluntary charity for the destitute poor relied, like the government's case, on exposing the collapse of the Dublin Mendicity Association. Moreover, he went on, the sheer scale of Ireland's poverty ruled out any reliance on parochial collections as in Scotland, while he thought it likely the bill would induce landowners to pay proper attention to the needs of the poor on their estates, as they did in England.[139] At the end of these 'exceedingly violent' debates, Fitzwilliam's amendment was in the end defeated by 107 to 41, although some verbal changes were made identifying first the old and infirm, then orphan children, and finally 'other destitutes' as suitable objects for relief in that order, and establishing a priority in admission of those destitutes resident in the union (as recorded in a union register) over those from elsewhere. This amounted to a preferential form of settlement, however diluted and ill-defined. Nicholls, who had observed from the public gallery, was scathing:

> It is difficult to describe the scene which took place, on the motion for going into committee on the bill. The confusion then, and indeed during the whole night, surpassed anything one could have expected in such a deliberative assembly. The alarms of the Irish peers as to the effects of the measure exceeded all bounds, and they were joined by several English peers who are supporters of the English Poor Law.[140]

The one amendment which Wellington had singled out as essential, the dropping of the £5 rating clause, was, along with the downgrading of the resident Dublin commissioner from a compulsory to a permissive element of the bill, the only other major amendment agreed by the Lords' committee.[141] Under pressure, Melbourne introduced a compromise motion allowing the lessee voluntarily to pay the rate for an occupier of land valued under £5, in return for a rate rebate of up to 10 per cent if agreed by the guardians.[142] This

138 *Ibid.*, 481–4, 493–5 [31 May]. There was a convention that the lord lieutenant should not comment in the Lords on Irish legislation currently under review.
139 *Ibid.*, 477–91 [31 May].
140 *Irish Poor Law*, p. 220.
141 *Hansard*, 3, xlii, 962–5 [22 June].
142 *Dublin Evening Mail* [*DEM*], 20 June 1838.

would prove a total dead letter in practice, and the failure to excuse impoverished small tenants from rates 'on account of poverty' turned out to be the Achilles heel of the measure in its early years.[143] Lesser and largely uncontroversial amendments introduced by Wellington and Ellenborough made townlands indivisible by poor-law boundaries; restricted the term of paid vice-guardians to one year; required the commissioners to inspect and report on the Irish medical charities; increased the maximum number of ratepayer votes for multiple properties from five to six; and made it easier for ratepayers in individual electoral divisions to press for the operation of the emigration clause.[144] Several added clauses for registering workhouse inmates as residents of electoral districts, and charging the districts for their relief, were welcomed by their supporters as introducing 'a kind of provisional law of settlement, with limitations'. Although denounced by Senior as rendering a bad bill worse, these clauses were not regarded by ministers as substantially altering its sense, and were welcomed by the liberal press. Nicholls had doubts about the workability of the latter provisions, but acceded to the duke's insistence upon them as necessary to localize responsibility for poverty.[145]

Despite serious reservations about dropping the £5 rating clause (which subsequent experience of ratepayer unrest fully justified), Russell was not prepared to risk losing the bill over it and thought it might be remedied later. After negotiations between Nicholls and Wellington preceding a conference of the two houses, the bill passed with this and the other Lords' amendments largely intact.[146] The final passage of the poor law bill in the Lords was accompanied by passionate rhetoric and formal protests from its opponents. The final majority for the bill was ninety-three to thirty-one, the bulk of the latter being Irish Tory peers; the poor relief bill was finally signed into law by the Queen on 31 July 1838 as 1 & 2 Vic. c. 56.[147]

143 In 1843 Lewis commented bitingly, 'The landlords think that the tenant will pay the rate if he can, and if he cannot, that he will be excused, or resist. In short, they don't care what happens: they leave the tenant to his fate': NLW: HCP, C/2860, Lewis to Graham [draft], Jan. 1843.

144 A *Bill [as amended by the House of Lords] for the More Effectual Relief of the Destitute Poor in Ireland*, PP 1837–38 (577), v.393.

145 *DEM*, 6 June 1838; NLW: NSP, C/595, Senior to Whately, 30 July 1838; *MC*, 8 June 1838; Willink, 'Nicholls', pp. liii–lv.

146 SUL: BP, MEL/RU/51, Russell to Melbourne, 20 July; *Hansard*, 3, xliv, 575–81 [24 July 1838]; Nicholls, *Irish Poor Law*, pp. 220–1. Nicholls had already conceded that he thought the £5 exclusion too high: CHP, J19/1/16/62, Nicholls to Morpeth, 10 Jan. 1838.

147 *Hansard*, 3, xliv, 11–31 [9 July].

The poor law and 'auxiliary measures'

Throughout the poor law debates the government had assured sceptics that 'auxiliary measures' would also be introduced to soften the impact of the new measure. These promises did not, however, meet the expectations placed upon them in 1838. Despite his attachment to the principle of public works for Ireland, as chancellor of the exchequer Spring Rice thought it his duty to ratchet down both the proposed expenditure and the principle of greater government initiative suggested by the Irish government. If, he warned Morpeth in June, the government were 'to interfere and undertake the execution of public works at the expense of the state, the whole principle on which Col. Burgoyne's Board was established by us must be abandoned'.[148] No new public works legislation was proposed in the 1837–38 session, and Lynch's bills were again postponed until 1839. Critics who had dismissed the latter as merely permissive and 'too unimportant to be government measures' were not surprised by this further delay.[149]

It would, however, be wrong to dismiss the government's interest in public works as a mode of relief and employment as mere window-dressing. Certainly some elements of the administration, especially in Dublin Castle, continued to see them as essential. Drummond clashed with Spring Rice in summer 1837 over the latter's veto on the clauses in the public works bill the Dublin administration thought essential to address the annual subsistence and employment crisis on the western seaboard. He indicated that additional powers were necessary to transfer the costs of famine to the responsible parties, and demanded powers to levy an emergency labour-rate on the 'rapacious and unfeeling landlords' who exported crops while the poor starved.[150]

On the more ambitious subject of railways as a developmental auxiliary, the second report of the railway commission was completed and formally passed to the government in March 1838. It recommended, as anticipated, a massive state-led railway construction initiative, which would both give direct employment to 'vast numbers of people', and pump-prime the Irish economy by stimulating commerce and opening up undeveloped resources.[151] As important as its recommendations were the arguments cited in their support by Drummond, unquestionably with the endorsement of his superiors at Dublin Castle. The report followed Lewis in recognizing that a 'transition' in

148 NLI: MP, Ms 535, Spring Rice to Morpeth, 14 June 1838.

149 *The Times*, 31 Jan. 1838.

150 Drummond to Spring Rice, 1 Aug. 1837, in O'Brien (ed.), *Drummond*, pp. 257–9.

151 *Second Report of Railway Commissioners.*

Irish agriculture from cottier to capitalist agriculture was vital to the interests of all classes – not least because the current system, while producing both exports and profits, had been accompanied by growing immiseration and a concomitant growth in social conflict. Consolidation was essential, but both practicalities and ethics required that it be carried out with 'judicious humanity' (i.e. gradually and with compensation), and be accompanied by state assistance to prevent a collapse of entitlements and to kick-start a more broadly-based cycle of growth. What was proposed was a policy strategy that combined both developmental and welfarist elements – and which sought to balance the respective responsibilities of the state and the landed class. The latter would be enforced through the new poor law. In language similar to that of his later admonitory letter to the Tipperary magistrates, Drummond observed:

> Of course we do not palliate the injustice and cruelty of turning families adrift helpless and unprotected upon the world. There is a compact, implied at least, between the landlord and the peasantry who have been brought up on his estate, by which the latter have as good a right to protection as the lord of the soil has to make arbitrary dispositions for the future management of his property. . . . [T]he country will now look to those who hold the property, having received it charged with all its moral as well as its legal engagements.

Unlike Lewis, however, he believed that the burden so imposed must be speedily distributed through other channels if the transition were not to be excessively prolonged and painful. Of the available alternatives, waste-land reclamation was desirable, but only as an investment rather than as a 'home colonization' exercise; settling cottier peasants on the land without wider economic development would only replicate existing problems. Emigration could not be undertaken on a scale commensurate with that of the social problem. Only great infrastructural projects would serve the multiple purposes of facilitating the introduction of the poor law, stimulating the economy, and raising the moral character of large numbers of the labouring poor through providing regular, well-paid, employment:

> The works necessary for completing such a system of railways as our report contemplates, would serve both these purposes, by affording present employment to vast numbers of the people, and by throwing open resources and means of profitable occupation, which are now inaccessible and almost unknown. The immediate effect would be to afford extensive relief to the most indigent portion of the population, and that in a manner the most acceptable to their feelings, and the most conducive to their moral improvement. . . . To that want of continuous employment and of adequate remuneration when employed, may be traced the cause, not only of the poverty of the Irish people, but, in a great measure, also of that heedless improvidence, and of those habits of lassitude and indolence, which it may possibly require years of a better system to eradicate wholly from their character.

The railway project would thus promote both the economic and moral regeneration of Ireland.

In an attempt to implement the report rapidly, Mulgrave and Drummond proposed in February 1838 that the tithe rent charge, a sum they thought amounting to around £400,000 per annum, be appropriated for five years for public works, principally railway-construction, to facilitate the introduction of the poor law (with the cost of the Anglican establishment transferred to the Consolidated Fund). However, this proved politically a non-starter. Russell concluded that, for all the inherent merits of the scheme, British opinion would not then swallow the increase in taxation involved in the transfer of the costs of the Irish Church to general taxation.[152] With widespread hostility to increased government expenditure evident in the Commons (especially from radicals who now held the balance of power), and the Conservative leadership in both houses openly antagonistic both to such a breach of *laissez-faire*, especially if it infuriated Tory-leaning private railway speculators in Ireland, and to the appropriation of Church revenues, the government seems to have suffered a loss of nerve on the topic in 1838. While still believing a state railway project desirable, Russell complained to the lord lieutenant that he doubted whether they 'could divide 150 in its favour' if connected to the tithe question.[153]

Drummond was reluctant to give it up and urged Russell to act on the Railway Commission's report to attain 'the great good [that] is within your reach': but the government had already suffered a series of embarrassing defeats following radical defections that session, and Russell appears to have opted, at least in the short term, for ministerial survival over pursuit of the original 'comprehensive plan' of tacking a major infrastructural project onto the introduction of the poor law.[154] Spring Rice, who still had hankerings after a massive Canadian colonization scheme, and hoped the revelation of the stark costs of poverty by the poor-rate would open eyes to its necessity, was reluctant to divert resources to other projects; he warned Morpeth that any fresh tax for railway construction (if this could be justified) must fall on Ireland not England.[155] The Railway Commission report was held over for publication until the end of the session, to allow the government a breathing space to decide what to do with it. Morpeth would seek to break the logjam over funding in the 1839 session.

152 NA: RP, PRO30/22/3A, fols 150–2, 159–60, 163, 165–72, Mulgrave to Russell, 21 Feb., Howick memo, [Feb.], Lansdowne memo, [Feb.], Drummond memo, 22 Feb.; MC: NP, M/902, Russell to Mulgrave, 26 Feb. 1838.

153 MC: NP, M/904, Russell to Mulgrave, 16 Mar. 1838.

154 NA: RP, PRO30/22/3A, fols 224–9, Drummond to Russell, 20 Mar. 1838.

155 NLI: MP, Ms 543, Spring Rice to Wilmot Horton, 7 Sept., Spring Rice to Morpeth, 26 Sept. 1838.

The legislative outcome of 1837–38 was thus less than had initially been anticipated. Moreover, the escalating degree of popular opposition expressed in Ireland had evidently disappointed and surprised the poor law's initiators. The lord lieutenant concluded that, under these circumstances, he was not over-sanguine as to its success, while sure it still represented 'a step in the right direction'.[156] Russell, ever the optimist, continued to defend the administration as having sought to provide 'in the spirit of the laws of Queen Elizabeth, for the subsistence of the poor', but was aware that this interpretation was hotly contested and opted to uphold the ministry's record mostly on other heads.[157] Much would depend on how the bill was now implemented and received in Ireland.

156 CHP, J/19/1/18/6, Mulgrave to Morpeth, 3 May 1838.
157 Lord John Russell, *The Government of Ireland* (London, 1839), p. 18.

7

Public reaction in Ireland and Britain, I: 1836–37

The publication of the third report of the Whately Commission, the commentaries upon it by Senior, Lewis and Revans, and the reports of George Nicholls, all attracted extensive public comment in Ireland and significant attention in Great Britain. The subsequent Irish Poor Law Bills of 1837 and 1837–38 likewise became the focus of heated public debate. The views of the 'public' in both countries were expressed through newspaper columns, pamphlet exchanges and public meetings, resolutions and petitions. This chapter considers the debates on the reports and commentaries of 1836; the public campaign led by Thaddeus O'Malley and others in support of a poor law in Ireland in 1836–37; Daniel O'Connell's counter-attack against this; and the critical response to the government's 1837 bill in Ireland and Britain. The following chapter reviews the response to the 1837–38 bill and the more polarized arguments of that session.

Public reactions to the Whately report

Newspapers which had long been committed to advocating a substantial poor law for Ireland not surprisingly found the conclusions of the Whately Commission inadequate. *The Times*, which continued to take an intense interest in the subject, had reacted to the commission's interim report in early January 1836 with impatience and hostility. It was clear from its 'strange astounding passages', the editorialist declared, that no public provision for the destitute was intended, although there was an attempt to obscure this reality behind 'mountains of irrelevant testimony'. The sympathies of the British people for the sufferings of their starving fellow-creatures would, however, be proof against such 'sophistry'. Quoting from the highly emotive evidence given by Catholic and Protestant clergy about deaths from hunger – 'accounts of deadly misery which make the blood run cold' – the paper demanded prompt rejection by the government of the findings of the 'learned leeches' of the commission.[1]

The staggered publication of the evidence accumulated by the assistant commissioners, which was widely reprinted in the British and Irish newspapers, provided ample ammunition for critics of Whately and his colleagues. *The Times* questioned rhetorically whether the commissioners could have read the evidence published under their name. For this paper it was axiomatic that the depth of destitution thus exposed demanded a measure modelled on the original English Poor Law Act – the 43rd of Elizabeth.[2]

The core recommendations of the third report were leaked to the press in the second half of March 1836; sympathetic papers, such as the *Observer*, praised the decision to reject the workhouse in favour of assisted emigration and employment for the able-bodied, not least because it believed that this is what the Irish poor themselves desired.[3] *The Times* printed the full report on 9 April, but opted now to denounce the ministry for delaying framing a measure rather than attack the report directly. Its subsequent comments likewise focused on the failure of other Whig measures to secure any real improvement in the condition of the poor, and the hypocrisy of 'the Big Beggarman' O'Connell and of Spring Rice on the poor-law question, rather than addressing the report as such.[4] Why such uncharacteristic hesitation in the 'Thunderer'? It is possible that the employment schemes bundled together in the third report may have been sufficient to appease (at least temporarily) a paper whose proprietor, John Walter, had strong preferences for a form of the old English poor law and whose hostility to both the workhouse system and Somerset House was notorious. At any rate, there was political capital to be extracted from goading the ministry with having denied any 'justice to Ireland' for the 'starving' poor, and the paper deployed long extracts from the volumes of evidence to prove the urgency of the case.[5] The *Morning Herald*, which like *The Times* had defected from the Whigs to the Conservatives in 1834, and which was also a staunch defender of the old English law against

1 *The Times*, 19, 23 Jan. 1836. True to the logic of its simultaneous campaign against the English Poor Law Amendment Act, *The Times* sought to identify the Irish commission's position as reflecting that of the English 'ultra-Liberal' utilitarians.

2 *Ibid.*, 28 Jan. 1836.

3 *Observer*, 20 Mar., 3 Apr. 1836.

4 *The Times*, 9, 20 Apr., 19 May, 2 Sept. 1836.

5 *The Times*, 9, 13 Sept., 19 Oct. 1836. The paper subsequently described the Whately Commission's employment recommendations as overcomplicated and encumbered with excessive machinery, but at least more commensurate with the scale of Irish destitution than the plans of the 'ignorant quacks' associated with the government; it rejected Whately's emigration proposals entirely: *ibid.*, 12 Dec. 1837.

the new, was more outspoken in rejecting the Whately recommendations as 'timid, unsatisfactory and ineffective', but welcomed the publication of evidence as forcing the question to the forefront 'in spite of the theories of political economists and starvation philosophers'.[6] For sections of the British press, the Irish poor-law question served chiefly as a proxy for their more central preoccupation with what they regarded as the Benthamite assault on venerable English paternalist institutions. If this entailed a rift with the bulk of their fellow Conservatives in Ireland who remained strongly opposed to any poor law, they were prepared to undertake it, not least because O'Connell proved a more convenient target as the embodiment of Irish propertied 'self-interest'.

The Whig *Morning Chronicle* was also initially ambivalent towards the Whately report, reporting its main points sympathetically, while criticizing Bicheno by name for his apparent lack of enthusiasm for state intervention in employment and emigration measures, and defending the report's emphasis on the waste-land reclamation against *laissez-faire* criticisms which had been made by the more orthodox liberal *Courier*.[7] The weekly *Examiner* was similarly uncertain, lamenting the 'wild speculations and one-sided schemes' that had been mixed up indiscriminately with the more sensible recommendations, while rejecting the Malthusian underpinnings it discerned in the report. While the paper accepted the arguments given in the report against workhouse relief in Ireland, it expressed no real confidence in the proposed alternatives.[8]

The *Chronicle* remained convinced that Morpeth would bring in an effective and 'civilizing' poor law bill in the next session, and it was scathing towards the 'monsters in human shape', as it characterized estate-clearing Irish landowners.[9] As with the Irish ministers, the paper's developing position on the ethical necessity of a poor law appears to have been stimulated by humanitarian outrage over the reported sufferings of the western poor in the seasonal crises of 1835 and 1836. In Donegal, it proclaimed, there were

> wretches, in comparison with whose lot even [a] hog's mess of potatoes and salt water might be accounted a luxury. For so utterly destitute are they, that their only food – if we may so abuse the term as to apply it to garbage taken into the stomach, not for sustenance but to prevent absolute inanition – is boiled sea weed. Disease has come to exaggerate the horrors, and typhus fever, the sure

6 *Morning Herald*, 2 Apr. 1836. A similar line was taken by the more reliably Tory *Standard*.

7 *MC*, 6, 25 Apr.; *Courier*, 18 Apr. 1836.

8 *Examiner*, 8 May 1836.

9 *MC*, 5, 13, 14 May 1836.

attendant upon every visitation of the kind, has struck down the enfeebled bodies of many of the sufferers.[10]

This appalling social state was the product, not, as Malthusians claimed, of unrestrained human passion, but of a landed indifference or oppression that must be curbed by the state. The *Chronicle*'s confidence in the government's intentions in this respect, combined with a strong preference for a scheme modelled on the 43rd Elizabeth (albeit suitably modified and accompanied by auxiliary measures) would later lead this and other British liberal papers to take a stronger line against the Whately report. By 1838 it had come to the conclusion that the archbishop's proposals had been 'wild and mischievous'.[11]

The radical *Sun* also thought the evidence had proved beyond doubt the necessity of a substantial poor law, ideally accompanied by a major railway-building initiative; only this, it decided, could bring about a true assimilation of the two countries in habits, sentiments and opinions, in essence a 'real union, in which Great Britain and Ireland would be linked together by the treble bond of law, interest and affection'.[12] A similar stance was taken by the radical *Tait's Edinburgh Magazine*, which reprinted extracts from the evidence to demonstrate the necessity of an Irish poor law for the wellbeing of the working classes of both islands.[13]

Perhaps the most enthusiastic reaction to Whately's report in the metropolitan press came from the *Spectator*, a weekly close to Brougham and associated with philosophical radicalism. Ireland was, its writer declared, an exception to the general rules of *laissez-faire*, not least as the scale of misery there posed urgent challenges to the security of the British state. Whately was right to declare Ireland too poor for a workhouse system, although he should have pronounced his own schemes 'preparatory' to the desired end of an ultimate attainment of equal laws between both countries. In the short-run only great public works and extensive emigration could render Ireland peaceful and allow capital to flow in to civilize the 'stagnant, monotonous and semi-barbarous people' of that country. The emigration plan in particular was 'a great, bold scheme, not unworthy of the enlightened intellect and high moral courage which have presided over the Commission of Inquiry'. This enthusiasm did not extend to all the proposals or to support for increased taxation in Britain – the *Spectator* subsequently insisted that any emigration

10 *MC*, repr. in *Scotsman*, 4 May 1836.

11 *MC*, 15 Feb. 1837, 3 Mar. 1838.

12 *Sun*, reprinted in *FJ*, 11 Feb. 1836.

13 The *Tait's* articles were reprinted as Christine Johnstone, *True Tales of the Irish Peasantry, as Related by Themselves* (2nd edn, Edinburgh, 1836).

fund for Ireland be raised in Wakefieldian mode from the profits of reclaiming colonial waste-lands.[14] This rhetoric of colonial improvement (on both sides of the Atlantic) was a far cry from the 'justice to Ireland' themes voiced elsewhere, and serves as a reminder of the variety of attitudes within the broad 'liberal' camp in Britain.[15]

Irish reactions to the third report were similarly divided. The most influential nationalist daily, the *Freeman's Journal*, was then seeking 'justice under the Union' and had long lobbied for an Irish poor law.[16] The paper's reaction to the release of the third report was one of acute disappointment. While it contained some useful suggestions, it declared, the whole fell far short of the benefits anticipated from the 'adoption of the comprehensive principle contained in the 43rd of Elizabeth' – the right of the destitute poor to relief from the produce of the soil they lived on. For the *Freeman*, the central failing of the third report (along with Musgrave and Smith O'Brien's bills) lay in the attempt to evade an unavoidable clash with the Irish landed class – the avowed 'enemy' of the poor: 'The . . . Commissioners will . . . find that the grappling-iron of a poor law must drag the heartless proprietor to the altar of charity, since he will not volunteer to approach it.'[17]

This confrontational and class-oriented approach echoed that already adopted by the Foxite ministers. However, it was not sustained with the same degree of intensity in the Irish popular press over the following months. Part of the reason for this was the hardening of O'Connell's line against an English-style poor law in the course of 1836, which led nationalist papers like the *Freeman* to be at times more circumspect in their support for it. Another, more immediate, reason was the surprisingly favourable stance on the third report initially taken by Poulett Scrope.

Scrope had for several years been regarded in Ireland as the standard-bearer in parliament for a comprehensive and effective Irish poor law, and indeed the *Freeman* had praised his 1836 bill in contradistinction to what it regarded as the inadequate alternatives of Musgrave and Smith O'Brien. In April 1836, however, Scrope rather unexpectedly announced his general approbation of the recommendations of the third report, if not the 'mystification' in its reasoning; if every individual was thereby secured a living by

14 Anon., 'Report on the Irish poor', *Spectator*, 9 Apr. 1836, 'The regeneration of Ireland', *ibid.*, 13 Apr. 1836, 'Irish poor-law question, and colonial waste lands', *ibid.*, 7 May 1836.

15 A similarly pro-colonization solution to the problem of Irish poverty had been posited by the free-trade radical Richard Cobden in his first major publication in 1835, *England, Ireland and America* (new edn, Philadelphia, 1980), pp. 63–6.

16 *FJ*, 10 Feb., 19 Mar. 1836.

17 *FJ*, 25 Mar. 1836.

employment on public works or by emigration, he wrote publicly to John Lawless, 'security against starvation' would be guaranteed.[18] This reflected Scrope's preference for labour-rate relief over a workhouse system, but also perhaps a rather superficial understanding of the real focus and intentions of the third report; he would later harden his opinions against it, not least in the context of a public disputation with O'Connell. With the government still silent on its own intentions, the *Freeman* subsequently hedged its bets, rejecting mass emigration as a panacea, but searching for positive items in the Poor Inquiry Commission's varied menu of proposals.[19]

The Irish Tory press in general received the Whately report with equanimity and probably some relief. The evidence presented, declared the *Dublin University Magazine* in an article that appeared just before the publication of the third report, removed any doubt that something must be done to raise the condition of the poor. While joining in the widespread condemnation of absentees and making clear its opinion that the cottier system must be eliminated, this organ of Irish Conservatism expressed a clear preference for the landlord-led voluntary approach, also noting the beneficial effects of emigrant remittances and praising the charitable feelings of the peasantry.[20] While Conservative writers might have been hesitant to fully endorse a report headed by the 'Whig' archbishop, subsequent events clearly demonstrated that most of their representatives were comfortable with its outlines.[21]

The conclusion of the Poor Inquiry Commission's labours and the renewed expectations of government action sparked an escalation of public meetings and petitioning activity in Ireland. One of the most widely reported meetings took place at the Royal Exchange, Dublin, on 29 March 1836. While this was convened by the lord mayor, the moving force was John ('radical Jack') Lawless, who appears to have stage-managed the proceedings, and who had been agitating for an Irish poor law since at least 1829.[22] Despite attempts by Fenton Hort and his supporters to have the debate postponed until after the third report was published, Lawless insisted that the leaked summary in the *Observer* was sufficient to demonstrate that it would be grossly inadequate to Ireland's needs. Nothing short of the poor-law principle of 43rd Elizabeth, 'the

18 Poulett Scrope to Lawless, 7 Apr., in *FJ*, 11 Apr. 1836.
19 *Ibid.*, 12, 16 Apr. 1836.
20 Anon., 'State of the Irish poor', *DUM*, 7 (Apr. 1836), pp. 349–64.
21 The liberal *Dublin Evening Post* (12 Apr. 1836) criticized the Tory press for its silence on the report, while giving its own opinion that the recommendations would restore landed ascendancy in the country.
22 'Petition from John Lawless for an Irish Poor Law', *Hansard*, 2, xxi, 1189 [May 1829]; *JHC*, lxxxv (1830), p. 414. See also Larkin (ed.), *Tocqueville's Journey*, pp. 78–9.

magna charta of England', would suffice, he contended. The law must drag the resistant landlords to the temple of charity and force them to perform their sacred duty, he declared, to the cheers of the audience. This assault on landed culpability was strongly echoed by John Dillon, and most of the other floor speakers, a number of whom pointed out that Ireland's lack of state provision for the able-bodied destitute was a marked deviation from the European norm. Hort's motion for postponement was heavily defeated and the meeting agreed to urge all parishes in Dublin and throughout the country to petition for a poor law on the model already presented by Poulett Scrope.[23] Scrope's subsequent welcoming of the Whately report might have somewhat dampened the ardour of the Dublin lobby, had it not been for the uncompromising support they received from the Ulster radical and Dundalk MP William Sharman Crawford.[24] The Dublin petition was presented to the Lords on 13 May by the duke of Leinster, where it provoked a sharp debate.[25]

Provincial meetings frequently tied demands for a poor law to the already heavily agitated question of tithe abolition, positing a link between the two. The key role played by parish priests in convening these joint meetings was reflected in the language used to justify the poor-law demand. One such resolution, agreed at a meeting of three parishes in west Wicklow, declared it 'repugnant to the ordinations of Divine Providence and the precepts of natural and written law, that any portion of our fellow-countrymen should perish for want while we possess the means of relieving them'. Reporting on a similar resolution from a meeting at Carlow, the *Freeman* commented that it was the 'cursed tithe system [which] has, more than all the other calamities of Ireland, rendered the introduction of poor laws necessary to the peace and welfare of the country'.[26] At a 'numerous and respectable' meeting held in the chapel yard at Westport, Co. Mayo, the curate Father William Feeny, in a fiery and well-received oration, declared that 'the rack rents were undoubtedly the great cause of Ireland's misery; and that they must have a poor law, if it were to be of any use, to strike at the root of the evil; no relief for the poor could be effective which did not cure the cause of poverty by striking at that master-mischief, and compelling the landlords to maintain the poor, whom their exactions made poor.' Other speakers also appealed to both natural rights and Christian ethics in making the case for the 'right of the poor' to a subsistence from the land. James Whittle of Castlebar added the

23 Anon., *Poor Laws for Ireland: (Resolutions and a Petition Adopted) at a Public Meeting held at the Royal Exchange, Dublin, on . . . 29th of March 1836* ([Dublin, 1836]); FJ, 30–31 Mar., *The Times*, 1 Apr. 1836.

24 *FJ*, 13 Apr. 1836.

25 *Hansard*, 3, xxxiii, 898–904.

26 *FJ*, 4 Apr., 24 Feb. 1836.

historicist case that the suppression of the Catholic religious houses during the Reformation had deprived the poor of their rightful property in alms, and that only the abolition of tithes and the institution of poor-rates could restore this (as the Elizabethan poor law had in England).[27]

Responses to Revans: Perrin, O'Malley and Alison

The public debate on the poor law was moved on by the publication of John Revans' *Evils of the State of Ireland* in autumn 1836 and the flurry of pamphlets that followed. The *Dublin Review* was quick to comment on Revans' 'excellent' pamphlet towards the end of the year. In an essay reviewing both Revans and the Whately report, Mark Perrin combined the established trope of depicting the 43rd Elizabeth as the source of the social 'rights and privileges' of the English people, with an enthusiastic (if not entirely slavish) endorsement of Revans' case for a workhouse-based Irish measure.[28] Emigration was rejected, except at the margin, as a costly and unproductive distraction from the real task of improving the agricultural infrastructure of Ireland, which Perrin agreed was both possible and desirable within a small-farm tenurial structure. On close inspection, he continued, many of the Whately recommendations revealed a desire more to 'gratify the proprietors of estates, than to relieve, or accommodate the poor straggling appendages of the soil'. Selected measures of national improvement, such as an arterial railway to the western ports of Ireland, were desirable, but must be supplemental to a genuine poor law.

The article took particular pains to defend the poor law from the charge, derived from Chalmers and others, that it would destroy the moral good of voluntary charity. In Ireland, Perrin argued, alms-giving was largely restricted to the peasantry – civic charitable institutions such as the mendicity associations were in decay everywhere except where disruptive sectarian enthusiasms were attached to them. The sense of religious obligation and the ancient customs of hospitality that led so many poor families to support wandering mendicants were admirable, but the existing system appeared less attractive when the phenomena of the 'beggar's curse' and the prudential dole given to buy protection from pillage were taken into consideration. Abuse of the goodwill of the poor alms-giver by the 'shameless, heartless and profane' was widespread, while the burden of supporting genuine destitution was unfairly

27 *Ibid.*, 9 May 1836.

28 [Mark Perrin], 'A poor law for Ireland', *DR*, 2 (Dec. 1836), pp. 51–95. Perrin was probably the son of the liberal-Protestant judge and former Whig attorney-general Louis Perrin.

heaped upon the poorer classes. Under such circumstances, the 'Scottish system' so lauded by the majority of the commissioners was plainly inapplicable; indeed, Revans had demonstrated that in fact it too was actually compulsory in practice in the Scottish lowlands. Only a rate-funded workhouse system would suffice, and it would be welcomed by the poor as a boon so long as relief conditions were not rendered too harsh.

Where Perrin deviated from Revans it was on points of implementation rather than principle. His preference for larger unions (of around 400 square miles) and for a local rather than national rate suggest a familiarity with the still unpublished Nicholls report, which was probably made available to him. The final pages of the essay feature an appeal to moderate Irish Catholics to place their trust in the Whig government for a decisive resolution of the question as part of the 'justice to Ireland' political project, while also hinting at some unresolved internal conflicts within the administration which might be resolved through judicious lobbying. Morpeth was praised as the kindly patron of the Irish poor:

> [H]e knows the country and its resources, – he knows what the poor have a right to expect, and what the affluent are able, and may be justly required, to contribute . . . The Government, *we hope*, is unanimous in its determination to give a cordial and energetic support to the act of the Secretary for Ireland. The *hearts* of the leading and influential members of the Cabinet are with us, upon this question; and if there be, amongst the usual supporters of the Government, any who entertain an opposite feeling, whatever deference may be due to their opinions, on other subjects, we trust it is unnecessary to warn Lord Melbourne against their arguments and representations upon this.

Melbourne was further instructed to consult Russell, '"*The* Secretary of State *for* Ireland," – the ardent and tried friend of our land, the protector and the advocate of oppressed and suffering humanity in every clime and country', along with Duncannon – an excellent Irish landlord ready and willing to impose greater taxation on himself for this good purpose – and the lord lieutenant, if he still had any doubts on the matter.[29]

A more radical Catholic case for an Irish poor law was made by Fr Thaddeus O'Malley in late 1836. O'Malley, who was then a curate at the pro-cathedral in Dublin, was already well known as one of the most radical and outspoken members of the clergy, and was an advocate of a rights-based national system of poor relief.[30] He published 'An Idea of a Poor Law for

29 *Ibid.*, pp. 93–4.

30 See Fergus A. D'Arcy, 'Federalist, social radical and anti-sectarian: Thaddeus O'Malley (1797–1877)', in Gerard Moran (ed.), *Radical Irish Priests 1660–1970* (Dublin, 1998), pp. 91–110.

Ireland' in ten lengthy instalments in the *Freeman's Journal* between 15 October 1836 and 11 January 1837, before bringing it out in pamphlet form with Dublin and London publishers.[31] This was a full-blooded and aggressive attack on the Whately Commissioners, which made effective use of Revans' critique of their calculations.

O'Malley began with a philosophical and theological discussion of the problem before moving on to dismiss the economic foundations of the third report. Social inequality, he believed, had been providentially ordained for the purpose of stimulating human endeavour towards self-improvement. But if such was 'the law of Providence in favour of social man', it followed that there should be a reciprocal social law in favour of Providence. The Scriptural prescript that 'the poor shall never cease out of the land' did not mean that society should or could tolerate the existence of a precarious class of beggars dependent on random charity for their very survival. All truly civilized societies since the ancient Hebrews had resolved this dilemma through resort to a poor law. While the pursuit of a balanced, socially-bonding measure should thus be the ethical goal of all societies, the Poor Inquiry Commission had, in contrast, offered only a socially divisive and delusive solution. At root it was an exercise in promoting class legislation – for the proposed improvements were intended solely for the improvement of the properties of the rich, merely offering prayers and sermons for the civilization of the poor. Aiming to frighten its readers from adopting a true poor law, it had really been motivated by a horror of high wages, with their corollary of lower rents. This would not do, O'Malley protested: nothing short of the principle of the English poor law would ensure social justice and satisfy the people of Ireland.[32]

O'Malley's attack on the emigration proposals in the report, on the grounds that the Malthusian case for a superabundant population in Ireland was based on 'the merest drivelling', was hardly out of line with the views of many (although by no means all) radicals. He upbraided Scrope for his apparent defection from true principles in giving time to this delusion. However, O'Malley's onslaught on the modes of waste-land reclamation and drainage advocated by the report was more incisive and innovative. The proposed board of improvement would prove both costly and a source of constant litigation. More importantly, it would not do, he argued, to provide temporary employment to the poor if this merely improved the estates of the existing proprietors at public expense without altering tenancy arrangements or the longer-term prospects of the peasantry. How would the poor benefit if the

31 Thaddeus O'Malley, *An Idea of a Poor Law for Ireland* (2nd edn, London, 1837).
32 'Idea of a poor law for Ireland', parts 1 and 2, *FJ*, 15, 26 Oct. 1836.

land reclaimed by their labour was then let to capitalists – perhaps (and here he revealed prejudices widespread in Ireland at the time) to a 'company of London Jews' or 'a few Scotch colonists'? Only the allocation of the reclaimed land to the labouring poor as small tenants could have the desired effect – and this could only be done through the mechanism of the poor law itself. Above all else, the measure must be about securing the principle of welfare entitlement as one intrinsic to the privileges and duties of social citizenship: 'I claim for my countrymen', he continued in impassioned vein, 'and I claim it peremptorily, a right to a subsistence out of the land in which Providence has cast their birth. The Scotchman enjoys this right – the Englishman enjoys this right – and if the state will not secure it to the Irishman, I for one, am ready to absolve him from all allegiance to it.'[33]

O'Malley proceeded to locate the failings of the third report in the preconceived bias and philosophical misconceptions of its principal authors. Why, he asked, had the Irish poor been subjected to the experimental doctrines of the 'Malthusian new lights', which the 'just and generous spirit of England' had rejected in 1834, despite all the strength of that 'virus' within the English commission of inquiry? The main culprit was, of course, Whately, whose 'abstract theories' and method of logical induction O'Malley mocked unmercifully. This 'distinguished mystifier' had determined the outcome of the Irish inquiry from its inception, making no secret of his hostility to compulsory relief, and his blinkered obsessions with non-interference, self-reliance and with what he saw as the absolute moral good of voluntaristic charity. The archbishop had been yoked with Bicheno, a man 'not of the hard Malthusian school, but only a sentimentalist of the exquisite Chalmers school; one of those who think, with the eloquent doctor, that it would be a pity to suffer any legislative provision for the poor to "disturb the beautiful process of gratuitous charity"'. Bicheno's 'pretty poetry', as expressed in his apologia in appendix H, was no substitute for a 'real charity' that was systematic, equitable and rights-based. O'Malley was careful to single out his superior, Archbishop Murray, from his general condemnation of the commission, and he ignored the others, with the exception of a swipe at Blake.[34]

In setting out his own model for an effective poor law, O'Malley respectfully noted Revans' proposals – which he believed to be 'something like semi-official' – and agreed with his preference for numerous local workhouses, a national rate and minimal local responsibility, but found Revans' plan 'too

33 'Idea of a poor law for Ireland', parts 3 and 4, *FJ*, 2, 9 Nov. 1836. *The Times* (29 Aug. 1837) denounced him as an Owenite utopian, but admitted the usefulness of his pamphlet in exposing the 'absurdities' of the government scheme.

34 'Idea of a poor law for Ireland', part 5, *FJ*, 22, 23 Nov. 1836.

simple' in conception and mistaken in locating the central authority in London. While not entirely coherent, O'Malley's own preferences were for a workhouse-based system under a strong Dublin commission, which would house the able-bodied destitute in the workhouses, but employ them in outdoor labour on waste-land reclamation and cultivation. The public lands so improved would subsequently be portioned into small farms at fair rent and allocated to the most deserving families, thus providing an incentive and aspiration to the destitute poor to improve themselves in return for state assistance, and escape the poverty trap. This plan bore some comparison to the 'poor colonies' instituted in Belgium and Holland, which O'Malley defended in principle against the unfavourable account provided by Senior in his report prepared for the 1834 English commission. He admitted that adverse contingencies and poor local management had led to partial failures on the continent, but argued this did not invalidate this mode of relief in Irish circumstances. O'Malley's most controversial (and to Irish Catholics, potentially most popular) proposal was that the poor law be funded through the appropriation of the tithe composition (worth, he believed, some £555,000 annually), with the costs of the established clergy being transferred directly to the Protestant landowners or to the Consolidated Fund. This centralized mechanism would, he concluded, be more equitable and effective in improving the country than a local rate aimed at obliging landowners to employ the poor on their estates, and prove less of an obstacle to the free movement of labour he believed essential to economic development.[35] While this preference for appropriated rather than additional revenue was clearly distinct from what Revans, Nicholls or the government had in mind, the publication of O'Malley's 'Idea', and the controversialist stance its author took against opponents of a poor law in Ireland, were nonetheless welcomed by some ministers as at least promoting a principle they held in common. Although he found much of O'Malley's views on the poor laws 'at variance with general principles', Mulgrave brought his writings to the attention of Russell and Nicholls, and endorsed the priest's comments on the importance of internal migration.[36]

Revans' arguments were also generally well received by a number of British commentators. Writing in the radical *London and Westminster Review*, the statistician Major George Graham reviewed his pamphlet along with Lewis's *On Local Disturbances* and the Whately Commission's reports.[37] Given that

35 'Idea of a poor law for Ireland', parts 5–10, *FJ*, 23, 30 Nov., 7, 14 Dec. 1836, 4, 11 Jan. 1837.

36 NA: RP, PRO30/22/2F, fols 149–50, Mulgrave to Russell, 8 Oct. 1837.

37 [George J. Graham], 'Poor laws in Ireland', *London and Westminster Review*, 25 (July 1836), pp. 332–65. Graham, the younger brother of Sir James Graham, was appointed registrar-general for England and Wales in 1842.

Revans' pamphlet had yet to be published at this point, it is probable that he was personally acquainted with Graham, who took his side strongly against Whately and Bicheno. The writer concluded that a workhouse-based poor law granting a right to relief to all the destitute was both safe and expedient (although the government might consider offering a fiscal guarantee for capping the poor-rates in the first instance to overcome landed fears). In contrast, Graham satirized the third report for its distortions and evasions: 'The Commissioners have made an off-hand Report, dictated by their prejudices, or the prejudices of some among them, and in which, for the sake of satisfying others, or the public, some little is said in favour of everybody's nostrum, and the one effectual remedy is the only one which is absolutely rejected.'[38]

Revans was also favourably reviewed by the Scotsman Dr William Alison in two lengthy articles in the Conservative monthly *Blackwood's*.[39] Like many of the English commentators, Alison tended to read the Irish poor law debate through the prism of the controversies surrounding poor relief in his own country. He was then engaged in a struggle for reform of the Scottish poor laws with the aim of granting a legal entitlement to the destitute poor and a more generous provision of relief, and had clashed with Thomas Chalmers on the optimum mode of poor relief and the underlying question of the applicability of Malthusian doctrine to social policy.[40] In 1836 Alison made the case that 'justice to Ireland' should be a Conservative as much as a Whig doctrine, and that its essence should lie in a good poor law. The evidence printed in Revans' pamphlet had merely confirmed his long-held opinions that Ireland's backwardness and unrest were rooted in the absence of such social provision, an absence he attributed to the insidious influence of the Malthusian economists on policy-makers. Irish demographic history clearly proved that 'below a certain grade of poverty the preventive check has no power'; in Ireland population had grown most rapidly in the poorest regions, whereas such an excess had been checked in England by the minimum entitlement existing under the law that had created the taste for 'artificial wants' that stimulated reproductive self-restraint. Chalmers' case for the moral and practical superiority of voluntary charity, which had previously proved so

38 *Ibid.*, p. 363.

39 [William P. Alison], 'Evils of the state of Ireland', *Blackwood's Edinburgh Magazine*, 40 (Oct. 1836), pp. 495–514; 'Justice to Ireland – a poor law', *ibid.* (Dec. 1836), pp. 812–31. Alison was professor of medicine at the University of Edinburgh.

40 For a summary of Alison's views on this, see his *Observations on the Management of the Poor in Scotland* (2nd edn, Edinburgh, 1840), and Mitchison, *Old Poor Law in Scotland*, pp. 173–5.

influential in Ireland, was 'a mere speculative delusion' that failed to stand up to empirical scrutiny.[41] Such was now, he asserted, the case in Ireland, and so it would remain if the Whately report was adopted. Ireland, like Scotland, needed only to grant a right to relief to the able-bodied poor within the workhouse (the infirm and helpless poor 'of good character' were best relieved in their own homes) to raise its standard of civilization and create the social security that would underpin rapid economic growth.

O'Connell and his enemies, 1836–37

Alison's articles were well received on the other side of the political spectrum, and regarded as authoritative refutations of claims that social differences between Ireland and the other 'home' countries rendered a standardized poor law inapplicable.[42] However, such an 'idea' of an extensive poor law for Ireland, articulated on both sides of the Irish Sea in later 1836, did not go unchallenged. The most disconcerting development for all advocates of a 'popular' poor law was the hardening stance adopted by O'Connell. The Irish leader was consistent in his long-standing scepticism towards a poor law encompassing relief to the able-bodied destitute, but notoriously inconsistent in his public utterances, mainly because of his desire to avoid alienating his supporters in the Catholic clergy and the Repeal party. As argued above, O'Connell's soft-pedalling on the question in 1835–36 led some to believe he had been converted, and gave pro-poor-law ministers false hope at a crucial moment in the formation of their policy that he would at least not oppose it. Even Sharman Crawford, who had serious doubts about O'Connell's sincerity on most matters, was persuaded in December 1835 that he would now 'go with the current' of public opinion for a poor law, and perhaps even put himself at the head of it. By the following April he had concluded that O'Connell would not after all give a bill any efficient support, but still anticipated no serious political antagonism from him on the matter.[43]

O'Connell's private comments on the Dublin meeting of 29 March 1836 reveal an irritable resignation to what now appeared inevitable, which he would tolerate reluctantly (for the moment) so long as what was proposed stopped short of the folly of a labour-rate:

> What a foolish meeting about poor laws! How strange it is that men will commit themselves on so awful a subject without knowing anything of the details; and

41 [Alison], 'Evils of the state of Ireland', p. 503.

42 *MC*, 7 Oct. 1836.

43 PRONI, Sharman Crawford Papers, D/856/D/44, 47, W. Sharman Crawford to J. Sharman Crawford, 31 Dec. 1835, 5 Apr. 1836.

> that most destructive of all experiments, employment for the able-bodied out of the poor rates!!! . . . A poor law we must have. We are come to it. We must have it as *the Repeal* slumbers. But not the 43d of Elizabeth, which directly led, as indeed a necessary consequence, to all the evils of the English poor laws . . . We *must*, however, have a poor law and *poorhouses*, and much of moral degradation and of change in the *mode* of suffering. The cause is injured by the silly, silly course taken at the meeting. I must take an entire part in future to keep them to rights. The last poor law in England is a great improvement; of course not perfect, but giving *us* a model wide indeed of the 43d Eliz. [sic][44]

This was hardly a declaration of war on the ministry or its putative measure, which appeared modelled precisely on the 1834 amendment act; indeed in a public letter to his constituents in September 1836 O'Connell was still expressing commitment to supporting any bill proposed by Morpeth, despite remaining persuaded that it must fail as a practical experiment.[45] Yet his letter does provide a clue to the abrupt shift in his public position towards the end of the year and the escalation that followed.

O'Connell was more sympathetic to the Whately recommendations (including both assisted emigration and public works) than some historians allow, but this was almost certainly not the prime reason for his renewed confrontation with his Foxite allies.[46] Only a perceived threat to his leadership of popular Catholic politics in Ireland could have provoked such an impolitic rift, and this was precisely what the agitation of the poor-law question by Lawless, Sharman Crawford and O'Malley (and to an extent also Poulett Scrope) increasingly appeared to represent in late 1836 and early 1837. O'Connell may also have been put more on edge by the very public defection of his former ally Feargus O'Connor in late 1836, and by the latter's publication of allegations that O'Connell had deviously sought to undermine his own attempts to attain an Irish poor law.[47]

Poulett Scrope's bitter exchange with O'Connell in May 1836 may have initiated this process. O'Connell had been absent from the discussion of Scrope's motion in the Commons, but, true to his commitment to answer what he regarded as the most absurd poor law proposals, had attacked it in

44 O'Connell to P. V. FitzPatrick, 1 Apr. 1836, in O'Connell (ed.), *Correspondence of O'Connell*, v, pp. 365–6.

45 O'Connell to the electors of Kilkenny in *FJ*, 1 Oct. 1836.

46 In May 1836 O'Connell joined H. G. Ward in a delegation to the prime minister requesting government support of a scheme to raise £3 million from the sale of colonial lands for assisting the emigration from Ireland of at least 100,000 families: 'Irish Poor-Law question, and colonial waste-lands', *Spectator*, 7 May 1836.

47 Feargus O'Connor, *A Series of Letters . . . to Daniel O'Connell* (London, 1836); *The Times*, 2, 10 Dec. 1836.

a letter published in the *Morning Chronicle.* Scrope counter-blasted with a long letter to the *Freeman's Journal*, which used highly emotive language to question O'Connell's political priorities. Would his pursuit of municipal corporations reform, he asked the Irish leader, 'put one potato into the mouth of a single starving child of misery, out of the three or four millions of your fellow-countrymen who rise every morning from their beds of damp earth or rotten straw, doubtful whether they can stave off famine for another day?' Scrope appealed to the 'facts' of English experience to prove his case for the 'improving' consequences of poor laws on all classes, but could not resist the temptation to attack O'Connell personally – as a landlord, Scrope charged, he had a selfish pecuniary interest in avoiding a poor-rate, and as a professional agitator he had opposed every measure to tranquillize and satisfy the people of Ireland. His opposition to a poor law could thus arise only from ignorance or interested bias (but more probably the latter).[48] This unwise attack on O'Connell's personal integrity provoked a flurry of letters and articles in the nationalist press attacking Scrope and his schemes, and had the desired effect for O'Connell of distancing the embarrassed Irish poor-law lobby from their former hero.[49] The subsequent onslaught on O'Connell as a self-interested oppressor of the poor, coming from both ends of the political spectrum in England – from the Cobbettite Major-General Charles Napier, to the constant jibes of *The Times* – merely allowed him to pose as a defender of true Irish interests against malign English interference.[50]

A much more serious challenge to O'Connell's hegemony came from within the Irish nationalist community, especially in the wake of the formation of the General Association of Ireland in July 1836. O'Connell intended this body to serve as a campaigning entity to rally support for 'justice to Ireland', principally by keeping public attention focused on the tithe and municipal corporations questions during the parliamentary recess.[51] In practice, however, it provided a platform for internal criticism of the leader, especially over the poor-law question. At the heart of this revolt was Sharman Crawford, with whom O'Connell had progressively fallen out over the former's refusal to compromise on the original demand for total abolition of tithes, and also the increasingly vocal Thaddeus O'Malley.

Sharman Crawford's alienation from O'Connell would lead him to give up his Dundalk seat in 1837 and later (in the wake of O'Connor) to embrace

48 O'Connell to Scrope, *MC*, 21 May, Scrope to O'Connell in *FJ*, 28 May 1836.

49 e.g. 'An Irishman' to Scrope, *FJ*, 28 May 1836.

50 Napier to O'Connell, 19 Jan., *The Times*, 24 Jan. 1837; leading articles in *ibid.*, 13 Jan., 22 Dec. 1837, 2 May 1838.

51 O'Connell to the People of Ireland, in *FJ*, 7 July 1836; Oliver MacDonagh, *The Emancipist: Daniel O'Connell 1830–1847* (London, 1989), pp. 153–5.

Chartism. In 1836, however, he was still within the nationalist tent, was regarded highly by the Catholic clergy, and was increasingly a thorn in O'Connell's side.[52] His public epistolary assaults on the leader's compromising stance on tithes, municipal reform and the franchise caused growing embarrassment. Moreover, his demand that the General Association and O'Connell take up the key question of the poor law in preference to all others could not but be regarded as a direct challenge to O'Connell's control of the movement's political strategy.[53] In his response, O'Connell took pains to warn Crawford of the dangers of public dissension and corrected his 'errors' of fact, but initially evaded any discussion of the poor law, which he observed Crawford had, 'as usual, lug[ged] into [his] letter'. O'Connell restated his general, if reluctant, consent to a government measure, and his desire to postpone giving his views until a forthcoming meeting of the Dublin Trades Political Union.[54] In a speech to that body on 13 November O'Connell made it clear that he would now support only an absentee tax linked to state relief to the aged, infirm and diseased. He added provocatively that, although he had voted against it, he now thought that the 1834 act had done great good in England, because 'it was a kind of repeal of the poor law': but even so the act was totally inapplicable to the problem of the '2,300,000 beggars in Ireland', not least as it would destroy the homely charity of the peasantry. A general poor law would increase pauperism, illegitimacy, vice and idleness, and depress wages; all evidence from European countries and North America pointed in this same direction. Only these convictions, he declared, rather than political calculation, had influenced him on this point; indeed his stance involved some potential danger, for if he had supported a poor law, he might forfeit the goodwill of the Catholic clergy, and possibly the wider public. However, he continued: 'I must do the people of Ireland this justice – I never lost any of my popularity by opposing them when they were wrong, if I had argument to show that I was right.' In response to those Catholics who favoured state relief of the able-bodied, O'Connell now articulated his own vision of social Catholicism:

> I call upon you all to deliberate on the subject, remembering that it is the command of God and the dictate of nature to be charitable to the poor. (Hear, hear.) I believe in a religion which tells me that I shall receive such spiritual

52 Archbishop Crolly of Armagh praised Sharman Crawford at a public meeting in Dundalk as proving that a Protestant and an Irish heart could be combined in the pursuit of true liberty for all, while deprecating any rift between him and O'Connell: *The Times*, 6 Oct. 1836.

53 e.g. Sharman Crawford to O'Connell, in *ibid.*, 2 Aug. 1836.

54 O'Connell to Sharman Crawford, in *ibid.*, 6 Oct. 1836.

> reward if I, by charity, earn the promise of my Redeemer. I profess a faith which teaches me that the tremendous sentence of eternal beatitude, or never ending woe, shall be pronounced on me because I visited the sick, gave food to the hungry, and clothed the naked, or for having neglected these duties. (Hear, hear.) At my time of life those thoughts cannot be absent from my mind, and I have not still to learn how uncertain is human existence. (Mr O'Connell here felt deeply affected for several minutes.) Forgive me, my friends, if I have forgotten you for a moment. I am bound by every tie to the poor, and their interest is a paramount object with me.[55]

While O'Connell may have been entirely sincere in the statement of these economic and religious doctrines, his motives in making the speech were almost certainly tactical.[56] The Trades Political Union was a more loyal body than the General Association (at least before he attacked trades-union combinations there the following year) and a safer platform for O'Connell to articulate his views. Yet while he received unanimous support therein on 13 November, he subsequently restricted himself to forming a trades deputation to consult Morpeth on his legislative intentions and to 'suggest' the best modes of proceeding.

The outcome of this meeting with the chief secretary, on 12 December 1836, was less than satisfactory – Morpeth gave little away and took the view that as O'Connell's 'Tail' on this occasion had been packed with opponents of a poor law it was less than representative of Irish opinion.[57] The lord lieutenant opined that, while he had been rather taken aback on reading the speech, he did 'not think [O'Connell] will be supported in his view by some of the most important of his usual adherents or by the middling classes generally'.[58] He would have been confirmed in this by reading the savage attack on O'Connell's speech published by the former MP John Richards, whose 1833 motion had sparked the formation of the Whately Commission, and by reports from Clare that even the usually ultra-loyal 'head pacificator', Tom Steele, was prepared on this matter to reject his master's voice and call for a poor law as the only way of undercutting agrarian violence. At a county meeting which had supported him unanimously, Steele declared that only a poor law could curb the Terry Alts, as 'this country can never enjoy peace nor

55 'National Trades Political Union', *ibid.*, 17 Nov. 1836. He repeated the same points at further meetings of this body on 20 November and 4 December, including in the latter a long attack on Revans, *ibid.*, 24 Nov., 9 Dec. 1836.

56 For the sincerity of O'Connell's Catholicism, see James Guilfoyle, 'The religious development of Daniel O'Connell, II: the making of a devotional Catholic', *New Hibernia Review*, 2 (1998), pp. 115–32.

57 NA: RP, PRO30/22/2D, fol. 141, Morpeth to Russell, 12 Dec. 1836.

58 Mulgrave to Russell, 14 Nov. 1836, *ibid.*, fol. 27.

progress in civilization, until every man is made to know that he has a right to support from the soil on which he stands as a freeman'.[59]

The ministers' more optimistic readings also appeared vindicated by the rougher ride O'Connell encountered in the General Association. He had hoped to keep public dissension to a minimum by referring the contentious matter to a private committee, but Crawford refused to include the poor law in the subjects so treated.[60] On 15 December O'Malley directly challenged O'Connell in the public forum by urging the body to support his plan for the appropriation of tithes in support of poor relief for the able-bodied. An obviously irritated O'Connell urged an adjournment to the debate on this motion, but not before provoking an ugly spat with Crawford and Lawless. The following day Crawford seconded O'Malley's proposal with some enthusiasm and greater aggression, challenging overtly the very economic dogmas and foreign case-studies that O'Connell had stressed in his speeches to the trades. The principle of poor laws was, he confidently proclaimed, founded upon eternal justice, upon religion, upon the positive right of the poor to subsistence; without conceding this fundamental truth, he was prepared to accept a compromise measure brought in by the government if it represented an instalment and would open the door to the achievement of full justice.[61] When the 'loud cheering' that followed died down, a clearly exasperated O'Connell was obliged to respond to a less than rapturous crowd. This was the first time he had faced such a confrontational public challenge on this matter within the bosom of his own movement. *The Times* immediately leapt on the events as marking 'the triumph of Father O'MALLEY, and the total defeat of Mr DANIEL O'CONNELL', although it was quick to point out that it was the victory of the principle of a poor law rather than the priest's 'wicked' assault on tithe that it welcomed.[62]

Further discussion of the question in the General Association revealed sharp divisions – Lord Milltown was a convinced advocate of a poor law and stated he would promote O'Malley's plan in principle; Sheil thought it a Tory-inspired distraction. The Repeal press was also divided – Staunton of the *Morning Register* was strongly for it, the ultra-loyal Richard Barrett of the *Pilot* decidedly against.[63] O'Connell's stronger stance did, however, have some effect. The previously enthusiastic *Freeman* now felt obliged to strike a more

59 Richards to O'Connell, *The Times*, 24 Nov.; *Examiner*, 18 Dec. 1836.

60 *MC*, 23 Nov. 1836.

61 'Meeting of the General Association', *The Times*, 19 Dec. 1836.

62 *Ibid.*, 21 Dec. 1836.

63 *Ibid.*, 27 Dec., *FJ*, 22, 23 Dec. 1836. Staunton had already made the case for a comprehensive poor law as part of 'justice to Ireland' in 'State and prospects of Ireland', *DR*, 1 (July 1836), pp. 281–312.

neutral stance, rejecting (at least temporarily) the O'Malley–Crawford argument for a 'right to relief' as incompatible with the existence of private property, and denying any real connection with the tithe question, while contending that an effective poor law was possible without these. Alarmed at the glee with which the Tory press had reported the divisions within the Association, the paper now sought to dampen down dissension and excitement on the issue.[64] Also, while O'Connell acknowledged that the bulk of the clergy were against him on this issue, with the obvious (but important) exception of Archbishop Murray, a few clerical voices were now raised in his defence.[65] The impression is one of sharp division within the Catholic-nationalist political community, but with a clear leaning still evident in favour of the poor law.

After an adjournment for the Christmas holidays, the 'war' over poor laws continued to rage in the General Association in the weeks preceding the opening of the session in February 1837, and was extensively reported and commented on by the press.[66] Lawless and Sharman Crawford again sought to set the agenda, with the latter publishing a series of confrontational letters to O'Connell. The indefatigable Lawless was active elsewhere – proposing a motion at the Mendicity Association's annual general meeting to submit a report critical of the Whately report and to endorse a poor law instead.[67] O'Malley stirred things further by attacking Sheil in print for his alleged attempt to smother the matter with a 'wet blanket', contrasting his hostility with the commitment of the 'truly benevolent and paternal government' to legislate, and reminding him that it was the Catholic clergy who had been responsible for the recent lauded victory at the Longford by-election, 'and as one of their order (and I write it proudly), I can tell you that they will cheerfully dispense with your barren vote of thanks, and would prefer in payment of your gratitude your vote for a poor-law'.[68]

This was not entirely rhetorical, for the Catholic clergy were indeed prominent voices at the parochial meetings in Dublin and elsewhere held to petition the government to enact a poor law, and the writings of Bishop Doyle were frequently cited in support of such motions.[69] At Newry in March, the Catholic bishop of Dromore, Michael Blake, and his clergy joined with the town's Anglican rector and Presbyterian minister in taking the lead at a

64 *FJ*, 19 Dec. 1836, 4, 20 Jan. 1837. The paper later swung back to an uncritical endorsement of O'Malley's plan, *ibid.*, 19 Apr. 1837.

65 Rev. J. Miley to O'Malley, 21 Dec., *ibid.*, 22 Dec. 1836.

66 *The Times*, 21 Jan., *MC*, 21 Jan. 1837.

67 *FJ*, 10 Jan. 1837.

68 O'Malley to Sheil, *The Times*, 10 Jan. 1837.

69 e.g. 'Poor laws – St Michael's and St John's Parish', *FJ*, 7 Feb. 1837.

meeting which recognized 'the divine right of the poor man to be fed out of the land on which he was born'.[70] It was impossible that the heat of the General Association debates should not spill over into these grass-roots meetings. In St Michan's parish in Dublin, a resolution read by Patrick O'Higgins (which a previous vestry meeting had sought to exclude) making the case for a right to relief as the 'gift of God', and praising O'Malley's writings, was challenged by the loyal O'Connellite minority:

> Mr Arkins – That is a stab at the character of Mr O'Connell. Mr O'Higgins is his enemy, and he brought forward this motion to stab Mr O'Connell (no, no, and great uproar).
>
> Mr Morrow rose to support the motion, because he knew that Mr O'Higgins was incapable of making any attack upon Mr O'Connell, and because this meeting would no[t] be held if the Rev. Mr O'Malley had not brought the subject before the public in the masterly manner which he did (hear, hear, hear).
>
> Mr Duggan – Does Mr Arkins think that we are all such dolts as to believe his assertion that Mr O'Higgins is the enemy of Mr O'Connell, because he proposes a vote of thanks to the reverend gentleman who has earned the gratitude of the whole country? When the late Dr Doyle wrote in favour of poor laws, and Mr O'Connell differed with him in opinion, if Mr O'Higgins or anyone else proposed a vote of thanks to Dr Doyle, would Mr Arkins consider that an attack or stab at Mr O'Connell (hear, hear, hear)?
>
> Mr Arkins – No, I would not; but this is an attack (order, order, question, question, Mr O'Higgins, Mr O'Higgins).
>
> Mr O'Higgins said, he disclaimed every idea of an attack, or slate, as it is called, at Mr O'Connell; on the contrary, he was more the friend of Mr O'Connell than those who were now following in his tail.[71]

This exchange is unlikely to have made pleasant reading for the Repeal leader. Nevertheless, Sharman Crawford's simultaneous reassertion of an uncompromising position on the tithe bill, thus threatening the survival of the ministry, gave O'Connell the opportunity to publicly disassociate himself from this troublesome rival, and subsequently to defeat him on an issue on which the latter had less public support. This loss of a key ally at a crucial moment weakened O'Malley's attempts to have the Association formally endorse his resolutions.[72]

70 O'Connell criticized this resolution as misguided, *ibid.*, 5 Apr. 1837.

71 'Poor Laws – St Michan's Parish', *ibid.*, 18 Jan. See also letter to O'Malley, in *ibid.*, 1 Feb. 1837.

72 'General Association', *The Times*, 17 Jan.; *FJ*, 21 Jan. 1837.

As the 1837 session opened, attention shifted back to Westminster. With Sharman Crawford now politically damaged, if still dangerous, and Lawless incapacitated through what appears to have been a mental breakdown, the threat to O'Connell on the poor-law question was now less direct.[73] Yet O'Malley's continuing activities, and the popular reception he had received from many clergy and grass-roots Repealers, continued to pose a threat, and the Irish MPs were clearly divided on the matter in parliament. O'Connell felt obliged to reassert his leadership by taking a strong stance against the government bill; crucially, the clear indication that Peel and the Conservative leadership would not reject it freed him to do so without risking the collapse of the ministry.

Public opinion and the 1837 bill

O'Connell was helped out of this difficult position by the limitations of the measure that appeared in the new session. Nicholls' tour of Ireland in autumn 1836 had been welcomed by many in Ireland as presaging a 'popular' measure.[74] However, the publication in mid-February 1837 of both the government's poor relief bill, and the first Nicholls report on which it was based, inevitably disappointed many members of the pro-poor-law lobby in Ireland. The measure fell far short of their demands in many respects, not least in denying a statutory 'right to relief', in rejecting any relief outside the workhouse, and in retaining a categorical distinction between poor relief and works of public improvement. O'Malley himself seems to have been in two minds about how to respond. In the preface to the second edition of his *Idea*, published in March 1837, he appears to have minimized the limitations of the bill:

> I find the ministerial measure is only a contraction of the plan which I here expound, and that it may be expanded without the slightest violence, so as to attain every purpose at which I aim. And as I was amongst the first, if not the very first to maintain those great principles which are the peculiar features of that measure, namely, its entire disenthralment from the embarrassments of settlements and bastardy provisions, I hope my claim to a patient hearing will be recognised by those who were engaged in concocting it.[75]

In the same month, however, O'Malley brought out a follow-up pamphlet with the same London publisher which, while hailing the government's bill

73 In March Lawless applied to the government for a place, rather to the lord lieutenant's embarrassment: CHP, J/19/1/14, fols. 29–30, Mulgrave to Morpeth, 19 Mar. 1837.

74 *Tipperary Free Press*, cited in *The Times*, 3 Oct. 1836.

75 O'Malley, *Idea*, p. i.

with 'pleasure', attacked both its core provisions and Nicholls personally. Not surprisingly, he objected to the proposed exclusion of the clergy from boards of guardians, as he thought their inclusion essential to ensuring that the 'popular element' was adequately represented; to the allocation of responsibility to the English commission; and the excessive size of unions (as well as the points raised above). He also favoured a two to one ratio that would impose the greater share of the rates burden on landowners, and dropping the £5 rating clause on the grounds that its inclusion would provoke evictions or rent increases. Despite these reservations, he continued to argue that amendment rather than rejection would be the best way forward.[76]

For its part, the *Freeman* was generally welcoming towards the bill, while agreeing with O'Malley on the danger of the £5 clause and the necessity of an Irish commission, and with O'Connell on the necessity of some (at least temporary) form of settlement while the system was being phased in across the country. Its more detailed analysis of the measure, in a series of leading articles in March 1837, again distinguished between the bill's principle, which it welcomed 'with pleasure and . . . gratitude', and specific clauses it found misguided and in need of amendment. Foremost amongst these was its support for Smith O'Brien's amendment to increase the amount of wasteland a union could appropriate on which to put to work the able-bodied paupers (the numbers of which it declared Nicholls had grossly underestimated). These articles are so close in structure and argument to O'Malley's (as yet unpublished) second pamphlet that it is probable they were actually written by him.[77] Perhaps inevitably, the serial defeat of the amendments proposed by the Irish members in the Commons placed increasing strain on the idea that the government's bill was cognate with the more 'popular' versions advocated in Ireland, and the enthusiasm of the *Freeman* dimmed as the session progressed.[78] By early June the paper was expressing disillusionment:

> [T]he more we see of the spirit and determination of the House, the more we are convinced that the bill will neither be an effectual remedy for Irish destitution, nor check the growth of Irish pauperism. We agree with the *True Sun* in

76 [Thaddeus O'Malley], *A Word or Two on the Irish Poor Relief Bill, and Mr Nicholls' Report; or, a Postscript to the Rev. Mr O'Malley's 'Idea of a Poor Law for Ireland'* (London, 1837).

77 *FJ*, 18 Feb., 9, 16, 19, 21, 22 Mar. Although he disagreed with him on certain points, O'Malley had written sympathetically to Smith O'Brien when the latter had been attacked by O'Connell, NLI: SOBP, Ms 429, O'Malley to Smith O'Brien, 23 Jan. 1837.

78 *FJ*, 12, 20 May 1837.

> thinking that it seems likely to turn out only a limited and experimental transfer to Ireland of portions of the English system, including such as are most objectionable and offensive. This is not what Ireland wants[.][79]

It appeared increasingly to his former critics that O'Connell might have been vindicated after all.

Initially, Irish Conservative reactions to the bill were mostly neutral or welcoming. The *Belfast News-Letter* commented positively on Russell's speech introducing the bill: the measure was 'so far guarded and modified, as to be at least worth trial in the shape of an experiment'.[80] While it also printed extracts from Nicholls' report without comment, the paper subsequently shifted its ground in the wake of public meetings in the north later in the year. The early tendency of the English Conservative press to either welcome or ignore the bill, and perhaps an initial reluctance to join O'Connell on a hostile platform, may have muted first reactions in Ireland.

Irish Whig-liberal voices were generally favourable to the government's proposal. The radical *Limerick Star* welcomed it as a real boon to the hungry poor of the west, but hoped also for auxiliary measures of employment. The support of the *Cork Southern Reporter* for the bill as it stood drew a sharp rebuttal from O'Connell.[81] Privately, the eminent novelist Maria Edgeworth wrote to Chadwick declaring that the Nicholls report had converted her opinion on the 'safety' of an Irish poor law featuring a destitution test and exclusion of any claim of 'right'.[82] Two very strongly supportive articles by the Roscommon MP Fitzstephen French must have added to the sense of satisfaction that Howick expressed on reading Edgeworth's letter. In January French announced himself 'with Revans and Lewis for a poor law' (eliding the differences between the two), for a 'limited' right to relief through the workhouse, and against the Whately Commission's plan to create places and patronage under the title of relief. Revans' book *should* have been 'the report', he concluded.[83] French appears not to have seen the 1837 bill as a significant deviation from Revans' principles, defending it vigorously against its critics and praising Russell as its real author. The bill combined, he argued, a just recognition of the moral and social claims of the poor on the rich with

79 *Ibid.*, 7 June 1837.

80 *Belfast News-Letter* [*BNL*], 17 Feb. 1837.

81 *Limerick Star*, quoted in *The Times*, 27 Mar.; O'Connell to the editor of the *Southern Reporter*, in *ibid.*, 27 Mar. 1837.

82 DUL: GP, 80/17, Maria Edgeworth to Chadwick, Mar. 1837 [extract]; UCL: CP, 887, Howick to Chadwick, 31 Mar. 1837.

83 [Fitzstephen French], 'Poor-laws for Ireland; Report of the Irish Poor Inquiry Commission', *British and Foreign Review*, 4 (Jan. 1837), pp. 1–25.

effective securities against idleness and moral hazard. Rather than deplete the wages-fund, it would call forth the hidden capital reserves in Ireland and indirectly stimulate reproductive employment.[84] On the key issue of the number of destitute poor in Ireland, the government received further statistical support from William Stanley, who published a pamphlet expanding the calculations he had supplied to Nicholls, and stressing both the carrot and stick respectively of Lynch's public works bills and the 'wise device' of the poor law in making the upper classes more interested in employing the poor.[85] Stanley, a former fisheries commissioner who had previously come to public attention as the author of a Cloncurry prize essay on a poor law for Ireland, became a target for vituperation second only to Nicholls for opponents of the government's bill, principally for his alleged careerism and 'Indianrubber elasticity to the wishes and measures of ministers'.[86]

The materials for a series of counter-attacks against the bill in Ireland were, however, being assembled. O'Connell again employed the reliable sounding-board of the Trades Political Union to launch his campaign on 29 March 1837; the points he made were similar to those he had rehearsed in parliament, albeit now spiced up for home consumption. The bill would, he alleged, introduce a new English tyranny under the London Commission, while its provision for *ex-officio* guardians would submit the people to control by an 'Irish Orange magistracy', and the weight of taxation would oppress and disfranchise the Catholic middle class. The Trades voted to condemn the measure and petition for a public works grant from the exchequer in its place.[87] On 4 April he felt strong enough to raise the matter without warning in the General Association. While suggesting carefully that he would not directly oppose the ministry on the bill, he turned his fire on the absent O'Malley's character and ideas. He asserted that all experiments in employing pauper labour in England, Europe and America had failed dismally – although even the bill, for all its faults, he noted, did not propose this fallacy. The sacred claims of the poor to subsistence should not be mixed up with any legal right, the allowance of which would immediately 'shut up the fountains of benevolence' and untie the bonds of society. Those who dared to challenge him on the subject, such

84 [Fitzstephen French], 'State of Ireland – projected poor law', *ibid.*, 5 (Oct. 1837), pp. 367–401.

85 Stanley, *Remarks on the Government Measure for Establishing Poor-Laws in Ireland. The Times* (5 Sept. 1837) alleged this pamphlet was published with secret service fund support.

86 *The Times*, 4 Dec. 1837. Stanley had originally been encouraged in taking up the subject by Bishop Doyle: see Doyle to William Stanley, 19 Jan., 20 Oct. 1832, in Fitzpatrick (ed.), *Doyle*, ii, pp. 372–3, 429–30.

87 *The Times*, 1 Apr. 1837.

as Staunton, were, he proclaimed, the victims of delusions and 'monomania'. This speech prefigured his more strident parliamentary opposition to the measure from late April 1837. For all O'Malley's subsequent protests that he had been wilfully misrepresented, O'Connell's tactical victory at this meeting may be taken as part of a successful fight back.[88]

O'Connellite pamphlets appeared following up his arguments, warning against the 'false popularity' of the measure and the added taxation on the farming class it threatened, and urging alternatives such as public works and loan funds to the 'poisonous snake' of poor laws.[89] A more sustained O'Connellite critique was subsequently penned by 'an MP for a western county' (possibly Sir William Brabazon of Co. Galway, who was particularly outspoken in the Commons debates in 1838). The author denounced Nicholls' 'Napoleonic' vision, and demanded the removal of the colonial status imposed on Ireland by the Union and the restoration of its legislative independence as the sole means to revive prosperity and eliminate poverty.[90]

Conservative, landed and provincial reactions against the bill were initially rather lacklustre. However, a campaign started slowly to gather steam from April 1837, taking up some of the critical themes identified by O'Connell and adding others specific to their respective constituencies. A committee of the landowners and landholders of Roscommon, under the chairmanship of William French of Clooniquin, presented their views to a county meeting on 8 April. At the heart of their list of objections were the excessive powers to be granted to the commissioners, which were suited only to the Spanish inquisition, the limitation of the rates burden to landed property only, and the absence of adequate plans for emigration and drainage.[91] The growing pressure from his constituents against the measure he had previously supported in print was probably responsible for Fitzstephen French's volte-face in the 1837–38 session. His fellow Roscommon MP the O'Conor Don had also swung against the bill.

The Roscommon meeting was, however, a relatively isolated event amid the spring 1837 assizes and grand jury meetings. Only the Cavan grand jury appears to have submitted a similar petition.[92] But there were other straws in

88 'General Association', *FJ*, 5 Apr.; O'Malley to Staunton, *ibid.*, 6 Apr. 1837.

89 Anon., *Thoughts on the Proposed Introduction of the Poor Laws into Ireland* (London, 1837); [P. Ryan], *Funds for the Poor of Ireland, without Taxation* [Thurles, 1837]; Anon., *A Substitute of a Poor Law in Ireland* (Dublin, 1837).

90 Anon., *A Few Cursory Observations on the Proposed Bill for Establishing Poor Laws in Ireland* (London, 1838). Brabazon had intended to move the motion against the third reading, and strongly supported O'Connell in this last-ditch debate: *MC*, 1 May 1838.

91 'Poor Laws – meeting of the County of Roscommon', *FJ*, 13 Apr. 1837.

92 *The Times*, 17 Apr. 1837.

the wind. The initially supportive stance of the *Belfast News-Letter* weakened in the wake of a series of public meetings in that town in April 1837. Intended by Belfast liberals to pass resolutions supportive of the government measure, these meetings were taken over by its opponents who upheld the moral and practical superiority of voluntarism, and attributed the attempt to get up a pro-poor-law petition to the interference of the itinerant English clergyman Tully Crybbace.[93] Many of Belfast's Presbyterian clerical and lay elite were strongly attached to the Chalmersian ideals of voluntary charity and moral improvement. The mathematician and schoolmaster James Bryce was sure that the ministry was reluctantly acceding to English clamour in bringing in the bill, and stated his preference for each church maintaining its own poor. His brother Rev. R. J. Bryce, principal of Belfast Academy, quoted Chalmers extensively and praised the successful experiment in parochial voluntarism he had initiated in Glasgow. Whatever their differences on doctrinal matters, the leaders of the two leading wings of Irish Presbyterianism, Henry Cooke and Henry Montgomery, were agreed in vigorously upholding these localist and voluntarist principles and rejecting any centralized and compulsory measure with or without the employment clauses which Crybbace had sought to add. A list of extensive amendments was agreed at the meeting, but Cooke's preference was for 'an optional Poor Law, of which they could [only] avail themselves in times of trial and scarcity'.[94] While the *News-Letter* was less dismissive of public-works employment than Cooke, it subsequently endorsed the clerically-led assault on the bill. The government's subsequent rejection of the amendments demanded looked set to spark a new series of protest meetings in Ulster, although this was cut short by the King's death in June.[95]

The anti-poor-law lobby in Ireland was given an important boost by the publication of a number of hard-hitting pamphlets in 1837. A number of these were by authors closely associated with members of the Whately Commission. Probably the most important, *Strictures on the Proposed Poor Law for Ireland*, if not by the archbishop himself, was certainly strongly endorsed by him.[96] The pamphlet began with some sarcastic swipes at Nicholls' 'flying

93 It was alleged that Crybbace had 'kicked up all the row in Belfast' after initiating similar public meetings at Drogheda and Newry. Although his own preferences were for a labour-rate rather than workhouses, he appears to have treated the poor-law campaign as something of a personal crusade: *BNL*, 18 Apr. 1837; [T. Tully Crybbace], *Provision for the Poor of Ireland* (n.p., [1837]).

94 *BNL*, 18 Apr. 1837.

95 *Ibid.*, 21 Apr.; 'Irish Poor Law – Meeting at Dromara', *ibid.*, 20 June 1837.

96 Anon., *Strictures on the Proposed Poor Law for Ireland*. While the authorship is unproven, the points made bear close similarity to Whately's critique of Nicholls and Revans in NLW: NSP, C/579, Whately to Senior 13 Nov.; and in Whately to Senior, 14 Nov. 1837, in Whately (ed.), *Life*, i, p. 396.

visit', but followed this up with a sustained and effective critique of the measure based on his report, which it contrasted slightingly with the authoritative and measured conclusions of the third report. The prolonged and thorough inquiries of 1833–36 had proven beyond question that the extent, causes and effects of Irish destitution were profoundly different from that of England. Only wilful blindness could confound the two and propose the same measure to redress these quite distinct problems:

> [Nicholls] saw from the window of his carriage rags and filth, as he had seen in the pauperized districts of England. He read in the public newspapers of outrages and resistance to lawful authority, and his imagination completed the picture of a pauperized district of England. But the destitute Irish peasantry, and even the Irish mendicants, are a different class of people, in every important feature of character, from the English pauper, as it is possible to imagine.[97]

Conscious that the same charge of ignorance could not be laid at the door of the other semi-official proponent of a poor law, Revans, the author then turned his fire on him. This 'young gentleman' was 'animated by as magnanimous a contempt for evidence, and [was] able to dispose of numbers and calculations with as much of easy legerdemain as Mr Nicholls . . . [he was] deplorably defective in knowledge of human nature, the character and habits of the people, and in patient investigation and accuracy of calculation'.[98] Moreover, despite their superficial similarities, Revans and Nicholls were proposing highly variant plans – the former envisaging indoor relief for able-bodied men (as a matter of right), while their families and the infirm (totalling upwards of 800,000 individuals) would receive outdoor relief. If Revans' calculations of need went well beyond Nicholls', the author continued, they still gravely underestimated the real scale of destitution in Ireland, while pointing towards an escalating scale of costs far beyond what Ireland could bear. Revans' sociological vision was also, he insisted, at variance with the Nicholls report: Revans envisioned an Irish rural society similar in form to the small-peasant society of Belgium, whereas Nicholls (unpersuasively) foresaw Ireland's 'transition' to an anglicized social model with a tripartite division of labour between landlord, capitalist farmer, and landless labourer.

In setting out a catastrophic projection of the consequences of a poor law, one calculated principally to arouse the 'terror' of Irish landowners, the author of the *Strictures* placed greatest emphasis on the likelihood that in practice the limited scheme proposed by Nicholls could not be a final solution – and that even Revans' more enlarged plan would also be swamped by the pressure of pauper numbers. Central to the dynamic of any poor law would

97 Anon., *Strictures on the Proposed Poor Law for Ireland*, pp. 20–1.
98 *Ibid.*, pp. 36–7.

be the corporate influence of the Catholic clergy, who were committed to a 'popular' extended system, and who would exploit mass dissatisfaction and the opportunities created by elections to boards of guardians to advance their agenda. The mobilization of such public pressure under clerical direction would quickly establish the reality of a 'right to relief'. Not even the despotic powers to be granted to the central commission could uphold a rigid workhouse test under such circumstances, and government would eventually give way in the face of chaos in Ireland – all Nicholls' 'fences and guards would be swept away like cobwebs before a hurricane'. The consequences for the landed order were too awful to contemplate – a universal transfer of landed property from the present possessors to the poor would mirror the effects of the French Revolution, and famine would stalk the land unhindered.[99] Whatever its effect on Irish opinion, the *Strictures* certainly needled certain commentators. Lewis, who was sure it was written by Whately and Blake, declared that it simply demonstrated their inability to understand the question, before denouncing the archbishop as acting 'like a shallow ignorant unprincipled demagogue'.[100]

Two of the 'efficient' Poor Inquiry Commissioners also contributed to the debate in 1837, namely John Corrie writing as 'Philo-Hibernus', and William Battie Wrightson (anonymously) in the pages of the heavyweight *Edinburgh Review*.[101] Corrie closely echoed the points made in (and the sarcastic tone of) the *Strictures*, warning interested parties – especially Irish landowners – that the 'triumphant procession' of the poor law bill must be halted if disaster was to be averted. The frustration of the spurned investigator was also evident – 'What mis-spent time! What useless toil!' he lamented, on witnessing the commission's report having been thrown, unheeded, under the table of the House. Alongside an attack on the 'missionary' Nicholls, Revans was accorded the honour of equal condemnation, not least because of his unorthodox economic views, which, 'soaring above the grovelling level of those dabblers in political economy, Adam Smith, or Malthus, or Ricardo, rejects the absurd doctrine that the rate of wages is regulated by the proportion between the demand and the supply. Wages, according to his brilliant discovery, may be

99 *Ibid.*, p. 85. A second edition appeared in February 1838 adding an attack on Nicholls' second report.

100 NLW: HCP, C/449, G. C. Lewis to T. F. Lewis, 3 July 1837. In a later letter he added: 'I have completely given up Whately: not only do I think his judgment utterly unsound, but I distrust his honesty. A man with Whately's lights who appeals in inflammatory language to the prejudices of the mob on such a subject as poor laws is, in my opinion, a scoundrel': Lewis to Villiers, 13 Dec. 1837, *ibid.*, C/2807.

101 [Corrie], *Remarks on the Bill*; [Wrightson], 'The workhouse system'.

raised to any given amount, by a judicious application of the workhouse system!'[102] No such sophistry could evade the established facts that 2.3 million were destitute in Ireland and that no poor law could be devised which would not render their fate worse rather than better.

Perhaps in answer to the continuing monopoly Poulett Scrope held over commentary on the Irish poor laws in the *Quarterly*, the *Edinburgh Review* turned over its pages to Wrightson in October 1837.[103] Despite his close relationship with Whately, Wrightson did not consult the archbishop on the article, and included criticisms of what he regarded as the lack of focus of the third report and its unfortunate admixture of recommendations on the categorically separate questions of employment, land improvement and assisted emigration. Nevertheless, at the core was a robust defence of the commission's recommendation of a 'Scottish' voluntarist system of relief on theoretical as well as practical grounds. Wrightson's chosen text for review was F. M. L. Naville's historical critique of workhouse systems, a convenient peg on which to hang both his assault on the government's Irish bill and his claim that the 1834 English act had failed to chain the 'monster pauperism'. Naville's evidence merely supported the conclusions of the Sturges Bourne committee of 1817, the third report of the Whately Commissioners, and the experience of Scotland, France and Prussia – that it was safe for the state to relieve only the infirm and incapable poor. Beyond this only a systematization of private charity was legitimate: 'It is no act of real kindness to teach the peasant to rely upon the public.'[104] Those who still entertained doubts were urged to re-read Senior's authoritative *Letter to Lord Howick*, and Torrens' neo-Malthusian case for emigration as an essential preliminary for any social improvement in Ireland.

Other former commissioners now also took a public stance. Naper, who had done so much to have the constructivist recommendations, of which Wrightson clearly disapproved, appended to the third report, defended the Poor Inquiry Commission (while demurring from some of its conclusions). He reinforced the key criticisms of Nicholls made by his former colleagues; Ireland was too poor for a poor law – it was wrong to punish the poor for their poverty by imprisonment – Nicholls' figures for destitution were gross under-representations.[105] Bicheno seems to have restrained himself

102 [Corrie], *Remarks on the Bill*, pp. 14–15.

103 The review had in 1834 carried an anti-poor-law article by a leading political figure, [Spring Rice], 'Proposed introduction of the poor laws into Ireland'.

104 [Wrightson], 'The workhouse system', p. 205; F. M. L. Naville, *De la charité légale* (2 vols, Paris, 1836). Naville (1784–1846) was a Calvinist pastor at Geneva sympathetic to Chalmers' moralistic opinions on charity.

105 Naper, *Address to the Landlords and Landholders of Meath*.

from contributing to the public debate, but appears to have been the author of a pamphlet-length private commentary on the bill produced for Lansdowne.

Several of the assistant commissioners, while not entirely vindicating the third report, also contributed critiques of the Nicholls report and the government bill. In a rather eccentric publication that combined romantic travelogue, vivid descriptions of rural poverty and political recommendations, the English Quaker Jonathan Binns rejected both the Whately and Nicholls reports in favour of a massive programme of relocating the impoverished peasants on waste-lands with twenty-year reclamation leases.[106] Binns expressed particular enthusiasm for the small-farm experiment developed by William Blacker on the Gosford estate in Armagh, and believed it to be applicable to the whole country and the basis of a bottom-up socio-economic rejuvenation which would do more than anything to address endemic poverty.[107] Workhouse relief would, he asserted, be an expensive distraction from agriculturally-focused development, and impossible to operate in a society so depressed in housing standards and diet.[108]

A later pamphlet by the Irish assistant commissioner (and radical) William Torrens McCullagh, was more damaging. Only the Lords, he angrily concluded, could save Ireland from the mockery of the government's bill, and satisfy the people's cry of 'WE WANT EMPLOYMENT NOT IMPRISONMENT'. Nicholls, as an ignorant mail-coach passenger, had flung aside not only the Whately report but the evidence published alongside it, and Russell was guilty of a measure which would simply imprison the Irish poor at the expense of the middle classes, while adding nothing to Irish national production.[109]

Other powerful critiques came from different parts of the political spectrum. Isaac Butt was the rising star of Irish Conservative politics, a founding editor of the *Dublin University Magazine*, and since 1836 Whately professor of political economy at Trinity College. In a May 1837 pamphlet he defended the reputation of his distinguished patron and the political

106 Binns, *Miseries and Beauties*. This plan was ridiculed as 'Quixotic' by the *Spectator*, but was more favourably received by other parts of the liberal and radical press: *Spectator*, 13 Jan. 1838, pp. 40–1; *Examiner*, 18 Feb. 1838, p. 100; *Tait's*, 5 (Feb. 1838), p. 131; *DR*, 4 (Apr. 1838), pp. 407–40.

107 Binns, *Miseries and Beauties*, i, pp. 153–4.

108 *Ibid.*, ii, pp. 440–1.

109 McCullagh, *Letter to the Representative Peers of Ireland*. McCullagh was subsequently reconciled to both the Whig ministers and the Irish poor law, serving as private secretary to the chief secretary in the later 1840s.

economy underlying the third report; less eligibility was impossible to apply in Ireland, he argued, and any measure without a law of settlement would lead to mass migration of paupers to the most generous unions. While Butt denied that Ireland was overpopulated, he stressed that only additional employment in food production would make any real difference to social conditions. His treatment of Nicholls was knockabout polemic – he was 'some holiday tourist' whose ignorant assumptions were not worthy of serious consideration – but Russell was identified as the true author of a measure designed mainly to meet legislative exigency.[110] Not surprisingly, Butt's case (along with the *Strictures*) were positively reviewed in his own journal, although the evangelical convert Rev. Samuel O'Sullivan could not resist adding the sectarian aside that pauperism and Popery were causally connected and that lifting the people out of the moral degradation of Catholicism must precede any real temporal improvement. In a subsequent article the journal predicted the poor law would kill charity, promote jobbing, and 'change good landlords into Jews'.[111]

The north Antrim landowner Sir Francis Workman MacNaghten, recently created a baronet by the Whig-liberal government, also published his own rival poor-law plan (essentially a labour-rate) and savaged both Revans and the ministerial scheme for their neglect of emigration and dismissal of voluntary relief. The excessive harshness of the English workhouse system (especially the separation of sexes) was, he declared, contrary to divine law and likely to produce widespread demoralization.[112] The remarkably thick-skinned Nicholls assured ministers that he saw nothing more of substance in MacNaghten's second pamphlet than in the many others he had read, although he admitted that his 'smartness and pungency of style' would procure it many readers.[113]

110 Isaac Butt, *The Poor-Law for Ireland Examined, its Provisions and the Report of Mr Nicholls contrasted with the Facts proved by the Poor Inquiry Commission* (London, 1837).

111 [Samuel O'Sullivan], 'Poor Law Bill for Ireland', *DUM*, 10 (July 1837), pp. 69–78. Anon., 'Thoughts on passing things – No. 1', *DUM*, 12 (Oct. 1838), pp. 451–5.

112 Francis Workman MacNaghten, *Some Observations on the Present State of Ireland* (London, 1837); *Poor Laws – Ireland. Observations upon the Report of George Nicholls* (London, 1838). Extracts from the latter pamphlet were published in *BNL* (5 Jan. 1838), and both were reviewed favourably in *The Times*, 9, 15 Jan. 1838.

113 CHP, J/19/1/16/62, Nicholls to Morpeth, 10 Jan. 1838.

From the Irish radical camp, McCullagh was joined by John Pitt Kennedy in attacking the ministerial plan. The latter's intervention was intended as an introduction to a new edition of his 1835 pamphlet, *Instruct; Employ; Don't Hang Them*, a constructivist case for the 'home colonization' of the Irish waste-lands on the model of the Belgian pauper colonies.[114] He defended the Poor Inquiry Commission report against the workhouse plan, ignoring its inconvenient Malthusian emphasis on emigration. Only mass employment on waste-land reclamation, he concluded, could lift Ireland free of the constant threat of famine, which even its advocates acknowledged no poor law could do.[115] This demand for employment measures, either as preparatory or as an alternative to a poor law, and listing of allegedly successful European precedents for this mode of relief, was echoed in other pamphlets.[116]

What is clear from these publications is the repetition of common themes – Nicholls' ignorance and miscalculations; the exceptionality of Irish poverty; the excessive burden of poor-rates on an impoverished society; the inapplicability and oppression of workhouse relief.[117] These simple (and potentially popular) arguments were widely disseminated across the political spectrum and made likely a more extensive and active opposition to the poor law bill when reintroduced in December 1837. At the same time, it is clear that the bill's opponents held widely divergent views on the alternatives which should replace the hated government bill (which even universal reference to the catch-all menu of the third report could only contain with difficulty and some evasion). Theoretically, the Malthusian-based minimalism and preference for

114 John Pitt Kennedy, *Instruct; Employ; Don't Hang Them: or Ireland Tranquilized without Soldiers, and Enriched without English Capital* (London, 1835). A protégé of the radical General Charles Napier, Kennedy (1796–1879), was a land agent in Co. Tyrone, and was appointed inspector-general of the national schools in 1837. For Napier's controversialist advocacy of his pamphlets, see Napier to O'Connell, 19 Jan., *The Times*, 24 Jan. 1837, Charles James Napier, *An Essay on the Present State of Ireland* (London, 1839).

115 John Pitt Kennedy, *Analysis of the Projects proposed for the Relief of the Poor of Ireland* (London, 1837).

116 e.g. Thomas Bermingham, *Remarks on the Proposed Poor Law Bill for Ireland* (London, 1838).

117 e.g. J. Stanley, *Poor Laws – Ireland. The Injustice of Assessing Landlords and the Impracticality of Assessing Landholders* (Dublin, 1837); James Connery, *The Reformer, or, an Infallible Remedy to Prevent Pauperism and Periodical Returns of Famine* (6th edn, Dublin, 1837); *Thomas Wright, To Lord John Russell* (Dublin, 1838).

emigration stated by Whately, Corrie and Wrightson was a world away from the interventionist public-works schemes of the Irish radicals McCullagh and Kennedy (which had more in common with O'Malley's plans). The 'Belgian' model of Irish rural society favoured by the latter was anathema both to the orthodox economists and defenders of the 'improving' landed interest such as Butt and Naper. Ultimately, if Nicholls' underestimation of the scale of destitution and the unpopularity of the workhouse were the weakest links in the government's case, the incoherence and inherent contradictions of the alternatives posed the same problem for his opponents.

8

Public reaction in Ireland and Britain, II: 1837–38

After the distractions associated with the death of William IV and the accession of the young Princess Victoria in summer 1837, the attention of the 'political public' in Ireland (and, to a lesser extent, Britain) was gradually drawn back to the Irish poor-law question. This chapter considers the public counter-attack launched against the government's reintroduced bill in 1837–38 by Richard Whately, Daniel O'Connell and much of the landed establishment in Ireland. Public opposition reached a higher level of intensity than in the previous year, and featured an extensive petitioning campaign, while 'outdoors' support for the measure in Ireland was divided and marginalized. Nevertheless, a number of influential voices in Ireland continued to make the case for the bill in print. This chapter considers their arguments, and the stronger currents in support of the measure in the effusions of British public opinion.

Despite the flurry of public attention it had received during the 1837 session, the Irish poor law bill was not a significant issue on the Irish election hustings during the general election of August 1837 that followed Victoria's accession to the throne. Russell praised Morpeth for 'having defeated the [English] anti-poor law cry' in his West Riding constituency, but noted that he had heard nothing stated either for or against the poor law in Ireland.[1] O'Connell later claimed that the Co. Cork election was nearly lost to the Tories because some Catholic clergy there opposed the rating clauses of the bill, but in fact the Whig-liberal candidates G. S. Barry and E. B. Roche, both at that point supporters of the bill, won with large majorities.[2] Apart from an isolated county meeting in Donegal which passed hostile resolutions (and

1 CHP, J/19/1/15/48, Russell to Morpeth, 25 Aug.; MC: NP, M/878, Russell to Mulgrave, 12 Sept. 1837.

2 NA: RP, PRO30/22/2F, fols 187–8, Warburton to Russell, 16 Nov. 1837. Barry and Roche both voted for the bill in February 1838, but Roche voted against and Barry abstained on the third reading, suggesting a shift in public attitudes in the course of 1838.

from which it was alleged Liberals and Catholics had been excluded), political excitement was directed elsewhere during the campaign.[3] The poor-law question clearly translated badly into the party-political polarities of 1830s Ireland. Nevertheless, the torrent of vituperation against Nicholls had left its mark, and the lord lieutenant was concerned at the hostility which any mention of his name seemed to raise at public meetings.[4]

As the start of the new session approached in autumn 1837, in which it was clear the government would reintroduce its bill, public controversy was reignited. Fr Thaddeus O'Malley reasserted his advocacy of a comprehensive measure in public letters of 15 September and 31 October, urging Russell to render the bill a 'final' and truly popular measure by acceding to amendments allowing outdoor agricultural work and substituting a national for the local rate.[5] After the experience of heavy defeats on these and other amendments in the previous session it proved much more difficult for O'Malley to arouse the same popular enthusiasm for the bill, even as a 'first step'. Even so, Dublin Castle regarded O'Malley's continuing support for the 'flawed' bill, his 'strenuous opposition to O'Connell', and his hostility to the principle of settlement, as among the remaining grounds for optimism.[6]

Against this, it was increasingly evident that the various elements of the anti-poor-law lobby in Ireland would now be better organized and more assertive. Richard Whately, excluded from the Lords in the 1837–38 session due to the rotating representation of Irish prelates, committed himself to promoting outdoor agitation. He was optimistic that the previous 'popular clamour' for a poor law was abating as the false simplicities of Nicholls' recommendations became progressively exposed, and took comfort from the stance taken by O'Connell – one which he doubted the Irish leader would have adopted if the movement for a poor law really was an 'irresistible stream'. Active resistance was now needed: 'I myself', he wrote to Senior, 'am ready to have any one's and every one's displeasure – am ready to expose myself to be torn in pieces by the rabble, or to forfeit all the favour of the great, rather than leave any means untried for preventing such a calamity to this island.' While this risk must be taken, he hoped that the worst danger would be averted by the simple stratagem of a cross-party initiative in the Commons or Lords for an amendment excluding the able-bodied from relief.[7] O'Connell's renewed outspokenness on the issue led Whately (rather to his own surprise)

3 *FJ*, 5 Aug. 1837.

4 NA: RP, PRO30/22/2F, fols 118–24, Mulgrave to Russell, 16 Sept. 1837.

5 *FJ*, 9 Sept., 1 Nov. 1837.

6 NA: RP, PRO30/22/3A, fols 30–5, Drummond to Morpeth, 6 Jan. 1838; Mulgrave to Russell, 10 Oct. 1837, *ibid.*, 2F, fols 149–50.

7 NLW: NSP, C/579, Whately to Senior, 13 Nov. 1837.

to praise the Irish leader's courage, although he still had some fear that O'Connell might be 'murdered by the mob' for his temerity.[8]

True to his word, the archbishop took a leading role in public meetings on the bill in Dublin in February 1838, and was delighted that a two-thirds majority now backed his case for confining relief to the impotent, and that, although a sizeable minority were vehemently for outdoor relief, no one appeared to be inspired by the government's bill. He urged his parliamentary allies to adopt delaying tactics while the petitioning movement was extended across the country, for, he told Wrightson, 'at the eleventh hour, men's eyes are getting opened – all are opposed, though on various grounds'.[9] Disappointed with the lack of interest in the Commons in 'the most important question that has been before parliament for many years', he placed his hopes in the Lords, and urged Lansdowne to pay attention to Irish opinion:

> Here, the eyes of all classes, poor as well as rich, are more and more opened every day to the hazardness of the experiment. I should suppose the government will hardly, in the face of continually fresh manifestations of this feeling, insist, *a l'outrance* [sic], on forcing the bill as it now stands, down the throats of the Irish nation, without any prospect of producing even that temporary satisfaction which alone could ever have been hoped for.

At the same time, he acknowledged that the opposition of the Catholic clergy was derived from an ambition opposite to his own – that of securing outdoor relief for the poor of their flocks.[10] While other ministers regretted the 'bile' Whately vented on the subject, his outspokenness was hardly unexpected given previous experience of his actions and opinions.[11] Far more worrying was the greater extent and politicization of public opposition in Ireland that faced the reintroduced bill.

The Conservative and O'Connellite campaigns against the 1837–38 bill

The Conservative press was much more hostile than in the previous year. Public opinion, the *Belfast News-Letter* declared, was now pretty well formed,

8 LPL, Whately Papers, MS 2164, fols 148–9, Whately to Senior, 25 Jan. 1838.

9 NLW: NSP, C/587, Whately to Senior, 22 Feb. 1838; Whately to Wrightson, 22 Feb. 1838, [Wrightson], *Irish Poor Laws*, pp. 7–8.

10 BL: BP, B/130, Whately to Lansdowne, 1 Mar., 24 Apr. 1838.

11 NA: RP, PRO30/22/3A, fols 161–2, Mulgrave to Russell, 21 Feb. 1838. Morpeth subsequently summed up the archbishop as 'a man of 1st rate genius, of very kindly feelings & a lover of truth perhaps beyond any one I ever met; he is very impracticable, apt to fly off at a target, the worst man of business ever born, and quite unconsciously full of self-worship': DRO: FP, 1262M/LI/27, Morpeth to Ebrington, 2 Apr. 1839.

and convinced that Russell's bill could only lead to confusion and inconvenience.[12] The *Dublin Evening Mail*, while rejecting O'Connell's opposition to any poor law as manifesting his 'aristocratic' contempt for the poor, attacked the government's 'Algerine' bill as creating a mechanism for robbing the landed without benefiting the destitute.[13] It endorsed Shaw's amendment to limit relief to the aged and infirm, and, when this was lost, it turned, like Whately, towards promoting a petitioning campaign to persuade the Lords to reject the 'Irish Bastille Bill'. The paper was outraged that only fourteen Irish Conservatives had voted against the third reading in the Commons and threatened them with retribution at the polls, but it put its faith in the peers.[14] The *Waterford Mail* was rather more ambivalent. It printed, approvingly, O'Malley's critiques of O'Connell, but made clear its own preference for a combination of relief of the impotent in asylums, and of the able-bodied by a labour-rate. Its rejection of the claim that Ireland was overpopulated put it at odds with the Whately–Senior viewpoint, but it saw nothing to support in the ministerial measure.[15]

On the nationalist side, O'Connell's unbending opposition was further signalled in correspondence published in the Irish papers celebrating the defeat of O'Malley's and other advocates' hopes for a sympathetic amendment of the bill in the 1837 session. He now announced his intention to agitate the subject to the hilt.[16] This was no idle threat. At a Dublin constituency meeting on 9 January 1838, which was thinly attended due to heavy snow, he publicly committed himself to supporting Sir Charles Styles's motion against the bill in principle, and to moving another such proposal himself in the Commons if necessary. At the same time he recommended that a report prepared by Staunton criticizing the limitations but not the principle of the bill should be sent to every clergyman in Ireland. O'Connell clearly now sought, if possible, to enlist those angered by the restrictions of the government measure in a campaign against what he considered an 'unamendable' bill.[17]

12 *BNL*, 8 Dec. 1837.
13 *DEM*, 1, 3, 31 Jan., 9 Feb. 1838.
14 *Ibid.*, 23 Feb., 26 Mar., 4 May 1838.
15 *Waterford Mail* [*WM*], 13, 20, 31 Jan., 21, 28 Mar. 1838.
16 O'Connell to his constituents, *FJ*, 19, 23 Dec. 1837. This inevitably provoked O'Malley and his allies to respond in kind, O'Malley to O'Connell, *ibid.*, 29 Dec. 1837, 5 Jan. 1838, Samuel Robinson to the people of Ireland, *ibid.*, 30 Dec. 1837, 28 Apr. 1838.
17 *FJ*, 10 Jan. 1838. Staunton's report criticized the powers given to the commissioners, the exclusion of clerical and inclusion of *ex-officio* guardians, the 'unnecessary' emigration clause, the ban on outdoor relief under all circumstances, and the 'unjust' rating clauses.

At a better attended petitioning meeting at the Corn Exchange on 23 January he sounded out the principal arguments he would later make in the Commons against the measure, lamenting that those who criticized part but not all of the bill still held back from endorsing his wholehearted opposition, while opining that the public enunciation of 'incontrovertible' facts must rally the public mind to him. This bill 'for imprisoning the poor and increasing the destitution of the country', grounded on the erroneous calculations of Nicholls and 'Stamp-office Stanley' (who bore the brunt of O'Connell's verbal assault), could not be allowed to proceed. He accepted the good intentions of Russell and Howick (necessarily, if the Lichfield House compact was to continue), but blamed them 'for looking to strangers for knowledge of our circumstances, and not for attending to the friends of Ireland'; naturally, that fact was taken to demonstrate the indispensability of the restoration of the Irish parliament. In a further move calculated to lure moderate Catholic (especially clerical) opinion away from the O'Malleyite position, O'Connell paid for the insertion of an article by his son John, attacking the Nicholls report and supporting Jonathan Binns's waste-land reclamation proposals as an alternative, in the previously pro-poor-law *Dublin Review*.[18]

O'Connell's full-blooded assault was not sufficient to silence O'Malley and Staunton, who responded vigorously, although they were now under the difficulty of justifying a measure of which they at best half-approved. O'Malley pointed out that William Stanley had no part in the drafting of the bill, but found himself in the awkward position of defending Nicholls from the charge of non-consultation. Revans and a number of assistant commissioners had come to the same conclusions as to the exaggerated numbers of destitute in the third report, he observed, although Nicholls had evidently gone too far the other way. Despite its flaws, O'Malley clung to the belief that the government bill provided an essential template, 'for we must begin with something . . . its structure is very simple, and it will on that account, be the more easily amended, should it not be found to work well'.[19]

O'Connell's initiative appears to have had an immediate effect, although perhaps not always as yet to the extent he wished; some parochial meetings in Dublin, dominated by the Catholic clergy, endorsed Staunton's critique of the 'obnoxious clauses' while continuing to uphold the principle of an Irish poor law.[20] Seeking to restore his authority over his grass-roots, O'Connell chose to be present in person at public meetings in Dublin's St George's and St Mary's parishes in January 1838, and endeavoured to swing opinion wholly

18 [O'Connell], 'Miseries and beauties of Ireland'.

19 'Mr O'Connell – Poor Laws', *FJ*, 26 Jan. 1838.

20 'Meeting of St Audeon's Parish', *ibid.*, 11 Jan. 1838.

against the bill and to identify the dissident O'Malley directly with the loathed Nicholls in an attempt to undermine his clerical opponent.[21]

The combined weight of O'Connell, Whately and the Conservative press, along with the negative focus on the bill thrown up by the pamphlet campaign and reports of the parliamentary debates of February 1838, appear to have had an impact on the cycle of county and borough meetings that began in that month. At Naas, Co. Kildare, two county meetings in which O'Connell's loyal lieutenant Peter Purcell took a leading role saw resolutions passed condemning Nicholls' scheme and recommending Purcell's alternatives of labour-rate employment on waste-land reclamation and relief of the impotent through reorganized medical charities. The second meeting, coinciding with a market day, saw large crowds assemble to hear and interact with the speakers. Purcell's insistence on the horrors of workhouse restrictions and diet (supported by English examples) aroused particular public ire:

> For your dinner you will get a pound of potatoes (a voice in the crowd, 'Why that would be only four.' Here the expressions of disapprobation became unanimous; there were loud cries of let them keep their bill, we won't have it, if it were good they would not give it to us, &c.) But you are to get supper, too; and what do you think it is? – Nicholls's gruel and an ounce of cheese (deafening cheers) . . . You see they take every care of you; but let me not be mistaken: I have told you what you are to get, under the humane provisions of this bill, as relief. There can be no exception made; any other treatment of food than I have specified would be illegal; all must be treated alike; the sick and the infirm – the unfortunate but industrious man, reduced to pauperism by the casualties of life – will be placed on the same level with the drunken and profligate, the reckless and the criminal. This will be the law, unless you adopt vigorous means to check its progress.

Yet even in these circumstances the Catholic clergymen present continued to take an O'Malleyite stance in support of the bill as an incremental step towards a state provision for the poor. 'In these workhouses, as they are termed,' the Rev. Mr Carney insisted, 'the poor will at least, get clean and comfortable lodgings – the children will be properly taken care of, and educated also, while the able-bodied will not live in idleness; for we find that each workhouse will have twelve acres of land, sufficient to employ them, while the wives and daughters of these men will be comfortably provided for . . . Talk of imprisonment indeed – is imprisonment worse than perishing with hunger and cold on the high way, covered with rags?' Rev. Gerald Doyle, parish priest of Kildare and a relative and close ally of the late Bishop Doyle, agreed that,

21 'Mr O'Connell – Combination', 'Meeting of St Mary's Parish', *The Times*, 30 Jan., 2 Feb. 1838.

imperfect as the bill was, he would support it as being better than nothing at all.[22] Lord Clements also wrote to thank the parish priest of Ballinamore for supporting him in the face of strong opposition to the poor law bill in Co. Leitrim.[23]

This stance reflected quite a different conception of the nature of destitution and the practicalities of addressing it – but one that could not compete in terms of popularity. Crudely put, while clerics' speeches received 'cheers' from the crowd, this was nothing like the 'deafening cheers' that greeted Purcell's rabble-rousing. Where the Catholic clergy dominated meetings, as at a parish meeting at Lemanaghan, King's County, called to protest against evictions, resolutions in favour of a poor law (on the government model) to protect the poor against landlord oppression could still be carried. This meeting began with a speech by Rev. Mr McKeon urging a poor law as the embodiment of both the divine precept and the 'natural law' that 'the landlord's title to his estate is bound by the conditions expressed or implied in the social compact, by which, when men give up a portion of their liberty, they are to receive that protection from the state which declares that no man shall perish from hunger in the land of his birth.'[24] Yet, this was increasingly a minority view. At other county meetings, stress was placed on both the bill's unsuitability to Ireland, and the damage the additional taxation would impose upon the improving classes – variously stated as the middle classes, the farmers, or the resident 'small gentry', depending on the social balance of the meeting. A Roscommon meeting stressed the 'despotic powers' granted by the bill; the Repeal MP and small landowner Cornelius O'Brien, presiding over a Clare meeting, claimed it would protect the 'great absentees' while imposing injury and insult on Ireland.[25]

A series of public meetings in Ulster reiterated the strong preference for the Scottish model of voluntarist parochial relief that had been expressed in the Belfast meetings of the previous year. In Belfast, the Presbyterian clergymen Cooke, Montgomery and Bryce were again at the forefront in demanding a voluntarist alternative to the bill. At a baronial assembly at Randalstown, Co. Antrim, resolutions deprecating the unnecessary costs of workhouse

22 'Poor Laws – Great Meeting in County Kildare', 'Adjourned Poor Law Meeting', *FJ*, 2, 28 Feb. 1838. Despite disagreeing with him over repeal, the bishop had described Gerald Doyle as 'the most popular clergyman in the County Kildare': James Doyle to Spring Rice, 29 Nov. 1832, in Fitzpatrick (ed.), *Doyle*, ii, p. 449–50. Not all of their fellow clerics agreed; an Ulster priest wrote in support of Purcell and against the 'Nichollite Bill', *FJ*, 17 Feb. 1838.

23 NLI: KP, Ms 14,298, Clements to Rev. J. Maguire, 11 May 1838.

24 *Athlone Sentinel*, cited in *FJ*, 12 Jun. 1838.

25 *The Times*, 14 Feb. 1838.

provision and urging an alternative of 'enabling the people to assess themselves at vestries, by parishes, half baronies, or such other unions as may be agreed on, for the support of our *Local Poor* alone', were agreed without opposition.[26] Similar points were made by local parochial meetings, such as that at Connor, Co. Antrim (where the local 'Sabbath day collections' for food, seed and clothing were praised as already providing what was necessary by means of charitable relief), and at county meetings with a more socially 'respectable' attendance. At the Co. Down meeting, Sharman Crawford's son John moved that parishes capable of demonstrating their capacity for meeting the needs of their poor by voluntary assessment be exempted from the national act. The grand juries of Co. Antrim and the borough of Carrickfergus agreed to similar petitions in March.[27] These meetings were usually well attended and vociferous; at Bushmills, Co. Antrim, the venue had to be changed twice to accommodate the large numbers who assembled to endorse the local landowner Sir Francis MacNaghten's protest against the measure. The petition agreed at this meeting received 800 signatures, including 'two deputy-lieutenants of the county, five magistrates, eight clergymen (including the Anglican archdeacon of Connor), and many hundreds of the most respectable inhabitants of the district'.[28] It was evident that, in the north at least, the government could expect little public support, even from most Whigs and radicals.[29]

Indicative of a more general shift in opinion was the outcome of the meetings of the combined committees of the charitable institutions of Dublin in February. In 1836 the Mendicity Association committee had strongly supported the proposed government measure. Now, however, Whately and his supporters dominated proceedings. The archbishop stated that, as an adoptive Irishman, he was outraged by the way in which 'our poor' were to be treated by English opinion (which had, he claimed, coerced the unwilling ministers into proposing the bill). Whately proposed what was essentially to become Shaw's amendment, that relief be restricted to the impotent, and was answered by the ubiquitous O'Malley, who instead urged an extension of the bill to allow guardians to grant outdoor relief with a labour test (as had recently been found indispensable in Nottingham and other distressed parts of England). Given the choice of pressing for a contracted or an expanded

26 *BNL*, 16, 27 Feb. 1838.

27 *Ibid.*, 16, 20 Mar. 1838.

28 'Poor-Laws – Public Meeting at Bushmills', *Belfast Chronicle*, reprinted in *FJ*, 26 Mar. 1838.

29 The *Northern Whig*, however, continued to adhere to the opinion that workhouse relief would be 'better, at least, than nothing', cited in *Liverpool Mercury*, 27 Apr. 1838.

provision, the meeting opted for the former in a proportion of two to one, with the resulting petitions to be presented by O'Connell and the duke of Leinster.[30] A further public meeting of the citizens of Dublin at the Mansion House on 13 March again saw O'Malley and his supporters beaten by a majority comprising an alliance of O'Connellites, Tories and radicals (the latter including W. T. McCullagh, who chaired the meeting, although the resolutions against the bill had been prepared by the Conservative banker David La Touche). Some face was saved by all agreeing on an additional motion for an immediate, additional, employment measure for Ireland, but this could hardly disguise the extent to which the pro-poor-law lobby had now been sidelined.[31] Another meeting during the Easter recess in April, convened and addressed by O'Connell, concluded in similar fashion, with a committee being formed to prepare an anti-poor-law petition to the Lords. Again the pro-poor-law minority, on this occasion including Staunton and Fr Toole, the parish priest of Narrowmore, Co. Kildare (whom Morpeth later quoted in parliament), were heavily defeated.

Sensing a distinct change in public mood, at this point the *Freeman's Journal* now renounced its previous O'Malleyite leanings and fell into line behind what was now clearly the majority view among Dublin nationalists.[32] The majorities against the Irish amendments now demonstrated, it declared, an English carelessness towards Irish feelings that might yet be redressed (paradoxically) by the House of Lords.[33] There was palpable disappointment in its columns when, instead of 'knocking the bill on the head', Wellington appeared to have strengthened the bill's 'landlordist' character by dropping the exclusion of £5 tenants from the rate while excluding mortgage payments from charges. The *Freeman* did, however, praise the amendment introducing a modified form of settlement.[34] Despite this defection, support for the measure did not disappear completely from the Dublin press. The *Post* remained loyal to the government, and represented a real, if minority, constituency. Despite his undisguised distaste for the tenor of the bill, the old radical Lord Cloncurry publicly urged its acceptance as better than nothing; indeed, he confided to the editor of the *Post*, the clear agenda of its enemies inclined him more favourably towards it: 'The government bill is certainly

30 'Meeting at the Mendicity Institution', *FJ*, 21 Feb., *The Times*, 27 Feb. 1838. Whately was supported by, amongst others, the Presbyterian representative on the Poor Inquiry Commission, James Carlile.

31 'The Poor Law Bill – Meeting of the Citizens of Dublin', *The Times*, 16 Mar. 1838.

32 *FJ*, 18 Apr. 1838.

33 *Ibid.*, 3, 4, 24 May 1838.

34 *Ibid.*, 4, 11 June 1838.

very faulty; but the opposition of our old taskmasters, the Grand Jury, jobbing landlords, &c., makes me suspect some essential virtue that I have not fully discovered.'[35]

It was certainly true that the county grand juries, meeting at the spring assizes of 1838, needed little encouragement to draw up Whatelyite petitions to the Lords, generally demanding the restriction of state relief to the 'impotent poor', along with some form of remunerative employment for the labouring poor. In March, the grand juries of Meath, Cavan, Wexford, Fermanagh, King's County, Down and Mayo all submitted similar resolutions, while, as *The Times* gleefully reported, there was not a single meeting in favour of the bill.[36] During the 1837–38 session, 116 petitions from various bodies, with 39,922 signatures, were presented against the bill; this swamped the paltry four (with 593 names) in its favour.[37]

The success of the petitioning campaign, and the rhetorical pyrotechnics which accompanied their presentation to parliament, convinced many in Ireland that the Lords would throw out the bill. Sensing an opportunity to promote the idea of Tory democracy, the *Dublin Evening Mail* sought to appropriate Sadler's mantle against 'the demoniac theory of MALTHUS' which it discerned as embodied in the government bill, and assured its readers that the landed interest would defend both its own and the poor's interests in the upper House.[38] On seeing these hopes disappointed, the paper also turned on the duke of Wellington for once again high-handedly disregarding the wishes of the Irish people.[39] This of course oversimplified the underlying problems of the Irish opposition. The *News-Letter* was more introspective in its interpretation, citing the lengthy delay in mobilizing opposition as the key failing: 'There was', the paper lamented, 'for a long time, an unaccountable apathy on the subject, which naturally led government into the error of supposing that their plan had been generally acquiesced in, if not directly approved of.'[40] This reading may have confused 'apathy' for intense division. Among the reasons for their defeat was the very heterogeneous character of the opposition in Ireland, which could agree on opposing the 'Irish Bastille Bill', but was at odds with itself on a suitable and workable alternative.

35 Cloncurry to Conway, 27 Apr. [1838], in Fitzpatrick (ed.), *Cloncurry*, pp. 458–9.

36 *The Times*, 12–13 Mar., *FJ*, 10, 29 Mar., *DEM*, 2 Mar. 1838.

37 Anon., *The Parliamentary Pocket Companion, for 1838* (London, 1838), p. 187. On 30 April Sir William Brabazon had counted 86 hostile petitions, containing 31,221 signatures: *Hansard*, 3, xlii, 676.

38 *DEM*, 14, 26 Mar., 4, 11 May. The *Waterford Mail* (5, 16 May 1838) was equally certain of the Lords' intentions.

39 *DEM*, 11 June 1838.

40 *BNL*, 4 May 1838.

Pro-poor-law voices in Ireland

There were some attempts in 1838 by the Irish supporters of the poor law to bolster what public support remained against the prevailing current. Some Irish Whigs continued to make a case for the bill as a 'just' tax on landlords – Winston Barron speaking at Waterford claimed it would oblige some landowners to pay rates of £500 to £1,000 a year for the relief of the poor.[41] In a lengthy pamphlet, the Galway MP A. H. Lynch defended his parliamentary vote for the bill (although not for all its clauses), on the grounds that it must precede other essential measures for employment. While the latter were indispensable, only the poor law could save the community from the disgrace of beggary and the evils of mendicancy. He appended a petition in support of it signed by the clergy and leading laymen in the town of Galway to demonstrate that it was not without public support, even at this stage.[42] Lynch's appointment to the lucrative post of Master in Chancery in February 1838 might have given ammunition to those inclined to read his support for the bill cynically as the pursuit of government favour – but his appointment was welcomed rather than denounced by elements of the Irish press as a reward for sterling public service.[43] As author of the auxiliary employment bills, Lynch retained a certain popularity despite his association with an unpopular measure. In 1839 he continued to uphold the new act as an essential first step towards national regeneration, and urged its rapid implementation and augmentation by the promised auxiliaries. The problems of destitution and mendicancy had been addressed by the poor law, he commented, but the separate issue of acute and widespread poverty remained to be tackled. The solution lay chiefly in the reclamation and cultivation of the Irish waste-lands, undertaken by a combination of public and private initiatives (the latter stimulated by the burden of poor-rates, and encouraged by the security for investment the poor law would promote). Like other radical advocates of Irish waste-land reclamation, Lynch regarded Belgium as a model both for public initiatives and as a social pattern for a dynamic small-farm economy.[44]

41 'Meeting of St Mary's Parish', *The Times*, 2 Feb. 1838. Barron also set out the reasons for his disagreement to O'Connell in a long letter to the press, *MC*, 29 Dec. 1837.

42 Lynch, *Address to the Electors of Galway*.

43 *FJ*, 2 Feb. 1838. Lynch was popular in Galway as an active local representative and an improving and employing landowner: see *Connaught Journal*, 12 Aug. 1839.

44 A. H. Lynch, *Measures to be adopted for the Employment of the Labouring Classes in Ireland* (London, 1839).

The other principal Irish Whig advocate of the bill in parliament, Lord Clements, also developed his views in print.[45] Like his fellow Connacht MP Lynch, Clements located the poor law within a developmental programme that recognized that the existing socio-economic condition of the Irish countryside was unsustainable, while rejecting the Lewis–Nicholls vision of a transition to an anglicized model of capitalist agriculture. He argued that Blacker's experiments in Armagh and his own experience as an improving resident proprietor in Leitrim proved that, under favourable tenancy arrangements, small-scale mixed farming could be profitable and draw out the many small capital sums currently hoarded unproductively within the countryside. Successful implementation of the poor law would promote an incremental consolidation of holdings without the violence and alienation associated with mass clearances for pastoral farming. Despite the bill's limitations, he still believed that the imposition of poor-rates would act beneficently, if gradually, to wean farmers away from granting rundale and conacre lettings to labourers, and to give instead cash wages sufficient for the labouring family's annual subsistence. At the same time it would identify to landlords the real monetary costs of evictions through 'the apprehension of a direct tax', and signify the preferable alternative of requiring 'fair rents' and giving profitable employment to their small tenants.

Crucial to the system's success, he concluded, would be its popular acceptance. This would best be achieved through widespread participation in the election of guardians, who would then 'partake in the feelings and interests of the people', and explain its beneficent workings to them. The farming classes collectively could and should take the lead in administering the system locally (with some, but limited, participation from *ex-officio* landlord guardians): Clements was anxious that the £5 rating clause be scrapped so as to encompass as large a proportion as possible of this class within the ratepayer-elector community, especially as in parts of the west nine-tenths of the tenantry would otherwise be excluded. He envisioned the tenants taking ownership of the system and using it to depauperize both themselves and their conacre-labourers, and to exert leverage over the landlords to co-operate to the rural community's mutual advantage. These beneficial consequences would take time; in the short-run the government must be prepared to face down the self-interested opposition of those who were now most vocal against the bill, and even more likely to resist its implementation:

45 Lord Clements, *The Present Poverty of Ireland convertible into the Means of Her Improvement, under a Well-Administered Poor Law* (London, 1838). The pamphlet was also serialized in the *Dublin Evening Post*.

> As long as visions of government works, and other popular projects, are afloat connected with the poor law, the unpopularity of the measure in Ireland among the farmers may be suppressed; indeed there are so many utopian projects for Ireland constantly *talked of*, but never seen, that they have such a very vague idea of what a poor law might be, that they have never yet begun (in the rural parts of Ireland) to occupy their minds seriously about it. But as soon as they discover that they are to be made to pay hard money, 'under the *pretext*' (as they will say) of supporting beggars in the workhouse, to whom they would much rather give a potato at home, and '*in reality*' (as they will say) to support a gang of jobbing parish officers, – that moment the general outcry will begin; and will be most violent, of course, among those classes who do not pay at present in proportion to their property. These are the higher, and hitherto the most influential class of farmers. The only way of meeting the outcry beneficially will be, by simply following the course pursued in England, – by making the representatives of the people very numerous, and by taking pains to convince their reason.[46]

For these reasons he favoured amendments to make the unions more numerous and compact, and to offer salaries to elected guardians who might not otherwise afford to spare the time or expense of attending board meetings at a distance from their homes. He envisaged the new boards as incipient agencies of quasi-democratic rural local government, with the landed grand juries reduced to residual courts of appeal. This radical vision of a poor law, with its emphasis on co-operation and the empowerment of the poorer tenantry, owed something to Revans, and was a serious attempt to develop what had become a rather sterile debate.[47] Clements sent his pamphlet to the organizers of the Belfast anti-poor-law meetings in the hope of persuading them that the bill would stimulate rather than quash charitable exertions, and its failure to make an impact on such opponents must have disheartened him.[48]

If Clements and Lynch were the most high-profile Irish defenders of the government measure in 1838, they were not alone. The former medical assistant commissioner William Borrett took issue with O'Connell's hostile letters, and urged support of the government bill (with the proviso that its 'objectionable' rating clause be modified) accompanied by a thorough reform of the Irish medical charities.[49] The Tory Irish landlords who supported Shaw's

46 *Ibid.*, pp. 151–2.

47 *Ibid.*, p. 168. He had previously described Revans as 'a conceited coxcomb', but also the author of 'the best book that has been published about poor laws': CHP, J/19/1/13/51, Clements to Morpeth, 18 Oct. 1836.

48 NLI: KP, Ms 14,298, Clements to Bruce, 20 Feb. 1838. His career as a parliamentarian was cut short by his sudden death the following year.

49 Borrett, *Three Letters*. For the medical charities issue, see below, pp. 322–3.

amendment were savaged for their 'selfish' opposition to a real poor law by another Irish liberal, although again not without the addition of criticism of the government for ignoring the views of its friends, especially on the desirability of outdoor relief to the aged and infirm, the restriction of the workhouse to providing a destitution test for the able-bodied, and the necessity of a 'comprehensive code of laws, suited to the magnitude of their wants'.[50] An unnamed member of the Dublin Mendicity Association also wrote in favour of the principle of the bill, while citing Revans and Doyle on the necessity of appending some law of settlement both to protect the port cities from the hordes of migrant labourers passing through en route to or from Great Britain and of localizing the responsibility for relief and agricultural improvement to individual landowners.[51] Thaddeus O'Malley's letters on the subject, which continued to appear in the Dublin press throughout the session, similarly offered at best a conditional and critical support for the ministerial measure, and included appeals for concessions that might 'neutralise the hostility to the measure' that was now so widely expressed and threatening to impede its successful implementation.[52] William Sharman Crawford, now out of parliament, also continued his active controversialism, but was even less willing to make allowances for the flaws of the government's bill than others. While he continued to attack O'Connell's ongoing resistance to any poor law whatsoever as a betrayal of his own proclaimed political principles, he now located the former's principal failure in his refusal to use his unparalleled public authority in Ireland to 'extort' the necessary concessions from government and parliament. He lamented that O'Connell had not thrown his weight behind key amendments, such as granting of a statutory right to relief, a law of settlement (by electoral division), removal of the emigration clause, the power to allow outdoor relief, and a rating clause that would impose a surcharge on rack-renting landlords.[53] Although Crawford participated in the Down petitioning meeting, he differed from other northern spokesmen (including his son) in still favouring a heavily amended compulsory measure over a local opt-out. His problem lay not only in O'Connell's fundamental

50 Anon., *An Address to the Lords embodying the Spirit of the Irish Grand Juries' Petitions on the Poor Relief Bill, with an Appeal in Favour of the Aged, Infirm and Destitute Agricultural Labourers* (London, 1838).

51 Anon., *The Necessity of Combining a Law of Settlement with Local Assessment in the Proposed Bill for the Relief of the Poor of Ireland* (Dublin, 1838).

52 O'Malley to Russell, 25 Apr., *FJ*, 26 Apr. 1838. O'Malley's preference was for the dropping of the maximum allowance of twelve acres of agricultural land attached to a workhouse, and the substitution of a national for a local rate.

53 Sharman Crawford, 'To the friends of "real justice" to Ireland', letters 1–4, *BNL*, 13, 16, 20 Feb.; Sharman Crawford to Daniel O'Connell, *FJ*, 27 Apr. 1838.

refusal to participate, but in the failure of those proposing amendments to agree on what these should be, and how they should be prioritized.

British public opinion and the Irish poor law bills

However fierce the Irish debate and marked the shift in opinion against the bill in the 1837–38 session, it was, as Whately had observed, in England that the fate of the bill would be decided. Public opinion in Great Britain was also divided over the Irish bill, but the preponderance of comment was always in favour of its principle, and on balance, supportive of the measure in hand. There was no hermetic seal separating the public debates in the two islands; parliament remained the focus of press, pamphlet and petitioning attention in each, and many pamphlets were published in both London and Dublin to address both audiences; Irish newspapers reprinted British press commentary, and vice versa. Also, many of the leading commentators in the Irish debate, such as Whately and Wrightson, were 'Irish' only by accident of association through the Poor Inquiry Commission. Nevertheless, there were certain distinct tendencies in the debates in the two public contexts.

There were two main foci for opposition to the measure in Britain. One was among last-ditch supporters of the old English poor law, who (for various reasons) wished its forms extended to Ireland at the same time as they sought the overthrow of the Somerset House Commission and dilution of the modifications introduced in England from 1834. As the English anti-poor-law movement gathered support in the context of the deteriorating economic conditions of 1837–38, Ireland served as something of a proxy for the battles simultaneously being contested in England by Tory and radical defenders of the 'rights of the poor man'. In contrast, the second focus was Malthusian, identifying, like Whately and his associates, the root of the social malaise of both islands in overpopulation, and regarding poor laws in their old or new forms as at best a necessary evil, at worst the fundamental cause of pauperism. These objections existed in stronger or weaker forms and were interwoven with other, especially party-political, considerations.

John Walter's *The Times* was, as observed above, a leading and influential voice in support of the old and against the new English laws. Yet, rather surprisingly and uncharacteristically, it appears to have taken a long time to take a position on the government's Irish bill. Between the bill's original introduction in February and the start of June 1837 there were no leading articles on the subject, comment being left to occasional pot-shots from its Irish correspondent.[54] Once it did commit itself, however, *The Times* proved a sustained and savage critic, combining its antagonism to the workhouse-test and

54 *The Times*, 3 Mar. 1837.

less-eligibility principles with a denunciation of what it took to be the cynical political objects of the ministry. In June 1837 the paper announced itself convinced that the bill was a con-trick, introduced as a show of conciliation to the 'Popish priests', but deliberately rendered so impracticable and inefficient in its prospective machinery that it could not pass the Lords (and thus risk alienating O'Connell).[55]

This rather convoluted high-political interpretation became more difficult to sustain as ministers' commitment to the measure became clearer in the following session. The paper changed tack to lambaste both the folly and incompetence of the measure and highlight the dangerous resistance it would arouse in Ireland. The fault lay with the 'fanatical simpleton' Lord John Russell, who hubristically had imagined his association with the introduction of the workhouse system in England had won him great laurels, and consequently had embraced the opinion on Ireland of such 'ignorant quacks' as Nicholls and William Stanley. Other ministers, although evidently antagonistic to the measure, had deferred to his obsession so as to keep going as long as possible the 'crazy machine' of the Whig government.[56] Just as the industrial downturn in England had provoked a growing outcry against the oppression of the new poor law, a violent reaction in Ireland would follow against this 'utterly hateful and condemnable abortion'.[57] The paper endorsed and summarized for a metropolitan audience the arguments of Irish writers such as MacNaghten, and echoed the most apocalyptic fears expressed across the Irish Sea. Yet as it became clear that Wellington would see it through with only relatively minor amendments, the paper's critical comments faded out.[58] Ironically, *The Times* would become one of the strongest defenders of the Irish poor law in the 1840s as a tool to discipline both the Irish landlords and peasants alike.

Although *The Times* would have been reluctant to admit it, the English writer who came closest to its position on the terms (as opposed to the politics) of the bill was the radical MP and heterodox political economist Poulett Scrope. As MP for Stroud, Scrope had multiple opportunities to voice his demand for the amendment of the measure to render it more similar to the 'Elizabethan' old poor law of England, but he also took his case to the public in pamphlet form.[59] To meet just Irish expectations and have any impact on

55 *Ibid.*, 2, 20 June 1837.

56 *Ibid.*, 4, 12 Dec. 1837, 10 Feb. 1838.

57 *Ibid.*, 16, 22 Dec. 1837.

58 The other Conservative and 'Tory-Radical' journals, such as *John Bull* and the *Poor Man's Guardian*, tended to follow *The Times*'s line on the Irish poor-law question: see *Examiner*, 19 Feb. 1837.

59 Scrope, *Remarks on the Government Bill.*

poverty, mendicancy and unrest, he insisted, the poor law must be compulsory, with a right to relief, settlement, powers of giving domiciliary relief to the crippled, sick and helpless, and outdoor employment relief to the able-bodied. Despite this critique, however, Scrope was ultimately to accept the government's bill rather than risk obtaining nothing at all.

Scrope gave some place in his alternative schema to assisted emigration, but some of his radical associates, especially those in the 'colonization lobby', placed this at the very heart of their projects for Ireland, rejecting or relegating other modes of relief and regeneration. First into the ring in 1837 was the St Albans MP H. G. Ward, whose Wakefieldian argument for the essential precondition of a Canadian colonization scheme drew the contempt of *The Times* but sympathy from parts of the liberal press.[60] A more heavyweight case for the primacy of assisted emigration was produced soon after by the political economist and promoter of Australian colonization Robert Torrens. While he welcomed the establishment of boards of guardians as the nucleus of local self-government in Ireland, Torrens agreed implicitly with Whately that the fundamental Irish problem lay in overpopulation, and that all other remedies would be futile without a rapid and large-scale removal of the 'surplus', as this alone could redress the adverse land–labourer ratio. At the same time he employed Ricardian arguments to demonstrate that land reclamation in Ireland could only bring the most marginal land into cultivation, with no effect on wages or consumption. He also took Nicholls to task for failing to recognize that any substitution of English tenancy arrangements and modes of agricultural production for the Irish cottier system must inevitably throw large additional numbers permanently out of employment and result in mass clearances. Rather than alleviating poverty, a poor law that successfully promoted the sociological aims of Lewis and Nicholls would thus vastly increase misery unless aided by other measures.[61] Ward and Torrens received support from A. C. Buchanan, the government's chief emigration agent at Quebec, who argued that a large-scale colonization project would be cheap, practicable and equally beneficial to Ireland and the Canadas (although the number he envisaged – some 40,000 a year – was less than that projected by the Wakefieldians).[62] Assisted emigration was still the focus of the bulk of orthodox economic opinion. In June 1837 the Political Economy Club of London

60 Ward, *First Step*; *The Times*, 4 Feb., *Examiner*, 5 Feb. 1837.

61 Torrens, *Letter to the Right Honourable Lord John Russell* (2nd edn, London, 1838). The first edition appeared in February 1837.

62 A. C. Buchanan, *Outline of a Practical Plan for the Immediate, Effective and Economical Relief of the Starving & Destitute Poor of Ireland* (Brighton, [1837]). An Irishman, Buchanan had the pamphlet published while on furlough.

(which included Torrens, Senior and Spring Rice) discussed the question: 'To what extent should emigration from Ireland be carried in order to dispauperise that country, and aid the introduction of poor laws; and from what sources should the expenses of such emigration be defrayed?'[63]

These economically orthodox conclusions were well received by the *Spectator*, long a sceptic on an Irish poor law. While it admitted the matter was now 'ripe' and hence politically unavoidable, it endorsed the Poor Inquiry Commission's case that auxiliaries and most especially emigration must take precedence. Ward and Torrens had successfully demonstrated that the latter could be undertaken with little permanent cost to the home exchequer, it observed.[64] Its criticism, unlike that of *The Times*, tended towards a despairing resignation at the failure of ministers (and indeed the opposition leaders) to grasp the obvious, and a somewhat misplaced stress on the role of Chadwick, Senior and Nicholls as the real authors of the bill.[65]

The other liberal weekly, the *Examiner*, although more defensive of the Irish government and 'justice to Ireland', took a similar line. The question of an Irish poor law was, its editorialist announced, no longer debatable, as '[t]he public has decided that there shall be one.' Thankfully the ministry had evaded the disastrous consequences for Ireland that would have ensued from a measure based on Sadler's motion of 1831, replete with all the evils of the then-unreformed English system. Where it thought the bill fell short of Nicholls' recommendations was on the matter of emigration – which it agreed with Lord Lansdowne in thinking absolutely essential for Irish regeneration.[66] Nevertheless, in 1838 it warmly recommended Clements' pamphlet to its readers as 'written in the masculine and unaffected style which befits the subject' and as 'remarkable for being hopeful without being visionary'.[67] The *Examiner* was at best a lukewarm and occasional supporter of the bill, rising to the government's defence only when the partisan speeches of Lyndhurst and Brougham strayed into a more generalized assault on its Irish policy, but attempting little by way of endorsement for the measure.[68]

63 *Political Economy Club*, pp. 46–7.

64 'The only reform for 1837', *Spectator*, 28. Jan.; 'The intended poor-law for Ireland', *ibid.*, 4 Feb., 'Colonel Torrens on the Irish poor-law question', *ibid.*, 25 Feb. 1837.

65 'The impracticable but inevitable poor-law for Ireland', *ibid.*, 28 Feb. 1837. Chadwick denounced its attack on subordinate officials as injurious and largely erroneous: UCL: CP, 23/414–17, Chadwick memo, n.d.

66 *Examiner*, 19 Feb., 18 June 1837.

67 *Ibid.*, 18 Feb. 1838.

68 *Ibid.*, 27 May 1838.

There were some attempts to formulate a more fundamentalist case against any poor law for Ireland, principally by active local poor-law administrators in England who, while briskly implementing the 1834 act in their own unions, continued to lean towards abolitionism. John Leslie of London had already made his name as an advocate of the new English act, but, like Wrightson, he continued to regard any poor law as at best a temporary evil, and 1834 as a step towards the eradication of state relief. All systems of poor relief were, he insisted, erroneous in principle – an immense insurance society founded on false premises and data, and in defiance of the divine precept of self-reliance. While the English act had 'virtually been an abolition of the poor laws to the able-bodied', the introduction of any plan to Ireland would have the opposite effect, depressing wages yet further and obscuring the 'present rising sun of prosperity' there. It was delusive to anticipate any social improvement in England from an Irish poor law, without a ban on Irish labour-migration.[69] Another English official, C. H. Bracebridge, also made the Whatelian case that poor laws generally should restrict themselves to the infirm, infants and incapable old, and that the able-bodied were outside its province and power, adding a long critique of the Nicholls report for ignoring these and other fundamentals.[70]

This position also found a voice in the press in the columns of some London periodicals. The *Morning Advertiser* proclaimed that '[i]t is very problematical to us whether the introduction of poor laws into any country has been advantageous to the bulk of the population, but it is quite clear to us, that so far as regards Ireland, their introduction would be a very great calamity.'[71] The *Monthly Review* also carried a lengthy and uncritical review of the *Strictures*, and declared itself convinced by the evidence that Nicholls must be 'a rash, an incompetent, and probably a selfish speculator'.[72]

These arguments were countered (and it appears outnumbered) by the productions of other British commentators. One clerical writer idealistically and explicitly identified the English 1834 act as embodying a purified and universally-applicable model for social cohesion consonant with Paley's moral philosophy, and praised Nicholls for successfully adapting it in a form practicably applicable to Ireland. Its success there was guaranteed, for '[w]hen a

69 John Leslie, Further Illustrations of the Principles upon which a Metropolitan Poor Rate is administered in the Parish of St George, Hanover Square (London, 1836).

70 [C. H. Bracebridge], *A Letter to the Right Hon. Lord John Russell on the Principles of the Irish Poor Law Bill* (London, 1837).

71 *Morning Advertiser*, cited in *FJ*, 12 Jan. 1838.

72 Anon., 'Poor law for Ireland', *Monthly Review*, 143 (1837), pp. 54–69.

healthy shoot from the primitive stock, well pruned, is transplanted into the rich soil, and genial clime of Ireland can it fail to be as the tree which will essentially tend to the healing of the nation?'[73]

Nicholls was also defended by a range of commentators. Leitch Ritchie, the Scottish novelist and travel writer, employed his recent sojourn in Ireland to illustrate his enthusiastic endorsement of the bill and the report on which it was based.[74] The 1834 English act had, he argued, established a model that was superior to that of Scotland or any in continental Europe, and was universally exportable. At its heart was the recognition that, while poverty was not a crime, it must be strictly treated as a misfortune and the pauper isolated from society by confinement in the workhouse. Allowance of anything more than a minimal form of indoor relief would threaten Ireland with the corruptions from which England had so recently been emancipated, and tempt the lower classes of Irish 'whose lives are, as it is, a tissue of make-shifts and expedients', to throw themselves upon the state.[75] Although no panacea, the positive sociological consequences of the bill would be transformative, not least in replacing the present 'castes' of Ireland with a distinct class system:

> It will afford numerous tangible points for laying hold of the minds of men, who are at present moved only in great masses, stirred by the views of religious or political enthusiasts. Civilization never comes in the lump. It works in detail; and, until Irish society is broken up into the small *selfish* circles of England, it will be impossible to operate upon it with advantage.[76]

Despite the 'ingenious' attempts of the *Strictures* and similar pamphlets to prove otherwise, Nicholls had based his argument for the practicality and safety of an Irish poor law on the facts collected by the assistant

73 J. Bosworth, *The Contrast: or, the Operation of the Old Poor Laws Contrasted with the Recent Poor Law Amendment Act, and the Necessity of a Legal Provision for the Poor Generally, but Especially in Ireland* (London, 1838).

74 Leitch Ritchie, *A Bystander's View of the Irish Poor Law Question* (London, 1837). Ritchie published his travelogue as *Ireland: Picturesque and Romantic* (London, 1837), which included long digressions on the poor-law question, which he defended in this text as appropriate for a female audience: 'A few years ago, I should not have ventured on this discussion in a picture-book, intended chiefly for the drawing-room table: but, in the present day, those who were formerly the mere ladies of England are ENGLISHWOMEN, and the sympathies that before were confined to a class of subjects, now embrace the whole interests of the human race.' The *Examiner* (29 Oct. 1837) approved of neither the confusion of genres, nor the presentation of a 'masculine' subject to a female readership.

75 Ritchie, *Bystander's View*, p. 47.

76 *Ibid.*, p. 52.

commissioners. Ireland's present 'virtual poor law', the cause of so much social disorganization and mendicancy, proved the country could support its own poor; the government deserved every praise for endeavouring to replace this with one that was equitable, rational and reflected the true designs of divine providence. Ritchie concluded by urging the Poor Law Commissioners to reflect on the nature of the 'high and holy mission' they had undertaken.[77]

An anonymous pamphlet of May 1837 also set out to rescue Nicholls from his detractors. While Scrope was dismissed for advocating what amounted to 'Captain Rock in a legal dress', this review focused chiefly on what it took to be the poor reasoning, self-contradiction and deliberate misreadings of the position embodied in the pro-Whately writers Torrens, 'Philo-Hibernus' (Corrie), Butt and the author of the *Strictures*. The government, rather than the defenceless Nicholls, was the real author of the bill, it asserted; Nicholls had been employed only to recommend a practical mode of proceedings in the wake of the confusions and contradictions of the third report and the division between Senior and Lewis. The outcome was the adoption of 'the purest form of poor laws'.[78]

Alongside these polemical responses to the critical literature, the bill received more extensive and heavyweight support from two important sources – the first from an English member of the corps of assistant commissioners under the Whately Commission, the second from one of the leading figures in the political economy establishment. The anonymous assistant commissioner, who had served in Co. Tipperary, denounced the third report as offering 'a few miserable palliatives' instead of a comprehensive remedy. This was hardly surprising, as

> their real object was to deter Parliament from entertaining any project of relief, by the abortiveness of some of their expedients, and the inapplicability of others. That such were the views contemplated, receives confirmation from the fact, that a majority of the Commissioners approved of the system of *voluntary* contribution, although it is well known that all attempts to legislate on that principle have hitherto lamentably failed.[79]

Again, Nicholls was defended as simply following out the instructions of a home secretary anxious to find a practicable scheme, and rightly concluding that a poor law proper would best be based on the reformed English model.

77 *Ibid.*, p. 55.

78 Anon., *Irish Poor: A Word for Mr Nicholls* (London, 1837).

79 Anon., *Remarks on the Application of the Workhouse System*, pp. 5–6. Walter Gisborne was the 'English' assistant who had taken evidence in Tipperary and the probable author of this pamphlet.

This did not preclude the necessity of some modifications and auxiliary measures – indeed without these, the workhouse test must fail. No poor law could prevent the incidences of famine consequent on the occasional failure of the conacre potato crop, although it would 'go a great way to relieve the aggravated symptoms of the disorder, and would serve as an index of the real condition of the poor, that timely measures might be adopted for their relief, before numbers perished from actual starvation, as is too frequently known to be the case'.[80] The poor law would thus serve as a kind of early-warning mechanism for triggering 'extraordinary' relief in such a crisis.

More generally, the author continued, the poor law would have some beneficial moral effect on Irish society, giving the poor labourer a guarantee against actual starvation, demonstrating that the law could serve as a protector and friend rather than a tool of the rich, and thereby loosening his grasp on the land; but these positive effects would be slow and contested, and a marked improvement in the material condition of the people required that the poor law be accompanied by increased agricultural employment on the waste-lands. The passage advocating this betrays some bitterness against the author's former superior and his prejudices and modes of reasoning:

> To leave everything to Providence and the landlords may be very well for an archbishop whose prayers are supposed to have a certain efficacy, but would be gross folly in a legislator, who must know the landlords better. The great body of the gentry in Ireland have never done one atom for the poor, and never will but on compulsion, and one of the most valuable results that may be expected from giving a right to relief in the workhouse, to all the poor without distinction, will be, that should the alarm now generally felt lest the able-bodied may avail themselves of the relief in too great numbers, turn out to be well-founded, the landlords will be driven by the pressure upon their incomes to turn their attention to 'those other circumstances' which at the time that they will diminish their burthens, will more than any direct system of poor laws tend to improve the condition of the people.[81]

Against this endorsement of the poor law as a measure of social retribution, the assistant commissioner also sought to provide a balanced reading of the difficulties of implementation, and the likelihood that the poor would continue their charitable support of seasonal vagrants. The system would acquire greater popularity and legitimacy if the 'really and permanently disabled' were provided for in infirmaries and almshouses operating on a more liberal scale than the workhouses proper, leaving the latter for temporary and coercive purposes only. A truly preventive poor law would also engraft the auxiliary

80 *Ibid.*, pp. 15–16.
81 *Ibid.*, pp. 30–1.

of a local loan fund system, providing seasonal credit at equitable rates to support the economy of makeshifts typical of the masses of rural poor, and help prevent them from slipping into a cycle of debt and ultimate destitution.[82] While reviewers noted this element, the nuances and sophistication of the assistant commissioner's contribution was generally overlooked in the desire to categorize him as a defender of the embattled Nicholls.[83]

The most prominent theoretical riposte to the political-economic critique of the Irish poor law bill (as well as to its radical advocates) came from Herman Merivale, who had been elected to the Drummond chair of political economy at Oxford in 1837.[84] Merivale's book, originating in a series of lectures delivered in late 1837 and early 1838, used his contribution to the controversy over the government's bill to discuss his other economic preoccupations. He was evidently reading Sismondi's *Études sur l'économie politique*, and was anxious to refute its critique of the English socio-economic order and advocacy of the superiority of a secure small-peasant agriculture, especially for Ireland.[85] This required a justification of the economic efficiency and social desirability of a transition to a tripartite division of labour and a capitalized agriculture in Ireland, not only against Sismondi, the Saint-Simonians and Owenites, but also against those protagonists of the Irish poor law who appeared to favour the enhancement rather than the supplanting of cottier farming; the 'fallacious' reasoning of Revans on wages was singled out for criticism.[86] However, he was prepared to admit that Revans was right, and

82 *Ibid.*, pp. 42–64. The proposed system of microcredit had, the author observed, successful precedents in the 'Monts de Pieté' projects operated by Barrington, Bagot and others.

83 *Examiner*, 22 Oct. 1837.

84 Herman Merivale, *Five Lectures on the Principles of a Legislative Provision for the Poor in Ireland* (London, 1838). In his later role as under-secretary for the colonies from 1847, Merivale proved an active opponent of Wakefieldian colonization schemes.

85 J. C. L. Simonde de Sismondi, *Études sur l'économie politique* (2 vols, Paris, 1837–38), quoted in Merivale, *Five Lectures*, p. 31. Merivale translated Sismondi's passage on Ireland as follows: 'The most desirable state of society is that in which the great body of cultivators are proprietors. It is not the state which yields the greatest net revenue or profit, but it is that which gives the greatest bulk of gross revenue; and which employs most labour, and recompenses it most amply. It is the state which maintains, in the greatest numbers, a happy population; for without increase of happiness, increase of population is only a calamity. The first thing to be done for this unhappy country [Ireland] is to assimilate, as far as possible, the condition of the peasant to that of a proprietor, and to open to him the means, by his own economy, of becoming absolute proprietor.'

86 Merivale, *Five Lectures*, p. 15.

Torrens' neo-Malthusian reading demonstrably wrong, in charging landlords with responsibility for holding down wages in the economically anomalous current condition of Ireland. This conclusion inclined him towards Lewis's prescription for a poor law as a precondition for the necessary transformation and capitalization of the rural economy, gradually raising the productivity of Irish labour, and with this the wages and the moral condition of the people. However, Merivale saw the poor law's effect as largely indirect and subsidiary to other agencies; he evaded all association of the measure with discussion of the rights or welfare of the poor and went out of his way to undermine what he saw as the myth of the Elizabethan poor law's beneficent effects. A sound measure could act as a measure of 'police and good order' in softening the pain of the essential 'period of transition', while also stabilizing wage fluctuations and fixing a minimum level of subsistence.

This was at best a conditional and prospective support for the principle of a poor law for Ireland, but Merivale endorsed the distinction drawn by Nicholls between poverty and destitution, and between the 'occasionally' and 'permanently' destitute, and endorsed a cautious measure to relieve only the last – comprising the able-bodied denizens of 'decayed' villages and suburbs, many of them ejected tenants, who could rarely find employment, and who lived by vagrancy and mendicancy. These, rather than the conacre-labourer families who might face occasional distress, were the 'absolutely destitute', and it was only these that a poor law could currently aid (although the wider peasant community would benefit from an equalization of the burden of supporting them). While he believed that Nicholls had estimated the numbers of such destitutes too conservatively, and that consequently the commissioners would be obliged to resort to outdoor relief for the impotent once the system was in full operation, it was right to begin 'experimentally' rather than bring this in too soon. A 'right to relief' and a law of settlement would also become indispensable in time and should be regulated by the workhouse test once the system was complete. He rebutted the views of the Genevan anti-poor-law writer Naville by insisting that the European workhouse systems he critiqued were institutions which had sought to profitably employ pauper labour, and thus bore no resemblance to the reformed English and proposed Irish institutions.[87]

Merivale was dismissive of auxiliary measures on orthodox *laissez-faire* lines. The assisted emigration advocated by Torrens and Whately could only be economically significant if carried out on a scale and speed that were physically impossible given the constraints of available shipping, the costs involved, and the availability of employment opportunities in the colonies. Moreover, 'a general plan of emigration would probably have the effect of causing much poor land to be abandoned, and only very slightly relieving the better'; it was

87 *Ibid.*, pp. 86–99.

the poor productivity of the Irish labourer, rather than a redundancy of his numbers, that had to be addressed.[88] Public works, on the other hand, simply drained the wages-fund through taxation, deranged the labour market, and produced unnecessary outcomes. Experience and theory alike indicated that private enterprise was always superior to state agency in any but the most elementary works; European examples – as Naville had shown – proved that waste-lands could only be profitably reclaimed under market conditions. If Merivale stripped the poor-law proposal of the optimistic hopes of its advocates, and provided ammunition for the enemies of 'auxiliaries', he at least promoted its passage by challenging the apocalyptic economic fears of its opponents.[89]

Greater enthusiasm for the bill remained the territory of the bulk of the liberal press. For radical papers, such as the *Leeds Times*, the issue was straightforward (if somewhat crude) – a poor law would be the only safety for the poor against the oppression of their 'cruel Orange landlords', obliging them to pay for the consequences of their actions.[90] While criticizing the 'centralization' inherent in certain clauses of the government's bill, the Yorkshire paper approved its general principle: 'This then is justice to Ireland – to feed its poor, and to put a bridle in the mouths of their oppressors.'[91] Similar anti-landlordist and moralist rhetoric – attacking O'Connell as a defender of the landed interest – was voiced by the *Edinburgh Advertiser* and the *True Sun*.[92] Feargus O'Connor's *Northern Star* enthusiastically damned O'Connell as the advocate of class-interest in Ireland and demanded an Irish poor law with provision for the able-bodied unemployed. His fellow Chartist Bronterre O'Brien was severely critical of the workhouse scheme and 'tyrannical' powers granted to the commissioners by the bill, but he also reserved his harshest invective for O'Connell and Irish landed opponents of poor laws.[93]

The *Morning Chronicle* was a more sophisticated and loyal voice on the ministerial side. Confident of the success (and ultimate popularity) of the English 1834 act, it was convinced its extension to Ireland would prove similarly effective.[94] Nicholls' report was, it alleged, 'drawn with the hand of a master'; if perhaps going too far in rejecting any form of settlement, it had

88 *Ibid.*, pp. 66–73.
89 *Globe*, cited in *FJ*, 14 Apr. 1838.
90 *Leeds Times*, cited in *FJ*, 10 Jan. 1837.
91 *Leeds Times*, cited in *FJ*, 21 Feb. 1837.
92 Cited in *FJ*, 14, 21 Jan., 1837.
93 *Northern Star*, 6 Jan., 12, 19 May 1838.
94 *MC*, 23 Jan., 25 Mar. 1837. Its line was echoed by organs of provincial middle-class liberalism, such as the *Manchester Guardian* (2 Feb. 1837) and *Liverpool Mercury* (1 June 1838).

successfully demonstrated the applicability of the workhouse system to Ireland.[95] Scrope's complaint that the bill contained no statutory right to relief was irrelevant, as in practice – as was already the case with the practice of the Dublin Mendicity Association and similar Irish bodies – no truly destitute person could be refused relief. Nicholls' estimates of the scale of actual destitution, as opposed to general poverty, were correct, and his recommendation of large unions and of supervision by the English commission were sound.[96] The *Chronicle*, like *The Times*, was also prepared to use the Irish case as a proxy in a controversy that was principally concerned with the English Amendment Act; the absolute limitation of relief to the workhouse in Ireland was defended not only as ensuring an indispensable test and proper treatment of the sick, aged and infirm poor in principle, but as following the best example set by those metropolitan unions who had gone furthest in implementing the ideas of 1834.[97] Its claim that Senior had now been converted to accepting the essentials of an Irish poor law in the same way that Chadwick's logic had converted him on the possibility of administrative reform in England was fiercely rebutted by *The Times*.[98] The ministerial *Globe* also engaged in such polemics, contrasting the 'Tory' case for a poor law as grounded in a selfish desire to exclude Irish labour from Britain, with the enlightened Whig plan to extend the new English system to Ireland, located within a broader reformist strategy for Ireland.[99]

The *Chronicle* remained equally combative after the publication of the second Nicholls report and reintroduction of the bill in late 1837. Wrightson's critique of the workhouse system was breezily refuted (for England) with reference to Chadwick's recent article in the same journal; Nicholls had effectively answered the question of its applicability to Ireland in the affirmative.[100] The popular opposition being whipped up by O'Connell was more problematic, obliging the paper to protest against his misrepresentations, and to urge the government to stand firm in the hope of retaining the confidence of the 'sensible and disinterested people' of Ireland. Despite growing evidence to the contrary, the paper insisted that O'Connell was risking his popularity in opposing the measure so prominently.[101] At the same time, his stance allowed

95 *MC*, 15 Feb., 25 Apr. 1837.

96 *Ibid.*, 27, 28 Apr., 1, 4 May 1837.

97 *Ibid.*, 1 June. In December the paper printed gleefully a letter from a London guardian and former *Times* subscriber denouncing that paper for its 'base and cowardly' falsehoods against the operation of the English act, *MC*, 26 Dec. 1837.

98 *Ibid.*, 21, 23 June, *The Times*, 22 June 1837.

99 *Globe*, cited in *FJ*, 2 Feb. 1837.

100 *MC*, 1 Dec. 1837; [Chadwick], 'New Poor Law', pp. 487–537.

101 *MC*, 26 Dec. 1837, 8 Jan., 10 Feb. 1838.

the paper to demonstrate to critics that the government was by no means O'Connell-ridden in its Irish policy. The government had wisely chosen to dismiss the contradictory and flawed cases made by O'Connell, Whately and the 'self-interested' grand juries, and ally themselves instead to more enlightened Irish figures, such as Lynch:

> We deny that the voice of the grand juries and of those landlords who oppose the measure is to be taken as the voice of the people of Ireland, or even as the voice of the majority of their own class. The prevalence of enlightened views amongst the Irish members was attested in a striking manner by the votes of a majority of the Irish members present for giving the control of the new measure to English commissioners, as the most skilled and impartial administrators.[102]

Thus the seemingly unpopular bill might yet be reconciled with the 'justice to Ireland' project. It would (albeit indirectly) prevent the recurrence of famine in Ireland.[103] While the *Chronicle*'s stance may have rallied British Whig and Irish reformist support for the bill, its confrontationalism towards O'Connell posed some problems for the government. One savage attack in early 1838, attributed to Nicholls but more probably penned by Chadwick, threw O'Connell into a fury and was deprecated as counter-productive by Dublin Castle.[104]

The *Sun*, also a liberal paper, was much less sanguine, but ultimately also fell into line behind the bill. While it would have preferred an employment-based bill similar to that suggested by the third report, it followed O'Malley and Staunton in accepting what was on offer as a first step, for 'once passed, there will be no possibility of adopting measures for its simple and unconditional repeal . . . it will give the poor a right in the soil of which it will be impossible ever to deprive them'.[105] For its part, the more moderate liberal *Scotsman* offered a cautious welcome, and praised the ministers for finding a safe *via media* through the minefield of relief policy and initiating 'an experiment scarcely less gigantic and hazardous than that of the abolition of slavery'.[106] This paper tended to emphasize G. C. Lewis's developmental thesis that an Irish poor law would be of greatest utility in creating safe conditions

102 *Ibid.*, 2, 21 May 1838.

103 *MC*, 28 May 1838.

104 While noting the necessity of a strong press campaign, Nicholls denied he had written the offending piece, and O'Connell subsequently withdrew his charges against him: NA: RP, PRO30/22/3A, fols 30–5, Drummond to Morpeth, 6 Jan.; CHP, J/19/1/16/62, 77, 80, Nicholls to Morpeth, 10, 19 Jan., O'Connell to Morpeth, 21 Jan. 1838.

105 *Sun*, cited in *FJ*, 10 Feb. 1838.

106 *Scotsman*, 18 Feb. 1837.

for the investment of private capital and obliging landowners to take an interest in improving their properties.[107]

Throughout these public debates in Britain the concerns about Irish labour migration and lower agricultural taxation which had been so prominent before 1834 were largely absent. Debate had shifted onto different ground, moulded by the continuing controversies over the English Poor Law Amendment Act and the government's political strategy for integrating Ireland into the United Kingdom. While enthusiasm for the limited measure of 1838 may have been constrained, there was some convergence between the views of Irish and English advocates of a more extensive measure that might at least establish a useful precedent and opportunity for future enhancement or augmentation. Whether these hopes were realistic would depend on the administrative and political history of implementation.

107 *Ibid.*, 14 Feb., 26 May 1838.

9

Implementation and adaptation, 1838–43

In early September 1838 George Nicholls and his team of four assistant commissioners arrived in Dublin to undertake the implementation of the Irish Poor Law Act. While Nicholls was always the most likely candidate for this mission, his appointment was not inevitable. Thomas Drummond had noted his personal unpopularity in early 1838 and urged Whitehall to be cautious about sending him over to carry the bill into effect. The lord lieutenant, shaken by the preponderance of hostile opinion expressed in Ireland against the measure during the 1838 session, also floated the idea of appointing an Irishman to the post to promote the measure's legitimacy.[1] Dublin Castle's attempts to nominate the Catholic Whig Thomas Wyse as a suitable Irish candidate in July were, however, thwarted, possibly by Somerset House.[2]

Meanwhile, Edwin Chadwick recommended himself as the prospective fourth Poor Law Commissioner who would undertake Irish business. He reminded Russell that, unlike Nicholls, he had always advocated a workhouse-based and comprehensive Irish measure, and warned that a firm hand would be required in both countries to prevent subversion by self-interested parties.[3] While Russell presumably agreed with Chadwick's argument that experienced English agency was essential in establishing the system in Ireland (and perhaps also with the rather more tendentious case that this 'neutral' oversight would prove more acceptable locally than Irish control), he was less persuaded by Chadwick's self-promotion and abrasive personality and opted instead to retain him in the subordinate position of secretary to the English commission. Chadwick's vigorous insistence that the appointment of another external member of the commission was unnecessary may have had more impact. In

1 NA: RP, PRO30/22/3A, fols 30–5, Drummond to Morpeth, 6 Jan.; CHP, J/19/1/18/6, Mulgrave to Morpeth, 3 May 1838. Some Irish papers went so far as to allege (falsely) that Nicholls had formerly been the mate or captain of a slave ship, *Tuam Herald*, repr. in *The Times*, 8 Sept. 1838.

2 *The Times*, 30 July, 3, 13 Aug. 1838.

3 UCL: CP, 1733/341–68, Chadwick to Russell [draft], 2 July 1838.

August 1838 Russell formally asked Nicholls to go to Ireland, leaving the regular English business to be transacted by the remaining commissioners, John George Shaw Lefevre and Thomas Frankland Lewis. Due to the latter's chronic illness, business was in fact usually transacted by Shaw Lefevre, assisted by Chadwick, until the appointment of George Cornewall Lewis in his father's place in January 1839.[4] While Nicholls had principal responsibility for Irish affairs, Chadwick initially kept a close watch on his proceedings, receiving copies of the assistant commissioners' weekly diaries and correspondence relating to the formation of the Irish unions. All orders and regulations prepared by the Irish board required the formal seal of the London commission for authorization.[5] With the appointment of G. C. Lewis and later Sir Edmund Head to the commission, however, Chadwick's influence declined, and Nicholls lost the close support of a key ally in London.[6]

Russell was insistent on vigorous and rapid implementation of the act, and assured Nicholls that he had full government support from both London and Dublin Castle.[7] The home secretary, characteristically, was over-optimistic as to the prospects of the enterprise. Nicholls' initial sojourn, he advised the commissioners, should not extend beyond two to three months, after which he could leave the daily business to the assistant commissioners while directing the Irish operation from Somerset House. Six additional assistants would be required to organize the Irish unions and establish the central administration in Dublin, combining experienced Englishmen with some fresh Irish appointments who would learn on the job. Political considerations were not to be forgotten, although Russell's injunction that the work should proceed so as simultaneously to 'obtain the concurrence of the men of property and to conciliate the good will of the Irish people' was asking a lot of his administrators.[8] Attempts to realize these conflicting aspirations would lead the poor law into difficulties in the following years.

4 NA: PLCP, MH1/15, pp. 83–4, 131–2, PLC Minutes, 3, 31 Aug.; NA: RP, PRO30/22/3B, fols 246–7, T. F. Lewis to Russell, 13 Aug. 1838. G. C. Lewis had been offered an Irish assistant commissionership in the interim, but declined this on the grounds of his health: NLW: HCP, C/2816, Lewis to Villiers, 10 Aug. 1838.

5 NA: PLCP, MH19/81, 63, W. Stanley to Chadwick, 17 Nov., Chadwick to J. Abercrombie, 1 Dec. 1838; *Fifth Annual Report of the Poor Law Commissioners*, PP 1839 [239], xx.1, pp. 23–4.

6 Anthony Brundage, *England's 'Prussian Minister': Edwin Chadwick and the Politics of Government Growth, 1832–1854* (University Park, PA, 1988), pp. 53–5.

7 Nicholls, *Irish Poor Law*, p. 234.

8 NA: PLCP, MH19/63, Russell to PLC, 11 Aug.; MC: NP, M/919, Russell to Normanby, 14 Aug. 1838. Russell's assurance may have been principally aimed at Nicholls himself, who had requested he not be kept in Ireland longer than required to organize the early proceedings: see Willink, 'Nicholls', p. li.

Russell himself made a brief visit to Dublin in September, shortly after Nicholls' arrival, thereby again demonstrating his personal commitment to the project.[9] Perhaps reassured by this, Nicholls appeared upbeat about the task ahead. Meeting him in Dublin, Lord Lansdowne found Nicholls 'sanguine . . . as to his act' (but added sarcastically 'when is he not so?'). Writing from Phoenix Park, Russell also declared Nicholls to be 'in high spirits – more confident than ever – and that is the way to succeed after all'.[10] Although this attitude may indeed have reflected Nicholls' rather buoyant personality, he was not the only English administrator who saw grounds for optimism. Richard Muggeridge, a poor-law official seconded to the hand-loom weavers' inquiry who had been gathering evidence in Ireland, assured his superiors that the act would be popular 'with that portion of the people for whose benefit it is most especially intended', and that the Catholic clergy, presently 'holding aloof', could be persuaded to co-operate in carrying it into effect.[11] If gentry resistance proved more of a problem, Russell was prepared to face it down. Indeed, he anticipated this as a necessary consequence of the act, and lectured the recalcitrant Spring Rice:

> I do not wonder at the antipathy to the poor law. It is as rational as the antipathy of the West Indians [i.e. planters] to the disuse of the whip. I still expect that if the unions are properly formed, and are in operation, the wretched tenants will find they have a security against their landlords which nothing but a poor law, or an agrarian law, will give them.[12]

Events would prove this expectation somewhat over-sanguine, but perhaps not entirely unwarranted. The comment demonstrated Russell's continuing adherence to the belief that, for all the anti-poor-law excitement of 1838, the measure would still be found to operate as a measure of 'justice to Ireland'.

Nicholls thus had the firm support of Russell and the Irish executive, but not of the entire Whig-liberal administration. Spring Rice at the Treasury (until his removal from office in summer 1839) remained implacably opposed, warning Russell that 'the word Union is an unlucky one, for you will make many persons repealers by these *Unions* who were steady friends to the Union of 1800.' He was now all the more convinced of the necessity of mass emigration to forestall the disorganization of Irish society, and privately urged Wilmot Horton to continue hammering at the principle of colonization from

9 NLI: MP, Ms 13,390/6, Russell to Spring Rice, 30 Aug. 1838.

10 NLW: NSP, C/597, Whately to Senior, 5 Nov.; SUL: BP, MEL/RU/59, Russell to Melbourne, 23 Sept. 1838.

11 NA: PLCP, MH19/81, Muggeridge to PLC, 9 Aug. 1838.

12 NLI: MP, Ms 13,390/6, Russell to Spring Rice, 16 Oct. 1838.

without the administration, while he would seek to assist it from within.[13] Nothing came of this before his withdrawal from the government, and indeed Nicholls explicitly rejected a proposal to promote Australian emigration under the poor law, and ignored the parallel efforts of Robert Torrens to promote it as an auxiliary measure. However, Spring Rice did his best to constrain poor law expenditure in Ireland. The commission's request for six additional assistant commissioners to cover the demands of Ireland was cut down to five (and this despite lobbying by Russell).[14]

Nicholls arrived in Dublin accompanied by four experienced English assistant commissioners, Edward Gulson, Richard Earle, William Hawley and William Voules. In addition, a number of 'Irish' assistant commissioners were freshly appointed – the first, Captain Charles Clements, apparently as a reward for his brother Lord Clements' resolute support for the bill in print and the Commons; despite this piece of patronage, the government tended to follow its practice in England of selecting 'men of business' to undertake the arduous duties of the office.[15] In the following month, Clements was joined by three more 'Irish' assistant commissioners, the land agent William John Hancock, the barrister and *Freeman's Journal* contributor John O'Donoghue and the Clonmel physician Dr Denis Phelan, the latter specifically with responsibility for investigating and reporting on the condition of the medical charities. There was a false rumour that Fr Thaddeus O'Malley would also be offered an assistantship, but the inclusion of two Catholics (O'Donoghue and Phelan) was surely intended to promote the measure's legitimacy among his supporters.[16] However, the fact that both Hancock and Phelan were openly identified with reformist or radical politics was held against them by Conservatives.[17]

13 Spring Rice to Russell, 27 Aug., *ibid.*, Ms 534, pp. 106–9; Spring Rice to Wilmot Horton, 7 Sept. 1838, *ibid.*, Ms 543, pp. 66–73.

14 NA: PLCP, MH19/81, PLC to Lords of Treasury, 17 Aug.; Baring to PLC, 31 Aug. 1838, *ibid.* [Robert Torrens], *Plan for an Association in Aid of the Irish Poor Law* (London, 1838); for Nicholls' rejection of Rev. William Blackwood's emigration scheme, see *Sixth Annual Report of the Poor Law Commissioners*, PP 1840 [253], xvii.447, pp. 40–2.

15 Brundage, *Making of the New Poor Law*, pp. 80–6.

16 *The Times*, 20 Aug., 17 Sept. 1838. O'Donoghue (1812–93) had been an assistant poor inquiry commissioner in 1833–36; he resigned in late 1843. Hancock (1791–1848) had been agent to Lord Lurgan, and would later die in service from a fever contracted during the Famine. For his 'great practical energy and resolution . . . [and] lively sympathy with the poor, the suffering and oppressed', see J. K. Ingram, 'Memoir of the late William Neilson Hancock', *Journal of the Statistical and Social Inquiry Society of Ireland*, 9 (1888–89), p. 385.

17 See NLW: HCP, C/2109, Nicholls to Lewis, 1 Nov. 1841. Hancock was married to Mary, daughter of the United Irishman Samuel Neilson of Belfast.

As significantly, the appointment of the pro-poor-law pamphleteer and Irish stamp-office official William Stanley as assistant secretary to the Dublin board indicated Nicholls' continuing reliance on this key local ally.[18] Nicholls and his team set up store in a wing of the Custom House, while his family took a house at Blackrock, south of Dublin.[19] Nicholls complained of the sacrifice his Irish secondment entailed for his family, but encouraged them also to become involved in his 'mission'. He persuaded Knight, the official publisher to the commission, to publish (anonymously) a 'little tale' by one of his daughters 'illustrating the working of the poor laws in England and Ireland'. This didactic text, clearly aimed at a domestic or juvenile audience, appeared as *Benevola* in 1840.[20]

On arrival, the assistant commissioners were allocated geographical regions, centred on the main towns of Belfast, Limerick, Cork and Dublin, within which they would have the responsibility for forming the unions and their component electoral divisions. Nicholls echoed the home secretary's preoccupation with winning hearts and minds in his initial instructions to his assistants. While the interests of private property were not to be disregarded, he wrote:

> It must always be borne in mind that the Irish people are peculiarly sensitive and ardent, quick in their perceptions, and hasty in their resolves; extremely sensible of kindness, but tremblingly alive to even the semblance of slight or neglect. The utmost caution will therefore be necessary on the part of every member of the Commission to conciliate their feelings and to gain their confidence. This will best be accomplished by a simple, straightforward line of conduct – a scrupulous fulfilment of promises of every kind – and the greatest care not to raise or encourage expectations, unless there is a reasonable prospect of their being fulfilled . . . We know, we are sure, that the object of the law we are called upon to administer is kind and beneficent, and calculated to better the condition and improve the social habits of the people; and knowing this, we cannot feel otherwise than confident in its application, and eagerly zealous in working out the results contemplated by the Legislature in its enactment.[21]

The assistants took seriously this injunction to dampen down the hostile excitement that had accompanied the parliamentary debates, and sought to mollify local opinion with what were often at best overly optimistic estimates

18 NA: PLCP, MH1/15, pp. 125, 131–2, Minutes of 28 and 31 Aug. 1838.

19 *The Times*, 17 Sept. 1838.

20 NLW: HCP, C/2098, Nicholls to Lewis, 15 Aug. 1840; *Benevola; A Tale* (London, 1840). The text relates the exploits of the (decidedly utilitarian) fairy 'Benevola' in shaping both the old and new English acts and the Irish Poor Law Act, and idealizes the positive consequences of the latter in a stereotyped Mayo village.

21 Nicholls to assistant commissioners, 11 Sept. 1838, *Fifth Report* (1839), p. 24.

of expenditure and income. At Newry, for example, Gulson assured a public meeting that no rates would be imposed for at least nine months, until after a workhouse had been constructed and opened; and that the anticipated costs had been exaggerated by the bill's opponents. Some three-quarters of the expense of relieving the inmates would, he claimed, be met from the produce of workhouse labour, while the remaining rate would be moderate and equitably imposed; generous government loans would allow easy repayments of the capital costs of the workhouse over twenty years, with interest charged only for the last ten years.[22] Such assurances appear to have been, on the whole, well received; after a public question and answer session at Derry, Clements received a unanimous vote of thanks from those present.[23] By spring 1839 Nicholls was, rather prematurely, expressing satisfaction that this mode of proceeding had led to the subsidence of all opposition, and reported that the law, 'if not universally popular in Ireland, is at least universally acquiesced in'.[24]

After about four weeks of touring to acquaint themselves with their districts, the assistant commissioners reassembled in Dublin on 9 October to discuss with Nicholls and the new 'Irish' appointments the best mode of proceeding. Nicholls declared himself more than satisfied with the encouraging reports they gave concerning feeling towards the law in the localities, and identified prospects of early success. He assured the duke of Wellington (whose support he clearly believed it desirable to cultivate) that the preliminary operations themselves had done much to alleviate hostility: '[T]he feelings of alarm and hostility with which the poor law measure was first regarded, have almost entirely subsided, and been followed by a spirit of acquiescence, and indeed very generally of approbation.' He hoped that a short tract he had nearly completed for distribution to magistrates and clergymen would remove any lingering reservations.[25]

Forming the Irish unions, 1838–40

In October 1838 the assistant commissioners, accompanied initially by their Irish apprentices, returned to their districts (with Derry now added as an

22 'The Poor Law Commissioners – Meeting at the Mendicity, Newry', *Newry Examiner*, in *FJ*, 8 Oct. 1838. In practice it proved impossible to render workhouse labour reproductive, see O'Brien, 'Workhouse management', pp. 116–17.

23 'Poor Law meeting in Derry', *Londonderry Journal*, in *FJ*, 25 Oct.

24 *Fifth Report* (1839), p. 31. For positive reports of the work of assistant commissioners elsewhere, see *Connaught Journal*, 12 Aug. 1839.

25 NA: RP, PRO30/22/3B, fols 313–14, Nicholls to Russell, 17 Oct.; SUL: WP, WP2/55/102–3, Nicholls to Wellington, 26 Dec. 1838.

independent base for Clements), armed with fresh instructions from Nicholls to create 'clusters' of unions emanating from these centres. District constabulary and coastguard officers were ordered to assist them in plotting the new boundaries. Meanwhile, the Dublin office sought the resolution of several technical problems that had been identified as potential sources of delay. Preliminary inquiries had revealed that, contrary to the assumption underlying the Lords' amendments, townland divisions were not universal in Ireland (particularly in the cities of Dublin and Cork), and that their boundaries were frequently imprecise and contested.[26] This error made necessary a summary amendment bill introduced and passed early in the 1839 session, giving the commissioners powers to declare townlands where these were absent and to determine disputed boundaries for the purposes of the Poor Law Act. They also received powers to create wards within urban electoral divisions that would combine wealthy and impoverished districts to share the rates burden.[27] The measure appeared uncontroversial, but the addition of a late government amendment tidying up potential uncertainties relating to the allocation of votes to ratepayers with property in more than one electoral division seems to have produced resentment on the part of Wellington (who had not been consulted on a matter touching on his amendment of 1838 and who subsequently believed it designed to give advantage to the government party). He later directed his pique on the matter against Nicholls personally.[28]

The hope that the new Irish poor law might yet prove 'popular' was not wholly delusional. Fr O'Malley, William Sharman Crawford and Michael Staunton continued to support the measure in public statements, treating it as a first stepping stone to a more advanced measure, and praising Wellington for assisting its passage in 1838. A. H. Lynch of Galway also defended its provisions, and noted that public meetings had demonstrated that the public 'appreciates the advantages of this most salutary measure'.[29] The liberal *Cork Southern Reporter* was enthusiastic as to its likely social effects; there was now, it commented:

26 SUL: WP, WP2/55/102–3, Nicholls to Wellington, 26 Dec. 1838. Senior derived some amusement from this absence of townlands in the towns – 'a very Irish nomenclature', NLW: NSP, C/599, Senior to Whately, 31 Jan. 1839.

27 *A Bill to amend an Act . . . for the more efficient Relief of the Destitute Poor in Ireland*, PP 1839 (18), iv.491, passed as 2 Vic. c.1; *Fifth Report* (1839), pp. 35–9.

28 Willink, 'Nicholls', pp. liii–lvi.

29 O'Malley to O'Connell, *FJ*, 31 July, Sharman Crawford to O'Connell, *The Times*, 7 Aug.; *Dublin Morning Register*, cited in *MC*, 1 Aug. 1838; Lynch, *Measures to be adopted*, p. 6. In 1844, however, O'Malley was quoted has having demanded a radical reform of the law as it stood, *Hansard*, 3, lxxiv, 1191–2 (14 May 1844).

> an identity of interest created between the landlord and the tenant, the rich man and the poor – between him who had much and him who had nothing. If the landlord, yielding to the insane impulses of party or sectarian frenzy, depopulates his estates, and drives forth his tenants to perish by the roadside, or seeks to prolong a precarious existence by crime, the poor laws offer an asylum, and the heartless aristocrat will be compelled to feed as paupers those whose labours would have added to his wealth. The poor man will now look for protection and advancement in the dread the rich man must entertain of undefined and unlimited taxation. . . . The Irish working classes are extremely shrewd. They will soon comprehend the bearing of the law, and regard it as their charter of maintenance.[30]

This comment was not untypical at the time.[31] This was in marked contrast to what had gone before, and reflects a loss of O'Connellite political interest in the subject (at least for the time being).

When combined with sensitive public relations management by the assistant commissioners, this continuing strand of substantive, if not overly enthusiastic, support for the measure could produce positive outcomes, at least in the first instance. In Co. Limerick, Smith O'Brien facilitated and presided over the public meetings that agreed the early formation of the Newcastle and Rathkeale unions. The former meeting saw the Newcastle courthouse 'completely thronged with all classes' to hear Hawley and Hancock explain their proposals. Both the general defence of the measure and the specific arrangements for the formation of the unions were, it was reported by the *Limerick Chronicle*, well received. After a vote of thanks moved by the Catholic and Anglican clergy of Newcastle West, the meeting 'separated, fully impressed with the importance of the information they had received, and convinced that the introduction of the law into the district will, without adding materially to the burdens of the owners and occupiers of property, confer one of the greatest benefits on the destitute poor'. The Rathkeale meeting was equally well attended and positive, and agreed that the best site for the union workhouse would be in that town.[32] These unions were the third and fourth to be 'declared', in late December, following hot on the heels of the predominantly urban unions of Belfast and Limerick.[33] Progress in Limerick was promoted by the enthusiastic support of a number of local landowners, including Lord Devon, who, although conscious that the rates would 'take some hundreds

30 Cited in *MC*, 19 Sept. 1838.

31 O'Brien, 'Establishment of poor-law unions', pp. 101–2.

32 *Limerick Chronicle*, in *FJ*, 26 Nov. 1838.

33 NA: HOP, HO100/258, fols 1, 9–10, 13–14, Nicholls to Russell, 26 Dec., Orders for Newcastle and Rathkeale Unions, 27, 28 Dec. 1838.

out of my pocket', was sure they would add to his son's future income by promoting social peace.[34]

Not all observers were so pleased. Spring Rice, whose Mount Trenchard estate lay within the prospective Rathkeale union, was initially complimentary about Hawley's early success in Co. Limerick, but rapidly turned against him.[35] Spring Rice had concerns that the proposed unions would be too large for effective operation and control, and about the location of workhouses in market towns (as opposed to the geographical centre of each union), but his principal objection related to the proposed electoral divisions. Like many landowners, Spring Rice was adamant that these should coincide with estate divisions, thus rendering the election of guardians more amenable to landlord control, and giving landowners a direct interest in improving the condition of the poor resident in 'their' electoral division (which under Wellington's amendment had been rendered the basic unit of rating). Hawley's decision to opt for larger electoral divisions, frequently overlapping estate boundaries, enraged the chancellor, who denounced the 'vapouring nonsense of a man who only wishes to add to his self importance', and warned Nicholls that the consequence would be landed resistance and ignominious failure.[36] Spring Rice was supported by his brother-in-law Aubrey de Vere (also a Rathkeale union proprietor) and, more significantly, the Dublin official Richard Griffith, but Nicholls proved either unwilling or unable to overrule his subordinates on this matter.[37]

The size of electoral divisions was a matter on which landed and 'popular' interest clearly diverged, and the decisions taken indicated a clear leaning in one direction. Larger divisions would require multiple guardians, making landed control over the annual elections potentially more difficult.[38] Nicholls admitted this in a letter to Wellington, citing the 'desire very generally evinced for large electoral divisions', and claiming that in Co. Limerick he had with difficulty overcome the popular demand for only four or six divisions per union to create fourteen or sixteen in each. Implicitly any further subdivision (as proposed by Spring Rice and his allies), or adherence to the original instruction that multiple-guardian divisions be exceptional, was politically

34 MC: NP, V/139, Devon to Normanby, 17 Mar. [1839].

35 NLI: MP, Ms 533, pp. 6–7, Spring Rice to Nicholls, 15 Nov. 1838.

36 Spring Rice to Nicholls, 9, 21 Dec. 1838, *ibid.*, Ms 533, pp. 189–93, Ms 543, pp. 144–5.

37 Griffith to Spring Rice, 4 Dec. 1838, *ibid.*, Ms 13,390/2.

38 Newcastle union, comprising 207 square miles and with 22 elected guardians, was divided into thirteen electoral divisions; five of these elected 2, and two elected 3 guardians.

impossible.[39] However, the chancellor was right to predict that large electoral divisions tended to promote fierce electoral battles.[40]

Local pressures and the compromises made by the assistant commissioners led to a considerable range of internal variants within and between unions. Whereas Nicholls had envisaged that the optimum number of elected guardians should range from ten to twenty-four, nearly half the unions exceeded this maximum, with a number being allocated many more; Cork was granted forty (including twenty for the city itself, which was divided into twelve wards), Kilkenny forty-seven (less than 20 per cent of these in single-guardian electoral divisions), and Sligo thirty-nine.[41] Londonderry, with twenty-seven guardians elected from twenty-two divisions, conformed (like many in Ulster) more closely to the original model, although this did not prevent the immediate and intense politicization of elections in the four-member urban division.[42] Nicholls later admitted that the commission had sought where possible to combine urban (or suburban) districts with their rural hinterlands in electoral divisions for a distinct sociological purpose. While the principle of individual proprietorial interest (as promoted by Wellington's amendment) was valuable, it risked promoting clearance and the social unrest associated with evictions:

> When we reflect ... on the thousands who depend for subsistence on the holding of a small portion of land, when we consider the extreme sensitiveness connected with anything like ejectment of a man from his holding, and the excitement which necessarily and naturally exists in Ireland on that subject, we cannot think that it would be consistent with sound policy or humanity to hold out a strong artificial inducement to the clearing of estates. As it is now, towns occasionally complain that persons formerly tenants on the estate of some neighbouring proprietor have been ejected in large numbers, that they have

39 SUL: WP, WP2/55/102–3, Nicholls to Wellington, 26 Dec. 1838. For the original instructions, see Minute of 9 Oct. 1838, in *Fifth Report* (1839), pp. 26–9.

40 For example, in the Kinsale union elections of March 1843, 19 candidates were nominated for the 15 single-member divisions, while 14 contested the six-member division of Kinsale itself; and while the majority of those nominated in the first category were listed as 'gentlemen' or 'esquires', the majority in the latter were tradesmen, merchants, doctors or farmers: *Copy of Correspondence between the Poor Law Commissioners for Ireland, on the Election of Guardians for the Division of Kinsale, March 1843*, PP 1843 (436) xlvi.639.

41 *Sixth Report* (1840), Appendix C.

42 Patrick Durnin, *The Workhouse and the Famine in Derry* (Derry, 2001), pp. 49–52. Both Clements at Derry and the Belfast-based assistant commissioner, Edward Gulson, appear to have been more sympathetic to the concerns of local elites and consequently the subject of less criticism than many of their colleagues.

> taken refuge in some wretched lodgings in the town, and after struggling on a short time these parties, who really had resided in some distant townland, apply for relief, are entered on the registry as residing in the town, and charged to the rate-payers of the town electoral division. A complete severance of the interests of town and country, whether effected by the formation of the Unions themselves or by that of the electoral division, must necessarily have increased this evil where it exists in reality, or at any rate have augmented the complaints on the subject where the grievance is said to be felt.[43]

These tensions between the principles of individual and collective responsibility, and over the allocation of the costs of poor relief, along with the confusions surrounding the boundaries of these unfamiliar tracts, remained unresolved and were a source of dispute throughout the life of the Irish poor law.

The size of unions was also an area of acute contention. Nicholls had initially envisaged around 100 unions, and at the start of proceedings had prepared a sketch map identifying ninety-seven market towns at the centres of circles of roughly ten statute miles radius. Noting that the absence of pre-existing relief structures rendered Ireland 'at present entirely a blank, and it is open to us to establish one rule, one system, in detail as well as in principle, throughout the whole country', Nicholls identified the market town and its commercial hinterland as the 'natural' unit of social organization. He was reluctant to multiply the number of unions excessively to avoid high establishment charges and the creation of large numbers of small workhouses. However, the mode of formation – with assistant commissioners working outwards from their urban 'bases' in an *ad hoc* fashion and engaging in dialogue and compromise with interested parties in the localities – made the initial blueprint difficult to adhere to.[44] While a deviation from the Benthamite ideal, it was a mode of proceeding that had worked well in extending the forms of the new poor law in England, and in which the transferred assistant commissioners were experienced.[45]

By March 1840 104 unions had already been declared, and a further thirty were contemplated, the divergence from the original scheme being explained by Nicholls as the result of 'a strong desire for small unions . . . [which], added to the want of convenient centres, and other local circumstances, led

43 *Ninth Annual Report of the Poor Law Commissioners*, PP 1843 [468], xxi.1, pp. 44–8.

44 *Fifth Report* (1839), pp. 24–5. It was impossible that all landed demands could be met regarding the drawing of union and electoral division boundaries or the location of workhouses: see O'Brien, 'Establishment of poor-law unions', p. 104.

45 Brundage, *Making of the New Poor Law*, pp. 105–44.

to an increase of the number beyond the original estimate'.[46] A considerable number of the new unions crossed county and barony boundaries, making co-ordination with other forms of local administration and taxation problematic.

Disputes with landowners over the boundaries of unions and location of workhouses delayed proceedings. One proprietor, for example, repeatedly petitioned Clements (unsuccessfully) into centring what became the Limavady union on the rival market town of Dungiven.[47] These problems were compounded in the west, which the commission left until last to organize. Many of the western unions far exceeded the nominal size Nicholls had initially envisaged. Here market towns were underdeveloped and sparse, and both resident landowners and the 'respectable' middle classes, the anticipated membership of the boards of guardians, relatively thin on the ground. Despite the lobbying of Dean Lyons of Binghamstown, the desire not to cede control over a board to 'the shopkeepers of Belmullet' led to the rejection of a separate union for Erris, and to divide that extensive and impoverished barony between the already huge unions of Ballina and Westport.[48] Time would demonstrate that the total of 130 unions formed in 1838–40 was inadequate for the country's needs, and a number of larger (mostly western) unions had to be subdivided to create an additional thirty-two unions in 1848–50; during the same revision the number of electoral divisions was also greatly expanded from 2,049 to 3,438.

Unions thus varied significantly in area and population, with a general tendency for both to be magnified in the western counties. In Ulster and Leinster, despite some notable exceptions (such as the unions of Cavan and Kilkenny), unions tended to be relatively small and compact. The average area of the forty-three Ulster unions was 122,000 statute acres; that of the thirty-four in Leinster 137,000 acres. The dense urban unions in Dublin and Belfast created some distortions, but the population of unions was also below the national average (an average of 54,900 inhabitants per union in Ulster, and 59,000 in Leinster, adjusted to the 1841 census returns). There were clusters of particularly non-populous unions in mid and south Ulster, the smallest nationally being Gortin in Co. Tyrone and Dunfanaghy in Co. Donegal, both with populations under 20,000 and small workhouses limited to 200–300 places.[49] The greatest contrast was with Connacht and western Munster,

46 Nicholls, *Irish Poor Law*, pp. 245–6.

47 O'Brien, 'Establishment of poor-law unions', p. 99.

48 *Ibid*., pp. 104–5; *Connaught Journal*, 20 Feb. 1840.

49 The smallest non-urban union by area was Carrickmacross in Co. Monaghan. Ulster also had a significant number of very small electoral divisions with populations under 1,000.

where dense areas of settlement were separated by extensive mountain and bogland tracts. In Connacht (divided into eighteen unions) the mean union size was 200,000 acres, but with an average population in each of 76,200. These averages were swamped by the massive extent of the unions such as Ballina (121,000 souls distributed over 498,000 acres), and Sligo (with 111,000 people on 255,000 acres). The former, one critic observed, was larger than some counties, and ten times the size of the smallest union. In Munster, Tralee union suffered from a similar gigantism, with 92,000 people spread over 351,000 acres. The long distances involved here (it was forty-three statute miles from Belmullet to the workhouse at Ballina, thirty-eight miles from the end of the Dingle peninsula to Tralee), were far out of line with the original plan of workhouses at the centre of unions of ten-mile radius, and would pose problems for the regular attendance of guardians from the further-flung divisions, and a fatal obstacle for the destitute in time of famine.[50]

Electing the guardians, 1839–43

The introduction of the partially-elected boards of guardians was a major innovation to the Irish body politic, and in a country as intensely politicized as Ireland, bound to cause great political excitement, especially in the early years. The system of multiple votes (a maximum of eighteen per individual in any union) gave added weight to larger property holders and the variable property qualifications restricted who could stand for the guardianship, but with nearly one million ratepayers registered by 1842 (around a quarter of the adult population, and including a number of women as ratepayers in their own right), the new poor-law boards were still by far the most representative bodies in the country.[51] Although both the allocation of a quarter of the seats on the boards to *ex-officio* magistrates (overwhelmingly landowners), and the greater likelihood of landed gentlemen (both *ex-officio* and elected) to have the time and resources to attend board meetings on a regular basis, tended to impose some check on the 'popular' character of boards, it did not

50 *Figures derived from Return of every Poor Law Union in Ireland, stating Population, Area and Number of Landholders*, PP 1845 (593), xxxviii.209. See *Hansard*, 3, lxvii, 1354 (23 Mar. 1843: O'Brien).

51 *Ninth Report* (1843), p. 43. The report enumerated 997,434 ratepayer-voters for the 108 unions rated in 1842–43; the addition of the 22 unions yet to be rated would have raised this total by 15–20 per cent to well over a million voters, but the major disfranchisement following the 1843 Poor Law Amendment Act precluded this. In contrast, the parliamentary electorate following the 1832 Irish Reform Act was about 90,000: see K. T. Hoppen, 'Politics, the law, and the nature of the Irish electorate, 1832–1850', *English Historical Review*, 92 (1977), p. 749.

eradicate it. In a number of union boards merchants, tradesmen, professionals and larger farmers outnumbered the landowners. In most unions the property qualification for guardians was set at or below £20, in many as low as £10.[52]

The partisan nature of many poor law elections was demonstrated at the very first contest held, that for the *ex-officio* guardians of the Belfast union in January 1839. To the outrage of the *Northern Whig*, the magistrates elected from their own number six Tories to only one Liberal.[53] 'Open' elections for the ordinary guardians would often prove yet more contentious. Shortly afterwards, a 'numerous and stormy' nomination meeting in Limerick town saw an attempt to restrict the power of nomination to a select committee of ratepayers (who sought to preclude a contest by nominating equal numbers of Protestants and Catholics), denounced by the lawyer Pierce Mahony, who reminded his audience that 'the law . . . gave the poor man the power of putting his hand in the pockets of the rich' and that the poorer ratepayers had as much right to representation as the wealthy.[54] This dispute gave rise to negative comments in parliament, and was the harbinger of troubles to come.[55]

Catholic clerics were heavily involved in electoral affairs, sometimes antagonistically, sometimes, in places where there was less political tension, more consensually. Devon observed that at Newcastle the elections had been fair and temperate, with limited clerical interference; his own agent had been elected chairman, with 'a very respectable R.C. magistrate' as vice-chair.[56] At Dungarvan, however, the Catholic bishop and his clergy took a close interest in electoral proceedings, implicitly in confrontation with the landed interest. At Kilbarron in Co. Tipperary a priest put himself at the head of a mob rioting against the 'partisan' actions of the local returning officer, while at Clogheen Fr Michael Tobin denounced Lord Glengall for nominating 'obnoxious individuals' for election.[57] In Carlow, already a cockpit for highly sectarianized politics, Bishop Doyle's protégé Fr James Maher denounced a Tory victory

52 *Report of the Select Committee of House of Lords, on Laws relating to Relief of Destitute Poor*, PP 1846 (694), xi.1, p. viii.

53 *Northern Whig*, cited *FJ*, 7 Jan. 1839.

54 *Limerick Chronicle*, repr. in *FJ*, 11 Jan. 1839.

55 O'Brien notes that even more trouble might have arisen had it been revealed that assistant commissioner Joseph Burke had been actively promoting the predetermination of elections in western unions on behalf of landed interests, 'Establishment of poor-law unions', p. 113.

56 DRO: FP, 1262M/LI/26, Devon to Ebrington, 26 Mar. 1839.

57 *Waterford Chronicle*, in *FJ*, 29 Apr. 1839; *Dublin Evening Post*, 28 Feb., 13 June 1839, cited in O'Brien, 'Establishment of poor-law unions', p. 111.

in 1840 as the consequence of sharp practice and urged ratepayers to vote only for Catholic candidates, as 'Protestants can have no sympathy with the poor'.[58]

In Dublin the *Freeman's Journal* took it as axiomatic that elections would be fought on party lines and urged Liberal candidates and electors to co-operate to prevent the 'corruption' and 'plunder' that must follow a Tory victory. For their part, the Conservatives claimed that the election had become a partisan contest due to Catholic pressure.[59] The highly acrimonious (and occasionally violent) competition of 1839 was followed by the resignation of the supervising assistant commissioner, Richard Earle, who subsequently expressed a jaded cynicism about Irish poor law affairs.[60] In Enniscorthy union in 1840 there were contests in nine of the fourteen divisions, producing twenty-six Liberal (lauded as 'the tried friends of the people') and four Tory guardians. Here again, attempts to prevent a contest had collapsed amid partisan animosity.[61] The outcome of the elections in Castlebar and Ballina in 1842 were similarly reported as anti-Tory triumphs.[62] Generalizing wildly from such evidence, *The Times* claimed in 1839 that such elections had turned the poor law into 'an engine of dirty, sordid, villainous efficacy, for subjecting both the rich and poor to the priesthood . . . [making it] another link in the national subjection to *political* Popery'. Its correspondent claimed that priestly influence had led to the near-exclusion of Protestants from many southern boards, and the election of 'the most noisy, troublesome and turbulent men . . . a very low class of Roman Catholic farmers being selected, instead of those possessing any interest in the land'.[63]

The commission at first sought publicly to play down assertions of irregularity or partisanship, and claimed the early elections (which had been facilitated by the constabulary as the agents for distributing and collecting votes) had been orderly and that no improper guardian had been elected. They observed that although contests had taken place in seventy-four of the ninety-nine extant unions in the first round of elections, these had been limited to 254 out of the 1,288 election districts therein. This conveniently ignored

58 *Carlow Sentinel*, 17 Oct. 1840.

59 *FJ*, 18, 25 June; 'Poor Laws – St Paul's Parish', *ibid.*, 19 June 1839.

60 NA: PLCP, MH19/81, Stanley to Chadwick, 22 June; UCL: CP, 1486/25–7, Nicholls to Chadwick, 28 Aug. 1839.

61 *FJ*, 6 Mar. 1840.

62 *Ibid.*, 29 Mar. 1842. At Castlebar tension was kept high by attempts of the chairman, Lord Lucan, to exclude Catholics from nomination: O'Brien, 'Establishment of poor-law unions', p. 118.

63 *The Times*, 2 Nov. 1839.

the facts that these districts tended to be the most heavily populated, that the pre-election nomination meetings were also often strongly politicized, and that a number of contests had been declared void.[64] The figures for the spring 1842 elections were similar.[65] However, in his 1841 report Nicholls could not avoid acknowledging that there had indeed been 'many irregularities', arising mostly, he claimed, from the imperfect lists of county cess payers (unavoidable until the new poor law valuations had been completed, but a source of great confusion given the chaotic state of cess records), and from the 'fireside' voting procedures whereby ballots were delivered to and collected from the homes of voters. Although some assistant commissioners had proposed the alternative of public voting at polling places, Nicholls rejected this as likely to lead to the popular excitement of electoral hustings.[66] Privately, he expressed hope that the political heat over elections would soon subside once the 'greatly exaggerated notions . . . [of] the power and influence attached to the office of guardian' were dissipated by experience.[67] This was wishful thinking. While the freedom of the guardians was indeed circumscribed by the prefectorial interventions of the assistant commissioners and the Dublin board, the office still combined both significant patronage powers over the appointment of workhouse staff, the admission of 'dependent' paupers, and the allocation of union contracts. Moreover, in the absence of other rural representative bodies, the guardianship was often regarded as a local political prize in its own right. Amid these concerns it should hardly be surprising that the 'management and comforts of the poor' were often relegated to a low place in electoral considerations.[68] This point should, however, not be overstated. The career of Thomas Synnott as an elected guardian in the North Dublin Union in 1839–

64 *Hansard*, 3, xlv, 347 [14 Feb. 1839: Shaw]; *Fifth Report* (1839), pp. 32–3; *Seventh Report* (1841), pp. 55–6.

65 *Eighth Annual Report of the Poor Law Commissioners*, PP 1842 [389], xix.1, p. [389]. A high proportion of the unions in which no contests took place were in Ulster.

66 *Seventh Report* (1841), pp. 54–5. For often chaotic consequences of basing the first elections on the cess returns, and the extent to which the constabulary were drawn into electoral sharp practice, see O'Brien, 'Establishment of poor-law unions', pp. 107–11. In practice, while the act of voting was private, ballot papers needed to be signed to be valid and were open to inspection by interested parties at the count, creating plentiful opportunities for electoral intimidation: see William L. Feingold, *The Revolt of the Tenantry: The Transformation of Local Government in Ireland 1872–1886* (Boston, 1984), p. 21.

67 MC: NP, V/739, Nicholls to Normanby, 26 May 1840.

68 *FJ*, 18 Feb. 1842.

43 suggests that O'Connellite political engagement need not be at odds with committed philanthropy.[69]

Another political issue concerned the admission of newspaper reporters to board meetings. Nicholls feared that, if they were permitted, 'a desire for popularity would be awakened, and individual guardians would too probably be led to address themselves to the passions of their hearers, or to party or sectarian feelings prevalent without doors, rather than to the sober disposal of the business in hand'. This was reasonable from an English perspective, but ran contrary to the desire of a majority on some Irish boards that their affairs be open to public view. Despite the strenuous efforts of Nicholls and assistant commissioner Voules, the commission was unable to enforce its prohibition on reporting, and after a power struggle with Cork and other recalcitrant unions, was obliged reluctantly to concede the point.[70]

Building the workhouses, 1839–46

Once the unions and electoral divisions had been formed and guardians elected, the provision of workhouse accommodation became the leading priority. The act had authorized the use of former barracks or the premises of existing charitable institutions as workhouses, but the clear preference was for a uniform model of workhouse, based on the architecture of classification and less eligibility pioneered by Nicholls and Rev. J. T. Becher at Southwell, Notts, from 1824, and gradually adopted in England and Wales from 1834.[71] Chadwick expressed a strong opinion that construction remain under the direct control of the commission and not the Irish Board of Works, and suggested that, once a model plan incorporating the most economical and health-promoting features had been produced, local construction could be entrusted to engineer officers rather than to expensive and frivolous professional architects.[72]

If Nicholls agreed with Chadwick's concerns about the Board of Works, he evidently did not think that the services of a professional architect could be dispensed with for preparing the 'model' on which Irish workhouses would

69 Bob Cullen, *Thomas L. Synnott: The Career of a Dublin Catholic* 1830–70 (Dublin, 1997), pp. 21–7.

70 NLW: HCP, C/2088, Nicholls to Lewis, 9 Dec. 1839; *Sixth Report* (1840), pp. 29–31; *Seventh Report* (1841), pp. 56–8.

71 Ultimately the only barracks to be so employed was at Fermoy, an experiment which 'turned out to be neither satisfactory nor economical': Nicholls, *Irish Poor Law*, p. 244. See also BL: GP, Add Ms 79,635, fols 40–2, 55–7, 127–8, Eliot to Graham, 1, 9 Nov., 20 Dec. 1841.

72 UCL: CP, 1486/14–20, Chadwick to Nicholls, 10 Dec. 1838.

be constructed, and nominated George Wilkinson for this purpose in December 1838. Wilkinson (1814–90) was a young English-born architect who had already designed a number of workhouses in England and Wales, starting with Witney, Oxfordshire, in 1835–36. The 'square' Tudor-style form he designed for the Abergavenny workhouse in 1837–38 would form the basis for his Irish work (indeed Wilkinson's Welsh experience was deemed ideal preparation for Irish circumstances). Wilkinson's estimate for preparing the plans of all the 130 Irish union workhouses of sizes varying from 300 to 1,300 inmates was submitted in late December, and won the approval of the commission, not least because his projected construction costs were one third lower than those of English houses of similar capacity.[73] His economy measures included the provision of mortar or earth rather than paved floors, which he thought appropriate for a people accustomed to living barefoot. The total capacity of the workhouse network when complete was anticipated to be 93,960 places, with an average of 723 inmates per workhouse.[74] Wilkinson believed his plan combined not only economy and durability with the necessary requisites for classification and ventilation, but that, while relatively unobtrusive, the proposed 'gabled roofs and elevated chimney shafts give [the workhouse] a pleasing and picturesque appearance'. He was subsequently criticized for the 'reckless extravagance' involved in his choice of such 'spurious Elizabethian' designs.[75] Russell agreed to the appointment of Wilkinson as a retained architect at £500 a year (for one year in the first instance, although his contract was renewed annually until 1855), and later acceded to the request for two salaried assistants. Wilkinson and his team were given responsibility not only for the design, but also for overseeing the construction of the edifices by local contractors.[76]

73 NA: PLCP, MH19/81, W. Stanley to Chadwick, 29 Dec. 1838; PLC to Russell, 8 Feb., *ibid.*, MH19/63; Minute of 10 Jan., PLC to Treasury, 8 Feb. 1839, in *Fifth Report* (1839), pp. 33–5.

74 *Hansard*, 3, lxvii, 1372 (23 Mar. 1843: Eliot). These numbers need to be treated with caution, as they were based on calculation of cubic space rather than beds, and later needed to be revised downwards: see Michael Gould, 'The administration of the workhouse and the Great Famine', *Ulster Local Studies*, 17 (1995), pp. 19–26.

75 Papers as to the providing of workhouses in Ireland, in *Fifth Report* (1839), pp. 81–3; *Hansard*, 3, lxvii, 1352 (23 Mar. 1843: Smith O'Brien).

76 NA: PLCP, MH19/81, Fox Maule to PLC, 11 Feb., 11 Apr. 1839. Russell later admitted that he doubted the expediency of giving Wilkinson sole responsibility for the Irish workhouse project, but the architect was retained until Treasury cutbacks obliged the commissioners to release him, and he turned to private practice in Dublin. *Hansard*, 3, lxx, 1377–8 (27 July 1843); Michael Gould, *The Workhouses of Ulster* (Belfast, 1983), p. 6.

Wilkinson's model workhouses took time to contract and build. They also had a tendency to run significantly over budget (to the fury of ratepayers saddled with the costs of repayment), and, while conforming to a fairly rigid design, varied widely in the quality of their materials and finishing. In 1842 the commissioners rationalized the overrun of £150,000 above the original estimate of one million pounds as a belated recognition that the workhouses could not, as initially intended, be finished to a standard inferior to those of England, in line with the assumed lower mode of living of the Irish people, not least as union boards had insisted on better standards.[77] Although a few landowners granted sites, most had to be bought or leased, and the commissioners experienced some difficulties in securing suitable level sites of adequate size adjacent to county towns and in dealing with the complexities of the Irish land market. Inexperience in these matters, and in working with a large number of local contractors, as well as obstacles placed in their way by some landed proprietors, undoubtedly led to some poor bargains; this proved a source of lasting conflict between Nicholls and the union boards, who were obliged to repay the building loans contracted by the commission on their behalf.

Nevertheless, by March 1840 sixty buildings were under construction and contracts were being prepared for another ten.[78] The first of these purpose-built establishments to be opened was that at Derry on 10 November 1840, followed over the next four months by those at Belfast, Clonmel, Lisburn, Lurgan, Balrothery, Kilmallock, Newcastle, Rathkeale, Castlederg and Waterford.[79] The initiation of the building projects was often the object for civic celebration. On the laying of the Galway workhouse foundation-stone in June 1840, speeches by assistant commissioner Burke and local dignitaries expressed the hope that the advance of the temperance crusade would restrict future occupancy to 'merely the deserted young and feeble old'. The local press was optimistic: 'The sun shone brightly, the day was beautiful, and this interesting ceremony passed off to the satisfaction of all present.'[80]

It took generally between twelve and thirty-four months to build and fit out each workhouse complex for the admission of inmates, with some suffering extensive delays for a variety of reasons including the default of

77 *Eighth Report* (1842), pp. 30–1.

78 *Sixth Report* (1840), pp. 35–7. The duke of Leinster granted the plot for Athy, Lord Midleton that at Midleton, the duke of Abercorn that for Strabane and Col. Knox the site at Ballinrobe: 'Statement of progress', *Tenth Annual Report of the Poor Law Commissioners*, PP 1844 [589], xix.57, pp. 312–15.

79 *Seventh Report* (1841), pp. 42–3.

80 *Connaught Journal*, 11 June 1840. For a similar event at Castlebar, see *ibid.*, 29 Oct. 1840.

contractors and the recalcitrance of individual boards to put the act into operation. Consequently the full implementation of the law was prolonged over more than six years until the completion of the final union workhouses (Clifden, Glenties and Milford) in late 1845. Local disputes further delayed the admission of paupers at Glenties until July 1846, and at Clifden until as late as March 1847.[81] The majority of workhouses opened for business, however, in the course of 1841 and 1842, with 110 (85 per cent) declared as fit for use by March 1843, and 98 (75 per cent) actually in operation.[82] Workhouse construction amounted to a significant public works project and provided much needed, if temporary and localized, employment in many areas. Devon commented on the positive, if temporary, effects of this boost to employment in Co. Limerick in 1839, but warned prophetically that attitudes might harden once the first rates were imposed.[83]

These delays in putting the act into operation caused some frustrations, not least in the context of the renewal of distress following partial crop failure in the western districts in 1838–39, and again in 1842–43. While the commission's refusal to countenance extraordinary relief was in conformity with the letter of the law, it dramatized the limitations of the measure in addressing crisis conditions and drew political criticism on the government and the measure.[84] This was not helped by Nicholls' retrospective gloss that the failure of 1839 had been exaggerated and that the salutary 'dread of scarcity' had induced more economical and prudential habits among the people.[85]

The authorities did, however, take some measures to accelerate implementation in response to public restiveness. In April 1839 Russell ordered a temporary increase of the assistant commissioners in Ireland to twelve; two further 'Irish' assistant commissioners, Joseph Burke and Caesar George Otway, were appointed by Nicholls.[86] Russell also urged his new Irish lord lieutenant, Lord Ebrington, to give the poor law all the attention he could spare and promote the rapid formation of the remaining unions.[87] The initial

81 The other unions which did not bring their workhouses into operation until 1846 were Milford, Cahirciveen, Swineford, Castlerea and Tuam.

82 *Ninth Report* (1843), p. 35.

83 MC: NP, V/139, Devon to Normanby, 17 Mar. [1839].

84 NLI: MP, Ms 13,392/5, Nicholls to Spring Rice, 26 June; *FJ*, 30 July 1839.

85 *Sixth Report* (1840), pp. 33–5.

86 *Ibid.*, p. 24; NA: RP, PRO30/22/3C, fols 296–7, Nicholls to Russell, 21 May 1839. Burke was formerly an honorary secretary to the Dublin Mendicity Institution and part of the pre-reform Dublin corporate establishment – his practice as assistant commissioner for the western unions reflected this bias; Otway (1809–67) was the son of the clergyman Caesar Otway.

87 DRO: FP, 1262M/LI/36, Russell to Ebrington, 11 Apr. 1839.

hopes of putting 'surplus' barrack accommodation into service had been abandoned in the face of resistance and over-charging by the military authorities, but the commissioners had better luck with existing charitable institutions, which had been vested in the commissioners by the 1838 act. Inquiries in spring 1839 found both the House of Industry and the Foundling Hospital in Dublin suitable for conversion, and these were adopted as the workhouses of the North and South Dublin unions respectively, their current inhabitants being moved to alternative accommodation. Both were ready to receive inmates under the new regime by 25 March 1840, and received the official endorsement of a viceregal visit shortly afterwards. Under the close personal supervision and 'constant care' of Nicholls, the Dublin institutions served as model schools for the training of workhouse masters and matrons for many of the provincial unions.[88] In Cork the House of Industry was also pressed into service as a temporary workhouse; it was declared fit on 15 February 1840, making this the first union in Ireland to come under the full operation of the poor law. The old building served until replaced by a purpose-built edifice in December 1841. At Clonmel the existing House of Industry was also adapted for use, and remained in operation until replaced by a Wilkinson-designed workhouse in 1853.[89] The commission considered co-opting the old poor-house in Belfast for the same purpose, but opted in the face of local resistance to wait instead until Wilkinson's new building was ready.[90]

Valuation, rating and vagrancy

The other major tasks facing the new boards lay in revising the valuation of the unions and setting a rate. Both were potentially controversial, and of acute interest to individuals as likely to affect directly their pockets. The gradual roll-out of the poor-law system meant that, along with the election of guardians and the formation of workhouses, valuation and rating matters were prolonged over a lengthy period and required constant attention from Nicholls and his staff. Under the 1838 act each board was given large discretion to either adopt the Griffith's valuation (where this existed locally) or order a union revision by a valuator. Finding that the Griffith's valuation did not take account of current letting value, and excluded houses valued under five pounds, the commissioners opted for the latter (although they later

88 *FJ*, 1 Apr. 1840; *Eighth Report* (1842), p. 32; UCL: CP, 1486/22–4, Nicholls to Chadwick, 31 July 1839. For a detailed study of the South Dublin union, see Burke, *People and the Poor Law*.

89 *Sixth Report* (1840), pp. 25–9.

90 O'Brien, 'Establishment of poor-law unions', p. 100; *BNL*, 19 Oct. 1838.

recommended using the Griffith's valuation as a uniform point of reference). Valuation was a highly-charged question not only because the precise allocation of rate between landlord and tenant would be affected by the relationship between the poor-law valuation and the actual letting value of a holding, but also because it was widely anticipated that the new poor-law valuation would be adopted as the basis of an anticipated revision of both the municipal and parliamentary franchise.[91] This created great temptations for boards to appoint valuators sympathetic to the political opinions of the majority of guardians. These 'much disputed valuations' were of enough importance to attract the attention of the lord lieutenant in autumn 1840, and led to the preparation of a report critical of local discrepancies. In March 1841 the viceroy dispatched a team of barristers selected by the Irish attorney-general to aid the assistant commissioners in regulating local valuation proceedings.[92] Nicholls reassured his masters that, with a couple of blatant exceptions (Ballina and Scariff), the valuations had been carried out in *bona fide* fashion and any errors had been within acceptable margins.[93] Despite these explanations the subject of valuation would form the basis of some of the growing assaults on the system from 1841 onwards. Landowners with political interests, such as Lord Downshire, took a close interest in the potential consequences of union valuations for their local constituencies.[94] Despite considerable apprehensions on the part of Nicholls and others concerning the first collections of rates, the initial levies provoked remarkably little concerted resistance.[95] Again, this was not to last.

In 1837–38 parliament had fudged the difficult question of the suppression of mendicancy and had ultimately dropped the putative vagrancy clauses from the act. As the poor law became established pressure grew to reopen the matter. In 1839 Devon warned that, while likely to offer 'an admirable asylum' for the old, able-bodied mendicants would not enter the workhouse unless

91 *Tenth Report* (1844), pp. 31–2; Morpeth's 1841 franchise bill included the 'revolutionary' proposal that the hitherto confused and contested county franchise be determined by the occupancy of property on a fourteen-year lease at a poor-law valuation of £5 (later raised to £8). While this bill failed, it was expected that any future revision would be founded on the poor-law valuation, and this was eventually adopted in the 1850 franchise act: see Hoppen, 'Politics', pp. 765–6.

92 DRO: FP, 1262M/LI/130, Ebrington to Pigot, 14 Mar. 1841.

93 *Seventh Report* (1841), pp. 50–4.

94 See, for example, PRONI, Belfast, Downshire Papers, D671/C/12/772–5: correspondence between Gulson and the agents of the Downshire estate on the valuation of the Lisburn union, February–March 1841.

95 NLI: MP, Ms 13,392/5, Nicholls to Spring Rice, 26 June 1839; *Eighth Report* (1842), pp. 32–3.

compelled to by some form of vagrancy law.[96] The commissioners endorsed this opinion, not least from a conviction that poor-rates would be accepted only as a replacement for rather than an addition to the unofficial 'tax' imposed by widespread begging. Many (although not all) boards of guardians agreed resolutions demanding such a prohibition, and ministers were lobbied strongly on the matter in the lead-up to the 1840 session.[97]

The Irish ministers demonstrated a distinct lack of enthusiasm for such a fresh measure. Nicholls complained that the promises made to him concerning a vagrancy bill had been ignored in 1839, and that Morpeth, a man 'full of doubts and afraid of his own shadow', and the solicitor-general Pigot, had subsequently back-pedalled on Russell's commitment to legislate. The Dublin executive was, he concluded, running scared of the anticipated hostility of O'Connell's 'tail' at a time of government weakness in the Commons.[98] When an Irish mendicity bill was finally introduced in March 1840, Nicholls' prognostications were realized. Morpeth's advocacy was half-hearted; he admitted that there were serious doubts about the judicial suppression of mendicancy in a country still lacking a right to relief, and stated that the government would allow extensive time for discussion. The repealer M. J. O'Connell protested that the repression of outdoor relief 'according to the custom of the country', without providing for it legally, was unacceptable. Nationalist opinion in Dublin agreed that the 'new starvation bill' was 'unnecessarily harsh and oppressive as regards the poor, [and] calculated to embarrass and retard the experiment of compulsory relief'.[99] In the face of widespread opposition in Ireland, the bill proceeded no further, prompting the cartoonist John Doyle to satirize what he saw as Morpeth's abject surrender to the importunate beggar-woman O'Connell and her numerous brood. Morpeth himself advised against reintroduction in the teeth of such resolute opposition.[100] Despite the protests of the commissioners, the measure fell into abeyance until revived in the very different circumstances of 1847. Its absence determined that pre-Famine Ireland would retain a dual form of poor relief, with alms to beggars paralleling the 'official' mode of assistance.[101]

96 DRO: FP, 1262M/LI/26, Devon to Ebrington, 26 Mar. 1839.

97 *Sixth Report* (1841), pp. 37–9.

98 NLW: HCP, C/2095, Nicholls to Lewis, 27 Jan. 1840.

99 *Hansard*, 3, lii, 1251–4 [20 Mar. 1840]; *FJ*, 23 Mar., 2, 4 Apr. 1840.

100 HB [John Doyle], *The beggar's petition* (9 Apr. 1840); NA: RP, PRO30/22/3E, fols 307–8, Morpeth to Russell, 28 Nov. 1840.

101 See *Seventh Report* (1841), pp. 48–9. Senior attempted to revive interest in the subject in 1843, but to no immediate avail: [Nassau Senior], 'Mendicancy in Ireland', *ER*, 77 (1843), pp. 391–411.

The assault on Nicholls, 1840–42

Behind the positive generalities of the annual reports, Nicholls and his staff seemed almost constantly employed in preventing the collapse or the 'perversion' of the new system. As one of the three Poor Law Commissioners, Nicholls was not immune from the growing crisis facing the institution in England and Wales following from the attempts to extend the workhouse principle to the north and to prohibit outdoor relief during a period of industrial recession, which provoked growing challenges to the commission from its parliamentary enemies.[102] The affairs of Ireland, however, absorbed most of his attention until his departure in late 1842, to an extent that – at least in Chadwick's opinion – damaged both his career and health.[103] Any hopes he might have entertained of a relatively short stay in the country evaporated as the Irish establishment lurched from crisis to crisis. The workhouse arrangements required, he informed his fellow commissioners in 1839, his constant care.[104] In 1840 he took on the added responsibility of making what became an annual tour of inspection of all workhouse buildings in preparation and operation, a mission that was onerous and potentially hazardous, given the poor state of many western roads. Indeed, Nicholls and Wilkinson nearly came to grief on a mountain road between Bantry and Tralee in August 1840: 'I have rarely seen a narrower escape – 'twas within an inch.'[105] The poor-law office in Dublin was, he complained to Lewis, chronically understaffed for the immensity of business required in establishing the novel and complex system.[106] 'We must work like coalheavers, day by day', he moaned, while suffering endless interruptions from visitors and enduring the completion of the constant stream of voluminous reports and returns demanded by parliament. The additional effort required to meet these 'extraordinary' demands threatened to disrupt the regular work of the office.[107]

102 See, for example, NA: RP, PRO30/22/3C, fols 381–2, Nicholls to Lewis, 24 July 1839, and discussion in Brundage, *Making of the New Poor Law*, pp. 174–9.

103 UCL: CP, 1486/92–108, Chadwick memo, n.d. [*c.*1851].

104 NA: RP, PRO30/22/3C, fols 395–6, Nicholls to Lewis, 3 Aug. 1839.

105 NLW: HCP, C/2097, C/2098, Nicholls to Lewis, 6 June, 15 Aug. 1840.

106 Nicholls to Lewis, 15 Oct. 1839, 11 Jan. 1840, *ibid.*, C/2083, C/2091.

107 UCL: CP, 1486/28–31, Nicholls to Chadwick, 25 Apr. 1840; BL: GP, Add Ms 79,635, fols 58–61, Nicholls to Eliot, 8 Nov. 1841. This problem persisted after Nicholls' departure; in 1843 the chief clerk Arthur Moore complained that the returns demanded by the Lords on workhouse buildings and contracts required sifting through 45,000 documents, many kept by the unions, and that even with all the clerks working until nearly midnight to prepare them on time, daily business was being neglected: SUL: WP, WP2/97/74, Graham to Wellington, 6 Feb. 1843.

Nicholls' resilience in the face of these pressures may have arisen in part from his reluctance to abandon a generally positive view of 'the Irish people generally, and of Irish boards of guardians and Irish assistant commissioners', and his underlying 'faith in the essential principles of the measure'.[108] He may also have been conscious that his personal standing in public life was now inextricably tied up with the success of the Irish poor law. He was less impressed by the Irish weather, not only for the toll it placed upon his own health, but for the constant risk that the consistently poor weather posed to the harvest and turf gathering and hence to the condition of the people. 'After fifteen months trial of the Irish climate,' he complained, 'I am compelled to say that it is not such as I should like to live in. England is bright and joyous by comparison!'[109]

Despite the growing volume of vituperation directed against him personally, and his (correct) sense that he lacked the full confidence of his fellow commissioners, Nicholls was assured that he retained the support of the Whig ministers. He was for the present, he believed, personally indispensable:

> [N]o one could take up and carry through what I have in hand here – I mean no new man – my quitting Ireland at this moment would cause serious embarrassment to the whole concern, and on this account (God knows no other) I wish to keep at my post for another year, when I think we shall have gotten matters into a fitting state for transference to other hands.[110]

The growing chorus of hostility to the law, and the change of government in 1841 was, however, to make his position much more difficult.

There were two distinct nodes of opposition to the poor-law administration in Ireland: a 'popular' antagonism given voice and weight by O'Connell and his supporters, and a 'landed' opposition which had similarly shown its teeth in the debates of 1837–38 without inflicting too much damage to the bill. Despite Nicholls' assurances that all forms of opposition had evaporated in the first year of implementation, both showed signs of resurgence from 1840 and were to pose a serious threat to the system in 1841–43. O'Connellite complaints were kept in check so long as the Whigs held office. O'Connell himself had publicly denounced the new system shortly after the passage of the bill, but subsequently allowed other matters to displace it from the top of his political agenda. His announcement in August 1838 that he now accepted

108 UCL: CP, 1486/25–7, Nicholls to Chadwick, 28 Aug. 1839.

109 NLW: HCP, C/2084, C/2087, Nicholls to Lewis, 20 Oct., 28 Nov. 1839.

110 Nicholls to Lewis, 31 July 1841, *ibid.*, C/2104. For his good relations with ministers, see Willink, 'Nicholls', pp. li, lvii, but also Normanby's comment that the experience of the last year had lowered his respect for Nicholls' judgement: NA: RP, PRO30/22/4A, fols 402–3, Normanby to Russell, 28 June 1841.

its existence and felt it his duty to make every exertion to render it as popular, useful and efficient as possible, did something to dampen down excitement.[111] O'Connell's stance was thus one of 'wait and see' rather than immediate confrontation.

A number of factors combined to restrict any overt and sustained nationalist opposition to the poor-law system before 1841. Firstly, a significant number of Catholics were either supportive or ambivalent towards the measure, and it retained a number of high-profile supporters, albeit usually combining defence of the 1838 act in principle with demands for its radical extension in practice. Some new voices were added to the debate. In one of his earliest journalistic forays, the future Young Irelander Thomas Davis denounced in 1839 the renewed campaign for promoting Irish emigration, and urged poor-law guardians to reject landed attempts to suborn them to act as agents for clearance projects. He was confident that the representative character of the institution would prevent this:

> Not even for a moment will we harbour the suspicion that the poor law guardians will be lured from that high and sacred duty that the people have elected them to fulfil. They are not mad enough, even were they unworthy enough, to forget the character of trustees, in which alone they stand to the people[.][112]

While this statement was made in hope and not always borne out in reality, the extent of engagement with the election of guardians in the early years of the system did much to 'domesticate' it and provide some sense of popular ownership.

Occasional public clashes between 'popular' boards and the central commission, such as the successful campaign by the Cork board to admit press reporters, also promoted this process.[113] For his part, G. C. Lewis was convinced of the underlying 'popularity' of the system, albeit for reasons of which he did not entirely approve. Inspecting the system in early 1843 he concluded that

> [T]he boards of guardians are extremely popular in their constitution, and are quite new. . . . Elected guardians are chosen annually by a suffrage nearly universal . . . Ratepayers can, if they wish, vote secretly by returning their voting paper in a sealed cover – a practice often followed. Consequently, the elected guardians are virtually returned by the priests and the landlords have no control.

111 *MC*, 30 Aug. 1838.

112 [Thomas Davis], 'Emigration – no remedy', *Citizen*, 1 (Dec. 1839), pp. 73–83.

113 *FJ*, 17 Sept. 1839, 19 Mar. 1840.

Landed hostility to the new system was stoked primarily by this democratizing tendency, as it had established 'the principle that certain municipal powers relating to the affairs of the poor are to be administered, not by landlords exclusively (as hitherto), but by boards consisting partly of landlords and partly of tenants; and in which, at present, the tenants have the majority. The Irish landlords (as is natural considering what was hitherto the rural regime in Ireland) cannot stomach this.' The system's strongest supporters were, he observed, the rural middle class – 'the strong farmers' – and the parish priests.[114] Lewis may have been right in his analysis, but popular attitudes toward the poor law were vulnerable to strong countervailing forces, especially when orchestrated by O'Connell.

A second reason why the response to the poor law remained muted before 1841 was the continuing hope that the promised 'auxiliaries' of railway construction and other public works would be introduced. The enactment of these, Lynch had reminded the public in 1839, had been the *quid pro quo* for his and many others' support of the poor law; the duty of the legislature was to 'proceed further; to pass measures for raising the condition of the people, and not only to provide against destitution, but to place the Irish peasant in that situation which the soil and the climate of Ireland, the physical and moral energies of her sons, entitle him to be placed in'.[115] In the wake of the passing of the Poor Law Act, anticipation was high in Ireland that the railway commission's recommendations would be enacted, and there were demands that the proposed system also be extended to Connacht.[116] Conversely, proprietorial and speculatory interests expressed intense alarm at such a large extension of state interference into the sphere of private enterprise, and great efforts were made to expose errors and inconsistencies in the findings of the commission and demonstrate its alleged 'favouritism' towards the government's political friends. The debate became further politicized as the English journals weighed in to support or oppose the proposals along broadly partisan lines.[117]

In the autumn of 1838 the lord lieutenant repeatedly pressed the 'urgency' of introducing a railway measure, citing political as well as developmental grounds for action. Irish circumstances dictated, he was confident, a bold departure from *laissez-faire*, and all parties would fall into line behind such a

114 Lewis to Grote, 11 Jan. 1843, in Lewis (ed.), *Letters*, pp. 128–30.

115 Lynch, *Measures to be adopted*, p. 8.

116 *FJ*, 10 Oct. 1838, 2 Feb. 1839.

117 e.g. *MC*, 17 Aug., 24 Sept., 27 Dec. 1838; *The Times*, 8 Oct. 1838; Anon., 'The Irish railway scheme', *Spectator*, 15 Sept. 1838, pp. 873–4.

measure of obvious national benefit.[118] He explicitly connected this to the successful implementation of the poor law and the relief of immediate distress. On this occasion the viceroy was supported by the chancellor, who arranged for Drummond and Burgoyne to address the cabinet on the matter in early 1839.[119] Russell's support was crucial; he endorsed the proposal enthusiastically, while expressing a preference for both a large loan and a guarantee against losses imposed on the county rates.[120]

Moving the Lords' address to the Crown at the beginning of the 1839 session, Lord Lovelace also linked the poor law and railway measures. The people of Ireland, he insisted, had received the poor law 'with a respect and attention highly creditable to the country', demonstrating both the people's confidence in the government and the responsiveness of parliament to the wants and wishes of that people. A further 'opportunity for acting in accordance with the wishes of that people', would be offered when the Irish railway report was presented.[121] During the course of 1839 Morpeth brought in a bill based on the report which, if it fell short of the full recommendations of the railway commissioners, went further than many observers had anticipated. 'In the first instance', a trunk line between Dublin and Cork, with branches to Limerick and Clonmel, would be built with a government loan of £2.5 million.[122] This was largely in line with the proposals mooted by the Irish railway engineer Charles Vignoles, who had advised the commission.[123] However, Conservatives and 'economical' radicals combined to oppose the initiative from a mixture of motives including suspicion of the ministry's political motives, the protection of English taxpayers and an adherence to *laissez-faire* principles. Peel's opposition, on orthodox economic grounds, was most damaging, and although the Commons motion was carried by a majority of forty-four, its prospects were limited. Given the parlous state of the ministry's majority the opposition alliance boded ill, and despite the efforts of its ministerial advocates, the bill was dropped in June.[124]

118 MC: NP, M/662, Normanby to Spring Rice, 14 Nov.; RA: MP, 100/101, Normanby to Spring Rice, 29 Nov.; NLI: MP, Ms 13,390/3, Normanby to Spring Rice, 5 Dec. 1838.

119 NLI: MP, Ms 13,392/5, Normanby to Spring Rice, 1 Jan. 1839; Spring Rice to Drummond, 15 Dec. 1838, *ibid.*, Ms 543, p. 127.

120 Russell to Spring Rice, 30 Jan. 1839, *ibid.*, Ms 13,392/6.

121 *Hansard*, 3, xlv, cols 7–12 [5 Feb. 1839: Lovelace].

122 *Ibid.*, 1060–81 [1 Mar. 1839: Morpeth]; *FJ*, 5 Mar. 1839.

123 [C. B. Vignoles], 'The railway system of Ireland', *DR*, 6 (Jan. 1839), pp. 207–69.

124 *Hansard*, 3, xlv, 1082–90 [1 Mar. 1839]; NLI: MP, Ms 536, pp. 150–1, Spring Rice to [Barrington], 1 Apr. 1839; NA: RP, PRO30/22/3C, fols 357–62, Ebrington to Russell, 26 June 1839.

This was unquestionably a setback for the ministry's Irish strategy and supporters of the Irish poor law. It was not helped by the additional failure of Lynch's much-vaunted measures to make any further progress that session. A grant of only £50,000 for Irish public works created further disappointment.[125] With Whig control over parliament slipping away (the ministry came perilously close to collapse in the 'Bedchamber Crisis' of May 1839), the prospect of major remedial measures dimmed. Nevertheless, despite O'Connell's drift towards a more provocative stance on repeal from 1839 and the much-lamented death in harness of Drummond in spring 1840, the alliance between repealers and the ministry remained relatively popular in much of Ireland and was embodied by the continuing presence of Morpeth (a full cabinet member from 1839) and the appointment of Ebrington as lord lieutenant in March 1839. The home secretary observed shortly before the 1841 election that the revival of repeal was not popular in Ireland, and that demotic politics was much more concerned with anti-Toryism.[126] For his part, Morpeth was unwilling to give up the railway plan and remained committed to reintroducing it when practicable; he sought to revive it in spring 1841 after Vignoles recommended a combination of private investment with government direction and a guaranteed rate of profit of 4 per cent per annum.[127] This railway bill (and an associated land drainage bill) disappeared on the fall of the administration, and subsequent attempts to revive the principle of state construction or ownership were vetoed by the Peel government.[128] Vain as these hopes of remedial measures proved to be, they held out the possibility of some relief to the poor law so long as the Whigs retained office, and contributed to the remarkable degree of support for the ministry in much of Ireland, evident as late as the elections of summer 1841.

The other significant check upon active resistance to the poor law had been the delay in imposing the first rates due to the staggering of the introduction of the system. As the workhouses began to come into operation in 1841 and 1842, the first rates were set and collected. The initial levies (often in urban or eastern unions) appear to have been relatively unopposed, but as the reach of the poor law extended into the western counties from 1842, and as the

125 *Hansard*, 3, xlviii, 1019–21 [28 June 1839].

126 NA: RP, PRO30/22/4A, fols 298–305, Normanby to Russell, 10 May 1841. After a brief period at the Colonial Office, Normanby had exchanged portfolios with Russell in August 1839.

127 *Hansard*, 3, xlix, 716 (24 July 1839); CHP, J/19/11/2, pp. 263–5, Morpeth to Devon, 25 May 1841; Anon., *Railways for Ireland* (London, [1841]).

128 BL: GP, Add Ms. 79,635, fol. 129, Graham to Eliot, 21 Dec. 1841; NLI: MP, Ms 13,394/1, Burgoyne to Monteagle, 4 Apr. 1843; *Hansard*, 3, lxx, 981–2 [11 July 1843].

country entered an agricultural recession in 1842–43, aggravated by the legacy of poor potato harvests in 1840 and 1841 and the collapse in demand for seasonal labour due to a British depression, the weight of the new rates was felt much more acutely. Nicholls noted that the fear of famine had dissipated with good weather in summer 1842, but failed to grasp that market fluctuations, and the sudden collapse of prices, might still impact on the small tenant's ability to pay both rent and rates.[129] There was an additional, temporary, factor tending to accentuate tenant resistance in 1842–44. The law required tenants to pay the whole rate in the first instance, subsequently deducting half the total from their landlord's rent; however, many smaller tenants were in arrears of six to eighteen months, and were being refused remission until the 'correct' gale of rent had been paid. This meant many tenants were initially saddled with the entire poor-rates bill until their rent arrears were paid off – a recipe for anger and confrontation not foreseen by the bill's framers. It was, as Lewis observed, no consolation to these small ratepayers that political economists held that all rates would ultimately devolve on landlord rents; they had to pay up in the first instance or suffer distraint of their goods, while the intense competition for land rendered bargaining with landlords very difficult.[130]

The O'Connellite revolt, 1842–43

In 1842 the combination of anger at the imposition of the rates, especially on the already overburdened smallholders of properties valued at under five pounds annually (i.e. those whom the original bills of 1837 and 1838 would have exempted), fear of the workhouse on the part of the able-bodied destitute, and the revival of a full-blooded repeal campaign, led to the emergence of a popular anti-poor-law movement. The initial flashpoint unions were in Skibbereen, west Cork and Waterford, where the first instances of violent resistance to the collection of rates were recorded in late 1842. Near Skibbereen a clash between the constabulary and an anti-poor-law crowd left two rioters dead and the neighbourhood tense and angry. When asked to calm the situation, a local priest is reported to have replied: 'I am favourable to a system of a compulsory tax for the poor, and desire to see it levied, but so determinedly hostile are the parishioners to it, that I should fear personal violence if I attempted to expostulate with them.'[131]

129 *Irish Poor Law*, pp. 285–6.
130 *Hansard*, 3, lxxi, 323 [7 Aug. 1843]; Lewis to Grote, 11 Jan. 1843, in Lewis (ed.), *Letters*, pp. 128–30.
131 *The Times*, 26, 28 Nov. 1842.

At Waterford in December, ratepayers were reported to have 'dug a large hole, and filled it up with the poor law papers, set fire to them, and covered them with clay, vowing they would never pay one half-penny of poor rates'; in March 1843 there were reports of large (and allegedly armed) gatherings in the vicinity of the town threatening to sack the workhouse and carry the inmates back to their homes. Resistance to the distraint of cattle, echoing the tithe war of the previous decade, was recorded.[132] While the commissioners were initially hopeful that these were isolated incidents, they were conscious that it was the imposition of rates on large numbers of poor smallholding tenants that was the principal problem, and the tone of their Irish reports from 1842–43 onwards was decidedly less upbeat than before.[133] Even in places where there was no physical resistance to the law, public meetings challenging its cost (especially the weight of the 'establishment charge' for the workhouse and the union staff) became widespread, there were many cases of passive resistance, and rate revenues declined. At Carrick-on-Shannon the guardians felt obliged to close the workhouse to new inmates in November 1843, leading to the highly publicized death of at least one rejected applicant.[134] Large numbers of petitions hostile to Nicholls and his policy of insensitive and expensive micromanagement were dispatched from boards and ratepayers' meetings.[135]

Violent resistance to poor-law rates spread outwards from Waterford, affecting the unions of Tipperary, Fermoy, Longford, Galway, Limerick, Carrickmacross and Ballinasloe, and reaching Donegal, Boyle and Westport by the end of 1843. Military forces were deployed in these eleven unions to assist centrally-appointed rate-collectors, with the constabulary employed similarly in another ten unions. This firm action by the authorities, especially in Waterford and Galway, appears to have been superficially effective, although the costs involved demonstrated how counter-productive would be the attempt to persevere with levying rates (or distraining goods in lieu) from the smallest occupiers, who were often themselves on the threshold of destitution. Additional problems were witnessed in the unions of Tuam, Dungarvan, Ballinrobe and Castlebar, where the guardians refused in whole or part to

132 *Ibid.*, 12 Dec. 1842; 13, 17, 25 Mar. 1843.

133 e.g. *Ninth Report* (1843), pp. 40–3.

134 O'Brien, 'Workhouse management', p. 127.

135 e.g. 'The Irish Poor Law – Cork Union', *The Times*, 12 Mar. 1842; *ibid.*, 13 Mar. 1843; *Hansard*, 3, lxviii, cols 1324–34 [5 May 1843: French]. Hostility towards Nicholls might yet have been greater had it been known that he had given permission for the use of unclaimed bodies from Irish workhouses for dissection: Bedfordshire and Luton Archives, Bedford, Wrest Park (Lucas) Manuscripts, L29/700/21/5, Lucas to de Grey, 7 Apr. 1842.

proceed with the setting or collection of a rate adequate for union needs.[136] Tuam proved particularly recalcitrant, a fact perhaps not unrelated to the open hostility of its prelate, John MacHale, towards the law; the board was only coerced into collecting a rate and opening its workhouse in 1846 after the commissioners had issued a writ of mandamus to compel them to appoint collectors, and subsequently dissolving the board and forcing fresh elections.[137]

Long-standing opponents of the poor law saw in this crisis evidence that many were now at last 'com[ing] round to the faith of the economists'.[138] However, the anti-poor-law unrest of 1842–44 had a serious impact only in a minority of unions, and was relatively short-lived (compared to the anti-poor-law campaign in northern England). Part of the reason for this lay with local or regional circumstances. The commissioners acknowledged that peasant resistance had arisen in part from 'just complaints' against corrupt rate-collectors in some unions, who were promptly replaced.[139] Many of the disturbed unions were in western districts with predominantly smallholding ratepayers suffering badly from the agricultural downturn and collapse of seasonal migrant labour markets. However, probably the most important determinant of the timing of the rates revolt arose from the instrumentalization of discontent by the O'Connellite campaign. In endeavouring to mobilize popular grievances behind repeal, O'Connell revived his populist anti-poor-law rhetoric dormant since 1838. He now sought, Nicholls observed, to excite 'deadly hostility to everything English, not excepting the poor law commissioners'.[140] In March 1842 O'Connell lectured the Repeal Association:

> [T]here was only one Poor Law for Ireland, and that was to give her back her Legislature and the income of her absentees, and then no Poor Law would be required for her. (Hear.) He understood that since he visited the North Dublin workhouse, the twenty poor children whom he saw there in such a bad state of health were in their graves. (Sensation.) The present system of Poor Laws was totally unfit for Ireland. (Hear, hear.) He would tell the government and the landlords that nothing would prevent an insurrection, if the Poor Law should continue, but his own personal exertions and influence over the people (cheers), and he doubted very much even of that influence if the Poor Law went on as it was going.[141]

136 *Tenth Report* (1844), pp. 27–8.

137 *Eleventh Annual Report of the Poor Law Commissioners*, PP 1845 [624], xxvii.247, pp. 22–3; *Thirteenth Annual Report of the Poor Law Commissioners*, PP 1847 [816], xxviii.1. For MacHale's involvement, see *Pilot*, 25 Jan. 1843.

138 BL: BP, B/96, Monteagle to Lansdowne, 12 Nov. 1842.

139 *Tenth Report* (1844), p. 28.

140 UCL: CP, 1486/37–9, Nicholls to Chadwick, 6 Jan. [1842].

141 *The Times*, 12 Mar. 1842.

His case was illustrated by the use of emotive arguments drawn from the parliamentary inquiry into the suffering of children in the North Dublin union.[142] The 'Liberator' continued to employ such inflammatory rhetoric on the poor law through 1842 and into the 'repeal year' of 1843, and found many ready listeners. O'Connell was on a collision course with the Conservative government, and exploitation of the poor-law question would serve as a useful weapon for enlisting disgruntled ratepayers behind his banner.[143]

The anti-poor-law movement did not, however, achieve hegemony over Catholic or nationalist opinion in 1842–43. The *Nation*, launched in October 1842 and part-edited by Thomas Davis, refused to condemn the system, for all its flaws, and insisted the poor-rate did more good than any other tax; this heterodoxy earned it the hostility of the slavishly O'Connellite *Pilot*.[144] Attempts within the Repeal Association to adopt a common platform against the poor law came awry in January 1843 when Davis and his fellow Young Irelander, John Blake Dillon, insisted on the addition of paragraphs to the report of its committee that dissented from the leader's line. Whereas John O'Connell, in his father's name, put the abolitionist case that 'private charity would be found equal to the support of the really indigent, if the regenerative influence of a native parliament were brought to bear upon the wealth, the industry, and the resources of the country', Dillon made a plea for retention and reform.[145] In answer to the neo-Whatelian tone of the younger O'Connell, he offered a fundamental restatement of the ethical, redistributive, case for a poor law:

> [A] state of things in which some members of the community were perishing from want of the common necessaries of life, while others were in the enjoyment of every luxury, and laden with superfluous wealth, was a state opposed to the providence of God, and as such calling loudly and imperatively for a change. To the objection that it is unjust and impolitic to tax the industrious for the support of the idle, [the reformers] reply, that when applied to this or any other country that is governed on aristocratic principles, this objection has no weight, because it rests upon an erroneous supposition. Those who rely on this objection must take for granted that idleness is in general the cause of poverty, and wealth the consequence of labour; whereas, in all countries whose people are

142 Ibid., 10 Dec. 1841; *Inquiry into the Treatment, Condition and Mortality of Infant Children in the Workhouse of the North Dublin Union*, PP 1842 [370], xxxvi.15.

143 See Lawrence J. McCaffrey, *Daniel O'Connell and the Repeal Year* (Lexington, KY, 1966), pp. 20–3, 33–8.

144 *Nation*, 31 Dec. 1842, 7 Jan., *Pilot*, 9 Jan. 1843; see also McCaffrey, *O'Connell*, p. 36.

145 [John O'Connell (ed.)], *Report of the General Committee of the Loyal National Repeal Association of Ireland, upon . . . the existing System of Poor Laws in Ireland* (Dublin, 1843), pp. 1, 16.

> the slaves of an aristocracy, but most of all in Ireland, because its people are the most enslaved, this wholesome rule of nature is reversed – the wealth which is produced by labour, and which ought to be its reward, being taken from its rightful owners, and monopolized by those who contribute in no way towards its production. While they fully admit the value of the principle, that labour ought not to be taxed for the support of idleness, the advocates of a poor law say that this principle, if acted upon at all, should be acted upon universally. . . . [T]hey insist that the Poor Rate is not correctly denominated a tax upon labour for the support of idleness; but should rather be described as a restoration to the labourer, of a small portion of that wealth of which he is deprived by unjust laws.

Before the introduction of the poor law, it was 'the unquestionable fact, that *the Poor have been allowed to die, while Dogs and Horses were consuming the food which God intended for their support*'. For all the urgent need for reform – granting greater powers to elected boards, permitting outdoor relief, and transferring more of the burden to the landowners – the 'good effects' of the existing law could even now be discerned.[146]

Although Young Irelanders and the liberal-Catholic clergy disagreed on many issues, on this they tended to converge. In some places priests took a leading part in protest meetings, while at the same time urging their audiences to pay their rates and petition for reform of the law rather than seeking wholesale revocation.[147] Indeed, the active intervention of the clergy was often credited with preventing violent confrontation with the authorities.[148] The *Dublin Review* continued to insist that 'a great diversity of opinion exists in Ireland on the subject of poor laws', while lamenting that the wasteful and authoritarian manner in which they had been introduced, and especially the neglect of representative boards of guardians, had lost the goodwill of the people and stirred up violent antipathy.[149] For his part Smith O'Brien, not yet a repealer but increasingly alienated from the British administration, also denied that the unrest amounted to a revolt against the principle of a poor law, but rather against the commission's attempts to administer it in opposition to Irish public opinion, and to specific and remediable elements of the 1838 act.[150] Given this degree of internal dissension, and the fluctuations over

146 *Ibid.*, pp. 4–7.

147 'Poor rates – important meeting in Dunkerrin', *Pilot*, 11 Jan. 1843; see also 'Letter from Mr O'Connell on the Irish poor law', *The Times*, 30 Dec. 1842.

148 *Pilot*, 30 Jan. 1843.

149 Anon., 'The grievances of Ireland', *DR*, 15 (Dec. 1843), pp. 341–5.

150 *Hansard*, 3, lxvii, 1347–69 [23 Mar. 1843]. Smith O'Brien resigned from the Newcastle board of guardians three months later in protest over British neglect of Irish grievances: *BNL*, 4 July 1843.

time and space in the manifestation of anti-poor-law feeling, it is difficult to accept without reservation the contention that this was 'perhaps the first Irish agitation that was both national *and* spontaneous'.[151]

The anti-poor-law movement faded in most parts of the country during late 1843 and 1844, due to a combination of political, economic and administrative developments. Having achieved mass mobilization through the 'monster meetings' of 1843 O'Connell had less reason to exploit the issue, and was preoccupied from October with preventing the collapse of the movement into chaotic violence and in preparing for the forthcoming state trials. Co-operation on the poor-law question between O'Connellites and Conservatives proved impossible in the circumstances, not least because they were pursuing different (albeit rather blurred) agendas, and Lewis took some comfort from the open feuding between the two anti-poor-law lobbies in January 1843.[152] Economic conditions in both countries tended to recover somewhat in 1843–44, with better harvests and stronger labour demand. The pressure on the poor law declined while the resources available to sustain it were augmented. Most importantly, the 1843 Poor Law Amendment Act removed a number of the most resented elements of the existing law, principally the direct rating of tenants valued at under four pounds per annum. By January 1844 under 8 per cent of the outstanding poor-rates remained uncollected, and by spring 1845 resistance to rate collection had collapsed in all but a handful of Connacht unions, with the system generally in a much healthier financial situation.[153] This hardly indicated a conversion of the populace to enthusiasm for the system, but rather a reluctant acceptance that it was now an established fact in the wake of the lifting of the burden from those least capable of paying. Nicholls' assertion that, given the novelty of the system, its teething troubles, and the introduction of new taxation at a difficult moment, 'the wonder perhaps is that the complaints have been so few, [and] the resistance so slight', may have been self-serving, but is a reminder that the anti-poor-law movement in Ireland needs to be kept in perspective.[154]

151 O'Brien, 'A question of attitude', p. 161.

152 BL: GP, Add Ms 79,661, Lewis to Graham, 23 Jan. 1843; see also *BNL*, 30 Dec. 1842.

153 *Tenth Report* (1844), pp. 30–1; *Eleventh Report* (1845), pp. 21, 25–6. In each of the biannual rates of 1844, just over £128,000 was collected in the fully-functioning unions. In both half-years over 30 per cent of expenditure was on establishment charges and repayment of workhouse loans.

154 BL: PP, Add Ms 40,533, fols 132–5, Nicholls to Peel, 14 Sept. 1843.

The landed campaign and the fall of Nicholls, 1840–43

The other strand of anti-poor-law sentiment in Ireland, sometimes in uneasy alliance with the popular wing, sometimes in confrontation with it, was the landed lobby. Predominantly, although not exclusively, Tory, this interest continued to protest against the new system along the lines set out in the 1837–38 debates, and used its political position in the House of Lords and the Conservative party, as well as its local majorities on grand juries and the magistrates benches, to keep the issue in the public eye. It was also able to rely on emergent lower-class Tory bodies, such as the Dublin Metropolitan Conservative Association, to promote its case more widely.[155] Although not all spokesmen for the landed interest supported the assault on the poor law, this appears to have been the predominant stance.[156]

One of the main objectives of the landed anti-poor-law lobby before 1841 was to establish that Nicholls and his staff had allowed or deliberately encouraged discrimination against Protestant and Conservative interests in the operation of the poor law, principally through their regulation of elections and valuations. To this end a multiplicity of local grievances and objections were brought to national attention through the agency of parliamentary questions and inquiries, and enthusiastic exposés were carried by anti-ministerial papers such as *The Times* and the *Dublin Evening Mail.*

Elections of guardians provided plenty of ammunition. In November 1839 *The Times* carried allegations that partisan returning officers had been appointed for a number of unions.[157] The threatened loss of landed control in a number of boards, to guardians characterized by some landowners as 'low publicans' and 'peasants', made this a charged issue. In the 1840 session a campaign for an inquiry was initiated by the Irish peers Glengall and Westmeath, placing growing pressure on the Dublin office to produce masses of papers and accounts in addition to their regular duties.[158] The electoral affairs of the Ennistymon union in Clare were raised in April, followed by the cases of Clonmel, New Ross and other unions.[159] The former Whately commissioner J. L. W. Naper also highlighted the issue of Catholic clerical activities in the elections at Oldcastle, Co. Meath, and the Lords insisted on the tabling

155 *The Times*, 11 May 1840.

156 For the dissentient case and condemnation of the 1842–43 protests by a landed advocate of outdoor relief, see Anon., *The South of Ireland and her Poor* (London, 1843).

157 *The Times*, 2 Nov. 1839.

158 MC: NP, V/741, Lefevre to Normanby, 15 Mar. [1840].

159 *Hansard*, 3, liii, 1004–5 [13 Apr. 1840]; MC: NP, V/739, Nicholls to Normanby, 26 May 1840.

of all relevant correspondence.[160] Many aspects of this campaign were blatantly sectarian; under parliamentary privilege Lord Westmeath accused Dr Denis Phelan, the Catholic assistant commissioner, of being a former member of the National Association of Ireland and directly under the control of the Catholic clergy.[161] After reviewing the relevant papers, Normanby defended Phelan's integrity, but also found it necessary to legitimize the role played by the clergy; given their pastoral and charitable role, it was natural that 'both the yeomanry and the peasantry, upon the introduction of a measure entirely new to them, should appeal to the priests for information and advice'. Any partisan inquiry into what were at most a marginal number of cases of misconduct would, he concluded, simply perpetuate this practice.[162] He was able to postpone the demanded inquiry, but only at the price of further antagonizing the Irish landed lobby and rendering them intent on mounting a stronger challenge in 1841.[163]

The onslaught in the 1841 session was better organized and more intense. The range of the campaign was now extended from the election of guardians to the allegedly anti-landlord bias in valuations carried out in unions such as Clogheen.[164] The epicentre of the political battle in 1841, however, soon emerged as the Clonmel union. Glengall, a prominent Co. Tipperary landowner who had been furiously engaged in partisan warfare in the union elections of his county, took the lead in agitating for a formal investigation of the part played by Phelan and the Dublin officials in union affairs.[165] Much turned on the dating and phrasing of correspondence by the board's assistant secretary, William Stanley, concerning the appointment of a Mr Butler as returning officer in 1839. While the lord lieutenant was satisfied after assurances that any discrepancies in the correspondence were inadvertent and harmless, and that Butler had been recommended in good faith (although he was later revealed to have been both a bankrupt and a repealer), the Tory majority in the Lords and their press supporters scented blood and opted to pursue the matter. The allegation of deliberate forgery by a Crown official, apparently to justify the appointment of a partisan returning officer, placed the home

160 NA: PLCP, MH19/81, J. W. Birch memo, 12 June 1840.

161 *Hansard*, 3, liii, 1005–6 [13 Apr. 1840].

162 *Ibid.*, 1010–14; MC: NP, V/737, 'Ennistymon union – copies of correspondence'.

163 *Hansard*, 3, lv, 1–5, 411–19 [23 June, 3 July 1840].

164 *Ibid.*, lvi, 738–41 [19 Feb. 1841].

165 Fr Michael Tobin alleged that Glengall had victimized those tenants who had voted against his direction in the union elections by serving immediate demands for payment of all rents due: Tobin to O'Connell, 7 Apr. 1839, in O'Connell (ed.), *Correspondence of O'Connell*, vi, p. 230.

secretary in a difficult position.[166] On this occasion Wellington clearly sympathized with the motion questioning the failure of the commissioners to 'do their duty' and agreed to press for a select committee which would proceed to interrogate Nicholls, Stanley and Phelan.[167]

The sympathetic Lord Devon thought this Lords inquiry both discreditable to the House and unfair to the Dublin officials, who were summoned to give evidence before it in an atmosphere of 'prejudice and bitterness' similar to the 'star chamber', but it undoubtedly had widespread support among the landed classes in Ireland.[168] Nicholls regarded it as a personal assault on himself and his officials, and believed the duke had been used by 'mischievous' interests.[169] He was dissuaded from resigning by the Whig ministers, who continued to believe him indispensable.[170] Wellington, however, now declared his regret at having so strongly supported the 1838 bill and insisted that the commission and not simply its clerk must be held to account, if justice was to be done to the property-holders of Ireland. He sought to extend the affair by adding (apparently incorrect) allegations that the returning officer of Naas union had illegally influenced the selection of a valuator for party purposes.[171]

Nicholls and the commission survived the 1841 assault, but not without cost. William Stanley was obliged to resign as secretary to the Dublin board, much to the disgust of his colleagues; he had been 'sacrificed', Nicholls lamented, 'to party violence'.[172] For his growing number of enemies, however, Nicholls' own fall was now only a matter of time, and was accelerated by the loyalty he continued to display to his officials, especially Phelan.[173] As

166 MC: NP, V/748, V/213a, V/214, Normanby to Nicholls, 5 Mar.; Ebrington to Normanby, 8, 9 Mar. 1841; *The Times*, 15 Mar. 1841.

167 *Hansard*, 3, lvi, 1344–6 [5 Mar.]; lvii, 3–8, 289, 334–6, 452–4 [8, 16, 18, 22 Mar. 1841].

168 DRO: FP, 1262M/LI/132, Devon to Ebrington, 21 Mar. 1840.

169 Willink, 'Nicholls', p. liii.

170 DRO: FP, 1262M/LI/184, Nicholls to Ebrington, 10 Mar.; MC: NP, V/216, Ebrington to Normanby, 13 Mar. 1841.

171 *Hansard*, 3, lvii, 806–7, 1398–1400 [2 Apr., 3 May 1841]; MC: NP, V/553, E. Vaughan to Normanby, 11 May 1841.

172 *Hansard*, lvii, 1244–5 [29 Apr.]; MC: NP, V/221, Ebrington to Normanby, 12 May 1841. Stanley was subsequently employed by the police board before eventually returning to the poor law office in Dublin 'with his character uninjured and a general admission of his truthfulness and integrity': NLW: HCP, C/2100, C/2104, Nicholls to Lewis, 4, 31 July 1841; Willink, 'Nicholls', p. liii.

173 NLW: HCP, C/2111, Nicholls to Lewis, 13 Nov.; BL: GP, Add Ms 79,635, fols 78–82, Eliot to Graham, 20 Nov. 1841.

significantly, his colleagues in the commission (especially following the resignation of the more sympathetic Shaw Lefevre in June 1841), increasingly regarded him as a cause rather than a victim of growing Irish agitation against the system. T. F. Lewis believed that Wellington's overt hostility rendered Nicholls' place untenable, and sought to persuade his son of this.[174] However, if the fall of the Whig government in August 1841 and its replacement by the Conservatives potentially undermined his position, Nicholls was unwilling to admit it. Unlike Chadwick (who had detected and criticized a Christian-economist antagonism to poor laws on the part of Peel), Nicholls rightly predicted the new prime minister would be 'prudent' and introduce no rash changes.[175] Peel's forbearance was, however, not shared by several other leading members of the incoming administration, especially the home secretary Sir James Graham, and Wellington, who now led the government in the Lords. Nor was it popular with the Irish Tory press.[176]

The duke in particular had developed a personal animus towards Nicholls and offered a sympathetic ear to the continuing torrent of complaints and allegations made by the Irish Tory peers. Wellington was obviously convinced by Glengall's claim that William Stanley, in an unguarded conversation with him, had admitted that 'the commissioners had endeavoured to work the poor law through the medium of the priests, because they were aware that the feeling of the farmers was hostile to the act, and that the priests were most likely to calm those feelings and prevent disturbances'; he passed the letter on to Graham with the observation that he had always suspected Nicholls of 'playing a game of [this] sort'.[177] He also acted as a conduit for more salacious allegations which Glengall collected from a 'young man just discharged from the Irish poor law office', which included charges that the office had systematically falsified its official returns to cover a trail of partisan activity.[178] Wellington exploded into a furious denunciation of Nicholls as a man who had betrayed his personal confidence: 'Mr Nicholls promised me that he

174 NLW: HCP, C/1705, T. F. Lewis to G. C. Lewis, 8 May 1841.

175 Nicholls to Lewis, 5 Aug. 1841, *ibid.*, C/2105; UCL: CP, 23/264, Chadwick memo [1841].

176 *BNL*, 28 Sept. 1841.

177 SUL: WP, WP2/79/117, Glengall to Wellington, 6 Oct.; Wellington to Graham, 8 Oct. 1841, *ibid.*, WP2/79/127. For his close relationship with the Irish representative peers, see Gray, 'Wellington', pp. 203–26.

178 SUL: WP, WP2/81/20, 102, Glengall to Wellington, 2, 17 Nov. 1841. Glengall's informant claimed he had been dismissed 'to make room for an ignorant nephew of Dr McHale', and gave Archbishop Whately as a character witness – both of which might have aroused some suspicion of the source.

would carry into execution fairly the provisions of the bill, particularly those which conferred powers upon the Commissioners. Instead of performing his promise, he appears to have acted in concert with those in Ireland whose object is to destroy all the rights and influence of property.' He urged Glengall to press the matter on the new home secretary.[179]

In this context Nicholls' attempts to persuade the duke of his good faith, and the necessity of a clear government endorsement of the commission if the growing resistance was to be countered, fell on deaf ears.[180] The Irish under-secretary Edward Lucas, himself a member of the Monaghan board of guardians, was openly hostile towards the commissioner.[181] Graham was equally convinced of his guilt in failing – through ignorance or design – to counteract the 'pernicious influence' of the priesthood.[182] Graham's first interview with the Irish commissioner was decidedly frosty, and he soon demonstrated a new determination on the part of the home office to pursue reports and explanations on the affairs of Ireland.[183] With the official relationship now one more of confrontation than co-operation, G. C. Lewis felt it opportune to follow his father's guidance and distance himself from his fellow commissioner.[184]

Nicholls was, however, not without supporters within the new administration. The chief secretary, Lord Eliot – a liberal-Tory with close connections to Peel – rapidly developed a rapport with the embattled commissioner and signalled a willingness to defend him in public. In response to Graham's charges that Nicholls had appointed assistant commissioners (i.e. Phelan and Hancock) close to the 'Catholic party' and hence under the influence of O'Connell and MacHale, and that he had allowed the provisions of the act relating to valuation (a highly sensitive matter given its connection with the franchise) to be violated, Eliot offered rational explanations. Like his Whig predecessors, Eliot treated the part played by the Catholic clergy as inevitable: 'As long as the great body of farmers, shopkeepers and other ratepayers are Roman Catholics, they will as a general rule elect guardians of their own

179 Wellington to Graham, 11 Nov., Wellington to Glengall, 18 Nov. 1841, *ibid.*, WP2/81/77–8, 103.

180 Nicholls to Wellington, 5 Oct. 1841, *ibid.*, WP/2/79/101.

181 NLW: HCP, C/2860, Lewis to Graham [draft], Jan. 1843.

182 SUL: WP, WP2/79/139, Graham to Wellington, 10 Oct. 1841.

183 NA: PLCP, MH19/81, Manners Sutton to PLC, 25 Sept. 1841; Willink, 'Nicholls', p. lviii.

184 NLW: HCP, C/1719, C/1720, T. F. Lewis to G. C. Lewis, 31 Nov., 16 Dec. 1841; BL: GP, Add Ms 79,661, Lewis to Graham, 6 Dec. 1841. T. F. Lewis attributed the failure of the Irish measure to the 'blunders' of Nicholls and his associates Gulson and Hall, and (typically) attributed this to their social inferiority: NLW: HCP, C/1730, T. F. Lewis to G. C. Lewis, 1 Jan. 1843.

persuasion.' Nicholls, he was convinced, had the success of the Irish poor law sincerely at heart, and had endeavoured in highly inauspicious circumstances to uphold the neutrality and authority of the Dublin office. While not always completely judicious in his actions and often 'blunt [and] plain spoken' in opinion, he was free from the influence of political feelings – indeed, Eliot added, 'if he has any they are conservative'.[185]

Eliot drew on the favourable opinions of a number of influential pro-poor-law Irish Tories to counterbalance Glengall's (more representative) opinion. The third Earl of Clancarty, in Eliot's opinion 'one of the most sensible men in the country', and an active guardian at Ballinasloe, expressed the view that Nicholls was 'a sincere and enthusiastic well wisher to the success of the poor law', who had 'by the production of the poor law done more for this wretched country than was ever done before'. If unfortunate in some of his appointments, he could not be blamed in the circumstances for appointing those favourable to the government of the day; even so, the admittedly partisan Phelan had been selected not for his politics but for the excellence of his book on medical charities.[186] Graham took note of Clancarty's views, and was aware of similar ones held by other moderate Conservatives such as Devon and Frederick Shaw.[187] However, with another parliamentary session approaching in which the Irish landed lobby would press even more heavily on the poor law issue, this merely delayed rather than prevented the fall of Nicholls. The 1842 session would indeed see another series of hostile motions and demands for inquiries, with the arrangements and costs of building the new workhouses (especially those in Ulster) added to the previous sources of complaint.[188]

185 BL: GP, Add Ms 79,635, fols 4–5, 8–11, 40–2, 78–82, Graham to Eliot, 12 Oct., Eliot to Graham, 16 Oct., 1, 20 Nov. 1841.

186 Eliot to Graham, 24 Oct., Clancarty to Eliot, 23 Oct. 1841, *ibid.*, Add Ms 79,635, fols 26–8. Clancarty's general support for the poor law did not extend to the arrangements for paying workhouse chaplains on a scale determined by the numbers of inmates they attended, and his support for a blatantly sectarian motion on this head embarrassed the government in 1842: Graham to Eliot, 18 Dec. 1841, 16 Jan. 1842, *ibid.*, fols 119, 150; *Hansard*, 3, lx, 626–34 [17 Feb. 1842].

187 For Shaw's sympathetic defence of Nicholls' integrity, see *ibid.*, lxvii, 1387 [23 Mar. 1843].

188 Ibid., lx, 191–2 [6 Feb.], lxiii, 963–4 [30 May 1842]; *Return of Sums which the Irish Poor Law Commissioners borrowed from the Exchequer Loan Office for building Workhouses*, PP 1842 (141), xxxvi.343; *Minutes of Proceedings of Lowtherstown Board of Guardians, respecting the Purchase of the Site and Building of the Union Workhouse, and Correspondence with Poor Law Commissioners*, PP 1842 (376), xxxvi.257.

In late November 1841 Graham decided on a course of action. Nicholls would be retained *pro tempore*, but checked by the deployment to the Dublin office of assistant commissioner Col. Charles A'Court, and the 'culling' of Phelan and Hancock. Although Eliot demurred, the proposals had support from Somerset House, with T. F. Lewis advising his son that A'Court as a gentleman (he was the brother of Lord Heytesbury) would do well in Ireland, if given full plenipotentiary powers to counter Nicholls.[189] Faced with a *fait accompli*, Nicholls accepted the enforced reorganization, and announced his intention to return to London by summer 1842. While he was allowed to save face in public, this amounted to a demotion, and was felt as such.[190] On his return to London, which was delayed by a tour of inspection until November 1842, he found his junior colleague Lewis (who had developed a good relationship with Graham and was related to the viceroy de Grey) very much the dominant member of the commission, and that Shaw Lefevre's replacement, Sir Edmund Head, was closely associated with him. In March 1842 the commissioners had determined to delegate all powers (except that of making general rules) to Lewis alone.[191]

Piqued by his humiliating treatment by both the Home Office and his colleagues, Nicholls considered resigning from the commission, but opted to remain in office to defend the continued existence of the Irish poor law, a project he felt neither Somerset House nor Whitehall was fully committed to: 'Their hearts', he lamented 'were not in the cause.' His position was further weakened when Graham made it clear that he would not support him if there was a general inquiry into the operations of the Irish poor law, indicating that Nicholls was likely to be made the scapegoat for its multiple failings.[192] T. F. Lewis crowed that by early 1843 Nicholls had subsided into a non-entity, albeit a busy one in small matters.[193] Nicholls could not prevent the government's shelving of a medical charities bill prepared on the basis of Phelan's 1841 report – which would have placed the existing fever hospitals, dispensaries and infirmaries under poor-law administration and funding – nor the consequent sacking of Phelan in January 1843. The latter step was intended precisely to indicate, in Lewis's words, that 'the Irish sceptre has passed from

189 SUL: WP, WP2/81/119, Graham to Wellington, 18 Nov.; BL: GP, Add Ms 79,661, Graham to Lewis, 2 Dec.; Eliot to Graham, 20 Nov., *ibid.*, Add Ms 79,635, fols 78–82; NLW: HCP, C/1719, T. F. Lewis to G. C. Lewis, 31 Nov. 1841.

190 BL: GP, Add Ms 79,635, fols 89–91, Graham to Eliot, 11 Dec. 1841.

191 NA: PLCP, MH19/81, Chadwick to Dublin PL Board, 7 Mar.; Lewis to Grote, 13 Mar. 1842, in Lewis (ed.), *Letters*, pp. 119–20.

192 BL: PP, Add Ms 40,533, fols 136–7, Graham to Nicholls, 22 Aug. 1843; Willink, 'Nicholls', pp. lviii–lx.

193 NLW: HCP, C/1730, T. F. Lewis to G. C. Lewis, 1 Jan. 1843.

Nicholls.'[194] It also served to further alienate Irish Catholic opinion from the system at a crucial time; the *Dublin Review* denounced Phelan's removal as signalling the wholesale Protestantization of the poor law administration, and 'an open proclamation of the anti-popery crusade'.[195]

It appears likely that the troubles which beset the poor law in 1842–43 were augmented by what could only be seen as a withdrawal of official favour from the Irish law and its architect.[196] Nicholls certainly believed this to be so, and pleaded his case to the prime minister in September 1843. Graham was wrong, he asserted, to personalize the failings of the Irish law:

> Sir James Graham seems to consider that the discontent which has been manifested in Ireland in reference to the poor law, and the resistance which in a few instances has been made to its working, are mainly or altogether attributable to me, and that if I had acted judiciously, all would have gone on without dissatisfaction or resistance. I do not wish to shrink from any of the responsibility fairly attendant on the position in which I was placed, and I am far from supposing that I have always acted right, or that we have avoided errors or escaped omissions; but I confidently assert that whatever might have been done, however perfect our plans and faultless the execution, dissatisfaction wd still have been manifested, complaints would still have been made, and resistance of some sort would have been attempted.

Nicholls' appointment had been at Russell's insistence, and his tenure had, he reminded Peel, involved considerable self-sacrifice. Resistance to the law had reflected the natural propensity of the Irish to resent new taxation, rather than any personal antagonism towards himself, and matters had slipped out of hand after rather than before his recall.[197] Nicholls was not granted his request to undertake a further tour of the Irish workhouses in autumn 1843, but – probably through the intervention of Peel – he was allowed a public right of reply to the critical report on the state of the workhouses in 1844. He remained out of official favour until his appointment as permanent secretary to the new Poor-Law Board established by the succeeding Russell government in 1847.

194 G. C. Lewis to T. F. Lewis, 15 Jan. 1843, *ibid.*, C/453. For the intense politicization of the medical charities question, involving the division of the Irish medical profession along generally confessional lines, see Geary, *Medicine*, pp. 155–80. Phelan was restored to an Irish assistant commissionership under the succeeding Whig-liberal government in March 1847.

195 Anon., 'The grievances of Ireland', p. 327.

196 This was Chadwick's conclusion: see UCL: CP, 1486/92–108, Chadwick memo, n.d. [1851?].

197 BL: PP, Add Ms, 40,533, fols 132–5, Nicholls to Peel, 14 Sept. 1843.

Following Nicholls' recall it was initially resolved that the Irish poor law should be administered through the occasional residence of one of the three commissioners, and Lewis arrived to take charge of affairs in January 1843. Although Lewis initially feared the critical condition of the system would detain him there all year (a prospect he did not relish), in fact he returned after a few weeks.[198] In his place two experienced English assistant commissioners, Edward Gulson and Alfred Power, were in April delegated the local responsibility for conducting Irish business. This at least had the benefit of appearing politically balanced: Gulson (although a Quaker and former protégé of Althorp) was seen as a Conservative, and close to the under-secretary Lucas, and thus acceptable to many landowners, while Power was a utilitarian radical friendly with Chadwick. This weaker central authority was questioned by the lord lieutenant, who despite his criticisms of both Nicholls and Lewis, thought firm administration of the poor law necessary. At the same time he was insistent that the conciliation of the gentry and landowners was the key to the success of the poor law.[199] Despite the personal capabilities of these individuals, this arrangement was administratively unsatisfactory (if politically useful), and Gulson complained about his absence of formal powers under the act; other assistant commissioners questioned the abilities of the duumvirate to keep the ship afloat if another storm arose.[200] In November 1845 a quasi-independent authority in Ireland was restored with the appointment of Edward Twisleton as a fourth 'English' Poor Law Commissioner and the resident commissioner for Ireland. On the formation of a separate Irish Poor Law Commission in 1847 he became its first chief commissioner.

The 1843 amendment and the domestication of the poor law

Despite the removal of Nicholls, the government still anticipated another round of anti-poor-law campaigning in parliament in the 1843 session, now fuelled by the active resistance to rates in many unions and the general alarmism affecting the Protestant gentry. Graham was committed to upholding what he regarded as the principles of the poor law, while making some timely

198 NLW: HCP, C/453, G. C. Lewis to T. F. Lewis, 15 Jan. 1843.
199 Cambridge University Library [CUL], Graham Papers, 2/IR, de Grey to Graham, 15 Feb. 1843.
200 NLW: HCP, C/1415, Gulson to Lewis, 1 May 1843; NLW: NSP, E/173, Edward Senior to Nassau Senior, 11 Oct. 1843. Gulson was one of the original English assistant commissioners appointed in 1834; Power subsequently served as chief commissioner in Ireland, 1849–72.

concessions to landed opinion. Peel also became seriously alarmed at the social disorder associated with the anti-poor-law campaign, as well the ammunition it was supplying to the repeal movement.[201] It was thus resolved to amend the 1838 act, addressing the most outstanding grievances. This, Lewis agreed, would be the best way of seeing off an O'Connell- or landlord-driven committee of inquiry which would further inflame passions in Ireland and demand more radical and destructive changes. The details of the bill were agreed between Lewis, Graham and the Irish executive in early 1843.[202] The central plank was the exemption of small occupiers holding land valued at under four pounds per annum from the direct payment of poor rate. This was intended to kill several birds with one stone. The removal of nearly half the total number of ratepayers (a clear majority in many western unions) would streamline collection and resolve the dilemma of extracting often very small sums from those least able to pay, and most prone actively to resist payment. If landowners found their rate bills increased in the first instance by the transfer of responsibility of paying the rates of these '£4 tenants', they would have the consolation – the lord lieutenant pointed out – of seeing the ratepaying electorate greatly reduced by the consequent exclusion of these often turbulent and priest-ridden smallholders.[203] Proportions of '£4 tenants' ranged from 85 per cent of ratepayers in Westport and 75 per cent in Ballina, to 37 per cent in the eastern union of Rathdown. In the electoral division of Belmullet, only 272 ratepayers remained by 1846, after nearly 2,500 '£4 tenants' were disfranchised.[204]

However, while Lewis had proposed the total exemption of £4 tenancies from rating, he had been overruled by the administration's preference for transferring these charges from occupier to lessor. The ministers' intention was to deny any incentive to further subdivision (a consequence Lewis had discounted); the effect in practice was to provide a further stimulus to landowners to clear these smallholders whose rates they were now obliged

201 CUL, Graham Papers, 2/IR, Graham to de Grey, 1 Feb. 1843; BL: PP, Add Ms 40,448, Peel to Graham, 14 Apr. 1843.

202 NLW: HCP, C/453, C/2860, G. C. Lewis to T. F. Lewis, 15 Jan., G. C. Lewis to Graham, Jan. 1843; BL: GP, Add Ms 79,661, Graham to Lewis, 26 Jan. 1843.

203 CUL, Graham Papers, 2/IR, de Grey to Graham, 15 Feb. 1843. In larger urban areas the bar was set at £8 annual value – a proposal regarded by Liberals as highly partisan.

204 *Return of the Valuation of every Union in Ireland*, PP 1843 (235), li.363; *Return of Name of each Union and Electoral Division in Ireland; Number of Occupiers, etc*, PP 1846 (262), xxxvi.469, p. 3.

to pay.[205] The restoration of 'the principal management, and the superintendence and working of the law' to the 'men of property', and away from the 'priests, demagogues and other blackguards' Nicholls had allegedly associated with, was Wellington's avowed objective in supporting the proposal.[206] When he introduced the bill he also proposed that the number of *ex-officio* guardians be raised to half the total on each board; although this was dropped, probably with a view to curbing parliamentary and outdoors opposition to such a politically provocative step; it was also opposed by G. C. Lewis.[207]

Most of the remainder of the bill involved procedural amendments, the most important being the definition of residence in an electoral division as the occupation of a tenement for eighteen months or having slept within the division for twelve months. This was calculated to transfer a greater number of paupers from the 'electoral division' to the 'union' lists, with the aim of resolving a confused situation which had caused great acrimony within unions, and to 'gradually equalize' the pressure of rates between electoral divisions. Another clause set the maximum proportion of rate that a tenant could deduct from his rent as one half, a device to counter the deliberate undervaluing of property by boards of guardians with the intention of imposing a heavier share on the landowner.[208] Conservatives had complained that the original clauses had threatened the very principle of private property by allowing tenants to transfer the entire rate to the landowner and even to compel rent reductions under certain circumstances.[209] Other amendments now allowed for the provision of separate institutions for deaf, dumb and blind children, and the institution of separate fever hospitals and insane asylums for the poor. There was a small change made to promote assisted emigration from the union rate.[210] After some thought, it was decided not to

205 NLW: HCP, C/2860, Lewis to Graham [draft], Jan. 1843; the stimulus to 'consolidation' was identified by Smith O'Brien, in *Hansard*, 3, lxvii, 1360–1 [23 Mar. 1843]. The full implications of the '£4 clause' would be seen in the massive clearances of the later 1840s: see James S. Donnelly, *The Great Irish Potato Famine* (Stroud, 2001), p. 151.

206 SUL: WP, WP2/97/9, Wellington to Graham, 26 Jan. 1843.

207 This proposal was strongly opposed by the Catholic MP for Dundalk, Thomas Redington, *Hansard*, lxix, 1305–8 [9 June 1843]; NLW: HCP, C/2860, Lewis to Graham [draft], Jan. 1843.

208 This clause drew protests from the Fermoy board as likely to lead to a much larger share of the rate being imposed on the tenantry: SUL: WP, WP/2/102/9, Thomas Dennehy to Wellington, 16 May 1843.

209 *BNL*, 18, 22 Sept. 1840; Henry Houghton, *The Poor Rate Payer's Guide* (Dublin, 1840).

210 *Hansard*, 3, lxviii, 1318–24 [5 May 1843]; 6th & 7th Vic. c. 92; *Tenth Report* (1844), pp. 33–4.

further antagonize O'Connellite opinion by inserting vagrancy clauses.[211] The bill was introduced after the Easter recess and passed through both houses relatively smoothly, although critics of the poor law took advantage of the debates to restate their arguments.[212]

Although the ministry had introduced the amendment bill with the intention of pre-empting a formal parliamentary inquiry, which would 'raise false hopes and fears', it was not able to prevent individuals again moving for extensive returns or forcing debates on the subject.[213] Typically, the 1843 assault came from two different directions, and although there was some overlap between the positions, with both exploiting the manifest discontent over the operation of the measure in Ireland, they were fundamentally at odds with each other as well as with the commission and the government. Smith O'Brien again offered a reformist and 'popular' critique, claiming the country was strongly for the principle of a poor law, if not for that currently in force. The regulatory harshness and financial incompetence of the commission had, he maintained, played a role in promoting unpopularity. His case was for an expansion of the system – to allow outdoor relief for the aged, sick and impotent poor, and to partner it with ameliorative measures of emigration or employment. The causes of failure, he concluded, 'lay upon the surface and . . . an effective remedy might be speedily applied'. Sharman Crawford, now the Chartist-sponsored MP for Rochdale, endorsed these core points.[214]

In contrast, Clanricarde's motion, which was backed by figures such as Glengall, Roden, Mountcashell and Whately, who had rejected the 1838 bill *in toto* and now declared their prognostications fully vindicated, was fundamentally hostile. While he apparently acknowledged that the system could not now practicably be abolished, Clanricarde implied that an inquiry would lead to radical changes to reduce its footprint as far as possible. Whately's claim that mendicancy had increased since 1838 because the poor-rate had squeezed out charitable donations and damaged the moral values of the poor, without providing any commensurate benefits, also pointed towards the need to withdraw state provision. It was clear that this lobby placed no faith in the government's amendment bill, and (as their critics feared) that only complete repeal would satisfy them.[215] However, faced with Wellington's waverings and

211 CUL, Graham Papers, 2/IR, Graham to de Grey, 27 Mar. 1843.

212 *Hansard*, 3, lxviii, 1324–36, 1340 [5 May 1843: French, Sharman Crawford, Smith O'Brien].

213 SUL: WP, WP2/97/74, WP2/107/52–3, Graham to Wellington, 6 Feb., 18 July 1843.

214 *Hansard*, 3, lxvii, 1347–69, 1387–91 [23 Mar. 1843].

215 *Hansard*, 3, lxviii, 1348–69, 1385–6 [8 May], lxxi, 918–26 [18 Aug. 1843].

strong feelings in the Lords, and the stirring up of fresh allegations of administrative abuses in the Edenderry union, Graham opted to permit an inquiry in the 1844 session if this were pressed for by the Irish peers.[216]

Despite this concession, most of the heat appears to have dissipated from the Irish poor-law controversies by 1844–45. The 1843 amendment act had the desired effect of removing much of the direct confrontation between rate-collectors and smallholders, while also reducing the virulence of elections by roughly halving the electorate (although with still over half a million electors the boards remained the most representative political bodies in the country). O'Connellite agitation had moderated, while Conservatives were increasingly drawn away to other, more emotive, controversies over agricultural protection and the grant to the seminary at Maynooth. The dissentient Whig peers Monteagle and Clanricarde, and the MPs Denham Norreys and Fitzstephen French, attempted to reopen parliamentary controversy in 1844, but had so limited an effect that Graham felt confident enough (with Russell's support) to withdraw his earlier promise of a general committee of inquiry.[217] What the ministry did permit was more tightly controlled committees to consider the report into the construction and financial arrangements of the Irish workhouses, prepared by their nominee James Pennethorne.[218] Pennethorne was critical of the siting and condition of a number of Irish workhouses, but his conclusions were counterbalanced by the inclusion in the published return of rebuttals by Nicholls and Lewis. Despite the best efforts of the commission's strongest critics, discussion of his report petered out inconclusively.[219]

When a select committee of the Lords finally met to review the workings of the act, in February–May 1846, it proved something of an anti-climax.

216 SUL: WP, WP2/109/66, 81–2, Wellington to Graham, 19 Aug., Graham to Wellington, 22 Aug. 1843; *Hansard*, 3, lxx, 1274–80 [20 July 1843: Clanricarde]. The Edenderry guardians had successfully sued against the commission's order that they pay for repairs to the workhouse which they claimed resulted from arbitrary decisions by the commission: see *Memorial and Papers from Board of Guardians of Edenderry Union in Ireland*, PP 1843 (382), xlvi.607.

217 *Hansard*, 3, lxxii, 272 [6 Feb. 1844], lxxiii, 325–6, 531–2, 1525–30 [27 Feb., 4, 25 Mar. 1844], lxxiii, 203–5, 510–16 [23, 30 Apr. 1844], lxxiv, 1181–1201 [14 May 1844].

218 *Ibid.*, lxxv, 222–3, 985–6 [3, 17 June 1844], lxxvi, 1–15 [27 June 1844].

219 A second inquiry in 1845 reported that about £46,000 excess expenditure had been incurred due to faulty contractors, and this sum was quietly remitted by the Treasury to the boards concerned: *Report of the Commissioner appointed to inquire into the Execution of the Contracts for certain Union Workhouses in Ireland*, PP 1845 (170), xxvi.399.

Presided over by the sympathetic Clancarty, it reported favourably towards the poor-law administration and recommended only minor amendments. If, its report observed, the poor law 'had failed of fulfilling the expectations that some too sanguine entertained of its success', it could not be said 'that it has failed of producing some important and very encouraging results that justify the wisdom of the legislature in its enactment, and should commend it, in its main principles, to public confidence'.[220]

Under the more amenable Gulson and the politically-savvy Lewis, the administration had been less confrontational than under Nicholls. Their correspondence was primarily procedural rather than crisis-driven in nature, although Gulson admitted he had felt obliged to intervene personally to prevent the free access of whisky and prostitutes to the Kilkenny workhouse in 1843.[221] A reduction in the number of assistant commissioners in Ireland inevitably reduced the oversight of the Dublin board over union boards, although this did not entirely eliminate complaints about centralized direction. The commissioners' one significant attempt to reassert their authority over the guardians – by attempting to prosecute the Limerick board for asserting the right (removed by the commissioners in 1843) to suspend their clerk – ended with an embarrassing climbdown.[222] After the constant crises of late 1842 to mid-1843, the commissioners reported that affairs had 'proceeded satisfactorily, upon the whole', in the 1844–45 season. This was generally true, although there were exceptions, requiring some continued military aid in rate collection and legal action to oblige recalcitrant boards to implement the act, in a number of Connacht unions.[223] By autumn 1843 assistant commissioner Edward Senior commented that 'we are now in smoother water on poor law matters', and in summer 1844 even the sceptical brother had become persuaded after a visit to Edward's district in Ulster that in certain parts of Ireland the poor law was working well.[224]

In the half-year ending 29 September 1844, 67,487 paupers had been relieved in the 103 functioning workhouses, with an average stay of ninety-two days, and an average weekly maintenance cost of one shilling and

220 *Report of the Select Committee of House of Lords, on Poor Laws . . . in Ireland*, PP 1846 (694), xi.1, p. iii.

221 NLW: HCP, C/1422, Gulson to Lewis, 13 Nov. 1843.

222 CUL, Graham Papers, 6/IR, Graham to Eliot, 20 Oct. 1843; O'Brien, 'A question of attitude', pp. 163–4.

223 *Eleventh Report* (1845), p. 21.

224 NLW: NSP, E/173, Edward Senior to Nassau Senior, 11 Oct. 1843; NLW: HCP, C/2375, Nassau Senior to Lewis, 1 Aug. [1844]. Edward Senior had been transferred to the north of Ireland in late 1841 despite Nicholls' objections: *ibid.*, C/2109, Nicholls to Lewis, 1 Nov. 1841.

ninepence per head.[225] On 1 January 1845, there were 39,175 inmates in 113 workhouses, just under a quarter of them 'able-bodied'. This amounted to well under half the capacity of the new system, and Nicholls had anticipated only a gradual and limited increase in numbers. The total relief expenditure for the preceding calendar year had been just under £270,000.[226] This rose slightly to £316,000 in 1845, amounting to an average rate of sixpence in the pound (or 2.5 per cent); with the charges so low, one assistant commissioner was certain that alarm at the 'great experiment' was sliding into acquiescence.[227]

The Malthusian fears of the poor law's opponents had been proved unfounded. But the limited resort to the workhouse suggested its success was partial at best. The evident reluctance of many of the Irish poor to seek refuge in the workhouse except *in extremis* may have offered some satisfaction to Nicholls and relief to Irish ratepayers, but for some British observers, this merely further demonstrated the 'otherness' of Ireland and undermined faith in the ability of 'British' social institutions to civilize it. The travel writer James Johnson, describing an Irish tour in 1844, mocked Irish paupers for their continued 'mania for begging' and their '*bastillo-phobia*' in resisting the aid proffered by the workhouse. He expressed despair at the cultural resistance of the Irish generally to the logic of the poor law.[228] Advocates of a more 'advanced' measure continued to maintain that only something closer to the 'old' English model could wean the Irish from such habits. The '*Times* Commissioner' into the condition of Ireland, T. C. Foster, argued that to render the law both popular and effective, a right to relief and discretionary outdoor relief must be allowed, and that this in turn (accompanied by a law of settlement) would facilitate the strict vagrancy measure necessary to tackle the continuing curse of importunate beggary.[229]

The Irish poor law had survived its first major crisis and was now in a period of lull before the onset of the second, and much more serious, challenge of the Great Famine. If it had fallen far short in practice of the high expectations of its advocates, and was still beset by many administrative problems intrinsic to the rushed and centralized mode of its introduction,

225 *Eleventh Report* (1845), p. 27.

226 Nicholls, *Irish Poor Law*, pp. 299–302. Numbers were still just under 51,000 on 28 March 1846, the eve of the onset of famine conditions: *ibid.*, p. 303.

227 [Alfred Power], *The Irish Poor Law: Past, Present and Future* (London, 1849), pp. 1–2.

228 James Johnson, *A Tour in Ireland: with Meditations and Reflections* (London, 1844), cited in *Scotsman*, 24 July 1844.

229 Thomas Campbell Foster, *Letters on the Condition of the People of Ireland* (London, 1846), pp. 552–60.

and the limitations of its provisions, it had neither collapsed nor been abandoned by its political masters, nor indeed by all strands of Irish society. Both Nicholls and his associates and the political rights of half the original ratepayer-electors had been sacrificed to assuage the revolts of 1842–43, with some success. If the reality was flawed in many ways, it is reductive to dismiss the poor law as a simple failure, of an institution wholly unsuited to the Irish environment.

10

Conclusion: the Irish poor law as idea and reality

The legislative initiatives of 1837–38 and the administrative processes that followed saw the poor law translated from the realm of ideas to that of reality. The 'idea of a poor law for Ireland', initially articulated as a moral imperative by Bishops Woodward and Doyle, enthusiastically developed by Thaddeus O'Malley, and radically envisioned by John Revans as the prime remedy for the 'evils of Ireland', bore only a very limited resemblance to the physical and bureaucratic superstructures raised by George Nicholls and George Wilkinson between 1838 and 1845. Many Irish and British advocates of a poor law inevitably felt acute disillusionment with the punitive and unpopular workhouse regime, and the absence of elements they had strongly advocated in print and during the parliamentary debates, including a statutory right to relief, outdoor relief to at least the elderly and incapable, reproductive employment for paupers, and the addition of 'auxiliary measures' (such as waste-land reclamation, railway construction and assisted emigration) to ease the burden of poverty and to provide alternative assistance. As late as 1846 there remained, however, considerable optimism on the part of many that a Whig government would 'complete the task' begun in 1838 of introducing the 'Elizabethan' poor law to Ireland.[1]

In evidence given before the 1846 inquiry into the operations of the Irish poor law, Sharman Crawford, Smith O'Brien and Denis Phelan continued to make the case for permitting outdoor relief, in opposition to G. C. Lewis and the poor-law administrators. Thaddeus O'Malley likewise took the 1838 act as a starting point, which now required vigorous amendment to bring it into line with 'the poor man's great charter' of the Elizabethan poor law of England. His preferences remained for an equitable national rate to replace an electoral district rating which he argued promoted class conflict and placed

1 e.g. Douglas, *Life and Property in Ireland assured*, p. 37; G. P. Scrope, *Letters to the Right Hon. Lord John Russell, on the Expediency of enlarging the Irish Poor Law* (London, 1846).

insupportable burdens on the poorest areas; for giving a right to relief 'to every poor person in the country'; and for 'workhouse out-door labour', putting the able-bodied to work on workhouse farms and the reclamation of waste-lands for their future settlement.[2] Even as his evidence was being presented in 1846, however, a crisis was building that would transform the context in which these debates were conducted.

In the half-decade following the first potato harvest failure of autumn 1845, the newly-implemented and already unpopular workhouse system was subjected to the rigorous test of famine on a scale not witnessed in Ireland for over a century. The degree to which it was found wanting is notorious. Both the number of workhouse inmates and the poor-rates levied to support them had reached saturation point in many unions by late 1846, and the system was already beginning to collapse (as O'Malley had predicted) in some heavily indebted western districts. In spring 1847 the government made the fateful decision to extend the poor law's provisions and transfer responsibility for relief to the system once the 'extraordinary' circumstances of the 1846–47 season were deemed to have passed. The extension bill was again vigorously opposed by Archbishop Whately and Nassau Senior, but passed by a Whig-liberal government with strong support from British public opinion and from the anti-landlord lobby in Ireland.[3] A good grain harvest, falling prices and the temporary disappearance of the potato blight in summer 1847 created the conditions in which direct rationing of the destitute through soup kitchens, implemented in late spring, could be wound up and responsibility transferred to the unions, with only very modest transitional assistance from state and charitable funds. The catastrophic consequences of this myopic policy, in terms of acute human suffering and extensive excess mortality, are widely acknowledged.[4] Not surprisingly, the horrendous failure of the extended poor law in the later years of the Great Famine accentuated the already hostile attitudes towards the system held by many contemporaries, and has shaped the acutely negative impression of the institution more generally in the historical literature.

2 *Report of the Select Committee of House of Lords, on Poor Laws ... Ireland*, pp. xxii–xxiv, 823–37.

3 For the opposition, see [Senior], 'Proposals for extending the Irish poor law', pp. 267–314, Richard Whately, *Substance of a Speech delivered in the House of Lords, on Friday, the 16th of March, 1847, on the Motion for a Committee on Irish Poor Laws* (London, 1847); for British public support, see Donnelly, 'Irish property must pay for Irish poverty', pp. 60–76.

4 For the failure of the poor law in 1847–50, see Kinealy, *This Great Calamity*, pp. 175–264, Gray, *Famine*, pp. 284–327.

This disastrous policy of almost total reliance on the poor law for famine relief ran counter to Nicholls' original contention that the 1838 system was not designed for and could not cope with a major disaster. The 1847 extension act provided both the legal responsibility of the boards to relieve all applicants, and the facility to offer relief outside the workhouse, that Irish supporters had demanded and which Russell and Morpeth had hinted at in 1836–38. However, this belated extension did nothing to augment the now grossly overloaded local taxation base or to deliver the auxiliary measures of employment and emigration the government had promised, and it came in the midst of a social implosion, mass evictions of defaulting smallholders and cottiers, and appalling levels of excess mortality due to starvation and famine-related disease. The concession of outdoor relief was further countered by harsh restrictions placed upon recipients, and the introduction of the 'Gregory clause' denying relief to families occupying more than a quarter-acre of land, which had been tacked on to the extension act to placate landed opposition in parliament.[5]

The unease with which many (although not all) Irish poor officials regarded the impossible responsibilities thrust upon them from late 1847 was reflected in the chief commissioner Edward Twisleton's abrupt resignation in March 1849, in protest at continued Treasury interference with the Irish Poor Law Commission's business, and the restriction of any further relief transfers to an inadequate 'rate-in-aid' imposed on the less impoverished eastern and northern Irish unions.[6] Although some semblance of stability was to be restored during the long reign of Twisleton's successor as chief commissioner, the more sanguine Alfred Power, the legacy of the Famine was devastating for the poor law.[7] Henceforth the institution, and in particular the workhouses which had frequently degenerated into charnel-houses in the later 1840s,

5 The act permitted guardians to give outdoor relief to three categories of paupers – the permanently disabled, those disabled by temporary sickness, and widows with two or more legitimate children; it also empowered the commissioners to permit outdoor relief (in food only) to other classes if the workhouse was full or if contagious disease prevailed: Alfred Power, *A Paper on Out-door Relief in Ireland* (London, 1875), p. 9.

6 Gray, *Famine*, pp. 314–16. The case that the Irish poor law must be saved by urgent reforms and Treasury assistance was also made by the recently resigned assistant commissioner John Ball, in *What is to be done for Ireland?* (2nd edn, London, 1849), p. 26.

7 Power, a close associate of Edwin Chadwick, was chief commissioner 1849–72 and then vice-president of the Irish local government board, 1872–80. For his preoccupation with reducing the numbers on outdoor relief and restoring the workhouse test as quickly as possible, see [Power], *Irish Poor Law*, pp. 42–59.

would be regarded with particular bitterness and dread by the Irish poor. Nationalist demagogues identified the poor law as the very engine of British genocide against the Irish people.

What may appear rather surprising in this context is the extent to which benign 'ideas' of an Irish poor law survived the disappointments of implementation and the trauma of the Famine, and even developed in reaction to these shocks. Indeed, the very disasters of the 1840s may, for some, have reinforced a vision of a purified or augmented poor law as a vital component in the regeneration of Ireland and the recasting of social relationships within it. Much of the Catholic clergy supported the 1847 extension act (albeit simultaneously demanding auxiliary measures and rejecting both the 'Gregory clause' and the increase in the proportion of *ex-officio* guardians to up to half each board's total), as it introduced the long-demanded elements of a statutory right, outdoor relief and a separate Irish commission.[8] The most extreme clerical voice in support of the poor law was that of Fr John O'Sullivan of Kenmare, who regarded its extension as a necessary and just act of retribution against an oppressive and largely absentee landed class. The poor law was, he wrote in O'Malleyite cadences at the height of the Famine, 'the only poor man's law that was ever passed for Ireland', which 'while it might press hard upon us, it must needs be utter ruin and destruction in the end to that heartless class who countenanced, and fostered, and encouraged the unnatural state of things in which we hitherto moved'.[9]

Such comments, shorn of their usual contextualizing demands for more immediate aid from the Treasury, were exploited by those with a rather different agenda. Charles Trevelyan (the recipient of many of O'Sullivan's letters) pronounced in his apologia, *The Irish Crisis*:

> For the first time in the history of Ireland the poor man has become sensibly alive to the idea that the law is his friend, and the exhortation of the parish priest of Dingle to his flock in September 1847 indicates an epoch in the progress of society in Ireland . . . 'Now for the first time, the poor man has an agent to collect *his* rent. That agent is the poor-rate collector, and he should be supported by the poor.'[10]

This theme of the poor law as the embodiment of a basic welfare entitlement for the poor continued to be widespread. Where Trevelyan and his associates in the government differed from the clergy was in insisting that heavy poor-rates must also be employed *unaided* as a coercive stick to force Irish

8 Gray, *Famine*, pp. 276–7.

9 NA: TP, T64/366A, O'Sullivan to Twisleton, 10 Dec. 1848, O'Sullivan to Trevelyan, 5 Feb. 1849.

10 C. E. Trevelyan, *The Irish Crisis* (London, 1848), pp. 162–3.

landowners into developmental expenditure, and to facilitate the bankruptcy and replacement of those who could not or would not comply with their developmental vision.

This instrumentalization of the system as an agent of forced modernization and behavioural transformation was rooted in a quite different 'idea' of an Irish poor law dating from the 1830s, albeit radicalized in the context of the apocalyptic conditions of 1846–50. Both Nicholls and G. C. Lewis had advocated the 1838 measure as a 'civilizing' force, calculated to lever Ireland and its people out of social backwardness by promoting the anglicization of the country's socio-economic structures. While neither man was comfortable with the more radical appropriation of this principle in the later 1840s, continuity was provided by the prominence of what have elsewhere been termed 'moralist liberals' in the debates of both periods. The third Earl Grey, who as Lord Howick had been one of the most forceful ministerial antagonists of Senior and Whately in 1836–38, took a particularly strident 'moralist' position on the Irish poor law from 1847.[11] For Grey, a punitive and unassisted poor law would both coerce the landed classes into development expenditure, and impose proletarianization and labour discipline on the labouring poor.[12] He lectured the lord lieutenant:

> The truth is if the Irish had industry and even the most ordinary knowledge of the arts of labour there would be no occasion for them emigrating. Ireland would afford them an ample field of employment. It is because they are rude, ignorant and turbulent savages that work cannot be found for them at home[.][13]

Only strict administration of the poor law could remedy these failings and enforce self-help, while simultaneously upholding the right of the poor to a minimum subsistence from the land. Grey's ideological allies Charles Wood and Charles Trevelyan at the Treasury, who were able to elicit strong support from influential sectors of the British public, agreed that the Famine was a providentially-ordained opportunity, and that the extended poor law, which was based on a 'principle of nature' was enacting a 'wonderful social revolution' in Ireland.[14]

While this 'moralist' construction of the Irish poor law was extremely powerful during the Famine, it was never hegemonic. Many of the Catholic clergy continued to follow the tradition of Doyle and O'Malley in regarding

11 See Gray, *Famine*, pp. 24–6, 54.

12 DUL: GP, 144/1, Earl Grey, 'Remarks upon poor law, emigration and Ireland', 18 Dec. 1848.

13 Grey to Clarendon, 4 Dec. 1847, *ibid.*, 81/3.

14 Gray, *Famine*, p. 319.

the idea of a poor law positively, while denouncing the failings of the existing legislation and the mode of administration as niggardly, oppressive and inhumane. Fr James Maher of Carlow, the inheritor of Doyle's mantle as a liberal-Catholic polemicist, was always amongst the most outspoken. A tireless relief worker during the Famine, he had repeatedly condemned the actual operation of the poor law as a betrayal of the absolute and 'divine' right of the poor to life.[15] At the same time, he vigorously denounced Whately for his public attempts to prevent the extension of outdoor relief in 1847, and subsequently held the archbishop responsible, through his 'teaching and great influence with the owners of the soil', for rendering it a dead-letter in practice.[16]

In 1862–63, in the context of a further depression in the Irish agricultural economy, Maher returned to the subject, damning both the landlord-dominated Carlow board of guardians and the Dublin commissioners for administering the act in a penny-pinching, vicious and 'exterminating' manner, and demanded higher rates and the allowance of outdoor relief as of right. At the root of the 'monster grievance' of current poor-law practice was the policy of pauperizing the occasionally destitute and 'deserving' poor through the workhouse test (and the waste of money on the dissolute and immoral minority of idle vagrants, or inmates corrupted by extended exposure to them). In short, for Maher the law needed urgent and radical reform to ensure that its original intention to provide legal rights to the honest and labouring poor was restored.[17]

As Anna Clark has documented, the post-Famine period saw a more general effort by the Catholic church to exert control over poor-relief policy, partly as a challenge to the power of government and local Protestant elites, and partly as a response to challenges to oppressive and 'immoral' treatment of workhouse inmates posed by the direct action of inmates themselves and by Catholic social reformers. Clark employs the public furore sparked by the South Dublin Union riots and petitions of 1860–61 to dramatize gendered, sectarian and nationalist resistance to the poor-law regime in a colonial context, but other themes are also apparent from her account. Both Catholic clergy and reformers and the 'wild workhouse girls' themselves collaborated (albeit with different motivations) in employing a language of the 'rights' of the poor to fair and humane relief under the law in their attack on the

15 'The sufferings of the Irish poor, Feb. 8th, 1848', in Moran (ed.), *James Maher*, pp. 14–34. Maher was also a leading theological controversialist, and uncle of Archbishop Paul Cullen.

16 'On the condition of the Irish poor, April 8th, 1847', 'To the Protestant archbishop of Dublin, on the Irish poor, October 23rd, 1862', in *ibid*., pp. 1–13, 303–9.

17 'The evils of the poor-law system, April 23rd, 1862', 'On the poor-laws, July 9, 1863', in *ibid*., pp. 289–94, 309–14.

guardians and Poor Law Commission. Not only did this attract significant public support, it provoked a public inquiry in 1861, and drew some public recognition from the Irish administration, which felt obliged to restore a workhouse chaplain previously dismissed by the South Dublin guardians for endorsing the inmates' charges.[18]

The poor-law authorities were fully conscious of this renewed post-Famine challenge to their authority. In 1863 chief commissioner Power informed Chadwick that he was wrong to think the Irish Catholic clergy opposed the poor law; indeed, the contrary was true of the lower clergy, who sought (against Power's policy) to extend outdoor relief as far as possible. Archbishop Cullen, however, being suspicious of all state institutions outside direct clerical control, was in his opinion thoroughly hostile to all poor laws and not just the current forms of administration.[19] This distinction observed by Power reflected an internal debate within the Catholic church over the relative merits of exclusively Catholic social provision, and of state provision rendered acceptable to Catholics, that would continue for the remaining decades of the century and beyond.[20] Significantly, however, alongside the development of the burgeoning Catholic welfare system of later nineteenth-century Ireland, the poor law itself became subject to a gradual 'Catholicization', not least through the increasing number of workhouse infirmaries staffed by nursing nuns from the 1860s.[21]

Nor was the case made for a reformed and humanized poor law entirely a Catholic concern. Isaac Butt, at this time a 'Liberal-Conservative' MP still uncommitted to home rule, took up the cause of the Dublin paupers and the dismissed chaplain in the House of Commons in 1860–61. A more sustained case was made by the political economist and statistician William Neilson Hancock, son of the former assistant commissioner W. J. Hancock, in a series of lectures and pamphlets. His central case, couched in liberal-unionist terms, was that the harsher Irish law must be brought into line with the more liberal and flexible English poor law, and that humane alternatives be found for the workhouse test for all but able-bodied men. The social fears and Malthusian doctrines prevalent in 1838 had now either been exploded, or rendered

18 Clark, 'Wild workhouse girls', pp. 389–410. Clark concludes that 'for all its many faults, the poor law system was accountable to the commissioners and to the court of public opinion, so that the horrors of the workhouse would be periodically exposed, even if few improvements transpired'.

19 UCL: CP, 1605/40–5, Power to Chadwick, 3 Oct. 1863.

20 For Cullen's 'Ultramontane' preoccupation with the Protestantizing tendencies of the Irish poor law, see Desmond Bowen, *Paul Cardinal Cullen and the Shaping of Modern Irish Catholicism* (Dublin, 1983), pp. 160–1.

21 Luddy, *Women*, pp. 49–51.

redundant by the social improvements that had followed from the Famine; in Hancock's opinion no legitimate obstacle now existed to prevent the creation of a 'real' poor law in Ireland.[22] This opinion was endorsed by some other members of Ireland's liberal intellectual intelligentsia, but remained highly contentious.[23]

The poor law made only limited steps towards realizing the more expansive vision of its advocates in the post-famine decades. Both Power and the boards of guardians were determined to ratchet down the levels of outdoor relief to a bare minimum from 1850. The 1847 act had rendered boards, and especially the key posts of chair and vice-chair, more securely in the hands of the landed classes by increasing the ratio of *ex-officio* to elected members, but this did not prevent continuing episodes of political agitation in board elections.[24] At the same time, however, the poor law expanded its sphere of welfare operations by taking control of the Irish dispensary system under the 1851 medical charities act, thereby implementing Denis Phelan's recommendations of a decade earlier. This created a new form of (non-pauperizing) outdoor relief under the poor law system, giving the poor access to more uniform and securely-funded medical relief. The expansion of medical provision was rapidly implemented and widely used.[25] Further legislation in 1862 allowed for admission of the 'outdoor' poor into workhouse infirmaries, and the boarding-out of orphan children under eight years old (as advocated by Hancock and others). Although the commissioners were reluctant to concede the demands of its critics for a regime less dependent on the workhouse test, Virginia Crossman observes that by this point the system was moving well

22 W. Neilson Hancock, 'The workhouse as a mode of relief for widows and orphans', *Journal of the Dublin Statistical Society*, 1 (1855), pp. 84–91; 'On the importance of substituting the family system of rearing orphan children for the system now pursued in our workhouses', *ibid.*, 2 (1859), pp. 317–31; 'Difference between English and Irish poor law, as to the treatment of women and unemployed workmen', *ibid.*, 3 (1862), pp. 217–35; *The Difference between the English and Irish Poor Law, as to the Treatment of Women and Unemployed Workmen* (Dublin, 1862).

23 For examples of support and opposition to Hancock within the Dublin learned societies, see, respectively, J. K. Ingram, 'A comparison between the English and Irish Poor Laws with respect to the conditions of relief', *Journal of the Statistical and Social Inquiry Society of Ireland*, 4 (1864), pp. 43–61; James Houghton, 'Observations upon a paper on poor relief, by Dr. Dowling of Tipperary', *Journal of the Dublin Statistical Society*, 3 (1862), pp. 156–62.

24 UCL: CP, 1605/35–6, 37–9, 110–11, Power to Chadwick, 28 Mar. 1859, 14 Mar. 1860, 22 Jun. 1877.

25 Crossman, *Poor Law in Ireland*, pp. 38–9.

beyond its residualist origins. Further reforms relating to the treatment of children, public hygiene and sanitation, and the provision of labourers' cottages, transferred increasing welfare responsibilities to the guardians and the Irish Poor Law Commission (after 1872 reorganized as the Local Government Board) in the ensuing decades.[26] Despite his best efforts, Power was incapable of preventing outdoor relief numbers from creeping up as unions proved increasingly willing to allow this; by 1875 a daily average of 30,319 persons were relieved outdoors, compared to 47,113 within the workhouses.[27]

This increase in the sphere of social responsibility, when combined with the revived mass agrarian and nationalist mobilizations of the 1870s–80s, created the context for the acute politicization of the boards of guardians depicted by William Feingold as 'the revolt of the tenantry'. The consequences of this shift from predominantly landed to nationalist-farmer control of boards in large swathes of the country have more recently been analysed by Crossman: the numbers allowed outdoor relief increased exponentially by the 1890s, and there was a marked increase in antagonism between these 'popular' boards and the Dublin authorities still intent on retaining the regime of 'less eligibility'.[28] What these accounts tend to underplay, however, is the extent to which that political revolt against landed control had been prefigured in the contested poor-law union politics of the pre-Famine period, when a combination of O'Connellite mobilization and a more conducive electoral regime (albeit tightened in 1843 and 1847) gave rise to significant local political excitement associated with annual poor-law elections. It also appears evident that the more liberal attitude towards allowing non-pauperizing relief to the 'respectable' poor (coupled with a continuing antagonism towards those deemed morally 'undeserving' demonstrated by 'popular' boards from the 1870s), drew on long-established demotic ideas of what an Irish poor law could and should do that predated the legislation of 1838 and which were regularly aired in the subsequent decades. The 1880s–90s saw in practice, over much of Ireland and in the face of determined resistance on the part of officials, the operation of a poor law in many ways closer to the vision of Doyle and O'Malley than to that of Nicholls. This did not save the poor law from denunciation in the revolutionary Dáil's 1919 'Democratic Programme' as an 'odious, degrading and foreign . . . system' that required replacement by 'a sympathetic native scheme' of care for the aged and infirm, nor prevent its abolition in the Irish Free State in 1923.[29] Nevertheless, this may represent

26 *Ibid.*, pp. 40–5.
27 Power, *Paper on Out-door Relief*, pp. 13–14.
28 Feingold, *Revolt of the Tenantry*; Crossman, *Politics, Pauperism and Power*.
29 *Dáil Éireann Debates*, i (21 Jan. 1919).

less a radical break with the past in reality than in appearance, albeit accelerated in the context of a more general critique of poor-law practice widespread in the early twentieth century.

The argument of this book is that the Irish poor law emerged from a messy combination of complementary and contradictory impulses. While it had an extensive hinterland in terms of pre-existing charitable institutions and debates on the disciplining of vagrancy and the relief of the 'deserving' poor, the poor law for Ireland emerged from the specific social, political and ideological conditions of the later 1820s and 1830s. The persistent voice of British labour-protectionism cannot be discounted, but the chief stimulus to legislation appears to have been the moral and social campaign for an equitable state provision of relief for the destitute poor led by prominent liberal-Catholic and 'popular' Whig-liberal figures, but shared by a wider coalition of supporters in Ireland and Britain. This in turn reflected a sociological turn in interpretations of the essential nature of the 'Irish problem' on the part of many Irish and British observers from the 1820s, along with a developing conception of the state as a potentially neutral and meliorist agency in Ireland. This changing perspective infiltrated popular Catholic politics in Ireland (somewhat to the dismay of Daniel O'Connell himself), and interacted with the 'justice to Ireland' political strategy developed by the Foxite Whigs in government from 1835 to produce a practical political initiative in 1837–38. The realities of parliamentary and cabinet politics combined with the self-confident model-building of Benthamite administrators (chiefly Nicholls and Chadwick), and the caution of some ministers, to limit the extent of the 1838 act and disappoint many of its advocates. There was, however, a widespread belief, promoted by both the comments of Russell and Morpeth in the Commons, and the popularity of John Revans' quasi-official intervention in print, that the 1838 measure was not necessarily a 'final' step and that further concessions could be extracted either legislatively or administratively.

The Whig ministers around Russell clearly perceived the introduction of a poor law to Ireland as comprising part of a broader 'justice to Ireland' policy, aimed at redressing the historic injustices in Irish society produced by previous British 'misgovernment'. In doing so they sought to blend the Foxite tradition of advancing popular rights with an economically heterodox understanding of Ireland's social disjunctures, and the model of meliorist state interventionism developed by Bentham's disciples. This, rather than any 'conservative' concern for cost or precedent, is what lay behind their rejection of Richard Whately's alternative report in 1836. At its core, Whately's proposal offered assistance to Irish landlords, chiefly through aiding the removal of their 'surplus' estate populations, while denying any direct welfare assistance to any but the most 'incapable' categories of poor. Russell's aim, however circumscribed by adverse political realities, was to create a statutory – if minimal – right of poor relief for the destitute poor. The associated Irish railways initiative suggests that this did not necessarily mean the neglect of developmental policies aimed at alleviating poverty alongside relieving destitution, although the failure of the government to deliver this 'auxiliary' before 1841 left the workhouse system dangerously exposed, just as the later collapse of the 'comprehensive measures' of 1847 (including waste-land reclamation and assisted emigration) left the extended poor law in an impossible position.

If there was a distinctly colonial dimension to the introduction of the Irish poor law, it was a complex and multi-dimensional one, reflecting the ambivalences of Ireland's quasi-colonial status in the British polity of the nineteenth century. Ireland was not the only colonized society that attracted such remedial attention from Whig ministers in the 1830s. Indeed, the Irish poor-law model was deemed exportable to the West Indian islands in the wake of the abolition of slavery in the British empire and a perceived necessity of extending some form of welfare entitlement to the freedmen. Mulgrave, who had served as the 'emancipatory' governor of Jamaica in 1832–34, may have been responsible for drawing the connection, but it was Russell who, hot on the heels of the passage of the Irish measure, ordered the Poor Law Commissioners to consider the practicalities of extending poor laws to the islands and to report to the colonial office, and urged the colonial authorities to follow the Irish initiative.[30] The colonial secretary, Lord Glenelg, although sceptical as to the necessity or urgency of the question, nevertheless admitted that 'society at large [has] now assumed the duty heretofore incumbent on private proprietors, of maintaining the destitute poor' in the colonies, and forwarded Shaw Lefevre's paper recommending a modified version of the Irish act.[31]

In 1839 several colonial assemblies and governors responded by preparing legislation, which required the approval of London to take effect. In November 1840 the commissioners reported to Normanby their opinion that the task in hand was similar to that in Ireland, and that a measure modelled on the 1838 act was desirable in preference to the more generous bill initially approved by the assembly of Dominica (which would have permitted outdoor relief).[32] A similar measure for St Kitts was also modified in line with the com-

30 NA: PLCP, MH19/63, Russell to PLC, 26 Sept. 1838.

31 Copy of circular dispatch addressed by Lord Glenelg to the governors of the West India Colonies, 1 Feb. 1839, *Papers relative to West Indies. Part 1*, PP 1839 (107-I), xxxv.143, pp. 36–42.

32 NA: PLCP, MH19/63, Commissioners to Normanby, 17 Nov. 1840.

missioners' preferences.[33] In the Caribbean, as in Ireland, the introduction of poor laws formed part of an attempted renegotiation of social relationships in place of an old and no longer tenable social order; but similar limitations were deemed essential to protect property from 'excessive' claims and to uphold the stimulus of 'less eligibility' to self-help and labour discipline.

In both Ireland and the Caribbean (as indeed in Scotland when its poor law was amended in 1845), it is too simplistic to regard these developments as a straightforward and uncomplicated extension of an 'English' system to subordinate territories. While the personnel of the Poor Law Commission sought (with some success in Ireland) to transfer their ideals of poor-law forms and administration, the political contexts of introduction were profoundly different from that of the English poor law extension act of 1834, and the coalitions that carried these new poor laws into operation were not the same. Indeed, the coalition was sharply at odds with that dominated by Christian political economists and liberal Tories which had drafted and carried the English measure and whose members clearly sympathized with the core recommendations of the alternative plan offered to Ireland by Archbishop Whately.[34] This was recognized even by the former commissioner T. F. Lewis in 1843, when he observed that 'in Ireland the measure was one of *Relief* not *restraint*, and the same odium as in England ought not to have been incurred – but Ireland has always a set of difficulties of its own, and O'Connell has set them off to the best advantage'.[35]

The underlying spirit and 'meaning' of an Irish poor law was thus quite different in the eyes of both its supporters (and despite the catastrophes of famine these remained influential) and detractors; and this shaped the patterns of resistance and acquiescence to the poor law into different forms to those in England and Scotland. Whether the experience of the poor law by the destitute (a subject outside the scope of the current study) was essentially different is another matter, although distinct Irish cultures of poverty and social expectation may have rendered this so. What is certainly the case is that the political context in which the poor law originated, emerged, and was contested was distinct and, despite the ambitions of poor-law officials, continued to provide an insuperable obstacle to the development of any uniform 'British' welfare institution.

33 J. M. Phillips to Commissioners, 26 Dec. 1840, Commissioners to Normanby, 6 Jan. 1841, *ibid*. However, when the case of Mauritius was referred to them under the Peel administration, the commissioners expressed themselves satisfied with the introduction of a more limited system of voluntary charity committees: Commissioners to Graham, 17 Feb. 1842, *ibid*., MH19/64.

34 Mandler, 'Tories and paupers', pp. 81–103.

35 NLW, HCP, C/1730, T. F. Lewis to G. C. Lewis, 1 Jan. 1843.

Ultimately, the Irish poor law might best be regarded as a hybrid institution, whose meaning and practical operations, both locally and centrally, were subject to regular contestations between competing lobbies and interests. The Famine period could be interpreted as an aberration, in which socio-economic collapse and political fracturing disempowered a number of Irish interest-groups (most fatally the swollen ranks of the destitute poor themselves, as well as to some extent also the landed lobby and the Catholic-nationalist lobby), and rendered an extraordinary degree of leverage to a clique of ideologues intent on manipulating the system to reconstruct Irish society according to their prescribed vision, whatever the human cost. Both before and after the catastrophe of the late 1840s no such monopoly of control was possible, and the relief of the Irish poor was the subject of vigorous exchanges and altercations.

Bibliography

Primary Sources

Archives

Aberystwyth: National Library of Wales
Harpton Court Papers
Nassau Senior Papers

Bedford: Bedfordshire and Luton Archives and Records Service
Wrest Park (Lucas) Manuscripts

Belfast: Public Record Office of Northern Ireland
Anglesey Papers
Downshire Papers
Sharman Crawford Papers

Cambridge: Cambridge University Library
Graham Papers (microfilm)

Chichester: West Sussex Record Office
Bessborough Papers

Doncaster: Doncaster Archives Department
Battie-Wrightson Papers

Dublin: National Library of Ireland
Killadoon Papers
Larcom Papers
Monteagle Papers
Smith O'Brien Papers

Durham: Durham University Library
Grey Papers

Exeter: Devon Record Office
Fortescue of Castle Hill Papers

Kew: National Archives
Home Office Papers

Poor Law Commission Papers
Russell Papers
Treasury Papers

Liverpool: Liverpool Record Office
Derby Papers

London: British Library
Althorp Papers
Bowood Papers
Broughton Papers
Graham Papers
Peel Papers

London: Lambeth Palace Library
Whately Papers

London: UCL Archives
Chadwick Papers
Ogden Mss

North Yorkshire: Castle Howard
Castle Howard Papers

North Yorkshire: Mulgrave Castle
Normanby Papers

Southampton: Southampton University Library
Broadlands (Melbourne) Papers
Wellington Papers

Stafford: Staffordshire Record Office
Hatherton Papers

Windsor: Royal Archives
Melbourne Papers (microfilm)

Official Publications

Hansard's Parliamentary Debates, 2nd and 3rd series
Dáil Éireann Debates
Journals of the House of Commons
Journals of the House of Lords
Report of the Select Committee on Legislative Provisions for Support of Aged and Infirm Poor of Ireland, Punishment of Vagrants, and Care of Lunatics, PP 1803–04 (109) v.771
Second Report of the Select Committee on State of Disease, and Condition of Labouring Poor, in Ireland, PP 1819 (409), viii.457
Report of the Select Committee on the Condition of the Labouring Poor in Ireland and Application of Funds for their Employment, PP 1823 (561), vi.331

Reports from the Select Committee on the State of Ireland with Reference to Disturbances, PP 1825 (129), viii.1

Select Committee of House of Lords appointed to inquire into State of Ireland more particularly with reference to the Circumstances which may have led to Disturbances in that Part of the United Kingdom: Minutes of Evidence, PP 1825 (181, 521) ix.1

First Report of the Select Committee on the State of the Poor in Ireland, PP 1830 (589), vii.278

Second Report of the Select Committee on the State of the Poor in Ireland, PP 1830 (654), vii.451

Third Report of the Select Committee on the State of the Poor in Ireland, PP 1830 (665), vii.649

Report of the Select Committee on the State of the Poor in Ireland, being a Summary of the First, Second and Third Reports of Evidence taken before that Committee: together with an Appendix of Accounts and Papers, PP 1830 (667), vii.1

A Bill to make provision for the Relief of the Poor in Ireland, in Certain Cases, PP 1831 (237), ii

Return of Number of Beggars, Vagrants and Foundlings relieved in Cork, Waterford, and Limerick, PP 1831–32 (565), xl

Commission and Instructions to the Commissioners on the State of the Poor in Ireland, PP 1834 (175), xliii.407

Return of Numbers of Existing Commissions of Inquiry, PP 1834 (291), xli.349

First Report from His Majesty's Commissioners for inquiring into the Condition of the Poorer Classes in Ireland: Appendix A, Supplement; Appendix B, Medical Relief, Dispensaries, Fever Hospitals, Lunatic Asylums; Supplement, Parts i. and ii, PP 1835 (369), xxxii.1

Select Committee on the Education of the People of England and Wales, and Grants in Aid: Report, Minutes of Evidence, Appendix, PP 1835 (465), vii.763

Accounts of Expenses of Commission for Inquiring into the State of the Poor in Ireland, PP 1835 (559), xlvii.1

First and Second Reports of the Select Committee appointed to inquire into the Amount of Advances made by the Commissioners of Public Works in Ireland, PP 1835 (573), xx.169

Poor Inquiry (Ireland): Appendix G: Report on the State of the Irish Poor in Great Britain, PP 1836 [40], xxxiv.427

Poor Inquiry (Ireland). Appendix H, Part i: Containing Reasons for recommending Voluntary Associations for the Relief of the Poor and Reasons for Dissenting from the Principle of raising Funds for the Relief of the Poor by the Voluntary System, as recommended in the Report, PP 1836 [41], xxxiv.643

Royal Commission for Inquiring into the Condition of the Poorer Classes in Ireland: Appendix H, Part ii. Remarks by J. E. Bicheno, PP 1836 [42], xxxiv.657

Third Report of the Commissioners for Inquiring into the Condition of the Poorer Classes in Ireland, PP 1836 [43], xxx.1

Return of Commissions issued since November 1830, PP 1836 (528), xxxvii.491

A Bill for the more effectual Relief of the Destitute Poor in Ireland, PP 1837 (38), iii.451

Second Report of the Commissioners for inquiring into the Condition of the Poorer Classes in Ireland, PP 1837 [68], xxxi.587

Report of George Nicholls, esq., to His Majesty's Principal Secretary of State for the Home Department, on Poor Laws, Ireland, PP 1837 [69], li.201

First Report of the Commissioners appointed to inquire into the Manner in which Railway Communications can be most advantageously promoted in Ireland, PP 1837 [75], xxxiii.283

Confidential Letter from Nassau W. Senior, Esq., to His Majesty's Principal Secretary of State for the Home Department, on the Third Report from the Commissioners for inquiring into the Condition of the Poor in Ireland, dated 14 April 1836, PP 1837, [90], li.241

Remarks on the Third Report of the Irish Poor Inquiry Commissioners; drawn up by the Desire of the Chancellor of the Exchequer, for the Purpose of being submitted to His Majesty's Government. By George Cornewall Lewis, PP 1837 [91], li.253

A Bill for the More Effectual Relief of the Destitute Poor in Ireland, PP 1837–38 (15), v.305

Second Report of Geo. Nicholls, esq., to His Majesty's Principal Secretary of State for the Home Department, on Poor Laws, Ireland, PP 1837–38 [104], xxxviii.657

Third Report of G. Nicholls, on Poor Laws, Ireland, containing Result of Inquiry into Condition of Labouring Classes, and Relief of Poor, in Holland and Belgium, PP 1837–38 [126], xxxviii.713

Second Report of the Royal Commission appointed to Inquire into the Manner in which Railway Communications can be Most Advantageously Promoted in Ireland, PP 1837–38 [145], xxxv.449

A Bill [as amended in Committee and on Re-commitment] for the More Effectual Relief of the Destitute Poor in Ireland, PP 1837–38 (238), v.345

A Bill [as amended by the House of Lords] for the More Effectual Relief of the Destitute Poor in Ireland, PP 1837–38 (577), v.393

Treasury Minute, dated 3 November 1836, respecting the Railroad Commission for Ireland, PP 1837–38 (654), xlvi. 481

A Bill to amend an Act . . . for the more efficient Relief of the Destitute Poor in Ireland, PP 1839 (18), iv.491

Papers relative to West Indies. Part 1: Circular instructions – Jamaica, British Guiana, PP 1839 (107–I), xxxv.143

Fifth Annual Report of the Poor Law Commissioners: with Appendices, PP 1839 [239], xx.1

Sixth Annual Report of the Poor Law Commissioners: with Appendices, PP 1840 [253], xvii.447

Seventh Annual Report of the Poor Law Commissioners: with Appendices, PP 1841 [327], xi.291

Return of Sums which the Irish Poor Law Commissioners borrowed from the Exchequer Loan Office for building Workhouses in Belfast, Londonderry, Castlederg, Strabane, Omagh and Banbridge, PP 1842 (141), xxxvi.343

Inquiry into the Treatment, Condition and Mortality of Infant Children in the Workhouse of the North Dublin Union, PP 1842 [370], xxxvi.15

Minutes of Proceedings of Lowtherstown Board of Guardians, respecting the Purchase of the Site and Building of the Union Workhouse, and Correspondence with Poor Law Commissioners, PP 1842 (376), xxxvi.257

Eighth Annual Report of the Poor Law Commissioners: with Appendices, PP 1842 [389], xix.1

Return of Valuation of every Union in Ireland, PP 1843 (235), li.363

Memorial and Papers from Board of Guardians of Edenderry Union in Ireland to Secretary of State for Home Department, complaining of Acts of Poor Law Commissioners, PP 1843 (382), xlvi.607

Copy of Correspondence between the Poor Law Commissioners for Ireland, on the Election of Guardians for the Division of Kinsale, March 1843, PP 1843 (436), xlvi.639

Ninth Annual Report of the Poor Law Commissioners: with Appendices, PP 1843 [468], xxi.1

Tenth Annual Report of the Poor Law Commissioners: with Appendices, PP 1844 [589], xix.57

Report of the Commissioner appointed to inquire into the Execution of the Contracts for certain Union Workhouses in Ireland, PP 1845 (170), xxvi.399

Return of every Poor Law Union in Ireland, stating Population, Area and Number of Landholders, PP 1845 (593), xxxviii.209

Eleventh Annual Report of the Poor Law Commissioners: with Appendices, PP 1845 [624], xxvii.247

Return of Name of each Union and Electoral Division in Ireland; Number of Occupiers, etc, PP 1846 (262), xxxvi.469

Return of Number of Inmates in each Workhouse in Ireland, March 1844–46, PP 1846 (297), xxxvi.505

Report of the Select Committee of House of Lords, on Laws relating to Relief of Destitute Poor, and Operation of Medical Charities in Ireland. Report, Minutes of Evidence, Appendix, Index, PP 1846 (694), xi.1

Thirteenth Annual Report of the Poor Law Commissioners: with Appendices, PP 1847 [816], xxviii.1

Newspapers

Athlone Sentinel
Belfast Chronicle
Belfast News-Letter
Carlow Sentinel
Citizen
Connaught Journal
Courier
Dublin Evening Mail
Dublin Evening Post
Examiner
Freeman's Journal
Globe
Leeds Times

Limerick Chronicle
Limerick Star
Liverpool Mercury
Londonderry Journal
Manchester Guardian
Morning Advertiser
Morning Chronicle
Morning Herald
Morning Register
Nation
Northern Star
Northern Whig
Observer
Pilot
Political Register
Scotsman
Spectator
Sun
Tait's Edinburgh Magazine
The Times
Tipperary Free Press
Waterford Mail

Printed Primary Sources

[Alison, William P.], 'Evils of the state of Ireland', *Blackwood's Edinburgh Magazine*, 40 (Oct. 1836), pp. 495–514

[Alison, William P.], 'Justice to Ireland – a poor law', *Blackwood's Edinburgh Magazine*, 40 (Dec. 1836), pp. 812–31

Alison, William P., *Observations on the Management of the Poor in Scotland; and its Effects on the Health of the Great Towns* (2nd edn, Edinburgh, 1840)

Anon., *Remarks on a Pamphlet recommending a National Provision for the Poor of Ireland* (Dublin, 1773)

Anon., *Resolutions of the Committee for managing the Charitable Fund, for the Relief of the Industrious Poor, in St George's Parish* (Dublin, 1814)

Anon., *Arguments in Proof of the Necessity and Practicability of Suppressing Street Beggary in the City of Dublin; Illustrated by Some Important Facts respecting Institutions which have been established in Other Places for that Purpose* (Dublin, 1817)

Anon., *Lachrymae Hibernicae, or, The Grievances of the Peasantry of Ireland, especially in the Western Counties. By a Resident Native* (Dublin, 1822)

Anon., *Society for Improving the Condition and Increasing the Comforts of the Irish Peasantry* (London, 1822)

Anon., *A Report of the British and Foreign Philanthropic Society, with Other Statements and Calculations explanatory of Mr Owen's Plan for the Relief of Ireland, and of the Poor and Working Classes generally in all Other Countries* (Dublin, 1823)

Anon., 'Remarks on some of the evils of Ireland, and their removal. By a Protestant inhabitant of the province of Ulster', *The Pamphleteer*, 25 (1825), pp. 141–59

Anon., *A Letter to a Friend, on the State of Ireland; with some Observations on the Best Mode of introducing Poor Laws into that Kingdom; Remarks on Absenteeism, and on the Cultivation of Waste Lands and Turf Bogs. By an Absentee Proprietor of Land in the South of Ireland* (Bristol, 1830)

Anon., *A Letter to the Agriculturalists of England on the Expediency of extending the Poor Law to Ireland. By a Landowner* (London, 1830)

Anon., *A Letter to the Right Hon. the Lord Mayor of Dublin, proposing an Wholesome and Improved System of Poor-Laws for Ireland, best calculated to ameliorate and better the Condition of the People, and to encourage the Industry and Prosperity of the Country. By Patricious* (Dublin, 1830)

Anon., *Hints suggesting the Possibility of essentially altering and amending the Poor Laws of Great Britain and Ireland* (London, 1830)

Anon., *The Desideratum, or, Ireland's Only Remedy; 'Poor Laws and Education', proved on Social, Political and Christian Principles. Addressed to the Citizens of Dublin. By P. E. H.* (Dublin, 1831)

Anon., *A Letter to the Right Hon. the Earl of Darnley, on the Introduction of a Labour Rate for the Employment of the Poor in Ireland* (Dublin, 1831)

Anon., 'Senior on the introduction of Poor-Laws into Ireland', *Fraser's Magazine*, 4 (1831), pp. 554–65

Anon., *Remarks on an Article in the* Quarterly Review, *for February, 1831; entitled 'Poor Law for Ireland', with Anecdotes of the Irish Character* (Dublin, 1831)

Anon., *Thoughts on the Poor of Ireland, and the Means of their Amelioration. By a Barrister* (Dublin, 1831)

Anon., 'The Scottish system of poor laws', *Dublin University Magazine*, 3 (May 1834), pp. 508–22

Anon., *Second Report addressed to the Directors and Proprietors of the London and Birmingham Railway Company, founded on an Inspection of, and Experiments made on, the Liverpool and Manchester Railway* (London, 1835)

Anon., *Poor Laws for Ireland: (Resolutions and a Petition Adopted) at a Public Meeting held at the Royal Exchange, Dublin, on . . . 29th of March 1836* ([Dublin, 1836])

Anon., 'The state of the Irish poor', *Dublin University Magazine*, 7 (Apr. 1836), pp. 349–64

Anon., 'Poor law for Ireland', *Monthly Review or Literary Journal*, 143 (1837), pp. 54–69

Anon., *Irish Poor: A Word for Mr Nicholls. By Looker On* (London, 1837)

Anon., *Remarks on the Application of the Workhouse System with Other Modes of Relief to the Irish Poor. By an Assistant Commissioner* (London, 1837)

Anon., *Strictures on the Proposed Poor Law for Ireland, as recommended in the Report of George Nicholls, Esq.* (London, 1837)

Anon., *A Substitute of a Poor Law in Ireland* (Dublin, 1837)

Anon., *Thoughts on the Proposed Introduction of the Poor Laws into Ireland* (London, 1837)

Anon., *An Address to the Lords embodying the Spirit of the Irish Grand Juries' Petitions on the Poor Relief Bill, with an Appeal in Favour of the Aged, Infirm and Destitute Agricultural Labourers* (London, 1838)

Anon., *A Few Cursory Observations on the Proposed Bill for Establishing Poor Laws in Ireland* (London, 1838)

Anon., 'Ireland', *Monthly Chronicle*, 2 (1838), pp. 31–9

Anon., 'The Irish railway scheme', *Spectator* (15 Sept. 1838), pp. 873–4

Anon., *The Necessity of Combining a Law of Settlement with Local Assessment in the Proposed Bill for the Relief of the Poor of Ireland* (Dublin, 1838)

Anon., *The Parliamentary Pocket Companion, for 1838* (London, 1838)

Anon., 'Thoughts on passing things – No. 1', *Dublin University Magazine*, 12 (Oct. 1838), pp. 451–5

Anon., *Railways for Ireland: From the 'Railway Monthly Journal' for June, 1841* (London, [1841])

Anon., 'The grievances of Ireland', *Dublin Review*, 15 (Dec. 1843), pp. 317–62

Anon., *The South of Ireland and her Poor* (London, 1843)

Aspinall, A. (ed.), *Three Early Nineteenth Century Diaries* (London, 1952)

Ball, John, *What is to be done for Ireland?* (2nd edn, London, 1849)

Barrington, Matthew, *An Address to the Inhabitants of Limerick, on the Opening of the Mont De Piété, or Charitable Pawn Office, for the Support of Barrington's Hospital, in that City* (Dublin, 1836).

Berkeley, George, *The Querist: Containing Several Queries, proposed to the Consideration of the Public* (2nd edn, London, 1750)

Bermingham, Thomas, *Remarks on the Proposed Poor Law Bill for Ireland, Addressed to George Poulett Scrope, Esq.* (London, 1838)

Bicheno, J. E., *An Inquiry into the Poor Laws, chiefly with a View to examine them as a Scheme of National Benevolence, and to elucidate their Political Economy* (London, 1824)

Bicheno, J. E., *Ireland and its Economy; being the Result of Observations made in a Tour through the Country in the Autumn of 1829* (2nd edn, London, 1830)

Binns, Jonathan, *The Miseries and Beauties of Ireland* (2 vols, London, 1837)

Borrett, W. P., *Three Letters upon a Poor Law and Public Medical Relief for Ireland to Daniel O'Connell, Esq., MP* (London, 1838)

Bosworth, J., *The Contrast: or, the Operation of the Old Poor Laws Contrasted with the Recent Poor Law Amendment Act, and the Necessity of a Legal Provision for the Poor Generally, but Especially in Ireland* (London, 1838)

[Bracebridge, C. H.], *A Letter to the Right Hon. Lord John Russell on the Principles of the Irish Poor Law Bill. By the Chairman of an English Poor Law Union* (London, 1837)

Brady, W. E., *A Letter and Suggestions for the Employment of the People, and the Amelioration of the Poor in Ireland, addressed to the Right Hon. Lord Morpeth* (London, 1835)

[Bruce, William], *Poor Rates, the Panacea for Ireland* (2nd edn, Bristol, 1828)

Bruce, W., *Poor Rates for Ireland* (3rd edn, London, 1829)

Buchanan, A. C., *Outline of a Practical Plan for the Immediate, Effective and Economical Relief of the Starving & Destitute Poor of Ireland* (Brighton, [1837])

Butt, Isaac, *The Poor-Law for Ireland Examined, its Provisions and the Report of Mr Nicholls contrasted with the Facts proved by the Poor Inquiry Commission, in a Letter to Lord Viscount Morpeth* (London, 1837)

[Chadwick, Edwin], 'The New Poor Law', *Edinburgh Review*, 63 (July 1836)

Clements, Lord, *The Present Poverty of Ireland convertible into the Means of Her Improvement, under a Well-Administered Poor Law* (London, 1838)

Cobbett, William, Cobbett's *Manchester Lectures, in support of his Fourteen Reform Propositions . . . To which is subjoined, a Letter to Mr O'Connell, on his Speech, made in Dublin, on the 4th of January, 1832, against the Proposition of establishing Poor-laws in Ireland* (London, 1832)

Cobden, Richard, *England, Ireland and America* ([1835] Philadelphia, 1980)

Connery, James, *The Reformer, or, an Infallible Remedy to Prevent Pauperism and Periodical Returns of Famine* (6th edn, Dublin, 1837)

[Corrie, John], *Remarks on the Bill for the more effectual Relief of the Destitute Poor in Ireland. By Philo-Hibernus* (2nd edn, London, 1837)

Craig, Edward Thomas, *An Irish Commune: The Experiment at Ralahine, County Clare 1831–1833* (Blackrock, 1983)

Cropper, James, *Present State of Ireland: with a Plan for improving the Condition of the People* (Liverpool, 1825)

[Crybbace, T. Tully], *Provision for the Poor of Ireland* (n.p., [1837])

Daly, Robert, *A Letter to the Editor of the Christian Examiner, on the Subject of a Legal Provision for the Poor of Ireland* (Dublin, 1829)

[Davis, Thomas], 'Emigration – no remedy', *Citizen*, 1 (Dec. 1839), pp. 73–83

de Beaumont, Gustave, *Ireland: Social, Political and Religious* ([edited and translated by W. C. Taylor, London, 1839] Cambridge, MA, 2006)

[de Coux, Charles], 'Christian political economy', *Dublin Review*, 3 (July 1837), pp. 165–98

[de Coux, Charles], 'Belgium and Holland', *Dublin Review*, 5 (Oct. 1838), pp. 463–96

[de Coux, Charles], 'Trade with France', *Dublin Review*, 6 (May 1839), pp. 357–95

de Sismondi, J. C. L. Simonde, *Études sur l'économie politique* (2 vols, Paris, 1837–38)

de Tocqueville, Alexis, *Memoir on Pauperism* (Chicago, IL, 1997)

de Villeneuve-Bargemont, Jean Paul Alban, *L'Économie politique chrétienne, ou recherches sur la nature et les causes du paupérisme, en France et en Europe, et sur les moyens de le soulager et de le prevenir* (3 vols, Paris, 1834)

Douglas, John, *Observations on the Necessity of a Legal Provision for the Irish Poor, as a Means of improving the Condition of the Irish People, and protecting the British Landlord, Farmer and Labourer* (London, 1828)

Douglas, John, *Life and Property in Ireland assured as in England by a Poor-rate on Land to provide Employment for the Destitute Poor on the Waste Lands of Ireland* (London, 1846)

Doyle, James, *Pastoral Letter addressed to the Roman Catholic Clergy of the Deanery of Kilcock* (Dublin, 1823)

[Doyle, James W.], *Important Letter from Bishop Doyle to – Robertson, Esq., MP, in Consequence of Some Observations which fell from that Gentleman in the Debate on*

Mr Hume's Motion for an Inquiry into the Church Establishment in Ireland (Dublin, [1824])

[Doyle, James W.], *Letters on the State of Ireland: Addressed by J. K. L. to a Friend in Ireland* (Dublin, 1825)

Doyle, James W., *Letter to Thomas Spring Rice, esq., M.P., on the Establishment of a Legal Provision for the Irish Poor, and on the Nature and Destination of Church Property* (Dublin, 1831)

[Doyle, James W.], *The Rt. Rev. Dr Doyle's Letter on Poor Laws in Reply to Mr Senior of London* (Dublin, 1831)

Ede, John, *Reflections on the Employment, Wages, and Condition of the Poor, showing the Fallacy and Injustice of recommending Emigration as a Remedy for the Lamentable State of the English Labourer, and tracing the Evils of Insufficient Wages and Ruinous Poor's Rates to their Natural Causes* (London, 1829)

Ensor, George, *The Poor and their Relief* (London, 1823)

Evans, G. H., *Remarks on the Policy of introducing the System of Poor Rates into Ireland* (London, 1829)

Fitzpatrick, William John (ed.), *The Life, Times and Contemporaries of Lord Cloncurry* (Dublin, 1855)

Fitzpatrick, William John (ed.), *Memoirs of Richard Whately, Archbishop of Dublin* (2 vols, London, 1864)

Fitzpatrick, William John (ed.), *The Life, Times and Correspondence of the Right Rev. Dr Doyle, Bishop of Kildare and Leighlin* (new edn, 2 vols, Dublin, 1890)

Flood, Henry, *Poor Laws. Arguments against a Provision for Paupers, if it be Parochial or Perpetual* (Dublin, 1830)

Foster, Thomas Campbell, *Letters on the Condition of the People of Ireland* (London, 1846)

[French, Fitzstephen], 'Poor-laws for Ireland; Report of the Irish Poor Inquiry Commission', *British and Foreign Review*, 4 (Jan. 1837), pp. 1–25

[French, Fitzstephen], 'State of Ireland – projected poor law', *British and Foreign Review*, 5 (Oct. 1837), pp. 367–401

[Graham, George J.], 'Poor laws in Ireland', *London and Westminster Review*, 25 (July 1836), pp. 332–65

Greville, C. C. F., *The Greville Memoirs (Second Part): A Journal of the Reign of Queen Victoria, from 1837 to 1852* (3 vols, London, 1885)

Grierson, George A., *The Circumstances of Ireland considered with Reference to the Question of Poor Laws* (London, 1830)

Hancock, W. Neilson, 'The workhouse as a mode of relief for widows and orphans', *Journal of the Dublin Statistical Society*, 1 (1855), pp. 84–91

Hancock, W. Neilson, 'On the importance of substituting the family system of rearing orphan children for the system now pursued in our workhouses', *Journal of the Dublin Statistical Society*, 2 (1859), pp. 317–31

Hancock, W. Neilson, 'Difference between English and Irish poor law, as to the treatment of women and unemployed workmen', *Journal of the Dublin Statistical Society*, 3 (1862), pp. 217–35

Hancock, W. Neilson, *The Difference between the English and Irish Poor Law, as to the Treatment of Women and Unemployed Workmen* (Dublin, 1862)

[Hickey, William], *The State of the Poor of Ireland briefly considered and Agricultural Education recommended, to check Redundant Population and to promote National Improvement* (Dublin, 1820)

[Hickey, William], Martin Doyle, *An Address to the Landlords of Ireland, on Subjects connected with the Melioration of the Lower Classes* (Dublin, 1831)

Hinchy, John, *General Observations on the State of Ireland, and Plans for its Improvement, with Remarks on Poor Laws* (Dublin, 1835)

Horton, R. Wilmot, *Causes and Remedies of Pauperism in the United Kingdom considered: Introductory Series. Being a Defence of the Principles and Conduct of the Emigration Committee against the Charges of Mr Sadler* (London, 1830)

Houghton, Henry, *The Poor Rate Payer's Guide; exhibiting the various Scales by which the Payment of the Rate is distributed between Landlord and Tenant* (Dublin, 1840)

Houghton, James, 'Observations upon a paper on poor relief, by Dr. Dowling of Tipperary', *Journal of the Dublin Statistical Society*, 3 (1862), pp. 156–62

Inglis, Henry D., *A Journey throughout Ireland, during the Spring, Summer and Autumn of 1834* (3rd edn, 2 vols, London, 1835)

Ingram, J. K., 'A comparison between the English and Irish Poor Laws with respect to the conditions of relief', *Journal of the Statistical and Social Inquiry Society of Ireland*, 4 (1864), pp. 43–61

Ingram, J. K., 'Memoir of the late William Neilson Hancock', *Journal of the Statistical and Social Inquiry Society of Ireland*, 9 (1888–89), pp. 384–93

Jacob, W., *Observations on the Benefits arising from the Cultivation of Poor Soils, by the Application of Pauper Labour; as exemplified in the Colonies for the Indigent, and for Orphans in Holland* (Lindfield, 1828)

Jennings, Louis (ed.), *The Croker Papers: The Correspondence and Diaries of the late Right Honourable John Wilson Croker* (3 vols, London, 1884)

Johnson, James, *A Tour in Ireland: with Meditations and Reflections* (London, 1844)

Johnstone, Christine, *True Tales of the Irish Peasantry, as Related by Themselves. Selected from the Report of the Poor-Law Commissioners* (2nd edn, Edinburgh, 1836)

Keating, M. I., *A Letter to Wilmot Horton, Esq., MP, on Emigration from Ireland* (Limerick, n.d.)

Kennedy, John Pitt, *Instruct; Employ; Don't Hang Them: or Ireland Tranquilized without Soldiers, and Enriched without English Capital* (London, 1835)

Kennedy, John Pitt, *Analysis of the Projects proposed for the Relief of the Poor of Ireland; more especially, that of Mr George Nicholls, embodied in a Bill now before Parliament; and that of the Commissioners for Inquiring into the Condition of the Poorer Classes in Ireland* (London, 1837)

Killarney, Frank [pseud.], *A Letter to the Earl of Mulgrave* (Cork, 1836)

Kingsley, William, *The Annual Medical Report of the Roscrea Fever Hospital and Dispensary, for the year 1827* (Roscrea, 1828)

Larkin, Emmet (ed. and trans.), *Alexis de Tocqueville's Journey in Ireland July–August, 1835* (Dublin, 1990)

[Leahy, David], 'Ireland and Lord Normanby', *Monthly Chronicle*, 3 (1839), pp. 289–301

Leslie, John, *Further Illustrations of the Principles upon which a Metropolitan Poor Rate is administered in the Parish of St George, Hanover Square; with a Few Desultory Observations on the Principle upon which Poor Rates are founded; and on the Proposed Extension of that System to Ireland* (London, 1836)

Lewis, George Cornewall, *An Examination of Some Passages in Dr Whately's Elements of Logic* (Oxford, 1829)

Lewis, George Cornewall, *On Local Disturbances in Ireland; and on the Irish Church Question* (London, 1836)

Lewis, Gilbert Frankland (ed.), *Letters of the Rt. Hon. Sir George Cornewall Lewis, Bart., to Various Friends* (London, 1870)

Longfield, Mountifort, *Four Lectures on Poor Laws, delivered in Trinity Term, 1834* (Dublin, 1834)

Lynch, A. H., *An Address to the Electors of Galway on the Poor-Law Bill for Ireland. With an Appendix, containing Extracts from the Evidence taken before the Commissioners of Poor Inquiry, Ireland* (London, 1838)

Lynch, A. H., *Measures to be adopted for the Employment of the Labouring Classes in Ireland; Detailed in an Address to the Electors of Galway; with an Appendix, containing Abstracts of the Reports of Some of the Provincial Assemblies in Belgium* (London, 1839)

[Macausland, John], *A Letter to the Right Hon. Lord Goderich, on the Deplorable Condition of the Helpless Poor in Ireland, with a Plan of Relief, as at Present partly in operation in several Districts of the Province of Ulster. By a Member of a Parochial Poor Relief Committee* (Dublin, 1827)

[MacDonnell, Eneas], *Practical Views and Suggestions, on the Present Condition and Permanent Improvement of Ireland, by Hibernicus* (Dublin, 1825)

MacNaghten, Francis Workman, *Some Observations on the Present State of Ireland* (London, 1837)

MacNaghten, Francis Workman, *Poor Laws – Ireland. Observations upon the Report of George Nicholls, Esq.* (London, 1838)

[Maginn, William], 'National economy: poor-laws for Ireland', *Fraser's Magazine* (March 1833), pp. 282–91

Martin, R. Montgomery, *Poor Laws for Ireland, a Measure of Justice to England; of Humanity to the People of Both Islands; and of Self-Preservation for the Empire* (London, 1833)

Maunsell, Henry, *The Only Safe Poor Law Experiment for Ireland: A Letter to the Right Honourable Lord Viscount Morpeth* (Dublin, 1838)

McCormac, Henry, *A Plan for the Relief of the Unemployed Poor* (Belfast, 1830)

McCullagh, W. T., *Letter to the Representative Peers of Ireland, on the Ministerial Measure of Irish Poor Laws* (Dublin, 1838)

McCullagh, W. Torrens (ed.), *Memoirs of the Right Honourable Richard Lalor Sheil* (2 vols, London, 1855)

[McCulloch, J. R.], 'Poor Laws', *Edinburgh Review*, 47 (May 1828), pp. 303–30

[McCulloch, J. R.], 'Sadler on Ireland', *Edinburgh Review*, 49 (June 1829), pp. 300–17

McGrath, Thomas (ed.), *The Pastoral and Education Letters of Bishop James Doyle of Kildare and Leighlin, 1786–1834* (Dublin, 2004)

Meagher, William, *Notices of the Life and Character of His Grace, Most Rev. Daniel Murray* (Dublin, 1853)

Merivale, Herman, *Five Lectures on the Principles of a Legislative Provision for the Poor in Ireland. Delivered in 1837 and 1838* (London, 1838)

Michaud, J. F., *Biographie universelle, ancienne et moderne* (Paris, 45 vols, 1843–65)

Mill, John Stuart, *The Principles of Political Economy* (3rd edn, 2 vols, London, 1852)

Molloy, Philip, *On Popular Discontent in Ireland* (Dublin, 1831)

Moran, Patrick Francis (ed.), *The Letters of Rev. James Maher, DD, late PP of Carlow-Graigue, on Religious Subjects; with a Memoir* (Dublin, 1877)

Naper, James Lenox William, *Practical Hints for the Relief and Employment of the Poor of Ireland* (Dublin, 1831)

Naper, James Lenox William, *An Address to the Landlords and Landholders of the County of Meath . . . on the New Poor Law Bill* (2nd edn, Dublin, 1837)

Napier, Charles James, *An Essay on the Present State of Ireland, showing the Chief Cause of, and the Remedy for, the Existing Distresses in That Country* (London, 1839)

Naville, F. M. L., *De la charité légale: de ses effets, de ses causes, et spécialement des maisons de travail et de la proscription de la mendicité* (2 vols, Paris, 1836)

Newsinger, John (ed.), *United Irishman: The Autobiography of James Hope* (London, 2000)

[Nicholls, George], *Eight Letters on the Management of the Poor. By an Overseer* (Newark, 1822)

[Nicholls, George], *The Farmer's Guide: Compiled for the Use of the Small Farmer and Cottier Tenantry in Ireland* (2nd edn, Dublin, 1842)

Nicholls, George, *A History of the Irish Poor Law in Connexion with the Condition of the People* (London, 1856)

Nicholls, George, *A History of the English Poor Law in Connection with the State of the Country and the Condition of the People* (new edn, 2 vols, London, 1898)

[Nicholls, —], *Benevola; A Tale: in Two Parts. Part the First – England. Part the Second – Ireland* (London, 1840)

O'Brien, R. Barry (ed.), *Thomas Drummond, Under-secretary in Ireland 1835–40: Life and Letters* (London, 1889)

O'Brien, William Smith, *Plan for the Relief of the Poor in Ireland; with Observations on the English and Scotch Poor Laws, addressed to the Landed Proprietors of Ireland* (2nd edn, Dublin, 1831)

[O'Connell, John], 'Miseries and beauties of Ireland', *Dublin Review*, 4 (Apr. 1838), pp. 407–40

[O'Connell, John (ed.)], *Report of the General Committee of the Loyal National Repeal Association of Ireland, upon the Various Remedies proposed for the Evils complained of under the existing System of Poor Laws in Ireland* (Dublin, 1843)

O'Connell, Maurice R. (ed.), *Correspondence of Daniel O'Connell* (8 vols, Dublin, 1972–80)

O'Connor, Feargus, *A Series of Letters from Feargus O'Connor, Esq., . . . to Daniel O'Connell, Esq. MP* (London, 1836)

O'Flynn, James, *Extracts from a Pamphlet on the Present State of the Irish Poor* (London, 1836)

O'Malley, Thaddeus, *An Idea of a Poor Law for Ireland* (2nd edn, London, 1837)

[O'Malley, Thaddeus], *A Word or Two on the Irish Poor Relief Bill, and Mr Nicholls' Report; or, a Postscript to the Rev. Mr O'Malley's 'Idea of a Poor Law for Ireland'* (London, 1837)

[O'Sullivan, Samuel], 'How is Ireland to be governed?', *Dublin University Magazine*, 4 (Oct. 1834), pp. 353–67

[O'Sullivan, Samuel], 'Poor Law Bill for Ireland', *Dublin University Magazine*, 10 (July 1837), pp. 69–78

Page, Frederick, *The Principle of the English Poor Laws illustrated and defended, by an Historical View of Indigence in Civil Society; with Suggestions relative to their Improved Administration* (3rd edn, London, 1830)

Page, Frederick, *Observations on the State of the Indigent Poor of Ireland, and the Existing Institutions for their Relief* (London, 1830)

Parker, C. S. (ed.), *Sir Robert Peel from his Private Papers* (3 vols, London, 1899)

Parker, William, *Observations on the Intended Amendment to the Irish Grand Jury Laws, now under the Consideration of the Honourable the House of Commons: to which is added, a Plan for the General Survey and Valuation of Ireland, and for the Commutation of Tithes; with Several Important Hints relative to the Internal Economy of Ireland, and the Distressed State of the Poor* (Cork, 1816)

Parker, William, *A Plea for the Poor and Industrious. Part the First, the Necessity of a National Provision for the Poor in Ireland; deduced from the Argument of the Rt Rev. R. Woodward, Late Lord Bishop of Cloyne: and from the present Deplorable State of the Lower Orders* (Cork, 1819)

Parker, William, *Letter from William Parker, to Earl Bathurst* (n.p., [1825])

[Perrin, Mark], 'A poor law for Ireland', *Dublin Review*, 2 (Dec. 1836), pp. 51–95

[Political Economy Club], *Political Economy Club, founded in London, 1821: Minutes of Proceedings, 1899–1920, Roll of Members and Questions discussed, 1821–1920* (London, 1921)

[Poor Inquiry Commission], *Instructions given by the Commissioners appointed to inquire into the State of the Poor in Ireland, to the Assistant Commissioners* (n.d. [1833])

[Poor Inquiry Commission], *Selection of Parochial Examinations relative to the Destitute Classes in Ireland* (Dublin, 1835)

[Power, Alfred], *The Irish Poor Law: Past, Present and Future* (London, 1849)

Power, Alfred, *A Paper on Out-door Relief in Ireland: Prepared at Earl Spencer's Request* (London, 1875)

[Quin, M. J.], 'Lynch's measures for Ireland', *Dublin Review*, 12 (May 1839), pp. 466–80

Revans, John, *Observations on the Proposed Alteration of the Timber-duties: with Remarks on the Pamphlet of Sir Howard Douglas* (London, 1831)

Revans, John, *Evils of the State of Ireland: Their Causes and Their Remedy – A Poor Law* (2nd edn, London, 1837)

Revans, John, *A Per Centage Tax on Domestic Expenditure, to Supply the Whole of the Public Revenue* (London, 1847)

Revans, John, *England's Navigation Laws no Protection to British Shipping* (London, 1849)

Revans, John, *Working Plan of the Administrative Reform Association* (London, 1856)

Revans, John, *List of the Present House of Commons, with the Degree of its Subjection to the House of Lords* (London, 1858)

[Rice, Thomas Spring], 'Mr Sadler's school – Italian economists', *Edinburgh Review*, 50 (Jan. 1830), pp. 344–63

[Rice, Thomas Spring], 'Ireland', *Edinburgh Review*, 57 (Apr. 1833), pp. 248–79

[Rice, Thomas Spring], 'Proposed introduction of the poor laws into Ireland', *Edinburgh Review*, 59 (Apr. 1834), pp. 227–61

Ritchie, Leitch, *A Bystander's View of the Irish Poor Law Question* (London, 1837)

Ritchie, Leitch, *Ireland: Picturesque and Romantic* (London, 1837)

Robinson, Samuel, *To the Right Honourable John Edward Littleton, MP, Secretary for Ireland: Remarks on the Advantages to be expected from a Compulsory Rate in Ireland* (n.p., 1833)

Russell, Lord John, *The Government of Ireland: The Substance of a Speech, delivered in the House of Commons, on Monday, April 15th, 1839* (London, 1839)

Russell, John, Earl, *A Letter to the Right Hon. Chichester Fortescue, MP, on the State of Ireland* (3rd edn, London, 1868)

Russell, John, Earl, *A Third Letter to the Right Hon. Chichester Fortescue, MP, on the State of Ireland* (London, 1869)

Russell, Rollo (ed.), *Early Correspondence of Lord John Russell, 1805–40* (2 vols, London, 1913)

[Ryan, P.], *Funds for the Poor of Ireland, without Taxation* [Thurles, 1837]

Ryan, Richard, *A Letter to the Right Hon. E. G. Stanley . . . in Answer to Doctor Doyle's Letter, to Thomas Spring Rice, Esq., MP, on the Subject of Poor Laws, and the Nature and Destination of Church Property* (Dublin, 1831)

Sadler, M. T., *Ireland: its Evils, and their Remedies: Being a Refutation of the Errors of the Emigration Committee and Others, touching on that Country* (London, 1828)

Sandys, Michael, *A Letter to the Right Honourable Henry Grattan, on the State of the Labouring Poor in Ireland, from the Rev. M. Sandys, AM, Minister of Powerscourt. With Mr Grattan's Answer* (Dublin, 1796)

[Scrope, George Poulett], 'The political economists', *Quarterly Review*, 44 (Jan. 1831), pp. 1–52

[Scrope, George Poulett], 'Poor laws for Ireland', *Quarterly Review*, 44 (Feb. 1831), pp. 511–54

[Scrope, George Poulett], 'Senior's *Letter on the Irish Poor*', *Quarterly Review*, 46 (Jan. 1832), pp. 390–410

Scrope, George Poulett, *Plan of a Poor-Law for Ireland, with a Review of the Arguments for and against it* (2nd edn, London, 1834)

Scrope, George Poulett, *Remarks on the Government Irish Poor-law Bill, in a Letter to Lord John Russell* (London, 1837)

Scrope, George Poulett, *Memoir of the Life of the Rt. Hon. Charles Lord Sydenham* (2nd edn, London, 1844)

Scrope, George Poulett, *How is Ireland to be governed? A Question addressed to the New Administration of Lord Melbourne in 1834, with a Postscript in which the Same Question is addressed to the Administration of Sir Robert Peel in 1846* (2nd edn, London, 1846)

Scrope, George Poulett, *Letters to the Right Hon. Lord John Russell, on the Expediency of enlarging the Irish Poor Law* (London, 1846)

Senior, Nassau W., *A letter to Lord Howick on a Legal Provision for the Irish Poor; Commutation of Tithes, and a Provision for the Roman Catholic Clergy* (London, 1831)

[Senior, Nassau W.], 'Mendicancy in Ireland', *Edinburgh Review*, 77 (Apr. 1843), pp. 391–411

[Senior, Nassau W.], 'Ireland', *Edinburgh Review*, 79 (Jan. 1844), pp. 189–266

[Senior, Nassau W.], 'Proposals for extending the Irish Poor Law', *Edinburgh Review*, 84 (Oct. 1846), pp. 267–314

Shackleton, Ebenezer, *Poor Laws the Safest, Cheapest and Surest Cure for Boyism of Every Kind in Ireland* (Dublin, 1832)

Simpson, M. C. M. (ed.), *Correspondence and Conversations of Alexis de Tocqueville with Nassau William Senior from 1834 to 1859* (2nd edn, 2 vols, London, 1872)

Stanley, J., *Poor Laws – Ireland. The Injustice of Assessing Landlords and the Impracticality of Assessing Landholders* (Dublin, 1837)

Stanley, William, *Remarks on the Government Measure for establishing Poor-laws in Ireland: Chiefly with Reference to the Existing Amount of Pauperism, as stated in the Report of the Irish Poor Inquiry Commissioners: and the Necessary Extent and Character of the Means for its Relief* (London, 1837)

Staunton, Michael, *Hints for Hardinge, being a Series of Political Essays published originally in the Dublin Morning Register; with an Appendix, containing Observations on the Report of Mr Spring-Rice's Committee on the State of the Poor in Ireland, and Letters to the Editors of the Times, Globe and Courier* (Dublin, 1830)

[Staunton, Michael], 'State and prospects of Ireland', *Dublin Review*, 1 (July 1836), pp. 281–312

Strickland, George, *A Discourse on the Poor Laws of England and Scotland, on the State of the Poor of Ireland and on Emigration* (London, 1827)

Swift, Jonathan, 'A proposal for giving badges to the beggars in all the parishes of Dublin', in Scott, Temple (ed.), *The Prose Works of Jonathan Swift, DD* (12 vols, 1897–1908), vii, pp. 325–35

Torrens, Robert, *A Letter to the Right Honourable Lord John Russell on the Ministerial Measure for Establishing Poor Laws in Ireland, and on Auxiliary Means which it will be necessary to adopt in carrying that Measure into Effect* (2nd edn, London, 1838)

[Torrens, Robert], *Plan for an Association in Aid of the Irish Poor Law* (London, 1838)

Trevelyan, C. E., *The Irish Crisis* (London, 1848)

[Vignoles, Charles B.], 'The railway system of Ireland', *Dublin Review*, 6 (Jan. 1839), pp. 207–69

Waller, Charles T., *A Plan for the Relief of the Poor in Ireland, in a Letter addressed to His Grace the Duke of Devonshire* (Bath, 1826)

Walsh, John Benn, *Poor Laws in Ireland, considered in their Probable Effects upon the Capital, the Prosperity and the Progressive Improvement of that Country* (London, 1830)

Ward, H. G., *The First Step to a Poor Law for Ireland* (London, 1837)

Whately, E. Jane (ed.), *Life and Correspondence of Richard Whately, DD* (2 vols, London, 1866)

[Whately, Richard], 'Emigration to Canada', *Quarterly Review*, 23 (July 1820), pp. 373–400

[Whately, Richard], *Letter to the Directors of the House of Industry at Bulcamp* (Halesworth, 1823)

Whately, Richard, 'Sermon XIV: Christ's example', in *Sermons on Various Subjects, delivered in Several Churches in the City of Dublin, and in Other Parts of the Diocese* (London, 1835), pp. 362–92

Whately, Richard, *Introductory Lectures on Political Economy, delivered at the University of Oxford, in the Easter Term, MDCCCXXXI* (3rd edn, London, 1847)

Whately, Richard, *Substance of a Speech delivered in the House of Lords, on Friday, the 16th of March, 1847, on the Motion for a Committee on Irish Poor Laws* (London, 1847)

Woodward, Henry, *A Letter on Tithe; addressed to the Editor of the Christian Examiner, in December, 1834; to which is prefixed, one on the same subject addressed in 1832, to the Right Hon. E. G. Stanley* (London, 1835)

[Woodward, Richard], *A Scheme for Establishing County Poor-Houses in the Kingdom of Ireland* (Dublin, 1766)

Woodward, Richard, *An Argument in Support of the Right of the Poor in the Kingdom of Ireland to a National Provision: in the Appendix . . . an Attempt is made to Settle the Measure of the Contribution due from Each Man to the Poor on the Footing of Justice* (Dublin, 1768)

Woodward, Richard, *An Address to the Publick, on the Expediency of a Regular Plan for the Maintenance and Government of the Poor: in which its Utility with Respect to the Industry, Morals and Publick Oeconomy is proved from Reason; and confirmed by the Experience of the House of Industry lately established in Dublin* (Dublin, 1775)

Wright, Thomas, *To Lord John Russell* (Dublin, 1838)

[Wrightson, W. B.], 'The workhouse system: the Irish poor law', *Edinburgh Review*, 66 (Oct. 1837), pp. 186–208

[Wrightson, W. B. (ed.)], *Irish Poor Laws: Additional Correspondence of Archbishop Whately 1837–1838* (n.p., [*c.*1867])

Secondary Sources

Books and articles

Akenson, Donald Harman, *The Church of Ireland: Ecclesiastical Reform and Revolution, 1800–1885* (New Haven, CT, 1971)

Akenson, Donald Harman, *A Protestant in Purgatory: Richard Whately, Archbishop of Dublin* (Hamden, CT, 1981)

Black, R. D. Collison, *Economic Thought and the Irish Question 1817–1870* (Cambridge, 1960)

Bowen, Desmond, *Paul Cardinal Cullen and the Shaping of Modern Irish Catholicism* (Dublin, 1983)

Boylan, Thomas A., and Timothy P. Foley, *Political Economy and Colonial Ireland: The Propagation and Ideological Function of Economic Discourse in the Nineteenth Century* (London, 1992)

Brandes, Inga, '"Odious, degrading and foreign" institutions? Analysing Irish workhouses in the nineteenth and twentieth centuries', in Gestrich, Andreas, Steven King, and Lutz Raphael (eds), *Being Poor in Modern Europe: Historical Perspectives 1800–1940* (Bern, 2006), pp. 199–228

Brogan, Hugh, *Alexis de Tocqueville: A Biography* (London, 2006)

Brown, Stewart J., *Thomas Chalmers and the Godly Commonwealth in Scotland* (Oxford, 1982)

Brundage, Anthony, *The Making of the New Poor Law: The Politics of Inquiry, Enactment and Implementation, 1832–39* (London, 1978)

Brundage, Anthony, *England's 'Prussian Minister': Edwin Chadwick and the Politics of Government Growth, 1832–54* (University Park, PA, 1988)

Brundage, Anthony, *The English Poor Laws, 1700–1930* (Basingstoke, 2002)

Burke, Helen, *The People and the Poor Law in Nineteenth-Century Ireland* (Littlehampton, 1987)

Cassell, Ronald D., *Medical Charities, Medical Politics: The Irish Dispensary System and the Poor Law, 1836–1872* (Woodbridge, 1997)

Clark, Anna, 'Wild workhouse girls and the liberal imperial state in mid-nineteenth century Ireland', *Journal of Social History*, 39 (2005), pp. 389–410

Collini, Stefan, Richard Whatmore, and Brian W. Young (eds), *Economy, Polity and Society: British Intellectual History 1750–1950* (Cambridge, 2000)

Comber, Maureen (ed.), *Poverty before the Famine: County Clare 1835* (Ennis, 1996)

Connolly, S. J., R. A. Houston, and R. J. Morris (eds), *Conflict, Identity and Economic Development in Ireland and Scotland 1600–1939* (Edinburgh, 1995)

Conway, Thomas G., 'The approach to an Irish poor law 1828–33', *Éire-Ireland*, 6 (1971), pp. 65–81

Crimmins, James E., 'Jeremy Bentham and Daniel O'Connell: their correspondence and radical alliance, 1828–1831', *Historical Journal*, 40 (1997), pp. 359–87

Crossman, Virginia, 'The New Ross workhouse riot of 1887: nationalism, class and the Irish poor laws', *Past & Present*, 179 (2003), pp. 135–58

Crossman, Virginia, *Politics, Pauperism and Power in Late Nineteenth-Century Ireland* (Manchester, 2006)

Crossman, Virginia, *The Poor Law in Ireland 1838–1948* (Dublin, 2006)

Crossman, Virginia, 'The humanization of the Irish Poor Laws: reassessing developments in social welfare in post-Famine Ireland', in Gestrich, Andreas, Steven King and Lutz Raphael (eds), *Being Poor in Modern Europe: Historical Perspectives 1800–1940* (Bern, 2006), pp. 229–50

Cullen, Bob, *Thomas L. Synnott: The Career of a Dublin Catholic 1830–70* (Dublin, 1997)

Cunningham, H. A. C., *The July Monarchy: A Political History of France 1830–1848* (London, 1988)

D'Arcy, Fergus A., 'Federalist, social radical and anti-sectarian: Thaddeus O'Malley (1797–1877)', in Moran, Gerard (ed.), *Radical Irish Priests 1660–1970* (Dublin, 1998), pp. 91–110

Dickson, David, 'In search of the old Irish poor law', in Mitchison, Rosalind, and Peter Roebuck (eds), *Economy and Society in Scotland and Ireland 1500–1939* (Edinburgh, 1988), pp. 149–59

Dickson, David, *Old World Colony: Cork and South Munster 1630–1830* (Cork, 2005)

Dickson, David (ed.), *The Gorgeous Mask: Dublin 1700–1850* (Dublin, 1987)

Donnelly, James S. jr, '"Irish property must pay for Irish poverty": British public opinion and the Great Irish Famine', in Morash, Chris, and Richard Hayes (eds), *Fearful Realities: New Perspectives on the Famine* (Blackrock, 1996), pp. 60–76

Donnelly, James S., *The Great Irish Potato Famine* (Stroud, 2001)

Durnin, Patrick, *The Workhouse and the Famine in Derry* (Derry, 2001)

Farrell, Michael, *The Poor Law and the Workhouse in Belfast 1838–1948* (Belfast, 1978)

Feingold, William L., *The Revolt of the Tenantry: The Transformation of Local Government in Ireland 1872–1886* (Boston, 1984)

Finer, S. E., *The Life and Times of Sir Edwin Chadwick* (London, 1952)

Foley, Tadgh, and Sean Ryder (eds), *Ideology and Ireland in the Nineteenth Century* (Dublin, 1998)

Geary, Laurence M., '"The whole country was in motion": mendicancy and vagrancy in pre-famine Ireland', in Hill, Jacqueline, and Colm Lennon (eds), *Luxury and Austerity* (Dublin, 1999), pp. 121–36

Geary, Laurence M., *Medicine and Charity in Ireland 1718–1851* (Dublin, 2004)

Geoghegan, Vincent, 'The emergence and submergence of Irish socialism, 1821–1851', in Boyce, D. G., R. Eccleshall and V. Geoghegan (eds), *Political Thought in Ireland since the Seventeenth Century* (London, 1993), pp. 100–23

Geoghegan, Vincent, 'Robert Owen, co-operation and Ulster in the 1830s', in Lane, Fintan, and Donal Ó Drisceoil (eds), *Politics and the Irish Working Class, 1830–1945* (Basingstoke, 2005), pp. 6–26

Gestrich, Andreas, Steven King, and Lutz Raphael (eds), *Being Poor in Modern Europe: Historical Perspectives 1800–1940* (Bern, 2006)

Ghosh, R. N., 'Malthus on emigration and colonization: letters to Wilmot-Horton', *Economica*, n.s. 30 (1963), pp. 45–62

Ghosh, R. N., 'The colonization controversy: R. J. Wilmot-Horton and the classical economists', *Economica*, n.s. 31 (1964), pp. 385–400

Goldstrom, J. M., 'Richard Whately and political economy in school books, 1833–80', *Irish Historical Studies*, 15 (1966–67), pp. 131–46

Gould, Michael H., *The Workhouses of Ulster* (Belfast, 1983)

Gould, Michael, 'The administration of the workhouse and the Great Famine', *Ulster Local Studies*, 17 (1995), pp. 19–26

Grace, Daniel, *The Great Famine in Nenagh Poor Law Union, Co. Tipperary* (Nenagh, 2000)

Graham, A. H., 'The Lichfield House Compact, 1835', *Irish Historical Studies*, 12 (1960–61), pp. 209–25

Gray, Peter, *Famine, Land and Politics: British Government and Irish Society 1843–1850* (Dublin, 1999)

Gray, Peter, '"Shovelling out your paupers": The British state and Irish Famine migration 1846–50', *Patterns of Prejudice*, 33 (1999), pp. 47–65

Gray, Peter, 'Wellington and the government of Ireland, 1832–46', in Woolgar, C. M. (ed.), *Wellington Studies*, III (Southampton, 1999), pp. 203–26

Gray, Peter, 'The peculiarities of Irish land tenure, 1800–1914: from agent of impoverishment to agent of pacification', in Winch, Donald, and Patrick K. O'Brien (eds), *The Political Economy of British Historical Experience, 1688–1914* (Oxford, 2002), pp. 139–64

Gray, Peter, '"Ireland's last fetter struck off": the lord lieutenancy debate 1800–67', in McDonough, Terrence (ed.), *Was Ireland a Colony? Economics, Politics and Culture in Nineteenth-Century Ireland* (Dublin, 2005), pp. 87–101

Griffiths, A. R. G., *The Irish Board of Works, 1831–1878* (New York, 1987)

Guilfoyle, James, 'The religious development of Daniel O'Connell, II: the making of a devotional Catholic', *New Hibernia Review*, 2 (1998), pp. 115–32

Harris, Jose, 'From poor law to welfare state? A European perspective', in Winch, Donald, and Patrick K. O'Brien (eds), *The Political Economy of British Historical Experience, 1688–1914* (Oxford, 2002), pp. 409–38

Hill, Jacqueline, and Colm Lennon (eds), *Luxury and Austerity: Historical Studies XXI* (Dublin, 1999)

Hilton, Boyd, *The Age of Atonement: The Influence of Evangelicalism on Social and Economic Thought, 1795–1865* (Oxford, 1988)

Hilton, Boyd, 'Whiggery, religion and social reform: the case of Lord Morpeth', *Historical Journal*, 37 (1994), pp. 829–59

Hilton, Boyd, *A Mad, Bad and Dangerous People? England 1783–1846* (Oxford, 2006)

Hollis, Aidan and Arthur Sweetman, 'Microcredit in prefamine Ireland', *Explorations in Economic History*, 35 (1998), pp. 347–80

Hoppen, K. Theodore, 'Politics, the law, and the nature of the Irish electorate, 1832–1850', *English Historical Review*, 92 (1977), pp. 746–76

Houghton, Walter E. (ed.), *The Wellesley Index to Victorian Periodicals 1824–1900* (5 vols, Toronto, 1966–89)

Howell-Thomas, Dorothy, *Duncannon: Reformer and Reconciler 1781–1847* (Norwich, 1992)

Innes, Joanna, 'The distinctiveness of the English poor laws, 1750–1850', in Winch, Donald, and Patrick K. O'Brien (eds), *The Political Economy of British Historical Experience, 1688–1914* (Oxford, 2002), pp. 381–407

Jenkins, Brian, *Era of Emancipation: British Government of Ireland 1812–1830* (Kingston, Ont., 1988)

Joannon, Pierre, 'O'Connell, Montalembert and the birth of Christian democracy in France', in O'Connell, Maurice R. (ed.), *Daniel O'Connell: Political Pioneer* (Dublin, 1991), pp. 89–109

Jones, Gareth Stedman, *An End to Poverty? A Historical Debate* (London, 2004)

Kidd, Alan, *State, Society and the Poor in Nineteenth-Century England* (Basingstoke, 1999)

Kinealy, Christine, *This Great Calamity: The Irish Famine 1845–52* (Dublin, 1994)

King, Stephen A., *Poverty and Welfare in England 1700–1850: A Regional Perspective* (Manchester, 2000)

La Berge, Ann F., 'A Restoration prefect and public health: Alban de Villeneuve-Bargemont at Nantes and Lille, 1824–1830', *Proceedings of the Annual Meeting of the Western Society for French History*, 5 (1977), pp. 128–37

Lane, Fintan, *The Origins of Modern Irish Socialism, 1881–1896* (Cork, 1997)

Lane, Fintan, *In Search of Thomas Sheahan: Radical Politics in Cork 1824–1836* (Dublin, 2001)

Lane, Fintan and Donal Ó Drisceoil (eds), *Politics and the Irish Working Class, 1830–1945* (Basingstoke, 2005)

Lavelle, Ruth, and Paul Huggard, 'The parish poor of St Mark's', in Dickson, David (ed.), *The Gorgeous Mask: Dublin 1700–1850* (Dublin, 1987), pp. 86–97

Lee, Joe, 'The social and economic ideas of O'Connell', in Nowlan, Kevin B., and Maurice R. O'Connell (eds), *Daniel O'Connell: Portrait of a Radical* (Belfast, 1984), pp. 70–84

Lees, Lynn Hollen, *The Solidarities of Strangers: The English Poor Laws and the People, 1700–1948* (Cambridge, 1998)

Levy, S. Leon, *Nassau W. Senior 1790–1864: Critical Essayist, Classical Economist and Advisor of Governments* (new edn, Newton Abbot, 1970)

Lindsay, Deirdre, 'The Sick and Indigent Roomkeepers' Society', in Dickson, David (ed.), *The Gorgeous Mask: Dublin 1700–1850* (Dublin, 1987), pp. 132–56

Luddy, Maria, *Women and Philanthropy in Nineteenth-Century Ireland* (Cambridge, 1995)

MacDonagh, Oliver, *The Emancipist: Daniel O'Connell 1830–1847* (London, 1989)

MacDonagh, Oliver, 'Ideas and institutions, 1830–45', in Vaughan, W. E. (ed.), *A New History of Ireland*, V: *Ireland under the Union*, I: *1801–70* (Oxford, 1989), pp. 193–217

MacDonagh, Oliver, 'The economy and society, 1830–45', in Vaughan, W. E. (ed.), *A New History of Ireland*, V: *Ireland under the Union*, I: *1801–70* (Oxford, 1989), pp. 225–8

Macintyre, Angus, *The Liberator: Daniel O'Connell and the Irish Party, 1830–47* (London, 1965)

Mandler, Peter, 'The making of the new poor law *redivivus*', *Past & Present*, 117 (1987), pp. 131–57

Mandler, Peter, *Aristocratic Government in the Age of Reform: Whigs and Liberals 1830–1852* (Oxford, 1990)

Mandler, Peter, 'Tories and paupers: Christian political economy and the making of the new poor law', *Historical Journal*, 33 (1990), pp. 81–103

McCaffrey, Lawrence J., *Daniel O'Connell and the Repeal Year* (Lexington, KY, 1966)

McDonough, Terrence (ed.), *Was Ireland a Colony? Economics, Politics and Culture in Nineteenth-Century Ireland* (Dublin, 2005)

McDowell, R. B., *Irish Public Opinion 1750–1800* (London, 1944)

McDowell, R. B., *Public Opinion and Government Policy in Ireland, 1801–46* (London, 1952)

McDowell, R. B., *The Irish Administration, 1801–1914* (London, 1964)

McGrath, Thomas, *Politics, Interdenominational Relations and Education in the Public Ministry of Bishop James Doyle of Kildare and Leighlin, 1786–1834* (Dublin, 1999)

Mitchison, Rosalind, 'Permissive poor laws: the Irish and Scottish systems considered together', in Connolly, S. J., R. A. Houston and R. J. Morris (eds), *Conflict, Identity and Economic Development in Ireland and Scotland 1600–1939* (Edinburgh, 1995), pp. 161–71

Mitchison, Rosalind, *The Old Poor Law in Scotland: The Experience of Poverty, 1574–1845* (Edinburgh, 2000)

Mitchison, Rosalind, and Peter Roebuck (eds), *Economy and Society in Scotland and Ireland 1500–1939* (Edinburgh, 1988)

Mokyr, Joel, and Cormac Ó Gráda, 'Poor and getting poorer? Living standards in Ireland before the famine', *Economic History Review*, 37 (1988), pp. 209–35

Moran, Gerard (ed.), *Radical Irish Priests 1660–1970* (Dublin, 1998)

Morash, Chris, and Richard Hayes (eds), *Fearful Realities: New Perspectives on the Famine* (Blackrock, 1996)

Nowlan, Kevin B. and Maurice R. O'Connell (eds), *Daniel O'Connell: Portrait of a Radical* (Belfast, 1984)

O'Brien, George, *An Economic History of Ireland from the Union to the Famine* (London, 1921)

O'Brien, Gerard, 'The establishment of poor-law unions in Ireland, 1838–43', *Irish Historical Studies*, 23 (1982), pp. 97–120

O'Brien, Gerard, 'Workhouse management in pre-Famine Ireland', *Proceedings of the Royal Irish Academy*, 86C (1986), pp. 113–34

O'Brien, Gerard, 'A question of attitude: responses to the new poor law in Ireland and Scotland', in Mitchison, Rosalind, and Peter Roebuck (eds), *Economy and Society in Scotland and Ireland 1500–1939* (Edinburgh, 1988), pp. 160–70

O'Brien, Gerard, 'Cosherers, wanderers and vagabonds: the treatment of the poor and insane in Ireland', *Saothar: Journal of the Irish Labour History Society*, 13 (1988), pp. 45–8

O'Brien, Seamus, *Famine and Community in Mullingar Poor Law Union, 1845–1849: Mud Huts and Fat Bullocks* (Dublin, 1999)

O'Carroll, Joseph, 'Contemporary attitudes towards the homeless poor 1725–1775', in Dickson, David (ed.), *The Gorgeous Mask: Dublin 1700–1850* (Dublin, 1987), pp. 64–85

Ó Ciosáin, Niall, 'Boccoughs and God's poor: the deserving and undeserving poor in Irish popular culture', in Foley, Tadgh, and Sean Ryder (eds), *Ideology and Ireland in the Nineteenth Century* (Dublin, 1998), pp. 93–9

O'Connell, Maurice R. (ed.), *Daniel O'Connell: Political Pioneer* (Dublin, 1991)

Ó Gráda, Cormac, 'The Owenite community at Ralahine, County Clare, 1831–33: a reassessment', in Craig, Edward Thomas, *An Irish Commune: The Experiment at Ralahine, County Clare 1831–1833* ([1830s] Blackrock, 1983), pp. 193–208

Ó Gráda, Cormac, *Ireland: A New Economic History 1780–1939* (Oxford, 1994)

O'Mahony, Michelle, *Famine in Cork City: Famine Life at Cork Union Workhouse* (Cork, 2005)

Ó Murchadha, Ciarán, *Sable Wings over the Land: Ennis, County Clare, and its Wider Community during the Great Famine* (Ennis, 1998)

O'Neill, Timothy P., 'Poverty in Ireland 1815–45', *Folk Life*, 11 (1973), pp. 22–33

O'Neill, Tim P., 'The charities and famine in mid-nineteenth century Ireland', in Hill, Jacqueline, and Colm Lennon (eds), *Luxury and Austerity* (Dublin, 1999), pp. 137–64

Opie, Redvers, 'A neglected English economist: George Poulett Scrope', *Quarterly Review of Economics*, 44 (1929), pp. 101–37

O'Toole, David, 'The employment crisis of 1826', in Dickson, David (ed.), *The Gorgeous Mask: Dublin 1700–1850* (Dublin, 1987), pp. 157–71

Ó Tuathaigh, M. A. G., *Thomas Drummond and the Government of Ireland, 1835–40* (Dublin, 1978)

Powell, Frederick W., *The Politics of Irish Social Policy 1600–1990* (Lampeter, 1992)

Poynter, J. R., *Society and Pauperism: English Ideas on Poor Relief, 1795–1834* (London, 1969)

Preston, Margaret H., *Charitable Words: Women, Philanthropy and the Language of Charity in Nineteenth-Century Dublin* (Westport, CT, 2004)

Quinn, James, 'The United Irishmen and social reform', *Irish Historical Studies*, 31 (1998), pp. 188–201

Rashid, Salim, 'Richard Whately and Christian political economy at Oxford and Dublin', *Journal of the History of Ideas*, 38 (1977), pp. 147–55

Riach, Douglas, 'Daniel O'Connell and American anti-slavery', *Irish Historical Studies*, 20 (1976), pp. 3–25

Robins, Joseph, *The Lost Children: A Study of Charity Children in Ireland, 1700–1900* (Dublin, 1980)

Robins, Joseph, *Fools and Mad: A History of the Insane in Ireland* (Dublin, 1986)

Roe, W. G., *Lamennais and England: The Reception of Lamennais's Religious Ideas in England in the Nineteenth Century* (Oxford, 1966)

Scherder, Ina, 'Galway workhouses in the nineteenth and twentieth centuries: function and strategy', in Gestrich, Andreas, Steven King and Lutz Raphael (eds), *Being Poor in Modern Europe: Historical Perspectives 1800–1940* (Bern, 2006), pp. 181–98

Sloan, Robert, *William Smith O'Brien and the Young Ireland Rebellion of 1848* (Dublin, 2000)

Stack, David, 'The "Secret Concatenation" in the mid-nineteenth century: the case of George Poulett Scrope, a still neglected political economist', *History of Political Economy*, 32 (2000), pp. 553–84

Stearns, Peter N., 'The nature of the *Avenir* movement (1830–31)', *American Historical Review*, 65 (1960), pp. 837–47

Strain, R. W. M., *Belfast and its Charitable Society: A Story of Urban Social Development* (London, 1961)

Vance, Norman, 'Improving Ireland: Richard Whately, theology and political economy', in Collini, Stefan, Richard Whatmore and Brian W. Young (eds), *Economy, Polity and Society: British Intellectual History 1750–1950* (Cambridge, 2000), pp. 181–202

Vaughan, W. E. (ed.), *A New History of Ireland*, V: *Ireland under the Union*, I: *1801–70* (Oxford, 1989)

Waterman, A. M. C., *Revolution, Economics and Religion: Christian Political Economy, 1798–1833* (Cambridge, 1991)

Willink, H. G., 'Life of Sir George Nicholls', in George Nicholls, *A History of the English Poor Law in Connection with the State of the Country and the Condition of the People* (new edn, 2 vols, 1898), vol. i, pp. i–lxxx

Winch, Donald and Patrick K. O'Brien (eds), *The Political Economy of British Historical Experience, 1688–1914* (Oxford, 2002)

Woods, Audrey, *Dublin Outsiders: A History of the Mendicity Institution 1818–1998* (Dublin, 1998)

Woolgar, C. M. (ed.), *Wellington Studies, III* (Southampton, 1999)

Electronic Sources

Higgenbotham, Peter, 'The Workhouse' <http://users.ox.ac.uk/~peter/workhouse/index.html>

Oxford Dictionary of National Biography <http://www.oxforddnb.com/>

Unpublished dissertations

Beale, George, 'Provision for the poor in south-east Ulster, c.1825–50' (PhD thesis, Queen's University of Belfast, 1995)

Fitzgerald, Patrick, 'Poverty and vagrancy in early-modern Ireland' (PhD thesis, Queen's University of Belfast, 1994)

Index

Note: 'n' after a page number indicates a note on that page.